# MEDIATION
# THEORY AND PRACTICE

# MEDIATION THEORY AND PRACTICE

## *Third Edition*

**James J. Alfini**
*Dean Emeritus & Professor of Law*
*South Texas College of Law*

**Sharon B. Press**
*Professor of Law & Director, Dispute Resolution Institute*
*Hamline University School of Law*

**Joseph B. Stulberg**
*Michael E. Moritz Chair in Alternative Dispute Resolution*
*The Ohio State University Moritz College of Law*

ISBN: 978–0–7698–6380–1 (casebook)
ISBN: 978–0–7698–6284–2 (looseleaf)
ISBN: 978–0–3271–8531–4 (ebook)

Library of Congress Control Number: 2013939482

> NOTE TO USERS
> To ensure that you are using the latest materials available in this area, please be sure to periodically check the LexisNexis Law School web site for downloadable updates and supplements at www.lexisnexis.com/lawschool.

Editorial Offices
121 Chanlon Rd., New Providence, NJ 07974 (908) 464-6800
201 Mission St., San Francisco, CA 94105-1831 (415) 908-3200
www.lexisnexis.com

MATTHEW◆BENDER

(2013–Pub.1179)

# Dedication

To Barry, Carol, and Midge.

# Preface to the Third Edition

In the seven years since we published the second edition of *Mediation Theory and Practice*, there have been a number of significant new developments in the mediation field and some changes in our personal lives. Jim Alfini transitioned to Dean Emeritus at South Texas College of Law. Sharon Press left the Florida Dispute Resolution Center to join the faculty at Hamline University School of Law and become the Director of the Dispute Resolution Institute. Our colleague and friend, Jean Sternlight, became immersed in multiple projects that commanded her time and talent, and so opted to withdraw from participating in developing the new edition; we continue to benefit from Jean's wise counsel and insights and we thank her for her extraordinary contributions to the first and second editions of this book.

Based on valued feedback from our colleagues in the mediation field who have used the text, as well as our experience with it, we have retained the primary content of the previous text but made significant changes to the manner in which we present and organize the materials. In particular, for this new edition, we importantly revised and updated the presentation of the materials in Chapter 1 and developed a new final chapter (Chapter 11) that captures in one place our previous discussion of the many contexts in which mediation is used and career possibilities in the field (previously Chapters 11 and 12). Further, we revised the order of presentation of materials in the following ways: Chapter 8 has been modified to focus exclusively on ethical issues in mediation, and the treatment of these materials is enriched by inclusion of notes and questions drawn from actual mediator grievances and advisory opinions. In addition, we moved the materials on mediator certification issues and judicial mediation to Chapter 9 (the institutionalization of mediation in the courts) and now follow that with Chapter 10, retitled as Mediation and the Lawyer as Advocate, with several new entries that reflect the increased focus on the lawyers' role as advocate for their clients who will be participating in mediation sessions and the resulting ethical issues.

Prominent among the new developments in the mediation field were an increased focus on the role of advocates in mediation and increases in the depth and breadth of advisory ethics opinions for mediators and mediation case law, especially in the area of good faith participation. In addition, mediation is increasingly being used to deal with major societal problems such as the foreclosure crisis. This new edition addresses these matters in enriched ways. As in previous editions, we have tried to include excerpts from both classic and new literature sources in this field as well as references and excerpts from new case law developments. We were greatly aided by our colleagues in the mediation field who continue to point us in the right direction and in some cases were very generous in granting us royalty-free permission to republish excerpts from their works.

Once again, our home institutions provided us with very helpful support. We thank our colleagues at Hamline University School of Law, The Ohio State University, Michael E. Moritz College of Law, and South Texas College of Law. Professor Stulberg also extends his deep appreciation to Ikerbasque, the Basque Foundation for Science, for awarding him a 2012 Ikerbasque Fellowship that partially supported his research in preparing this new edition Our students also provided us with excellent feedback in the classroom, letting us know of the strengths and weaknesses of the previous edition. We owe a great deal of thanks to Ben Lowndes, a second year student at Hamline University School of

## Preface to the Third Edition

Law and South Texas College of Law students Alanna Beck (3L) and Martin Pytlewski (2L) each of whom provided us with extraordinary research assistance in producing this third edition. Jennifer Beszley at Lexis Publishing also deserves our thanks for her editorial assistance and helpful direction through the publishing process.

# Table of Contents

# Table of Contents

# Table of Contents

## Table of Contents

# Table of Contents

# Table of Contents

# Table of Contents

# Table of Contents

# Table of Contents

# Table of Contents

# Table of Contents

# Table of Contents

# Table of Contents

# Chapter 1

# HISTORICAL CONTEXT AND CONCEPTUAL FRAMEWORK

## A.  INTRODUCTION

### 1.  Why Study Mediation?

Lawyers are problem solvers. They are professionally trained and committed to helping persons deal with differences in a constructive, principled way.

There are many ways to solve a problem: submit it to a judge for a decision; negotiate a deal; flip a coin; go to war. Mediation is one more process that people use to resolve disputes.

Consider the following situations:

• A family sues a doctor and hospital alleging that malpractice occurred when, in the course of the defendants performing surgery on their 12-year-old son for testicular cancer, the procedure became complicated by a hemorrhage and cardiac failure, leaving their child in an irreversible vegetative state.

• A school district, pursuant to federal law, develops an individualized education plan for one of its students who is hearing impaired. The district proposes to provide the student with a sign language interpreter for whichever classes the student would like; the student's parents object to the proposed plan, claiming that their preferred solution is for the district, at its expense, to send their child to a private school that could provide their child with comprehensive support services.

• Hundreds of home owners who suffered partial or complete losses of their home and personal belongings due to a hurricane challenge their insurance company's denial of policy coverage reimbursement, with the insurance company claiming that their loss was caused by water, not wind, and thus not covered under the standard homeowner's insurance policy.

• A consumer completes the purchase of a piece of jewelry valued at $4,500 through an Internet site but then never receives delivery of the item.

• A proposal is made to build a 13-story Islamic Community Center on a vacant lot located two blocks from the World Trade Center site in New York City; the Center will include a mosque. The proposal ignites instant, highly publicized, and often vitriolic rhetoric from politicians, pundits, and concerned citizens in support of or in opposition to the plan.

- A parent contests the attempt by a child welfare agency to remove her three children, all under the age of eight, from her apartment, claiming that the agency's allegation that the children are not safe in her presence is false. A court-appointed guardian ad litem supports the agency's assessment.

If you, as a lawyer, were asked by any of the parties in these situations to represent them and help "solve their problem," how would you proceed? You might explore using mediation. Why?

Mediation is a process in which an independent, neutral intervener assists two or more negotiating parties to identify matters of concern, develop a better understanding of their situation, and, based upon that improved understanding, develop mutually acceptable settlement proposals. The mediation process has four distinctive features: first, the negotiators identify, as broadly as they choose, each issue they want to address; second, the mediator acts as a neutral; third, the mediator has no authority to impose a binding decision on the parties; and fourth, the parties reach agreement — settle the matter — only if every party accepts the proposed settlement terms for each issue. Stated negatively, no one party must agree to an outcome and no mediator, in the absence of party agreement, can impose a decision on the parties. Stated positively, mediation requires individual engagement in and responsibility for resolving disputes.

## 2.  Historical Perspective

Mediation has a distinguished history. In international affairs, political leaders and institutions have long assumed a mediating role to promote negotiations to stop hostilities among warring parties or to create economic development packages among national partners. In Central America and Africa, family elders in indigenous tribal groups assume a mediating role to promote problem solving among disputing community members. In China, mediation has been a primary process for resolving a range of interpersonal controversies. And, in 2008, the European Union mandated its member nations to develop implementing legislation to support using mediation to resolve cross-border civil and commercial disputes.

In the United States, religious, immigrant and trade groups in colonial New England sustained their ethical and religious traditions in part by using mediation to resolve conflicts among group members. More formal use of mediation took hold in the early 20th century with the emergence of union-management relations in the railroad industry, and following World War II, the United States Congress created the Federal Mediation and Conciliation Service (FMCS) to provide mediation services to private sector union and management personnel engaged in collective bargaining.

But mediation's prominence and expanded use emerged in the United States in the late 1960s as part of the "movement" known as "Alternative Dispute Resolution" (ADR). ADR proponents advocated using such dispute resolution procedures as negotiation, mediation, arbitration, elections, summary jury trials — that is, "alternatives" to traditional trials and accompanying litigation processes — to resolve disputes for which the traditional court procedures appeared ill-suited or ineffective.

Since ADR's foundational history so importantly shaped its subsequent trajectory, it is examined more thoroughly below. No one disputes that ADR's basic impact has transformed the nature of today's justice system; mediation — and its dispute resolution partner, negotiation — emerged as the "darling children" of this ADR movement, with policy makers, scholars, and practitioners citing their flexibility and efficiency, along with party control over the outcome, as salient reasons for encouraging, indeed, mandating, their use. Mediation has been used to resolve a broad range of controversies, including neighborhood disputes, divorces, complex business transactions, mass tort claims, intellectual property conflicts, bankruptcies, and controversies resulting from natural disasters.

The dramatic growth and breadth of mediation's use in the United States has served as the basis for recent widespread adaptations internationally. Many U.S. scholars, mediation trainers, and court administrative experts have served as consultants to groups and governments engaged in democracy building and court reform initiatives throughout Europe, Latin America, selected African nations, the Middle East and the Far East.

People interact in a global environment. The background culture, social practices and human values of a particular group importantly influence how its members design and implement their dispute resolution procedures. While it is culturally myopic to believe that one can understand mediation by studying only the United States' experience, there are three compelling reasons that support our almost exclusive focus on it: first, today in the United States, many state and federal courts systematically refer cases to mediation before a party can schedule a trial date; every practicing lawyer in any U.S. court system must know its dynamics in order to effectively represent their clients in it. Second, the U.S. experience in using mediation has itself been shaped by its own rich diversity of participants and perspectives, so important questions regarding how differing values impact the design, fairness, and professionalism of mediation are matters that U.S. mediation policy makers have addressed and that mediation proponents elsewhere find valuable when adapting mediation practices to their own country's setting. And third, there is no question but that much of the material regarding mediation theory and practice, including statutory provisions and court rules, professional codes of conduct, and education and training materials that are studied and adapted by persons in countries other than the United States were written by U.S. policy makers and scholars who were reflecting on the U.S. experience.

What follows, then, is the United States' story. We examine the foundational years of its contemporary history in order to highlight those important issues around which current practice and controversy pivot.

## B.  THE FOUNDATIONAL YEARS OF THE CONTEMPORARY ADR MOVEMENT: 1960s AND 1970s

### 1.  The Challenges

Beginning in the late 1960s, people used mediation to resolve many different conflicts, and the three challenges described below illustrate their striking breadth.

### a.  A Hot City Night

Police officers are conducting a routine patrol of a city street that teems with people in bars and entertainment centers. Young car owners cruise the streets strutting their wheels. Crowds mingle. It is a typical, hot Saturday evening in August in one of the nation's medium-sized urban areas. Suddenly, two Caucasian police officers are involved in a scuffle with three female African American teenagers. Amid screaming and shouting of "pigs" and "honkeys go home," police try to wrestle the three girls to the ground to handcuff and arrest them on charges of drug dealing. They fiercely resist. Police aggressively use billy clubs to subdue them. By the time police officers shove them into the car, the girls' faces are notably bruised and one girl is spitting up blood. Thirty onlookers, all shouting hate slogans at the police, begin to "rock" the police car before it can pull away. The police officers fire warning shots into the air, and then accelerate the car; regrettably, one protester did not jump back in time and is fatally injured.

Pictures of the three arrested women appear in the next day's newspaper. Two have swollen jaws, later determined to be broken. The third has a swollen eye; it is reported that this third individual, a 15-year-old, was six months pregnant but suffered a spontaneous abortion during the prior night's activity.

On Sunday morning, through church sermons and local news programming, the leadership of the African American community action agency calls upon all "decent members of the community" to participate in a mass demonstration in front of police headquarters on the following day, Monday, at 12:00 noon. Their goal is to "protest acts of police brutality" and demand that "the Police Commissioner create an independent citizen review board to investigate the Saturday night incident and all future citizen complaints of police misconduct." The Police Commissioner, in a Sunday night television interview, states that "all citizens have a right to engage in free speech and assembly, but if they are disruptive, they will be arrested." He further noted that the internal affairs division of the police department was already investigating the Saturday night situation and that an independent citizen board was both unnecessary and contrary to guidelines contained in the collective bargaining agreement negotiated between the City and the police officers' union. In a different television interview that night, the family of the fatally injured individual announces it will sue the city and the individual police officers.

You are a lawyer and concerned citizen of the community. You receive a telephone call from the Mayor late Sunday evening. She describes the above scenario and then asks: Can you help us solve these matters? How would you respond?

## b.  Neighborhood Citizenship

As the new academic year began, four seniors who were living in an off-campus apartment for the first time in their college career decided to host a "welcome-back-to-campus" party. The party started on Friday evening and concluded Sunday afternoon! As the hosts described it: "lots of fun — football in the backyard, and food, television, dancing, music, booze, and sex throughout the house."

The party did not endear the students to the Smiths, their neighbors and thirty-three-year residents of the neighborhood. Several times during the weekend, the Smiths visited the house and requested that the noise abate; that effort seemed only to generate the opposite response: enhanced volume. Complaints to the police, as far as the Smiths were concerned, were ineffective. Officers stopped by to talk with the students, but no arrests were made and the noise seemed to increase as soon as the police left.

Similar incidents continued throughout the fall. Tensions were exacerbated by the fact that the Smiths and their college neighbors shared a common driveway. The Smiths often left their car in the middle of the driveway close to their side-entrance door; only when students complained to them that they could not get their cars out of the driveway would the Smiths move their car to their garage in the back.

One morning in mid-October, a student resident bolted from the house to his car, needing to get to the university to take a mid-term exam. The Smith's car was blocking the driveway. The student frantically rang the doorbell. Mr. Smith answered, said that he would move the car as requested, but then took five minutes "to find his car keys." That delay caused the student to arrive at the university close to the beginning of classes, making it difficult for him to find an available parking spot. As a result, he arrived at the mid-term exam 15 minutes after the test had started, and he felt rushed and upset when completing the exam. The following week, he learned that he had failed the exam. Since he was certain that Smith had been slow to find his keys just to harass him, the student hosted "a very loud party for Mr. and Mrs. Smith's benefit" on the following Saturday evening. That night was an uncomfortable, aggravating one for the Smiths.

On the Sunday afternoon following the party, three of the student residents were playing catch with a football on their front lawn. An errant pass landed on Mr. Smith's front lawn. As a student went to retrieve the football, Mr. Smith, standing by his porch with his metal-prong rake, threw the rake at the student, yelling: "get off our lawn." By all accounts, the rake's prongs narrowly missed hitting the student's face.

The next day, Mr. and Mrs. Smith filed a criminal complaint for harassment against their college-student neighbors. The Smiths must prove beyond a reasonable doubt that the defendants, with the requisite mental culpability, committed the acts of which they are accused.

The trial court administrator contacts you, describes the situation, and asks for your advice on "how to handle this — and lots of cases like it that don't seem to belong in court." What is your response?

## c.  Working for Local Government

A group of 275 persons work for the sanitation department of a large city in the northern United States. Their working conditions are multifaceted. In brutally cold weather, workers find it difficult to keep their trucks operating and their hands warm; heavy snowfall complicates picking up garbage containers as well as making each container heavier to lift. During the summer months, their challenge is to beat the heat: hot, humid weather makes sustained physical activity difficult; garbage left on hot sidewalks becomes infested with rodents; and, at a day's end, employees reek of garbage aroma and their clothes are frequently not salvageable.

Workplace operations also involve personal dynamics. Tempers routinely flare among co-workers who approach their tasks with varying degrees of persistence. Supervisors generate animosity and low morale by assigning overtime work to their friends or by rewarding favored employees with desirable vacation schedules. Some employees complain that their health insurance coverage is inadequate, while others assert that intemperate supervisor treatment of employees is grounded in racial bias.

A group of these employees decides that they could improve their working conditions if they addressed their employer with a unified voice, so they seek recognition as a union. The city leaders balk, claiming that such recognition would undercut their sovereign prerogative. The employees respond by engaging in a work stoppage. For one week, employees refuse to collect garbage; it piles up on the streets and avenues of the city and its neighborhoods, generating a concern about citizens' health. News media reports are split: some editorialize that the employees are greedy and should be terminated while others accuse the city administration of promoting sub-optimal workforce productivity by ignoring legitimate concerns regarding working conditions.

The Mayor contacts you, a local leader of the Bar Association, and asks for your thoughts about the most constructive way to proceed. How would you respond?

## 2.  The Grand Experiment

### a.  Diagnosing the Challenge

These challenges, in the 1960s and 1970s, were typically handled in the following ways:

In "A Hot City Night," the physically injured parties or their estates would hire a lawyer to initiate litigation against the appropriate parties for damages; the leaders of the community action agency who wanted to address the policy matters reflected in the alleged acts of police brutality would organize and conduct a mass citizen sit-in at city hall, demanding to talk to the Chief of Police and Mayor about policing practices in their neighborhood — and when these citizens refused to leave city hall after being ordered to do so by the police, they would immediately be arrested for trespassing.

For the disputing neighbors in "Neighborhood Citizenship" situations, one neighbor, as did the Smiths, would file criminal misdemeanor charges against the other neighbor, with the penalties, upon conviction, ranging from fines or probation to a maximum one-year prison sentence. And for situations recounted in "Working for Local Government," public employees would work in partnership with supervisors to secure incremental change on a unit-by-unit basis within individual governmental jurisdictions while simultaneously pursuing new statewide legislation that would make it lawful for public employees to form unions.

These responses are understandable and predictable. And, on one version of political theory, they were correct: the court is the appropriate forum for handling legal controversies between identifiable parties but is not designed to handle all social or political disputes; for those broader controversies, citizens should resort to active participation in the political process, including efforts to achieve legislative reforms.

Although compelling in theory, these responses, in a significant sense, failed to serve the public good. Why? In a nutshell, they prevented persons who were involved in the controversy and had to live with its resolution from discussing directly with one another what mattered to them, and then taking responsibility for developing acceptable and responsive solutions. The leadership of the community action agency wanted to talk with — work with — the police department to strengthen community acceptance of law enforcement activities; it did not want to defend themselves in a criminal court action for allegedly refusing to disperse a lawful order to leave a public space. The senior citizen neighbors wanted the students' parties to be conducted in a way that enabled the students to have fun while also permitting them to enjoy some peace and quiet — they were not interested in, or satisfied by, incarcerating the students for their conduct. And the public employees wanted to discuss working conditions.

But the legal and political systems did not permit these direct dialogues; the responses, instead, prompted those with power to hide behind the law's authority and those without it to resort to using hostile rhetoric toward the very persons with whom they had to strike a resolution.

Using mediation, by contrast, permitted and required those involved in the dispute to meet with one another and, with the assistance of a third-party neutral, engage directly in discussions about issues that mattered to them and work responsibly to develop solutions acceptable to all. Further, mediation program leaders worked diligently to ensure that those persons serving as mediators were capably trained and reflected meaningful racial, ethnic, gender, and economic diversity with whom multiple parties could feel instant empathy and respect. And, those same mediation program leaders, by actively promoting mediation's use to resolve neighborhood conflicts, prison hostage negotiations, environmental disputes, Native American land claims, and other public policy challenges, took mediation outside the courtroom, thereby making it a visible, accessible, timely, and effective forum for resolving controversies in a non-violent manner.

Mediation's use during this formative historical period can be viewed, then, as an experimental, affirmative effort to "take mediation to the fuss" in order to meet this fundamental challenge of stimulating citizens to participate in their justice system. How was this accomplished?

## b.  The Building Blocks of Mediation Services

*1. "Hot Disputes."* To respond to the "hot disputes" — those controversies that simply erupted without warning — there were both public and private sector initiatives. In the 1964 Civil Rights Act, Congress created the Community Relations Service (CRS) of the U.S. Department of Justice. The purpose of CRS is to recruit, train, and deploy persons skilled at developing and advancing the use of conciliation and mediation to resolve controversies in which racial and ethnic tensions pierce the environment. Throughout its important history, CRS personnel have intervened in such matters as the citizen disruptions and chaos surrounding the implementation of the Boston School desegregation orders, the march of the Ku Klux Klan in the predominantly Jewish suburb of Skokie, Illinois, and Native American land claim negotiations; its contemporary services focus on matters ranging from strengthening police community relations to assisting communities address the dynamics of hate crimes.

In the private sector, the Ford Foundation and the William and Flora Hewlett Foundation assumed the leadership role in providing substantial financial support to not-for-profit organizations to experiment with using mediation to resolve these social conflicts. Additionally, many religious and civic organizations as well as community leaders, motivated by a passion to secure civil stability and promote social welfare, seized the initiative to become neutral interveners — "peacemakers" — in their efforts to resolve community tensions. The persons who assumed leadership roles in these early efforts came from strikingly different backgrounds: James Laue, an eminent theologian and activist academician; Theodore Kheel and Ronald Haughton, each nationally prominent labor mediators and arbitrators; Sam Jackson and Willoughby Abner, two African American community and political activists who became the first and second directors of the National Center for Dispute Settlement of the American Arbitration Association; Linda Singer and Michael Lewis, attorneys with a commitment to experimenting with mediation's use in prison settings; Raymond Shonholtz, a former public defender who became founder and first director of the nationally acclaimed, albeit controversial, Community Boards Program in San Francisco; and George Nicolau and Joseph B. Stulberg, each of whom directed regional, then national, comprehensive mediation centers and became widely known as preeminent mediation trainers.

These persons, and others like them, intervened in disputes involving controversies between police departments and citizen groups, environmentalists and builders, school districts and parents, universities and protesting students, and Native Americans and United States citizens. Their involvement was fluid; defining and measuring what constituted "success" was part of the experiment. Results were uneven, though everyone appreciated how significant a resource investment was required to sustain such efforts. What energized such experiments was a common vision that fostering direct engagement of disputing parties to resolve their differences enhanced human dignity, engendered accountability, and unleashed citizen imagination to resolve significant controversies effectively and non-violently.

*2. "Neighborhood Citizenship."* To respond to the need for effectively resolving interpersonal disputes among neighbors and not simply "processing" cases, many court systems created experimental mediation programs, using trained citizen volunteers to mediate such cases. Beginning with the experimental Night Prosecutor's Program in Columbus, Ohio, the Arbitration as an Alternative ("4-A") program of the American Arbitration Association (AAA), and the Citizen Dispute Settlement (CDS) programs in selected Florida counties, mediation proponents and sympathetic judicial personnel offered a new approach and philosophy for servicing the "Neighborhood Citizenship" cases. This alternative approach can be simply described: Bring all the neighbors into a room. Have them meet with one another in the presence of a community resident trained in conducting problem-solving dialogues. Try, through that discussion, to have the parties discuss their concerns, communicate their aspirations to one another, and work out arrangements acceptable to each. If the matter can be resolved in this manner, the case is removed from the (already crowded) court docket. Such programs quickly established dramatic results: settlement rates often exceeded 75% of the cases, and numerous studies provided striking evidence of party satisfaction with both the process and the results.

These court-related mediation experimental programs received critical impetus from Harvard Law Professor Frank Sander's presentation entitled "Varieties of Dispute Processing" at the 1976 Pound Conference; Sanders clarion call was endorsed and amplified by the comments of then-U.S. Supreme Court Chief Justice Warren Burger, who encouraged all lawyers and judicial administrators to resolve disputes. In 1977, the U.S. Department of Justice gave prominence to the early local initiatives by launching experimental Neighborhood Justice Centers (NJC) in Kansas City, Missouri; Atlanta, Georgia; and Los Angeles, California. Though each program adopted a differing design model, all shared two features: using mediation to resolve "neighborhood problems" and using citizens from a broad range of backgrounds and training as volunteer mediators.

*3. Public Employment: State and Local Government.* The most explosive, structured growth in the use of mediation during this historical period occurred in public sector labor relations. Historically, laws in the United States separated the treatment of private enterprise employment practices from those operative when the government is employer; put cryptically, unions of employees in the private sector were acceptable but unions for such public employees as teachers or police officers were not. Social attitudes changed notably during the 1960s, as leading voices articulated workplace concerns that seemed common to all working women and men: workplace safety; wages and benefits levels; policies governing job promotions or layoffs; and the use of dispute resolution systems (notably, arbitration) for efficiently and fairly addressing employer or employee concerns.

Various state legislatures, while recognizing important differences between public and private sector workplace operations, passed laws authorizing public sector employees to join unions and engage in collective bargaining over wages, hours, and other terms and conditions of employment. The statutes created administrative agencies, variously referred to as Public Employment Relations Boards (PERB) or Public Employment Relations Commissions (PERC), to implement collective negotiations among state and local government personnel. To address predictable bargaining deadlocks between employers and employee representatives, these statutes provided for "impasse procedures," including mediation, which parties could use to resolve their disputes. Administrative agencies quickly recruited and trained staff employees to serve as mediators and also developed "panels" of individuals whom administrative agency personnel would appoint to serve as mediators on a per case basis.

## 3. Lessons of the "Grand Experiment"

The concentrated use of mediation during this period importantly shaped the trajectory of its subsequent development. The lessons learned included the following:

a.  *Using mediation could be effective in helping resolve a broad range of controversies.* The experiment established that one of the distinctive strengths of using mediation was that one could deploy it in disputes of varying complexity. Whether the dispute involved two parties or two hundred, one issue or many, or claims of limited or significant public interest, using mediation as the forum for addressing them was viable.

b.  *Mediation was efficient.* In most settings, using mediation was more efficient than available alternatives on such key measures as time, economic resources, emotional costs, and compliance with the outcomes.

c.  *The "value-add" of mediation was predicated on mediator neutrality.* Though many persons were skeptical that controversies could be resolved without there being someone "with authority" to decide the matter, disputing parties and policy makers appeared willing to try or mandate mediation because they viewed it as a "low-risk" option: no mediator could impose an outcome and the potential existed that the parties might actually resolve their dispute. Mediator neutrality strengthened party confidence in the integrity of the process by reinforcing the truth that the mediator was not an "agent of the system."

d.  *Mediator competence was broadly defined.* History demonstrated that persons of multiple backgrounds and training capably served as mediators. Substantive expertise was broadly defined; racial and ethnic diversity created access to multiple disputants, and diverse life experiences fostered credibility. Since non-lawyers, significantly more so than lawyers, advocated mediation's use and were involved in its implementation during this period, many lawyers, not without justification, initially perceived the "mediation movement" as being an anti-lawyer movement.

e.  *Mediation, as a subject matter of knowledge, was multidisciplinary.* Dispute resolution scholarship, from World War II through the 1970s, focused primarily on the dynamics of collective bargaining, mediation, and arbitration involving private sector unions and management. Scholars trained as economists, political scientists, and psychologists conducted that scholarship, while legal scholars focused primarily on the interplay between the courts and the arbitration process. With mediation's broad-based use during these foundational years, scholars trained in international relations, peace studies, communication theory, urban planning, environmental science, law, and business joined those from the traditional disciplines.

f.  *Funding mediation services was problematic.* Providing mediation services required resources — minimally, of time and talent of the mediator or provider agency. Most mediation programs were financially supported by public or private grants, with the Law Enforcement Assistance Administration (LEAA) of the U.S. Department of Justice being the primary provider for court-annexed mediation programs and the Ford Foundation and Hewlett Foundation supporting private sector initiatives. The grants, appropriately, were time-limited; required evaluative components; and were disbursed to existing entities, such as courts or not-for-profit agencies that were positioned to design and implement conflict resolution services. Three features shaped these grants: first, the monies supported organizational professional staff and affiliated personnel to provide mediation services without charge to the disputing parties; second, not-for-profit agency personnel had discretion, in implementing direct service delivery, to use some monies to support party participation in mediation, ranging from covering their transportation or housing expenses to providing meals during the negotiations; and third, all mediation services for court-annexed programs servicing the "neighborhood case" or "minor dispute" were provided on a volunteer basis by community residents. The funding philosophy of both the governmental and philanthropic organizations was targeted to short-term support, theorizing, "If the program is valued by the community it serves, then the locality would develop and provide its own funding sources to sustain it." For many dispute resolution programs, that transition would prove illusory.

g.  *Success — and measuring success — varied.* Measuring success or failure was a challenge. Program grant recipients had understandable motives for professing success, but such rhetorical claims as "the parties, by participating in an effective problem-solving process, will be better able to resolve future conflicts by themselves" remained uncorroborated. Social scientists were challenged to develop credible evaluation protocols to assess how a particular program performed and how it compared with other dispute resolution systems: for example, was the resolution of three of five issues in mediation a success or failure? Was an agreed upon resolution by parties the only relevant measure for success or failure? How could one compare the quality of mediated outcomes with court-adjudicated outcomes? And, particularly for agencies servicing "the hot disputes," it was problematic to define what constituted a "case," let alone assess whether or not it was successfully resolved.

h.  *Professionalism.* There were no existing professional organizations for mediators that served as a forum for establishing codes of conduct, identifying best practices, or establishing minimum competencies. The National Academy of Arbitrators had been established as a preeminent professional organization for private sector labor arbitrators, but there was no comparable professional organization for mediators. The Society of Professionals in Dispute Resolution (SPIDR) was created in 1974 to meet that need. Its early membership consisted primarily of mediators working in the rapidly expanding environment of public sector labor relations;

Robert Helsby, SPIDR's first president, was the Chair of New York State's Public Employment Relations Board. But persons serving as mediators in social policy and court-annexed programs were eligible for membership as well.

In 1977, stemming from the considerable excitement and publicity surrounding the Pound Conference of the previous year, the American Bar Association created a Special Committee to study the growth of court-annexed citizen dispute settlement programs. Its first chair, Talbot D'Alemberte, later to be President of the ABA, helped shape the Committee and its staff to be a comprehensive, national resource for providing materials and technical assistance to lawyers, judges, and court personnel interested in developing program initiatives in this area.

## C. MEDIATION'S GROWTH AND IMPACT ON THE JUSTICE SYSTEM

### 1. Introduction

During the 1980s, mediation's use would accelerate onto a flight path that would make its presence pervasive in the judicial system and, in more limited fashion, among federal government agencies. By the decade's end, mediation would be regularly used to resolve a broad range of conflicts, including family problems, disputes over disaster relief claims, intellectual property disputes, bankruptcy claims, tax challenges, and mortgage foreclosure controversies; and, with increasing regularity, mediation transnational commercial disputes or post-war relief controversies. No lawyer can conduct a traditional law practice today without counseling clients about mediation or representing them in a mediation conference. The practice of mediation has become more professionalized; for some individuals, the prospect of developing a career as a mediator is now viable. And the study of mediation has garnered broad-based academic research interest.

### 2. Practice

#### a. The Rise or Decline of the Dominant Practice Areas of the Foundational Years

The decade of the 1980s developed in significantly different ways for each of the three practice areas that dominated the foundational years. Most mediation initiatives survived and transformed, but others withered.

For *Public Sector Labor Relations*, as noted previously, many legislatures passed statutes granting targeted public employees the right to form and join unions and engage in collective bargaining. The statutory framework created administrative agencies to administer activities and provide, among other things, mediation services to resolve bargaining impasses. Such agencies at the state and local government level are now conventional elements of government service.

Similarly, efforts to stabilize mediation's use for handling *Neighborhood Citizenship* cases received strong judicial endorsement; some state legislatures passed statutes providing for mediation's use and allocated funding to judicial budgets or not-for-profit organizations to sustain these programs; Colorado, New York, and Florida were among the jurisdictions to lead this movement. Variously referred to as Neighborhood Justice Centers, Citizen Dispute Settlement programs, or Community Dispute Resolution Centers, these programs now number more than 400 throughout the country; all retain the feature of using mediation with volunteer citizens to handle these disputes.

But sustained financial support for mediation of community disputes — "hot disputes" — has largely disappeared. Although CRS remains intact, mediation experiments funded through private foundation grants receded. In recent times, there have been important initiatives by such not-for-profit organizations as the Public Conversation Project and Deliberative Democracy to organize and promote public dialogue and "deliberation" about controversial public policy issues, such as health care practices or immigration law reform, but these efforts tend not to be organized to resolve concrete disputes among identifiable stakeholders.

## 3.    Expanded Areas of Practice

### a.    Areas of Emerging and Expansive Growth

Not all mediation experiments from the Foundation years survived, but a breathtaking range of new practice areas have emerged since the 1980s. These new practice areas have accelerated into the present time. Here is a sample.

*1. Public Disputes.* Public regulatory agencies have found themselves challenged to resolve differences among the multiple stakeholders. Some federal government agencies have changed its administrative "publish and comment" procedure for developing regulations to a process entitled Regulatory Negotiation ("reg-neg"); in the "reg-neg" process, the agency and its private sector stakeholders hire a private mediator to facilitate their collective negotiations of acceptable rules. Similar activity at the state level has been more episodic: the Office of Dispute Resolution in the State of New Jersey, located within the Department of the Public Advocate, operates in a manner similar to CRS, whereas Minnesota, through a statutory scheme, provides for mediation services to resolve land-use disputes.

*2. Corporate Initiatives.* The shifting economic climate continually triggers private sector initiatives that are designed to enable a company to compete effectively in a rapidly developing global economy; many businesses welcome any effort to improve total quality management, including those targeted at the effective, efficient, and satisfactory resolution of disputes involving customers, suppliers, or employees. Large organizations, such as insurance companies, have developed and implemented mediation programs to handle a variety of customer complaints. General counsel of large corporations have publicly subscribed to the Center for Public Resource's "Pledge" to explore using alternative dispute resolution procedures, including mediation, to resolve their business and legal controversies. Trade and professional organizations within the construction industry, a prominent user of arbitration processes, have developed and encouraged the use of mediation as a "pre-arbitration" step to resolve disputes arising from the construction of residential and commercial projects.

These initiatives, though tentative at first, are now widespread.

The most significant growth for mediation activity, particularly during the 1980s, targeted individual cases that arose in one of three general categories: education, the family, and, ultimately, general civil litigation.

*3. Mediation in Education.* In 1973, Congress passed the Rehabilitation Act. It required school districts to develop individualized educational plans (IEPs) for each student certified to be in need of special services, with the overall goal of integrating that student into the normal tempo of school life to the maximum feasible extent. The statutory framework required that the district's proposed plan be acceptable to the student's parents. If the parties could not agree to a plan, the statute encouraged them to use mediation to resolve their differences. While some school districts hired lawyers to serve as mediators, others trained school-based staff to mediate these situations. Taking a different tack, states such as Massachusetts hired full-time staff mediators into their education department to service these controversies.

While mediation of special education cases was developing with increasing visibility, mediation proponents also entered the school system via a different route.

A typical day in a middle school or high school often involves such incidents as students getting into a hallway fight because one student angrily threatened another for not having returned his iPod. Or, more provocatively, in response to a "bully" who mercilessly teased a new student about her physical appearance, the new student's brother might confront the "bully" on the playground and attempt to gain revenge by physically attacking him. How does a school effectively address such matters? A common response was to suspend the offending students, typically for a minimum five-day period; the obvious drawback to that response was that the parent or parents of those students were often working so the student's non-school suspensions day were unsupervised, leaving the dispute unresolved and often more pronounced. That environment led mediation advocates to explore using mediation in innovative ways.

Community Boards (San Francisco) and Safe Horizon (New York City) developed programs in which they trained high school students to become mediators; these student mediators, under supervised conditions, mediated cases involving students — their "peers" — who had been involved in disruptive behavior. The mediation process became a safety valve for the school: it was an affirmative response for dealing with student conflicts, a viable alternative to suspension, and a learning process for all participants. While questions have surfaced regarding the focus and effectiveness of peer mediation programs, their presence today is ubiquitous in middle schools and high schools in the United States.

*4. Family Mediation.* Mediation is widely used to resolve disputes involving families in at least three distinct ways.

Divorce mediation is now a profession; that was not true in 1980. To obtain a civil divorce in the United States, parties must fulfill the statutory requirements of a particular state's jurisdiction. Even though the widespread presence of "no-fault" divorce makes securing a divorce less onerous, the divorcing couple must still resolve matters relating to the division of real and personal property, payment of debts, and matters such as pension benefits, health care coverage, spousal and child financial support, and, where appropriate, parenting arrangements. As the divorce rate in the United States increased, the experience of securing a legal divorce became more visibly excruciating. Stereotypically, clients reported that after each had retained a lawyer, direct discussion between them ceased. As lawyers communicated offers and counteroffers, the estranged partners developed increasingly bitter pictures of how their spouse was being selfish, manipulative, or mean. If the parties contested the proposed arrangements and submitted their controversy to a judge for adjudication, parties frequently perceived the judicial decision to be neither fair nor congruent with their own values. In addition to the process for securing a legal divorce being financially and psychologically costly, those burdens escalated during the post-divorce period that was frequently checkered by one party petitioning the court to secure or contest compliance with various provisions of the divorce decree. And the impact of this entire process on the psychological health of the affected children remained troublesome.

This adversarial climate paralleled those social controversies from the foundational period: participants felt that legal arguments prevented them from discussing their central concerns; resolutions were not crafted to meet the parties' particular circumstances; and those individuals who had to live with the outcome were removed from important aspects of the negotiating and decision-making process. Mediation proponents cautiously urged its experimental use to resolve these matters. The practice grew in both the public and private spheres.

The Association of Family and Conciliation Courts (AFCC), was originally organized in California by a group of court employees who were trained as mental health professionals and had responsibility, within the California statutory framework, for protecting the welfare of children whose parents were seeking a legal divorce; to the extent possible, their charge was also to explore with the divorcing couple the possibility or desirability of reconciliation. As the divorce rate became more ubiquitous, counselors expanded their focus to include helping family members resolve financial and parenting issues in a manner that enabled each affected party to retain maximum dignity, strength, and respect as they moved on to their separate lives. That new dimension quickly led AFCC members to embrace a mediation model for assisting families. AFCC, expanding into a national organization of practitioners, court personnel, and scholars, assumed a leadership role in advancing this emerging field; individuals, including Jay Folberg and Alison Taylor, contributed early scholarship to this emerging field, and AFCC triggered the development of statements of best practices, ethical codes of conduct, and continuing research. From a private-provider perspective, O.J. Coogler, based in Atlanta, Georgia, was the first person to design and use a "structured mediation process" for handling divorces. Leaders of the AAA soon developed its Family Mediation programs. Dr. John Haynes, a psychologist, encouraged its development and use by practicing mental health professionals. All persons aligned with these initiatives believed that using mediation to assist parties seeking a divorce would be a more attractive option than the default forum. Private fee-paying practices developed, representing the first steps into a new financing model for the delivery of mediation services.

Mediation, especially under court sponsorship, has been used to address other recurring cases involving family members. Two areas are prominent. The first targets the parent-child relationship that is riddled with tension and complexity, leading the parent to seek court assistance to supervise their child. A parent, for example, might disapprove her teenage child's boyfriend or girlfriend, so the parent imposes rules prohibiting their socializing or at least limiting it to before particular curfew hours. The child, protesting the rule, leaves the house and moves in with a friend — or simply lives on the street. A parent seeks court assistance to structure a parent-child relationship that attempts to stabilize the relationship; many courts have created mediation programs to address these matters (the cases often being referred to as PINS (Persons in Need of Supervision) or CHINS (Children in Need of Supervision) cases).

But parents themselves might behave in way that endangers their child's well being. A parent's abuse of drug or alcohol or experiencing depression might trigger conduct that jeopardizes their child's safety. A public agency charged with protecting children welfare must secure court assistance to protect the child, including their removal from the parent's home; multiple participants, including lawyers, guardian *ad litem*, and others meet in a "family conference" setting to attempt to work out sustainable living arrangements.

5. *Civil Lawsuits with Represented Parties.* Given the expanded, though targeted use of mediation in court-related settings, it was only a matter of time until parties involved in virtually any civil action filed in court would be encouraged or required to use mediation. And that dam broke in Florida in 1988.

By 1988, multiple mediation initiatives dotted the Florida landscape: citizen dispute settlement programs; family and divorce mediation; peer mediation; consumer mediation; and public policy mediation. In 1988, the legislature assumed a leadership role in promulgating legislation that authorized civil trial court judges to promote pre-trial settlement by referring almost any civil court filing to mediation. The message was clarion: any case, large or small, "simple" or "complex," "important" or "unimportant," might be resolved through mediated negotiations. Disputes involving breach of contract, business dissolutions, catastrophic personal injuries, medical malpractice, construction projects, or trust and estates were all eligible for mediation referral. The Florida Supreme Court was responsible for implementing the statute. It created a committee comprised of practicing lawyers, judges, mediators, and court administrators and charged it with creating proposed rules and standards for realizing the statute's promise. Professor James Alfini, then of Florida State University School of Law, together with Michael Bridenback and Sharon Press, then Director and Associate Director of the Dispute Resolution Center of the Florida Supreme Court, served as the Court and Committee's technical faculty and staff to design and implement this unprecedented initiative. The committee worked rapidly, and, in consultation with a broad range of professionals from across the nation, developed its governing framework for implementation. That framework included the following features, several of which remain controversial:

    a.    *Eligible Cases.* With very limited exceptions, a trial court judge can refer any civil case to mediation.

b.  *Referral Method.* Mandating party participation in mediation does not constitute a denial of a party's state constitutional right to a jury trial. If a trial judge orders a case to mediation, the burden shifts to the party seeking an exemption to file a motion setting forth the grounds as to why mediation for that particular case is ill-suited or unwarranted.

c.  *Mediator Qualifications.* Parties and their counsel may select whomever they wish as their mediator as long as they do so within 10 days of the court's referral to mediation. Thereafter, the court appoints a mediator from a pool of court-certified mediators. To become a court-certified mediator, a person must meet those standards that the Florida Supreme Court believes will ensure competent, quality mediation practice. Those standards, having evolved over time, now include the following requirements:

To be a Florida court-certified mediator, an individual must successfully complete a Florida Supreme Court certified mediation skills training program of the type for which he or she is seeking certification. Persons serving as mediators for county court (case below $15,000 in dispute) and small claims cases must complete a minimum of 20 instructional hours; those mediating family matters, civil cases involving claims of $15,000 or greater, and dependency cases (abuse and neglect) must complete 40 hours of training in each area; those mediating appellate cases must already be certified as a circuit, family, or dependency mediator and complete an additional seven hours of mediation training. In addition to this training, each applicant (except for appellate mediators) must observe mediation or conduct supervised mediations in a mentorship component. Finally, for each certification area, except county, a person must obtain a minimum number of "points" accrued via education training and mediation experience. *See* Appendix E.

d.  *Fees.* For cases involving claims below a prescribed dollar amount, mediators generally provide their service on a volunteer basis. For family cases and larger civil cases, mediators can establish their own fee structure, subject to court approval of those fees as "reasonable fees." The standard practice is to charge an hourly rate.

e.  *Program Administration.* State and local court offices supervise, coordinate, and monitor the delivery of mediation services. For family and dependency cases involving parties with low to modest incomes, court personnel or contract mediators paid by the court conduct the mediation hearings. For standard civil court cases that are mediated by a mediator in private practice, no public reporting requirements exist and the competitive market place determines successful and unsuccessful mediator practices.

Within 10 years of operation, Florida reported that more than 3,000 persons had completed the required training programs and been certified as mediators, and it also reported that more than 125,000 mediation cases were conducted annually. The legal culture in Florida embraced its use, routinely using mediation to resolve cases ranging from smaller personal injury and breach of contract cases to catastrophic torts, medical malpractice claims, and multi-party construction project disputes.

The Florida experience, with suitable adjustments, has been replicated in multiple state court systems. This expanding awareness and support has led court-administrators and appropriate external stakeholders, in some jurisdictions, to design and implement a broad range of mediation initiatives connected to court services. Victim Offender Reconciliation Programs, for example, bring together the crime victim and perpetrator to discuss ways of engaging in reconciliation initiatives; students who are inexcusably absent from school now meet in mediation sessions with parents, school counselors, social workers, and teachers to develop positive, realistic steps to correct the problem; family conferencing, referenced previously, is yet another development.

In sharp contrast to the use of mediation during the Foundational years, this explosive growth for court-connected cases has been strongly supported and guided by judges, Bar association personnel, and many private legal practitioners. That participation has contributed importantly not only to process acceptability but also to the development of full-time private mediation practices for some lawyers.

Florida's approach has served as an important benchmark against which other state initiatives have been measured. Its comprehensive use of mediation for all matters of court-connected cases raised policy and practice challenges not even envisioned during the Foundational years. These matters include such questions as:

*i.* If all mediation sessions are conducted in a confidential setting, how is the public to learn about, and gain confidence in, this segment of the justice system?

*ii.* If a court system effectively mandates parties to use mediation before parties can go to trial, what does the court do to ensure that parties have qualified mediators to serve them?

*iii.* How do persons who are trained in one profession — law or mental health — simultaneously perform their mediating role and maintain fidelity to possibly competing norms of professional responsibility? For example, how does a lawyer serving as mediator conduct herself so as not to violate the lawyer's professional prohibition against representing parties with conflicting interests? How does the mental health professional mediate issues involving property division or pension benefits without transgressing the prohibition against practicing law without a license?

*iv.* While lawyers represent parties in many cases that go to mediation, are special rules or protections required in mediation to protect the pro se (unrepresented) party?

*v.* Does the practice of charging fees for service, particularly fees based on an hourly rate, undermine the public's access to, or confidence in, the integrity of the mediation process?

*vi.* If the parties fail to reach resolution in mediation and proceed to trial, is it appropriate for the judge to ask the mediator for his or her insights about the case so that judicial time and resources can be effectively utilized?

*vii.* What standards can court personnel use to assess the quality of a mediator's performance other than knowing whether or not the case was resolved in mediation?

*viii.* If parties and their counsel select their mediator based on that mediator's expertise and experience, will they want — or demand — that the mediator use her expertise to recommend appropriate outcomes rather than facilitate the development of party-acceptable solutions?

*ix.* What impact will various qualifications for serving as a mediator have on the diversity of persons serving as mediators?

*x.* What impact will the presence of "repeat players" in the mediation process, such as insurance companies or large employers, have on the fairness of the process?

As multiple state court systems incorporate mediation referrals into its case processing procedure, there has been continued experimentation as to how each system answers these and related questions.

*6. Expanding Practice Areas.* While mediating civil trial cases in various state judicial systems has become widespread, the expanding use of mediation in three other sectors — the Federal judiciary; the Internet; and court systems in foreign jurisdictions — warrant discussion.

a.    *Federal Courts.* The U.S. federal government, as noted previously, legitimized and endorsed the use of mediation when it created federal processes for using mediation to resolve bargaining impasses in the transportation and private business sectors. It reaffirmed and expanded its public policy commitment by creating and funding the Community Relations Service of the U.S. Department of Justice.

But the commitment of the federal government to use mediation within the federal court system or throughout the executive agencies was, until the 1990s, subdued. That has now changed. In 1990, Congress passed two laws affecting the use of alternative dispute resolution processes in federal agencies. The Negotiated Rulemaking Act made permanent the experimental uses of the "Reg-Neg" process referenced above. The Act establishes a framework whereby a federal government agency responsible for issuing various rules (e.g., the Environmental Protection Agency or the Federal Communications Commission) could engage a neutral third-party intervener (mediator) to facilitate rule development. Though the use of the "Reg-Neg" process has been uneven, it continues.

Congress also passed the Administrative Dispute Resolution Act in 1990. The Act authorizes and encourages each federal agency to consider using various dispute resolution processes, including mediation, to resolve any of the multiple conflicts that arise in the course of their work, from intra-agency controversies to agency/public interactions. This initiative received additional support from Executive Orders by Presidents George H.W. Bush (1991) and Bill Clinton (1998), directing or encouraging agencies and their litigation counsel to explore various resolution procedures in addition to traditional litigation. Currently, many federal agencies require the agency and its sub-contractors to use mediation as a first step in resolving alleged contractual breaches in service delivery.

With the passage of the Civil Justice Reform Act of 1990 and the Alternative Dispute Resolution Act in 1998, Congress aligned the federal district courts with the ADR movement. Unlike the state court initiatives which encouraged or mandated the use of mediation, the federal statutory framework required federal district courts to establish a more general ADR program; mediation, advisory arbitration, mini-trials, or summary jury trials were among possible processes that district courts could make available to litigants. The 1998 Act also mandated that litigants consider using ADR processes at an appropriate time. Several district courts quickly adopted advisory arbitration programs; soon thereafter, selected district courts adopted experimental mediation programs using volunteer attorneys as mediators. One important, unusual twist that first developed in the federal sector, and is now replicated in many state court systems, is the use of mediation within the federal circuit courts of appeal; a designated court employee serves as a full-time mediator of cases that are on appeal from the trial court's initial case disposition, conducting some mediation conferences in person and others by telephone.

b.    *The Internet.* Technology has impacted the context in which mediation is used and the forms in which it is practiced. While digital telephones, fax machines, and cable television bands permit rapid communication or dialogue among multiple parties, the Internet revolution increases that capacity in ways not yet fully explored. Electronic mail, chat rooms, mobile communication apparatus, and videoconferencing permit people to communicate from virtually anywhere in the world. These tools secure multiple economic efficiencies, including minimizing the challenge of finding mutually acceptable meeting dates, eliminating delays in document transmissions, and reducing travel costs. They also facilitate broad-based community participation in discussing policy matters. In the aftermath of Hurricane Katrina, for example, many "public meetings" about issues related to the reopening of public schools, including student school assignments, teacher appointments, and resumption of school transportation services, took place through facilitated meetings supported by videoconferencing and other technologies. Their participants included New Orleans public school officials, Louisiana political and governmental leaders, and concerned parents who participated from their forced relocation residences in Houston, Texas.

But Internet technology also promises to take the need for dispute resolution — and possibly mediation — into uncharted waters. The dispute resolution program developed and used by eBay, for instance, invites parties to a consumer-merchant dispute to submit their controversy to resolution using mediation, with all communication conducted entirely via the computer. Parties identify their concerns, advance proposed solutions, and then, through guided questioning and discussion by a mediator, consider possible outcomes; if none are acceptable, the mediator proposes settlement terms based on what she considers to be a fair outcome. While this approach retains the public structure of a mediation conversation, it exhibits distinctive differences, including the parties' concentrated focus on resolving only financial claims and the design of the electronic program so that it shifts the mediator's role into one of a mediator/advisory arbitrator role. What impact this model will have on the more traditional approach used in in-person mediation conferences remains unanswered. At the international level, the United Nations Commission on International Trade Law (UNCITRAL) established a working group in 2011 to develop rules and practices to govern online dispute resolution for cross-border electronic commercial transactions. The Working Group's proposed rules, published in August 2012 for public discussion and further analysis, apply only to those cross-border commercial disputes that are business-to-business or business-to-consumer and that are low value and high-volume. The rules are designed to govern the procedural aspects of whichever dispute resolution process, including mediation, the parties choose to use.

c.   *Mediation in a Global Environment.* The use of mediation in multiple international settings is expanding. Court systems in Argentina and Brazil are aggressively developing and implementing mediation programs. Courts in Great Britain systematically support its use to resolve family and civil matters. Each European Union member nation, pursuant to the 2008 EU Directive that supports the use of mediation to resolve trans-border commercial disputes, is promulgating implementing legislation. And, much like responding to the "hot disputes" in our Foundational years, NGOs such as Partners for Democratic Change and Mediators Without Borders have developed the infrastructure for training and supporting indigenous mediators to assist their fellow citizens in resolving broad-based social controversies, ranging from disputes involving Roma (Gypsy) relocation practices to governmental budget allocation decisions.

In summary, the mediation process is a significant component of the fabric of a 21st century justice system in which lawyers participate. That factor requires accountability.

## 4.   Promoting Quality Practice

Mediation practitioners, policymakers, and the court systems supporting its use are obligated to deliver a professional, quality service; program users expect no less. Since mediation practice does not require a license, policy makers and practitioners have shaped professional development using multiple strategies.

Many court systems have adopted minimum qualifications regarding training and development for persons who seek to be appointed to a court roster of mediators. Most require a mediator to participate in a court-approved intensive basic mediator performance-skill training program and in continuing mediator education programs; the program framework that Florida developed has become the standard model. In addition to completing a basic mediation skills training program, some courts have imposed professional training qualifications to mediate particular kinds of cases, such as being a licensed attorney in that state to mediate complex civil litigation or having received advanced graduate training in a helping profession to mediate matrimonial cases.

Practitioners and policy makers have created professional organizations to encourage practitioner dialogue, advanced training, and public education. As noted previously, AFCC was established in 1963; SPIDR was created in 1974. The Academy of Family Mediators (AFM) was formed to monitor and establish performance standards for mediating family disputes. The National Association for Mediators in Education (NAME) (later re-named Conflict Resolution Education Network (CRENet)) was created for practitioners in educational programs. In 2001, SPIDR, AFM, and CRENet merged to form the Association for Conflict Resolution (ACR), importantly providing a home for dispute resolvers from all disciplines. In addition to these professional organizations, many state supreme courts have established advisory committees of lawyers, judges, court personnel, and community leaders to recommend the development of appropriate mediation program rules and standards of professional conduct. Provider organizations, such as the American Arbitration Association and, later, CPR (officially known as International Institute for Conflict Prevention and Resolution) and JAMS (Judicial Arbitration and Mediation Services) offer training and education programs about mediation to the business and legal community. Community Dispute Resolution Center Program Directors formed their own statewide organizations to share information and adopt strategies to ensure program growth and quality, and community dispute resolution centers themselves created the National Association for Community Mediation (NAFCM). Finally, Bar Associations at the local, state, and national levels have established committees to explore and monitor mediation's growth in their respective jurisdictions. In less than 20 years, the ABA organizational commitment grew from its initial status as a Special Committee on the Resolution of Minor Disputes to become the Section on Dispute Resolution Section with more than 19,000 members. All of these organizations, and other "subject-specific" groups, sponsor annual conferences, publish magazines, support studies, and engage in education initiatives to advance public understanding of the mediation process.

Importantly, these professional organizations often collaborate on joint initiatives. A striking example of such partnership was the development of the Model Standards of Conduct for Mediators (*see* Appendix A). The three major national professional organizations — the American Arbitration Association, the American Bar Association's Section on Dispute Resolution, and the Association for Conflict Resolution — partnered, first in 1994 and then again in 2005, to draft, discuss, and adopt the governing standards of ethical conduct for mediation practice. Professor Sharon Press served as one of the ACR Representatives to the 2005 Committee, and Professor James Alfini served as one of the ABA Representatives to the 1994 Committee. Professor Joseph Stulberg served as the 2005 Committee's Reporter. These Standards have served as the model ethical code not only for multiple state court systems and private organizations in the U.S. but also for the European Union's Code of Conduct for Mediators. Another example of significant professional partnership, though more loosely structured, was the collaborative participation of member representatives in the joint project with the National Conference of Commissioners on Uniform State Laws (NCCUSL) to develop the Uniform Mediation Act (*see* Appendix F). *Mediation: Law, Policy, and Practice*, the primary treatise on mediation reported in 1997 that more than 2,200 statutes and court rules referenced "mediation." That situation posed important challenges for lawyers practicing across state jurisdictions who had to know which law governed their mediation process and whether different states approached mediation with a consistent vision. In an attempt to provide clarity and consistency to these and other challenges, NCCUSL and the American Bar Association's Section on Dispute Resolution initiated in 1997 an unprecedented partnership to develop a Uniform Mediation Act. The final Act, developed through multiple public sessions and public comment over a four-year period, was adopted by NCCUSL in July 2001. Amended in 2003 to address matters involving international controversies, the Uniform Mediation Act (UMA) and its remarkable reporter's notes prepared by Professor Nancy H. Rogers constitute an important benchmark in the development of law, policy, and practice in mediation.

## 5.   Scholarship

Scholarship on mediation bears two distinctive features: first, in significant ways, scholarship has transformed practice; second, the scholarly home disciplines for studying mediation have shifted significantly over a 40-year period. These features emerged in three distinct ways.

### a.   Theory Centers

Beginning in the 1980s, the William and Flora Hewlett Foundation provided leadership and financial support to create Theory Centers in Dispute Resolution; it wanted to advance the knowledge of the dispute resolution field beyond "sharing experiences" to a more nuanced understanding of its basic structures and values. The Foundation provided financial support to a limited number of universities at which there were multidisciplinary groups of scholars — from law, political science, economics, psychology, philosophy, industrial relations, organizational behavior, communication, urban planning, and international relations — who were interested in studying the design and use of dispute resolution processes in multiple settings. This interdisciplinary commitment was distinctive; coincidentally, many of the persons engaged in this scholarship were also active practitioners.

The Program on Negotiation (PON), a consortium of faculty from Harvard University, Massachusetts Institute of Technology, and Tufts University, was created with this Hewlett Foundation support and remains, perhaps, its best known center. Other universities among the initial Theory Centers were Northwestern University (based at its Kellogg Business School), Stanford University, the University of Michigan, and George Mason University.

PON was located administratively at Harvard Law School, where pre-eminent professors Roger Fisher and Frank E.A. Sander were engaged in path-breaking scholarly work. Among the early work products supported by PON was *Getting to Yes* by Roger Fisher and William Ury; *The Art and Science of Negotiation* by

Howard Raiffa; *The Manager as Negotiator* by David Lax and James Sebenius; *Getting Disputes Resolved* by Jeanne Brett and Stephen Goldberg, and *When Talk Works* by Deborah Kolb. Mediator practitioners could no longer complain that there were no "standard" materials in the field that they should read.

The Hewlett Foundation ultimately created and sustained 18 university Theory Centers. The Centers' work importantly increased the visibility and academic credibility of this scholarly field. Although the Foundation's financial support for this initiative concluded in December 2004, some collaborations still operate with independent revenue sources. While Theory Centers provided important impetus for scholarship, they were not its only source.

## b.  Legal Scholarship

In the years following the 1976 Pound Conference, legal scholars and law schools became active, significant contributors to the study and practice of the emerging field of dispute resolution. In 1984, the Ohio State University Moritz College of Law and the Benjamin Cardozo School of Law implemented the nation's first clinical mediation programs using law students as mediators to resolve neighborhood citizenship disputes and small claims court cases. The first law school courses in dispute resolution, and their accompanying casebooks, emerged in the middle 1980s. And in the late 1980s, the faculty at the University of Missouri-Columbia School of Law, led by Professor Leonard Riskin, developed a broad-based curriculum in which materials for studying ADR processes were introduced into each course of the traditional first-year curriculum.

Two law reviews devoted exclusively to dispute resolution scholarship were launched during the 1980s: *The Journal of Dispute Resolution* was started at the University of Missouri-Columbia School of Law, and *The Ohio State Journal on Dispute Resolution* was published at the Ohio State Moritz College of Law. Together with PON's *Negotiation Journal* and AFM's *Mediation Quarterly*, these journals became the focused, dedicated resources for scholarship and practice commentary. Today the number of ADR specialty journals operating at law schools has significantly increased.

Dispute resolution scholarship, whether through law review articles or books, has significantly shaped mediation theory and practice. Three contributions, each excerpted in this text, are illustrative. In 1994, Professor Leonard Riskin wrote a short article entitled, *Understanding Mediators' Orientations, Strategies, and Techniques: A Grid for the Perplexed* (*see* Chapter 4). In it, he described mediator orientations on one dimension as being either "facilitative" or "evaluative." Those terms instantly became the established vocabulary to describe or criticize particular mediator conduct, and it became a crucial distinction in the development of various mediator behavior ethical codes and ethical opinions. Similarly, in 1994, Professor Robert A. Baruch Bush, a law professor, and Professor Joseph Folger, a professor of communication, published their celebrated book, *The Promise of Mediation* (*see* Chapter 4). In it, they advanced a comprehensive account of mediation theory and practice that they labeled, Transformative Mediation. That conception differs on several important theoretical principles and practice strategies from those consti-tuting either the "evaluative" or "facilitative" approach denoted in Riskin's terminology, and it has emerged as a distinct approach to mediation practice; the U.S. Postal Service, among the nation's largest employers, adopted the Transformative Mediation framework and training materials when implementing its mediation program to address internal employment discrimination claims. Finally, Professor Lawrence Susskind, a professor of urban planning at Massachusetts Institute of Technology and active mediator of environmental disputes, wrote a compelling article for the *Vermont Law Review* in which he asserted that mediators of environmental disputes had a ethical duty to represent the interests of persons affected by the decision but who did not participate in the negotiations; Professor Stulberg, also an active mediator practitioner, wrote a rebuttal to Susskind, arguing that a mediator's neutrality regarding outcomes was the defining value of the mediator's role (*see* Chapter 4). That debate has shaped professional discussion, ethical codes, and mediator practice since 1981.

Recent scholarly contributions to this field, such as Professors Hal Abramson's *Mediation Representation: Advocating a Creative Problem-Solving Process*, Robert Mnookin's *Beyond Winning: Negotiating to Create Value in Deals and Disputes*, Nancy H. Rogers's *Designing Process and Systems for Managing Disputes*, and Ellen Waldman's *Ethics: Cases and Commentaries* — continue to share this important interest in grounding scholarly analysis to applied settings.

### c.  Degree Programs

The Foundational Years galvanized interest in the study and practice of alternative dispute resolution processes. The development of university M.A. and Ph.D. degree programs in conflict resolution began in the 1980s and many universities created various certificate programs in dispute resolution at the undergraduate, graduate, and professional school levels. This development was important for several reasons: first, it signaled the traditional academic community's growing acceptance and legitimacy of this subject matter as a scholarly discipline. Second, these programs represented a distinctive shift from the traditional academic home for dispute resolution scholarship, Industrial Relations, to a new multi-disciplinary or eclectic approach. George Mason University, for example, established the first Master of Arts and Doctor of Philosophy degree programs in Conflict Resolution. The degree programs were offered through its newly established Institute of Conflict Analysis and Resolution (ICAR). Its faculty members reflected multiple areas of traditional academic training, including political science, law, sociology, international relations, and communication; the curricular offerings combined theoretical and applied coursework to examine how dispute resolution processes, actors, and theories became operationalized in social conflicts, court-annexed cases, business operations, and international relations. That curricular shape has been replicated in most conflict resolution degree and certificate programs established thereafter; notably absent is the study of labor relations and its rich history of using negotiation, mediation, arbitration, elections, and other dispute settlement systems which, from post World War II until the 1970s, had been the primary focus of dispute resolution scholarship.

## 5. The Challenges of Growth

All practicing lawyers in the United States must know about mediation because they counsel their clients about its dynamics, represent clients in such conferences, or serve as mediators themselves. Lawyers are trained to analyze and shape human interactions in a manner congruent with principles of fair treatment, resourceful problem solving, and fidelity to community ideals. Lawyers have contributed significantly to mediation's recent development, and they must continue their responsible stewardship of its use.

The enthusiasm which accompanied the meteoric rise of mediation must be tempered by an appropriate demand for accountability. Important studies raise questions regarding the degree to which mediation meets some or all of its goals, beginning fundamentally with concerns about whether parties are treated fairly in mediation. Other accountability questions focus on: financing mediation services; ensuring access; balancing party confidentiality with a public's right to know; licensing mediators; monitoring mediator performance; ensuring mediator diversity; and improving public understanding of mediation. These and other important policy and practice topics are raised throughout this text.

# Chapter 2

# NEGOTIATION

## A.  OVERVIEW

It is essential that the students of the mediation process have some familiarity with negotiation theory and practice strategies. Mediation is generally defined by relating it to negotiation. Some commentators, for example, have defined mediation as negotiation in the presence of a third-party neutral (the mediator). Moreover, the parties to a mediation will often have attempted to negotiate a settlement prior to the mediation and may therefore arrive at the mediation with firmly entrenched negotiation postures and positions.

This chapter introduces some of the thinking about the negotiation process, particularly those commentaries that would be helpful to the lawyer mediator or the lawyer representing a party in mediation. During the past few decades, an extensive literature on the subject of negotiation has evolved. A rich scholarly literature explores such topics as psychological barriers to settlement, cross-cultural issues, and negotiator styles. As well, neighborhood bookstores carry popular treatments of negotiation that offer tips on how to negotiate on a wide range of subjects and from a number of different perspectives.

As you read through the materials on negotiation theory, pay particular attention to the vocabulary that emerges. Phrases such as "win-win solutions," "integrative versus distributive bargaining," "cooperative versus competitive negotiations," "positional bargaining," and "collaborative problem-solving" are used extensively throughout the mediation literature.

This chapter is arranged into three sections that offer a sampling from the literature on negotiation intended for lawyers. Section B focuses on negotiation strategies and behavior. Section C addresses the ethics of negotiation, particularly the issue of lying in negotiations. Section D explores psychological and economic analyses of negotiation. Finally, Section E looks at negotiating in the Internet age.

## NOTE ON NEGOTIATION TERMINOLOGY

As noted above, negotiation theorists have developed a distinctive vocabulary. Although this terminology may initially seem somewhat confusing, each of the authors whose writings are excerpted in this chapter views the negotiation process somewhat differently and is seeking to develop a conceptual framework for understanding how people *negotiate*, or *bargain*. Indeed, commentators generally use the terms *negotiation* and *bargaining* as if they are interchangeable. We mention some of these terms at the outset to emphasize that these words and phrases are not necessarily interdependent but merely represent varying perspectives on how to describe or analyze the negotiation process.

In Section B of this chapter, we will encounter the notion of *principled negotiation*. As espoused by Fisher and Ury, particularly in their landmark book, *Getting to YES, principled negotiation* is an approach to bargaining that permits "the pie" that is the subject of the negotiation to be expanded, resulting in so-called *win-win solutions*. This approach is often also referred to as *integrative bargaining*.

Fisher and Ury also introduced the concept of *BATNA* (Best Alternative to a Negotiated Agreement). The term *BATNA*, when encountered in the literature, should not be confused with one's *bottom line*. *Bottom line* generally refers to the very minimum for which you will settle. *Bottom line* is also sometimes referred to as your *reservation price*. *BATNA*, on the other hand, is not the minimum that you think you should get but what you will do if you don't get that minimum. What will you do if you are unable to negotiate an agreement? For attorneys attempting to negotiate a settlement in a court case, their clients' *BATNA* is often that of trying the case in court.

Those who ascribe to *principled negotiation*, or *integrative bargaining*, generally distinguish it from other forms of negotiation that are focused on dividing a limited resource. Specifically, *integrative bargaining* can be contrasted to *distributive bargaining, positional negotiations* or *hard bargaining*, where parties are more rigidly locked into positions as they attempt to split up a fixed pie.

*Principled negotiation* has been criticized because it fails to consider the *distributional* aspects of negotiation. Rather than assuming that the pie is expandable, *distributive bargaining* assumes *zero-sum negotiations*, where plus one for me equals minus one for you.

The *integrative-distributive* dichotomy may be juxtaposed with the *cooperative-competitive* dichotomy discussed by Gerald Williams and Gary Goodpaster. Do the *cooperative* negotiators fit neatly into the *integrative bargaining* package and the *competitive* negotiators into the *distributive bargaining* package? Not necessarily. Each of these commentators on the negotiation process is using a different framework for discussing negotiation behavior. What is important is that you understand the author's use of each term and phrase well enough to be able to consider how they overlap and how they can be distinguished from one another.

Some theorists distinguish negotiation behaviors from negotiation processes. For example, in explaining *problem-solving negotiation*, Carrie Menkel-Meadow states that *cooperative* or *collaborative negotiation* are terms that refer to behaviors that people exhibit while negotiating. The *problem-solving* approach to negotiation, on the other hand, refers to a more comprehensive process. She suggests that "[t]he conceptualization used in planning problem-solving negotiation is useful in all negotiation, regardless of the particular behaviors chosen in the executory stages."

Having a clear understanding of these terms and phrases is crucial to an attorney's being able to adopt a comprehensive, flexible approach to representing a client's interests in a negotiation or mediation. Indeed, some lawyers may use multiple, seemingly inconsistent, approaches in a single negotiation. For example, a lawyer may decide that her client's interests can best be served by taking an *integrative* approach at the outset of a negotiation and then switching to *distributive bargaining*. Or, a lawyer might commence a negotiation using an *adversarial competitive approach* and then become more *problem-solving* when it appears that no deal is forthcoming. As you read through the materials in this chapter, consider whether and how such combination of approaches might be sensible.

## B.  NEGOTIATION STRATEGIES AND BEHAVIOR

The materials below introduce some of the more prominent prescriptions and descriptions of negotiation strategy and behavior. Readings discussing and critiquing "principled negotiation" are excerpted in Section 1. Section 2 presents materials on cooperative versus competitive negotiation, and Section 3 outlines the "problem solving" approach to negotiation, which calls upon lawyers to rethink certain basic assumptions about lawyering. Finally, the article excerpted in Section 4 asks us to look beyond labels and focus on the skills necessary for effective negotiation.

### 1.  Integrative Versus Distributive Negotiation

*Getting to YES: Negotiating Agreement Without Giving In*, by Roger Fisher and William Ury, is perhaps the most well-known work in the extensive negotiation literature. While it can usually be found in the neighborhood bookstore, *Getting to YES* has also been the focus of considerable commentary by legal scholars. It argues for a "principled" approach to negotiation. The essential method presented by Fisher and Ury calls upon the negotiator to *"separate the people from the problem," "focus on interests rather than positions," "invent options for mutual gain,"* and *"insist on using objective criteria." Getting to YES* also introduced the acronym *BATNA* — Best Alternative to a Negotiated Agreement — into the ADR vocabulary.

Proponents of principled negotiation discredit the "positional" approach to bargaining that is perhaps most consistent with a lawyer's training. In our adversarial system, lawyers are trained to develop and advance "positions" on behalf of their clients with adversarial zeal. Principled bargainers urge lawyers to abandon negotiation strategies and behaviors that require rigid adherence to their positions and argue that they adopt the precepts of the "principled" approach to negotiation.

Thus, the Fisher and Ury framework is often referred to as the win-win approach to negotiation because of its goal of "expanding the pie." It is also referred to as integrative bargaining, as opposed to distributive bargaining, which assumes a fixed pie.

The following commentaries offer critiques of the principled negotiation framework. In the first excerpt, Russell Korobkin criticizes what he labels "the integrative supremacy claim." He does not argue that lawyers should not engage in integrative bargaining, but rather that legal negotiations are often distributive in nature and therefore "lawyers would be better served, on balance, to think of distributive bargaining as the cake and integrative bargaining as the frosting, rather than the reverse." In the second commentary, Ebner and Kamp focus on the relationship aspect of principled negotiation, analyzing and critiquing the "separate the people from the problem" precept.

# AGAINST INTEGRATIVE BARGAINING
## 58 Case W. Res. L. Rev. 1323 (2008)[*]
## By Russell Korobkin

Integrative bargaining, also known as "problem-solving," "value-creating," or "win-win" negotiation, is the centerpiece of normative negotiation scholarship and negotiation teaching. It has held this position at least since the publication of "Getting to Yes" by Fisher and Ury in 1981. . . .

To begin, let me admit that the title of this essay is somewhat misleading, or at least lacks the subtlety that I hope to convey. I am not really against integrative bargaining, by which I mean structuring negotiated agreements in such a way as to increase the joint value of a deal to the participating parties. As a matter of fact, I am firmly in favor of it. Through integrative bargaining, negotiators can make everyone involved in a transaction better off than they would otherwise be.

But the value of integrative bargaining, although substantial, has been oversold. This is true, I believe, with regard to negotiation generally, and especially concerning legal negotiations, the term I use for the negotiation contexts in which lawyers most routinely find themselves. For the past quarter century, the primary normative message of negotiation theory literature has been that negotiators will achieve better outcomes by focusing their attention on the integrative aspect of bargaining rather than its distributive aspect, by which I mean the division of resources in a way that makes one party worse off to the same extent that the other party is made better off. I call this the "integrative bargaining supremacy" claim.

In some cases, the dedication to the value of integrative bargaining often takes on a kind of missionary zeal. Practitioners of integrative tactics are seen as modern, sophisticated negotiators. In their search for "win-win" outcomes, they display subtlety, creativity, intelligence, and sophistication. In contrast, negotiators who employ distributive tactics are surly Neanderthals who try to use brute force and other boorish, knuckle-dragging behavior to subjugate their opponents. Teaching negotiation is viewed by many as the task of civilizing the great unwashed horde of naive, instinctive negotiators and convincing them to renounce their backward, distributive ways.

Integrative bargaining supremacy is often defended with the assertion that, while most everyone has an intuitive sense of how to use some distributive tactics, such as taking a firm position and grudgingly making concessions, individuals who lack formal negotiation training are less likely to intuitively grasp the fundamental concepts of integrative bargaining. This point is probably accurate, but it can obscure the fact that negotiations generally, and legal negotiations specifically, have more distributive potential than integrative potential. For this reason, lawyer-negotiators would be better served, on balance, to think of distributive bargaining as the cake and integrative bargaining as the frosting, rather than the reverse.

. . .

I. Integrative and Distributive Value

An agreement is integrative to the extent that it creates additional cooperative surplus compared to some alternative. Because integrative value is relative, identifying it requires the specification of a baseline case for purposes of comparison.

Suppose that Bonnie Buyer is negotiating to purchase a house from Sam Seller. Bonnie's reservation price, defined as the maximum that she would be willing to pay, is $100,000. Sam's reservation price, defined as the minimum amount he would be willing to accept, is $90,000. An agreement, if one is reached, will create $10,000 in social value, or what I will call "cooperative surplus," relative to no deal, because Bonnie subjectively values the house $10,000 more than does Sam. How that $10,000 is split between them — whether, for example, the price agreed to is $90,000, $95,000, or $100,000 — is a matter of distributive bargaining; any gain for Bonnie means a loss for Sam, and vice versa. We can thus say that the deal will produce $10,000 in distributive value, divided based on distributive bargaining ability.

Now let's also assume that Sam is an excellent handyman and enjoys tinkering with things around the house. Bonnie, in contrast, cannot fix anything, and she hates having to call service people to the house because she fears that they will take advantage of her. These facts suggest that more cooperative surplus might be created by the sale of the house if Sam will promise to repair any item that breaks for one year after the sale. Let us assume, for example, that this would cause Bonnie's reservation price to increase to $110,000, while Sam's reservation price would increase only to $92,000. Any deal that included the repair agreement would be integrative because it would create more cooperative surplus than the parties could obtain through the sale of the house alone — the baseline case. The extra $8,000 can be understood as the value that can be generated by the negotiators' integrative bargaining ability.

This example demonstrates what an integrative agreement might look like, but it does not provide an analytically precise description of what the baseline point of comparison should be for a judgment whether an agreement is integrative. Let me suggest the following definition: for an agreement to be appropriately labeled integrative, it must create more cooperative surplus than the terms of whatever type of agreement would be customary under the circumstances. If houses were customarily sold with a one-year repair agreement, agreeing to a sale with such a repair agreement would still create $18,000 in cooperative surplus — which would have to be divided between the parties — but it would not be an example of an integrative agreement. This definition underscores that integrative bargaining requires creativity on the part of the negotiators — the ability to think "outside the box" rather than simply agree to customary terms.

II. Achieving Integrative Bargains

With this definition in place, it becomes possible to describe a set of tactics, or techniques, that negotiators can employ to reach integrative agreements: adding issues, subtracting issues, substituting issues, and logrolling. All four are variations on the theme of searching for ways to reconfigure the terms of a deal to increase its joint value.

## A. Adding Issues

The simplest way to make an agreement integrative is to add one or more issues that the buyer values more than the seller to the customary set of terms, or what I will call the "negotiation package." The seller of a used car might add a warranty, the seller of a company might add his services during a transitional period of time, or a plaintiff in litigation might add a non-disclosure clause, promising to keep the generous settlement price secret to protect the defendant from subsequent nuisance suits. Of course, adding issues to the negotiation package is only integrative if the buyer values them more than the seller. Adding issues that the seller values more than the buyer would reduce the cooperative surplus. Assuming that Sam loves the antique chair that sits in the living room, whereas Bonnie considers it the ultimate example of poor taste, adding it to the transaction would reduce the cooperative surplus rather than increase it: Sam's reservation price would increase (because he values the chair), while Bonnie's would stay the same (because she does not) or maybe even increase slightly (because she would have to dispose of it).

## B. Subtracting Issues

The opposite of adding an issue that the buyer values more than the seller is subtracting something from the negotiation package that the seller values more than the buyer. Opportunities to profit from this integrative tactic are often more difficult to spot than opportunities to add issues because the negotiators first have to identify ways to unbundle what often appears to be a unitary, indivisible item. If the negotiation package consists of a single house, as in the example I used involving Sam and Bonnie, what is there to subtract? As it turns out, ownership of a house can be sliced and diced in many different ways, as can the contents of almost any negotiation package. Two examples: First, ownership can be divided into physical parts: if Sam loves the original chandelier in the dining room and Bonnie is indifferent, the chandelier can be subtracted from the package. Second, ownership can be divided temporally: if Sam wants to keep the house until his relatives visit in the spring and Bonnie is in no hurry to move, cooperative surplus can be created by subtracting ownership for the next six months from the negotiation package.

## C. Substituting Issues

Sometimes, parties can determine in the course of negotiations that the cooperative surplus they could create by entering an agreement would be greater if they completely changed the subject of the negotiation from what they originally assumed it would be. Perhaps when Bonnie visits Sam's house, she learns that he has another, similar property nearby. The main difference is that the second house is located on a main street and has associated traffic noise, so Sam would be willing to sell it for $85,000. The location makes it far more convenient to public transportation, however, which Bonnie values highly because she doesn't own a car, so she is willing to pay up to $110,000 for it. In this case, substituting the noisy, convenient house for the quiet, inconvenient house — which could be understood alternatively as subtracting one issue and adding another — should be considered an integrative move.

## D. Logrolling

Finally, in many bargaining contexts, the baseline, or customary deal includes multiple issues, but the terms that deal with those issues can be changed. In this case, it provides conceptual clarity to think in terms of logrolling — that is, trading one issue for another — rather than adding or subtracting issues. For example, either Bonnie's or Sam's real estate agent might produce a copy of a standard form contract drafted by the local association of realtors that specifies that the sale will close in thirty days and provides the buyer with ten days in which to conduct a home inspection and cancel the transaction if defects are discovered. If Bonnie is leaving on vacation and wants to conduct the inspection when she returns, and Sam wants at least two months before he has to move, the parties can logroll by agreeing to extend the inspection contingency to twenty days and the number of days until closing to sixty.

. . .

## V. Integrative vs. Distributive Bargaining in Legal Negotiations

From the standpoint of negotiation theory, there is no such category as "legal" negotiation. There are, however, some negotiation contexts in which the participation of lawyers is ubiquitous. Certain characteristics of these contexts suggest that lawyer-negotiators, in particular, will have more to gain for their clients through their skill in distributive tactics than through their skill at integrative bargaining.

## A. Litigation Settlement

Perhaps the prototypical bargaining context involving lawyers is the out-of-court settlement negotiation, in which the negotiators seek to exchange the waiver of the legal claims of the plaintiff (effectively the "seller") for some consideration, usually money, offered by the defendant (effectively the "buyer"). Since the large majority of all lawsuits are resolved through negotiation rather than adjudication, settlement negotiations might be called the primary business of litigators.

With a few very narrow exceptions, settlement negotiations reflect nearly perfect bilateral monopoly conditions, which suggests that distributive potential is likely to be substantial. If Walker files a lawsuit against Driver for negligent operation of her automobile, neither has the option of settling the claim with a third party instead of the other litigant . . .

The distributive potential is reinforced by the fact that the transaction costs of pursuing adjudication are high, and the outcome of adjudication is always uncertain.

Assuming that litigants are risk averse, both factors suggest that not only are the plaintiff and defendant likely to have divergent reservation prices in settlement negotiations, in most cases the defendant's reservation price should be higher than the plaintiff's. In such circumstances, the cooperative surplus that can be produced by the baseline agreement — the exchange of cash for a waiver of claims — will often be large.

While the distributive potential of settlement negotiations is, on average, large, their integrative potential will usually be small. Where the litigants have an ongoing relationship, it is conceivable that they could add issues concerning that relationship to the negotiation package and create substantial value — for example, a defendant could promise to place future orders with the plaintiff in return for the plaintiff dropping his breach of contract suit — but this can increase joint value relative to the baseline transaction only if the dispute has not sufficiently poisoned the relationship to the point that continued dealings aren't feasible (that is, the benefits of an ongoing relationship must outweigh the costs), and the parties would not have independently entered the same agreements concerning the future (because if they would have negotiated the same future arrangements regardless, the integrative bargaining tactics would not create any marginal value). And this possibility of integrative value, of course, does not exist at all when the lawsuit is between strangers or near-strangers.

A common example of an integrative tactic that can be used in a settlement negotiation between strangers is the addition to the negotiation package of an apology by the defendant. Adding an apology often will be more valuable to the recipient plaintiff than costly to an issuing defendant, so it has the possibility of creating cooperative surplus. But except in cases where reputational damage has caused long term harm to a plaintiff's financial interests, apologies usually have a small amount of value in comparison to the issue of damages.

Consider a wrongful death plaintiff willing to accept $1 million to settle his claim out of court, and a defendant with a reservation price of $1.5 million. If the defendant offers to add a formal apology to a settlement, the plaintiff's reservation price is likely to decline only slightly. A gratuitous apology — that is, one provided without the explicit condition that it be considered part of the compensation package — offered by the defendant at the outset of negotiations is likely to be a very good distributive tactic, because it is likely to engender goodwill and cause the plaintiff to be less recalcitrant when the parties bargain over the $500,000 in cooperative surplus. But the apology probably has only modest potential to expand the bargaining zone and increase the total cooperative surplus.

Structuring settlement payments over a period of time (effectively adding the issue of a financing arrangement to the baseline transaction) can create joint value by taking advantage of differences in discount rates and/or tax status, but this also will usually expand the bargaining zone only modestly compared to the amount of cooperative surplus at stake in a baseline transaction that assumes an immediate cash payment.

B. Business Transactions

Perhaps settlement negotiations have more distributive than integrative potential, on average, but what about the transactional negotiations conducted by business lawyers that grease the wheels of commerce? . . . [T]he relative potential of integrative bargaining tactics is far greater, on average, in transactional negotiations than in distributive ones. But the relative potential of integrative bargaining can easily be overstated even in this context.

One reason is that in many transactional negotiations, the clients agree on the foundational structure of the negotiation package, including price, before the lawyers become involved. At this point, the business executives call on their legal department or their outside attorneys to "paper the deal" with a formal contract, and it is only at this point that the lawyers become involved in the negotiation.

Under these conditions, the negotiation context looks more like a bilateral monopoly, and the value of distributive skill increases. Although both parties technically retain the option to walk away from the negotiation and enter into an agreement with a different party, the transactional and reputational costs of doing so at this point can be substantial. In addition, the lawyer, as an agent, faces high personal costs of recommending this course of action to her client, because she risks being labeled as a deal-killer. In this situation, there will tend to be a large bargaining zone, which is to say that both the buyer's and seller's lawyers will prefer to sacrifice a substantial amount of the cooperative surplus that a completed transaction will create rather than break off negotiations and recommend cancellation of the deal to their clients. This feature, common in business transactions at the time the lawyers enter into the picture, suggests that distributive tactics will often be quite valuable.

While the distributive potential of transaction negotiations is often greater than it initially appears, the integrative potential of transactional negotiations is often relatively less than it first appears because the widespread adoption of efficiencies into the baseline negotiation package through the development of trade custom. This is true for large-scale business transactions generally, and for industry-specific negotiations in which transactional lawyers develop specializations.

Take, for example, a merger negotiation, in which a large conglomerate, Alpha Company, seeks to purchase a small, high-technology company called Beta. Beta's value to Alpha is primarily in the former's portfolio of technology patents. Because Beta has more information than Alpha about whether competitors might seek to challenge the validity of these patents on the grounds that they are not sufficiently novel or non-obvious, Alpha's reservation price is likely to increase more than Beta's will if Beta provides a contractual representation that it has no knowledge of any current challenges to its patents and agrees to indemnify Alpha for harms suffered if such a challenge is subsequently mounted by a third party.

On its face, this looks like an excellent example of integrative potential, and indeed it would be if we were to assume that the baseline transaction between Alpha and Beta would include no such representation or indemnification provision. This probably was a fair description of the situation the first time one company purchased another principally for the latter's patent portfolio and consulted a lawyer for assistance in structuring the terms of the deal. In most cases, however, lawyers do not begin negotiating the terms of complicated transactions from scratch. Instead, they draw on a large base of institutional memory and industry custom. Where this is the case, the value of providing these terms is captured by customary practice, and the integrative potential that depends on the skill of the negotiators will be correspondingly limited.

Complex transactions in which terms are negotiated to some degree — as opposed to deals in which one party offers an adhesion contract to the other on a take-it-or-leave-it basis — will always offer some potential for integrative bargaining, because the preferences, needs, and cost structures of the parties are unlikely to be precisely the same from one transaction to the next. But the amount of value that can be gained only if the lawyers negotiating the deal's terms are personally skilled at using integrative bargaining tactics is often much less than what is assumed in the typical negotiation classroom, where the acquired wisdom of industry-specific custom that informs the baseline for transactions in the real world is rarely assumed.

Notwithstanding the provocative title of this essay, my criticism is of the integrative bargaining supremacy claim, not integrative bargaining itself. The point is one of emphasis. My argument is not that integrative bargaining has no value or even minimal value, but more modestly, that the majority of legal negotiations will have more distributive than integrative potential. I have tried to support this claim, admittedly circumstantially, by showing that the types of negotiations in which lawyers typically participate will usually have substantial distributive potential, and at the same time that their integrative potential will tend to be more limited than often assumed.

What has been most obviously lacking, perhaps, is a description of the tactics negotiators might use to take advantage of the distributive potential that I claim is ubiquitous. Distributive bargaining is itself a complex activity that deserves its own nuanced analysis. Proponents of integrative bargaining supremacy sometimes caricature distributive tactics as being limited to making unreasonable demands and then refusing to make concessions. Although aggressiveness and stubbornness do have their place as tactics, distributive bargaining is not limited to these stereotypic behaviors. A savvy bargainer who focuses attention on distribution devotes resources to improving her options away from the bargaining table, understands the needs of her counterpart, invokes external norms as the basis for decisions, uses social norms of fair bargaining to reach agreement, and builds a reputation as a fair and honorable business partner. Unfortunately, a discussion of how a negotiator can best combine these approaches to achieve success at capturing cooperative surplus from her counterpart — that is, at distributive bargaining — is a topic for another essay.

# RELATIONSHIP 2.0*

*In* Rethinking Negotiation Teaching: Venturing Beyond the Classroom
(Christopher Honeyman, James Coben & Giuseppe De Palo, Eds., 2010)
By Noam Ebner & Adam Kamp

*Getting to Yes* purports to address a core problem: negotiators often find themselves cornered into a trade-off. . . . By exerting pressure on two fronts at once, demanding a better deal while threatening to withhold or damage a good relationship, negotiators try to maneuver their opposites into a concession on the former in return for an easing of the pressure in the latter. However, making these concessions or being "nice," as the authors state correctly, is no answer. On the contrary — it may make a negotiator vulnerable, perceived as weak, and open to manipulation (Fisher, Ury, and Patton 1991: 8-9).

In essence, this is a relationship problem, and in that perspective one might say *Getting to Yes* is a relationship-oriented book. In order to avoid the relationship/ substance trade-off, the *Getting to Yes* model suggests that negotiators *separate the people from the problem*. By dealing with their opposite in a respectful and open manner, while not going any easier on the substance of the deal, negotiators can avoid paying a price for relationship.

Separating the people from the problem is, in essence, the core framing of relationship in negotiation in the *Getting to Yes* model. Relationship exists *alongside* the substance of the negotiation. It should be a *working* relationship, one whose costs might be measured in terms of time, patience and communication, but not in concessions on the substance of the deal. Taken in context of the complete model the book presents, the essence of a "good" negotiation relationship would then be one that supports open communication, sharing of interests, exploration of options, and presentation of and comparison of standards.

. . .

We suggest that in attempting to create a clear scheme . . . to follow ("Form a good working relationship with the other without paying a price for it") we are actually sweeping a very challenging tension under the carpet. This separation between relationship and substance is a very tricky precept to master, practically speaking. As the *Getting to Yes* authors themselves state, negotiators are humans, and human nature and the dynamics of negotiation challenge our ability to separate relationship and substance. Manipulative negotiators you face — be it your boss or your three year old daughter — will *always* attempt to tie the two elements of relationship and substance together. More challenging, manipulative negotiators will often be supported in their behavior by internal and external forces affecting you.

. . .

[I]t would seem that no sooner have we been offered a way out by striving towards a separation between people and problem, than we are once again sucked back into people-issues. Instead of leaving this notion of separation as a stand-alone, overarching precept, the authors attempt to simplify things by becoming prescriptive, breaking down just how this separation might be accomplished. We suggest that in this breakdown of do's and don'ts, the authors lead negotiators along a relationship-tightrope walk, along which human nature beckons them to fall into relationship-traps (or to use Fisher, Ury, and Patton's own terminology, situations in which negotiators will be tempted to pay a substantive price for maintaining the relationship) at every turn.

The *Getting to Yes* authors recommend four things regarding relationship:

1)   You need to listen well, allowing the other to express themselves as best as they can;

2)   You need to give the other space and allow them to vent, without reacting to emotional outbursts;

3)   You need to step into the other's shoes, enabling yourself to see things from their perspective, and then reconsider your position; and

4)   You need to view the other as a partner, not a competitor or enemy.

Each of these recommendations (intended to be "universally applicable") is hazardous to some extent in itself; in the aggregate, they are almost certain to cause the negotiator to fall into the very relationship traps he or she is attempting to avoid. We will briefly discuss some of the reasons we consider each of these recommendations to be hazardous, and then focus on the list as a whole.


Listen

Can it really be that the prescription to listen is *always* suitable, context notwithstanding? For example, this approach assumes an honest, straightforward speaker, and one who lacks the self-awareness to doctor one's statements for the benefit of one's counterpart. This is hardly the case. Such uncritical listening to a manipulative negotiator frames the entire discussion in a context that may have little bearing to the counterpart's actual reality, and can build sympathy for a situation that is in fact mostly or entirely illusionary. While it may of course be possible to counter this, later on, through reframing, it is setting the negotiator up for the challenge of applying that complex skill successfully. In any event, few teachers of negotiation discuss any potential value in *not* listening to the other party, or consider other models of discussion.


Allow venting, avoid reacting

Not only is the expectation that we try to forego emotionality in the face of a heated outburst a sheer impossibility, but here in particular the suggestion that negotiators should allow the other party emotions they deny themselves has the result of valuing the other's feelings over their own. If venting serves a purpose in negotiation, then it might be something we should consider allowing ourselves to do as well — passing the onus to be accepting, understanding, forgiving (and perhaps even conceding) over to the other party. While there may be an advantage to recognizing a counterpart's emotions and stake in the game, this should not come at the cost of one's own emotional interests — yet that might be just the result of such a one-sided process-concession.

## Recognize partisan perceptions

. . . [D]espite the *Getting to Yes* authors' protestations that one can understand another's perception without adopting it — is that necessarily true? Remember, we are being advised to understand the other's perception in a reality in which the other might not be concerned about understanding our own. This creates an imbalance: two parties understand Party A's perceptions, but only one party understands Party B's perceptions. Might this not have the effect of shifting the balance towards Party A's perceptions — which both parties can appreciate? For example, consider that better outcomes are generally a product of setting high values for oneself. When the *Getting to Yes* authors suggest that understanding another's perceptions may cause one to re-evaluate the merits of one's own claim, doing so is counter to keeping one's own goals high, and may result in unnecessarily lowering one's expectations.

Of course, whether one has a competitive or a cooperative bargaining style, one might still find it useful to understand the other's perceptions in order to better cast one's own response in terms one's counterpart may understand. But without clarifying the dangers of understanding those partisan perceptions so profoundly that they become the dominant frame of the conflict, this advice might lead the unwary reader awry.

## Partnerize the other

This is potentially the most dangerous trap, because it assumes mutuality of purpose. If the other side is treating you as a partner, then in most cases the most productive solution is going to be to treat the other as a partner as well. The book treats the creation of trust necessary to create such a partnership as simple, taken in stride. However, especially when considering an experienced and manipulative negotiator, those same overtures can be used to create a false sense of partnership; the trappings of trust-building, such as gifts or friendly statements, can lead us to make concessions based on preserving the relationship that we have assumed to exist.

## Aggregate hazards

Taken all together, these recommendations lead students down an even more hazardous path regarding relationship, owing to the potential implication of one party adopting this general mode of behavior regardless of their opposite's actions. If these recommendations (and others offered in Chapter Two of *Getting to Yes*) were made by a mediator speaking to both parties at once, or if one could promise that all negotiators would read *Getting to Yes* and adopt it to the same degree, these would be wonderful recommendations. As the authors say in their introduction to the method:

Dealing with a substantive problem and maintaining a good working relationship need not be conflicting goals if the parties are committed and psychologically prepared to treat each separately on its own legitimate merits. However, these recommendations are made to *individual negotiators*, who (in the rest of the chapter following the above quote) are charged with taking responsibility to conduct an effective negotiation for *both* parties, to ensure effective and productive communication between *both* parties, and for understanding the other party and where they are coming from. As a cluster of recommendations, this package seems highly likely to send the average negotiator . . . right back down the path of being *more concerned about the relationship than the other* — and falling into the same old trap of paying a price for it.

The risk associated with these recommendations might well be worthwhile if following them could be guaranteed to deliver the desired combination of a working relationship with no associated substantive costs, and the best deal possible for the individual negotiator following them. Obviously, that cannot be guaranteed in any individual case. . . .

. . .

For all these reasons, then, the foundational text for many negotiation classes is very much incomplete in the picture it paints of relationship. It admonishes readers not to pay a price for a good relationship — yet, at the same time, it extols the value of a good relationship to such an extent that it seems it is worth paying almost *any* price in order to obtain one! In a real-life situation, this might easily translate into even the most wary "separate the people from the problem" novice making seemingly small concessions in the deal in order to obtain a good relationship.

## NOTES AND QUESTIONS

(1) Korobkin's general criticism of Fisher and Ury's "principled," or "integrative," approach to negotiation is that it fails to account for the "distributional" aspects of a negotiation. The integrative approach is oriented toward achieving a win-win solution, while distributive bargaining assumes a zero-sum game where plus one for me means minus one for you. Is Korobkin correct when he argues that although one may wish to begin a negotiation with an integrative approach, ultimately one needs to reckon with the distributive aspects of the negotiation, and one should thus view the distributive as the cake and the integrative as the frosting, rather than vice versa? Even in those negotiations where the distributive aspects are clear, is it possible to take an integrative approach? That is, although integrative and distributive approaches to bargaining provide distinct communication frameworks, are they reconcilable? How? Which of these communication frameworks do you think would be most suitable for a mediation? Why?

(2) James White, another scholar of the negotiation process, criticizes Fisher and Ury's insistence on the use of "objective criteria." Instead, White argues in favor of "persuasive rationalizations." Is this more in line with what a lawyer is trained to do?

(3) Ebner and Kamp criticize Fisher and Ury for insisting on "separating the people from the problem," particularly because it requires concession-making to preserve relationships that "may make a negotiator vulnerable, perceived as weak,

and open to manipulation." However, there is no doubt that people problems, such as a growing dislike for the personality or attitude of the lawyer for the other side, may get in the way of one's ability to stay focused on one's client's interests. One of the more difficult people problems to deal with during a negotiation may arise when the lawyer for the other side makes offensive or demeaning comments. For a helpful analytical framework for dealing with such comments, see Andrea Kupfer Schneider, *Effective Responses to Offensive Comments*, 1994 Negotiation J. 107.

(4) As you read the material in the next section, consider how the integrative/distributive dichotomy meshes with the cooperative/competitive dichotomy.

## 2. Cooperative Versus Competitive Negotiation

The behaviors that people exhibit when they negotiate or bargain have been the subject of considerable interest to social scientists. One set of research has sought to identify styles or patterns of negotiating behavior that might be deemed most "effective." Although there has never been a clear consensus over what is meant by negotiation effectiveness, these earlier studies have been very helpful in identifying varying negotiation styles or types. In particular, the identification of cooperative versus competitive negotiating styles emerged from this research. In the selections that follow, Professor Gerald Williams discusses the distinguishing characteristics of competitive and cooperative negotiators; Professor Gary Goodpaster argues for a clearer understanding of competitive behavior in negotiation; and Professor Williams reports on the similarities between effective, cooperative negotiators and effective, competitive negotiators.

## LEGAL NEGOTIATION AND SETTLEMENT
### 48–54 (1983)*
### By Gerald R. Williams

The experimental literature on negotiation contains a running debate between two opposing schools of thought: one arguing generally for a "cooperative" approach to negotiation and the other for a "tough" or "competitive" approach . . .

What are the ingredients of a "tough" approach? As defined in social psychological literature, they include:[16]

1. making high initial demands;

2. maintaining a high level of demands in the course of the negotiation;

3. making few concessions;

4. making small concessions (when concessions are made); and

5. having a generally high level of aspiration.

What we have learned so far about competitive negotiators is brought to life by

---

[16] I. MORLEY AND G. STEPHENSON, THE SOCIAL PSYCHOLOGY OF BARGAINING (1977).

the insights of Herbert W. Simons. In *Persuasion: Understanding, Practice and Analysis*, pp. 133-134 (1976), he observes that the underlying dynamic of combative strategies is to move psychologically against the other person by word or action. Videotapes of competitive lawyers engaged in negotiating do show a definite pattern of behavior of moving psychologically against the other (non-competitive) attorney. They make very high demands and few (if any) concessions. They use exaggeration, ridicule, threat, bluff, and accusation to create high levels of tension and pressure on the opponent.

What are the effects of these tactics? If used effectively, the tactics cause the opposing attorney to lose confidence in himself and his case, to reduce his expectations of what he will be able to obtain in the case, and to accept less than he otherwise would as a settlement outcome. As Simons observed, the combative approach is a manipulative approach, designed to intimidate the opponent into accepting the combative's demands . . .

The elements of the cooperative approach also come from insights of Simons. The basic dynamic of the cooperative negotiator is to move psychologically *toward* the opposing attorney. Cooperative negotiators seek common ground. They communicate a sense of shared interests, values, and attitudes using rational, logical persuasion as a means of seeking cooperation. They promote a trusting atmosphere appearing to seek no special advantage for self or client. The explicit goal is to reach a fair resolution of the conflict based on an objective analysis of the facts and law.

Osgood observed a crucial dynamic here: the cooperative negotiator shows his own trust and good faith by making unilateral concessions. Making unilateral concessions is risky, but cooperative negotiators believe it creates a moral obligation in the other to reciprocate. The cooperative strategy is calculated (subconsciously) to induce the other party to reciprocate: to co-operate in openly and objectively resolving the problem; to forego aggression, and to make reciprocal concessions until a solution is reached.

Cooperative negotiators feel a high commitment to fairness, objecting to the competitive view of negotiation as a game. To a cooperative, the gamesmanship view is ethically suspect. They feel that to move psychologically *against* another person to promote one's own interest is manipulative and an affront to human dignity. On the other hand, cooperatives move psychologically *toward* other people to achieve their preferred outcome. Competitive negotiators have reason to ask whether this is any less manipulative. Their manipulation is designed to induce or permit the opponent to trust, cooperate with, and make concessions to the manipulator.

The strengths of the cooperative approach as identified in the literature are that cooperative strategies are often more effective than tough strategies for two primary reasons: they produce more favorable outcomes, and they result in fewer ultimate breakdowns in bargaining (in the legal context, resort to trial)..

The cooperative strategy, like the competitive, has limitations. Its major disadvantage is its vulnerability to exploitation, a problem compounded by the apparent inability of some cooperative types to recognize it when it happens. When a cooperative negotiator attempts to establish a cooperative, trusting atmosphere, in a negotiation with a tough, non-cooperative opponent, the cooperative attorney has an alarming tendency to ignore the lack of cooperation and to pursue his cooperative strategy unilaterally. The strategy requires him to continue discussing the case fairly and objectively, to make concessions about the weaknesses of his case, and refrain from self-serving behavior. In this situation, the tough negotiator is free to accept all of the fairness and cooperation without giving anything in return. In fact, it would be irrational to do anything else. On these facts, the cooperative has placed himself at a serious disadvantage. He has forgone attacking the other's position, he has conceded the weaknesses of his own position, and he has received no reciprocal value in return.

# A PRIMER ON COMPETITIVE BARGAINING
1996 J. Disp. Resol. 325, 325–26, 341–43, 370–77[*]
By Gary Goodpaster

One cannot understand negotiation without understanding competitive behavior in negotiation. It is not that competing is a good way to negotiate; it may or may not be, depending on the circumstances. Understanding competition in negotiation is important simply because many people do compete when they negotiate, either by choice or happenstance.

Competitive bargaining, sometimes called hard, distributive, positional, zero-sum or win-lose bargaining, has the purpose of maximizing the competitive bargainer's gain over the gain of those with whom he negotiates. He is, in effect, trying to "come out ahead of," or "do better than," all other parties in the negotiation. For this reason, we sometimes refer to this competitive bargaining strategy as a *domination* strategy, meaning that the competitive bargainer tends to treat negotiations as a kind of contest to win.

The competitive negotiator tends to define success in negotiation rather narrowly. It is simply getting as much as possible for himself: the cheapest price, the most profit, the least cost, the best terms and so on. In its simplest form, this strategy focuses on immediate gain and is not much concerned with the relationship between the negotiating parties. A more complex version of this strategy focuses on long-term gain. This focus usually requires some effort to maintain or further a relationship and usually moderates the competitive, often aggressive, behavior that jeopardizes relationships and possibilities of long-term gain . . .

People bargain competitively essentially for three reasons, which often overlap. First, by inclination or calculation, they view the negotiation as a kind of competition, in which they wish to win or gain as much as possible. Secondly, they do not trust the other party. Where parties are non-trusting, they are non-disclosing and withhold information, which leads to further distrust and defensive or self-protective moves. Parties may be non-trusting because they are unfamiliar with the other party or because they are generally or situationally non-trusting. Finally, a party may bargain competitively as a defense to, or retaliation for, competitive moves directed at it.

. . . The competitive negotiator adopts a risky strategy which involves the taking of firm, almost extreme positions, making few and small concessions, and withholding information that may be useful to the other party. The intention, and hoped-for effect, behind this basic strategy is to persuade the other party that it must make concessions if it is to get an agreement. In addition to this basic strategy, competitive negotiators may also use various ploys or tactics aimed at pressuring, unsettling, unbalancing or even misleading the other party to secure an agreement with its demands.

In an important sense, the competitive negotiator plays negotiation as an information game. In this game, the object is to get as much information from the other party as possible while disclosing as little information as possible. Alternatively, a competitive negotiator sometimes provides the other party with misleading clues, bluffs, and ambiguous assertions with multiple meanings, which are not actually false, but nevertheless mislead the other party into drawing incorrect conclusions that are beneficial to the competitor.

The information the competitive negotiator seeks is the other party's bottom line. How much he will maximally give or minimally accept to make a deal. On the other hand, the competitive negotiator wants to persuade the other side about the firmness of the negotiator's own *asserted* bottom line. The competitive negotiator works to convince the other party that it will settle only at some point that is higher (or lower, as the case may be) than its *actual* and unrevealed bottom line . . . . Taking a firm position and conceding little will incline the other party to think the competitor has little to give. Thus, if there is to be a deal, then the other party must give or concede more.

. . . Competitive and cooperative bargaining strategies conflict. A simple cooperative strategy leaves the cooperator vulnerable to exploitation by a competitor. There is also good evidence that competitive negotiators who use the high demand, firmness, small concession strategy get better negotiation results than cooperators, at least where "better" means getting the most immediate gain.

Cooperative bargainers vary greatly in their sophistication. Innocent cooperators who, consciously or unconsciously, uncritically adopt the premise that cooperation begets cooperation may unwittingly engage in behavior that exposes them to possible exploitation. Potentially detrimental information disclosures, unilateral concessions, or excessive concession making are all examples of this kind of behavior. Some cooperators may even exhibit invariant, non-adaptive or "pathological" cooperation. That is, they either consistently and detrimentally misinterpret the other party's exploitive moves, or otherwise always respond to persistent hard bargaining with increasing deference or reasonableness and with more, or greater, concessions.

If the hard bargainer overreaches too much, the cooperator may feel pushed beyond his own boundaries of reasonableness and cooperation and break off the negotiations out of frustration and anger at the other party's unreasonableness. A canny, hard bargainer, however, who is skilled in reading the other party and sensitive to the possibility of pushing too far, can always take advantage of a naïve and inexperienced cooperative negotiator. Innocent or naive cooperators tend to assume that the other party is bargaining non-exploitively. They want to be trusted and tend to trust others. In their desire to be reasonable and friendly, they assume that the other party will act the same way, even in the face of contrary evidence.

Cooperators may worry more about having a good relationship and keeping things calm, reasonable, and agreeable than they do about getting exactly what they want. Indeed, going into the negotiation, they may not specifically know what they would deem a good disposition. Instead, rather than enter the negotiation with certain figures or positions in mind as desirable results, they may enter with vaguer, more malleable and manipulable notions that they only want "what's fair" or "what's reasonable" under the circumstances. The lack of a clear reference point makes them less able to discern their own interest and, therefore, more vulnerable to competitive claiming.

The cooperator's desire to be a certain kind of person — noncompetitive, nonaggressive, fair, decent, honorable — may also result in turning the other cheek to the other party's hard-bargaining tactics. In fact, naive cooperators may undercut getting what they want by assuming that they must make unilateral concessions or compromises without a return just to get an agreement. They sometimes fail to distinguish between their behavior toward others and their behavior toward the problem they are trying to resolve. In other words, they are "soft on the people" and "soft on the problem."

The cooperator faces a dilemma: the reasonable, compromising conduct in which he wishes to engage in order to obtain a fair and just agreement also puts him at risk. If the other party is also cooperative, all is well and good. The other party, however, may not be cooperative. Instead, the other party may either be overtly competitive or cooperative in demeanor and competitive in substance. If, for example, to be reasonable and attempt to have the union understand its point of view, management volunteers important information, such as planning a plant expansion, the union may simply take the information and use it to its advantage without volunteering information in return or reciprocating in any other way. Similarly, if Susan, being cooperative, makes a concession hoping to trigger a concession from Jerry, Jerry may simply take the concession and either give nothing in return or give a non-commensurate concession. Indeed, the cooperator's concession may encourage the other side to seek more or greater concessions. In this situation, the truly naïve cooperator may respond by conceding more in the hope of inducing a concession and movement toward an agreeable settlement rather than by noting the lack of reciprocity and adjusting his own behavior to protect himself.

The cooperator faces the dilemma that the way he wants to negotiate may put him at risk of being taken or exploited. Obviously, cooperative negotiators should not naïvely *assume* that the other party will also act cooperatively. Indeed, they must recognize that they cannot successfully bargain cooperatively unless the other party cooperates. They also need to devise ways to protect themselves from the other party's possible competitive moves that are often masked or hidden by a genial, reasonable, or cooperative demeanor.

Aware of the potential risks involved in their cooperative behavior, a negotiator could adopt a hard bargaining strategy. This strategy would certainly not be necessary in all cases. In fact, many negotiators might object to hard bargaining in principle. How does a wise and careful cooperative negotiator protect herself from competitive bargainers?

*Defensive cooperativeness.* During the initial stages of a negotiation the parties feel each other out, not only to gain information respecting positions, wants, and desires, but also to get a sense of whether, and how far, they can trust one another. Since trust, or providing security that one can trust, is a key issue, cooperators should try to anticipate negotiations, develop information about the other party, and build a relationship with the other party prior to negotiation.

Because cooperative behavior promotes trust, it tends to induce reciprocal cooperative behavior. Once in a negotiation, the careful cooperator adopts a cooperative, yet wary, demeanor and indicates a general posture of flexibility on issues. This may signal or hint at a willingness to make concessions on certain issues. Nevertheless, the defensive or cautious cooperator does not make significant concessions before determining whether the other party is trustworthy.

*Fractionating concessions.* A careful negotiator can, in part, fashion a self-protective concession strategy by fractionating concessions. One fractionates concessions by dividing an issue into smaller issues and, therefore, into smaller concessions where one gives on an issue. Using this method, the negotiator can make a small concession and wait to see how the other party responds. If the other party makes an equivalent concession, the negotiator can proceed.

*Ambiguous or disownable signals.* A negotiator makes a "disownable" concession move by making an ambiguous statement that suggests a willingness to make a concession but which can also be plausibly interpreted as not expressing such willingness. If the other party interprets the statement as offering a concession and reciprocates, then the negotiator confirms the other side's interpretation in some way. If the other party seeks to grab the assumed concession without offering a return, the negotiator denies making it. Suppose, for example, that one party has repeatedly argued that two conditions had to be met before he would consider changing his position. After a time, however, he begins to mention only one condition, thereby, signaling a willingness to drop the unmentioned condition.

This sort of signaling is, in effect, a testing of the other party. This test, however, does not run the actual risk of making a concession or exposing weakness. At most, it is an unclear expression of a contingent willingness to concede. As another example, consider two parties negotiating over contract terms. The buyer wants the seller to give her the same discount on equipment that the seller gives some of its other, much larger customers. The seller says, "We can write something like a 'favored nations' clause into the contract." The buyer responds, "I'll take that, and I appreciate getting the same discount as your larger customers," but he makes no concession in return. The seller then responds, "Well, you can have the clause, but it doesn't apply to discounts." Alternatively, had the buyer shown a willingness to concede, the seller could let the buyer's first interpretation of the statement stand.

If there is little trust, this process of signaling can be quite subtle because the target of the signal may be uncertain whether to interpret a statement as expressing a willingness to concede. If the target is uncertain, he may fear responding in a way which clearly shows his willingness to reciprocate because that may put him at risk. Consequently, the parties sometimes engage in trading ambiguous statements until one party feels secure enough to make a clear proposal or until both parties simultaneously make a clear move.

*"Directional" information.* Sometimes a negotiator may encourage cooperative bargaining simply by indicating on which issues the other party should improve its proposals. This tactic provides the other party with some information about the negotiator's priorities but without clearly committing to anything.

*Demanding reasoned justifications.* A negotiator should make a practice of asking the other party to justify its positions in terms of some objective criteria. If the other party simply behaves competitively and attempts to extract whatever gains it can, it may have difficulty in stating satisfactory justifications for its positions.

*Contingent cooperativeness and the reformed sinner strategy.* There is good evidence that even those who wish to bargain cooperatively can succeed with competitive negotiators by adopting a shifting "competitive to cooperative" or "reformed sinner" strategy. This strategy involves making a high, initial demand, remaining firm initially, and then moving to a "contingently cooperative" strategy. Contingent cooperativeness involves behaving cooperatively if the other party reciprocates cooperative behavior and increasing cooperative behavior as the other party does so. Interestingly, the cooperator's initial firmness may signal to the other party that competitive behavior will not work.

. . .

The contingently competitive strategy appears to work by giving the other party evidence that its own cooperative behavior, but not its competitive behavior, has a desirable effect. In carrying out this general strategy, the cooperator may expressly negotiate over the negotiation ground rules and seek the other party's commitment to negotiate cooperatively as well, but, in any case, asserting a norm and expectation of cooperative behavior. The cooperator may then attempt to structure the negotiation to handle small issues first, where the risk of loss is not great. When ready to take some risks, the cooperator makes contingent proposals. The proposal expressly offers a concession or adopts a position closer to the other party's demands yet contingent on some specific concession or change of position from the other party.

*Strategy imitation or tit-for-tat.* Response — in-kind or tit-for-tat — is a form of contingent cooperation a negotiator can use to handle a competitor. If the cooperator observes competitive tactics, she can call attention to them and state that she knows how to bargain that way too and will respond in kind unless the other party bargains cooperatively. Alternatively, the cooperator can just respond in kind by using tit-for-tat to discipline the other party.

Tit-for-tat is a negotiation strategy designed to shape the other party's bargaining behavior. One dilemma negotiators face is figuring out whether to bargain cooperatively or competitively. If one wishes to be reasonable and bargain cooperatively, there is a risk that the other party will bargain competitively and gain an advantage. Using tit-for-tat, a negotiator solves that problem by competing just as the other party does and, in effect, sends the message that "I will bargain the way you bargain and will use the same tactics you use." This teaches the other party that it cannot get away with anything, and may lead to cooperative behavior.

In general, using a tit-for-tat or matching strategy appears to be an effective way to induce cooperation. The strategy makes it clear to the other party that it risks retaliation and increasing conflict if it continues to bargain competitively.

*Time-outs.* Negotiating parties deadlock when no party is willing to make a further concession to bring the parties closer together. When the parties are nearing a deadline and are deadlocked, they may realize that the negotiation will fail completely unless they cooperate. Declaring a time-out when a dead-lock is apparent gives the parties time to assess the situation without continued conflict, reconsider their reading of the negotiation thus far, and determine more rationally whether to risk trusting the other party. Often enough, when the parties return to formal negotiation, each side signals a willingness to move towards an agreement or make concessions leading to an agreement.

Because people bargain competitively for various reasons, negotiators and mediators need to understand competition in negotiation in order to respond appropriately. Some people bargain competitively without giving much conscious attention to the matter. Others compete in response to the other party's competitive behavior. In this response, they follow the common pattern that a particular kind of behavior elicits a similar behavior in response. In other words, one party frames the negotiation as a contest, and the other party picks up the competitive cues and behaves accordingly. Further, people naturally incline to competitive bargaining when they are non-trusting. In such situations, in order to avoid putting themselves at risk, non-trusting people act guardedly and adopt elements of the competitive strategy, for example, withholding information or misrepresenting a position. Finally, one can readily imagine ambiguous bargaining situations, in which at least one party is non-trusting, quickly devolving into a competitive negotiation between both parties. The non-trusting party acts defensively, and the other party senses this as competitive behavior and, therefore, acts in a similar fashion.

Negotiators, however, can also consciously adopt a competitive strategy. Negotiators are most likely to compete purposefully when

- the parties have an adversarial relationship;

- a negotiator has a bargaining power advantage and can dominate the situation;

- a negotiator perceives an opportunity for gain at the expense of the other party;

- the other party appears susceptible to competitive tactics;

- the negotiator is defending against competitive moves; or

- there is no concern for the future relationship between the parties.

This list suggests that competitive bargaining most likely occurs in situations such as labor and lawsuit negotiations, insurance and similar claims type settlements, and in one-time transactions between a relatively experienced party and a relatively inexperienced party. One would, for example, expect to see it in sales transactions where the parties will probably not see each other again.

Representative bargaining or bargaining for a constituency may also prompt competitive bargaining even when there will be future negotiations between equally sophisticated parties. The negotiator's accountability may override relationship concerns and reasons for cooperation. The concerned audience, consisting of a client, constituency, coalition partner, or other phantom party at the table, is, in effect, looking over the negotiator's shoulder. The negotiator, therefore, takes positions and makes moves she believes her client either expects or would approve. International negotiations between countries, union-management, lawsuit negotiations, and negotiations between different parties in interest-group coalition negotiations sometimes evidence this pattern.

Aside from circumstantial or situational pressures, there are some parties who bargain competitively because they believe that is the way to conduct business. There are also parties who are simply predisposed to bargain competitively and will incline to do so opportunistically in any bargaining situation if possible.

Finally, it is important to note that one can bargain competitively in a negotiation on some issues and cooperatively on others. In other words, a negotiator can selectively use competitive strategy or tactics on particular issues, while using a cooperative or problem-solving strategy on other issues. In such a case, extracting gain competitively may not greatly endanger future relationships. At least, there is a judgment call concerning this. The negotiator attempts to calculate the net effect of the overall results and skews the benefits, insofar as possible, to his side. In this kind of calculation, it is clear that there is some kind of assessment or balancing of short-term versus long-term gain. Again, there is no formula to calculate these gains, and the parties probably follow rules of thumb prevalent in the industry and developed from prior experience, or they calculate these gains based on hopes or individualized assessments.

Similarly, it is possible for negotiators to use an integrative or problem solving bargaining strategy in order to increase the amount of gain possible to the parties. At some point, however, notwithstanding cooperation to produce greater gain, the parties will have to distribute or divide the gain. Therefore, they may also engage in competitive bargaining.

Obviously, competitive bargaining covers a continuum of behaviors from the simplest, unreflective adversarial actions to highly conscious and virtually scripted contests. As such, competitive bargaining moves are natural responses in some negotiation situations and advantageous or profitable actions in others. This being so, what are the downsides to competitive negotiation?

At least in its full-blown form, competitive negotiation is risky bargaining. The competitor takes risks in order to secure gains. Among these is the risk that there will be no gains at all. The competitive strategy of staking out a position and holding firm, particularly when joined with various devious tactics, runs the risk of alienating, frustrating, or angering the other party and, thus, precluding a possible agreement.

Even if there is an agreement, it may not be a sustainable one. On reflection, the other party may conclude that it does not really like the deal or feels that it was "taken" in some way. Furthermore, even if there is a deal and it survives, the bargaining that occurred may adversely affect future relations between the parties. This is certain to happen if one party discovers that the other party actively misled or manipulated it. It may also happen just because of residual hard feelings or mistrust arising from the tactics used.

Beyond these concerns, competitive bargaining is neither efficient nor productive bargaining. It is inefficient and nonproductive because parties who withhold and manipulate information miss possibilities of cooperating to find or create additional value to divide between them. As a result, they can be said "to leave gains on the table."

Along this line, genuine cooperation and positive relationships are two real gains that competitive negotiators are unlikely to ever realize and bring to bear in immediate or prospective negotiations between themselves and others. Put another way, although a competitive negotiator may realize a gain in a particular negotiation, he may forgo far greater possible gains in doing so.

## LEGAL NEGOTIATION AND SETTLEMENT
### 25–30 (1983)[*]
### By Gerald R. Williams

[Ed. Note: Gerald Williams' research studied the negotiating behaviors of practicing attorneys in Denver, Colorado and Phoenix, Arizona. While Williams found that these lawyers could generally be placed in either the cooperative or the competitive category in terms of their negotiating behaviors, he concluded that there were effective and ineffective negotiators in both categories. That is, use of a cooperative style could, in and of itself, no more guarantee negotiating effectiveness than the use of a competitive style.]

In contrast to the friendly, trustworthy approach of cooperative effectives, effective/competitives are seen as dominating, competitive, forceful, tough, arrogant, and uncooperative. They make high opening demands, they use threats, they are willing to stretch the facts in favor of their clients' positions, they stick to their positions, and they are parsimonious with information about the case. They are concerned not only with maximizing the outcome for their client but they appear to take a gamesmanship approach to negotiation, having a principal objective of outdoing or outmaneuvering their opponent. Thus, rather than seeking an outcome that is "fair" to both sides, they want to outdo the other side; to score a clear victory . . .

While there are differences in approach between the two types of effective negotiators, both types are, in fact, rated as highly effective. Our interest is in what makes them effective, *i.e.*, what traits they have in common. Common traits have particular importance, since law students and attorneys can seek to understand and emulate them irrespective of which pattern they prefer to follow . . . .

Both types of effective negotiators are ranked as highly experienced. This comes

---

as no surprise, since we normally assume that negotiating effectiveness improves with experience. Its meaning here is illuminated by the comment of a responding attorney, who wrote: "it is important to have enough experience in order that you have confidence in yourself and be able to convey that confidence."

More importantly, both types are seen as ethical, trustworthy and honest, thus dispelling any doubt about the ethical commitments of effective/ competitives. However, the priority of these traits is ranked much higher for cooperatives (3rd, 6th and 1st in priority) than for competitives (15th, 20th and 11th in priority). Given the current interest and concern about professional responsibility in the Bar, the high ratings on ethical and trustworthy for both effective groups are worthy of notice. Although literature on professional responsibility generally argues that high ethical standards are a precondition to success in practice, many law students and some practicing attorneys continue to believe or suspect that they must compromise their ethical standards in order to effectively represent their clients and attain success in practice. The findings of this survey suggest such compromises may be not only unnecessary, but actually counterproductive to one's effectiveness in negotiation situations.

In the same vein, we see that both types are careful to observe the customs and courtesies of the bar. While some attorneys have argued that there are tactical advantages in deliberately departing from the etiquette of the profession, as a general rule effective negotiators observe it . . . .

Although effective/competitives were seen as taking unrealistic opening positions, in general they share with cooperatives the traits of being realistic, rational, and analytical. These three attributes become very important in interpreting negotiator behavior. They mean more than the idea of "thinking like a lawyer"; they impose limits on how far a negotiator may credibly go in such things as interpretation of facts, claims about damages and other economic demands, and levels of emotional involvement in the case.

Both effective types are seen as thoroughly prepared on the facts and the law of the case. They are also described as legally astute. This, again, is something to be expected. But it bears emphasis because, as we shall see, ineffective negotiators lack these qualities. One attorney had these traits in mind when he wrote, "In my experience, the most important part of negotiation is thorough preparation and a complete knowledge of the strengths and weaknesses of your position . . . . I feel individual personality traits (e.g., loud, forceful, quiet, reserved) are unimportant."

Legal astuteness means they have not only done their homework by informing themselves about the legal and procedural ramifications of the case, but they also have acquired good judgment about how and when to act with respect to this information.

Both types of effective attorneys are rated as creative, versatile, and adaptable. This is true even though competitive effectives are also labeled rigid. Apparently there is a distinction between being tough (which competitive attorneys are) and being obstinate. An attorney should not be so rigid that he is unable to seek creative solutions to problems. The flavor of the terms is suggested in a comment by an attorney representing a party who was involved in a very acrimonious dispute with a neighbor over an irrigation ditch. He wrote, "Our problem was solved by a simple relocation agreement executed by the parties and recorded. The opposition attorney and myself, after great study and much effort, came up with the simple solution of simply relocating the ditch."

Both types are self-controlled . . . .

One of the more important marks of effective negotiators is skill in reading their opponent's cues. This refers not only to the ability to judge an opponent's reactions in negotiating situations, but to affirmatively learn from the opponent. The old saying is that experience is the best teacher. Experience is only a good teacher for those who are skillful at learning from it. In the course of interviews connected with Denver attorneys, they were routinely asked what they did when they were faced with an inexperienced opponent — an opponent fresh out of law school. Their responses were very informative. One group of attorneys would get a sly grin on their face, their eyes would light up, and they would say "I hammer them into the ground." By far the larger number of attorneys responded quite differently, however. They said that when they had a "green" opponent, they slowed the case way down, tried to spell everything out as they went, and tried generally to show the younger attorney the right way to go about handling a case.

Consider this problem from the perspective of law graduates recently admitted to the bar. During the first few months of practice, they encounter some attorneys who hammer them into the ground, exploiting and taking advantage of them at every turn, and others who are trying to teach them how to be good lawyers. The experience is not calculated to engender trust in fellow officers of the court. Rather, the tendency in young lawyers is to develop a mild paranoia and to distrust everyone. This is unfortunate, because *some* opponents are providing valuable information, albeit in subtle ways. The key, then, is to learn to observe and "read" the opposing attorney and know who can be trusted and who cannot and then learn from both types without being misled by either.

Competitive and cooperative effectives are rated as perceptive, a term that goes hand in hand with skill in reading cues. It relates in part to the ability to perceive an opponent's strategy and his subjective reaction to your strategy. It also has a larger connotation, referring to the accuracy of one's perception of the whole case. One attorney in our study gave a telling description of his perception of a recently completed case: "I lost the case. Though my opponent was ineffective in preparation and presentation — and was a drunk — the judge *disbelieved* my key witness, a fundamentalist Minister, and the plaintiff got every cent he had wrongly demanded from my client."

Finally, it must be stressed that both types of effective negotiators are also rated as effective trial attorneys. As mentioned earlier, the alternative to settlement is trial. If an attorney is known as a weak trial attorney, it will often be more profitable for his opponent to take him to trial than agree to a reasonable settlement. This creates an awkward and troublesome dynamic, because the weak trial attorney knows that his client would be poorly served by an inept trial of the case. The weak attorney discounts the case as an inducement to the other side to settle and avoid the costs (and benefits) of trial. The interplay between fear of trial and discounting of the case is not healthy. There appears to be only one solution: to be taken seriously, lawyers who negotiate legal disputes (as opposed to non-actionable matters) must either develop substantial expertise as trial attorneys, or must openly associate themselves (whether by partnership, a referral system, or some other way) with very effective trial counsel.

## NOTES AND QUESTIONS

(1)   Would you characterize your negotiation style as cooperative or competitive? Why?

(2)   Do Professor Goodpaster's suggestions for dealing with a competitive negotiator ("defensive cooperativeness," etc.) make you feel more comfortable about adopting a cooperative bargaining posture? Why or why not?

## 3.   Problem-Solving Negotiation

## TOWARD ANOTHER VIEW OF LEGAL NEGOTIATION: THE STRUCTURE OF PROBLEM-SOLVING
31 UCLA L. Rev. 754, 817–29 (1984)*
By Carrie Menkel-Meadow

### C. *The Process of Problem-Solving Negotiation*

The process of problem-solving negotiation is likely to be very different from the linear, reciprocal concession patterns leading to compromise in adversarial negotiation. This section reviews how problem-solving negotiation processes are likely to differ from adversarial negotiation.

### 1. Planning

As the discussion thus far should indicate, the crux of the problem-solving approach is the conceptualization and planning which precede any execution of the negotiation. A problem-solving conception of negotiation should be distinguished from cooperative or collaborative negotiation. The latter refers to particular behaviors engaged in during the negotiation, such as "being flexible, disclosing information and establishing good relationships with the other negotiator." These behaviors may be useful in problem-solving negotiations, but they can also be used as tactics in adversarial negotiations where their purpose is to achieve greater individual gain. The conceptualization used in planning problem-solving negotiation is useful in all negotiation, regardless of the particular behaviors chosen in the executory stages. Planning may indicate that needs are truly incompatible and call for the use of adversarial strategies to maximize individual gain, or that resort to adjudication is necessary.

Although economic evaluation of the case and some prediction of how a court

---

would rule in a dispute resolution will still be appropriate, potential solutions need not be limited to some prediction of the mid-point compromise between estimated first offers. Instead, the planning stages of a problem-solving negotiation resemble the brainstorming process described by Fisher & Ury in *Getting To YES*. The process emphasizes exploring and considering both parties' underlying needs and objectives and the devices suggested earlier in this Article for expanding resources. The problem solver who has engaged in a brainstorming planning session is likely to approach a negotiation with a number of possible proposals which can be offered for two-sided brainstorming with the other party. While the planning stages of an adversarial negotiation may narrow and make the offers more precise, the problem-solving planning stages are more likely to result in a broadening of solutions. As Fisher & Ury point out, the key to creative problem-solving is to separate the creative stages of planning from the necessarily more rigid judgment stages.[257] The more potential solutions a negotiator is able to bring to the bargaining table, the more probable it is that agreement will be reached; stalemate and rejection are less likely to occur. In the legal context these brainstorming sessions should include the client, as she may have some solutions of her own, as well as important insights into what the other party desires.

The planning discussed above is primarily substantive planning focused on potential solutions rather than strategic planning focused on what positions to take in the negotiation. Strategic planning may depend on how willing the other party is to depart from the more familiar adversarial negotiation process. At the intersection of substantive and strategic planning are considerations of what information about the other party's needs is necessary to plan for solutions acceptable to the other party. An example best illustrates this point.

Suppose that in a lawsuit based on concealment of a leaky roof in the sale of a residence, the plaintiff has sued for $10,000, the cost of repairing the roof. However, a more extensive portion of the roof was repaired than that which seemed necessary to prevent leaks. The plaintiff has been forced to take out a bank loan in order to repair the roof. This is a further encumbrance on the property, and the plaintiff is having a great deal of difficulty making all of the payments on the house. In addition, the plaintiff is concerned that her parents will learn she bought the house without following their advice to have an inspection made. The defendant seller of the house needs to make payments on her own house and is worried about the possibility of rescission. A bona fide dispute about the facts is whether the defendant misrepresented the facts, and if so, whether he did so negligently or intentionally. The seller holds a second mortgage on the house and the plaintiff now threatens to withhold payment. The plaintiff has taken the deposition of the defendant's former housekeeper who does remember a leaky roof when the defendant was in possession.

Assuming that we represent the plaintiff in this case, there are a number of needs that can be identified. Economically, the plaintiff would like to recover the cost of the roof repair, probably with a minimum of transaction costs. Depending on her dealings and relationship with the defendant, the plaintiff might wish to have the defendant's actions declared legally fraudulent. Recall, however, that in this

---

[257] R. FISHER & W. URY at 62-66. [R. FISHER & W. URY, GETTING TO YES (1981).]

example the defendant holds a second mortgage on the house so that the plaintiff and the defendant will have a continuing relation-ship if the plaintiff remains in the house. The plaintiff's social needs may include preventing her parents from discovering that she bought the house without an inspection. Psychologically, it is possible that the plaintiff feels both foolish for not discovering the leak and angry because it was hidden. Furthermore, the plaintiff may feel that the defendant's deception was morally wrong and she may want an apology, payment as punish-ment, and/or an assurance that this is the only undisclosed defect.

At this point all we know of the defendant's needs may be what we learned from our client, the plaintiff. We know, for example, that the defendant needs the money from the second mortgage to pay the mortgage on her own new home. We may know that the defendant would prefer not to have a legal judgment of fraud entered against her because it will damage her credit rating. Similarly, the defendant may not want a lawsuit for fraud to become public because it could damage her relationship with business associates or her reputation in the community. Finally, it is possible that because the house-keeper has already given testimony against her, the defendant fears losing a lawsuit and may feel regretful or guilty about what she has done. Note that many of the assumptions or speculations about the defendant's needs have to be more fully discovered, either in pretrial discovery or in informal investigation, or tested in the negotiation.

Having identified the parties' needs, we can now begin to consider a number of general solutions. These may include such things as settling the case privately because both parties fear publicity, an apology and new promise that nothing else is defective, and perhaps a delayed or installment payment from defendant to plaintiff, or a reduction on the plaintiff's obligation on the second mortgage. The one remaining issue which is likely to result in conflicting views, the amount of the settlement, can be made less difficult either by having an independent determina-tion of the proper amount to repair the original damage or by expanding the resources through time payments and tax structures that may permit the plaintiff to realize more dollars than the defendant actually pays out.

The structure of this example may not work in all cases, but it illustrates how the analysis of both parties' needs may lead to a number of possible solutions.

## 2. Execution

To the extent that both parties engage in a problem-solving negotiation structure, the negotiation is likely to resemble a fluid brainstorming session. Even if only one party has engaged in a problem-solving planning process, the negotiation need not be reduced to an adversarial exercise. First, the parties may begin with a greater number of possible solutions simply because two heads are better than one. In addition, as empirical research has demon-strated, when both parties approach negotiation with the objective of working collaboratively, more of the information reflecting the parties' needs may be revealed, facilitating the search for solutions. Thus, in the case of the leaky roof, the amount of damages might be easier to determine if both parties approached the problem by looking for ways to reach agreement than if one approached the problem as simply maximizing or minimizing payment, using litigation as a threat. On the other hand, even a single problem solver can propose alternative ways of measuring liability that may eventually be successful, if she has accurately determined the other party's needs.

When the problem solver is able to present a number of different solutions which potentially satisfy at least some of the other party's needs, it is more likely that the adversarial concession and argumentation pattern can be avoided than if she presents a single demand. The parties can consider variations of each of the proposals using the techniques of game theorists who simply alter the coordinates slightly at each play to see if a more efficient solution can be achieved. Thus, the negotiation game may be played on a multi-dimensional field rather than on one that is linear, or two-dimensional. In the leaky roof case one party may suggest a number of different methods of payment, such as reduction of the second mortgage, lump-sum, or installment payments at different discount factors, rather than simply demanding $10,000.

In addition to the different offer structure, problem-solving negotiations are likely to have different information sharing processes. As discussed above, many conventional works on negotiation urge the negotiator not to reveal information. The problem solver recognizes that he is more likely to develop solutions which meet the parties' needs by revealing his own needs or objectives, while at the same time trying to learn about the other party's. In short, there is no incentive to dissemble. When this is the goal, the process consists of asking questions in search of clarification and information, rather than making statements or arguments designed to persuade the other party to accept one's own world view.

On the other hand, totally uninhibited information sharing may be as dysfunctional as withholding information. In experimental simulations Pruitt & Lewis found that there was not necessarily a correlation between free information exchange and joint profit.[268] Instead, joint profit was associated with information processing — that is, the ability to listen to, receive, and understand the information and how it related concretely to the problem. Furthermore, information sharing in a thoughtless and unrestricted fashion may lead to the sharpening of conflict as value differences are revealed in competing goals and needs. In problem-solving negotiation it is crucial to understand the usefulness and function of particular pieces of information — such as exploring how strongly one party desires something — because each piece is related to possible solutions. Problem solvers must determine what information is needed and why, and must be able to absorb information from the other side to test assumptions about needs, goals or objectives.

An example taken from my negotiation course can illustrate. In negotiating a partnership agreement, students are given information about each of the prospective partners. One partner has an immediate need for a relatively high salary because he must provide for a disabled child. The other partner would also like a high salary, but is more concerned about creating the partnership because he is excited about entering a new business. Students, who in my experience are more likely to be adversarial negotiators, have tended to approach the salary negotiation

---

[268] Pruitt & Lewis at 170–72. [Pruitt & Lewis, *The Psychology of Integrative Bargaining, in* NEGOTIATIONS: SOCIAL-PSYCHOLOGICAL PERSPECTIVES (D. Druckman ed. 1977).]

as a conventional zero-sum negotiation. When, as happens occasionally, one side reveals why the salary is needed, a greater variety of solutions seem to come unlocked, such as sliding scales, deferred versus immediate compensation, special provisions for the child, and salary trade-offs for other items. In this situation the party who learns of the disabled child either may be moved by sympathy or by the more instrumental realization that if this is of concern to his future partner it should be dealt with now so it is not a future drain on the partnership. Whatever the motivation, the new information can serve as a source of new solutions ending an otherwise stalemated salary negotiation. Obviously, not all negotiation problems will contain such useful information, but the problem solver is willing to share information about needs that may facilitate such solutions. Thus, problem solving produces a more sophisticated calculus concerning what information should be revealed.

Related to the information flow is the process by which the proposals are evaluated during the negotiation. Fisher & Ury describe this process in a problem-solving environment as principled movements which are reasoned, justified statements about why a particular proposal is important. Fisher & Ury distinguish such movements from the arguments over position which occur in conventional adversarial negotiation. In conventional negotiation, each party takes a position such as the first offer or target position, argues for it, and then makes unprincipled concessions to reach a compromise.

Even conventional adversarial negotiation, however, may be justified by principled movements. One of the most valuable contributions of the growing clinical literature on legal negotiation has been the analysis of using reasons for concessions. Thus, in order to avoid the pitfalls of totally unjustified concessions, negotiators are told that "it is important that the pattern and content of . . . justifications [for concessions] will be well thought out in ad-vance" as "the justification offered for a particular concession invariably will be assessed by one's opponent . . . ."[276] These suggestions about principled movement in the adversarial context, however, have been used largely to justify movements up and down the limited linear plane. Thus, although useful even in adversarial negotiation, principled movements are of a different sort and used for different purposes in a problem-solving negotiation.

According to Fisher & Ury, in the problem-solving context the negotiator will use principled movements to justify proposals and suggestions in terms of their relationship to the parties' underlying interests or objectives. Reconciling interests will be more effective than arguing over positions, they say, because "for every interest there usually exist several possible positions that could satisfy it . . . . Reconciling interests rather than compromising between positions also works because behind opposed positions lie many more shared interests than conflicting ones."[278]

In the process of considering possibilities, the problem solver articulates reasons why a particular solution is acceptable or unacceptable, rather than simply rejecting

---

[276] G. BELLOW & B. MOULTON. [G. BELLOW & B. MOULTON, THE LAWYERING PROCESS: NEGOTIATION (1981).]

[278] R. FISHER & W. URY at 11, 41-57. [R. FISHER & W. URY, GETTING TO YES (1981).]

an offer or making a concession. Articulating reasons during the negotiation facilitates agreement in a number of ways. First, it establishes standards for judging whether a particular solution is sensible and should be accepted. If the reason is focused on the parties' underlying needs, the negotiator can consider whether the proposal is satisfactory to the parties. She need not be concerned with such conventional evaluation as "Is this the most I can get?" or its counterpart, "Is this the least I can get away with?" Second, principled proposals focus attention on solving the problem by meeting the parties' needs, rather than winning an argument. Furthermore, continuously focusing justification on the parties' needs may cause negotiators to see still other solutions, rather than simply to respond with arguments about particular offers. The use of principled proposals can decrease the likelihood that unjustified and unnecessary concessions will be made simply to move toward agreement. Finally, the use of principled proposals causes the parties to share information about their preferences that they might otherwise be reluctant to reveal.

Principled negotiations in the legal context may be more complex, however. In addition to proposals based on the parties' underlying needs, negotiators can focus on the legal merits as a justification for a particular proposal. In-deed, negotiators are told to use "the law" or "the facts" to make arguments or justify positions in analyzing how concessions can be justified in adversarial negotiations. For example, in deciding whether to accept a particular settlement offer a negotiator might say: "We might not agree on the percentage of responsibility, but in this jurisdiction there is comparative negligence so it is unlikely that our contributory negligence will bar recovery. My client is entitled to something." In some sense, all legal negotiations are measured against the legal merits because, in deciding whether to accept a particular proposal, the negotiator must also decide whether the negotiated agreement is better than the one which would be achieved at trial or in a form contract. In Fisher & Ury's parlance this is termed one of the BATNAs (Best Alternative to a Negotiated Agreement). All proposals in litigation negotiations will be measured against predictions about what the court might order.

Proposals justified by the legal merits can be problematic. Given a dispute where the parties have widely divergent views of the merits and how they will be determined by a fact-finder, negotiators may find themselves involved in precisely the sort of unproductive argumentation inherent in adversarial negotiation. Indeed, as some have argued, one of the primary advantages of negotiation over adjudica-tion is that no judgment need be made about whose argument is right or wrong. Parties can agree to settle on principles such as community norms or values that are broader than those the court can consider. On the other hand, focusing on the merits as a justification still may be more productive than adhering to arbitrary positions simply out of competitive stubbornness.

Ideally, of course, proposals should be justifiable on a basis which integrates the parties' needs and the legal merits. Returning to the leaky roof example, consider how a demand by the plaintiff for $10,000 "because your client defrauded mine" contrasts with the following proposal to the defendant:

"One solution here might be for your client to pay my client $7,000 by reducing the monthly payment on the second mortgage over the term of the five-year mortgage. It seems to me that this is fair because if we go to trial I think the court will find the defendant liable for at least $7,000 of the damages to the roof. The housekeeper's testimony will make it clear the defendant knew of the leak and the court will believe the housekeeper because she has no reason to lie. A payment of $7,000 is fair because it cost $3,000 to repair the roof, $3,000 to re-plaster the room and $1,000 to replace the ruined rugs. The proposal seems fair because it fits the needs of both of the parties. My client needs a reduction in her total monthly payments to meet all of her obligations, including the second mortgage payment to your client, and your client won't be out of any immediate cash to settle this case. If you prefer some other method of payment or other formulation, I'd be happy to discuss it with you."

The defendant's lawyer is now able to respond to the assessment of the legal merits and his client's needs and may modify this proposal, perhaps by offering a small cash payment with less of a reduction on the second mortgage to insure some future income. In addition, by presenting proposals with such justifications, each party reveals its assumptions about the other party's needs and legal positions, and can be corrected where wrong. When proposals are not justified in this way, the problem-solving negotiator should ask on what basis the proposal is made to be sure the principles are articulated and not assumed. Notice that the proposal is sufficiently flexible and indeterminate in terms of how the $7,000 second mortgage reduction will be structured. Both parties, therefore, can modify the proposal and contribute to the final solution without having to accept or reject the general principle of the solution.

Thus, although the relationship of the legal merits to the parties' underlying needs may be more problematic and complex than a simpler justification on the basis of the parties' underlying interests, these articulated rationales for negotiation proposals may be more likely to produce acceptable solutions.

Finally, a word should be said about the process of problem-solving negotiation from the perspective of the behavior of the parties. Problem-solving conceptions of negotiation do not necessarily result in weak or conciliatory strategies or tactics. As Fisher & Ury have stated, "being 'nice'" is not the answer to unproductive adversarial negotiations. Negotiating styles and behaviors are the means or procedures by which negotiation results and solutions are achieved, but they are not synonymous concepts. An overly coop-erative negotiator may be just as likely to produce an ineffective compromise by giving in without basis as would a competitive negotiator who stubbornly holds to an unreasonable position. Some game theory suggests that cooperative strategies positively affect joint outcomes. Empirical studies of the effectiveness of cooperative versus competitive behaviors, however, are more complex and as yet inconclusive, both in legal negotiation and in more general negotiations studied by social psychologists. It is beyond the scope of this Article to discuss particular behaviors, other than in the context of negotiation structure. Furthermore, the state of negotiation art and science is not sufficiently advanced to permit accurate generalizations about specific behavioral choices.

Because problem-solving negotiations are likely to result in a greater number of potential solutions not contemplated in advance, the client in such negotiations is more likely to become involved in evaluating proposals. This will be particularly true where a client's objectives or needs may change over time, or need to be reevaluated as new proposals are forthcoming. Thus, the increased fluidity and emphasis on the parties' underlying interests may result in greater client involvement in the legal negotiation process. One of the key differences between the conventional adversarial model and the problem-solving model is the extent to which the parties and their lawyers engage in a continually interactive negotiation process, using the opportunity to seek new solutions rather than simply moving along a predetermined linear scale of compromise.

## NOTES AND QUESTIONS

(1) Professor Menkel-Meadow states that the planning stage of problem-solving negotiation resembles a "fluid brainstorming session" and that in the execution stage the problem-solving negotiator should offer reasons why a solution may be acceptable or unacceptable. How are these aspects of the two stages related?

(2) May a problem-solving approach be used in connection with both integrative and distributive bargaining? By both cooperative and competitive negotiators?

## 4.  What's in a Label?

In the following commentary on negotiation pedagogy, Andrea Kupfer Schneider argues that rather than focus on negotiation styles (e.g., integrative, distributive, competitive, cooperative), we should be teaching the skills that make for effective negotiation.

### TEACHING A NEW NEGOTIATION SKILLS PARADIGM
39 Wash. U. J.L. & Pol'y 13 (2012)[*]
By Andrea Kupfer Schneider

Imagine the following description of a negotiator: In the most recent sales negotiation, this negotiator was open, friendly, warm, she schmoozed at the beginning of the negotiation, asserted her legal and policy arguments as to her position, asked questions for information about the situation, asked the other side about their interests, avoided answering a few challenging questions, conceded slowly, demonstrated respect for the other side and that she was listening to them, created options, found trade-offs that became part of the solution, grabbed a larger percentage of the pie that she created, held absolutely unmovable on the delivery date, added a promise of better quality follow-up in the future, and then, to get the deal done, split the difference at the end on the insurance cost. What negotiation style is this? Collaborative because she schmoozed and created options? Competitive because she was unmovable on the date and grabbed more of the pie? Compromising because she made trade-offs?

And herein lays the problem with negotiation style labels: they hide the reality

---

of what negotiators actually do, and need to do, in order to be effective. Effective negotiators need to choose skills that are appropriate given the context, client, and counterpart. The selection of skills is what matters, not the label given to them. And while the use of labels might provide guidance . . . through a framework at the outset, these same labels hamstring us later . . .

. . .

### 1. Assertiveness

The ability to assert yourself in a negotiation can depend on your alternatives, your goals, your research or knowledge in the area, and your ability to speak persuasively. In order to assert oneself, a minimal skill might be some level of competence and knowledge. An average skill would be to have fully researched the situation and be well-prepared. Best practices would include confidence based on competence and knowledge.

In measuring your skills using the concept of BATNA, a minimal level of skill would be to know your BATNA in advance of a negotiation. The average skill level would be to then set your reservation price for the negotiation based on that BATNA. And best practices would be to work on improving your BATNA before and during the negotiation. You could also work to worsen their BATNA.

A minimal skill would be to set a realistic, specific goal. Average skill would perhaps be to set this goal optimistically high with sufficient research into criteria to back this up. And best practices would include having mapped out framing arguments or other persuasive tools that would help sell your goals. For example, . . . [some] argue that the key to success is a good story. And, as they define it, "A story is a fact, wrapped in an emotion that compels us to take action that transforms our world." Minimal skill in speaking would be the ability to explain your client's position. Average skill would include speaking clearly about why this position is worthwhile. Best practices would include researching in advance what types of arguments, criteria (legal precedent, industry practice, etc.), and salesmanship techniques work best with your particular counterpart. There are, no doubt, other skills as part of assertiveness that could be similarly mapped.

### 2. Empathy

Empathy is linked to success in a variety of careers. The skill of "empathic accuracy," according to William Ickes, is what creates "the most tactful advisors, the most diplomatic officials, [and] the most effective negotiators." Even lawyers and economists now recognize that separating decision-making from emotions is detrimental.

Being empathetic in a negotiation requires a complex mix of skills — a willingness to hear the other side, open-mindedness or curiosity, good questioning and excellent listening, among others. First, one needs the belief and understanding that your counterpart might have something to contribute. And so a minimal skill would be to distinguish between the rare win-lose negotiations and those that might have room for joint gain. An average skill would be the ability to find integrative potential. Best practices would be to translate the parties' interests into realistic integrative proposals.

Second, one needs the skills to gather information about one's counterpart to build the relationship in order to work together substantively. A minimal skill might be to ask questions of the other side in order to get information about them to help move the process along. An average skill would perhaps be to ask questions to uncover the counterpart's interests and needs. Best practices would include having a learning conversation in order to better understand the counterpart's client and that client's situation in order to propose solutions that respond to those needs.

Similarly, a minimal skill in listening would be to let the other side explain their case without interrupting. An average skill would be to ask questions when they are done to both clarify and demonstrate one's listening. Best practices would include looping or active listening to confirm that you accurately understand their perspective and that, even if you don't agree with their position, you respect their position.

### 3. Flexibility

Talented negotiators work to find a variety of ways to get the job done both in their strategic choices as well as more flexible outcomes. Being flexible in negotiation allows a stylistic move from simple compromising to more sophisticated integrative solutions. It also helps to prevent stalemate. And so a minimal skill on flexible strategic choices might be choosing a style based on a particular context or counterpart. An average skill would be shifting your strategy or tactics in the course of the negotiation to respond to your counterpart. Best practices would include careful thinking about the reputation of your counterpart, selecting skills on that basis as well as your own skill set and your client's situation, and then adapting your skills as needed based on your counterpart and newly acquired information in the course of the negotiation.

In terms of finding creative outcomes, Leigh Thompson writes about three types of creativity: fluency (the ability to create many solutions); flexibility (the ability to generate different solutions); and originality (the ability to come up with a unique solution). A negotiator will want to work on all three of types in order to be most effective and to think about the processes (for example, brainstorming) that might assist in creating different solutions. A minimal skill would be simply knowing your priorities so that you could do trade-offs at the table. An average skill could be preparing one or two different tradeoffs that might work (cash payment in exchange for earlier settlement, length of contract in exchange for lower salary, etc.) Best practices would be to examine a variety of creative processes both before and during a negotiation — non-specific compensation, contingent agreements, adding issues, etc. — that could provide additional solutions.

### 4. Social Intuition

We know that having a pleasant and welcoming personality helps effectiveness in life. The work of Daniel Goleman on emotional and social intelligence has made it clear that successful people manage their emotions and social skills in order to get along with others. As Goleman notes from studies of primates, outgoing monkeys have lower levels of stress hormones, stronger immune function, and are best able to integrate into new social groups. In short, "[t]hese more sociable young monkeys are the ones most likely to survive." While we are unlikely to deny another negotiator life-sustaining food because they are not outgoing, Goleman outlines the significant business and life advantages to being more socially intelligent. And recent articles have focused on the importance of teaching these skills to lawyers.

Social intelligence itself is defined as both social awareness (much of this falls under empathy discussed above) and social facility, which includes interacting and presenting ourselves to others. Others have also written about the importance of being nice and of the "No-Asshole" rule in business as being exceedingly successful.

In a more specific negotiation context, we have seen this from several angles. The research on tone in negotiation shows that positive moods can make people more creative and more likely to use integrative strategies. The converse is also true — negotiators in bad moods are more likely to be competitive.

Similarly, in rating negotiators as effective, . . . many adjectives covering social skills fit into effectiveness: personable, rational, perceptive, self-controlled, sociable, helpful, smooth, etc. Unsurprisingly, these adjectives could be mapped onto a measure of social intelligence.

Some students might argue that a more effective personality cannot be taught — we are or are not, by the time we are adults, outgoing and sociable. Yet a closer reading of the skills should overcome that hesitancy. This is not an issue of personality but rather of working on social skills that can be taught and improved. For example, in relation to setting the tone of the negotiation, a minimal skill might be to have a basic greeting. An average skill could be to think about how to set a better tone by having food, or ambiance. Best practices could include a conscious attempt to enter the negotiation in your own good mood and actively work to ensure that the other side is similarly situated.

In terms of setting rapport, for example, Leigh Thompson suggests that a "[s]avvy negotiator[] increase[s her] effectiveness by making themselves familiar to the other party." A minimal skill would be to have a level of cordiality. An average skill level would be to schmooze with the other side, asking questions about them, and breaking the ice. Best practices would include advance research to find areas of commonality and to be genuinely friendly & curious.

## 5. Ethicality

Perceptions of a negotiator's ethicality — his trustworthiness and willingness to follow the ethical rules — has a direct impact on reputation. And reputation — the perception of ethicality — is directly linked to effectiveness in negotiation. A minimal level of skill would be to follow the professional rules of responsibility and not actively deceive the other side. An average level of skill would be to also view possible deceptive behavior through the lens of likely ramifications including your reputation. Best practices would include being actually trustworthy and treating the other side fairly.

The levels of trust, outlined by Roy Lewicki, could also be used to measure skills as we want to be trustful as well as trustworthy. A minimal level of skill would be to create calculus-based trust between oneself and one's counterpart. An average level would work on knowledge-based trust, where repeated interactions create more predictable responses. Finally, best practices might be striving for identification-based trust where the parties create a mutual understanding of each other's needs and can act on their behalf. This latter level of trust might not be realistic in between opposite sides of the negotiation but understanding the incentives that create this level of trust can be very helpful, particularly in repeated interactions.

Being both trustworthy and trustful includes defending yourself against the unethical. A minimal level of skill would be to assume that others might lie to you and contemplate what you can do about that. An average level of skill would include asking defensive questions to double check their assertions and writing compliance measures into the contract. Best practices could include building a sufficiently strong relationship so that it is more difficult for others to lie to you.

6. Putting the Skills Together

Ideally, we could create a three dimensional figure that demonstrates how all these skills relate to one another.

. . .

Each person could measure themselves on each skill independently while working to broaden their skill arsenal. Each skill might not be utilized in each negotiation but the skill-set itself would always be available.

Negotiation books generally provide . . . a framework for how to decide which style to engage. Similarly, the use of a framework for organizing our skill choices remains important. As the negotiator is the constant, at whatever level of skills the negotiator is going into the negotiation, the choice of which skills to use should be determined by examining three key "C" variables: the Client, the Counterpart, and the Context of the particular negotiation. In the legal context, the interests of our clients should have an impact on our behavioral choices. How important are the relationships among the parties? What are their past interactions? What are the client's interests in communication, reputation, and future dealings?

We also need to be aware of how certain skills interact with the other side and the stylistic and skill choices that our counterparts make in the course of the negotiation. Different skills respond better or mesh more effectively depending on the situation. Much has been written, for example, of the concern that problem-solving behavior will be taken advantage of by a more competitive approach. The addendum to the second edition of Getting to Yes primarily answered questions about how to deal with someone who is not problem-solving. . . . [I]t is extremely helpful to review how different styles might interact and, therefore, what skills should be utilized to increase effectiveness in any given interaction.

Finally, the context should have an impact on the skills chosen. What type of case is this? We would imagine that family, personal injury, neighborhood dispute, business deals, or government regulation cases would all have different expectations and different skills might be highlighted in each case. Under what substantive shadow of the law does this negotiation occur? How strong are the facts or law or finances on each side? And, what process is likely to occur if these negotiations do not bear fruit? All of these key questions influence the choice of skills and styles chosen in the course of the negotiation.

So perhaps labels aren't so terrible after all. More, it is that labels can hide or overshadow the real focus of negotiation skills training. We know that we need to categorize in order to convey a significant amount of complex information. We also know that style labels are pithy and easy to understand. At the same time, we need to teach the weaknesses of labels and be sure that our students are not over reliant on the simplification that labels provide. Students need to struggle with the nuances of skills — the fact that skills can seem contradictory or counterintuitive leads us to want to oversimplify (e.g. all competitive negotiators are jerks, all accommodators are nice) rather than more effectively parsing each skill to stand on its own. This is particularly important in the areas of social intuition and ethicality which have, up to this point, been subsumed in discussions of style without holding their own style "label."

When we focus on skills, we can provide students clear goals for improving in all areas while making them more aware of their particular strengths and weaknesses. Further, we can highlight the choices that they must make along the course of negotiation in terms of using each skill rather than sending them off with guidance only at the style level. Finally, we can give students a different construct on how to choose among the skills based on client, counterpart, and context that will give them a more sophisticated understanding of the evolving and nuanced process of negotiation.

## NOTE AND QUESTION

While Professor Schneider's perceptive article offers an important new perspective on teaching negotiation, does she ultimately conclude that labels are still necessary for providing a framework for teaching essential negotiation skills?

## C.  NEGOTIATION ETHICS

Although a number of ethical issues may confront a lawyer who is negotiating on behalf of a client, the most troubling is the extent to which a lawyer may engage in deception. A number of commentators have argued that the ABA Model Rules of Professional Conduct do not offer adequate guidance to the practicing lawyer. The materials in this section wrestle with this notion. Ruth Fleet Thurman argues that Model Rule 4.1 does not present a clear standard as to what is acceptable in negotiations. She suggests that lawyers should generally adhere to a higher standard of truth-telling. Charles Craver is more accepting of Rule 4.1 and draws a line between deception and dishonesty. While he also believes that lawyers should avoid deception and adhere to high standards, he would apparently leave it up to lawyers to police themselves.

## CHIPPING AWAY AT LAWYER VERACITY: THE ABA'S TURN TOWARD SITUATION ETHICS IN NEGOTIATIONS
### 1990 J. Disp. Resol. 103, 103–15*
### By Ruth Fleet Thurman

Should the legal profession permit lawyers to lie when negotiating on behalf of clients? The virtually unequivocal position of the profession and commentators is "no," and such a position is generally followed by the American Bar Association Model Rules of Professional Conduct (Model Rules).** The Preamble to the Model Rules states, "[a]s a negotiator a lawyer seeks a result advantageous to the client but consistent with the requirements of *honest dealings with others*." Model Rule 8.4(c) declares that dishonesty, fraud, deceit, and misrepresentation constitute professional misconduct, and is based on a similar rule in the earlier American Bar Association Code of Professional Responsibility (Model Code). The Model Code also mandates that a lawyer shall not knowingly make a false statement of law or fact.

When the American Bar Association (ABA) adopted the Model Rules in 1983, the Model Code provision was included. However, the Model Rules language reads, "false statement of *material* law or fact" in Model Rule 3.3, Candor Toward the Tribunal, and in Model Rule 4.1, Truthfulness in Statements to Others. The narrowing of the veracity requirement in negotiations is clearly set forth in the official Comment to Model Rule 4.1. (Comments are intended as 'guides to interpretation.') The Comment declares, "A lawyer is required to be truthful when dealing with others on a client's behalf, but generally has no affirmative duty to inform an opposing party of relevant facts." The Comment continues, "[w]hether a particular statement should be regarded as one of fact can depend on the circumstance. *Under generally accepted conventions in negotiations* certain types of statements ordinarily are not taken as statements of material fact." The Comment then singles out three exceptions to the veracity requirement for negotiators: (1) Estimates of price or value placed on the subject of a transaction; (2) a party's intentions as to an acceptable settlement of a claim; and (3) the existence of an undisclosed principal except where nondisclosure of the principal would constitute fraud. The reason for developing these three particular items as exceptions is unclear and is certainly inconsistent with the Preamble's *honest dealings with others* precept, and Model Rule 8.4's proscription against dishonesty, deceit and mis-representation . . . .

. . . .

. . . The error in . . . the exception for lying in negotiations provided in Rule 4.1, is in the notion that rules of ethics must be set so that they accommodate the lowest possible threshold of professional behavior. Lawyers should abide by high and aspirational standards of conduct. Lawyers' influential position in society, together with their fiduciary responsibilities, demand uncompromising levels of trust, integrity, and veracity. Countenancing puffery, exaggeration, distortion and out-right lying in negotiations is inconsistent with this high standard, especially in light of the indispensable role of lawyers in our legal system. Lawyers ought not be compelled to lie for clients or to compensate for the lies of opposing counsel who comfortably exploit the exception to veracity as set out in the Comment to Model Rule 4.1.

[Professor James] White suggests that truthfulness ought to be determined contextually by the subject matter of the negotiation, and the region and background of the negotiators, and type of law practice. This thinking represents another outgrowth of a *situational ethics* framework of analysis. The difficulty of devising standards applicable to the wide range of activities embraced by negotiation and the wide range of proficiency, skill, and sophistication among lawyers from divergent backgrounds, contrary to White's suggestion, does not justify relaxing requirements of integrity and veracity in negotiations.

Is White correct in his assertion that successful negotiators must be able to mislead like poker players and that even the most honest and trustworthy do so? Is misleading the same as lying? What is a lie? What is the harm in a little lying? Webster defines a "lie" as "an assertion of something known or believed by the speaker to be untrue with intent to deceive . . . an untrue or inaccurate statement that may or may not be believed true by the speaker. something that misleads or deceives."

Philosopher Sissela Bok defines a "lie" as "an intentionally deceptive message in the form of a *statement*."[89] When she began her study of lying, Bok wrote that she looked to moral philosophers for guidance and concluded that in addition to hurting the liar and the victim, lies harm society by lowering the level of trust and social cooperation. Relations among human beings are founded on some degree of veracity, without which institutions collapse.

Bok recommends a "test of publicity"[92] which asks which lies, if any, would reasonable persons justify. The test requires reasonable persons to look for non-deceptive alternatives and moral reasons for and against the lie from the perspective of those potentially deceived or affected by the lie. The test also considers the value to society of veracity and accountability, and whether informed consent to be deceived has been freely given (as in playing poker or bargaining in a bazaar where each tries to outwit the other). The reasonable persons would consider the harm to persons outside the deceptive situations, such as distrust, loss of personal standards, and spreading of deception by others in retaliation or limitation.

Consent, Bok observes, must be based on adequate information, ability to make a choice, and freedom to opt out. Informed consent eliminates the discrepancy between liar and dupe. Thus, reasonable persons would probably have no objection to buyer and seller trying to outwit each other by bargaining deceptively in a bazaar.

Even if Bok's test of publicity countenanced lying in a bazaar or a poker game, the question remains whether negotiations by lawyers should be placed on a par with bargaining in a bazaar or playing poker. Looking beyond the liars and dupes

[89] S. Bok, LYING: MORAL CHOICE IN PUBLIC AND PRIVATE LIFE 15 (1978) (emphasis in original).
[92] *Id.* at 100.

to the harm to persons outside the situation, one can see that lying spreads and multiplies the harm and abuse, thereby increasing the damage. Moreover, the absence of clear-cut standards as to what is acceptable increases the likelihood of abuse.

It is easy to see that blatant deception in negotiations can produce these harmful results. Even trivial puffery, if told with the objective of shading the truth or in an effort to distort or mislead, undermines the integrity of the liar, who will then find it easier to slide into a more serious level of lying and distortion. Like pedestrians crossing the street against red lights or automobile drivers exceeding the speed limit, law-abiding citizens find themselves falling into the same practices when they observe large numbers of persons violating the law. If many lawyers shade the truth when they negotiate in behalf of clients, the practice will spread by imitation or retaliation and will spill over into more serious distortions. The ultimate outcome is loss of trust and goodwill toward lawyers and the law. Bar association public relations campaigns may be able to dispel *myths* about lawyers, but not matters for which there is a *factual* basis.

To avoid this insidious cycle, lawyers engaged in negotiations should make it a practice to weigh their statements before speaking and ask themselves: Is this statement true? Is it necessary? Do I have an alternative? May I say nothing or tell the truth? Like the social white lie, told usually out of good intentions to be polite or save someone's feelings, puffery, exaggeration, or simple misstatements in negotiations can become ingrained and habitual. At that point, duplicity becomes a way of life. These types of deception can be reduced by consciously looking for alternatives, even without clear-cut standards as to what is acceptable.

## NEGOTIATION ETHICS: HOW TO BE DECEPTIVE WITHOUT BEING DISHONEST/HOW TO BE ASSERTIVE WITHOUT BEING OFFENSIVE
38 S. Tex. L. Rev. 713, 714–15, 718–20, 724–31, 733–34 (1997)*
By Charles Craver

. . . Although the ABA Model Rules unambiguously proscribe all lawyer prevarication, they reasonably, but confusingly, exclude mere "puffing" and dissembling regarding one's true minimum objectives. These important exceptions appropriately recognize that disingenuous behavior is indigenous to most legal negotiations and could not realistically be prevented due to the nonpublic nature of bargaining interactions.

If one negotiator lies to another, only by happenstance will the other discover the lie. If the settlement is concluded by negotiation, there will be no trial, no public testimony by conflicting witnesses, and thus no opportunity to examine the truthfulness of assertions made during the negotiation. Consequently, in negotiation, more than in other contexts, ethical norms can probably be violated with greater confidence that there will be no discovery and punishment.

One of the inherent conflicts with regard to this area concerns the fact that what

---

people label acceptable "puffing" when they make value-based representations during legal negotiations may be considered improper mendacity when uttered by opposing counsel.

Even though advocate prevarication during legal negotiations rarely results in bar disciplinary action, practitioners must recognize that other risks are created by truly dishonest bargaining behavior. Attorneys who deliberately deceive opponents regarding material matters or who withhold information they are legally obliged to disclose may be guilty of fraud. Contracts procured through fraudulent acts of commission or omission are voidable, and the responsible advocates and their clients may be held liable for monetary damages. It would be particularly embarrassing for lawyers to make misrepresentations that could cause their clients additional legal problems transcending those the attorneys were endeavoring to resolve. Since the adversely affected clients might thereafter sue their culpable former counsel for legal malpractice, the ultimate injury to the reputations and practices of the deceptive attorneys could be momentous. Legal representatives who employ clearly improper bargaining tactics may even subject themselves to judicial sanctions.

Most legal representatives always conduct their negotiations with appropriate candor, because they are moral individuals and/or believe that such professional behavior is mandated by the applicable ethical standards. A few others, however, do not feel so constrained. These persons should consider the practical risks associated with disreputable bargaining conduct. Even if their deceitful action is not reported to the state bar and never results in personal liability for fraud or legal malpractice, their aberrational behavior is likely to be eventually discovered by their fellow practitioners. As other attorneys learn that particular lawyers are not minimally trustworthy, future interactions become more difficult for those persons. Factual and legal representations are no longer accepted without time-consuming and expensive verification. Oral agreements on the telephone and handshake arrangements are no longer acceptable. Executed written documents are required for even rudimentary transactions. Attorneys who contemplate the employment of unacceptable deception to further present client interests should always be cognizant of the fact that their myopic conduct may seriously jeopardize their future effectiveness. No short-term gain achieved through deviant behavior should ever be permitted to outweigh the likely long-term consequences of those improper actions.

. . . .

When lawyers are asked if negotiators may overtly misrepresent legal or factual matters, most immediately reply in the negative. Many lawyers cite Model Rule 4.1 and suggest that this prohibition covers all intentional misrepresentations. While attorneys are correct with respect to deliberate misstatements by negotiators concerning material legal doctrines, they are not entirely correct with respect to factual issues. Almost all negotiators expect opponents to engage in "puffing" and "embellishment." Advocates who hope to obtain $50,000 settlements may initially insist upon $150,000 or even $200,000. They may also embellish the pain experienced by their client, so long as their exaggerations do not transcend the bounds of expected propriety. Individuals involved in a corporate buy out may initially over-or under-value the real property, the building and equipment, the inventory, the accounts receivable, the patent rights and trademarks, and the goodwill of the pertinent firm.

It is clear that lawyers may not intentionally misrepresent material facts, but it is not always apparent what facts are "material." The previously noted Comment to Rule 4.1 explicitly acknowledges that "estimates of price or value placed on the subject of a transaction and a party's intentions as to an acceptable settlement of a claim" do not constitute material facts under that provision. It is thus ethical for legal negotiators to misrepresent the value their client places on particular items. For example, attorneys representing one spouse involved in a marital dissolution may indicate that their client wants joint custody of the children, when in reality he or she does not. Lawyers representing a party attempting to purchase a particular company may understate their client's belief regarding the value of the goodwill associated with the target firm. So long as the statement conveys their side's belief — and does not falsely indicate the view of an outside expert, such as an accountant — no Rule 4.1 violation would occur.

Legal negotiators may also misrepresent client settlement intentions. They may ethically suggest to opposing counsel that an outstanding offer is unacceptable, even though they know the proposed terms would be accepted if no additional concessions could be generated. Nonetheless, it is important to emphasize that this Rule 4.1 exception does not wholly excuse all misstatements regarding client settlement intentions. During the early stages of bargaining interactions, most practitioners do not expect opponents to disclose exact client desires. As negotiators approach final agreements, however, they anticipate a greater degree of candor. If negotiators were to deliberately deceive adversaries about this issue during the closing stage of their interaction, most attorneys would consider them dishonest, even though the Rule 4.1 proscription would remain inapplicable.

The relevant Comments to Rule 4.1 are explicitly restricted to negotiations with opposing counsel. Outside that narrow setting, statements pertaining to client settlement objectives may constitute "material" fact. ABA Commission on Ethics and Professional Responsibility, Formal Opinion 370 indicated that knowing misrepresentations regarding client settlement intentions to judges during pretrial settlement discussions would be impermissible because the misstatements would not be confined to adversarial bargaining interactions.

When material facts are involved, attorneys may not deliberately misrepresent the actual circumstances. They may employ evasive techniques to avoid answering opponent questions, but they may not provide false or misleading answers. If they decide to respond to inquiries pertaining to material facts, they must do so honestly. They must also be careful not to issue partially correct statements they know will be misinterpreted by their opponents, since such deliberate deception would be likely to contravene Rule 4.1.

A crucial distinction is drawn between statements of lawyer opinion and statements of material fact. When attorneys merely express their opinions — for example, "I think the defendant had consumed too much alcohol" and "I believe the plaintiff will encounter future medical difficulties" — they are not constrained by Rule 4.1. Opposing counsel know that these recitations only concern the personal views of the speakers. Thus, personal view statements are critically different from lawyer statements indicating that they have witnesses who can testify to these matters. If representations regarding witness information is knowingly false, the misstatements would clearly violate Rule 4.1.

A frequently debated area concerns representations about one's authorized limits. Many attorneys refuse to answer "unfair" questions concerning their authorized limits because these inquiries pertain to confidential attorney-client communications. If negotiators decide to respond to these queries, must they do so honestly? Some lawyers believe that truthful responses are required, since they concern material facts. Other practitioners assert that responses about client authorizations merely reflect client valuations and settlement intentions and are thus excluded from the scope of Rule 4.1 by the drafter's Comment. For this reason, these practitioners think that attorneys may distort these matters.

Negotiators who know they cannot avoid the impact of questions concerning their authorized limits by labeling them "unfair" and who find it difficult to provide knowingly false responses can employ an alternative approach. If the plaintiff lawyer who is demanding $120,000 asks the defendant attorney who is presently offering $85,000 whether he or she is authorized to provide $100,000, the recipient may treat the $100,000 figure as a new plaintiff proposal. That individual can reply that the $100,000 sum suggested by plaintiff counsel is more realistic but still exorbitant. The plaintiff attorney may become preoccupied with the need to clarify the fact that he or she did not intend to suggest any reduction in his or her outstanding $120,000 demand. That person would probably forego further attempts to ascertain the authorized limits possessed by the defendant attorney!

. . . .

Many practicing attorneys seem to think that competitive/adversarial negotiators — who use highly competitive tactics to maximize their own client returns — achieve more beneficial results for their clients than their cooperative/problem-solving colleagues — who employ more cooperative techniques designed to maximize the joint return to the parties involved. An empirical study, conducted by Professor Gerald Williams, of legal practitioners in Denver and Phoenix contradicts this notion. Professor Williams found that sixty-five percent of negotiators are considered cooperative/problem-solvers by their peers, twenty-four percent are viewed as competitive/adversarial, and eleven percent did not fit in either category.[43] When the respondents were asked to indicate which attorneys were "effective," "average," and "ineffective" negotiators, the results were striking. While fifty-nine percent of the coopera-tive/problem-solving lawyers were rated "effective," only twenty-five percent of competitive/adversarial attorneys were rated effective. On the other hand, while a mere three percent of cooperative/problem-solvers were considered "ineffective," thirty-three percent of competitive/adversarial bargainers were rated "ineffective."

In his study, Professor Williams found that certain traits were shared by both effective cooperative/problem-solving negotiators and effective competitive/adversarial bargainers. Successful negotiators from both groups are thoroughly prepared, behave in an honest and ethical manner, are perceptive readers of

---

[43] GERALD R. WILLIAMS, LEGAL NEGOTIATION AND SETTLEMENT 19 (1983).

opponent cues, are analytical, realistic, and convincing, and observe the courtesies of the bar. The proficient negotiators from both groups also sought to maximize their own client's return. Since this is the quintessential characteristic of competitive/adversarial bargainers, it would suggest that a number of successful negotiators may be adroitly masquerading as sheep in wolves' clothing. They exude a cooperative style, but seek competitive objectives.

Most successful negotiators are able to combine the most salient traits associated with the cooperative/problem-solving and the competitive/ adversarial styles. They endeavor to maximize client returns, but attempt to accomplish this objective in a congenial and seemingly ingenuous manner. They look for shared values in recognition of the fact that by maximizing joint returns, they are more likely to obtain the best settlements for their own clients. Although successful negotiators try to manipulate opponent perceptions, they rarely resort to truly deceitful tactics. They know that a loss of credibility will undermine their ability to achieve beneficial results. Despite the fact successful negotiators want as much as possible for their own clients, they are not "win-lose" negotiators who judge their results, not by how well they have done, but by how poorly they think their opponents have done. They realize that the imposition of poor terms on opponents does not necessarily benefit their own clients. All factors being equal, they want to maximize opponent satisfaction. So long as it does not require significant concessions on their part, they acknowledge the benefits to be derived from this approach. The more satisfied opponents are, the more likely those parties will accept proposed terms and honor the resulting agreements.

These eclectic negotiators employ a composite style. They may be characterized as competitive/problem-solvers. They seek competitive goals (maximum client returns), but endeavor to accomplish these objectives through problem-solving strategies. They exude a cooperative approach and follow the courtesies of the legal profession. They avoid rude or inconsiderate behavior, recognizing that such openly adversarial conduct is likely to generate competitive/adversarial responses from their opponents. They appreciate the fact that individuals who employ wholly inappropriate tactics almost always induce opposing counsel to work harder to avoid exploitation by these openly opportunistic bargainers. Legal negotiators who are contemplating the use of offensive techniques should simply ask themselves how they would react if similar tactics were employed against them.

. . . .

Despite the contrary impression of some members of the general public, I have generally found attorneys to be conscientious and honorable people. I have encountered few instances of questionable behavior. I would thus like to conclude with the admonitions I impart to my Legal Negotiating students as they prepare to enter the legal profession. Lawyers must remember that they have to live with their own consciences, and not those of their clients or their partners. They must employ tactics they are comfortable using, even in those situations in which other people encourage them to employ less reputable behavior. If they adopt techniques they do not consider appropriate, not only will they experience personal discomfort, but they will also fail to achieve their intended objective due to the fact they will not appear credible when using those tactics. Attorneys must also acknowledge that they are members of a special profession and owe certain duties to the public that transcend those that may be owed by people engaged in other businesses. Even though ABA Model Rule 1.3 states that "[a] lawyer shall act with reasonable diligence," Comment One expressly recognizes that "a lawyer is not bound to press for every advantage that might be realized for a client. A lawyer has professional discretion in determining the means by which a matter [shall] be pursued."

Popular negotiation books occasionally recount the successful use of questionable techniques to obtain short-term benefits. The authors glibly describe the way they have employed highly aggressive, deliberately deceptive, or equally opprobrious bargaining tactics to achieve their objectives. They usually conclude these stories with parenthetical admissions that their bilked adversaries would probably be reluctant to interact with them in the future. When negotiators engage in such questionable behavior such that they would find it difficult, if not impossible, to transact future business with their adversaries, they have usually transcended the bounds of propriety. No legal representatives should be willing to jeopardize long-term professional relationships for the narrow interests of particular clients. Zealous representation should never be thought to require the employment of personally compromising techniques.

Lawyers must acknowledge that they are not guarantors — they are only legal advocates. They are not supposed to guarantee client victory no matter how disreputably they must act to do so. They should never countenance witness perjury or the withholding of subpoenaed documents. While they should zealously endeavor to advance client interests, they should recognize their moral obligation to follow the ethical rules applicable to all attorneys.

Untrustworthy advocates encounter substantial difficulty when they negotiate with others. Their oral representations must be verified and reduced to writing, and many opponents distrust their written documents. Their negotiations become especially problematic and cumbersome. If nothing else moves practitioners to behave in an ethical and dignified manner, their hope for long and successful legal careers should induce them to avoid conduct that may undermine their future effectiveness.

Attorneys should diligently strive to advance client objectives while simultaneously maintaining their personal integrity. This philosophy will enable them to optimally serve the interests of both their clients and society. Legal practitioners who are asked about their insistence on ethical behavior may take refuge in an aphorism of Mark Twain: "Always do right. This will gratify some people, and astonish the rest[!]"

## NOTES AND QUESTIONS

(1)   In the excerpt from her article, Professor Thurman states: "If many lawyers shade the truth when they negotiate in behalf of clients, the practice will spread by imitation or retaliation and will spill over into more serious distortions. The ultimate outcome is loss of trust and goodwill toward lawyers and the law." Is this concern heightened with the increased use of mediation by lawyers? In his thoughtful article, *Telling the Truth in Mediation: Mediator Owed Duty of Candor*, Disp.

Resol. Magazine, Winter 1997, Bruce E. Meyerson quotes a prominent mediator: "Don't believe anything a lawyer will tell you during a mediation!" Meyerson goes on to argue for a higher standard of truth-telling in the mediation setting. Do you think it is feasible to have one standard of truth-telling in mediation, another in negotiation, and still another in court?

(2) The question of whether the dictates of Rule 4.1 apply to mediation, or whether an attorney is held to a higher truthfulness standard akin to Rule 3.3's requirement of absolute candor to a tribunal will be discussed in Chapter 10.

(3) In a path-breaking study, Professors Art Hinshaw and Jess K. Alberts sought to determine empirically whether attorneys actually follow the requirements of Rule 4.1. They surveyed 734 lawyers, asking them what course they would take "if a client asked them to assist in a fraudulent pre-litigation settlement scheme":

> Nearly one-third indicated they would agree to one of the client's two requests to engage in the fraudulent scheme. Half of the respondents indicated that they would refuse both of the client's overtures. And the remaining twenty percent of respondents either indicated that they were not sure how to respond to both requests or refused one request and indicated that they were not sure how they would respond to the other request. Furthermore, this study identified multiple failures in the respondents' understanding and application of Rule 4.1.

Because these findings suggest apparent widespread violations of the requirements of Rule 4.1, the authors conclude that, "certain beliefs and attitudes about lawyer negotiation responsibilities need to be adjusted" and make recommendations that include clarification of Rule 4.1's requirements, greater attention to education on negotiation ethics in law school and CLE programs, and increased enforcement of the rules. 16 Harv. Negot. L. Rev. 95, 147–63 (2011). Do you think that the organized bar and the law schools will be willing to address this problem head-on, and take the steps suggested by Hinshaw and Alberts?

## D. PSYCHOLOGICAL AND ECONOMIC ANALYSES

In recent years, social science researchers, particularly from psychology and economics, have offered new insights into negotiation behavior. Much of this research is referred to as "barriers" research, because it seeks to identify and analyze various barriers or obstacles to the settlement of cases. The authors of the materials in this section apply these research findings to the negotiation practice setting.

# PSYCHOLOGICAL PRINCIPLES IN NEGOTIATING CIVIL SETTLEMENTS

4 Harv. Negot. L. Rev. 1, 2–4, 39–56 (1999)*
By Richard Birke & Craig R. Fox

This article focuses on psychological obstacles to the rational resolution of legal disputes. Our purpose is to alert legal scholars and practitioners to the psychological principles most relevant to legal negotiation, particularly those that apply to civil litigation. In so doing, we adapt a well-established body of psychological literature to legal negotiations. Because there have been few attempts to date to adapt these principles specifically to the realm of legal decisionmaking, our applications of some of these principles to legal negotiations are necessarily speculative. Nonetheless, we believe that awareness of these principles will help practitioners achieve more efficient and desirable settlements. The psychological principles that we present in this article operate in a similar manner to optical illusions in that they typically involve automatic, subconscious processes that are difficult to subvert. However, we think that increased awareness of psychological principles will make any lawyer a better negotiator, as awareness can help lawyers identify situations in which they might consciously choose to override or attempt to compensate for their instinctive reactions. Moreover, understanding of these tendencies can help lawyers anticipate bias in the behavior of others.

. . . .

This article is organized around a series of questions that lawyers are likely to ask themselves as they guide cases from intake through to settlement.

. . . .

Question 7· Should I make the first offer, and if so, what should it be?

*Your wrongful death case is proceeding. A pre-trial ruling has made the possibility of punitive damages near zero, and given that the heirs are distant relatives, the likelihood of any "loss of consortium" damages is slight. The death came relatively quickly, so you estimate that "pain and suffering" will not yield vast amounts of money from a jury.*

*Nonetheless, because your case on liability is strong, the other side has offered to settle, upon conditions. They will admit to liability if you can agree to actuarial damages (the amount she would have earned over the rest of her life) plus some token amounts for the other aspects of the case. In preparation for negotiation over the amount of actuarial damages, you have discovered some interesting facts. The deceased had worked as a waitress, earning approximately $20,000 per year, but she had finished two years of law school at a reasonably prestigious school, and was on the "Dean's list" every term. She was enrolled and ready to start her final year of school at the time of her death.*

*Attorneys in the case have a meeting with you later this week to discuss possible*

---

*settlement. Will you make the first offer? Will you invite them to make it? If you do, what will it be?*

When considering the question of whether to make the first offer or wait for an opponent to make the first offer, the traditional practice has been for the moving party (the plaintiff or the prosecution) to make a proposal that is rejected by the defendant, and the rejection is followed by a counter. Positional bargaining may cause an iterated chain of steps toward a mid-point, and if the mid-point is agreed upon, a settlement occurs. Otherwise, a trial is likely.

The first "offer" is generally the demand stated in the complaint as the request for damages. However, this amount is often an overstated figure that is included to prevent a jurisdictional challenge and to get the attention of the defendant. It is rarely seen by defendants as a credible settlement offer. Similarly, some defendants respond to the complaint with an offer to settle the case for its nuisance value. Again, this figure is so starkly low relative to the ultimate settlement value of most cases that it is not a perceived as an offer to settle. It is an announcement of aspiration, not valuation.

When the time comes to make sincere offers, someone has to go first, but most attorneys prefer to hold their cards close to their vests. The question looms — how to start?

## 1. Psychological Considerations

There is little empirical research on the question of whether it is best to make the first offer. Two psychological phenomena may be relevant. In situations where one's counterpart has only a vague sense of what is reasonable (*e.g.*, because there is little or no judicial precedent), making the first offer may afford an opportunity to exploit . . . anchoring bias, and draw the counterpart into an order of magnitude that is more favorable to the offeror before the counterpart makes an offer that anchors both parties in a range that favors him. On the other hand, a pervasive norm that governs negotiation behavior is that of reciprocity, according to which one should reciprocate concessions made by others. In fact, distributive negotiations typically settle roughly midway between the opening offers to the extent that this midpoint is feasible for both sides. Hence, making the second offer can afford the negotiator an opportunity to define where that midpoint lies. In general, whether one makes the first offer in order to exploit anchoring, or makes the second offer in order to leave room for concessions and exploit reciprocity, it is good strategy to make as extreme an opening offer as can be gotten away with, but not so extreme that the offeror appears to be negotiating in bad faith.

In cases where opposing counsel has no clear notion of the value of the claim, she will be more susceptible to anchoring bias. The case of the "waitress/lawyer," for example, might provide an opportunity to anchor opposing counsel to a higher number than she might otherwise have considered. Valuing the career worth of a law student is a highly speculative enterprise, as her chosen career path may have been a lucrative corporate career or a lower-salaried career in public interest law. Furthermore, long-term success in her chosen path is largely a matter of guesswork. Hence, a high first offer might draw opposing counsel into a debate about how successful a law career the deceased would have had, rather than a discussion on whether she would have finished law school at all.

In cases where opposing counsel has a reasonable idea concerning the value of the claim, it may behoove the lawyer to wait for the other side to make the first offer so that the lawyer can respond with a counter-offer that defines a midpoint favorable to him. Had the deceased been an established attorney with a stable income, it might make sense to let opposing counsel make the first offer. In such an instance, if opposing counsel offered four million dollars as a settlement, and the lawyer aspired to settle at eight million, she should counter at twelve.

## 2. Remediation

To protect against being exploited by one's counterpart, we suggest that attorneys gather as much information as possible that might help them assess the value of the claim in question. The more information one has at his fingertips, the less likely he is to be drawn into accepting an inequitable offer due to an anchoring bias. Furthermore, we suggest that attorneys decide in advance on their reservation price (in consultation with the client, of course), and that they base this price on a carefully researched estimate of what is likely to happen if the case goes to court. Adjustments are appropriate only as relevant new information comes to light. Finally, we suggest that attorneys can use the norm of reciprocity to their advantage by insisting that their own concessions be followed by concessions from their counterpart. In our experience, people tend to be more sensitive to the rate of concessions than they are to the magnitude of those concessions.

## Question 8: How should I frame the offer?

*The wrongful death case is close to settlement. They've agreed that if you will compromise on the expected wages then they will compensate you for other aspects of the claim — provided that they "feel okay with the offer." The other attorney wants to see your offer in writing.*

*There are a number of aspects of your demand — loss of consortium, expected wages, medical bills, funeral costs, attorneys fees, etc. Some of the bills are in — e.g., funeral costs — and you are waiting for others — e.g., medical bills. Furthermore, although you can compile some of your attorney's fees, you haven't gotten all the hourly work bills from your associates, and you still have bills coming in from expert consultants and investigators. Do you send the information piecemeal, or wait to collect all the information and send one bill?*

Traditional economic analysis suggests that people should be sensitive to the impact of offers on final states of wealth, and that the particulars of how those offers are communicated should not matter. Empirical studies of attorneys suggest that describing an offer in terms of gains versus losses can affect a lawyer's willingness to accept the offer. Certainly, lawyers choose words carefully, and this tendency extends to the crafting and communication of offers. However, for the most part, attorneys use this skill to avoid admitting or denying liability, or to avoid the accidental creation of exploitable weaknesses in their cases. Less thought goes into the question of how to frame an offer so that it is most likely to be accepted.

### 1. The Psychology of Value and Framing

Behavioral decision theorists have documented systematic violations of the standard economic assumption that people evaluate options in terms of their impact on one's final state of wealth. In particular, prospect theory assumes that people adapt to their present state of wealth and are sensitive to changes with respect to that endowment.

Second, people exhibit diminishing sensitivity to increasing gains and losses. For example, increasing an award from zero to $1000 is more pleasurable than increasing an award from $1000 to $2000; increasing an award from $2000 to $3000 is even less pleasurable, and so forth. Similarly, increasing a payment from zero to $1000 is more painful than increasing a payment from $1000 to $2000, and so on. One key implication of this pattern is that people's willingness to take risks differs for losses versus gains. For example, because $1000 is more than half as attractive as $2000, people typically prefer to receive $1,000 for sure than face a fifty-fifty chance of receiving $2,000 or nothing (*i.e.*, they are "risk-averse" for medium probability gains). In contrast, because losing $1000 is more than half as painful as losing $2000, people typically prefer to risk a 50-50 chance of losing $2,000 or losing nothing to losing $1,000 for sure (*i.e.*, they are "risk-seeking" for medium probability losses).

. . . .

Third, prospect theory asserts that losses have more impact on choices than do equivalent gains. For example, most people do not think that a fifty percent chance of gaining $100 is sufficient to compensate a fifty percent chance of losing $100. In fact, people typically require a 50% chance of gaining as much as $200 or $300 to offset a 50% chance of losing $100.

Taken together, the way in which a problem is framed in terms of losses or gains can have a substantial impact on behavior in negotiations. First, loss aversion contributes to a bias in favor of the status quo because relative disadvantages of alternative outcomes loom larger than relative advantages. Hence, negotiators are often reluctant to make the tradeoffs necessary for them to achieve joint gains. To illustrate, consider the case of two partners in a failing consulting firm. The joint office space and secretarial support costs are unduly burdensome, and each could operate productively out of their homes with minimal overhead costs. If they could divide their territory and agree not to compete, each could have a profitable career — but each would have to agree to give up half the firm's client base. Each partner may view the territory they retain as a gain that doesn't compensate adequately for the territory they must relinquish. Yet failure to make such a split consigns them to continuation in a losing venture.

Second, both loss aversion and the pattern of risk seeking for losses may lead to more aggressive bargaining when the task is viewed as minimizing losses rather than maximizing gains. Indeed, in laboratory studies, negotiators whose payoffs are framed in terms of gains (*e.g.*, they were instructed to maximize revenues) tended to be more risk-averse than those whose payoffs are framed in terms of losses (*e.g.*, they were instructed to minimize costs): the first group tended to be more concessionary but completed more transactions. Recently, Professor Rachlinski documented greater willingness to accept settlement offers in legal contexts when the offer is perceived as a gain compared to when it is perceived as a loss.[182]

Third, the attractiveness of potential agreements may be influenced by the way in which gains and losses are packaged and described. In particular, if a negotiator wants to present a proposal in its best possible light to a counterpart, he or she should attempt to integrate each aspect of the agreement on which the counterpart stands to lose (in order to exploit the fact that people experience diminishing sensitivity to each additional loss) and segregate each aspect of the agreement on which the counterpart stands to gain (in order to avoid the tendency of people to experience diminishing sensitivity to each additional gain). For instance, in the partnership dissolution example, it would be most effective to describe the territory forgone as a single unit (*e.g.*, "everything west of highway 6 is mine") and the territory obtained in component parts (*e.g.*, "and you will have the Heights neighborhood, the eastern section of downtown, everything north of there to the river, South Village, etc."), and least effective to describe the territory foregone in component parts (*e.g.*, "I keep the west side of downtown, the riverfront, North village, and everything between downtown and Ballard Square . . .") and the territory obtained as a single unit (*e.g.*, "everything east of highway 6 is yours").

### 2. Remediation: Protecting Against Framing Effects

Knowledge of the psychology of value can help a negotiator make offers appear more desirable to her counterpart, as described above. As for defending against inconsistency or manipulations by others, a negotiator should be aware that aspirations, past history, or previous offers may influence the frame of reference against which a negotiator perceives losses and gains; as a result, risk attitudes may be influenced by these transitory perceptions, which in turn influence how aggressively a negotiator bargains. Furthermore, negotiators must consciously overcome their natural reluctance to make concessions in order to exploit opportunities for trades that make both sides better off. Finally, in order to protect against mental accounting manipulations by others, a negotiator might develop a scoring system for each of the issues under consideration or translate everything into a unified dollar metric. By adding up points or dollars across all issues, the negotiator can focus on the value of the aggregate outcome to her client, rather than a piecemeal mélange of incremental gains and losses that may have been creatively framed by her counterpart.

Returning to our hypothetical question of whether to wait and send one bill or to send the bills as they come in, our advice is to wait and send one bill. If one bill came in for expenses to date and then a second bill came in for medical expenses and so forth, the recipient of the bills would have to endure a series of segregated losses rather than a single, integrated loss.

Question 9: How should I evaluate their offers?

[182] *See* Rachlinski at 128. [Jeffrey J. Rachlinski, *Gains, Losses, and the Psychology of Litigation*, 70 S. Cal. L. Rev. 113, 13–58 (1996).]

*You have been discussing with your client two possible settlement packages in your "hot pie" case. Package A would require the company to pay a cash amount of $100,000, and Package B would require an agreement by the company to pay all of your client's current and future medical bills, change the temperature at which they serve their pies, and give her a cash payment of $50,000. Your client has expressed, in confidence, a mild preference for the $100,000 cash.*

*While you are out of town on other business and before you could communicate these offers to your counterpart, the opposing counsel leaves you a message offering $100,000 to settle the case. When you call your client to communicate this news, rather than show elation, she expresses concern and suggests that the other deal now seems more appealing. How do you counsel your client?*

When an attorney receives an offer from the other side, he is ethically obligated to transmit that offer to his client.[185] He is not obligated to show the client a letter or play a voice-mail message or recite verbatim the offer with appropriate inflections. As the lawyer communicates the offer, the lawyer inevitably, if unwittingly, introduces a spin on the offer that may influence the client to consider it favorably or unfavorably. Usually the attorney's impression (and indeed, the client's) of the offer will be influenced to some degree by the identity of the offeror. In particular, if the attorney's dealings with the other side have been rancorous, the attorney may view any offer with a great deal of suspicion. Sometimes the relationship impedes impartial evaluation of an offer, causing a negotiator to reject an offer from an adversary that he should have accepted.

## 1. Psychology of Reactive Devaluation

Fixed-pie bias (i.e., the assumption that what is good for my counterpart must be bad for me) may contribute to reactive devaluation, which is a tendency to evaluate proposals less favorably after they have been offered by one's adversary. In one classic study conducted during the days of Apartheid, researchers solicited students' evaluations of two university plans for divestment from South Africa.[187] The first plan called for partial divestment, and the second increased investments in companies that had left South Africa. Both plans, which fell short of the students' demand for full divestment, were rated before and after the university announced that it would adopt the partial divestment plan. The results were dramatic: students rated the university plan less positively after it was announced by the university and the alternative plan more positively.

We hasten to note that the source of an offer may be diagnostic of its quality. It may be reasonable to view an offer more critically when the source is one's opponent, particularly if there is an unpleasant history between the parties. However, evidence from the aforementioned studies suggests that people tend to experience a knee-jerk overreaction to the source of the offer. If negotiators

---

[185] Model Rules Of Professional Conduct Rule 1.2(a), 1.4 (1995).

[187] *See* Stillinger et al. [Constance Stillinger et al., The Reactive Devaluation Barrier to Conflict Resolution, unpublished manuscript, Stanford University (1990) (on file with authors).] For a description of the study, see Mnookin & Ross [Robert H. Mnookin & Lee Ross, *Introduction* to BARRIERS TO CONFLICT RESOLUTION 3 (Kenneth J. Arrow et al., eds, 1995).]

routinely under-value concessions made their counterparts, it will inhibit their ability to exploit tradeoffs that might result in more valuable agreements.

Consider an example of how reactive devaluation might manifest itself in a negotiation between lawyers. Imagine a simplified environmental cleanup action in which the parties are a governmental enforcement agency (represented by a single person) and a single responsible polluter. There may be two solutions to their problem. In one, the government effectuates the cleanup and sends a bill to the polluter. In the second, the polluter does the cleanup and the government inspects. Perhaps solution one meets more of the polluters' interests than solution two. One might suppose that the polluter would prefer this solution regardless of how it emerges as the agreed method. However, studies of reactive devaluation suggest that once the government tentatively agrees to that particular solution, the polluter may view the alternative solution more favorably. The apparent thought process is "if they held it back, it must be worse for them and therefore better for me than the one offered." The polluter may irrationally reorder her priorities and reject a deal simply because it was offered freely by an opponent.

## 2. Remediation

Resisting the destructive effects of reactive devaluation will require negotiators to unlearn a pervasive assumption that most people carry with them. Negotiations are rarely fixed-sum and it is simply not true that what is good for one side is necessarily bad for the other. As mentioned above, both parties often have congruent interests or a mutual interest in exploiting tradeoffs on issues that they prioritize differently. To resist reactive devaluation, one must short-circuit a deeply ingrained habit. It is natural to react against freedom to choose, and when an opponent holds back one offer in favor of another, it's natural to yearn for the alternative option. However, it would be wise to critically examine this natural impulse and ask if this impulse is a rational response to a truly inferior offer or an emotional reaction against the other side's initiative.

Even if a lawyer can restrain herself from reactive devaluation, it may be very difficult to buffer this response in his counterpart. Certainly, it first may help to cultivate a cordial relationship with one's counterpart to the extent that this is possible, so that offers are regarded with less suspicion. Second, it may be helpful to ask a mutually trusted intermediary to convey a proposal. Some commentators have suggested that reactive devaluation can be overcome with the help of a mediator. Finally, if a party crafts a settlement package that would be mutually beneficial, it may be helpful to work with opposing counsel to make them feel as if the solution was jointly initiated or even that it was the opposing counsel's idea.

Returning to the hypothetical, the client may be experiencing reactive devaluation. It may behoove the attorney to counsel her client to consider whether her change of heart was a result of the fact that her original package was offered by her opponent in the litigation or is a result of other factors. If her reaction was driven by its source, the attorney should make sure she understands that she is rejecting her formerly-preferred deal solely because it was offered by an adversary, and not necessarily because it fails to meet her interests.

Question 10: How can I get people to accept my offers?

*You are submitting your offer on the harassment case. To what extent do you think that each of the following might help get your offer accepted by opposing counsel? Why?*

*1) "Of course, we put a lot of time and energy into crafting this offer, and we've conceded at least five different times on the amount that we are willing to take. We're asking you to concede just once from your initial offer."*

*2) "You once told me that money was a secondary issue, that it was confidentiality that mattered most to your client. We've agreed to give you that. Isn't your statement still true?"*

*3) "I've run this offer by six other people in this firm, all of whom used to work with you before you took your present job. They all thought that the offer was one that your client should accept."*

*4) "We've been friends for a long time, so how about helping me make this one go away? Once we get it done, I'll take you out for a beer."*

*5) "And while I don't want to put any pressure on you, you probably know that we hired Justice Brown from the local court where our case is filed. I showed him our offer just to get his feedback, and he thought your client would be foolish not to accept."*

*6) "This offer is open for forty-eight hours. After that, all bets are off."*

Negotiation is, in part, a game of mutual influence. Many attorneys are naturally gifted in the art of social influence while others are less comfortable with this dimension of lawyering. We believe that the study of social influence tactics can help attorneys protect them selves against exploitation.

## 1. Psychology of Social Influence

A vast literature in social psychology examines how individuals persuade others to accede to their requests. Psychologist Robert Cialdini[191] organizes the literature into six pervasive principles of social influence that we describe below. Cialdini observed these tactics in his study of salespeople, fund-raisers, advertisers, and other professionals.[192] We believe that these principles apply with equal force to negotiations of civil settlements by attorneys.

### a. Reciprocation

One should repay, in kind, what another person has provided. Even uninvited favors and gifts leave people with a sense of indebtedness that they feel they must reciprocate. In negotiation, there is a strong norm that a party should respond to each concession that his or her counterpart makes with a concession of his or her own, even if the initial offer was rather extreme.

---

[191] *See* Cialdini. [ROBERT B. CIALDINI, INFLUENCE: THE PSYCHOLOGY OF PERSUASION (1993).]

[192] *See id.*

The tendency to reciprocate is not in itself problematic, but when one side reciprocates relatively trivial concessions with meaningful concessions, such as a significant reduction in what was already a reasonable request, she may be committing a negotiation error. A skillful negotiator knows that people tend to reciprocate acts of kindness, even when the original kindness is uninvited and of no value to the recipient. Lawyers bargain over both substantive and logistical matters, such as discovery schedules, stipulations, deposition schedules, compliance with orders, and the possible settlement of the action. They rarely get everything they want, and the result of these interactions generally involves some degree of compromise from both sides. Occasionally, a logistical concession from one attorney may elicit a substantive concession from opposing counsel.

Two suggestions are in order. First, as noted in Question 7, the lawyer should make an optimistic first offer in order to leave room for concessions that will be expected by the other side (in response to concessions that they will make). Second, it is important to resist the temptation to reciprocate meaningless or negligible concessions.

Returning to our hypothetical, it is easy to see that the first phrase employed by the attorney is an attempt to exploit the reciprocation norm. The speaker draws attention to previous concessions, thereby putting pressure on the respondent to reciprocate.

### b. Commitment and Consistency

Once a person makes a choice or takes a stand, she encounters personal and interpersonal pressure to behave consistently with that commitment. There are at least three manifestations of this principle in negotiation. First, a public commitment to a statement of principles, an aspiration, or a criterion of fairness is difficult to abnegate at a later time. Second, after a negotiator gets her "foot in the door" by having her counterpart accede to a small initial request, later cooperation becomes more likely. Third, after investing significant time and energy into crafting a tentative agreement, negotiators are more likely to give in to last-minute requests by their counterparts.

Sometimes lawyers decrease the possibility of negotiated settlement by publicly committing to an unrealistic aspiration. They often promise an optimistic result before they have all of the relevant facts, typically in an effort to get retain a potential client. For example, a plaintiff's attorney might tell his client that the case should not settle for less than $100,000. The client and attorney may then become wedded to this aspiration level. Suppose the lawyer later discovers that the objective value of the case is $50,000. It may be an embarrassment at this point for the attorney to recommend accepting an offer that is even as high as $80,000.

In addition to commitments made in valuation, commitments made in reaction to offers can be detrimental to the negotiating process. A lawyer often rejects offers made by the other side, or prematurely commits to an unrealistic "walk-away" price. If she later wishes to accept the offer or relax her reservation price, she must either admit that she was wrong or come up with a reason why circumstances have changed. We recommend that lawyers be circumspect in making public commitments, and that they help provide opponents with face-saving reasons to back down from commitments opponents may have made (*e.g.*, provide reasons why circumstances have changed).

It is quite common for negotiators to force endgame concessions. For instance, when a real estate deal is near consummation, it is common for sellers and mortgage companies to reveal myriad small costs that were not discussed earlier. Lawyers may try at the last moment to tack on attorney's fees and court costs to a settlement. Provided that these costs are small relative to settlement amounts, the recipient of such a request may feel that it is better to concede rather than to scuttle the whole deal and "go back to square one." Again, one useful means to defend against such exploitation is to decide in advance on a reservation price and to resist temptations to back off of this value unless additional information justifies doing so.

Returning to the hypothetical, it is easy to see that the use of the phrases "You once told me that . . ." and "Isn't your statement still true?" are attempts to pressure the recipient to remain consistent with prior statements and offers.

### c. Social Proof

People view a behavior as correct in a given situation to the degree that they see others performing it. The reactions of others thus serves as "proof" that the behavior is appropriate. For example, canned laughter has been shown to elicit more laughter in audiences and cause them to rate material as funnier than they do in its absence. In general, people are more likely to follow the behavior of others when the situation is unclear or ambiguous or when people are unsure of themselves. Moreover, people are more likely to follow the example of others whom they perceive to be similar to themselves. Senior lawyers in large firms inculcate junior associates into practice, in part, by modeling a great many behavioral characteristics that are not necessarily effective, but which are nonetheless deeply ingrained. When and where to meet for negotiations, how to dress for work, and how to interview clients are all matters that are typically transmitted uncritically from one generation of firm lawyers to the next.

In settlement negotiations, lawyers can exploit past precedents and examples of other litigants who have accepted similar terms in attempts to gain compliance. In order to defend against such tactics, we encourage lawyers to seek out for themselves information concerning comparable cases and values in order to effectively evaluate the case at bar.

Returning to our hypothetical, the reference to the "other six people" who approved the offer is an attempt to influence the recipient to conform to social proof. These former colleagues provide cues for appropriate behavior in a circumstance in which the proper response is unclear.

### d. Liking

People prefer to say yes to others they know and like. Several factors promote liking: physical attractiveness, similarity, compliments, cooperation, and familiarity. Contrary to the popular belief that a successful negotiator ruthlessly intimidates and exploits her counterparts, a positive relationship can be more effective for achieving mutually beneficial and equitable outcomes. Moreover, leading economists have argued that cooperation and honesty tend to promote long-term success in bargaining. And studies of lawyers negotiating prove that those who are cooperative (a trait that engenders liking) are rated as more effective, on average, than lawyers who are not.

The fourth statement in our hypothetical is a transparent attempt to leverage "liking" in order to influence the recipient to accept the settlement offer. The more the recipient likes the offeror, the more likely she will be to accept.

### e. Authority

People are more likely to accede to the request of a perceived authority figure. The best known illustration of this principle is Milgram's work, which demonstrated the willingness of ordinary people to administer what they thought were dangerous levels of electrical shocks to a person with an alleged heart condition merely because an "experimenter" in a white laboratory coat insisted that "the experiment requires that [they] continue."[206] Equally sobering is the demonstration by Hofling and his colleagues in which a researcher identified himself over the phone as a hospital physician and asked hospital nurses to administer a dangerous dose of an unauthorized drug to a specific patient; in this case 95 percent of the nurses attempted to comply.[207] Not only do titles tend to promote compliance and deference, but so do uniforms and other trappings, such as fancy automobiles. Certainly, most trial attorneys will agree that the judge's physically elevated status and somber, traditional robe reinforce a courtroom hierarchy in which the judge enjoys the greatest status. Even a retired judge or a sufficiently senior partner may lend an air of authority to a position or an offer, as might a "home turf" advantage.

In our hypothetical, the reference to Justice Brown is meant to lend an air of authority to the offer. To the extent that the recipient regards the Justice in esteem or believes him to be a figure of authority in the community, the offer may be more readily accepted.

### f. Scarcity

Opportunities often seem more valuable when they are less available. According to psychological reactance theory, when people are proscribed from making a certain choice, they desire that choice more and work harder to obtain it. This is the principle underlying the success of the ubiquitous "limited time offer" in consumer advertising. Threats to freedom can take the form of time limits, supply limits, and competition. In negotiation, these tactics can be a particularly effective means of gaining compliance. Savvy negotiators can dramatize their alternatives by entertaining competing bids, or they can strategically impose artificial time limits for negotiation.

---

[206] *See* STANLEY MILGRAM, OBEDIENCE TO AUTHORITY (1974).

[207] *See* Charles K. Hofling et al., *An Experimental Study of Nurse Physician Relationships*, 143 J. NERVOUS & MENTAL DISEASE 171 (1966).

In our hypothetical, the time limit attached to the offer may trigger a response by the other side. They may be more willing to accept the offer in reaction to the threat of its imminent disappearance.

# WHY NEGOTIATIONS FAIL: AN EXPLORATION OF BARRIERS TO THE RESOLUTION OF CONFLICT
8 Ohio St. J. on Disp. Resol. 235, 238–49 (1993)*
By Robert H. Mnookin

Why is it that under circumstances where there are resolutions that better serve disputants, negotiations often fail to achieve efficient resolutions? In other words, what are the barriers to the negotiated resolution of conflict?

. . . I will explore four such barriers. Each of these barriers reflect somewhat different theoretical perspectives on negotiation and dispute resolution. The first barrier is a *strategic barrier*, which is suggested by game theory and the economic analysis of bargaining. The barrier relates to an underlying dilemma inherent in the negotiation process. Every negotiation characteristically involves a tension between: (a) discovering shared interests and maximizing joint gains, and (b) maximizing one's own gains where more for one side will necessarily mean less for the other. The second barrier arises as a result of the *principal/agent* problem. In many disputes, principals do not negotiate on their own behalf but instead act through agents who may have somewhat different incentives than their principals. This work draws on research concerning the "principal/agent" problem in law and economics and transaction cost economics. The third barrier is *cognitive*, and relates to how the human mind processes information, especially in evaluating risks and uncertainty. My discussion here draws on recent work in cognitive psychology, especially the path-breaking research of my colleague, Amos Tversky and his collaborator, Daniel Kahneman.[14] The fourth and final barrier, "*reactive devaluation*," draws on the social psychological research of my colleague Lee Ross, and relates to the fact that bargaining is an interactive social process in which each party is constantly drawing inferences about the intentions, motives, and good faith of the other.[15]

As should be obvious, I am not attempting to provide a comprehensive list of barriers or an all-encompassing classification scheme. Instead, my purpose is to show that the concept of barriers provides a useful and necessarily interdisciplinary vantage point for exploring why negotiations sometimes fail. After describing these four barriers and their relevance to the study of negotiation, I will briefly suggest a variety of ways that neutral third parties might help overcome each of these barriers.

## A. Strategic Barriers

[14] *See* JUDGMENT UNDER UNCERTAINTY: HEURISTICS AND BIASES (Daniel Kahneman et al., eds., 1982).

[15] Constance A. Stillinger et al., *The Reactive Devaluation Barrier to Conflict Resolution*, J. PERSONALITY & SOC. PSYCHOL. (under review).

The first barrier to the negotiated resolution of conflict is inherent in a central characteristic of negotiation. Negotiation can be metaphorically compared to making a pie and then dividing it up. The process of conflict resolution affects both the size of the pie, and who gets what size slice.

The disputants' behavior may affect the size of the pie in a variety of ways. On the one hand, spending on avoidable legal fees and other process costs shrinks the pie. On the other hand, negotiators can together "create value" and make the pie bigger by discovering resolutions in which each party contributes special complementary skills that can be combined in a synergistic way, or by exploiting differences in relative preferences that permit trades that make both parties better off. Books like "Getting to Yes" and proponents of "win-win negotiation" emphasize the potential benefits of collaborative problem-solving approaches to negotiation which allow parties to maximize the size of the pie.[17]

Negotiation also involves issues concerning the distribution of benefits, and, with respect to pure distribution, both parties cannot be made better off at the same time. Given a pie of fixed size, a larger slice for you means a smaller one for me.

Because bargaining typically entails both efficiency issues (that is, how big the pie can be made) and distributive issues (that is, who gets what size slice), negotiation involves an inherent tension — one that David Lax and James Sebenius have dubbed the "negotiator's dilemma."[18] In order to create value, it is critically important that options be created in light of both parties' underlying interests and preferences. This suggests the importance of openness and disclosure, so that a variety of options can be analyzed and compared from the perspectives of all concerned. However, when it comes to the distributive aspects of bargaining, full disclosure — particularly if unreciprocated by the other side — can often lead to outcomes in which the more open party receives a comparatively smaller slice. To put it another way, unreciprocated approaches to creating value leave their maker vulnerable to claiming tactics. On the other hand, focusing on the distributive aspects of bargaining can often lead to unnecessary deadlocks and, more fundamentally, a failure to discover options or alternatives that make both sides better off. A simple example can expose the dilemma. The first involves what game theorists call "information asymmetry." This simply means each side to a negotiation characteristically knows some relevant facts that the other side does not know.

Suppose I have ten apples and no oranges, and Nancy Rogers has ten oranges and no apples. (Assume apples and oranges are otherwise unavailable to either of us.) I love oranges and hate apples. Nancy likes them both equally well. I suggest to Nancy that we might both be made better off through a trade. If I disclose to Nancy that I love oranges and don't eat apples, and Nancy wishes to engage in strategic bargaining, she might simply suggest that her preferences are the same as mine, although, in truth, she likes both. She might propose that I give her nine apples (which she says have little value to her) in exchange for one of her very valuable oranges. Because it is often very difficult for one party to know the underlying preferences of the other party, parties in a negotiation may puff, bluff,

[17] Roger Fisher, William Ury & Bruce Patton, Getting to Yes (2d ed. 1991).

[18] David A. Lax & James K. Sebenius, The Manager as Negotiator (1986).

or lie about their underlying interests and preferences. Indeed, in many negotiations, it may never be possible to know whether the other side has honestly disclosed its interests and preferences. I have to be open to create value, but my openness may work to my disadvantage with respect to the distributive aspect of the negotiation.

Even when both parties know all the relevant information, and that potential gains may result from a negotiated deal, strategic bargaining over how to divide the pie can still lead to deadlock (with no deal at all) or protracted and expensive bargaining, thus shrinking the pie. For example, suppose Nancy has a house for sale for which she has a reservation price of $245,000. I am willing to pay up to $295,000 for the house. Any deal within a bargaining range from $245,000 to $295,000 would make both of us better off than no sale at all. Suppose we each know the other's reservation price. Will there be a deal? Not necessarily. If we disagree about how the $50,000 "surplus" should be divided (each wanting all or most of it), our negotiation may end in a deadlock. We might engage in hardball negotiation tactics in which each tried to persuade the other that he or she was committed to walking away from a beneficial deal, rather than accept less than $40,000 of the surplus. Nancy might claim that she won't take a nickel less than $285,000, or even $294,999 for that matter. Indeed, she might go so far as to give a power of attorney to an agent to sell only at that price, and then leave town in order to make her commitment credible. Of course, I could play the same type of game and the result would then be that no deal is made and that we are both worse off. In this case, the obvious tension between the distribution of the $50,000 and the value creating possibilities inherent in any sale within the bargaining range may result in no deal.

Strategic behavior — which may be rational for a self-interested party concerned with maximizing the size of his or her own slice — can often lead to inefficient outcomes. Those subjected to claiming tactics often respond in kind, and the net result typically is to push up the cost of the dispute resolution process. (*Buchwald v. Paramount Pictures Corp.*[21] is a good example of a case in which the economic costs of hardball litigation obviously and substantially shrunk the pie.) Parties may be tempted to engage in strategic behavior, hoping to get more. Often all they do is shrink the size of the pie. Those experienced in the civil litigation process see this all the time. One or both sides often attempt to use pre-trial discovery as leverage to force the other side into agreeing to a more favorable settlement. Often the net result, however, is simply that both sides spend unnecessary money on the dispute resolution process.

## B. The Principal/Agent Problem

The second barrier is suggested by the recent work relating to transaction cost economics, and is sometimes called the "principal/agent" problem. Notwithstanding the jargon, the basic idea is familiar to everyone in this room.

The basic problem is that the incentives for an agent (whether it be a lawyer, employee, or officer) negotiating on behalf of a party to a dispute may induce

---

[21] No. C 706083, 1990 Cal. App. LEXIS 634 (Cal. Superior Jan. 31, 1990).

behavior that fails to serve the interests of the principal itself. The relevant research suggests that it is no simple matter — whether by contract or custom — to align perfectly the incentives for an agent with the interests of the principal. This divergence may act as a barrier to efficient resolution of conflict.

Litigation is fraught with principal/agent problems. In civil litigation, for example — particularly where the lawyers on both sides are being paid by the hour — there is very little incentive for the opposing lawyers to cooperate, particularly if the clients have the capacity to pay for trench warfare and are angry to boot. Commentators have suggested that this is one reason many cases settle on the courthouse steps, and not before: for the lawyers, a late settlement may avoid the possible embarrassment of an extreme outcome, while at the same time providing substantial fees.

The Texaco/Pennzoil dispute may have involved a principal/agent problem of a different sort. My colleague Bob Wilson and I have argued that the interests of Texaco officers and directors diverged from those of the Texaco shareholders in ways that may well have affected the conduct of that litigation.[25] Although the shareholders would have benefited from an earlier settlement, the litigation was controlled by the directors, officers, and lawyers whose interests differed in important respects. A close examination of the incentives for the management of Texaco in particular suggests an explanation for the delay in settlement.

The directors and officers of Texaco were themselves defendants in fourteen lawsuits, eleven of them derivative shareholder actions, brought after the original multi-billion Pennzoil verdict in the Texas trial court. These lawsuits essentially claimed that Texaco's directors and officers had violated their duty of care to the corporation by causing Texaco to acquire Getty Oil in a manner that led to the multi-billion-dollar Texas judgment. After this verdict, and for the next several years, the Texaco management rationally might have preferred to appeal the Pennzoil judgment and seek complete vindication, even though a speedy settlement for the expected value of the litigation might have better served their shareholders. Because they faced the risk of personal liability, the directors and officers of Texaco acted in such a way as to suggest they would prefer to risk pursuing the case to the bitter end (with some slight chance of complete exoneration) rather than accept a negotiated resolution, even though in so doing they risked subjecting the corporation to a ten-billion-dollar judgment. The case ultimately did settle, but only through a bankruptcy proceeding in which the bankruptcy court eliminated the risk of personal liability for Texaco's officers and directors.

## C. Cognitive Barriers

The third barrier is a by-product of the way the human mind processes information, deals with risks and uncertainties, and makes inferences and judgments. Research by cognitive psychologists during the last fifteen years suggests several ways in which human reasoning often departs from that suggested by theories of rational judgment and decision making. Daniel Kahneman and Amos

[25]  Mnookin & Wilson at 295, 315-323. [Robert H. Mnookin & Robert R. Wilson, *Rational Bargaining and Market Efficiency: Understanding* Pennzoil v. Texaco, 75 Va. L. Rev. 295 (1989).]

Tversky had done research on a number of cognitive biases that are relevant to negotiation.[29] This evening, I would like to focus on two aspects of their work: those relating to loss aversion and framing effects.

Suppose everyone attending this evening's lecture is offered the following happy choice: At the end of my lecture you can exit at the north end of the hall or the south end. If you choose the north exit, you will be handed an envelope in which there will be a crisp new twenty-dollar bill. Instead, if you choose the south exit, you will be given a sealed envelope randomly pulled from a bin. One quarter of these envelopes contain a $100 bill, but three quarters are empty. In other words, you can have a sure gain of $20 if you go out the north slightly more. This is a well known phenomenon called "risk aversion." The principle is that most people will take a sure thing over a gamble, even where the gamble may have a somewhat door, or you can instead gamble by choosing the south door where you will have a 25% chance of winning $100 and a 75% chance of winning nothing. Which would you choose? A great deal of experimental work suggests that the overwhelming majority of you would choose the sure gain of $20, even though the "expected value" of the second alternative, $25, is higher "expected" payoff.

Daniel Kahneman and Amos Tversky have advanced our understanding of behavior under uncertainty with a remarkable discovery. They suggest that, in order to avoid what would otherwise be a sure loss, many people will gamble, even if the expected loss from the gamble is larger. Their basic idea can be illustrated by changing my hypothetical. Although you didn't know this when you were invited to this lecture, it is not free. At the end of the lecture, the doors are going to be locked. If you go out the north door, you'll be required to *pay* $20 as an exit fee. If you go out the south door, you'll participate in a lottery by drawing an envelope. Three quarters of the time you're going to be let out for free, but one quarter of the time you're going to be required to pay $100. Rest assured all the money is going to the Dean's fund — a very good cause. What do you choose? There's a great deal of empirical research, based on the initial work of Kahneman and Tversky, suggesting that the majority of this audience would choose the south exit — i.e., most of you would gamble to avoid having to lose $20 for sure.[30] Kahneman and Tversky call this "loss aversion."

Now think of these two examples together. Risk aversion suggests that most of you would not gamble for a gain, even though the expected value of $25 exceeds the sure thing of $20. On the other hand, most of you would gamble to avoid a sure loss, even though, on the average, the loss of going out the south door is higher. Experimental evidence suggests that the proportion of people who will gamble to avoid a loss is much greater than those who would gamble to realize a gain.

Loss aversion can act as a cognitive barrier to the negotiated resolution of conflict for a variety of reasons. For example, both sides may fight on in a dispute in the

---

[29] For a discussion of various cognitive barriers, see Daniel Kahneman and Amos Tversky, *Conflict Resolution: A Cognitive Perspective, in* BARRIERS TO CONFLICT RESOLUTION (K. Arrow et al., eds.).

[30] Amos Tversky & Richard Thaler, *Anomalies: Preference Reversals*, 4 J. ECON. PERSPECTIVES 201 (Spring 1990); Amos Tversky et al., *The Causes of Preference Reversals*, 80 AM. ECON. REV. 204 (March 1990).

hope that they may avoid any losses, even though the continuation of the dispute involves a gamble in which the loss may end up being far greater. Loss aversion may explain Lyndon Johnson's decision, in 1965, to commit additional troops to Vietnam as an attempt to avoid the sure loss attendant to withdrawal, and as a gamble that there might be some way in the future to avoid any loss at all. Similarly, negotiators may, in some circumstances, be adverse to offering a concession in circumstances where they view the concession as a sure loss. Indeed, the notion of rights or entitlements may be associated with a more extreme form of loss aversion that Kahneman and Tversky call "enhanced loss aversion," because losses "compounded by outrage are much less acceptable than losses that are by misfortune or by legitimate actions of others."[31]

One of the most striking features of loss aversion is that whether something is viewed as a gain or loss — and what kind of gain or loss it is considered — depends upon a reference point, and the choice of a reference point is sometimes manipulable. Once again, a simple example suggested by Kahneman and Tversky, can illustrate.

Suppose you and a friend decide to go to Cleveland for a big night out on the town. You've made reservations at an elegant restaurant that will cost $100 a couple. In addition, you've bought two superb seats — at $50 each — to hear the Cleveland orchestra. You set off for Cleveland, thinking you have your symphony tickets and $100, but no credit cards. for $100. You have a choice. You can use the $100 you intended for the fancy dinner to buy Imagine that you park your car in Cleveland and make a horrifying discovery — you've lost the tickets. Assume that you cannot be admitted to the symphony without tickets. Also imagine that someone is standing in front of the Symphony Hall offering to sell two tickets the tickets to hear the concert, or you can skip the concert and simply go to dinner. What would you do?

Consider a second hypothetical. After you park the car, you look in your wallet and you realize to your horror that the $100 is gone, but the tickets are there. In front of the Symphony Hall is a person holding a small sign indicating she would like to buy two tickets for $100. What do you do? Do you sell the tickets and go to dinner? Or do you instead skip dinner and simply go to the concert?

Experimental research suggests that in the first example many more people would skip the symphony and simply go out to dinner, while in the second example, the proportions are nearly reversed; most people would skip dinner and go to the concert. The way we keep our mental accounts is such that, in the first instance, to buy the tickets a second time would somehow be to overspend our ticket budget. And yet, an economist would point out that the two situations are essentially identical because there is a ready and efficient market in which you can convert tickets to money or money to tickets.

The purpose of the hypotheticals is to suggest that whether or not an event is framed as a loss can often affect behavior. This powerful idea concerning "framing" has important implications for the resolution of disputes to which I will return later.

---

[31] Kahneman et al.

### D. "Reactive Devaluation" of Compromises and Concessions

The final barrier I wish to discuss is "reactive devaluation," and is an example of a social/psychological barrier that arises from the dynamics of the negotiation process and the inferences that negotiators draw from their interactions. My Stanford colleague, psychology Professor Lee Ross, and his students have done experimental work to suggest that, especially between adversaries, when one side offers a particular concession or proposes a particular exchange of compromises, the other side may diminish the attractiveness of that offer or proposed exchange simply because it originated with a perceived opponent. The basic notion is a familiar one, especially for lawyers. How often have you had a client indicate to you in the midst of litigation, "If only we could settle this case for $7,000. I'd love to put this whole matter behind me." Lo and behold, the next day, the other side's attorney calls and offers to settle for $7,000. You excitedly call your client and say, "Guess what — the other side has just offered to settle this case for $7,000." You expect to hear jubilation on the other end of the phone, but instead there is silence. Finally, your client says, "Obviously they must know something we don't know. If $7,000 is a good settlement for them, it can't be a good settlement for us."

Both in laboratory and field settings, Ross and his colleagues have marshaled interesting evidence for "reactive devaluation." They have demonstrated both that a given compromise proposal is rated less positively when proposed by someone on the other side than when proposed by a neutral or an ally. They also demonstrated that a concession that is actually offered is rated lower than a concession that is withheld, and that a compromise is rated less highly after it has been put on the table by the other side than it was beforehand.[33]

. . . Ross has described a range of cognitive and motivational processes that may account for the reactive devaluation phenomenon.[35] Whatever its roots, reactive devaluation certainly can act as a barrier to the efficient resolution of conflict. It suggests that the exchange of proposed concessions and compromises between adversaries can be very problematic. When one side unilaterally offers a concession that it believes the other side should value and the other side reacts by devaluing the offer, this can obviously make resolution difficult. The recipient of a unilateral concession is apt to believe that her adversary has given up nothing of real value and may therefore resist any notion she should offer something of real value in exchange. On the other hand, the failure to respond may simply confirm the suspicions of the original offeror, who will believe that her adversary is proceeding in bad faith and is being strategic.

### III OVERCOMING STRATEGIC BARRIERS: THE ROLES OF NEGOTIATORS AND MEDIATORS

The study of barriers can do more than simply help us understand why

---

[33] *See* Stillinger et al. *See also* Lee Ross & Constance Stillinger, *Barriers to Conflict Resolution,* 7 NEGOTIATION J. 389 (Oct. 1991).

[35] *Id.* [Rob J. Robinson et al., *Misconstruing the Views of the "Other Side": Real and Perceived Differences in Three Ideological Conflicts, Stanford Center on Conflict and Negotiation Working Paper No. 18* (June 1990).]

negotiations sometimes fail when they should not. It can also contribute to our understanding of how to overcome these barriers. Let me illustrate this by using the preceding analysis of four barriers briefly to explore the role of mediators, and to suggest why neutrals can often facilitate the efficient resolution of disputes by overcoming these specific barriers.

First, let us consider the strategic barrier. To the extent that a neutral third party is trusted by both sides, the neutral may be able to induce the parties to reveal information about their underlying interests, needs, priorities, and aspirations that they would not disclose to their adversary. This information may permit a trusted mediator to help the parties enlarge the pie in circum-stances where the parties acting alone could not. Moreover, a mediator can foster a problem-solving atmo-sphere and lessen the temptation on the part of each side to engage in strategic behavior. A skilled mediator can often get parties to move beyond political posturing and recriminations about past wrongs and to instead consider possible gains from a fair resolution of the dispute.

A mediator also can help overcome barriers posed by principal/agent problems. A mediator may bring clients themselves to the table, and help them understand their shared interest in minimizing legal fees and costs in circumstances where the lawyers themselves might not be doing so. In circumstances where a middle manager is acting to prevent a settlement that might benefit the company, but might be harmful to the manager's own career, an astute mediator can sometimes bring another company representative to the table who does not have a personal stake in the outcome.

A mediator can also promote dispute resolution by helping overcome cognitive barriers. Through a variety of processes, a mediator can often help each side understand the power of the case from the other side's perspective. Moreover, by reframing the dispute and suggesting a resolution that avoids blame and stresses the positive aspects of a resolution, a mediator may be able to lessen the effects of loss aversion. My colleague Tversky thinks that cognitive barriers are like optical illusions — knowing that an illusion exists does not necessarily enable us to see things differently.[36] Nevertheless, I believe that astute mediators can dampen loss aversion through reframing, by helping a disputant reconceptualize the resolution. By emphasizing the potential gains to both sides of the resolution and de-emphasizing the losses that the resolution is going to entail, mediators (and lawyers) often facilitate resolution.

With respect to the fourth barrier, reactive devaluation, mediators can plan an important and quite obvious role. Reactive devaluation can often be sidestepped if the source of a proposal is a neutral — not one of the parties. Indeed, one of the trade secrets of mediators is that after talking separately to each side about what might or might not be acceptable, the mediator takes responsibility for making a proposal. This helps both parties avoid reactive devaluation by allowing them to accept as sensible a proposal that they might have rejected if it had come directly from their adversary.

---

[36] Tversky & Thaler, *supra* note 30.

## NOTES AND QUESTIONS

(1)  Although the usefulness of interdisciplinary research to negotiation practice is well demonstrated in the foregoing articles, certain limitations have also been noted. Some commentators have pointed to less tangible factors that may influence negotiation behavior but have not been considered by social science researchers. In *The Role of Hope in Negotiation*, 44 UCLA L. Rev. 1661, 1684–85 (1997),[*] Jennifer Gerarda Brown criticizes economic theories of negotiation for failing to recognize a role for hope:

> Hope is part emotion, part preference structure, part cognitive process. Hope affects people's behavior, as much in negotiation as in any other context . . . .
>
> Hope may not be easily subject to manipulation. Even if hope is not fixed, we may be unable to find and operate the mechanism that moves hope up or down. So if hope is not malleable — or if we are unable to change malleable hopes — why focus on it? Why not just take hope as a psychological wildcard — like pride, anger, or love — that may affect the negotiation, but not in a manner that economists would study or care about?
>
> Even if we cannot manipulate hope, we might want to include it in models of negotiation because more inclusive models will be better predictors of negotiation processes and outcomes . . . .
>
> Similarly, hopeless models that fail to incorporate optimism will overestimate the probability of settlement, because they will wrongly assume that negotiators accurately calculate the probable distribution of the other side's reservation price. Realizing that an optimistic seller might inflate the range of the buyer's possible reservation prices will show that such parties are less likely to come to terms than we might at first predict.
>
> Measuring hope — even if we cannot manipulate it — might also be useful. Negotiators should try to assess the other side's optimism or satiation point if these variables might affect behavior in negotiation. For example, if a buyer was able to discover that a seller might be sated easily, this could affect the buyer's first and subsequent offers. Or if the buyer knew that the seller had an unrealistically optimistic view of the buyer's reservation price, the buyer might plan to bring to the negotiation some "proof" that would educate the seller away from her optimism. In either case, measuring hope prior to a negotiation might help a negotiator prepare more thoroughly.

For an argument that economists should move away from the standard neoclassical assumptions by recognizing that people exhibit bounded rationality, bounded self-interest, and bounded willpower, see Christine Jolls et al., *A Behavioral Approach to Law and Economics*, 50 Stan. L. Rev. 1471 (1998). For interdisciplinary commentary on negotiation, see *Symposium: The Emerging Interdisciplinary Canon of Negotiation*, 87 Marq. L. Rev. 637 (2004); The Negotiator's Fieldbook: The

---

[*] Copyright © 1997 by William S. Hein & Co. and UCLA Law Review. Reprinted with permission.

Desk Reference for the Experienced Negotiator (Andrea Schneider & Christopher Honeyman, eds., 2006); and *Rethinking Negotiation Teaching Series* published by DRI Press (2009–2012), at http://law.hamline.edu/rethinkingNegotiation.html.

(2)   Professor Mnookin explores different ways in which the addition of a third-party neutral (a mediator) to the negotiation setting may overcome barriers to settlement. For other discussions of the value of adding a mediator, see Robert A. Baruch Bush, *"What Do We Need a Mediator For?": Mediation's "Value-Added" for Negotiators*, 12 Ohio St. J. on Disp. Resol. 1 (1997), and Jean R. Sternlight, *Lawyers' Representation of Clients in Mediation: Using Economics and Psychology to Structure Advocacy in a Nonadversarial Setting*, 14 Ohio St. J. on Disp. Resol. 269 (1999).

(3)   As you read, analyze, and discuss the materials in the following chapters, consider how mediation may "add value" to negotiations.

# E.   ONLINE NEGOTIATION

## YOU'VE GOT AGREEMENT: NEGOTI@TING VIA EMAIL*
*In* Rethinking Negotiation Teaching: Innovations for Context and Culture
(Christopher Honeyman, James Coben & Giuseppe DePalo, Eds., 2009)
By Noam Ebner, Anita D. Bhappu, Jennifer Gerarda Brown,
Kimberlee K. Kovach & Andrea Kupfer Schneider

Email is a fact of life for any negotiator and we ignore its potentials and pitfalls at our peril. . . .

### *Interactivity*

On the receiving side, email imposes high "understanding costs" on negotiators because it provides little "grounding" to participants in the communication exchange. Grounding is the process by which two parties in an interaction develop a shared sense of understanding about a communication and a shared sense of participation in the conversation. Without the clues provided by shared surroundings, nonverbal behavior, tone of voice, or the timing and sequence of the information exchange, negotiators may find it challenging to accurately decode the messages that they receive electronically. In addition, the tendency of email negotiators to "bundle" multiple arguments and issues together in one email message can place high demands on the receiver's information processing capabilities.

. . .

### Part II: Media Effects: Implications of Email Communication for Negotiation

Comparison of face-to-face negotiation and email negotiation gives rise to five major implications — incorporating both challenges and opportunities for parties negotiating by email:

1)   Increased contentiousness

2)   Diminished information sharing

3)   Diminished process cooperation

4)   Diminished trust

5)   Increased effects of negative attribution

### 1) Increased Contentiousness

Even before the advent of Internet-based e-communication, research showed that communication at a distance via technological means is more susceptible to disruption than face-to-face dialogue. . . .

In Internet-based communication, these findings not only hold true, they are intensified. Communication in cyberspace tends to be less inhibited; parties ignore the possible adverse consequences of negative online interactions because of physical distance, reduced social presence, reduced accountability and a sense of anonymity. The lack of social cues in e-communication causes people to act more contentiously than they do in face-to-face encounters, resulting in more frequent occurrences of swearing, name calling, insults, and hostile behavior.

Research shows that these findings on e-communication also hold true in e-negotiation. Early research showed that negotiators are apt to act tough and choose contentious tactics when negotiating with people at a distance. . . .

Hence, email negotiators are contending on a much rougher playing field than face-to-face negotiators. Still, the better we understand the nature of email . . . the greater our abilities to turn the potentially hazardous characteristics of email to good use — i.e., *reducing* contentiousness. Used properly, lean media may facilitate better *processing* of social conflict exactly because these media do *not* transmit visual and verbal cues. . . .

### 2) Diminished Inter-party Cooperation

. . . [T]he potential for integrative outcomes grows as parties become more aware of each other's needs and capabilities, and areas of potential joint gain emerge. Email negotiations make information exchange likely to be constrained, analytical, and contentious. This diminishes negotiators' ability to accurately assess differential preferences and identify potential joint gains. . . . The use of email may, therefore, accentuate competitive behavior in negotiations.

However, when used properly, email could *increase* information exchange. Lean media may work to promote more equal participation among negotiators. Diminished social context cues and resulting reduction in the salience of social group differences can reduce social influence bias among individuals and encourage lower-status individuals to participate more rather than discounting or ignoring information provided by lower-status individuals, as they might in face-to-face encounters, negotiators may be receptive to this additional information when using email. Attention to this "new" information may subsequently enable negotiators to identify optimal trades and create more integrative agreements. . . .

### 3) Reduction in Integrative Outcomes

. . . If email somehow encourages negotiators to become more contentious and confrontational in the way they communicate, this can lead to spiraling conflict and the hardening of positions. This problem is made even more severe by the difficulty of establishing rapport in email, which we will expand on below. The development of rapport has been shown to foster more mutually beneficial settlements especially in lean media contexts perhaps because it engenders greater social awareness among negotiators.

On the other hand, the media effects of email negotiation include one feature that might promote integrative thinking and outcomes. . . . [N]egotiators tend to exchange long messages that include multiple points all in one "bundle" when using asynchronous media like email. Argument-bundling may facilitate integrative agreements by encouraging negotiators to link issues together and consider them simultaneously rather than sequentially. This can promote log-rolling, a classic tool for reaching integrative outcomes. However, negotiators should avoid "over-bundling:" too many issues and too much information delivered at one time can place higher demands on the receiver's information processing capabilities. Nego-tiators may, therefore, have more difficulty establishing meaning and managing feedback in asynchronous media further hindering their efforts to successfully elicit and integrate the information that is required to construct a mutually beneficial agreement.

### 4) Diminished Degree of Interparty Trust

Trust between negotiating parties has been identified as playing a key role in enabling cooperation, problem solving, achieving integrative solutions, effective-ness, and resolving disputes. Negotiators are trained and advised to seek out and create opportunities for trust-building whenever possible, and as early as possible in the course of a negotiation process.

Communication via email, however, is fraught with threats to trust that are inherent in the medium and in the way parties approach and employ it. . . . Email negotiators enter the process with a lower level of pre-negotiation trust in their counterparts than do participants in face-to-face negotiations. This initially low expectation regarding interpersonal trust may exacerbate the fundamental attri-bution error by reinforcing the tendency to seek out reasons to distrust rather than to recognize trustworthy actions. This becomes a self-fulfilling prophecy: expecting to find counterparts untrustworthy, email negotiators share less information; this reinforces their counterparts' expectations. As a result, participants in email negotiation also experience lower levels of *post*-negotiation trust than do partici-pants in face-to-face negotiations.

### 5) Increased Tendency Towards Sinister Attribution

The media effects of email negotiation exacerbate the tendency toward the sinister attribution error: the bias toward seeing negative events as the outgrowth of others' negative intentions rather than unintended results or conditions beyond their control. The lack of social presence and of contextual cues lends a sense of distance and of vagueness to the interaction. The asynchronous dynamic of email negotiations adds to this challenge. Research shows that e-negotiators ask fewer clarifying questions than face-to-face negotiators do. Instead of gathering information from their counterparts, email negotiators may be more likely to make assumptions. If those assumptions later prove unfounded, the negotiators may perceive the other's inconsistent actions or preferences as a breaking of trust. The power of the sinister attribution error in e-negotiation is clearly demonstrated by experiments showing that e-negotiators are more likely to suspect their opposite of lying than are face-to-face negotiators, even when no actual deception has taken place. Analysis of failed email negotiations shows that they tend to include unclear messages, irrelevant points, and long general statements each of which provides ample breeding ground for the sinister attribution error.

## Part III: Repacking the Negotiator's Toolbox: Recommended Skill-Sets for Email Negotiators

In this section, we will briefly introduce four basic skill-sets that email negotiators need to acquire in order to cope with the media effects of email discussed in the last section. These four skills are discussed as initial proposals, and are certainly not suggested as an exhaustive list; no doubt, others will emerge.

### *Skill-Set #1: Writing Ability*

A central skill that may seem both so obvious and so crucial that we need not address it is the ability to write — clearly, persuasively, and (at times) movingly. For most lawyers, fortunately, writing is a skill used and developed daily. Much of their legal training has been devoted to developing clear, effective writing. For some lawyers as well as other professionals, however, writing is not considered a central activity in their employment. Skills become rusty from lack of use, or a particular style of writing (marketing, for example, in the management context; brief writing in the legal context) may not lend itself well to email. Particularly when it comes time to establish rapport, defuse tension, or even apologize, some email negotiators may find that their writing skills are simply not up to the task at hand. Thus, a central skill set for effective email negotiation may be to improve the clarity and emotional power of writing. And when writing skills fall short of the task's requirements, email negotiators need the wisdom to discern their own limitations, pick up a phone, or make an appointment to meet in person with their negotiation counterparts.

### *Skill Set #2: Message Management*

### Managing Our Own Anxiety

The art of negotiating solely by exchanging written messages through postal mail is a long-forgotten one. We have become accustomed to exchanging opinions through synchronous communication, either face-to-face or over the telephone. Email negotiators need to relearn the art of asynchronous communication. This may not be intuitive, for one of the Internet's promises is instant access to anything and anyone. Our synchronous-communication upbringing, combined with our expectations of instant access, clash with the basic nature of asynchronous communication. As a result, email communication often involves an anxiety that blends distrust of the channel with distrust of the other. When we send messages and do not receive responses promptly, not only do we question whether our counterparts received the messages, we begin to wonder why (if indeed they *have* received them) they are taking so long to respond. To manage this anxiety and prevent a downward spiral of distrust, e-negotiators need to understand and bear in mind the limitations of the medium they are using. They also need to develop gentle but effective ways to follow up when counterparts do not respond in what seems to be an appropriate period of time, generously calculated. . . .

**Managing the Other's Anxiety**

Research has shown that frequent message exchanges, as opposed to communication broken by intervals, are conducive to trust-building within groups. This is also true for the dyadic group formed by two people negotiating. Responding to an email within 24 hours, even if only to say that we are considering what a negotiation counterpart has written, might be a useful standard. On the other hand, delivering a strongly negative response or a total rejection of the counterpart's proposal should not be done too hastily. Negotiation counterparts want to know that we have carefully read and processed their proposals to us. But when a negotiator realizes that she has taken an inexcusably long time to respond in an email negotiation exchange, she should usually acknowledge that fact in the interests of preserving the relationship. . . .

**Utilizing Asynchronicity**

Once we become aware of, and overcome, the challenging characteristics of asynchronous communication, we can focus on the potential it offers for improved communication dynamics. It can be a very conducive channel for reasoned discussion, careful responses, and trust-building moves. It can help control our response time — to our own advantage. Asynchronous communication allows us to avoid knee-jerk reactions or escalatory cycles of contentious behavior, and to think proactively. . . . We can read a received message twice, or ask a colleague to take a look at it and tell us what she thinks, before we reply to it, lowering the effect of sinister attribution. We can do the same with a message we have written, before sending it. By learning when *not* to click "Reply," and when to delay clicking "Send," email negotiators can use the medium to maximum effect.

*Skill-Set #3: Relationship Management*

**Setting the Stage: Unmasking**

. . . The sense of anonymity and distance created between email negotiators leads both to assumptions that one can get away with aggressive or trust-breaking behavior, and to a lowering of moral inhibitions against doing so. This necessitates that negotiators consciously adopt a proactive agenda of unmasking themselves *toward* the other. The more negotiation counterparts perceive us as *people they know* rather than anonymous, faceless email addresses, the more likely they are to share information, rely on us, and trust in us.

## Building Rapport

. . .

In face-to-face encounters, introductions and light, social conversations come naturally; in e-negotiation, this tendency diminishes. As we have discussed, negotiators tend to remain on topic, task-oriented, and analytic, leaving little room for social lubrication. As a result, e-negotiators need to *consciously* dedicate time and effort to the unmasking process. Experiments have indicated that even minimal pre-negotiation contact, at the most basic level of "schmoozing" via preliminary email introductory messages or brief telephone exchanges, has the potential for building trust, improving mutual impressions, and facilitating integrative outcomes. By inviting the other to reply, we are initiating a cycle of unmasking which not only transcends physical distance but also reshapes the process into one allowing for recognition and empathy, which can continue to develop as the negotiation progresses.

We would suggest building rapport through words rather than emotions. A negotiator could write the business part of the email first — working for absolute clarity and thoroughness — and then back to insert the schmooze factor at the beginning of the email, e.g., "lovely to see you last week," "thanks much for getting back to me," etc. We habitually begin in-person conversation with some ice breaking or small talk, but often forget to include it when using the medium that needs it the most. Exceptions to this guideline exist, of course. When negotiators are engaged in rapid-fire exchange of short, clarifying emails, it could become quite annoying to wade repeatedly through a paragraph of schmooze before reading the point of the email.

Because email lends itself to informal communication, negotiators should be urged to think carefully about the level of formality they want to establish when negotiating by email. Though e-negotiators need to establish rapport and unmask their own humanity, it would be a mistake to open informally, e.g., using the counterpart's first name or simply opening with "Hey Bill!" for many negotiations. For some email recipients, a greater level of formality will actually *increase* rapport and trust. A good way for negotiators to manage this is to note their counterpart's tone and formality level, and reflect this in their next message, taking care to err on the side of caution.

## Showing E-empathy

Demonstrating empathy is universally described as a powerful tool and important skill for any negotiator. This has been found to hold true in online communication as well: e-negotiators who show empathy are trusted by their negotiation opposites more than those who do not. This trust might cause the empathic negotiator's actions and intentions to be construed more positively, diminishing the tendency towards sinister attribution. Negotiators will be more likely to share information with a trusted counterpart, opening the door for more integrative agreements.

. . .

. . . Many of the most basic communication tools negotiators are advised to employ facilitate the showing of empathy to one's negotiation opposite. Three examples might be active listening, reflecting (or summarizing), and asking questions focusing on the counterparts' needs and concerns. . . .

### Skill-Set #4: Content Management

The absence of contextual cues focuses email negotiators on the actual *content* of messages. This necessitates particular skills with regard to three issues:

### Clarity

As we have seen, message clarity helps avoid sinister attribution and allows for precise information sharing. Clear messages allow e-negotiators to focus on what their counterparts have written, reply to their points and consider their proposals. Clarity in reply creates a virtuous cycle.

To achieve such clarity, e-negotiators should avoid unnecessary length. "In summary" sentences might be useful. Negotiators should always remember that, in contrast to a telephone or face-to-face conversation, email creates a searchable file of information. The downside is that this can give rise to "gotcha" opportunities; the upside is that searchability disciplines both sides to stay honest about their representations and commitments. . . . Mindful use of the subject field helps with searchability and message clarity, and also presents a valuable opportunity for framing. Further, even before drafting the text of an email, negotiators should think carefully about each field. To whom should the email be sent? Should anyone appear in the "cc", or disappear in the "bcc" field? Is the negotiator inadvertently offending someone by leaving them out of the exchange or relegating them to the "cc" field when they ought to appear in the "to" field.

### Bundling

Email negotiators tend to bundle multiple points and multiple arguments in a single message. While on the one hand we have noted how this tendency might potentially facilitate the identification of integrative agreements by encouraging negotiators to link issues together and consider them simultaneously rather than sequentially, it might also clash with basic message clarity. Additionally, even if clearly written, an excessive amount of data might send the message recipient into an information overload. Email negotiators need to learn and practice balanced bundling. Judicious use of the "subject" line in an email helps both negotiators and their counterparts to search for and to frame the content of emails they receive.

Thus, negotiators should craft subject lines that are sufficiently general that a broad search will produce a list that includes them (e.g., "Smith v. Jones") but also specific enough that they alert the recipient to what they contain and facilitate targeted searches (e.g., "Smith v. Jones — concerns about Smith deposition").

### Framing

With the bulk of a message's impact shifted to its content, language and wording become paramount. This is especially important in the framing of issues and discussion topics. Asynchronous communication allows for careful framing of issues and well thought-out revision of frames proposed by the other party. As we have noted, opportunities for using an email message to frame an issue begin with the wording of the subject field.

Part of framing is also thinking about the formatting of the email, which affects the perceptual frame through which the other recipient takes in the message content. In the body of the email, negotiators should alter default settings for style and font with caution and only for good reason. Wallpaper might be too informal for business contexts, including negotiations. Colored fonts should be used only for distinguishing comments written into an earlier document; some email programs will do this automatically when replying or forwarding. Most of the time, however, a simple black typeface is most appropriate. Times Roman, Arial, or other default fonts are preferable to the more exotic options; as Shipley and Schwalbe hilariously point out, some fonts (such as "Chalkboard") "create a homey effect," while others (such as "Blachmoor") "indicate to the reader that a necklace of garlic, a silver bullet, and a wooden cross should be kept close at hand". A negotiator should also think carefully about using all caps — IT IS THE EQUIVALENT OF SCREAM-ING in email. Finally, we would suggest not using too many !!! to make a point or too many to try and lend "tone" to a particular comment — unless negotiators are certain that the relationships they have with their opposites make this suitable.

## NOTE AND QUESTIONS

Do you think the concerns of Ebner and his colleagues are consistent with your experiences in your use of email, or are they overstated? As you read the materials on mediation in the following chapters, consider how their observations and suggestions might be extended to online mediation. Might a specially trained mediator be able to mitigate some of the problematic effects of online communication?

# Chapter 3

# MEDIATION PROCESS AND SKILLS

## A. INTRODUCTION

This chapter will highlight the substantive skills and strategies which shape the distinctive role of the mediator. It identifies possible contributions and constraints of taking an impartial role in dispute resolution, points out deliberate strategies which the mediator may adopt in attempting to build a settlement and indicates the activities which the mediator must avoid. Beyond the skills required for effective mediation, additional characteristics are important, because mediation is mostly an art, not a science. While mediation, at its core, is based on a set of foundational values, each mediator has a distinctive mediation style, which will be defined by the mediator's individual personality traits.

As you will read in Chapter 4, *infra*, there are many different styles and orientations to which mediators subscribe. The most widely used approaches are facilitative, evaluative, and transformative. For purposes of understanding the skills of the mediator, this chapter will focus primarily on the facilitative style of mediation for several reasons. First, the facilitative style of mediation most underscores the differences between the role a mediator plays and that of an attorney or judge. As such, the facilitative style emphasizes skills that generally are not learned in law school. Second, the facilitative style is the conventional, presumptive approach used by mediators in many settings; even some of the most evaluative mediators acknowledge that their first efforts in a mediation are usually facilitative and that they move into an "evaluative" framework only if the parties desire that type of intervention. The final section of this chapter briefly highlights the transformative and evaluative approaches for comparison purposes.

## B. INITIAL CONSIDERATIONS

### 1. Mediation Process

There are many different theories concerning the number of steps within the mediation process. Some scholars identify three or four stages, and others assert 12 or more. At a minimum, it is helpful to consider certain discrete stages of a mediation, as set out below.

### a. The Beginning

This includes any review the mediator makes of preliminary information about the facts and circumstances of the mediation, planning for the location and set-up of the mediation, and the mediator's opening statement. If the mediation is scheduled after the parties have filed a lawsuit, some mediators will review the court file or a pre-mediation memorandum prepared by the parties. If the mediation is conducted either "pre-suit" or under the auspices of a mediation program, an intake person or the mediator may have had some preliminary conversations with the parties, and possibly their attorneys, if the parties are represented.

### b. Accumulating Information

This includes the parties, and possibly their attorneys (if represented), recounting what happened to bring them to mediation and sharing what is important to them. A mediator accumulates information throughout the process.

### c. Developing an Initial Agenda

Based on the initial identification by the parties of their needs, interests, and concerns, the mediator will assist the parties in organizing their conversation. Providing structure will often assist the parties to keep focused. The agenda is always subject to revision as the mediation proceeds.

### d. Generating Movement

Often parties in dispute are trapped in the way they are thinking about their dispute. One of the benefits a mediator brings to the process is the ability to help the parties understand their situation in a new way and consider creative alternatives for addressing their issues. In addition, the parties may find it useful during the mediation to meet with the mediator individually in a separate session (caucus). This too can happen at varying times during the mediation and may occur more than once.

### e. Ending the Mediation

This includes any of the following possible endings (or some combination): a full resolution with a written agreement signed by all of the parties; a full resolution of the dispute with no written agreement (may include a dismissal of the underlying case if one had already been filed in court); a partial resolution which is written and signed by the parties; a cessation of the mediation session with an agreement to return to mediation and continue the discussion at a scheduled future date; or no agreement with no future plans to mediate further.

In learning the skills of the mediator, it is easier to understand the process in a linear format, i.e., you start at the beginning, gather information, develop the agenda, generate movement and finally reach a conclusion. In actuality, the middle stages of mediation are often cyclical rather than linear. The mediation will always have a beginning and an ending, but in the middle it may loop back and forth between these artificial stages. For purposes of learning the process, we will discuss each phase as a separate and distinct part of the mediation. Keep in mind, however, that when mediating a "real" case, the phases will often meld together. Although this segmented approach to understanding and learning mediation is widely held, it has not been universally adopted. For example, mediators who subscribe to the transformative school of mediation, reject this stage model as a means of understanding the process since a mediation will follow the needs of the individual parties rather than some pre-determined model.

## 2.  The Mediator

Before returning to the mediation process to study it in greater depth, we will focus on the mediator — both the role and qualities or characteristics of the individual which contribute to his/her effectiveness. The role of the mediator and the definition of the term can vary depending on the type of mediation, program goals, and local practice. According to one state statute, "the role of the mediator includes, but is not limited to, assisting the parties in identifying issues, fostering joint problem solving, and exploring settlement alternatives." Section 44.1011(2), Florida Statutes. By contrast, the Uniform Mediation Act (Appendix F) defines a "mediator" as "an individual, of any profession or background, who conducts a mediation."

A definition, however, cannot capture the wide range of dynamics, strategies, and techniques a mediator employs when attempting to assist parties in negotiating their dispute. In discussing the role of a mediator, it is fitting to examine the skills, abilities, and other attributes that are required to perform the role effectively. While the following is not an exhaustive list, it represents the thinking of a diverse group of mediators who worked for five years in a consensus-based effort as part of the Test Design Project to provide mediation programs, courts, and other interested parties with improved tools for selecting, training, and evaluating mediators. While the desired traits were normally referred to as KSAOs or Knowledge, Skills, Abilities and Other Attributes, the Test Design Project chose not to identify particular types of required legal or procedural subject matter knowledge because "they are specific to the situation (*e.g.*, type of mediation program, state law), and because for some types of program little or no substantive knowledge is required prior to selection."

### PERFORMANCE-BASED ASSESSMENT: A METHODOLOGY, FOR USE IN SELECTING, TRAINING, AND EVALUATING MEDIATORS
The Test Design Project 19 (1995)[*]

Skills, Abilities, and Other Attributes

1. Reasoning: To reason logically and analytically, effectively distinguishing issues and questioning assumptions.

---

2. Analyzing: To assimilate large quantities of varied information into logical ideas or concepts.

3. Problem Solving: To generate, assess and prioritize alternative solutions to a problem, or help the parties to do so.

4. Reading Comprehension: To read and comprehend written materials.

5. Writing: To write clearly and concisely, using neutral language.

6. Oral Communication: To speak with clarity, and to listen carefully and empathetically.

7. Non-verbal Communication: To use voice inflection, gestures, and eye contact appropriately.

8. Interviewing: To obtain and process information from others, eliciting information, listening actively, and facilitating an exchange of information.

9. Emotional stability/maturity: To remain calm and level-headed in stressful and emotional situations.

10. Sensitivity: To recognize a variety of emotions and respond appropriately.

11. Integrity: To be responsible, ethical and honest.

12. Recognizing Values: To discern own and others' strongly-held values.

13. Impartiality: To maintain an open mind about different points of view.

14. Organizing: To manage effectively activities, recordsand other materials.

15. Following procedure: To follow agreed-upon procedures.

16. Commitment: Interest in helping others to resolve conflict.

## 3. Mediator Functions

The functions of a mediator are very much tied to the goals and expectations of the parties or mediation program, the context in which the mediation takes place, and the style of the mediator. In underscoring this point, the Test Design's Report stated in bold print "The resulting lists [of mediator tasks and KSAOs] are not exhaustive, and they do not reflect reality for every program. They are intended merely as a starting point to encourage any given program to prepare a modified list that reflects its actual practices." The Report identified seven major tasks, which each involved several sub-tasks:

Gathering Background Information

Facilitating Communication

Communicating Information to Others

Analyzing Information

Facilitating Agreement

Managing Cases

Documenting Information

# NOTES AND QUESTIONS

(1)   What other characteristics do you think would be important for a mediator to possess? Of those that are listed, which are the most important to the mediation process? How do these correspond to ethical duties of a mediator?

(2)   Some claim that anyone can be a good mediator, if suitably trained. Do you agree?

(3)   It was noted in the Test Design's publication that the terms used "arise out of the predominant North American culture, and may not apply to another society or even to indigenous or minority cultures within North America." What are the cultural assumptions made in identifying the list of attributes and the tasks? Are there other attributes which may be important in other cultural contexts?

## 4.   Beginning the Mediation Process

There are no restrictions on where a mediation can be held. Usually, though, a mediation takes place in a conference room — either the mediator's or one of the attorney's. If the mediation is court-ordered, it may take place in a courthouse. As with traditional negotiation practices, a mediator must give thought to the location (neutrality of the setting, accessibility, comfort, etc.) and room set-up for the mediation.

Normally, when the mediator invites the parties into the room, the mediator will tell them where to sit (either verbally or by motioning to a particular grouping of chairs on one side of the table). The seating should reflect a structure conducive to the process of communication which the mediator is trying to create; if one party sits at the table but the other sits in the corner, the process is skewed. A mediator will often sit so that, from the parties' perspective, the mediator is "in the middle." Sometimes, parties bring other people with them to mediation, such as an attorney. If other people are in the mediation room, they should sit with the persons whom they are accompanying. Here are some options:

Possible Seating Arrangements (mediator and two disputants)

D= Disputant; M=Mediator

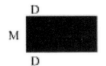

Possible Seating Arrangements (mediator, two parties and an attorney)
P = Party, M = Mediator, A = Attorney

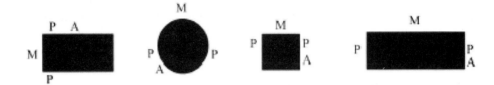

Note that there are many different possibilities; to some extent the decision will depend on the mediator's own personal style and preference, as well as what shape table is available. Some mediators prefer not to use any table at all or only a low coffee table in a "living room" type setting. This is most commonly seen in divorce or other family — issue type mediations. It is important to keep in mind the following general principles when determining seating:

- the mediator should be equidistant between the disputants (and everyone should be seated on similar chairs);

- the parties should be able to look at each other and the mediator comfortably;

- the parties should be far enough apart that they are not bumping into each other, nor able to read each other's notes, but close enough that the mediator can see both parties even while providing focused attention on one.

But how does the mediator decide whether someone should be in the mediation room or not?

Typically, the following persons are "entitled" to be in the room:

- the mediator;

- the people in dispute (if there is a court case, this will usually be defined as the "named parties");

- attorneys for the disputants (if applicable) *Note*: in a state which has adopted the Uniform Mediation Act, see *Chapter 5*, this is expanded to include "an attorney or other individual designated by a party";

- a sign language interpreter or other representative necessitated under the Americans with Disabilities Act (if applicable);

- foreign language interpreter (if necessary).

Other individuals often appear at mediation; these include family members, bailiffs, members of the media, friends, moral supporters, observers, and witnesses. Whether these individuals are admitted into the mediation usually is dependent upon agreement of the disputants. Any of the disputants has a right to object to their inclusion at the mediation. The mediator may wish to discuss with the disputants the ramifications of such a disagreement by noting that mediation requires active participation by the disputants, that participation in mediation is voluntary, and that if one or more of the disputants are unwilling to proceed because of someone's presence or absence, the mediation might be immediately concluded.

Whether to permit such persons into the mediation session is a decision for the parties to make. However, the extent of their participation, once admitted, is strongly influenced by the mediator's responsibility for conducting a constructive dialogue. How these decisions are made and by whom is dependent on the mediator's style and orientation. For example, the more evaluative orientations would view these decisions as the sole responsibility of the mediator, while those who practice from a transformative perspective would view these decisions to be the sole responsibility of the parties. *See* Chapter 4, *infra*.

## NOTES AND QUESTIONS

(1)   The illustrated seating arrangements when an attorney is representing one of the parties suggest that the attorney sit next to his or her client and that the parties (or disputants) sit between the attorney and the mediator. What are the pros and cons of such an arrangement from the perspectives of the parties, the mediator, and the attorneys?

(2)   Identify additional people who may participate in the mediation and how you would set up the room to accommodate their participation (*e.g.*, interpreters, co-mediators, moral supporters, etc.).

(3)   Note that in some cultures it is expected that members of the extended family or community will attend the mediation. What are the pros and cons for including extended family members in the mediation session?

## C.   MEDIATION PROCESS

### 1.   Mediator's Opening Statement

A mediation will typically begin with the mediator providing an "opening statement." Even if all parties have previously participated in a mediation, it is not advisable to skip this step. There are several reasons for beginning the mediation in this fashion:

- to establish the procedures and the mediator's role;

- to put people at ease;

- to convey a sense of mediator competence and skill, thereby inviting trust and comfort with the process and the mediator;

- to reconcile any conflicting expectations regarding what will happen in mediation;

- to satisfy ethical requirements (if applicable).

Typically, there are six basic components to an opening statement:

- Introducing the mediator, disputants, and others present.

- Establishing credibility and impartiality of the mediator.

- Explaining the process of mediation and the role of the mediator.

- Explaining the procedures which will govern the process (including, if applicable the possibility of meeting separately with the parties).

- Explaining the extent to which the process is confidential or inviting parties to set terms of confidentiality.

- Asking the parties if they have any questions.

The mediator's opening statement should be clear and concise. A mediator should try to avoid using "jargon" or technical words that the disputants are unlikely to understand (*e.g.*, plaintiff, defendant, claimant, respondent, pro se). Even if the parties are represented by attorneys and the attorneys are present, it is a good idea for the mediator to focus the opening statement on the parties, to talk directly to them, and to ensure their understanding of the process. Although delivering an opening statement should not consume a lot of time, a mediator should not rush through it. The mediator's opening statement is important — it must be long enough to cover all of the elements clearly and completely, and short enough not to lose the interest of the parties.

Delivering the mediator's opening statement is deceptively difficult. One cannot underestimate the importance of starting the mediation in an articulate, informative, and calming manner. This is the one part of the mediation that can be practiced in advance.

In developing an opening statement, a mediator should recognize that while an opening statement need not be structured in any particular order, it should flow and sound like the individual mediator. Its precise content and tone also may vary depending on the type of mediation and the context of the mediation. With these caveats in mind, a mediator should consider the following suggestions.

### a.   Introductions

Before the mediation begins, the mediator should decide how he or she wants to be addressed. For example, are first names appropriate? What about titles or degrees (*e.g.*, Dr., Colonel, attorney . . .)? As a general rule, the mediator should only tell the parties the information they need to know. Generally, parties do not need to know the titles or degrees a mediator holds. In fact, sometimes this information can be harmful to the mediation process as the disputants may look to the mediator for legal or technical advice rather than just facilitation. On the other hand, if the parties are represented by attorneys who are present, it might make everyone more comfortable to know the legal qualifications of the mediator. Also, mediators who practice in a more evaluative or directive style may have been chosen for their subject matter expertise, and therefore should disclose this information. In addressing the disputants, generally the mediator will use last names; however, this is not a firm rule. For example, if the disputants are on a first name basis and request that the mediator use first names, it would be appropriate to do so. In any case, the mediator should be certain of the pronunciation of the parties' names.

## b.  Establishing Credibility and Impartiality

It is important for the mediator to establish credibility in order to give the disputants confidence that the mediator and the process of mediation may be of assistance to them. The focus should be on the mediator's mediation experience — not the mediator's unrelated experience or expertise. As noted above, depending on the circumstances, lawyers and law students might want to refrain from revealing their legal expertise. The easiest (and safest) way for the mediator to establish credibility is to provide the disputants with information about the mediator's experience as a mediator. For example, if the mediator is "certified" as a mediator, stating that fact would be a quick and easy way to establish credibility. Mediators should not be falsely modest about their experience, but they must not forget that the disputants are there to resolve their disputes and not listen to a long dissertation about the mediator's experience, no matter how impressive it may be.

In order to gain the disputants' trust and confidence, a mediator should assure the disputants of the mediator's impartiality about the dispute and the individuals involved. The most concise, credible way to do this is to provide the participants with information regarding the mediator's previous experience and knowledge about the dispute and then let the parties draw their own conclusion. This can be accomplished with this simple sentence: "I have not met either of you before and have no previous knowledge of the events which brought you to mediation today." Most people will conclude that the mediator is impartial if the mediator does not know either of them and has no preconceived notion about the dispute. This approach works best when mediating community or small claims disputes. For more complex disputes, the mediator may have received information in advance from the parties to review and may have been chosen by the parties and/or their attorneys based on their previous experience with the mediator; this requires a modified approach.

In situations in which the mediator knows one or more of the parties or attorneys, the mediator should conduct a two-part analysis. First, the mediator should assess how well he/she knows the individual and if this relationship raises any concerns for the mediator regarding his/her ability to remain impartial. If the mediator believes that his or her impartiality might be compromised, or perceived to be so, then the mediator should not conduct the mediation. A mediator should attempt to make this assessment as soon as possible in order to create the least disturbance for the disputants. When in doubt, it is better to err on the side of caution and decline the mediation.

If the mediator analyzes the prior relationship and concludes that it does not jeopardize the integrity of the process, then the mediator moves to the second part of the test, namely disclosing the contact to the parties. While the exact requirements of ethical rules vary, a mediator is often prohibited from mediating any case in which the parties express concern regarding previous contact or in some cases if the relationship is "too close." The ethical constraints placed on the mediator will be discussed in greater detail in Chapter 8, *infra*.

### c.   Explaining Mediation and the Role of the Mediator

Next the mediator will explain what mediation is and what the disputants can expect in this process. The mediator should try to include this explanation early in the mediator's opening statement. In defining mediation, and depending on the circumstances, the mediator typically strives to use the simplest terms possible. Often it is helpful to highlight the difference between mediation and the traditional court process since most people are more familiar with litigation as a form of dispute resolution. It might also be helpful to discuss the mediator's and the parties' roles in the process. If one or more of the parties are represented by counsel, the mediator should modify the opening to include the role of the party's (or parties') attorney(s).

For example:

> *Mediation provides you with an opportunity to talk with one another with the help of another person, a mediator, who is not involved in the dispute. As mediator, my job is to assist you in talking to each other so that you can gain a better understanding of what happened. It is not my job, nor am I permitted, to decide who is right or wrong or to tell you how to resolve your conflict. Rather, in mediation you have the ability to develop a resolution that makes sense to each of you. If you develop options that each of you find acceptable, we will write them into an agreement that each of you can sign and the matter will then be closed. If you are unable to resolve it here, you will [return to the judge who will make a decision for you — if court-ordered] or [need to choose another means of handling your dispute — if private].*

### d.   Explaining the Procedures That Will Govern the Process

The mediator should discuss the following procedural guidelines:

• *Speaking Order*: If the mediation involves a case already filed in court, generally, the mediator will invite the plaintiff to speak first. Typically, the person who filed the claim has the obligation to let the other person know why he/she filed the case. If the mediation is taking place prior to or in lieu of a case having been filed in court, the mediator may ask the person who requested mediation to begin or alternatively, ask the disputants who would like to begin. The person who begins has an advantage in framing the dispute; therefore, whoever speaks second should be given latitude to share not only a response, but also to describe concerns which the disputant has. See Chapter 8, *infra*, for a further discussion of how an attorney might divide these responsibilities with a client.

• *Separate Sessions (Caucus)*: Sometimes it will be useful for the mediator to meet with the disputants (and their attorneys, if represented) separately during the mediation. If the mediator might do so, he/she should discuss this during the opening statement so that no one is alarmed if it later occurs. Since there may not be a separate session, the mediator should not spend too much time in the opening statement discussing its procedural aspects. Mediators often refer to this separate session as a caucus; most people do not regularly use that term, so a mediator should gauge the disputants' sophistication with the process to decide whether it may be better to refer to it simply as a separate session.

• *Note-Taking*: If the mediator plans to take notes, the mediator should let the disputants and attorneys know. It is generally a good idea to provide pen and paper for the disputants and encourage them to listen for new information and to take notes, if necessary, while the other is talking. This enables the parties to remember issues they want to discuss without having to interrupt each other.

• *Explaining the Confidentiality of the Process*: The mediator should be well-versed in the level of confidentiality which applies to the mediation and review this with the disputants. Some mediators have a confidentiality agreement prepared for parties (and attorneys, if applicable) to sign prior to beginning a mediation so that everyone is clear on the level of confidentiality that attaches. Others provide an opportunity for parties (and their attorneys, if applicable) to discuss and agree upon the level of confidentiality they want. *See* Chapter 5, *infra*.

The following is an example of the portion of a mediator's opening statement that addresses the procedural aspects of the process. When possible, a mediator should use the parties' names and invite their responses and commitment to the procedures suggested by the mediator.

> *Let me explain how this process will work today. When I finish speaking and have answered any questions you may have, we will begin. [I see that each of you are here with your attorney. It has been my experience that mediation works best when the parties themselves actively participate in the process. Mr. Green, have you and your attorney discussed your respective participation? . . . Ms. Kodly, have you and your attorney discussed your respective participation?]*

> *Since Mr. Green sought this mediation [or brought this case to the attention of the court], we will begin by having him describe his concerns. Ms. Kodly, you will then have an opportunity to share your concerns [which I understand will be through your attorney]. Please feel free to add additional information or concerns. At some point, I may find it useful to meet with each of you individually. If such a situation arises, I will explain the process in greater detail.*

> *I have found it best if each of you treat the other with courtesy and respect during this mediation so that when one of you is speaking, I would ask that the other listen carefully. Is that guideline acceptable to each of you? I have provided each of you with paper and pen to jot down any new information you may hear, as well as any issue you wish to discuss and are afraid you may forget while the other person is speaking. I, too, may*

*be taking some notes. This is merely to help me keep information straight.*

*At the end of this mediation, I will discard my notes and encourage you to do the same because the discussions we have here are confidential. [NOTE: this will need to be tailored to the specific circumstances under which the mediation is conducted, see Chapter 5, infra.]*

• *Asking the Parties if They Have Any Questions*: The parties have just received a lot of information to think about so it is important to pause and let them ask any questions about the information which has been provided.

After answering any questions or determining that the disputants have none, the mediator should be ready to hear from them. Begin by asking the party who brought the claim (or the party's attorney) to describe the events that led to the mediation.

## 2. Accumulating Information

In order to assist parties in mediation, mediators need to learn what the issues are that brought the parties to mediation. This is true regardless of whether they have come to mediation voluntarily, by contract, or by order of the court in which they filed their dispute. In addition to listening to parties' descriptions of the actual circumstances surrounding their dispute, mediators observe the behavior of the parties toward one another before, during, and after a mediation as a means of accumulating useful information. People communicate through more than just the spoken word. Nonverbal cues, posture, and tone of voice all convey a wealth of information.

A mediator should try to establish an atmosphere in which the possibility of constructive dialogue is enhanced. Frequently, the parties have let their concerns simmer, exchanged heated words, and then avoided each other. Assisting the parties in communicating with one another constitutes an important first step toward building a resolution.

The mediator's role in the information gathering process combines structure and patience. With the mediator's assistance, the parties may be able to reorient their perspectives from an adversarial posture to one of collaboration. The mediator's role, while not that of a decision-maker, need not be passive. The mediator listens for many things, including (a) the interests of the parties; (b) the issues in dispute (*see* Section C.3., *infra*); (c) proposals that the parties may have as to how the issues may be resolved; (d) principles and values that each party holds; and finally (e) emotions or feelings associated with the conflict. It is important to note that the parties usually do not clearly identify each of these items, and thus the mediator must listen carefully in order to "hear" them. The mediator tries to help the parties reestablish trust so that practical solutions do not evade them. The mediator's role is not to endorse each person's perception as "right or wrong" but to acknowledge their concerns as ones which they possess and which constitute the benchmarks of settlement possibilities. Since all parties are different and bring different perceptions to a situation, the mediator should not assume all parties fit in the same box. The mediator must listen carefully and appreciate the unique strands which individuals will highlight if given the appropriate forum for doing so.

## a.   Pre-Mediation Information/Case File

Determining whether to review pre-mediation information by seeking summaries or memos from the attorneys or the case file is an individual mediator's decision and varies by context. In some instances there will not be any pre-mediation information; in a court-ordered case, the mediator may not have the right to access the court file or there simply may not be any time to do so prior to beginning the mediation. In complex cases, mediators will often ask the attorneys to produce confidential pre-mediation statements which may include the theory of the case, negotiation efforts to date, and areas of concern for the attorneys and parties. If pre-mediation information is available, it may be useful, in advance of the first meeting, for the mediator to review it in order to obtain an orientation to the context within which the contested issues might be discussed. For example, if mediating a divorce, the mediator might want to be aware, in advance, of the length of the marriage and the number and ages of any children. A mediator may also wish to conduct some pre-screening to ensure that mediation will be appropriate, for example, to determine if there is a history of domestic violence that could compromise the mediation process. If the mediator chooses to review pre-mediation information, the mediator must remember that the information provided may only represent the issues from one disputant's perspective. Secondly, reliance on documents should not replace the opportunity for the disputants to describe in their own words (or their attorney's) what has brought them to mediation.

## b.   The Disputants' Opening Statements

The disputants or their attorneys will articulate their concerns. The mediator must listen carefully. What they say, the manner in which the information is shared, and the order of presentation are all important pieces of information. The mediator should usually let each disputant take as much time as needed without interruption from the other party or the mediator.

When the first party is finished, the mediator should not ask the other to "respond," but rather should invite a description or explanation of that party's issues and concerns. The second person to speak often feels defensive — the mediator's job is to put the parties at ease enough to share what is important to them.

Mediators should usually refrain from asking any questions until all the disputants and/or their attorneys have spoken. While it may be tempting to ask "just a quick question" before each disputant has spoken, one never knows how long the answer may be to even a quick question. Further, if the first person's opening statement was long, a significant amount of time may have elapsed from the point the mediation began. By the time the second or third disputant has an opportunity to speak, he or she may have already given up any hope of this being a fair process. Finally, the comments of the remaining parties usually help clarify matters, thereby answering questions before the mediator asks them.

After each party has spoken, the parties often will look to the mediator to identify the next step in the process and to provide some structure. A helpful intervention is for the mediator to identify the issues as the parties have put them forth. To perform that important task requires a mediator to organize the information accurately and constructively. Taking good "mediator notes" can be most helpful for executing that task, and a discussion of their role and status is warranted.

## c. Notes

A mediator's notes serve three important purposes:

- identification of the issues which the disputants wish to address;

- clarification of statements/issues for the mediator;

- record of "movement" with regard to offers and solutions.

The mediator's notes *should not* be a transcript of the mediation. Notes, by definition, are selective. Three practical dangers arising from taking too many notes are:

- If the disputants observe the mediator taking voluminous notes, they may become more cautious in what they say. If they are represented by counsel, questions may be raised about future use of those notes.

- In taking copious notes, the mediator must look at what is being written rather than devote eye contact, concern, and attention to the person who is speaking. This undermines the personal rapport that the mediator wants to establish.

- If a mediator takes too many notes, it will be difficult for the mediator to locate helpful information and follow up questions the mediator may have.

In general, mediators should trust their memories for the larger details. A mediator's notes are an organizational tool and should permit the mediator to recall a particular issue by a quick glance.

In addition to using notes as an organizational tool, notes can help mediators assure the disputants that they have been heard. This is particularly useful when one disputant is repeating a thought over and over. The mediator can read the areas of concern which the mediator has noted and then ask if there is anything other than what the mediator has already captured in the notes which the disputant wishes to discuss at the mediation. This approach assures the disputant that the mediator has heard the concerns and allows the disputant to add anything which has not yet been included. When attorneys present the issues, it is generally easier to identify clearly and concisely the legal areas of discussion; however, the mediator may need to delve deeper into some of the other interests of the disputants. For example, attorneys may focus on monetary issues and potential outcomes in court, while omitting other concerns that are very important to the parties.

It is also important in taking notes that the information be recorded in neutral, simple terms. It is probable that the disputants will be able to see the mediator's notes during the mediation. One of the problems in recording exact words is that the mediator is confirming that person's characterization of the issue. One of the reasons mediation is an effective dispute resolution technique is that the mediator can "see" the dispute differently than the disputants. For example, one person may describe activities as "noise," while the other may describe it as "music." A mediator needs to think of a neutral term to describe it which both can accept. For example, "drum playing." In general, a mediator's notes should include as few modifiers as possible.

The following paragraph summarizes the information that the parties shared with the mediator during their opening statements in a small claims action:

> Upon meeting with two parties, the mediator learned from Mr. Watkins that he is a landlord and is suing Mr. Goodwin for back rent of $750; the lease allows tenants to keep only "small" pets; Mr. Goodwin has obtained a large dog; and Mr. Watkins has had frequent complaints from other tenants regarding Mr. Goodwin's late evening, early morning parties on the weekends. Mr. Goodwin has responded that the rent has not been paid as the oven has been broken for two months; Mr. Watkins has not fixed the oven despite requests by Mr. Goodwin to do so; and he objects to Mr. Watkins' unannounced presence in his apartment several times in the past month.

The mediator's notes may look something like this:

| **Mr. Watkins** | **Mr. Goodwin** |
|---|---|
| rent ($750) | oven (two months) |
| dog | landlord visits |
| parties | |

Accumulating information and taking effective notes depends heavily upon the mediator's ability to listen. In the following excerpt, Joseph Stulberg and Lela Love detail these required listening skills for the mediator.

### d. Listening Skills

## THE MIDDLE VOICE: MEDIATING CONFLICT SUCCESSFULLY
### 64, 70–72 (Carolina Academic Press, 2013)*
### By Joseph B. Stulberg & Lela P. Love

Listening effectively to what someone is saying consists of more than just hearing sounds. One listens to understand the message the speaker is trying to communicate. To listen well is to capture the entire message. Listening skills prevent one from short-circuiting or contaminating that message-sending process. Here are some guidelines that a mediator can follow to insure he receives all that is sent:

*Concentrate.* Minimize distractions . . . .

---

*Maintain Focus.* People cannot talk as fast as others can listen. A mediator should not use the overlapping time to daydream or worry about something else . . . .

*Be patient.* One cannot hear, let alone be certain he has captured what someone else is saying, if that person is not given a chance to complete his statements. Sometimes parties repeat themselves. Some speakers are hard to understand. A patient listener allows a speaker the freedom to tell his story — even if the telling is less than perfect.

*Don't interrupt.* One cannot listen while talking. It is tempting to interrupt a party by asking questions or providing information, but such behavior both disrupts a speaker's chain of thought and exhibits unhelpful conduct that other participants might copy.

*Understand without judgment.* . . . A mediator cannot argue mentally with the speaker. Understand first; evaluate later — much later. . . .

A mediator actively seeks to ensure he understand the parties' communications and to demonstrate that understanding to them. In doing so, he displays a level of interest and respect that encourages disclosure and further communication.

A mediator can ask questions in order to clarify previous statements. He can attempt to summarize in his own words what was said. He can, in a separate session with the party, try to confirm his understanding of what the party said by identifying the emotion that the statement exhibits or the priority ranking the party attaches to particular items.

However, a mediator should never try to show his understanding of what was said by simply repeating back to the parties in their own words what they just said . . . .

[A] mediator is not simply a tape recorder with a playback button; if he understands what was said, he should show it by summarizing the statements in his own words.

Second, from the moment a person begins to serve as mediator, he should try to reorient the way the parties view their situation. He starts to do this by always describing the dispute in less explosive, non-judgmental language. Harsh language is an important barometer of parties' feelings, but restating insults rarely helps promote party dialogue and collaboration . . . .

Third, disputing parties have strong emotions. Despite what the mediator has said about his neutrality, if one party hears the mediator repeat allegations, assertions of fact, or conclusions in the language of his adversary, then he will conclude, fairly or not, that the mediator believes everything the other has said . . . . If that occus, the mediator's potential contribution may be irreversibly diminished . . . .

---

Listening is hard work. It appears easy because there is not much physical activity involved. But the parties will know whether the mediator is listening to them; the following signs confirm it:

- Effective and appropriate eye contact

- Appropriate facial gestures

- Appropriate affirmative head nods (Remember that the nod of the head can be interpreted as agreement or acknowledgment. A mediator should try to be consistent with any nods to avoid concerns regarding lack of impartiality.)

- Avoidance of actions or gestures that suggest boredom (such as yawning and leaning on your hand)

- Asking clarifying questions

- Paraphrasing using neutral words

- Not interrupting the speaker

- Not talking too much

- Acknowledging and validating feelings and thoughts (having empathy)

## e.    Questioning

Part of accumulating information may take place through the mediator's use of questions. Set out below are descriptions of the types of questions that are effective for a mediator to ask and the contexts in which asking them is most appropriate. Consider how a mediator's use of questions is similar to and distinct from that of a lawyer.

*Open*: This question is designed to get or keep the disputants talking. This form of question should be used predominantly in the early stages of the mediation when the mediator is gathering information. Asking open questions gives the disputants the opportunity to share their experiences and shape the dialogue.

Example:

Can you please elaborate on that statement?

The mediator usually will begin by asking broad questions which require explanations. As the session progresses, the mediator can ask narrower questions, such as:

How do you see the situation being resolved?

*Clarifying*: Commonly used to gather a clearer understanding or to confirm a piece of information. Clarifying questions are typically used at the beginning of mediation when the mediator is gathering information to understand the issues for discussion.

Examples:

Mr. Stockmeyer, can you explain in greater detail the injuries you suffered?

OR

Ms. Jones and Ms. Stoon, how would you like for that payment to be made?

*Closed*: These are questions which can be answered with merely a "yes" or "no" response. While this technique may extract some information, it should be used infrequently and with discretion because it does not elicit a complete response. The best use of closed questions is toward the end of a mediation or with disputants who volunteer a lot of information and the mediator is trying to limit their domination of the mediation.

Examples:

I have noted that your daughter Terry's religious upbringing and participation are important concerns for you. Would you be satisfied with the proposal that she attend a religious camp this summer?

OR

Does this written agreement completely satisfy your original claim?

*Justification*: This type of question usually begins with "Why" and calls on someone to justify his/her position (*e.g.*, past behavior, actions, feelings). Since this type of question tends to make people feel defensive and is often judgmental in nature, mediators should try to avoid using it. Often the question can be asked in another way to obtain the same useful information.

Example:

Instead of "Why did you fire Ms. Benk?" try, "What were the reasons for Ms. Benk's discharge?"

*Compound*: This is typified by multiple questions being asked as one question. The problem with using a compound question is that it is confusing to the person who has been asked the question and thus leads to a confusing answer. As a result, mediators should try to avoid using these questions.

Example:

Were you wearing your seat belt and talking on your cell phone at the time of the accident?

Use of good questioning techniques can help the mediator learn and clarify information. More importantly, it can help the parties understand more about the dispute from each other's perspective. A good exchange of information and joint problem solving can be fostered by the mediator's approach. A mediator should use questions to clarify, to help parties better understand their own interests and risks, to explore possibilities and to confirm movement or agreement. A mediator should not use questions merely to satisfy his or her own curiosity. Facilitative and evaluative mediators differ over whether a mediator should use questions to judge the situation. *See* Chapter 4, *infra*.

## f.  Non-Verbal Communication

Non-verbal communication is a vital part of our overall communication. Experts estimate that 55% of the information we gather is from non-verbal behavior; 38% from the tone and sound of the speaker's voice and only 7% from the actual words that the speaker uses. Paying attention to the silent cues and observing the communication between the parties will be valuable to the mediator. These cues help the mediator to identify such matters as the priorities, deeply held values, and areas that might be negotiable.

Non-verbal cues will serve as guide posts and indicators, but a mediator should be careful not to make assumptions based on a single non-verbal action. For example, traditionally, body language experts identified standing with one's arms crossed in front as a "closed" posture that indicates that individual's unwillingness to participate or hostility to the person or issue being discussed. Today, we understand that there might be many different reasons for assuming such a posture — *e.g.*, one is cold, one is comfortable like that, one is missing a button and trying to cover it up, and on and on. Experts now say that we should look at the total package of behaviors that an individual exhibits and, more importantly, at changes in behaviors.

Non-verbal communication may not be obvious. As in all aspects of the mediation, the mediator must be careful not to assume too much. These issues should be explored with the party or parties if the mediator thinks that the party is signaling something or if cues from one of the parties or the party's demeanor do not match what the party is verbalizing. The mediator should be sensitive to and aware of the impact that cultural differences may have on how parties react to conflict and the process of mediation. It may be appropriate to meet separately with the party to validate the feedback.

Mediators also need to be sensitive to their own non-verbal cues. A party may conclude that a mediator whose arms are folded is someone who is simply not interested in what the parties have to say, rather than someone who has simply achieved a comfortable physical position.

## 3.  Agenda Development

The parties have told their respective versions of the events that brought them to mediation. They probably have shared their reaction and evaluation of the other party's stated version of the events. The mediator should now lend a degree of structure to the discussion of the issues.

### a.  Characterizing the Issues

As opposed to the traditional way lawyers and law students think about "issues," in mediation an issue is some matter, practice, or action that enhances, frustrates, alters, or in some way adversely affects some person's interests, goals, or needs.

Mediation focuses on "negotiating issues," which are issues that people are capable of, and have the resources for, resolving. By definition, not all issues can be negotiated because the parties do not have all the resources necessary to resolve every problem for every person.

An example of an issue that is not a negotiating issue is "prejudice" or "bigotry." If one party has a prejudice or hatred against a particular group of people, mediation will not alter that party's deeply held attitudes and beliefs — no matter the length of the mediation session or the skill of the mediator. By contrast, the parties may be able to gain a greater understanding of how each views the situation.

In addition, the parties may be able to discuss and reach agreements on particular behaviors that may be causing difficulties between them, behaviors which themselves are negotiable and may be rooted in, or shaped by, prejudicial attitudes. The specific incidents are negotiating issues, while the general attitudes of prejudice and bigotry are not.

As the parties and/or their attorneys speak, the mediator will listen carefully to what is said (and not said) and note the issues which the parties (or their counsel) have identified as needing to be discussed in order for them to resolve the dispute which brought them to mediation.

Unrepresented parties to a dispute will typically speak in plain English and not in the language commonly referred to as "legalese." Typically, they will relate a series of events and it will be up to the mediator to cull through the information to succinctly state what has been heard as the issues. It is important to realize the range of flexibility that the mediator possesses when characterizing the dispute.

Example:

Fred Student housed his German Shepherd puppy at Al's House of Pets for 60 days over the summer and incurred a bill of $360. Fred has not made any payments on the bill and it is past due by six months. Fred has promised to drop off payments twice in the last two months to Al and has not done so.

What are the issues in this dispute?

A mediator, particularly one who is legally trained, might be tempted to characterize the issues as: "bad debt and broken promises." That is a mistake, for it simply invites parties to become defensive in arguing the merits of their claims. The more constructive approach is to characterize the issues as: "payment due and method of payment." By framing the issue in more neutral, future-oriented terms, the mediator reduces party defensiveness, invites party communication, and assists the parties to think creatively about possible resolutions.

When parties are represented in mediation, the statement of the issues will generally be in legalistic terms similar to how a cause of action would be presented to a court. A mediator's challenge in these circumstances is to help the parties (and their attorneys) identify the interests behind these issues, as well as, where appropriate, those non-legal issues which are of importance to them.

A mediator shapes both the way in which the parties talk with each other and the range of discussion. It may be tempting to limit the mediation discussion to the legal issues or four corners of the complaint if the mediation is of a case already filed in court. However, very often when people are embroiled in conflict, they get stuck. They keep talking about the same issues and ignoring the fact that previous difficulties may have an impact on the current dispute. Sometimes, the greatest assistance a mediator can provide is to help the parties expand their discussion. The common misconception about negotiation and mediation is that the most difficult disputes to resolve are those that involve a lot of money and multiple issues. In fact, frequently the most difficult conflicts to resolve are those that involve a single issue and very little money; in these situations there is little room for the disputants to maneuver and there are few concessions to offer.

## b.  Priorities

The disputants and their attorneys will talk about many things. By definition, some will be more important to them than others. Assisting them in identifying what matters most and what matters least to them establishes an environment which invites negotiation. Note that disputants will often discuss what is most important to them first and then repeat it several times in different ways. Listening carefully may reveal the attachment an individual has to an issue, and tactful questioning can confirm the level of interest on a particular topic.

## c.  Structuring the Discussion

As human beings, each of us is limited by the fact that we can only talk about one thing at a time. Hence, the order in which issues are discussed is an important element of the process. Generally, the guiding principle when setting an agenda is that you want to order the discussion in a way that will assist parties to move toward resolution. Note, however, that mediators who practice from a transformative perspective would view setting the agenda as a decision for the parties to make, not the mediator.

Some mediators will listen to the opening statements of the disputants with an ear toward identifying the "easy" issues. In the event that the parties and/or their attorneys do not choose a place to start their discussion, the mediator could then suggest one of these "easy" issues as a place to begin. The theory at work here is that individuals in dispute tend to feel frustrated and believe that their dispute will never be resolved — certainly not by talking with the other person. By helping disputants experience success rapidly, even if it is only a relatively minor matter, they become more optimistic and develop some momentum for productively discussing the more difficult issues.

By contrast, other mediators listen to the opening statements with the goal of identifying the core issue. Their theory is that by having the parties first bargain on the issue that they view as central to the dispute, the smaller (and easier) issues then fall into place. Finding a good place to start will come with practice and often will be driven by the preferences of the individuals involved in the mediation and the specific circumstances of the mediation.

Here are some guides mediators may use to find a starting place and structure the discussions.

*Categories*: Often the issues can be divided according to various subject matters or principles. Typical categories are: economic matters and non-economic matters or financial and behavioral. Appropriate categories will vary according to the nature of the dispute. By dividing multiple issues into a limited number of categories, the mediator assists the parties in breaking down the dispute into manageable parts.

*Nature of Remedies*: Some concerns raised by the parties will invite remedies which are mutual, *e.g.*, require both to do something for the other.

Other concerns require one party to do something and the other party merely to accept it, *e.g.*, one party pays the other party a sum of money. Often, mutual remedy issues are easier for the parties to discuss and agree to than are those for which one party has the burden of compliance.

*Time*: Sometimes the issues will break into categories according to time. For example, the disputants may wish to discuss the issues in chronological order (what happened first) or reverse chronological order (what happened last). In addition, sometimes an issue has a time constraint attached to it; the parties might find that discussion of those issues which are most constrained by time is constructive because there are outside interests pushing them toward resolution.

*Relationship of the Party to the Issues*: Some issues will be particularly difficult to resolve if the party or parties have a strong philosophical or personal attachment to the issue. It may be best to defer discussion of these matters until other issues are resolved and the parties have built some momentum toward resolution.

*Logic*: In some instances, issues will come up which are logically related to each other. In using this manner of organization, be careful not to focus unduly on past events instead of future possibilities.

While there are many ways to structure the agenda of discussion, the mediator must be prepared to take responsibility for setting an agenda based on what the parties have said if they do not do so for themselves. One of the greatest assets a mediator brings to the mediation is an ability to create structure and develop a process to assist the parties' communication. If the parties themselves or the mediator neglect to create an agenda, the possibility increases that the discussion will degenerate into impasse not because the parties necessarily disagree on all matters, but rather because no one focused on separating those items on which the parties agree from those about which they remain in substantial disagreement.

## 4. Generating Movement

Even after an agenda for discussion has been agreed to and the first issue to discuss has been selected, the parties may still be stuck. At this point, the mediator's job is to assist the parties in thinking about their dispute in other ways to help them move forward. It is important to keep in mind that disputants and their attorneys may not want to resolve their dispute in mediation. They may believe it is in their (or their client's) best interest to pursue the traditional legal process, some other means of resolution, or no resolution at all. The mediator's job is not to make sure that every situation is resolved in mediation, but rather to help the parties consider their options and make an informed decision as to how to resolve their dispute.

In addition to considering the topics developed in Chapter 2, *supra*, on negotiation, there are additional ways a mediator may be helpful to the parties in generating movement. The following sections present some options to consider for keeping the mediation discussions moving.

## a.   Procedural Items

*Alternate Discussion of Issues.* This is useful so that one party does not perceive himself/herself as "winning" or "losing" everything. A sure way for someone to become recalcitrant is if he/she believes that the other person is the only one who needs to make concessions; or conversely, if someone feels that he/she is the only one who is making any concessions.

*Focus on the Future.* It is helpful to remind parties that they cannot change what happened in the past, but they can decide how they want things to be in the future. As a means of comparison, the traditional litigation process focuses on the past, determining what happened, and who was wrong or right. In mediations involving an ongoing relationship, what happened in the past need only be relevant in helping parties determine how they want to behave in the future.

*Be Positive.* When disputants come to a mediation, they are often frustrated, nervous about being in mediation, and stressed about having a dispute which has not been resolved. As mediator, you may be the only one who remembers that conflict can be positive — that it can offer an opportunity for the parties to learn from each other. By maintaining a positive atmosphere in the mediation, the mediator can help the parties view their dispute as a learning endeavor.

*Use of Silence.* Most people are not comfortable with silence. Silence can be very powerful in helping parties and their attorneys reflect on the effect of a particular proposal or statement. As mediator, do not be afraid of silence. In particular, use silence when one party or his or her attorney has made an offer or counteroffer. The mediator should not be the person who breaks the silence — give the other party or attorney an opportunity to respond.

*Use of Humor.* People become more flexible when they are laughing because laughter often reveals some comfort with oneself and the situation. However, humor should never be used at the expense of anyone involved in the mediation.

## b.   Informational Items

*Create Doubts.* A great question for the mediator to pose to the parties and their attorneys is: "Is it possible . . . ?" If the parties acknowledge that something is possible, even if they say it is unlikely, they already are less rigid in their position and may then be able to consider other options. A corollary to this technique is to challenge assumptions. Often we will assume the worst of people with whom we are in conflict. A mediator can be very helpful to the parties and their attorneys, by asking them to consider whether their assumptions may not be accurate.

*Integrative Solutions.* If the mediator helps the parties and their attorneys to identify their interests (not just their positions) and think creatively, they may be able to identify issues in which they both can achieve the "win-win" solution that they want. If one considers mediation as negotiation in the presence of a mediator, then the techniques and theory found in Chapter 2, *supra*, on negotiation will also be useful to a mediator.

*Use of Facts.* Often the disputants have not spoken for a significant period of time prior to the mediation, or perhaps ever. It is often helpful for the mediator to encourage the parties to listen for "new information" from the other and to consider that as a possible rationale for adopting a different "position."

*Establish Priorities and Trade-Offs.* Not everything that the parties or their attorneys present at mediation will be of equal importance to them. Helping them identify which items are most important will help them see that other items are less important. This may yield greater flexibility and ideas regarding items to "trade-off." While we often think that disputes arise when individuals disagree about what is most important, in actuality those differences may lead to an easy agreement. For example, if one person puts a high value on an issue such as full payment of the amount owed while the other puts a high value on a different issue, such as that there be no lump sum payment, these individuals may be able to reach an agreement which results in full payment over time and addresses both of their "high priority" issues.

*Use Role Reversal.* Helping parties and attorneys see the situation from the other person's perspective is often very helpful. This technique is most useful when meeting separately with the parties and they are able to react with greater honesty.

*Point Out Possible Inconsistencies.* A mediator should never embarrass or berate a party, attorney, or other person involved in the mediation, but sometimes a mediator can note gently that there may be inconsistencies within comments or proposals that have been made.

*Identify Constraints on Others.* Everyone operates under some constraints — be they resource, psychological, or political. Proposed solutions must account for these constraints or the solution will not be acceptable. Assisting the disputants and their attorneys to see each other's constraints may be useful in helping them understand the dynamics at work in reaching an agreement and lead to greater creativity.

*Be the Agent of Reality.* The mediator should never force the parties to settle their dispute or any portion of it in mediation. The mediator may, however, help the parties to think through the consequences of not resolving the dispute in mediation (what is the party's BATNA and WATNA, i.e., best and worst alternatives). The parties may want to consider monetary costs, time lost, relationship issues, and the uncertainty of a court outcome when evaluating the acceptability of the proposed negotiated settlement terms so that their decision to settle or not is as informed as possible.

## c. Relationship Issues

*Appeal to Past Practices.* Sometimes the parties will have had a prior good relationship. In such cases, it may be useful for the mediator to explore with the parties how they have resolved similar issues in the past. If the parties have no prior relationship (or no positive prior relationship), this will probably not be a useful technique.

*Appeal to Commonly Held Standards and Principles.* Sometimes both parties will express a common theme, for example, to be treated respectfully or that they are concerned about the "best interest of their child." While acknowledgment of this notion will not "solve" their issues, it is often helpful for the mediator to point out to the parties (and their attorneys) that they do agree on some matters. A corollary to this technique is to utilize "peer pressure" (what would the general public do in a situation) as a way of helping parties to identify commonly held standards.

These techniques can help trigger flexibility. But the mediator must remember that making progress is normally done incrementally. The mediator may select a place for the parties to begin their discussions, but quickly discover that resolving it is more complex or difficult than originally envisioned. The mediator can deploy several different approaches for generating movement (three different attempts is generally good because using more may make the parties feel inappropriately pressured) but then move on to another issue if the parties remain in disagreement. The mediator will return to that issue at some later point.

Sometimes the mediator will want to meet with the parties separately. This can be another effective way of generating movement. Because there are many issues to consider when using this technique, it warrants separate discussion.

## 5.   The Separate Session (Caucus)

At some point during the mediation session, the mediator, a party, or an attorney, may decide that it would be useful for the mediator to meet separately with each of the parties. A caucus may also be called for the mediators, in the event there are co-mediators, or for an attorney and client to meet alone. For the purpose of this section, we focus on the separate meetings a mediator conducts with the parties.

The extent to which caucuses are used varies tremendously. Some mediators believe that it is more desirable to use joint sessions, whenever possible, to allow the disputants to communicate directly with one another. They are reluctant to use caucuses for fear of breaking the flow of the joint session. Other mediators rely on the technique extensively, and only use joint sessions at the very beginning and perhaps the end of a mediation. Some mediators do not declare an impasse unless they have had an opportunity to meet with the parties separately. As a generalization, evaluative mediators tend to be more enthusiastic about caucuses than are facilitative mediators. Similarly, attorney mediators tend to use caucus more frequently than non-attorney mediators. However, many mediators break with these generalizations and vary their use of caucus depending on the nature of the particular mediation. In any event, mediators' varied approaches to caucus are neither inherently right nor inherently wrong.

Regardless of mediation style, there is general agreement that a mediator should have a reason and a purpose in calling a caucus. What follows are some reasons (using the acronym ESCAPE) why the mediator might decide to meet privately with each party.

### a.   Rationale and Sequence of Separate Sessions

*Explore Settlement Options.* Sometimes the mediator will sense that the parties may be more open to discussing potential options if the other party is not present. In this situation, the mediator will usually begin with the party who appears to be willing to negotiate.

*Signal Warning Signs.* During the session, one party may exhibit behaviors which threaten any possibility of agreement. For example, one party may be continuing to refer to the other in an insulting manner or not allow the other to finish a thought without interrupting. If a party is represented, the unhelpful behavior may be that of the attorney. If the mediator senses that any of this is occurring, the mediator should meet first with the party (and attorney, if represented) who is exhibiting the behavior to discuss the mediator's observations.

*Confirm Movement:* At the start of the session, one party — for example, a landlord — may have indicated that the only acceptable resolution is for the other party — the tenant — to move. As the discussion progresses, the landlord appears to signal a change in that position but the mediator is not certain; the mediator needs to know if there is flexibility but does not want to explore that directly the landlord while in the presence of the tenant for fear that the landlord would try to "save face" by immediately denying any willingness to adjust. The mediator would declare a caucus and meet first with the party who had signaled possible movement to learn if the signal were accurate or a misstatement.

*Address Recalcitrant Party.* Every so often, one party will take a position early in the session and not move from it. It may become apparent to the mediator that the session will quickly conclude unless the other party is willing to meet the demand or the recalcitrant party is willing to consider movement. In such instances, the mediator should meet first with the "recalcitrant" party. As used here, the term "party" is not limited to named parties. A "recalcitrant party" may be an attorney or other representative.

*Pause.* At times, emotions can run high and the mediator may sense that the parties need a break to collect themselves, stop crying, or calm down. Separate meetings can provide this opportunity. The mediator should use his/ her judgment as to whether to meet first with the person who is upset or to meet first with the other party, thereby allowing the distraught individual an opportunity to calm down privately.

*Evaluate.* Finally, a caucus may be deemed necessary to evaluate the proposals that are currently being discussed. A private session affords the parties the opportunity to take a few moments to assess the impact of accepting or rejecting a potential resolution without the pressure of having the other party in the room. It also provides private time for reflection when the mediator is meeting with the other party. In situations in which there are multiple parties with shared interests or a party is represented, meeting alone enables them to consult with one another before making decisions. Generally, in this situation, the mediator can meet with either party first.

## b. Why Not Meet Separately?

Some mediators follow a set sequence in their mediation conference. They start by making an opening statement, ask each party to make their opening remarks, and then immediately call for caucus sessions. But there are important reasons why a mediator might decide not to meet separately with the parties, so the better practice is for the mediator to assess each situation and proceed accordingly. Set out below are reasons why the mediator might not want to meet separately with the parties:

*It Is Unnecessary.* If the parties are making progress and working together, there may be no need to stop them and meet separately. In fact, doing so might disrupt the momentum that has developed and have the effect of interrupting rather than assisting the process.

*Low Level of Trust Between the Parties.* Sometimes the parties have developed a very low level of trust between them. There will be no resolution to the dispute unless each party sees and hears from one another exactly why they accept particular settlement terms. Negotiating breakthroughs that happen while one party is out of the room will be viewed with suspicion and not accepted. In such circumstances, it might be best to keep the parties together.

*Physical Arrangements.* Sometimes the physical set-up of the mediation does not lend itself to meeting separately with the parties. For example, if there is no place for the parties and their attorneys to wait while the mediator is meeting with the others, calling a caucus might not be prudent.

### c.  Principles of the Separate Session

*The Mediator Should Have an Identifiable Reason for Meeting Separately with the Parties. See* Section C.5.a., *supra.* Non-agreement between the parties and "not knowing what else to do" are not reasons to meet separately. It seems overly simple to point out that the parties will not be in agreement from the outset of mediation. However, one of the most common misuses of caucus occurs when the parties state in their opening statements that they do not agree, so the mediator immediately, or very soon after the mediation begins, calls for separate sessions. Many mediators believe that when the caucus is called so early in the process, each party will simply repeat in caucus what was said in joint session. By calling an early caucus, the mediator has not provided the parties with the opportunity to negotiate for themselves, and thereby has not fostered joint problem solving. However, as noted above, some mediators (often those who use a more evaluative approach) do believe in the early use of caucus.

*Confidentiality.* Many mediators take the approach that unless the caucusing party and attorney authorizes the mediator to share the content of what was said with the other party, the mediator must keep all information gained in a separate session private. Some other mediators take the reverse approach, which is that they are permitted to share all information they learn in caucus *except* where instructed otherwise by the caucusing party. A third approach would be to inform the parties at the beginning that nothing said in caucus would be considered confidential. Therefore, the parties would be on notice not to share any information they were unwilling to tell the other party. While any of these approaches may be acceptable, depending on applicable ethical and procedural standards, it is crucial that the mediator adequately explain what the parties should expect in terms of confidentiality prior to asking the party to share information.

*The Mediator Meets with Each Party Every Time a Separate Session Is Called.* Meeting with each party every time a caucus is called serves two purposes. First, it reduces the level of suspicion about what happened during the caucus in which one party participated and the other did not. Second, it provides each party an opportunity to share information with the mediator. There are many reasons why parties may be reluctant to share full information in the presence of the other party; a caucus allows them to speak freely.

*The Amount of Time a Mediator Spends with Each Party in Caucus Need Not Be Identical.* The mediator should promise *equal opportunity* to meet separately, *not equal time.* Although the mediator must provide the opportunity for each party to meet separately with the mediator, the length of their meetings need not be identical. In fact, it will rarely be equal. If after meeting with one party, the mediator discovers that there is no strategic reason for meeting with the other party, the mediator should still meet with the waiting party, or that party's attorney, because the party or attorney may have a reason for wanting to meet with the mediator. The mediator would begin the second meeting by indicating that the mediator does not have anything he/she needs to ask or share but before reconvening, would willingly discuss anything the party or his/her attorney would like to share. Thus, the second meeting might last only a minute or two if the party (and his/her attorney) has nothing to say. Nonetheless, since the mediator provided the opportunity to meet separately with the mediator and it was the party's decision to end the meeting, the mediator preserves the appearance of impartiality and the party will be less likely to be concerned that the other caucus was longer. The party and attorney will be empowered to determine how long a caucus they desire.

## d.    The Mechanics of the Separate Session

When the time comes to meet separately, the mediator should:

- State the intention to meet separately with each party. The mediator should avoid using the term "caucus" if the term is not familiar to the disputants.

- Indicate the meeting sequence. If the parties are represented, the mediator will typically meet with the attorneys and their clients together. In some circumstances, the mediator might chose to meet with the attorneys without their clients. It would be unusual, for the mediator to meet with represented parties without their counsel; however, a mediator could do so if such a meeting were requested by a party.

- Indicate the approximate length of the meeting. In mediations involving unrepresented individuals, such as small claims mediation, a mediator should strive to keep separate meetings to no more than 10 minutes apiece. In complex cases, or those in which the party is represented by an attorney, a caucus may last considerably longer. One reason the length is less problematic when a party is represented is that the "waiting time" will not seem as long if the party has someone with whom to talk and plan strategy when the mediator is meeting with the other participants.

- Excuse one party and counsel from the room in which the mediator will conduct the caucus.

When declaring the caucus, the mediator should provide directions as to the location of a suitable waiting area. The mediator might encourage the parties to use their waiting time to attend to personal matters or, in a structured fashion, assign them a task to complete. While time may go quickly for the mediator and the party inside the room, it can seem like an eternity to the party who is waiting outside. If the caucus is taking longer than initially predicted, the mediator should let the party and attorney waiting outside know that more time is required.

When alone with one party in the room, a mediator will often employ the following practices:

- *Record the Time That the Caucus Began*. The mediator may think that she will remember how long the meeting with each party has been, but time moves very quickly and it is important not to lose track of it — the party waiting won't!

- *Separate Caucus Notes from Regular Notes*. The mediator can use either a separate piece of paper or the back of the joint information notes to record caucus insights. In any case, the mediator must record caucus information in such a way as to avoid inadvertently revealing confidential information.

- *Review the Rules of Confidentiality of the Separate Meeting and the Purpose for Meeting with the Party*. Remind the parties at the beginning and at the end of the each separate session of the level of confidentiality which attaches to information revealed and discussed in caucus. Often, caucus information is considered confidential unless the mediator has permission to share. The parties and their attorneys, however, can agree to a different level of confidentiality for caucuses. Therefore, it is critical that the degree of confidentiality be reviewed so that everyone is clear. This can be done jointly before the mediator excuses one of the parties, but more typically will be done individually with each party.

- *The Language Used By the Mediator in Caucus, as in Full Session, Must Remain Neutral*. Since the mediator is alone with one party, it is easy to get trapped into using the language of that party or the attorney. Even though the other party is not in the room, the mediator must maintain neutrality, and the choice of language is one of the most obvious ways to demonstrate that stance.

- *The Reason for Calling the Caucus Should Shape the Agenda*. Before beginning a caucus, the mediator should have a clear sense of what to try to accomplish in the caucus; this enables the mediator to know how to both start and end the caucus. For example, if the caucus was called to evaluate settlement options on targeted issues, the mediator generally would start with a discussion of that single issue that is most important to the parties (and attorneys) and prod them to asses the strengths and weaknesses of various options. The mediator need not invite discussion of every issue in every caucus. The mediator should use caucus time strategically.

When the mediator has accomplished the reason for meeting separately, the mediator should conclude the meeting. Before doing so, the mediator may want to check with the party and the attorney to ascertain if there is anything else they would like to share. As the caucus ends, if confidentiality has been assured, the mediator must ask the party and the attorney if there is anything that the mediator is permitted to share with the other side. The party and attorney may give the mediator blanket authority to share everything discussed, permission to share some amount of information, or ask that nothing they shared be discussed. If the mediator believes that some information which has been identified as non-public may be beneficial to building a settlement, the mediator may ask the party (and attorney) if they would be willing to share the information themselves. Alternatively, the mediator may ask for specific permission to share the information and explain to the party (and attorney) why it would be useful. In the end, whether the mediator agrees with the party and his/her attorney regarding non-disclosure, the mediator must respect the party's decision. Once the mediator's authority to share caucus information has been established, the mediator declares the caucus closed and escorts the party and attorney to the waiting area.

### Second Caucus

To begin, the mediator should go get the other party and attorney in the waiting area and escort them to the mediation room. Once settled, the mediator begins the second meeting in the same fashion as the first (separate notes, record the time, and invite the party's and attorney's confidence). The difference is that the mediator has just spent time alone with the "other side" and presumably has gained some additional information or insight, and everyone knows it. The mediator must fight the temptation to immediately reveal information which was learned in caucus, even if the mediator has permission to do so. The mediator's role has not changed. After the first separate meeting, the mediator should not become an advocate for settlement options proposed by one side or compromise a party's position by immediately revealing that party's concerns and interests. The mediator's focus in the second caucus is to invite the second party and attorney to share their perspectives and concerns on the topics under review. It is also useful to remember the negotiation principles, such as "reactive devaluation," introduced in Chapter 2, *supra*, that may be at work in this situation.

A good technique to use in caucus is to ask questions as hypotheticals. For example, a mediator might ask, "If the other party were willing to do X, would you be willing to do Y?" This allows the mediator to assume the scapegoat role if a suggestion is unacceptable. The party or attorney can reject the "hypothetical" without getting angry at the other side for proposing the idea. It also protects offers of movement made by one side.

The second caucus ends in identical manner to the first caucus by establishing with the party and attorney what information may be shared. Sometimes the mediator continues meeting with the parties in separate sessions, if additional developments or proposals regarding negotiating issues have occurred in caucus and they require clarification or exploration. Many mediators, however, after meeting once with each party, reconvene all parties and counsel in joint session to continue the discussion.

Sometimes as a result of the information shared in separate sessions, the parties and attorneys will be in substantial agreement. Other times, the parties are still very far apart. Regardless of where the parties are on that continuum, the mediator should begin the joint session with some encouraging words. Specifically, the mediator should thank the parties and the attorneys for the opportunity to meet with them separately. If the parties are still far apart, indicate that is the case but that this does not mean that the session needs to end immediately. The parties and attorneys may want to add additional information or ideas.

If the parties are close together or even in substantial agreement, the mediator might continue (after thanking them) with a statement along the lines of, "As a result of my individual conversations with each of you, it appears that you may be close to reaching an agreement on the following issues, but the precise terms need to be worked out."

Even if the mediator is certain the parties and attorneys are at the same point, the mediator must decide how to reveal this potential consensus. Basically, there are three options:

> (1) The mediator announces the terms of the agreement: "After speaking with each of you, there appears to be agreement regarding the matter of rent arrears. Both Ms. Jones and Mr. Smith agree that payment by Mr. Smith to Ms. Jones of $250 will constitute complete satisfaction of the claim for rent arrears. Is that correct?"

> (2) The parties/attorneys reveal the agreement to each other: "Ms. Jones, will you please share with Mr. Smith and me your proposal for resolving the rent issue?"

> (3) Some combination of (1) and (2), above.

If the parties are unrepresented, it is usually preferable to allow the parties to reveal the agreement to each other since it is their agreement. This allows the parties to assume greater ownership over the agreement. However, if the parties are highly emotional or extremely angry at one another, or the agreement is very complicated, the mediator may choose to reveal some or all of the terms in the manner noted in (1), above. If the agreement is conveyed by the mediator, the mediator should check with each party after each term is revealed to ensure that there is agreement. At a minimum, the parties should at least be nodding their affirmation as the mediator speaks. If the parties are represented, the attorneys may want to take a more active role in discussing the settlement terms.

## 6.   Concluding the Mediation

It is the mediator's responsibility to end the session, whether or not the parties have settled their dispute. There are four ways in which a mediation session might end:

> 1.   *The Parties Do Not Reach Any Agreement.* If the case was ordered by the court to mediation, the mediator will probably be required to file a report of "impasse" with the court. Most courts will accept a report from the mediator which states when the mediation occurred, who appeared at the mediation, and that no agreement was reached. While some judges may want to know why no agreement was reached, rules of confidentiality will

often prevent mediators from providing this information. See Chapter 5, *infra*, for a more detailed discussion. If the case was mediated voluntarily or pursuant to an agreement of the parties, there is normally no need for the mediator to write a report. The parties will merely decide on another means of resolving the dispute.

2. *The Parties Request to Continue Mediation After a Specific Period of Time.* A continuation is usually requested when one or both of the parties want to resolve their dispute, but need additional time to gather information that has bearing on their decisions and actions. Typically, the mediator who began the mediation will complete the mediation.

3. *The Parties Have a Partial Agreement, Meaning That They Have Resolved Some Issues but Need Some Other Type of Dispute Resolution for Helping Them Address Issues Which They Were Unable to Settle.* In this situation, the parties may draft an agreement in which they identify both the substantive settlement terms they have reached as well as the procedural agreements they have reached for addressing the unresolved issues. Any item included in the signed mediation agreement is typically not confidential, and thus, could be discussed with a judge or other dispute resolver.

4. *The Parties Reach Agreement on All the Issues.* Generally, if an agreement is reached, it is reduced to writing in order to preserve the parties' ability to enforce the agreement. *See* Chapter 6, *infra*. When attorneys are present at mediation, typically one of the attorneys will draft the mediated agreement. If attorneys are not involved, the mediator will typically provide to the parties a document outlining their settlement terms. In some states, it is the mediator's ethical responsibility in a court-ordered mediation to ensure that the terms of agreement are memorialized (written and signed). However, the potentially critical issue of unauthorized practice of law (UPL) has been raised against some mediators who have drafted written agreements. See Chapter 8, *infra*, for a more detailed discussion. Regardless of who writes the final agreement, the parties often leave with a signed "Memorandum of Understanding."

## a. No Agreement

Some parties will decide not to resolve their dispute in mediation because they believe their case was not suitable for mediation, they need more time to reflect, or there are strategic reasons for wanting to take a case to trial or another form of dispute resolution. If the parties do not reach a consensus in mediation, the mediator should still try to end the session in an upbeat manner. Many times, disputes which do not resolve at mediation do settle at some point before trial, with or without the further assistance of the mediator.

Before concluding, mediators typically do the following:

- Review with the parties and attorneys any issues that were resolved and explore the possibility of a partial agreement outlining what issues have been resolved and which issues are still unresolved.

- Encourage post-mediation communication between the parties by asking the parties or attorneys if they wish to exchange contact information. Absent such an exchange, unrepresented parties often lack the ability to contact one another even if they wanted to reach out after the mediation.

- Encourage the parties and attorneys to consider returning to mediation (with the same or different mediator) if they think it would be helpful.

- End on a positive note by thanking the parties for their time and effort at the mediation. The mediator often accepts the scapegoat role by saying, "I regret that I was not able to assist you in resolving your dispute today," thereby encouraging the parties to have confidence that it is still within their capacity to end their controversy in a mutually satisfactory way.

### b. Agreement

Regardless of who writes the agreement (the parties, attorneys or mediator), it must be done carefully and accurately, for the agreement most likely will become legally binding and enforceable. The parties also need to understand it and be able to refer back to it. And if the mediation itself had been court-ordered, a court-ordered mediation, a judge may have to review and enforce the settlement terms.

### i. Format of an Agreement

The written agreement should be clear and concise. Here are some guidelines:

- Separate the different elements of the agreement, assign a number to each and list them sequentially. Do not write a long narrative.

- Do not include "confessions."

- Use the names of the parties, not legal jargon (e.g., complainant or respondent) and make certain the names are spelled correctly. The first time a name is referenced, write it out completely, and then when referring to the parties later in the agreement, use just the first or last names (depending on the context of the dispute).

- Write out dates rather than use the numerical equivalents (e.g., March 4, 2015 rather than 3/4/15). In addition, be precise; avoid using ambiguous phrases such as bi-weekly, monthly, at the end of the month, the end of the week, in the summer, etc.

- When the agreement involves a monetary settlement, write out the dollar amount. This may appear very old-fashioned, but it is easy to misread numbers or misplace a decimal. In addition, specify the place, method (e.g., by means of cash with receipt, bank check, money order, etc.) and timing of payments. If there is a payment schedule agreed to of less than five payments, write out each payment date and amount.

- Keep the tone positive and prospective. A mediation agreement should not retell the dispute's history but be forward looking. A useful phrase to include is "in the future" particularly if a party has agreed to do (or not do) something in the future, but is unwilling to acknowledge that he or she did not (or did) do it in the past.

- If unrepresented, the mediator should invite the parties to assist in writing the document by reading each element of the agreement as it is written. Ask them if the words used accurately capture their agreement. Pride of authorship belongs to the parties not the mediator.

- When writing the terms of the agreement, the mediator should never change the substantive settlement terms the parties have adopted. If related issues come up during the drafting of the agreement which were not previously discussed, the mediator should raise the matters with the parties for their negotiation and decision as to how they wish to handle the issues.

- Just as the mediation must be conducted in a neutral manner, the agreement or memorandum of understanding must be written in a fair and balanced manner. It is useful to start with those items which are mutual obligations, alternating, where possible, whose name appears first in each sentence. The goal is for the agreement to reflect an appropriate sense of balance between the parties. If the mediation is successful, everyone should feel as though they achieved something from it, and the written agreement should reflect that fact.

## ii.   Enforcement

One advantage of a mediated agreement is in compliance. Since the parties have worked out the settlement terms themselves, they are more likely to understand them, believe they are fair and workable, and feel compelled to honor them.

But what happens if the agreement is not fulfilled? If the case was mediated pursuant to a court order, the parties can often enforce their mediated agreement in the same manner as any court order. In order for the court to enforce the agreement, it must be clear and unambiguous. In addition, the court probably will only be able to enforce monetary terms. Settlement provisions such as, "The parties agree to treat each other respectfully in the future" are often helpful and fundamental in mediation agreements, but are not ones which a court can effectively enforce. Parties may wish to include such terms, but they should understand that a court cannot enforce specific performance obligations such as "respect."

If the mediation is the result of a voluntary submission, the parties still have an enforceable agreement. If there is alleged non-compliance, then one party must take the additional step of filing a court case to enforce the mediation agreement as a contract.

If the parties are expressing a great deal of concern about enforcement, the mediator may want to explore with them whether there are issues which remain unresolved in the mediation. See Chapter 6, *infra*, for a more complete discussion of enforcement issues.

# D.   OTHER FORMS OF MEDIATION

The facilitative, problem-solving approach to mediation is not universally adopted. The other two major schools of thought on mediation are transformative and evaluative. Read the following excerpts focusing on the differences and similarities between these approaches and what has been described above.

## 1.   Transformative Mediation

The following excerpt from an article written by Robert A. Baruch Bush and Joseph P. Folger highlights the hallmarks of a transformative approach to mediation.

### TRANSFORMATIVE MEDIATION AND THIRD-PARTY INTERVENTION: TEN HALLMARKS OF A TRANSFORMATIVE APPROACH TO PRACTICE
13 Mediation Q. 263, 266–75 (1996)*
By Robert A. Baruch Bush & Joseph P. Folger

When mediators are effectively putting the transformative approach into practice, the ten patterns or habits of practice discussed below are evident in their work . . . . Each of the ten points describes, in part, what the work of a mediator implementing the transformative framework looks like . . .

**Hallmark 1:** *"The opening statement says it all": Describing the mediator's role and objectives in terms based on empowerment and recognition.*

Mediators . . . following a transformative approach begin their interventions with a clear statement that their objective is to create a context that allows and helps the parties to (1) clarify their own goals, resources, options, and preferences and make clear decisions for themselves about their situation; and (2) consider and better understand the perspective of the other party, *if* they decide they want to do so.

. . . .

**Hallmark 2:** *"It's ultimately the parties' choice": Leaving responsibility for outcomes with the parties.*

. . . An important hallmark of the transformative approach is that its practitioners consciously reject feelings of responsibility for generating agreements, solving the parties' problem, healing the parties, or bringing about reconciliation between them. Instead, third parties following a transformative framework sensitize themselves to feeling responsible for setting a context for, and supporting, the parties' own efforts at deliberation, decision making, communication, and perspective taking.

Thus, the mediator feels a keen sense of responsibility for recognizing and calling attention to opportunities for empowerment and recognition that might be missed by the parties themselves, and for helping the parties to take advantage of these opportunities as they see fit. In practice, calling attention to these opportunities means inviting the parties to slow down and consider the implications or questions that follow from a statement one of them has made . . .

. . . .

When mediators firmly grasp the transformative framework, they recognize and feel strongly that *only the choices or changes that the parties freely make*, regarding what to do about their situation or how they see each other, will be of real or lasting value . . .

**Hallmark 3:** *"The parties know best": Consciously refusing to be judgmental about the parties' views and decisions.*

The value placed on empowerment within the transformative framework motivates third parties who follow this approach to consciously avoid exercising judgment about the parties' views, options, and choices.

. . . .

The sign of transformative practice is that the third party's actions are responsive to the disputants' moves. A shift of power is not an outcome prompted or justified by third-party judgment; rather, it is one possible result of a series of moves that the parties themselves initiate, based on their own judgments.

**Hallmark 4:** *"The parties have what it takes": Taking an optimistic view of parties' competence and motives.*

. . . Third parties who successfully implement a transformative approach are consistently positive in their view of the disputants' fundamental competence, their ability to deal with their own situation on their own terms. Likewise, the third parties take a positive view of the disputants' motives, of the good faith and decency that underlie their behavior in the conflict situation, whatever the appearances may be . . . .

. . . .

This commitment to assuming the disputants' underlying competence and decency is actually quite critical to a transformative approach because it directly affects the steps the mediator will and will not take in practice. If a mediator believes that the parties are incapable of making good decisions about how to deal with their situation, the mediator will take over responsibility and act directively, instead of supporting the parties' own decision making.

. . .

**Hallmark 5:** *"There are facts in the feelings": Allowing and being responsive to parties' expression of emotions.*

In transformative practice, third parties view the expression of emotions — anger, hurt, frustration, and so on — as an integral part of the conflict process. Intervenors therefore expect and allow the parties to express emotions, and they are prepared to work with these expressions of emotion as the conflict unfolds.

. . . .

. . . [W]hen parties express emotions, the mediator does not just wait until it is over and then go on with the issue discussion. Instead, the mediator asks the parties both to describe their feelings and, perhaps more important, to describe *the situations and events that gave rise to them.* These descriptions of the facts behind the feelings very often reveal specific points that the parties are struggling with, both to gain control over their situation and to understand and be understood by the other party . . .

. . . .

**Hallmark 6:** *"Clarity emerges from confusion": Allowing for and exploring parties' uncertainty.*

Intervenors who understand the transformative framework expect that disputants will frequently be unclear and uncertain about the issues underlying their conflict, what they want from each other, and what would be the "right" choices for them. Indeed, the intervenors recognize that such unclarity presents important opportunities for empowerment . . .

In practical terms, this means that the intervenor is willing to follow the disputants as they talk through and discover for themselves what is at stake, how they see the situation, what each believes the other party is up to, and what they see as viable options . . . .

**Hallmark 7:** *"The action is 'in the room' ": Remaining focused on the here and now of the conflict interaction.*

In the transformative approach to practice . . . the intervenors attend to the discussion that is going on "in the room," to each statement made by the disputants and to what is going on between them, rather than "backing up" to a broader view on the identification and solution of the problem facing the parties. The third party avoids looking at the unfolding conflict interaction through a problem-solution lens because doing so would make it hard to spot and capture opportunities for empowerment and recognition.

Instead, the mediator focuses on the specific statements (verbal and nonverbal) of the parties in the session about how they want to be seen, what is important to them, why these issues matter, what choices they want to make, and so on. The mediator uses this focus to spot precisely the points where parties are unclear, where choices are presented, where parties feel misunderstood, where each may have misunderstood the other — that is, the points where there is potential for empowerment and recognition. When the mediator spots such points, he or she attempts to slow down the discussion and to take time to work with the parties, together or separately, on clarification, decision making, communication, and perspective taking, that is, the processes of empowerment and recognition.

. . . .

**Hallmark 8:** *"Discussing the past has value to the present": Being responsive to parties' statements about past events.*

. . . Parties' comments about the past can be highly relevant to the present, in the unfolding conflict interaction. In talking about what happened, each disputant reveals important points about how he or she sees, and wants to be seen by, the other party . . . .

. . . .

[I]f third parties view the history of conflict as evil, as something that the session quickly must move beyond, then important opportunities for empowerment and recognition will almost certainly be missed. An important hallmark of transformative practice is a willingness to mine the past for its value to the present — in particular, for the opportunities such review offers parties to help clarify their choices and reconsider their views of one another.

**Hallmark 9:** *"Conflict can be a long-term affair": Viewing an intervention as one point in a larger sequence of conflict interaction.*

. . . [T]hird parties, following the transformative approach are more likely to believe that no single intervention can address all the dimensions of a conflict in their entirety . . . . This outlook is crucial in enabling the intervenor to avoid a directive stance aimed at only one measure of success: settlement.

Seeing the intervention as one point in a stream of conflict interaction also gives third parties an awareness of the *cycles* that conflict interaction is likely to go through. Third parties following a transformative approach expect disputants to move toward and away from each other (and possible agreement) as the conflict, and the intervention unfolds . . .

**Hallmark 10:** *"Small steps count": Feeling a sense of success when empowerment and recognition occur, even in small degrees.*

. . . Third parties committed to this approach are careful to mark for themselves (as well as for the parties) the micro — as well as the macro — accomplishments of sessions, and they do not define success solely in terms of the final agreements reached. Instead they see and value the links between parties' micro-accomplishments and their macrocommitments . . . .

## QUESTIONS

(1)  How are Test Design's list of skills, abilities, and other attributes of a mediator, set out in Section B of this chapter, *supra*, consistent with, and how are they different from, the transformative form of practice?

(2)   If one subscribes to the transformative school of thought, how would the skills covered above differ (*e.g.*, mediator's opening statement, setting the agenda, etc.)?

(3)   What are the pros and cons for the parties in participating in a "transformative mediation"?

(4)   Do you believe that the facilitative and transformative approaches are inconsistent with each other?

## 2.   Evaluative Mediation

The following excerpt highlights some of the different approaches that might be employed by a mediator who practices from an evaluative framework. As you read this excerpt, consider whether this approach would be appropriate in all circumstances. For example, is attorney representation necessary if the mediator proceeds in an evaluative manner?

### DO'S AND DON'TS FOR MEDIATION PRACTICE
Disp. Resol. Magazine, Vol. 11, No. 2, 19–22 (Winter 2005)*
By Marjorie Corman Aaron

This is practical advice for mediators, gleaned from years of experience — and too many mistakes . . . .

At the joint mediation session, the mediator plays many roles: moderator, master of ceremonies, questioner, alter ego, persuader, dealmaker.

DO

*Set the appropriate tone with an opening statement* . . . .

*Remind the parties and counsel of the confidentiality of the mediation process.*

*Remind the parties that they own the mediation and its outcome is theirs to determine* . . . .

*Ask the parties and counsel to try to listen objectively to the other side's opening presentation.* Suggest that, rather than scribbling responses, they try to imagine how jurors listening for the first and only time would view the dispute.

*Explain to the parties that mediators are agents for settlement.* If appropriate, explain that a mediator might help them evaluate their options and alternatives. What you bring to the process that no one else has is neutrality. Because you have no stake in either side winning or losing, the parties might want to ask for your evaluation — and then give it some weight. The process may give the parties some perspective, perhaps some reality testing, so that they can decide whether a proposed settlement makes sense.

*Develop an opening "patter" that fits your personality and your philosophy . . . .*

*Listen and take notes during the presentations* — even if you have heard it all before. Be proactive and eager about examining architects' plans and photographs, medical reports, loan agreements and other original critical documents in the case.

*By the end of the presentations, strive to have a real and detailed understanding of all parties' legal and factual arguments . . . .*

*Ensure that the issue of damages is addressed . . . .* Get the parties' theories of damages and supporting evidence out on the table. Ask questions to focus the issues. You might probe to demonstrate where the parties agree on the facts or the law and identify the sources of disagreement.

*Ask questions gracefully, without indicating bias . . .* If you are going to ask a particularly difficult question, soften it by saying that you are playing devil's advocate. Provide a graceful exit route, such as: "Of course, if you were preparing for trial, you would have developed this issue further."

*Ask questions and make comments that anticipate the reactions or feelings of the side listening to the presentation . . . .*

*Reframe negative comments toward the more positive, if possible.*

*Use active listening techniques from time to time . . . .*

## DON'T

*Act like a judge or permit the parties or counsel to treat you like one.*

*Allow cross-examination or disruptive interruptions or objections.*

*Lose control of the proceedings unless the parties have "taken over" to engage in real dialogue and problem solving.*

*Indicate that counsel could have done a better job of analyzing the case, advising a client or preparing for the mediation . . . .*

*Omit a joint session focused on the parties' perspectives or on what gives rise to the dispute,* except in very unusual circumstances . . . if you are called upon to provide an evaluation, it is important for both sides to have seen and heard the presentation upon which it is based.

*Interrupt the presentations too much . . . ..*

*Ask questions that indicate you favor one party's argument or position . . . .*

*Make one side's case stronger by asking questions or making statements in joint sessions . . . .* In private sessions, you may point out how the other side's case could be even stronger and note that he or she will probably figure this out before trial.

The private caucus is often an important opportunity for parties and counsel . . . .

DO

*Start the private caucus by asking the parties and counsel what they are thinking*, what they might want to say that they were not comfortable saying in the joint session.

*Feel free to empathize with each party's perspective, while maintaining neutrality in the dispute . . . .* Use jokes, war stories, any common ground to indicate that you can see their points of view . . . . This is called manipulation . . . and it is clearly part of the mediation process.

*Reiterate that you will not reveal information to the other side unless you are expressly authorized to do so.*

*Help the parties see that, whatever the past perceived injury or wrong, they are now faced with making choices going forward . . . .*

*Ask the parties to begin focusing on solutions,* including but not limited to dollars. In some cases, you may suggest a number of options for them to tinker with and ponder. Then it is your job to shuttle back and forth, trying to put a deal together.

*Try to get a sense of the settlement numbers the parties have in mind.* You might ask them to estimate the chances of a liability finding or of various levels of damages awards. Do a thumbnail risk analysis with the parties and counsel, using their numbers to see what settlement might make sense for them . . . .

*Find the tiebreaker.* As you get down to the last issues, as the number gap narrows and the parties look as if they are drawing a line in the sand over the last dime, suggest a solution and ask both parties to consider it. Explain that you will tell each party if and when the other side agrees to the proposal. The other side will not be able to come back and shave the deal up or down. Make sure your proposed solution is one that the parties can and should accept.

*Wait to offer your own evaluation until you see no other way to achieve progress toward settlement.* Evaluation carries a great risk — primarily, that the party on the negative side of the evaluation will no longer view you as being neutral or as being very smart. The "winning" party in the evaluation, of course, will think you are brilliant. But this will undermine the mediation and cause you to lose credibility.

*Make sure, before you evaluate, that the party would like to hear what you think of the case.* Be explicit about what relevant experience and expertise you do or do not have. Provide consistent evaluations to both sides in private sessions.

*Provide any evaluations very gently* — and in private caucus only. Couch your evaluation in terms of what an average jury might do, how jurors' sympathies might lie. Encourage dialogue and listen to it. Don't argue, but explain, from a neutral's perspective, why you might reach a different solution. If your evaluation is unfavorable to one party, provide a face-saving reason. Try to prevent an unfavorable evaluation from turning a party against you or the process.

*Make sure, before you evaluate, that the rules of all ADR providers, court programs and controlling statutes permit case evaluation.*

*Pay attention to the bargaining styles of all parties and counsel* . . . .

*Keep the numbers and the options rolling.* If people must eat, it's generally best to order in rather than break the momentum . . . .

*Have patience.*

## DON'T

*Ask for anyone's bottom line* . . . . Most of the time, the parties won't tell you the truth and, as soon as they announce their bottom line — usually, a fake one — they may become entrenched. If you later have to ask them to negotiate past an announced bottom line, it looks as if you didn't really listen or respect their limits.

*Assume that you will be delivering an evaluation* . . . .

*Deliver an inconsistent evaluation to both sides.* It is always tempting to tell both sides they have a terrible case and find an easy settlement in the middle. That may settle one case, but it will quickly ruin your reputation as a mediator . . . .

*Give up on the bidding* . . . . Never believe a number is final until the parties have walked out the door — threatening to walk out isn't good enough . . . A better approach is to communicate the last number and encourage a counter. Help the parties test each other.

*Allow the parties to dig in on a position or a number as a matter of ego* . . . .

Since a final agreement is mediation's goal, there are no don'ts to offer — only do's.

## DO

*Write up the deal then and there* . . . .

*Include a provision stating that the agreement is valid and enforceable,* if the parties intend it to be . . . .

*Tackle ambiguities or inconsistencies* in the parties understanding of the deal and in the nitty-gritty of getting it done . . . .

*Make sure the parties read the agreement aloud* . . . .

# QUESTIONS

(1)   How are the Test Design's list of skills, abilities, and other attributes of a mediator consistent with, and how are they different from, the evaluative form of practice?

(2)   What were the similarities and differences between Ms. Aaron's description of mediation with an evaluative component and the description of both the facilitative and transformative processes of mediation?

(3)   What are the pros and cons for the parties in participating in a mediation conducted by "an evaluative mediator"?

(4)  Would an evaluative mediator need to incorporate different practices if one or more of the parties are unrepresented?

# Chapter 4

# MEDIATOR ROLES, ORIENTATIONS, AND STYLES

## A. INTRODUCTION

This chapter focuses on the mediator. It presents varying perspectives relating to the functions to be served by the mediator and his or her overall orientation toward the parties in mediation. Section B contains excerpts from theorists and commentators with different philosophical notions of the proper *role* to be served by the mediator. Section C views the mediator's role from a practice perspective by reviewing the overall *orientations* that have been recommended or identified by commentators on the mediation process. Section D presents an empirical perspective and reviews the *styles* of mediation that have been identified by researchers. You should consider carefully how these various *roles*, *orientations*, and *styles* interrelate. Which ones are consistent with one another? Which are inconsistent?

## B. MEDIATOR ROLES

### 1. Role Conceptions

In the following two excerpts, Lon Fuller and Robert A. Baruch Bush develop their conceptions of the mediator's role by first emphasizing the unique character of mediation. They then argue for a conception of the mediator's role that is most consistent with mediation's true character. Fuller sees mediation's "central quality" as "its capacity to reorient the parties toward each other." He thus views the mediator's role (or "function") as that of assisting the parties "to free themselves from the encumbrance of rules and of accepting, instead, a relationship of mutual respect, trust and understanding." Similarly, Bush examines "the special powers of mediation" in developing his "empowerment-and-recognition" conception of the mediator's role. He rejects two popular conceptions of the mediator's role — the "efficiency" conception and the "protection-of-rights" conception — because they are not in line with mediation's unique character.

# MEDIATION — ITS FORMS AND FUNCTIONS
## 44 S. Cal. L. Rev. 305, 307–08, 315, 318, 325–26 (1971)*
### By Lon L. Fuller

. . . [O]f mediation one is tempted to say that it is all process and no structure.

Casual treatments of the subject in the literature of sociology tend to assume that the object of mediation is to make the parties aware of the "social norms" applicable to their relationship and to persuade them to accommodate themselves to the "structure" imposed by these norms. From this point of view the difference between a judge and a mediator is simply that the judge orders the parties to conform themselves to the rules, while the mediator persuades them to do so. But mediation is commonly directed, not toward achieving conformity to norms, but toward the creation of the relevant norms themselves. This is true, for example, in the very common case where the mediator assists the parties in working out the terms of a contract defining their rights and duties toward one another. In such a case there is no pre-existing structure that can guide mediation; it is the mediational process that produces the structure.

It may be suggested that mediation is always, in any event, directed toward bringing about a more harmonious relationship between the parties, whether this be achieved through explicit agreement, through a reciprocal acceptance of the "social norms" relevant to their relationship, or simply because the parties have been helped to a new and more perceptive understanding of one another's problems. The fact that in ordinary usage the terms "mediation" and "conciliation" are largely interchangeable tends to reinforce this view of the matter.

. . . When we perceive how a mediator, claiming no "authority," can help the parties give order and coherence to their relationship, we may in the process come to realize that there are circumstances in which the parties can dispense with this aid, and that social order can often arise directly out of the interactions it seems to govern and direct.

. . . Where the bargaining process proceeds without the aid of a mediator the usual course pursued by experienced negotiators is something like this: the parties begin by simply talking about the various proposals, explaining in general terms why they want this and why they are opposed to that. During this exploratory or "sounding out" process, which proceeds without any clear-cut offers of settlement, each party conveys — sometimes explicitly, sometimes tacitly, sometimes intentionally, sometimes inadvertently — something about his relative evaluations of the various items under discussion. After these discussions have proceeded for some time, one party is likely to offer a "package deal," proposing in general terms a contract that will settle all the issues under discussion. This offer may be accepted by the other party or he may accept it subject to certain stipulated changes.

Now it is obvious that the process just described can often be greatly facilitated through the services of a skillful mediator. His assistance can speed the negotiations, reduce the likelihood of miscalculation, and generally help the parties to reach a sounder agreement, an adjustment of their divergent valuations that will produce

---

something like an optimum yield of the gains of reciprocity. These things the mediator can accomplish by holding separate confidential meetings with the parties, where each party gives the mediator a relatively full and candid account of the internal posture of his own interests. Armed with this information, but without making a premature disclosure of its details, the mediator can then help to shape the negotiations in such a way that they will proceed most directly to their goal, with a minimum of waste and friction.

[T]he central quality of mediation . . . [is] its capacity to reorient the parties toward each other, not by imposing rules on them, but by helping them to achieve a new and shared perception of their relationship, a perception that will redirect their attitudes and dispositions toward one another.

This quality of mediation becomes most visible when the proper function of the mediator turns out to be, not that of inducing the parties to accept formal rules for the governance of their future relations, but that of helping them to free themselves from the encumbrance of rules and of accepting, instead, a relationship of mutual respect, trust and understanding that will enable them to meet shared contingencies without the aid of formal prescriptions laid down in advance.

## EFFICIENCY AND PROTECTION, OR EMPOWERMENT AND RECOGNITION?: THE MEDIATOR'S ROLE AND ETHICAL STANDARDS IN MEDIATION
### 41 Fla. L. Rev. 253, 255–57, 259–73 (1989)*
### By Robert A. Baruch Bush

[V]oices on all sides are calling for uniform standards for mediator qualifications and practice. The concern for standards is especially urgent not only because of the growth of voluntary mediation in recent years, but also because of a growing trend toward state legislation providing for mandatory, court-connected mediation of civil disputes.

[T]he adoption of common standards, no matter how urgent, requires as a first step the acceptance of a common conception of the mediator's role on which to base such standards. Unfortunately, no such common conception exists today, nor has one even been sought before now. On the contrary, until now pluralism has reigned in mediation practice. Mediation has been seen by some as a vehicle for citizen empowerment; by others as a tool to relieve court congestion; and by still others as a means to provide "higher quality" justice in individual cases. These and other visions of mediation have coexisted and produced very different conceptions of the mediator's role. But no one conception had found general acceptance. Therefore, even if the public interest urgently demands common standards, we cannot reasonably meet this demand without first choosing which conception of the mediation process and the mediator's role should govern.

. . . [M]ediators occupy a unique role which they are ethically obligated to understand and fulfill.

---

. . . [U]nder the common definition of mediation, a neutral third party works with the disputing parties to help them reach a mutually acceptable resolution. This definition might itself appear to answer the question of what the mediator's role should be. However, this standard definitional language can be read in different ways, and it does not reflect in practice any common conception of the mediator's role in the process. On the contrary, as discussed above, many different conceptions exist. Among these, however, two call for special and critical discussion. Both the efficiency and protection-of-rights conceptions of the mediator's role are quite popular today; both have greatly influenced the operation of mediation programs and the articulation of mediation standards. Nevertheless, neither merits such popularity or influence. Despite their prevalence, both conceptions are deeply flawed, and for similar reasons.

The efficiency conception holds that the mediator's primary role, and the main value of the mediation process, is to remove litigation from the courts by facilitating settlement agreements in as many cases as possible. This reduces court congestion, frees scarce judicial time, and economizes on public and private expense. Sometimes this conception is framed more narrowly by saying that the mediator's role is simply to facilitate agreements. However, this characterization is usually only a surrogate for the efficiency conception, since the value of agreements in this view is that they represent conservation of public and private resources. Therefore the efficiency conception usually is accompanied by a focus on mediators' settlement rates and time-and-cost figures. This conception is advanced most commonly by judicial administrators and planners, and by the business-law community, as part of the search for "alternatives to the high costs of litigation." By contrast, the protection-of-rights conception holds that the mediator's primary role, and the main value of the mediation process, is to safeguard the rights of the disputing parties and potentially affected third parties by imposing various checks for procedural and substantive fairness on an otherwise unconstrained bargaining process. This prevents settlement agreements from compromising important rights. Sometimes, this conception is expressed by saying that the mediator's role is to ensure that agreements are based on informed consent and that they are not fundamentally unfair to either side. This characterization, however, is really only a surrogate for the protection-of-rights conception, for the primary concern is avoiding unknowing waivers of legal rights, including the right to fundamental fairness inherent in legal doctrines such as unconscionability. Therefore, the protection-of-rights conception usually engenders a focus on mediator duties, especially on the duty to advise and urge parties to obtain independent legal counsel and the duty to terminate a mediation that threatens to produce an unreasonably unfair agreement. Advocates of disadvantaged groups and the trial practice segment of the bar are among those advocating this conception. It has heavily influenced most of the mediation practice codes proposed in recent years.

. . .

The first flaw in both conceptions is that efficiency and protection of rights are both interests that third parties other than mediators can promote much more effectively than mediators themselves. Therefore, why give either of these jobs to mediators in the first place? If efficiency is the concern, an arbitrator can be more effective than a mediator in removing cases from court and disposing of them expeditiously and finally. The greater structure of the arbitration process, and the arbitrator's decisional authority, make speedy and final disposition much more likely in arbitration than in mediation. On the other hand, if protection of rights is the primary concern, a judge can do so far more effectively than a mediator. As many have observed, the informality and privacy of mediation, and its de-emphasis on substantive rules of decision, inevitably place rights and fairness at risk. By contrast, adjudication's emphasis on procedural formality, substantive rules, and neutral supervision of zealous advocates assures greater protection of rights and fairness than mediation could possibly afford. In short, if the concern is efficiency or protection of rights, mediation can be dismissed altogether as superfluous, because other processes can perform both these functions much more effectively.

One answer to this criticism is that mediation can accomplish something else of value that these other processes cannot. If so, however, then this value and not the two in question should define the mediator's role . . . . Another answer is that, while other processes can more effectively promote either efficiency *or* protection of rights, mediation somehow can combine both functions as those other processes cannot . . . [I]n practice these two functions are bound to conflict with one another. Thus, it is difficult to see how mediation, or any process, could effectively serve both.

In fact, this leads to the second flaw common to both the efficiency and protection-of-rights conceptions. Not only are mediators incapable of serving *both* these roles simultaneously, they actually are incapable of serving *either* of them separately. Indeed, the attempt to serve either will render the mediation process either useless or abusive.

If we adopt the efficiency conception, under which the mediator's primary role is simply to reach agreements as expeditiously as possible, the effect is to create a role devoid of any clear ethical constraints on mediator behavior. Mediators become little more than case-movers; the only performance standards are their agreement rates and time/cost figures. Such a conception creates perverse incentives; it opens the door to, and indeed encourages, manipulative and coercive mediator behavior, especially in a process unconstrained by procedural or substantive rules or fear of publicity. Mediation becomes the "forced march to settlement" that many of its critics have rightly decried. . . .

On the other hand, if we adopt the protection-of-rights conception, mediators cannot effectively serve this role without undermining their usefulness altogether. As Professor Stulberg has argued, mediators who try to protect substantive rights and guarantee that agreements are fair must adopt substantive positions that inevitably compromise their impartiality, either in actuality or in the parties' eyes.[31] Yet impartiality is crucial to the mediator's many tasks. . . .

To summarize, the mediator cannot effectively and coherently fulfill the role envisioned by either the efficiency or the protection-of-rights conception. On the other hand, neutral third parties in other processes, such as arbitration and

---

[31] *See* J. STULBERG, TAKING CHARGE/MANAGING CONFLICT 141-49 (1987); Stulberg at 87, 96-97 [J. Stulberg, *The Theory and Practice of Mediation: A Reply to Professor Susskind*, 6 VT. L. REV. 85, 88-91 (1981)]; *see also* McCrory, *Environmental Mediation — Another Piece for the Puzzle*, 6 VT. L. REV. 49, 80-81 (1981).

adjudication, *can* fulfill these roles. Therefore, neither the efficiency nor the protection-of-rights conception offers a sound basis for establishing uniform standards for mediator qualifications, training, and practice. For this reason, it is important to resist the tendency to gravitate toward either conception, both of which remain extremely influential despite their deficiencies. The only basis for resisting them, however, is the articulation of another conception of the mediator's role which is sounder, more fruitful, and more in touch with the positive essence of mediation. This is the . . . empowerment-and-recognition conception.

. . . The basis for a sounder conception of the mediator's role lies in examining what mediation *can* do that other processes cannot. In other words, what important powers or capacities are unique to mediation that are not found to the same degree, if at all, in other methods of dispute resolution? The mediator's role should then be to act in ways that fulfill these unique capacities.

. . . Thoughtful mediation theorists and practitioners have given much consideration to identifying mediation's unique powers. In their comments, two points consistently are expressed regarding the capacities of the mediation process.

The first special power of mediation, and what some call "[t]he overriding feature and . . . value of mediation," is that "it is a consensual process that seeks self-determined resolutions."[36] . . . Mediation places the substantive out-come of the dispute within the control and determination of the parties themselves; it frees them from relying on or being subjected to the opinions and standards of outside "higher authorities," legal or otherwise. Further, mediation not only allows the parties to set their own standards for an acceptable solution, it also requires them to search for solutions that are within their own capacity to effectuate. In other words, the parties themselves set the standards, and the parties themselves marshal the actual resources to resolve the dispute. When agreement is reached, the parties have designed and implemented their own solution to the problem. Even when the parties do not reach an agreement, they experience the concrete possibility, to be more fully realized in other situations, that they can control their own circum-stances. They discover that they need not be wholly dependent on outside institutions, legal or otherwise, to solve their problems. I call this the empowerment function of mediation: its capacity to encourage the parties to exercise autonomy, choice, and self-determination.

. . . Mediated outcomes empower parties by responding to them as unique individuals with particular problems, rather than as depersonalized representatives of general problems faced by classes of actors or by society as a whole.

The second special power of mediation was described classically by Professor Lon Fuller . . . Fuller sees mediation as evoking in each party recognition and acknowledgment of, and some degree of understanding and empathy for, the other party's situation, even though their interests and positions may remain opposed. Of course, such mutual recognition often will help produce concrete accommodations and an ultimate agreement. But even when it does not, evoking recognition is itself an accomplishment of enormous value: the value of escaping our alienated isolation

---

[36] J. Folberg & A. Taylor at 245. [J. Folberg & A. Taylor: Mediation: A Comprehensive Guide to Resolving Conflicts Without Litigation (1984).]

and rediscovering our common humanity, even in the midst of bitter division. Professor Leonard Riskin observes accordingly that one of the great values of mediation is that it can "encourage the kind of dialogue that would help . . . [the disputants experience] a perspective of caring and interconnection."[45] Others also have stressed this special power of mediation to "humanize" us to one another, to translate between us, and to help us recognize each other as fellows even when we are in conflict. I call this the recognition function of mediation.

. . . Here, then, are the special powers of mediation: It can encourage personal empowerment and self-determination as alternatives to institutional dependency, and it can evoke recognition of common humanity in the face of bitter conflict. Both powers involve restoring to the individual a sense of his own value and that of his fellow man in the face of an increasingly alienating and isolating social context. These are valuable powers indeed. Further, they are unique to mediation. These are functions mediation can perform that other processes cannot.

As for evoking empathetic recognition of the other fellow, adjudication and arbitration at best treat such recognition as irrelevant. More often, they destroy the very possibility of empathy by encouraging strong, frequently extreme, adversarial behavior. While in negotiation, recognition may occur, but only haphazardly, for no one stands above the fray to encourage and help the parties rise above their own positions and acknowledge those of their opponents. As for empowerment, it is almost by definition impossible in adjudication and arbitration. Both disempower the parties in differing degrees, whether by their authoritative and legalistic character, or by their heavy reliance on advice and representation by professional advocates. Although empowerment is more of a possibility in negotiation, the difficulty of reaching settlement in unassisted negotiations often frustrates this possibility, and negotiation through professional advocates again involves disempowerment in its own way.

Thus, what mediation can do that other processes cannot is to encourage empowerment of the parties and evoke recognition between them. These are its unique and valuable capacities. The mediator's role is to act so as to fulfill these unique capacities. Accordingly, in general terms, the mediator's role is: (1) to encourage the empowerment of the parties — i.e., the exercise of their autonomy and self-determination in deciding whether and how to resolve their dispute; and (2) to promote the parties' mutual recognition of each other as human beings despite their adverse positions. I emphasize here that this role can and should be performed successfully whether or not the parties reach an agreement, and whether or not any agreement reached satisfies some external standard of right or fairness. In other words, it is not the mediator's job to guarantee a fair agreement, or *any* agreement at all; it *is* the mediator's job to guarantee the parties the fullest opportunity for self-determination and mutual acknowledgment. Mediators who ignore this job have not fulfilled their professional responsibilities, even if the parties reach an

---

**45** Riskin at 354 [Riskin, *Toward New Standards for the Neutral Lawyer in Mediation*, 26 ARIZ. L. REV. 329 (1984)]; *see also id.* at 332, 347-49, 352, 359 (*referring to the value of caring and interconnection*); *Riskin, supra* note 6, at 56-57 (*relating mediation* to the shift in public values from self-fulfillment to the ethic of commitment) [Riskin, *Mediation and Lawyers*, 43 OHIO ST. L.J. 29, 30-34 (1982)].

agreement. Conversely, mediators who do this job *have* fulfilled their responsibilities, even if the parties reach *no* agreement.

. . .

## NOTES AND QUESTIONS

Bush was obviously influenced by Fuller in developing his "empowerment and recognition" conception of the mediator's role. When Fuller was writing in the early 1970s, mediation was most widely used in the field of labor-management relations. Arguably, that field is less bound by rules of law and may therefore be more conducive to having the mediator eschew a protection of rights conception of the mediator's role and to assist the parties in creating their own norms during the mediation and defining their rights and duties toward one another. Does the rejection of a protection of rights conception become more difficult as mediation is used: (a) in substantive areas that are more traditionally defined by the parties' legal rights; (b) in areas in which a dispute has been transformed into a law suit filed in court and that case has been referred by a judge to mediation to be conducted by a lawyer-mediator?

## 2.   Mediator Accountability

Should the mediator feel a sense of responsibility or accountability for the outcome of a mediation? Should the mediator seek to insure that the result is fair or just? Lawrence Susskind and Joseph Stulberg present us with a now classic debate over mediator accountability in the following excerpts. In focusing on the role of the environmental mediator, Susskind expresses concern not only for the rights of the disputants but also for those unrepresented at the table. Arguably, agreements made at an environmental mediation affect individuals not represented at the mediation, including future generations. Building on this protection-of-rights conception of the environmental mediator's role, Susskind argues that the mediator must feel responsible not only for the mediation *process*, but also for the *outcome* of the mediation. Stulberg challenges such a conception of the mediator's role. He argues that Susskind's notion that a mediator should be accountable for the fairness of the outcome of a mediation is inconsistent with the essential functions and qualities of a mediator, particularly that of mediator neutrality. He then presents his conception of the seven essential functions and three desirable qualities of a mediator. This 1981 debate is then made current by the excerpt from the Susskind/Stulberg discussion at the Marquette symposium three decades later.

# ENVIRONMENTAL MEDIATION AND THE
# ACCOUNTABILITY PROBLEM
6 Vt. L. Rev. 1, 14–16, 18, 42, 47 (1981)*
By Lawrence Susskind

One analysis of environmental mediation suggests nine steps that must be completed for mediation to be successful: (1) all the parties that have a stake in the outcome of a dispute must be identified; (2) the relevant interest groups must be appropriately represented; (3) fundamentally different values and assumptions must be confronted; (4) a sufficient number of possible solutions or options must be developed; (5) the boundaries and time horizon for analyzing impacts must be agreed upon; (6) the weighting, scaling, and amalgamation of judgments about costs and benefits must be undertaken jointly; (7) fair compensation and mitigatory actions must be negotiated; (8) the legality and financial feasibility of bargains that are made must be ensured; and (9) all parties must be held to their commitments. Although these steps will ensure a fair and efficient process, the success of a mediation effort must also be judged in terms of the fairness and stability of agreements that are reached. From this standpoint, a mediator should probably refuse to enter a dispute in which the power relationships among the parties are so unequal that a mutually acceptable agreement is unlikely to emerge. In addition, environmental mediators should probably withdraw from negotiations in which any of the parties seek an agreement that would not be just from the standpoint of another participant or from the standpoint of a party not at the bargaining table.

To achieve just and stable agreements, mediators may have to find ways of enhancing the relationships among the parties so they will be better able to reconcile future differences (that threaten implementation) on their own. Mediators may also have to build the basic negotiating capabilities of one or more of the parties to ensure more equal bargaining relationships.

Agreements are sometimes reached because one party with substantial power holds out for what it wants while other parties, with less leverage, realize that they can either accept a small gain or wind up with nothing at all. Under these circumstances, all sides may sign such agreements but with unequal degrees of enthusiasm. This result sends a message to the community-at-large that it is acceptable for the most powerful interests to pressure opponents into accepting less than completely fair outcomes. Mediators should avoid setting such precedents, if only because they undermine the chances of attracting less powerful but obstructionist parties to the bargaining table in the future.

It is also quite possible that short-term solutions with which the parties to an environmental dispute are quite pleased can generate new and different problems for other groups outside the bargaining process. It would be irresponsible to ignore these problems if they are indeed foreseeable; if only because implementation may be obstructed by those outside groups later on.

The classic model of labor mediation places little emphasis on the mediator's role as a representative of diffuse, inarticulate, or hard-to-organize interests. All the appropriate parties to a labor-management dispute are presumed to be present at the bargaining table. Thus, the problems of protecting unrepresented segments of the society or reducing impacts on the community-at-large receive little, if any, attention. Joint net gains are presumed to be maximized through the interaction of the parties and their ability to know for themselves how best to achieve their objectives. No effort is made to bolster the claims or abilities of the weaker stakeholders. Precedent is not a concern; indeed, one of the presumed strengths of labor mediation is that parties are free to devise agreements of their own design. Finally, spillovers, externalities, and long-term impacts are, for the most part, ignored since the time frame for implementing most labor-management agreements is relatively short. The parties will usually face the same adversaries again in a few years which makes it easier for them to hold each other to their agreements.

Although procedural fairness and ethical behavior on the part of labor mediators and self-interest maximizing behavior on the part of the participants in labor-management negotiations are presumed to be sufficient to ensure just and stable agreements, these assumptions are inappropriate in the environmental field. Just and stable agreements in the environmental field require much closer attention to the interests of those unable to represent themselves. Joint net gains can be achieved only if the parties attempt to understand the complex ecological systems involved and to generate appropriate compromises that go beyond their self-interests. In short, self-interested negotiation must be replaced by "principled negotiation."

> . . . [E]nvironmental mediators ought to accept responsibility for ensuring (1) that the interests of parties not directly involved in negotiations, but with a stake in the outcome, are adequately represented and protected; (2) that agreements are as fair and stable as possible; and (3) that agreements reached are interpreted as intended by the community-at-large and set constructive precedents.

> . . . Environmental mediators, to the extent that they adopt the broader view of their responsibilities suggested in this article, will probably need to possess substantive knowledge about the environmental and regulatory issues at stake. Effective environmental mediation may require teams composed of some individuals with technical background, some specialized in problem solving or group dynamics and some with political clout.

> . . . An environmental mediator should be committed to procedural fairness — all parties should have an opportunity to be represented by individuals with the technical sophistication to bargain effectively on their behalf. Environmental mediators should also be concerned that the agreements they help to reach are just and stable. To fulfill these responsibilities, environmental mediators will have to intervene more often and more forcefully than their counterparts in the labor-management field. Although such intervention may make it difficult to retain the appearance of neutrality and the trust of the active parties, environmental mediators cannot fulfill their responsibilities to the community-at-large if they remain passive.

# THE THEORY AND PRACTICE OF MEDIATION:
# A REPLY TO PROFESSOR SUSSKIND
6 Vt. L. Rev. 85, 86–87, 91–97, 114, 115–16 (1981)*
### By Joseph B. Stulberg

The basis of this article is that Susskind's demand for a non-neutral intervenor is conceptually and pragmatically incompatible with the goals and purposes of mediation. The intervenor posture that Susskind advocates is not anchored by any principles or obligations of office. The intervenor's conduct, strategies or contribution to the dispute settlement process is, therefore, neither predictable nor consistent. It is precisely a mediator's commitment to neutrality which ensures responsible actions on the part of the mediator and permits mediation to be an effective, principled dispute settlement procedure.

Susskind maintains, in four distinct ways, that a mediator of environmental disputes should not be neutral. Environmental mediators ought to be concerned about:

1. The impacts of negotiated agreements on under-represented or unrepresentable groups in the community.

2. The possibility that joint net gains have not been maximized.

3. The long-term or spillover effects of the settlements they help to reach.

4. The precedents that they set and the precedents upon which agreements are based.

At a substantive level, Susskind argues that the mediator must ensure that the negotiated agreements are fair.

. . . What functions of office does the mediator have that enable him to fulfill that objective? A brief listing would include the following functions.

A mediator is a catalyst. Succinctly stated, the mediator's presence affects how the parties interact. His presence should lend a constructive posture to the discussions rather than cause further misunderstanding and polarization, although there are no guarantees that the latter condition will not result. It seems elementary, but many persons equate a mediator's neutrality with his being a non-entity at the negotiations. Nothing could be further from the truth. Susskind, borrowing from the writings of a distinguished mediator, notes that the mediator performs some procedural functions and, if necessary, assumes an active role. Even the mediator's assumption of a procedural role, however, is an important action that, in itself, may be sufficient to reorient the parties towards an accommodation. Susskind implies that the procedural role is passive whereas an active role would include suggesting substantive resolutions to an issue. The active/passive distinction, however, seriously misrepresents the impact of the mediator's presence on the parties. Much as the chemical term, catalyst connotes the mediator's presence alone creates a special reaction between the parties. Any mediator, therefore, takes on a unique responsibility for the continued integrity of the discussions.

---

A mediator is also an educator. He must know the desires, aspirations, working procedures, political limitations, and business constraints of the parties. He must immerse himself in the dynamics of the controversy to enable him to explain (although not necessarily justify) the reasons for a party's specific proposal or its refusal to yield in its demands. He may have to explain, for example, the meaning of certain statutory provisions that bear on the dispute, the technology of machinery that is the focus of discussion, or simply the principles by which the negotiation process goes forward.

Third, the mediator must be a translator. The mediator's role is to convey each party's proposals in a language that is both faithful to the desired objectives of the party and formulated to insure the highest degree of receptivity by the listener. The proposal of an angry neighbor that the "young hoodlum" not play his stereo from 11:00 p.m. to 7:00 a.m. every day becomes, through the intervention and guidance of a mediator, a proposal to the youth that he be able to play his stereo on a daily basis from 7:00 a.m. to 11:00 p.m.

Fourth, the mediator may also expand the resources available to the parties. Persons are occasionally frustrated in their discussions because of a lack of information or support services. The mediator, by his personal presence and with the integrity of his office, can frequently gain access for the parties to needed personnel or data. This service can range from securing research or computer facilities to arranging meetings with the governor or President.

Fifth, the mediator often becomes the bearer of bad news. Concessions do not always come readily; parties frequently reject a proposal in whole or in part. The mediator can cushion the expected negative reaction to such a rejection by preparing the parties for it in private conversations. Negotiations are not sanitized. They can be extremely emotional. Persons can react honestly and indignantly, frequently launching personal attacks on those representatives refusing to display flexibility. Those who are the focus of such an attack will, quite understandably, react defensively. The mediator's function is to create a context in which such an emotional, cathartic response can occur without causing an escalation of hostilities or further polarization.

Sixth, the mediator is an agent of reality. Persons frequently become committed to advocating one and only one solution to a problem. There are a variety of explanations for this common phenomenon, ranging from pride of authorship in a proposal to the mistaken belief that compromising means acting without principles. The mediator is in the best position to inform a party, as directly and as candidly as possible, that its objective is simply not obtainable through those specific negotiations. He does not argue that the proposal is undesirable and therefore not obtainable. Rather, as an impartial participant in the discussions, he may suggest that the positions the party advances will not be realized, either because they are beyond the resource capacity of the other parties to fulfill or that, for reasons of administrative efficiency or matters of principle, the other parties will not concede. If the proposing party persists in its belief that the other parties will relent, the question is reduced to a perception of power. The mediator's role at that time is to force the proposing party to reassess the degree of power that it perceives it possesses.

The last function of a mediator is to be a scapegoat. No one ever enters into an agreement without thinking he might have done better had he waited a little longer or demanded a little more. A party can conveniently suggest to its constituents when it presents the settlement terms that the decision was forced upon it. In the context of negotiation and mediation, that focus of blame — the scapegoat — can be the mediator.

. . . One way to generate a list of the desirable qualities and abilities a mediator should possess is to adopt the posture of a potential party to a mediation session and analyze the type of person that it would want in the role. The following qualities and abilities would probably be included: capable of appreciating the dynamics of the environment in which the dispute is occur-ring, intelligent, effective listener, articulate, patient, non-judgmental, flexible, forceful and persuasive, imaginative, resourceful, a person of professional standing or reputation, reliable, capable of gaining access to necessary resources, non-defensive, person of integrity, humble, objective, and neutral with regard to the outcome. Three of these qualities merit further analysis.

It is very important that a mediator have the capacity to appreciate the dynamics of the environment in which the dispute is occurring. The objective of negotiation and mediation is to have parties agree to do something. Discussions are to result in action. The mediator must be able to appreciate the real world constraints, pressures, and frustrations under which the parties act. Only then can he establish the tempo of discussions and range of settlement possibilities in a manner commensurate with the urgency of the dispute. Parties with vital interests at stake will not be persuaded to reorient their perspectives towards one another by the intervenor who simply admonishes them to love one another.

Second, the mediator must be intelligent. The question remains, however, whether the mediator must be knowledgeable about the substantive area in dispute. In an environmental dispute involving nuclear reactor plants, what should the mediator know about the science of nuclear energy? This question, touched upon by Susskind, has been framed in ways that are seriously misleading. We do not know what constitutes technical knowledge nor in which subjects the mediator should have such knowledge. Should the mediator, for example, know about the science of nuclear energy, the science and economics of alternative energy resources, the legal regulatory process governing the licensing of nuclear plants, or the politics of energy development? Are all of those items of technical knowledge? If so, which type or types should the mediator possess?

That this question even surfaces reflects an insidious example of a straw man argument. Susskind correctly suggests that an environmental mediator needs to possess substantive knowledge about a dispute. His conclusion intimates, when combined with his suggestions that mediators traditionally assume primarily a passive role and are concerned predominately with procedural matters, that the traditional mediator need not possess equivalent substantive knowledge. Nothing could be further from the truth. The mediator of a labor-management negotiation session who is not familiar with the intricacies of budgets, work schedules, personnel practices, legal guidelines stipulating mandatory bargaining subjects, arbitration awards which interpret particular phrases of contract language and the like, is ineffective and even becomes a stumbling block to an agreement. Susskind's argument hints of the distinction between communication skills and substantive knowledge in a particular subject area.

From the perspective of the potential party to the mediation sessions the mediator should possess both process (communication) skills and content knowledge. The content knowledge a mediator should have depends on the specific type of dispute into which the mediator might intervene and what the parties believe will be the most useful to them. The parties at least want the mediator to be intelligent enough to become educated about the matters in dispute as the talks progress. The knowledgeable mediator can ask penetrating questions, be sensitive to when parties are erecting artificial constraints on their conduct, and avoid becoming an obstacle in the discussions of the more subtle nuances of the matters in dispute. The mediator does not possess such knowledge, however, for the purpose of serving as an expert who advises the parties as to the "right answers."

The third major characteristic is that a mediator must be neutral with regard to outcome. Parties negotiate because they lack the power to achieve their objectives unilaterally. They negotiate with those persons or representatives of groups whose cooperation they need to achieve their objective. If the mediator is neutral and remains so, then he and his office invite a bond of trust to develop between him and the parties. If the mediator's job is to assist the parties to reach a resolution, and his commitment to neutrality ensures confidentiality, then, in an important sense, the parties have nothing to lose and everything to gain by the mediator's intervention. In these two bases of assistance and neutrality there is no way the mediator could jeopardize or abridge the substantive interests of the respective parties.

How is this trust exemplified in practice? Suppose a party advocates certain proposals because of internal political divisions which might impede discussions. For tactical reasons, however, the party does not want to reveal these internal divisions to the other parties. A mediator to whom such information is entrusted can direct discussions so that such a dilemma can be overcome. The mediator's vigorous plea made in the presence of all parties to remove the proposal from further discussions, for example, might provide a safe, facesaving way for that party to drop its demand.

There is a variety of information that parties will entrust to a neutral mediator, including a statement of their priorities, acceptable trade-offs, and their desired timing for demonstrating movement and flexibility. All of these postures are aimed to achieve a resolution without fear that such information will be carelessly shared or that it will surface in public forums in a manner calculated to embarrass or exploit the parties into undesired movement. This type of trust is secured and reinforced only if the mediator is neutral, has no power to insist upon a particular outcome, and honors the confidences placed in him. If any of these characteristics is absent, then the parties must calculate what information they will share with the mediator, just as they do in communicating with any of the parties to the controversy.

. . . If we were to accept the obligations of office that Susskind ascribes to the environmental mediator with regard to insuring Pareto-optimal outcomes, then the environmental mediator is simply a person who uses his entry into the dispute to become a social conscience, environmental policeman, or social critic and who carries no other obligations to the process or the participants beyond assuring Pareto-optimality. It is, in its most benign form, an invitation to permit philosopher-kings to participate in the affairs of the citizenry.

. . . A final note is in order regarding the propriety of a mediator having a substantive commitment to a particular outcome or range of outcomes for a given dispute. It appears that the impetus for Susskind's prescription, that an environmental mediator not be neutral, emanates from the understandable reluctance to accord conclusive weight to the preferences of the parties in every conceivable situation. For example, if parties to a collective bargaining session agree to adopt a racially-discriminatory hiring policy, the mediator, Susskind would argue, should object. Although the stated principle is correct, the mediator's role is not thereby converted into that of an advocate, even if the parties find acceptable an arrangement that is contrary to important principles of public policy or morality.

How should the mediator respond to such a situation? The answer seems relatively straightforward. The mediator should press the parties to examine whether or not they believe that (1) they would be acting in compliance with the law or with principles they would be willing, as rational agents, to universalize; (2) their activities will be acceptable to their respective constituencies and not overturned by public authorities; and (3) in the short and long run, their proposed actions are not contrary to their own self-interest. If the parties listen to these arguments and still find the proposed course of action acceptable, then the mediator can simply decide as an individual that he does not want to lend his personal presence and reputation, or the prestige of the mediation process, to that agreement and he can withdraw. That judgment is one for the mediator *qua* moral agent, not mediator, to make. It is comparable to the dilemma faced by a soldier who is given an order to commit a morally heinous act.

It is certainly the case that each of us is not neutral with regard to everything. Each of us has preferences, interests, commitments to certain moral principles and to an evolving philosophy of life which, when challenged or transgressed, will prompt us into advocating and acting in a manner that is faithful to these dictates. There is clearly no reason to be apologetic or hesitant about defending or advocating such considered judgments. It is also true, however, that mediation as a dispute settlement procedure can be used in a variety of contexts, not all of which would meet approval with everyone's considered judgments. What is important is that one keep distinct his personal posture of judgment from the rule defined practice of the mediator and act accordingly.

# CORE VALUES OF DISPUTE RESOLUTION: IS NEUTRALITY NECESSARY?***

95 Marq. L. Rev. 805 (2012)

PANELISTS

. . .

Joseph ("Josh") B. Stulberg
Lawrence ("Larry") Susskind

. . .

**LARRY SUSSKIND:** . . . If the institutional context that tees up the mediation doesn't define who is or who isn't a party, whether they come with advocates, what the responsibilities of those advocates might be, whether the product of the discussion is binding, whether it sets a precedent, etc. — if all these things aren't defined by the system you're in, what are the mediator's responsibilities?

*Don't look to me if the parties don't show up; don't look to me to be responsible if there are enormous inequalities among the parties; don't look to me to be responsible if the parties have a hard time representing themselves or the category of stakeholders they're supposed to represent; don't look to me if the parties don't understand the scientific, technical, or other complexities surrounding the decisions they're making; I'M NEUTRAL!*

In my world, you must be responsible, or at least accountable, for how these considerations get addressed. If the parties start to talk, and it's clear from the way they're talking that someone not present is going to be adversely affected, I would say, *Gee don't you think that group should be represented at the table?* And for each of the points I'm raising, I'm interested in what it means to have a theory of practice — a way of answering these different questions on a case-by-case basis.

To bring it back to today's discussion, maybe the system that you're mediating in, which has taken care of all this for you, ought to be questioned. Maybe it's not doing what it should do relative to who gets to the table, what their negotiating capacities are, whether they are prepared to pursue their own interests effectively, what other parties should be there, what other information they might need, what kind of accountability they ought to have to the community at large, whether an informal precedent is being set, etc. Maybe you should be asking yourself these questions. Maybe it is the mediator's responsibility to be highly attentive in every case to issues like these and not just say, *I'm in a court-connected context, the system is the way it is, it just tees up the cases for me, and I don't have to worry about any of that.*

**JOSH STULBERG:** . . .

Let me try to come at the question . . . in a slightly different way than the way in which Larry has set it up. At a conceptual level, I think of mediation as embracing the following elements. First, mediating is a justice event. It is not a casual

---

\* The following discussion is an edited version of a panel discussion that occurred at Marquette University Law School on September 23, 2011.

\*\* Copyright © 2012. All rights reserved. Reprinted with permission.

conversation; it is not a conversation to create a business deal. It is a justice event, and so needs to be conducted with those values in mind. Second, participants are members of the political community. While I certainly want to support the central value of personal autonomy, that value cannot skew or escape the fundamental fact that we are all members, in an important sense, of a political community. How I want and choose to live my life is, to some extent, clearly and appropriately shaped and constrained by how others want to live their lives. It is simply not true that one's "self-determination" licenses him or her to do whatever she wants. Third, at least at a conceptual level, there is an important difference between concepts of impartiality, objectivity, and neutrality. My argument years ago — and I still believe it — is that neutrality is distinctive. It is neutrality with respect to outcome, not process. Being neutral means adopting an unswerving commitment to structure and guide a conversation that simultaneously embraces the values of a justice event and that encourages and cultivates disputing parties to work out matters in a way that they want to live their lives as members of a political community. That may sound like an abstract or "highfalutin" theory, but I am confident that it plays out in practice. I think if I were rewriting what I wrote thirty years ago, I would emphasize more strongly that mediation's central values systematically support not only party self-determination, but also, crucially, party responsibility.

The mediator's posture, then, must be congruent with promoting each of those central values. Let me end this way. With characteristic elegance, Larry talks about mediators who are working in public policy contexts. The image portrayed there, of course, is that parties are making decisions that foreclose options both for people not at the table and as well as for members belonging to future generations. If someone bulldozes a particular plot of land, it is hard, if not impossible, to recapture it. Given that substantive context, Larry argues in our *Vermont Law Review* exchange that a mediator should be held accountable for the negotiated outcomes in the ways that he prescribes. But he also claimed that mediators working in other contexts, particularly those who mediated labor-management collective bargaining impasses, did not confront that same challenge. I tried to argue that he was incorrect factually about that claim; I believe that disputes involving labor — management collective bargaining matters, as well as other explosive community disputes, share the feature that the parties' collective decision at a particular moment in time significantly forecloses some (though not all) future possibilities. But that fact, I argued, does not change the core values of the mediator's role, including the duty to be neutral.

. . .

**LARRY**: Let me put a finer point on the kinds of choices that I think mediators have to make, whether in well-structured processes or less well-structured processes. I think most mediators believe that a good process almost always yields a good outcome. At the heart of what we do as mediators is trying to structure a good process — whether we gin it up ourselves or let the system tee it up. But notice, that means we are taking responsibility for a good outcome by ensuring that the process is organized and managed properly. So, if a good process yields a good outcome — if we believe that — then we are obligated to say what we mean by a good outcome.

So, what would a good outcome be in a mediated case? I argue that (1) the outcome must be viewed as fair by the parties; and (2) the process and outcome ought to be as *efficient as possible* — that is the parties ought to think that whatever time and money was spent, was well-spent. Now, I'm not sure that the parties are the only ones who have a right to assess the outcome. The system managers might want to say something about that as well. So a good outcome is fair and efficient, and then Bernie [Mayer — a third symposium participant] mentions that the result should be stable — we don't want unhappy participants to shun their negotiated commitments. This doesn't mean results can't be revised, but if an outcome is not stable, it probably wasn't a good process because the outcome wasn't one that people were willing to abide by.

Fair, efficient, stable, and now I would suggest a fourth indicator of the quality of a mediated outcome — and that is, it ought to be *wise*. Now what is a wise outcome? In retrospect, you could say that if the parties used the information available to them they probably reached as wise an outcome as they could. What a pity if they reached an outcome that didn't work well because they didn't bother to take account of the information or resources available to them. Fair, efficient, stable, wise — for me, these are the four qualities of a good mediated outcome.

As mediators, we need to be prepared to say what we think a good outcome is. If I take responsibility for a good outcome — or these four qualities of an agreement — then I've got to do something during the process to try to help the parties produce such outcomes. I have to remain impartial, but I can take responsibility in various ways for the management of the process. I can do this without taking sides, but I can make clear my commitment to helping the parties reach a high-quality outcome. I don't think that's a contradiction. I think I can ask questions that cause participants to think about choices they are making and whether those choices will lead to a "high quality" outcome.

. . .

**JOSH (interrupting Larry)**: But, Larry, there is no requirement to be impartial in order for someone to help disputing parties promote a fair outcome that is efficient and wise . . . . So when you say that you, the intervener, need to remain impartial in order to promote "the good outcome," I can challenge that by saying, "no, you, the intervener, do not need to be impartial. You need to be really smart; you need to be savvy in terms of how to facilitate a conversation that yields a good outcome." We don't disagree that a good process generates a good outcome . . . Let me restate my point. On those criteria you cite — fair, efficient, stable, wise — I don't think the intervener being impartial is a necessary condition for effectively serving the parties' goals that fare well on those standards. As a practical matter, it might be prudent to be impartial so people work with you, but there is nothing in principle that requires the mediator, the intervener, to be, in your words, "impartial," and in mine, "neutral," in order to help them reach such outcomes. You and I agree that good process generates good outcomes, where good process reflects just that — it is fair, efficient, and stable; but the standard of "wise" introduces a substantive, not process, criterion — you accept it but I reject it.

Just one final point . . . I understood your earlier comments — both those in the Vermont article and what you said today — to be that one of the real challenges is who the parties are. And if not all the parties — people affected by the outcome —

are in the room, you don't have a good process, even though everybody who actually is there does view it as "fair." I'm not sure how —

**LARRY (interrupts)**: Substitute "stakeholders" for "parties."

**JOSH**: Okay. My question can be stated: *If all the stakeholders are not in the conversation, then is it the mediator's duty — in terms of being responsible for the outcome, accountable for the outcome — that the intervener in some sense represents those interests?*

**LARRY**: I don't think the neutral can represent those interests. I think that the neutral, in an effort to take responsibility for the quality of the outcome, can do a number of things to help ensure that all the appropriate stakeholding interests are represented, not by representing them but by saying, *Do you think a draft of this agreement ought to be reviewed before it's finalized by a group that hasn't been at the table? Aren't you worried that those groups that have been left at the sidelines might try to block implementation of the agreement? Let's at least give them a chance to review it before you finalize it. Maybe you want someone else sitting in, not in the same role as everyone else, but in some other related role. Maybe you want to make transparent what it is you're doing while you're doing it, so those groups can at least have a say.*

I never imagined the mediator saying: *For the next half hour I'm going to represent a hard-to-represent group that isn't here. Watch me transform myself chameleon-like into that group and speak for them.* That's not what I'm saying. But there are a whole variety of ways in which I can take responsibility for the quality of an outcome without speaking for a missing group: a mediator can ask leading questions, suggest ideas and options, or offer to carry a draft of an agreement to others who are not present and try to incorporate their reactions into a final version of the agreement.

**JOSH**: So what should a mediator do if a fourteen-year-old single child doesn't want to participate in the mediation of a divorce between her parents, though she will clearly be affected by the outcome?

**LARRY**: I can suggest that a [guardian ad litem] be appointed for them and I could say to the parents, "Don't you think the interest of your child should at least be discussed here, through eyes other than yours and you have the option of a proxy to represent your child?"

**JOSH**: And the mother says, "No, I know exactly how my daughter feels."

**LARRY**: If both of them say that and I say, "Well it's my obligation to try and point this out to you, and if I can't convince you, then I can't convince you." But my responsibility for trying to ensure a fair outcome goes as far as aggressively trying to think of ways to suggest that interests not represented at the table could be represented — not to represent them myself.

. . .

# NOTES AND QUESTIONS

(1) Did Stulberg or Susskind change or modify their views on mediator accountability over the three decades between the Vermont symposium and the Marquette symposium?

(2) How is the classic debate between Susskind and Stulberg over mediator accountability affected by the increased use of mediation by the courts and the entry of lawyers into the mediation field? In *Public Values and Private Justice: A Case for Mediator Accountability*, 4 Geo. J. Legal Ethics 503, 508–09, 521 (1991), Judith Maute argues:

> The extent of mediator accountability for fairness varies by whether or not the mediator is a lawyer, and by whether the parties are independently represented by counsel.
>
> . . . Mediators intercede to facilitate an agreement the parties could not reach on their own. If it produces agreement, the mediation may substitute for public adjudication, often a desirable and appropriate end. When mediation intercedes to settle a legal dispute, additional safeguards are needed to protect for two important values at risk with private settlement: public values of fairness and authoritative public resolution of legal conflicts. The mediator is properly held to a higher standard of accountability. The process should enable both parties to obtain relevant information about the law and how it might apply to the instant facts. When disparities in power or knowledge disable a weaker party from effective bargaining, the mediator must intervene to avoid a patently unfair agreement at odds with the probable outcome of adjudication.

Although a lawyer-mediator may possess general legal knowledge that may suggest to her that the unrepresented disputants are headed toward an agreement that would be an unlikely outcome if the dispute were adjudicated in court, how might the lawyer mediator assure herself during the mediation that her legal assessment is correct? That is, aside from the theoretical concerns that Bush and Stulberg would have with Maute's position, are there practical concerns?

In *Informed Consent in Mediation: A Guiding Principle for Truly Educated Decisionmaking*, 74 Notre Dame L. Rev. 775, 812 (1999),* Jacqueline Nolan-Haley argues for acceptance of a principle of informed consent in mediation that would promote fairness:

> A robust theory of informed consent requires that parties be educated about mediation before they consent to participate in it, that their continued participation and negotiations be voluntary, and that they understand the outcomes to which they agree. Informed consent serves the values of autonomy, human dignity, and efficiency. It guards against coercion, ignorance, and incapacity that can impede the consensual underpinnings of the mediation process.

---

Nolan-Haley takes pains to point out that she is not advocating an adversarial model for mediation sessions nor, unlike Judith Maute, is she suggesting that mediation outcomes approximate likely adjudicated outcomes. Rather, she argues for a "sliding-scale model of informed consent disclosure," where mediators would owe a greater duty of informed consent disclosure to unrepresented parties than to those parties represented by counsel. Recognizing the value of neutrality in mediation, she considers the research of Cobb and Rifkin and others:

> Perhaps the real question should be: when is absolute neutrality called for and when is a modified approach preferable? I argue that when court programs require unrepresented parties to enter the mediation process, fairness demands that these parties know their legal options before making final decisions in mediation. A modified approach to mediator neutrality permits mediators to employ an *informative* decisionmaking model and give unrepresented parties such information.

*Id.* at 837.

But how is this information to be supplied to the parties? Will the lawyer-mediator simply make a threshold decision that one or both parties need legal information and then suggest that they consult a lawyer? Although such an approach would be less likely to compromise a mediator's neutrality than having the mediator supply the information, is it realistic to expect that many unrepresented parties will be able to afford lawyers?

(3)   Does Judith Maute's argument for mediator accountability go beyond that of Susskind? It certainly is contrary to traditional notions of mediator neutrality. Recall that a mediator's ability to "be neutral with regard to outcome" is high on the list of Stulberg's desirable qualities of a mediator. Recognizing the tension between accountability and neutrality, Maute offers the following viewpoint that is clearly premised on a protection of rights conception of the mediator's role: "When a mediated agreement avoids adjudication, traditional mediator neutrality undermines protection of the parties' legal rights." Maute, *supra*, at 503. What does it mean to be neutral? Stulberg recognizes that mediators will have "preferences, interests, commitments to certain moral principles and to an evolving philosophy of life," but argues that a mediator must keep this "personal posture of judgment" distinct from his or her role as a neutral dispute resolver.

The complexity of the concept of mediator neutrality is demonstrated by Sara Cobb and Janet Rifkin in their study of mediator neutrality, *Practice and Paradox: Deconstructing Neutrality in Mediation*, 16 Law & Soc. Inquiry 35, 37 (1991): "[L]ike other folk concepts, neutrality is both 'transparent' *and* 'opaque': transparent because it operates on the basis of widely held assumptions about power and conflict, and opaque because it is exceedingly difficult to raise questions about the nature and practice of neutrality from *within* this consensus." Is neutrality then more of an aspirational goal of the mediator? Consider the following:

> For ourselves we recommend a strictly neutral settlement strategy as an initial position. Deviating from this stance should be explicitly and deliberately chosen and justified. We are impressed with the difficulty of making such powerful value decisions for others. Should mediators attempt to do

so, they should act openly and with the obligation to explain their judgment to the parties.

Sydney E. Bernard, Joseph P. Folger, Helen R. Weingarten & Zena R. Zumeta, *The Neutral Mediator: Value Dilemmas in Divorce Mediation*, 4 Mediation Q. 61, 73 (1984).

(4)   Susskind's notion of mediator accountability is premised to a large extent on the perceived need to protect the interests of unrepresented third parties to an environmental mediation by ensuring that the outcome is fair to all relevant interests. Arguably, there are similar concerns in a divorce mediation, where interested third parties such as the children, grandparents, and other relatives often are not represented at the table. Should a divorce mediator be concerned with the fairness of the outcome? In *Mediation and Therapy: An Alternative View*, 10 Mediation Q. 21 (1992),[*] John M. Haynes, a prominent divorce mediator and mediation trainer, argues that while a therapist or lawyer exercises power over both process and content when rendering professional services to a client, when acting as a mediator the therapist or lawyer must separate his or her role as professional (therapist or lawyer) from his or her role as mediator. He offers the following advice to divorce mediators:

> [W]e actually assert power in controlling the process but deny power in relation to the content. The assumed contract in mediation is that the mediator will assist the clients to resolve specific problems *on their own terms.* In divorce, these problems include the amount and duration of child and maintenance support, the appropriate division of assets, and future parenting roles. . . .

> [T]he mediator does exercise power when managing the process because true process neutrality can often benefit one side at the expense of the other. Families choose mediation because they want someone to regulate a dispute and provide an environment in which a self-determined solution can be found. The mediator cannot proclaim process neutrality. He or she cannot stand aside while one party verbally abuses the other, cannot permit secrecy, and must intervene to assure that all parties understand the issues and the data that determine the issues . . . . The mediator's neutrality is confined to the content of the agreement. He or she is not neutral on the process; indeed, he or she continually exercises power to control the process to assure a mutual problem definition, a neutral environment, and a joint decision that is mutually acceptable.

*Id.* at 23, 24.

Is the line Haynes draws between process neutrality and content (outcome) neutrality a clear one? Keep this in mind as you consider the discussion of mediator orientations in the following section.

---

## C.  MEDIATOR ORIENTATIONS

With the increased entry of lawyers into the mediation field, issues concerning the orientation of the mediator have become more salient. Because lawyer-mediators possess substantive legal knowledge and often have considerable litigation experience, there is a temptation to apply this knowledge and experience during the mediation and offer the mediator's personal evaluation of the case. Many have argued that an *evaluative* orientation is inconsistent with the notion of the mediator as a communication facilitator and that the mediator's orientation should be a strictly *facilitative* one. Moreover, with the publication by Robert A. Baruch Bush and Joseph Folger of *The Promise of Mediation: Responding to Conflict Through Empowerment and Recognition*, there has been an increasingly strong interest in having the mediator adopt a *transformative* orientation. Consider how the following descriptions and arguments for these various orientations are consistent or inconsistent with the mediator roles previously discussed.

### 1.  Facilitative vs. Evaluative

The debate over the efficacy of a facilitative versus an evaluative mediator orientation was sparked in large part by the publication of the "Riskin grid." In a 1994 article at 12 *Alternatives to the High Cost of Litigation* 111, Leonard Riskin sought to "propose a system for classifying mediator orientations." Riskin's system is based on the answers to two questions: "1. Does the mediator tend to define problems *narrowly* or *broadly*? 2. Does the mediator think she should *evaluate* — make assessments or predictions or proposals for agreements — or *facilitate* the parties' negotiation without evaluating?" Riskin explains this classification scheme in the following excerpt from his longer article on the same subject. Note that Riskin is not advocating either style, but simply seeking to describe the mediator orientations in current practice. The excerpt from the article by Lela Love presents her arguments against an evaluative orientation, and Donald Weckstein presents the counter-argument that mediator activism in the form of evaluation or other interventions may actually enhance party self-determination. In the final excerpt in this section, Professor Riskin reconsiders the "Riskin Grid."

### UNDERSTANDING MEDIATORS' ORIENTATIONS, STRATEGIES, AND TECHNIQUES: A GRID FOR THE PERPLEXED
1 Harv. Negot. L. Rev. 7, 24–32, 34–38 (1996)*
By Leonard L. Riskin

. . . Most mediators operate from a predominant, presumptive or default orientation (although, as explained later, many mediators move along continuums and among quadrants). For purposes of the following explication of mediator orientations, I will assume that the mediator is acting from such a predominant orientation. For this reason, and for convenience, I will refer to the "evaluative-narrow mediator" rather than the more precise, but more awkward, "mediator

---

operating with an evaluative-narrow approach."

---

## MEDIATOR ORIENTATIONS

### Role of Mediator

### EVALUATIVE

| Problem Definition NARROW | EVALUATIVE NARROW | EVALUATIVE BROAD | Problem Definition BROAD |
|---|---|---|---|
| | FACILITATIVE NARROW | FACILITATIVE BROAD | |

### FACILITATIVE

---

A mediator employs strategies — plans — to conduct a mediation. And a mediator uses techniques — particular moves or behavior — to effectuate those strategies. Here are selected strategies and techniques that typify each mediation orientation.

### 1. Evaluative-Narrow

A principal strategy of the evaluative-narrow approach is to help the parties understand the strengths and weaknesses of their positions and the likely outcome of litigation or whatever other process they will use if they do not reach a resolution in mediation. But the evaluative-narrow mediator stresses her own education at least as much as that of the parties. Before the mediation starts, the evaluative-narrow mediator will study relevant documents, such as pleadings, depositions, reports, and mediation briefs. At the outset of the mediation, such a mediator typically will ask the parties to present their cases, which normally means arguing their positions, in a joint session. Subsequently, most mediation activities take place in private caucuses in which the mediator will gather additional information and deploy evaluative techniques, such as the following, which are listed below from the least to the most evaluative.

a. *Assess the strengths and weaknesses of each side's case* . . . .

b. *Predict outcomes of court or other processes* . . . .

c. *Propose position-based compromise agreements* . . . .

d. *Urge or push the parties to settle or to accept a particular settlement proposal or range* . . . .

## 2. Facilitative-Narrow

The facilitative-narrow mediator shares the evaluative-narrow mediator's general strategy — to educate the parties about the strengths and weaknesses of their claims and the likely consequences of failing to settle. But he employs different techniques to carry out this strategy. He does not use his own assessments, predictions, or proposals. Nor does he apply pressure. He is less likely than the evaluative-narrow mediator to request or to study relevant documents. Instead, believing that the burden of decision-making should rest with the parties, the facilitative-narrow mediator might engage in any of the following activities.

  a. *Ask questions* . . . .

  b. *Help the parties develop their own narrow proposals* . . . .

  c. *Help the parties exchange proposals* . . . .

  d. *Help the parties evaluate proposals* . . . .

The facilitative nature of this mediation approach might also produce a degree of education or transformation. The process itself, which encourages the parties to develop their own understandings and outcomes, might educate the parties, or "empower" them by helping them to develop a sense of their own ability to deal with the problems and choices in life. The parties also might acknowledge or empathize with each other's situation. However, in a narrowly-focused mediation, even a facilitative one, the subject matter normally produces fewer opportunities for such developments than does a facilitative-broad mediation.

## 3. Evaluative-Broad

It is more difficult to describe the strategies and techniques of the evaluative-broad mediator. Mediations conducted with such an orientation vary tremendously in scope, often including many narrow, distributive issues . . . .

In addition, evaluative-broad mediators can be more-or-less evaluative, with the evaluative moves touching all or only some of the issues.

The evaluative-broad mediator's principal strategy is to learn about the circumstances and underlying interests of the parties and other affected individuals or groups, and then to use that knowledge to direct the parties toward an outcome that responds to such interests. To carry out this strategy, the evaluative-broad mediator will employ various techniques, including the following (listed from least to most evaluative).

  a. *Educate herself about underlying interests* . . . .

  b. *Predict impact (on interests) of not settling* . . . .

  c. *Develop and offer broad (interest-based) proposals* . . . .

  d. *Urge parties to accept the mediator's or another proposal* . . . .

If the mediator has concluded that the goal of the mediation should include changing the people involved, she might take measures to effectuate that goal, such as appealing to shared values, lecturing, or applying pressure.

#### 4. Facilitative-Broad

The facilitative-broad mediator's principal strategy is to help the participants define the subject matter of the mediation in terms of underlying interests and to help them develop and choose their own solutions that respond to such interests. In addition, many facilitative-broad mediators will help participants find opportunities to educate or change themselves, their institutions, or their communities. To carry out such strategies, the facilitative-broad mediator may use techniques such as the following.

a. *Help parties understand underlying interests* . . . .

b. *Help parties develop and propose broad, interest-based options for settlement* . . . .

c. *Help parties evaluate proposals* . . . .

Figure 3 highlights the principal techniques associated with each orientation, arranged vertically with the most evaluative at the top and the most facilitative at the bottom. The horizontal axis shows the scope of the problems to be addressed, from the narrowest on the left to the broadest on the right.

Role of the Mediator

| Evaluative | | |
|---|---|---|
| Problem Definition **NARROW** | **Urges/pushes parties** to accept narrow (position-based) settlement<br>**Proposes** narrow (position-based) agreement<br>**Predicts** court or other outcomes<br>**Assesses** strengths and weaknesses of each side's case | **Urges/pushes parties** to accept broad (interest-based) settlement<br>**Develops and proposes** broad (interest-based) agreement<br>**Predicts** impact (on interests) of not settling<br>**Educates self** about parties' interests | Problem Definition **BROAD** |
| | **Helps parties** evaluate proposals<br>**Helps parties** develop & exchange narrow (position-based) proposals<br>**Asks** about consequences of not settling<br>**Asks** about likely court or other outcomes<br>**Asks** about strengths and weaknesses of each side's case | **Helps parties** evaluate proposals<br>**Helps parties** develop & exchange broad (interest-based) proposals<br>**Helps parties** develop options that respond to interests<br>**Help parties** understand interests | |
| Facilitative | | |

*Figure 3.*

D. Movement along the Continuums and Among the Quadrants: Limitations on the Descriptive Capabilities of the Grid

Like a map, the grid has a static quality that limits its utility in depicting the conduct of some mediators.

It is true that most mediators — whether they know it or not — generally conduct mediations with a presumptive or predominant orientation. Usually, this orientation is grounded in the mediator's personality, education, training, and experience. For example, most retired judges tend toward an extremely evaluative-narrow orientation, depicted in the far northwest corner of the grid. Many divorce mediators with backgrounds or strong interests in psychology or counseling — and who serve affluent or well-educated couples — lean toward a facilitative-broad approach. Sometimes, the expectations of a given program dictate an orientation;

for example, narrow mediation tends to dominate many public programs with heavy caseloads.

Yet many mediators employ strategies and techniques that make it difficult to fit their practices neatly into a particular quadrant. First, some mediators deliberately try to avoid attachment to a particular orientation. Instead, they emphasize flexibility and attempt to develop their orientation in a given case based on the participants' needs or other circumstances in the mediation.

Second, for a variety of reasons, some mediators who have a predominant orientation do not always behave consistently with it. They occasionally deviate from their presumptive orientation in response to circumstances arising in the course of a mediation. In some cases, this substantially changes the scope of the mediation. A mediator with a facilitative-broad approach handling a personal injury claim, for instance, normally would give parties the opportunity to explore underlying interests. But if the parties showed no inclination in that direction, the mediator probably would move quickly to focus on narrower issues.

In other cases, a mediator might seek to foster her dominant approach using a technique normally associated with another quadrant. Thus, some mediators with predominantly facilitative-broad orientations might provide evaluations in order to achieve specific objectives consistent with their overall approach. [For example,] Frances Butler, who mediates child-custody disputes for a New Jersey court, . . . uses a mixture of facilitative and evaluative techniques in the service of a broad, facilitative agenda: she asks questions (a facilitative technique) to help her understand the situation, then makes proposals (an evaluative technique), and then solicits the parties' input (a facilitative technique) in order to modify the proposals.

A narrow mediator who runs into an impasse might offer the parties a chance to broaden the problem by exploring underlying interests. This might lead to an interest-based agreement that would enable the parties to compromise on the distributive issue as part of a more comprehensive settlement. Similarly, a broad mediator might encourage the parties to narrow their focus if the broad approach seems unlikely to produce a satisfactory outcome.

For these reasons it is often difficult to categorize the orientation, strategies, or techniques of a given mediator in a particular case . . . .

## NOTES AND QUESTIONS

(1)  Some mediation practice books and materials are now distinguishing between facilitative and evaluative mediation and offering advice on when these forms of mediation are most appropriate. For instance, Marjorie Corman Aaron discusses the many factors that should be considered by the mediator before providing the parties with an evaluation. M.C. Aaron, *Evaluation in Mediation, in* Mediating Legal Disputes 267–305 (Dwight Golann ed., 1996).

(2)  Since its initial publication in 1994, the "Riskin grid" has provoked considerable commentary and controversy. In "Evaluative" Mediation is an Oxymoron, 14 *Alternatives to High Cost of Litigation* 31 (1996), Kimberlee Kovach and Lela Love argue that "evaluative mediation" is an oxymoron because anyone who

engages in the activities Riskin describes as "evaluative" is not engaged in mediation. They do not argue that these "evaluative" activities are wrong or unhelpful, but rather that they should not be labeled mediation because they are inconsistent with the distinctive attributes of the mediation process. Kovach and Love would therefore draw a line that clearly distinguishes evaluation from mediation. On the other side, James Stark has argued that "case evaluation, performed competently, has a useful place in certain forms of mediation practice." James Stark, *The Ethics of Mediation Evaluation: Some Troublesome Questions and Tentative Proposals, from an Evaluative Lawyer Mediator*, 38 S. Tex. L. Rev. 769 (1997). John Bickerman takes the position that the parties often want and expect an evaluative mediator: "Without sacrificing neutrality, a mediator's neutral assessment can provide participants with a much-needed reality check . . . . Sophisticated parties ought to have the freedom to choose the mediation style that best suits their needs." John Bickerman, *Evaluative Mediator Responds*, 14 *Alternatives to High Cost of Litigation* 70, 70 (1996). Of course, Kovach and Love would respond that such an approach is fine — give the parties what they want, just don't call it mediation. Consider the arguments of Professors Love and Weckstein in the following excerpts.

(3)   For a symposium addressing these issues, see 2000 Journal of Dispute Resolution, issue 2.

(4)   Does Professor Riskin's reassessment of his grid in the final article in this section assist in resolving the facilitative/evaluative debate? How?

# THE TOP TEN REASONS WHY MEDIATORS SHOULD NOT EVALUATE
24 Fla. St. U. L. Rev. 937, 937–48 (1997)*
By Lela P. Love

. . . The debate over whether mediators should "evaluate" revolves around the confusion over what constitutes evaluation and an "evaluative" mediator.

. . . .

An "evaluative" mediator gives advice, makes assessments, states opinions — including opinions on the likely court outcome, proposes a fair or workable resolution to an issue or the dispute, or presses the parties to accept a particular resolution. The ten reasons that follow demonstrate that those activities are inconsistent with the role of a mediator.

I. THE ROLES AND RELATED TASKS OF EVALUATORS AND FACILITATORS ARE AT ODDS

Evaluating, assessing, and deciding for others is radically different than helping others evaluate, assess, and decide for themselves. Judges, arbitrators, neutral experts, and advisors are evaluators. Their role is to make decisions and give opinions. To do so, they use predetermined criteria to evaluate evidence and arguments presented by adverse parties. The tasks of evaluators include: finding

---

"the facts" by properly weighing evidence; judging credibility and allocating the burden of proof; determining and applying the relevant law, rule, or custom to the particular situation; and making an award or rendering an opinion. The adverse parties have expressly asked the evaluator — judge, arbitrator, or expert — to decide the issue or resolve the conflict.

In contrast, the role of mediators is to assist disputing parties in making their own decisions and evaluating their own situations. A mediator "facilitate[s] communications, promotes understanding, focuses the parties on their interests, and seeks creative problem solving to enable the parties to reach their own agreement."[9] Mediators push disputing parties to question their assumptions, reconsider their positions, and listen to each other's perspectives, stories, and arguments. They urge the parties to consider relevant law, weigh their own values, principles, and priorities, and develop an optimal outcome. In so doing, mediators facilitate evaluation by the parties.

These differences between evaluators and facilitators mean that each uses different skills and techniques, and each requires different competencies, training norms, and ethical guidelines to perform their respective functions. Further, the evaluative tasks of determining facts, applying law or custom, and delivering an opinion not only divert the mediator away from facilitation, but also can compromise the mediator's neutrality — both in actuality and in the eyes of the parties — because the mediator will be favoring one side in his or her judgment.

Endeavors are more likely to succeed when the goal is clear and simple and not at war with other objectives. Any task, whether it is the performance of an Olympic athlete, the advocacy of an attorney, or the negotiation assistance provided by a mediator, requires a clear and bright focus and the development of appropriate strategies, skills, and power. In most cases, should the athlete or the attorney or the mediator divert their focus to another task, it will diminish their capacity to achieve their primary goal. "No one can serve two masters." Mediators cannot effectively facilitate when they are evaluating.

II. EVALUATION PROMOTES POSITIONING AND POLARIZATION, WHICH ARE ANTITHETICAL TO THE GOALS OF MEDIATION . . . .

III. ETHICAL CODES CAUTION MEDIATORS — AND OTHER NEUTRALS — AGAINST ASSUMING ADDITIONAL ROLES . . . .

IV. IF MEDIATORS EVALUATE LEGAL CLAIMS AND DEFENSES, THEY MUST BE LAWYERS; ELIMINATING NONLAWYERS WILL WEAKEN THE FIELD . . . .

V. THERE ARE INSUFFICIENT PROTECTIONS AGAINST INCORRECT MEDIATOR EVALUATIONS . . . .

---

[9] John Feerick et al., *Standards of Professional Conduct in Alternative Dispute Resolution*, 1995 J. DISP. RESOL. 95 app. at 123.

# IN PRAISE OF PARTY EMPOWERMENT — AND OF MEDIATOR ACTIVISM

33 Willamette L. Rev. 501, 502–04, 532–35, 539–40, 547–50,
552–53, 559 (1997)*
By Donald T. Weckstein

. . . I come to praise party empowerment, not to bury it! The success and effectiveness of mediation is dependent upon the free choice of disputants in determining how best to resolve their conflicts . . . . A coerced settlement is inconsistent with a legitimate mediation process, as is any resolution that lacks voluntary and informed consent of the disputants. A party who is unaware of important information or available alternatives to an offered settlement is prevented from exercising effective self-determination . . . .

This article attempts to answer questions concerning when, if ever, a mediator should give an opinion, evaluation, suggestion, recommendation, or prediction, or offer pertinent information or advice . . . . [T]his article contends that in several situations these interventions enhance rather than deny party self-determination.

The key to self-determination is informed consent. A disputant who is unaware of relevant facts or law that, if known, would influence that party's decision cannot engage in meaningful self-determination. A mediator generally should encourage parties to seek such information from other sources. However, if a party cannot or will not do so and looks to the mediator for guidance, it should not be considered improper for the mediator to serve as a source of pertinent information. Likewise, if the mediator's style is to offer that information unless the parties decline it, the mediator should be free to do so ethically. Self-determination extends to the disputants' willingness or unwillingness to be exposed to a mediator's educational efforts or evaluations. Accordingly, when consistent with the parties' expectations and the mediator's qualifications, activist intervention by the mediator should be encouraged rather than condemned . . . .

---

The decision of whether and how to use this information are determinations for the parties to make. If they choose to ignore it, it will be their intentional choice and not a default made in ignorance. Accordingly, the relevant inquiry should not be *whether* to inform the parties but *how* to inform them.

One option is for the mediator to volunteer "information" short of professional "advice . . . ."

Assuming the mediator is qualified by training and experience to give relevant information concerning wrongful discharge rights and remedies, at least two major problems must still be resolved: (1) Can the mediator give such information without sacrificing his or her impartiality? (2) Is there really a difference between offering such information and offering professional advice, assuming the latter to be impermissible?

If the mediator had anticipated the problem of the unrepresented status of the claimant, the mediator, at the outset of the mediation, and with concurrence of both parties, might have provided a brief summary of the applicable law . . . .

Even if the mediator had missed the opportunity to educate the parties in advance, information concerning legal norms still can be made available in the course of the mediation. One possibility is for the mediator to ask the parties at the beginning of each mediation whether they would object to the mediator informing them of relevant principles of law, as the need may arise.

Another practice, usable by the mediator . . . is to ask counsel for the respondent to briefly state his understanding of the main principles of the law . . . in the applicable jurisdiction. Because counsel knows that the mediator is familiar with the law, the presentation is not likely to be too one-sided . . . . A variation of this scenario would be for the mediator to ask the claimant to try to explain her understanding of the law in this area, and then ask respondent's counsel whether that also is his understanding . . . .

When one or more parties are represented by legal counsel, allowing a qualified mediator to offer legal information probably is more acceptable since counsel can correct any inaccuracy or imbalanced recital of relevant law. Nevertheless, some parties and mediators may still regard this type of mediator intervention as raising an *appearance* of partiality . . . .

Even if one party may benefit more than another in a particular matter, each party in every case has the opportunity to benefit from an activist mediator's offer of neutral, professionally competent information. There is no bias for or against either party, only a bias in favor of the integrity of the process so that all parties have the opportunity to be informed and, thus, empowered to engage in true self-determination . . . .

Mediator evaluations, although controversial, are little more than another way of making a suggestion or recommendation. When an evaluation is made in terms of how a court or arbitrator might evaluate all or part of a disputant's case, it is, in effect, a prediction. Predictions and evaluations go a step beyond a mediator's offer of abstract information. They speculate how a third-party decisionmaker or the mediator would apply that information.

[P]redictions of likely arbitral outcomes are common and expected in labor grievance mediations. Predictions of how a court might determine issues in other proceedings also can be useful in overcoming impasses or establishing a framework for the parties to develop a resolution that meets their own notions of fairness . . . . While represented parties can receive that type of information from their legal counsel, a knowledgeable mediator's prediction provides more objective information with probably greater utility in the negotiations . . . .

Whether a mediator's prediction will be considered ethical likely will be influenced by one's preconceptions of the mediation process, the parties' expectations, the mediator's explanation of the nature of the prediction, and the way the particular jurisdiction treats other information-based interventions, such as professional evaluations and advice.

Since a predicted outcome that favors one party may raise questions of the mediator's impartiality in the eyes of others, the mediator is well-advised to phrase the prediction as one based on experience and study of relevant data, and not as a personal opinion. To avoid party misinterpretation, the mediator should explain that the prediction is only an estimate and the actual outcome may differ for various reasons, including, for example: (1) differences in the orientations and perceptions of judges, juries, and arbitrators; (2) the actual evidence offered and admitted in the adjudication; and (3) other environmental factors that might influence the tribunal. The mediator must emphasize that the prediction is not a directive or recommendation, and that the parties should reach their own agreement of a fair resolution, with or without reference to the prediction . . . .

Like predictions, other evaluations frequently relate to the strengths and weaknesses of a party's case . . . .

Mediation . . . initiates a facilitated negotiation process, during which a mediator's evaluation may become one of many factors used to aid the parties' self-determination of their dispute.

Evaluations, especially of a predictive nature, generally should be resorted to only after other more facilitative measures have failed to break an impasse. The manner in which the evaluation is presented may be critical to its reception by the parties. A "gestalt" impression of the value of a disputants' case, or general sense of how the mediator feels a court would determine the matter, is more likely to engender resistance from the party whose case is devalued, and to raise suspicions of partiality. A more effective — and acceptable — approach would be an issue-by-issue evaluation, particularly if combined with a decision analysis which seeks to establish probabilities of success at each step of a potential judicial proceeding. Normally, a mediator can minimize resistance to an evaluation by delivering it, with explanations, in caucus. If a decision analysis is used, however, the choices that would need to be made might be presented to all parties in a joint session, with the percentages of success and bottom-line settlement values worked out collaboratively by the mediator with each party in private caucuses.

Among the more controversial activistic interventions is the propriety of mediator evaluations or predictions raising questions of the fairness of proposed settlement offers . . .

A mediator, like other professional practitioners, is obligated to subordinate his or her own interests to that of the parties served — subject only to the overriding interest of the profession's social function. Pursuant to this professional obligation, in certain circumstances, the mediator's role to assure the disputant's informed self-determination would ethically justify a greater degree of activistic intervention. Among the circumstances favoring enhanced interventions are: (1) when the parties request their use or appear to need or expect activist assistance from the mediator, and (2) when the dispute resolution context calls for accountability by the mediator to third parties or overriding legal principles. For example, activist intervention commonly would be justified if the mediator believed that the best interest of children of a divorcing couple were not being considered adequately.

As a general practice, perhaps incorporated in a standard of ethics, a mediator, at the outset of the mediation, should consult with the parties regarding their expectations and the mediator's usual style of mediation. Unless the parties indicate a preference for purely facilitative mediation or reject or limit the applications of specific types of activistic intervention, the mediator should be free to offer such interventions as he or she deems appropriate.

## DECISIONMAKING IN MEDIATION: THE NEW OLD GRID AND THE NEW NEW GRID SYSTEM
### 79 Notre Dame L. Rev. 1, 29–33, 52–53 (2003)*
### By Leonard L. Riskin

. . . .

[B]oth the structure and terminology of the facilitative-evaluative/role-of-the-mediator continuum have caused confusion . . . . [T]he narrow-broad/ problem-definition continuum remains useful, even though it may not be capable of describing certain kinds of mediation behaviors, and even though many commentators have ignored or misunderstood it. In addition . . . the grid misses important issues because it: fails to distinguish between the mediator's behaviors with respect to substance and process; has a static quality that ignores both the interactive nature of mediation decisionmaking and the elements of time and persistence; is grounded on the idea of overall mediator orientations — an unrealistic notion that excludes attention to many other issues in mediator behavior, obscures much about what mediators do, and ignores the role and influence of parties.

. . . .

*A. Revising the Grid: A "New Old Grid" of Mediator Orientations Using "Directive" and "Elicitive"*

. . . . I believe the terms "directive" and "elicitive" would serve better than "evaluative" and "facilitative" to anchor the role-of-the-mediator continuum. First, they more closely approximate my goal for this continuum, which was to focus on the impact of the mediator's behavior on party self-determination. Second, the term "directive" is more general and abstract than "evaluative" and therefore may cover a wider range of mediator behaviors. a "new old grid" on which the terms "directive" and "elicitive" substitute for "evaluative" and "facilitative."

# FIGURE 3. THE "NEW OLD GRID": MEDIATOR ORIENTATIONS

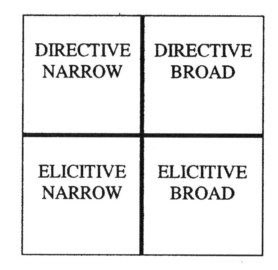

This "New Old Grid" of mediator orientations can better help us understand a range of mediator behaviors by focusing on the extent to which *almost any conduct* by the mediator *directs* the mediation process, or the participants, toward a particular procedure or perspective or outcome, on the one hand or, on the other, *elicits* the parties' perspectives and preferences — and then tries to honor or accommodate them. Thus, it gets much closer to the fundamental nature — and intent and impact — of various kinds of mediator behaviors, especially as they affect party self-determination.

I do not mean to assert that all elicitive behavior enhances party autonomy and all directive behavior undermines it. Directive mediator behavior almost always impairs party autonomy in the very short run; however, sometimes it also may be essential for fostering party autonomy. For example, a mediator may have to be directive in establishing and enforcing certain ground rules and pursuing particular lines of inquiry in order to protect one or more of the parties' ability to exercise their influence. Using the terms "directive" and "elicitive" also can help us recognize that mediators can direct (or push) the parties toward particular outcomes through "selective facilitation" — directing discussion of outcomes the mediator favors, while not promoting discussions of outcomes the mediator does not favor — without explicitly evaluating a particular outcome.

Although I proffer this "New Old Grid" of mediator orientations, I have substantial reservations about using it, because it retains many of the limitations of the old grid. First, the very idea of an overall orientation could imply, to some, a kind of rigidity in a mediator, an unwillingness to respond to circumstances. Thus, it may impair the mediator's ability, and that of the parties and their lawyers, to approach situations with an open mind. Second, as demonstrated above in connection with the old grid, it is nearly impossible — and generally unwise — to label a particular mediator with an overall orientation . . . . For example, almost every mediator will direct on some issues and elicit on others. And nearly any move by a mediator can have both directive and elicitive aspects or intents or effects. Thus, a mediator might direct the parties toward a particular understanding of their situation in order to elicit options from them. Similarly, when a mediator asks whether one party would consider a future business relationship with the other, this obviously has an elicitive thrust. But merely asking the question can be directive, too, in the sense that it directs the party's attention toward a particular issue and, at least for the moment, away from other issues.

In other words, there is a complex, dynamic quality in the relationships between directive and elicitive mediator moves. They often travel in tandem, and a particular move can have both directive and elicitive motives and effects.

. . . .

The "New Old Grid" of mediator orientations is more useful than the old one in providing a quick overview. Yet, like the old grid, it resembles a map that shows only major highways and large cities. On such a map, additional information — such as smaller towns, smaller roads, rivers, airports, recreation areas and ball parks, topography, and weather — could inform and remind travelers of choices and decisions that can enrich their journeys. People concerned about mediation — mediators, consumers, trainers, regulators — also could benefit from maps of mediation that highlight particular issues. With this in mind, I put forth a series of other new grids.

[NOTE: Professor Riskin proceeds to offer three additional substantive decision-making grids, two procedural decisionmaking grids, and one metaprocedural decisionmaking grid which highlight that a mediator may have different orientations depending on whether one is considering substance, procedures or the way decisions about procedures will be made. So for example, a mediator may have facilitative orientation to substantive decisionmaking while also being highly directive with regards to procedural issues.]

. . . .

. . . The old grid's greatest virtue, its simplicity, is also its greatest vice. The original system — based on just one static image of the mediator's orientation —

fostered valuable dialogue and useful debate, but it also obscured our vision of many important issues and may have prompted an unproductive polarization in the academic literature. The "New New Grid" System is much more complex. I hope this complexity will produce more insight than confusion.

## 2.  Transformative Mediation

Recall that Professor Bush had argued in the excerpt from his 1989 article, appearing above, that mediators should see their role as one of "empowerment and recognition." In his book with Joseph Folger, *The Promise of Mediation*, the empowerment and recognition role forms the basis for an argument that mediators should adopt a *transformative* orientation so that mediation can reach its full potential. A transformative mediation offers the parties opportunities for personal empowerment and encourages the parties to give and receive recognition of each other's interests, concerns, and needs. Bush and Folger distinguish transformative mediation from problem-solving mediation. They argue that the mediator's activities in a problem-solving mediation are too directed toward achieving the goal of an outcome that will satisfy the parties rather than providing the parties with opportunities for empowerment and recognition. As you read the following excerpt from *The Promise of Mediation*, consider how the transformative orientation compares to the facilitative or evaluative orientations. Is it consistent with one or both?

## THE PROMISE OF MEDIATION: THE TRANSFORMATIVE APPROACH TO MEDIATION
### 45–46, 49–56, 62, 64–72 (2d ed. 2005)*
### By Robert A. Baruch Bush & Joseph P. Folger

The Transformative Theory of Conflict

The transformative theory of conflict starts by offering its own answer to the foundational question of what conflict means to the people involved. According to transformative theory, what people find most significant about conflict is not that it frustrates their satisfaction of some right, interest, or pursuit, no matter how important, but that it leads and even forces them to behave toward themselves and others in ways that they find uncomfortable and even repellent. More specifically, it alienates them from their sense of their own strength and their sense of connection to others, thereby disrupting and undermining the interaction between them as human beings. This crisis of deterioration in human interaction is what parties find most affecting, significant — and disturbing — about the experience of conflict.

Negative Conflict Interaction: A Case in Point

The transformative theory starts from the premise that interactional crisis is what conflict means to people. And help in overcoming that crisis is a major part of

---

what parties want from a mediator . . . .

. . . [R]esearch suggests that conflict as a social phenomenon is not only, or primarily, about rights, interests, or power. Although it implicates all of those things, conflict is also, and most importantly, about peoples' interaction with one another as human beings . . . .

### The Picture of Negative Conflict Interaction — and the Evidence Behind It

. . . Conflict, along with whatever else it does, affects people's experience both of self and other. First, conflict generates, for almost anyone it touches, a sense of their own *weakness* and incapacity . . . [C]onflict brings a sense of relative weakness, compared with their preconflict state, in their experience of self-efficacy: a sense of lost control over their situation, accompanied by confusion, doubt, uncertainty, and indecisiveness. This overall sense of weakening is something that occurs as a very natural human response to conflict; almost no one is immune to it, regardless of his or her initial "power position." At the very same time, conflict generates a sense of *self-absorption*: compared with before, each party becomes more focused on self alone — more protective of self and more suspicious, hostile, closed, and impervious to the perspective of the other person. In sum, no matter how strong people are, conflict propels them into relative weakness. No matter how considerate of others people are, conflict propels them into self -absorption and self -centeredness.

. . . .

[T]he experiences of weakness and self-absorption do not occur independently. Rather, they reinforce each other in a feedback loop: the weaker I feel myself becoming, the more hostile and closed I am toward you; and the more hostile I am toward you, the more you react to me in kind, the weaker I feel, the more hostile and closed I become, and so on. This vicious circle of *disempowerment* and *demonization* is exactly what scholars mean when they talk about *conflict escalation*. The transformative theory looks at it more as *interactional degeneration*. Before conflict begins, whatever the context, parties are engaged in some form of decent, perhaps even loving, human interaction. Then the conflict arises, and propelled by the vicious circle of disempowerment and demonization, what started as a decent interaction spirals down into an interaction that is negative, destructive, alienating, and demonizing, on all sides.

. . . When nations get caught up in that spiral, the outcome is what we've seen all too often in the last decades — war, or even worse than war, if that's possible. For organizations, communities, or families who get caught up in the conflict spiral, the result is the negative transformation of a shared enterprise into an adversarial battle . . . .

### What Parties Want from a Mediator: Help in Reversing the Negative Spiral

Taking the transformative view of what conflict entails and means to parties, one is led to a different assumption, compared with other theories of conflict, about what parties want, need, and expect from a mediator. If what bothers parties most about conflict is the interactional degeneration itself, then what they will most want from an intervenor is help in reversing the downward spiral and restoring constructive interaction. Parties may not express this in so many words when they first come to a mediator. More commonly, they explain that what they want is not just agreement but "closure," to get past their bitter conflict experience and "move on" with their lives. However, it should be clear that in order to help parties achieve closure and move on, the mediator's intervention must directly address the interactional crisis itself.

The reason for this conclusion is straightforward: if the negative conflict cycle is not reversed, if parties don't regenerate some sense of their own strength and some degree of understanding of the other, it is unlikely that they can move on and be at peace with themselves, much less each other. In effect, without a change in the conflict interaction between them, parties are left disabled, even if an agreement on concrete issues is reached. The parties' confidence in their own competence to handle life's challenges remains weakened, and their ability to trust others remains compromised. The result can be permanent damage to the parties' ability to function, whether in the family, the workplace, the boardroom, or the community . . . .

From the perspective of transformative theory, reversing the downward spiral is the primary value that mediation offers to parties in conflict. That value goes beyond the dimensions of helping parties reach agreement on disputed issues. With or without the achievement of agreement, the help parties most want, in all types of conflict, involves helping them end the vicious circle of disempowerment, disconnection, and demonization — alienation from both self and others. Because without ending or changing that cycle, the parties cannot move beyond the negative interaction that has entrapped them and cannot escape its crippling effects.

This is transformative theory's answer to the question posed previously: What kind of help do people want from a mediator? As transformative theory sees it, with solid support from research on conflict, parties who come to mediators are looking for — and valuing — more than an efficient way to reach agreements on specific issues. They are looking for a way to change and transform their destructive conflict interaction into a more positive one, to the greatest degree possible, so that they can move on with their lives constructively, whether together or apart . . . .

### The Theory of Mediation as Conflict Transformation

. . . [T]ransformative mediation can best be understood as a process of *conflict transformation* — that is, changing the quality of conflict interaction. In the transformative mediation process, parties can recapture their sense of competence and connection, reverse the negative conflict cycle, reestablish a constructive (or at least neutral) interaction, and move forward on a positive footing, with the mediator's help.

### Party Capacity for Conflict Transformation: Human Nature and Capacity

. . . The critical resource in conflict transformation is the parties' own basic humanity — their essential strength, decency, and compassion, as human beings. As discussed earlier, the transformative theory of conflict recognizes that conflict tends to escalate as interaction degenerates, because of the susceptibility we have as human beings to experience weakness and selfabsorption in the face of sudden challenge.

However, the theory also posits, based on what many call a *relational theory* of human nature, that human beings have inherent capacities for *strength* (agency or autonomy) and *responsiveness* (connection or understanding) and an inherent *social* or *moral impulse* that activates these capacities when people are challenged by negative conflict, working to counteract the tendencies to weakness and self-absorption . . . . The transformative theory asserts that when these capacities are activated, the conflict spiral can reverse and interaction can regenerate, even without the presence of a mediator as intervenor. In fact, the same research that documents the negative conflict cycle also documents the power of the human capacities for strength and understanding to operate in the face of challenge and conflict, and ultimately to transform conflict interaction . . . .

Figure 2.2 expands the picture presented earlier and illustrates this positive potential of conflict interaction. It is true, as we have seen with hundreds of parties in all of the different contexts that we've worked in, that people in conflict tend to find themselves falling into the negative cycle of weakness and self-absorption. But it is equally true that people do not necessarily remain caught in that cycle. Conflict is not static. It is an emergent, dynamic phenomenon, in which parties can — and do — move and shift in remarkable ways, even when no third party is involved. They move out of weakness, becoming calmer, clearer, more confident, more articulate, and more decisive — in general, *shifting from weakness to strength*. They move away from self-absorption, becoming more attentive, open, trusting, and under-standing of the other party — in general, *shifting from self-centeredness* to *responsiveness* to other. Just as studies document conflict's negative impacts and the downward conflict spiral, they also document the dynamics of these positive shifts and the upward, regenerative spiral they engender.

The arrows moving from left to right in Figure 2.2 represent these shifts: the movements parties make from weakness to strength and from self-absorption to understanding of one another. In transformative theory, these dynamic shifts are called *empowerment* and *recognition*. Moreover, as the figure suggests, there is also a reinforcing feedback effect on this side of the picture. The stronger I become, the more open I am to you. The more open I am to you, the stronger you feel, the more open you become to me, and the stronger I feel. Indeed, the more open I become to you, the stronger I feel in myself, simply because I'm more open; that is, openness not only requires but creates a sense of strength, of magnanimity. So there is also a circling between strength and responsiveness once they begin to emerge. But this is not a vicious circle, it is a "virtuous circle" — a virtuous circle of conflict transformation.

Why conflict transformation? Because as the parties make empowerment and recognition shifts, and as those shifts gradually reinforce in a virtuous circle, the interaction as a whole begins to transform and regenerate. It changes back from a negative, destructive, alienating, and demonizing interaction to one that becomes positive, constructive, connecting, and humanizing, even while conflict and disagreement are still continuing. This reversal of the conflict cycle from negative and destructive to positive and constructive is what the spiral line ascending at the right of Figure 2.2 represents.

The keys to this transformation of conflict interaction are the empowerment and recognition shifts that the parties themselves make. No matter how small and seemingly insignificant, as these shifts continue and accumulate, they can transform the entire interaction. Is it hard for those shifts to occur? It most certainly is, especially for parties who have been overcome by the sense of weakness and self-absorption that conflict first brings. It's hard, but it's eminently possible.

. . . .

The Role of the Mediator in Conflict Transformation:

A Case in Point

Mediators provide important help and support for the small but critical shifts by each party, from weakness to strength and from self-absorption to understanding . . . .

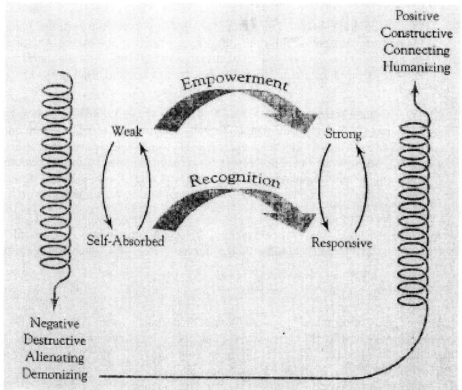

**FIGURE 2.2 CHANGING CONFLICT INTERACTION**

[T]he mediator . . . offer[s] specific forms of support that help the parties make empowerment and recognition shifts, when and as they choose, and thereby change the quality of their conflict interaction. This is perhaps the central claim of the transformative theory — that mediators' interventions can help parties transform their conflict interaction . . . .

### Mediation as Conflict Transformation: Definitions and Guiding Principles

The previous discussion brings us to the definition of mediation itself, and the mediator's role, in the transformative model. Both of these definitions differ markedly from the normal definitions found in training materials and practice literature — in which mediation is usually defined as a process in which a neutral third party helps the parties to reach a mutually acceptable resolution in some or all of the issues in dispute, and the mediator's role is defined as establishing ground rules, defining issues, establishing an agenda, generating options, and ultimately persuading the parties to accept terms of agreement . . . .

By contrast, in the transformative model:

- Mediation is defined as a process in which a third party works with parties in conflict to help them change the quality of their conflict interaction from negative and destructive to positive and constructive, as they explore and discuss issues and possibilities for resolution.

- The mediator's role is to help the parties make positive interactional shifts (empowerment and recognition shifts) by supporting the exercise of their capacities for strength and responsiveness, through their deliberation, decision-making, communication, perspective taking, and other party activities.

- The mediator's primary goals are (1) to support empowerment shifts, by supporting — but never supplanting — each party's deliberation and decision-making, at every point in the session where choices arise (regarding either process or outcome) and (2) to support recognition shifts, by encouraging and supporting — but never forcing — each party's freely chosen efforts to achieve new understandings of the other's perspective.

[I]t is important to introduce here a few important principles that should guide the mediator in supporting empowerment and recognition shifts — all of which grow out of a proper understanding of the dynamics through which these shifts occur.

First, these are shifts that the parties, and the parties alone, can make. No mediator can "get" parties to shift out of weakness or self-absorption, nor should he try. Parties gain strength and openness by making decisions by and for themselves, in their own way and at their own pace. A mediator who tries to "get" shifts to happen actually impedes this process by removing control of the interaction from the parties' hands. In other words, this mediator violates the defined goal of supporting empowerment by *supplanting* party decision-making.

Second, the mediator should expect that parties do not normally begin to shift out of self-absorption until they have first shifted out of weakness and gained strength in some degree. Simply put, people are likely to extend themselves to others when they are still feeling vulnerable and unstable. Empowerment shifts are therefore usually the first to occur, as the desire and capacity for strength reasserts itself, and supporting them is where the mediator's help is likely needed first. When such shifts do occur, however, they are often followed quickly by recognition shifts, as the desire and capacity for connection reasserts itself. Thus gains in strength often lead directly and quickly to gains in responsiveness . . . .

Third, even though there is likely to be a dynamic interplay of empowerment and recognition, the move toward conflict transformation is unlikely to be smooth and even. Rather, empowerment and recognition shifts are often followed by retreats back into weakness and self-absorption, as the interaction reaches new or deeper levels; and the retreats are then followed by new shifts into strength and openness, and so on. In pursuing the goal of supporting shifts, the mediator has to be prepared for this back and forth, in order to follow along and be ready to provide support for new shifts as the opportunities for them arise. Ultimately, the cycling shifts and retreats tend to move forward, and the overall interaction changes in quality from negative to positive — but great patience is required of the mediator in *allowing* that movement rather than trying to "move" the parties forward.

Fourth, even though the mediator's job is to support empowerment and recognition shifts, the transformative model does not ignore the significance of resolving specific issues. Rather, it assumes that if mediators do the job just described, the parties themselves will likely make positive changes in their interaction and find acceptable terms of resolution for themselves where such terms genuinely exist. Consider the strong logic of this claim: if empowerment and recognition shifts occur, and as a result the parties are interacting with clarity and confidence in themselves (strength) and with openness and understanding toward each other (responsiveness), the likelihood is very high that they will succeed in finding and agreeing on solutions to specific problems, without the need for the mediator to do that for them. More important, they will have reversed the negative conflict spiral and will have begun to reestablish a positive mode of interaction that allows them to move forward on a different footing, both while and after specific issues are resolved and even if they cannot be resolved . . . .

Finally, it is important to point out that to focus on and successfully pursue the goal of supporting interactional shifts, two fundamental things are required of the mediator . . . . The first requirement is that the mediator never lose sight of the overall point of his or her mission: to help the parties transform their conflict interaction from destructive and demonizing to positive and humanizing. Maintaining this clear perspective is not all that easy in a professional culture that generally views attainment of agreement or settlement as all important. One thing that can help is to have a firm mental anchor that keeps the mediator on course . . . .

The other requirement is a deep acceptance of the premises about human motivation and capacity that constitute the ultimate foundation of the transformative theory. It will be very difficult for a mediator to stop trying to get the parties to make shifts, unless the mediator is firmly convinced that doing so is not only impossible but *unnecessary* — because the parties have both the desire and the capacity to make those shifts for themselves. Indeed certain hallmarks of transformative practice show how a transformative mediator's approach reflects the premises about human nature that underlie the model, including these: leaving responsibility for outcomes with the parties, refusing to be judgmental about the parties' views and decisions, and taking an optimistic view of the parties' competence and motives . . . .

Holding in mind clearly both the picture of the conflict transformation mission and the premises about human nature that underlie it, the mediator can steer clear of a few serious missteps that are easy to make. First, she is reminded that empowerment is independent of any particular outcome of the mediation. If a party has used the session to collect herself, examine options, deliberate, and decide on a course of action, significant empowerment shifts have occurred, regardless of the outcome. Whether the outcome is a settlement that the mediator finds fair and optimal or unfair or even stupid, or a decision not to settle at all, the goal of supporting empowerment shifts has been achieved. And as a result, the party has gained increased strength of self from the process of self-awareness and self-determination enacted in the mediation session.

So even if a mediator is tempted to think, "Perhaps steering the party to what I know is a better outcome is really more empowering," the clear understanding of empowerment as a shift from weakness to strength reminds the mediator that even a "poor outcome" produced by the party's own process of reflection and choice strengthens the self more than a "good outcome" induced by the mediator's directiveness or imposition. That is, such "good outcomes" do not engender strength of self, unless accompanied by the process of empowerment. Solving problems *for* parties is not transformative media-tion, because it fails to support — and probably undermines — genuine party empowerment. It is the concrete steps toward strengthening the self within the session that constitute empowerment, not the nature of the outcome or solution.

In addition, we put "good outcome" in quotation marks in the foregoing discussion, because even beyond the empowerment effects of the process, the quality of an outcome must itself be measured not only by its material terms but also by the process through which it was reached. Outcomes that are reached as a result of party shifts toward greater clarity, confidence, openness, and understanding are likely to have more meaning and significance for parties than outcomes generated by mediator directiveness, however well-meant . . . .

Similarly, clarity about mission, premises, and goals can help avoid mis-steps in supporting recognition. As discussed earlier, recognition is not recognition at all unless it is freely given. It is the *decision* of the party to expand his focus from self alone to include the other that constitutes the recognition shift. If that decision is itself the result of pressure, cajoling, or moralizing, it represents nothing but self-preservation. Forced recognition, in short, is a contradiction in terms. When parties have made only slight recognition shifts, the mediator may be tempted to push for more, especially if he thinks he can get the party to see things differently. Yet when force is applied, recognition vanishes altogether. The key is for the mediator to under-stand that the goal of supporting recognition shifts is fulfilled through whatever degree of recognition the parties are genuinely willing to give.

This actually points back to the critical point made earlier about the interplay between the two kinds of movement: recognition shifts are almost always based on empowerment shifts. Until the point is reached where parties are consciously choosing their steps, recognition is unlikely to occur or to be genuine or meaningful.

## NOTES AND QUESTIONS

(1)   The practice of transformative mediation got a boost in 1994 when the world's largest employer, the United States Postal Service, adopted transformative mediation for its REDRESS (Resolve Employment Disputes Reach Equitable Solutions Swiftly) program, in which postal service employees opt for mediation as an alternative to the Equal Employment Opportunity (EEO) complaint process. In *Upstream Effects from Mediation of Workplace Disputes: Some Preliminary Evidence from the USPS*, 48 Lab. L.J. 601 (1997), Jonathan F. Anderson and Lisa Bingham report on a preliminary study of the REDRESS program in three pilot cities: "Ninety-two percent of supervisors and 41% of employees experienced recognition of the other's perspective. Over two-thirds of all participants felt increased empowerment over their situation. There is evidence that mediation is having a transformative effect on participants." For other commentary and studies of the REDRESS program, see Antes, Folger & Della Noce, *Transforming Conflict Interactions in the Workplace: Documented Effects of the USPS REDRESS (TM) Program*, 18 Hofstra Lab. & Emp. L.J. 429 (2001); Bingham, Kim & Raines, *Exploring the Role of Representation at the USPS*, 17 Ohio St. J. on Disp. Resol. 341 (2002).

(2)   For articles that discuss and analyze the themes and concepts of transformative mediation from various practice and theoretical perspectives, see *Transformative Approaches to Mediation*, Special Issue, Mediation Q., Vol. 13, No. 4, Summer 1996; Folger, Bush & Della Noce (eds.), *Transformative Mediation: A Sourcebook* (Association for Conflict Resolution and Institute for the Study of Conflict Transformation, 2010).

(3)   For critical reviews of Bush and Folger's mediation model, see Carrie Menkel-Meadow, *The Many Ways of Mediation: The Transformation of Traditions, Ideologies, Paradigms, and Practices*, 11 Negotiation J. 217, 235–38 (1995); and Michael Williams, *Can't I Get No Satisfaction?: Thoughts on The Promise of Mediation*, 15 Mediation Q. 143 (1997). In *Transformative Mediation: In Search of a Theory of Practice*, 22 Conflict Resol. Q. 397 (2005), Lisa P. Gaynier argues that there are fundamental weaknesses in Bush and Folger's theoretical construct for transformative mediation and proposes a Gestalt-based theory to support mutual recognition and empowerment.

## 3.   Other Mediator Orientations

### a.   Understanding-Based Mediation

Another approach to mediation is the understanding-based mediation model. This orientation was pioneered by Gary Friedman and Jack Himmelstein. In their book, *Challenging Conflict Mediation Through Understanding* (2008), Friedman and Himmelstein introduce this form of mediation. Understanding-based mediation focuses on parties' increased understanding and resolving the conflict together. As you read the following article excerpt, consider the positive and negative impacts of not using caucuses during mediation.

# RESOLVING CONFLICT TOGETHER: THE UNDERSTANDING-BASED MODEL OF MEDIATION
2006 J. Disp. Resol. 523[*]
By Gary Friedman & Jack Himmelstein

. . .

Four interacting principles guide this work:

1. Developing Understanding: The overarching goal of this approach to mediation is to resolve conflict through understanding. Deeper understanding by the parties of their own and each other's perspectives, priorities, and concerns enables them to work through their conflict together. With an enhanced understanding of the whole situation, the parties are able to shape creative and mutually rewarding solutions that reflect their personal, business, and economic interests.

We therefore rely heavily on the power of understanding rather than the power of coercion or persuasion to drive the mediation process. We want everything to be understood, from how we will work together, to the true nature of the conflict in which the parties are enmeshed, where it came from, how it grew, and how they might free themselves from it. We believe the parties should understand the legal implications of their case, but that the law should not usurp or direct our mediation. We put as much weight on the personal, practical, or business related aspects of any conflict as on the legal aspect. In finding a resolution, we want the parties to recognize what is important to them in the dispute, and to understand what is important to the other side. We strive for a resolution to satisfy both.

2. Going Underneath the Problem: Experience has shown us that conflicts are best resolved by uncovering what lies underneath them. Conflict is rarely just about money, or who did what to whom. It also has subjective dimensions: the beliefs and assumptions of the individuals caught in its grasp, their feelings, such as anger and fear, the need to assign blame, and the desire for self-justification. There are also assumptions about the nature of conflict itself, which support the conflict and keep it going — like the theory of the exclusivity of right and wrong. And there are ideas about how conflicts must be resolved, such as the belief that the other person must change his position or that an authoritative third party must decide the outcome.

We need breadth and depth of understanding to hope to break out of such a complex and multilayered situation, what we call a "Conflict Trap." Repeatedly, we find that the basis for resolution comes from discovering together with the parties what lies at the very heart of their dispute, which is often a surprise to the parties, and which often has a profound affect on their work together.

3. Party Responsibility: This approach is also grounded in the simple premise that the person in the best position to determine the wisest solution to a dispute is not a third party, whether a court or judge or mediator, but the individuals who

---

created and are living the problem. Therefore, we ask the disputants to assume the primary responsibility for working things through, and we ask that they work things through together. As we like to think about it: Let the parties own their conflict.

4. Working Together: When we promote working together, we mean that all meetings with the mediator occur with all parties present (including lawyers if they have a role). There is no caucusing, no shuttling back and forth; no secrets to keep from one party or the other; and no private meetings, except for those between the parties and their counsel. Instead of being responsible for fashioning an acceptable solution, the mediator's job is to enable the parties to reach a mutually agreeable solution together.

We believe the impulse to work through conflict together is a natural part of the human condition, though it may be nascent, buried, or blocked. It is hardly recognized in the legal community, but we have seen it, waiting to be tapped and given room for expression. We have seen it succeed for many thousands of individuals and organizations . . .

## B. Parties' Responsibility and Non-Caucus Approach

In the Understanding-Based Model, the emphasis is on the parties' responsibility for the decisions they will make. In this approach, the assumption is that it is the parties, not the professionals, who have the best understanding of what underlies the dispute and are in the best position to find the solution. It is their conflict and they hold the key to reaching a solution that best serves them both. Meeting together with the parties (and counsel) follows from these assumptions about parties' responsibility.

Many other approaches to mediation recommend that the mediator shuttle back and forth between the parties (caucusing), gaining information that he or she holds confidential. Our central problem with caucusing is that the mediator ends up with the fullest picture of the problem and is therefore in the best position to solve it. The mediator, armed with that fuller view, can readily urge or manipulate the parties to the end he or she shapes. The emphasis here, in contrast, is on understanding and voluntariness as the basis for resolving the conflict rather than persuasion or coercion.

We view the mediator's role in the Understanding-Based Model as assisting the parties to gain sufficient understanding of their own and each other's perspective so as to be able to decide together how to resolve their dispute. The parties not only know first hand everything that transpires, but they have control over fashioning an outcome that will work for both. They also participate with the mediator (and counsel) in designing a process by which they can honor what they each value and help them reach a result that reflects what is important to both of them. As mediators, our goal is to support the parties in working through their conflict together, in ways that respect their differing perspectives, needs, and interests, as well as their common goals.

To work in this way is challenging for both the mediator and the parties. The parties' motivation and willingness to work together is critical to the success of this approach. Mediators often assume that the parties (and their counsel) simply do not want to work together, and therefore keep the parties apart. In our experience, many parties (and counsel) simply accept that they will not work together and that the mediator will be responsible for crafting the solution. But once educated about how staying in the same room might be valuable, many are motivated to do so. If the parties (and the mediator) are willing, working together throughout can be as rewarding as it is demanding.

## C. Role of Law and Lawyers

. . . [I]n this model, we welcome lawyers' participation, and we include the law. But we do not assume that the parties will or should rely solely or primarily on the law. Rather, the importance the parties give to the law is up to them. Our goals are: 1) to educate the parties about the law and possible legal outcomes, and 2) to support their freedom to fashion their own creative solutions that may differ from what a court might decide. In this way, the parties learn that they can together reach agreements that respond to both their individual interests and their common goals while also being well informed about their legal rights and the judicial alternatives to a mediated settlement.

In these and other respects, the Understanding-Based Model seeks to utilize mediation's potential to resolve conflict in ways that honor the parties, their differences, and their relationship.

. . .

Bottom line, the essential point of the entire exercise of the legal conversation is to make the law "people-size" or, more precisely, "party-size." We want the parties to understand how the law might apply to their conflict so that they can give it as much or as little weight as they choose in the decisions they make together. We are constantly aware of the distorting potential of the legal lens, and we work hard to give the parties the means to use the "the control knob" over the disempowering intensity of that lens. We do this in a variety of ways.

In terms of the content of the law, we often ask the lawyers to slow down or to state in plain English some of the concepts spoken in classical legalese. We may try to translate ourselves by looping in straightforward language what the lawyers are saying in legal terminology. We also check to confirm that the parties understand, reemphasizing that that is the goal, and give them the chance to ask questions that will help them understand.

Asking the lawyers to explain the principles and reasoning that underlie the law's potential application may help resonate with the parties' direct experience while reducing the law's potentially confusing and literal application. Once freed from the traditional legal lens, the parties can see the law for what it's supposed to be: society's effort to guide and regulate personal and business relationships from going awry, and to help put them back on track when they do.

Through all of the above, mediators must maintain bifocal vision, with one eye on content and one eye on the impact that the legal conversation is having on the parties. Is it helping or not? Is the law "party-size?" Are the parties confused, overwhelmed, or frustrated? Are they losing focus on what is important to them that may be embodied in other reference points than law? Are they surrendering their own perspectives and responsibility to the lawyers or to the law? We tell by watching the parties' reactions, listening to their concerns, and inquiring of the parties with the shared goal of increasing their understanding. . . .

## NOTES AND QUESTIONS

(1)   Another mediator orientation that has been identified is narrative mediation. In *Narrative Mediation: A New Approach to Conflict Resolution*, John Winslade and Gerald Monk explain that people view things from a perspective that is influenced by their culture and their life experiences. These elements shape a person's story about their life's events. Since each party to a conflict has formed their own conflict story based on their perspectives, the goal of narrative mediation is to introduce different perspectives and descriptions, with the goal of helping parties to rewrite and agree on a new alternative, conflict-free narrative. Toran Hansen, in the following excerpt, offers a concise summary and explanation of the process of narrative mediation:

> Coming out of the tradition of Narrative Family Therapy, the Narrative Mediation adopts a profoundly therapeutic style of mediation, which contrasts against the bargaining style. In therapeutic mediation, mediators emphasize increasing understanding among the disputants and overcoming relationship problems. Face-to-face contact between parties is maximized during the intervention, as are attempts to uncover underlying issues and veiled interests. The goal is not simply to reach agreements but to use the intervention as an opportunity to improve communication and to develop a foundation for addressing problems in general. In the bargaining style, settlements are more heavily emphasized, caucuses are more frequent, and attempts to narrow issues, promote compromise, and synthesize arguments are more common. The narrative approach seeks to better conflict parties as people, as much as it attempts to deal with the specific conflict at hand and generate a settlement.

Toran Hansen, *The Narrative Approach to Mediation*, 4 Pepp. Disp. Resol. L.J. 297, 300–07 (2004).

(2)   In what types of conflicts do you think narrative mediation or understanding based mediation would be most effective? Both models emphasize face-to-face negotiations, and eliminate caucusing. Would this be influential?

(3)   In Chapter 3, *supra*, it was suggested that a mediator begin each mediation conference by delivering a mediator's opening statement. How, if at all, might the content of an opening statement differ from that set forth in Chapter 3 if one were: (a) a transformative mediator? (b) an Understanding-Based Mediator?

(4)   Other mediation orientations have also been suggested by scholars and practitioners. Some might be characterized as hybrids. In *Adapting Mediation to What Users Want*, 45 Md. B.J. 55 (2012), John Bickerman introduces an orientation he labels *analytical mediation*. In this orientation "the mediator adjusts his or her style based on the needs of the parties." And, "uses the style best suited to the

dispute at each moment of the process." The style of mediation "should fit the circumstance of the moment and adapt as the circumstances change."

(5) As you read through the materials that follow, consider the potential interplay between certain orientations or mediator styles and critical issues relating to the use of mediation such as diversity, power, and justice.

## D.  MEDIATOR STYLES

A few empirical studies of mediators in operation have sought to identify and characterize the varying styles employed by individual mediators. Although the settings for these studies varied widely by type of dispute and locale, there are bases for comparison. In her book, *The Mediators* (1983), Deborah Kolb reported on a study of public sector labor mediators working for the Wisconsin Employee Relations Commission and the Federal Mediation and Conciliation Service. Kolb identified two distinct mediator styles — *dealmakers* and *orchestrators*. The state mediators tended to adopt a *deal-maker* style that placed a heavy reliance on caucusing and having the parties communicate through the mediator rather than directly with each other. One *dealmaker* described the basic tactic used to strike a deal as "hammering." The federal mediators, on the other hand, tended to use an *orchestrator* style that emphasized flexibility and direct communication between the parties, putting the burden on the parties to come to an agreement. Susan Silbey and Sally Merry studied mediators in three Massachusetts-based community and family mediation programs. In their article, *Mediator Settlement Strategies*, 8 Law & Pol'y 7 (1986), Silbey and Merry identified two modal styles of mediation, *bargaining* and *therapeutic*. The *bargaining* style tended to be more structured and controlling, employing caucuses, and discouraging direct communication among the parties. It ignored emotions and concentrated on the bottom line. The *therapeutic* style, on the other hand, encouraged the parties to fully and freely express their feelings to one another. In the excerpt that follows, James Alfini surveys the styles of lawyer-mediators handling relatively high stakes civil cases in the Florida court-connected mediation program. He identifies three mediator styles: *trashing, bashing,* and *hashing it out*. The student should consider and compare these styles in light of the settings in which the mediators operated.

## TRASHING, BASHING, AND HASHING IT OUT: IS THIS THE END OF "GOOD MEDIATION"?
### 19 Fla. St. U. L. Rev. 47, 66–73 (1991)*
### By James J. Alfini

. . . Our interviews with the circuit mediators and lawyers revealed three distinct styles. These three approaches to the mediation process are characterized as (1) trashing, (2) bashing, and (3) hashing it out.

### 1. Trashing

---

* Copyright © 1991 by the Florida State University Law Review. Reprinted with permission.

The mediators who employ a trashing methodology spend much of the time "tearing apart" the cases of the parties. Indeed, one of these mediators suggested the "trasher" characterization: "I trash their cases. By tearing apart and then building their cases back up, I try to get them to a point where they will put realistic settlement figures on the table."

To facilitate uninhibited trashing of the parties' cases, the overall strategy employed by these mediators discourages direct party communication. Following the mediator's orientation and short (five to ten minutes) opening statements by each party's attorney, the mediator puts the parties in different rooms. The mediator then normally caucuses with the plaintiff's attorney and her client in an effort to get them to take a hard look at the strengths and weaknesses of their case. One plaintiff's lawyer described the initial caucus:

> The mediator will tell you how bad your case is . . . try to point out the shortcomings of the case to the parties and try to get the plaintiff to be realistic. They point out that juries aren't coming back with a lot of money anymore on these types of cases. They ask you tough questions to get you to see where you might have a liability problem or the doctor says you don't have a permanent injury so you may get nothing. They will try to get you to take a hard look at the deficiencies in your case that obviously I already know, but sometimes it enlightens the plaintiff to hear it from an impartial mediator.

Having torn down the case in this manner, the mediator will try to get the plaintiff and plaintiff's attorney to consider more "realistic" settlement options. The mediator then gives the plaintiff's lawyer and her client an opportunity to confer, while the mediator shuttles off to caucus with the defense.

The defense caucus is similar to that conducted with the plaintiff, except that the mediator may present the defendant with a new settlement offer if the plaintiff caucus has resulted in one. A defense attorney described the caucus:

> During the defense caucus, the mediator will usually say, "Well, you know they've asked for this figure and they think they have a strong case in this regard. Their figure is 'x.' They're willing to negotiate. They have told me that they'll take this amount which is obviously lower than the original demand" — if he has authority from the plaintiff to reveal that to you. If he doesn't, he won't say anything about that. He asks, "What do you think the case is worth? Why?"

> He'll then work through the case with us, pointing out outstanding medicals, lost wages and other special damages, then tallying them up and a certain percentage of pain and suffering and come up with a figure. And then they may discuss the strength of the case. I've had mediators say things to me in the caucus such as, "I was impressed by the plaintiff; I think they're going to be believable. Have you factored that into your evaluation of the case?"

If the trasher gets the defense to put a figure on the table that is closer to the plaintiff's current offer, the mediator will then shuttle back to the plaintiff.

Once the trasher has achieved the goal of getting both sides to put what she believes to be more realistic settlement figures on the table, she will shuttle back and forth trying to forge an agreement. If this is accomplished, the mediator may or may not bring the parties back together to work out the details of the agreement. One trasher explained that, once separated, he never brings the parties back together even at the final agreement stage.

On the whole, the attorneys appeared to accept, if not appreciate, the extreme caucusing methodology of the trasher. As one defense lawyer whose practice is limited to personal injury actions explained:

> We communicate through the mediator. Personal injury is a very emotional type of practice where emotions run high. What we find is that the personalities of the attorneys come into conflict, the personality of the carrier comes into conflict and the personality of the adjuster comes into conflict. So it's best to bring in a distance of parties. To walk back and forth and give some insight to each other.

Mediators who employ a trashing methodology tend to draw on their own experiences with the litigation process to get the parties to take a hard look at their cases. Indeed, all of the trashers that were interviewed are experienced trial lawyers. They call upon their own experiences not only to expose procedural and substantive weaknesses on both sides, but also to get the parties to consider the costs of litigation. One defense attorney explained that once the mediator points out the weaknesses and has the party assess the costs of litigation, the mediator will say, " 'Do you guys really want to spend all this money to take this case to trial?' I see a lot of that which, for your typical insurance company, is a very fruitful approach." This same lawyer, however, saw this approach as less effective when representing government agencies: "It's not nearly as fruitful because governmental agencies, especially the sheriff, are such easy targets for lawsuits that nuisance value doesn't really exist. If we don't think we have done anything wrong, we generally fight to the bitter end even if we get clobbered."

If the trashing methodology is to be effective, the importance of having a mediator with litigation experience was underscored by this same attorney:

> I've had two occasions where we had a mediator that had never really litigated and had not dealt with the type of issues we were dealing with. In both cases, he, I felt, completely misperceived the issues and the possible exposure and liability. In one case, he thought we had horrible exposure and we really didn't, at least in my opinion. In the other case, he thought we had a great defense because there was a whole lot of things against us and we really needed to settle.

### 2. Bashing

Unlike the trashers, the mediators who use a bashing technique tend to spend little or no time engaging in the kind of case evaluation that is aimed at getting the parties to put "realistic" settlement figures on the table. Rather, they tend to focus initially on the settlement offers that the parties bring to mediation and spend most of the session bashing away at those initial offers in an attempt to get the parties to agree to a figure somewhere in between. Their mediation sessions thus tend to be shorter than those of the trashers, and they tend to prefer a longer initial joint session, permitting direct communication between the parties.

Most of the bashers interviewed were retired judges who draw on their judicial experience and use the prestige of their past judicial service to bash out an agreement. One of the retired judges explained that he emphasizes his judicial background during his opening statement to get them in the right frame of mind:

> I introduce myself and give them my background because I think that's very helpful to litigants to know they're before a retired judge with a lot of experience . . . . I tell them that even a poor settlement, in my judgment, is preferable to a long and possibly expensive trial together with all the uncertainties that attend a trial.

This mediator described the mediator's role as "one who guides," and explained why he believed that a retired judge makes an effective mediator: "If you're a retired judge you bring much more prestige to the mediation table than just an attorney because the people look at this attorney and say, 'I have an attorney; what do I need this guy for?' A 'judge' they listen to."

The notion that a mediator is "one who guides" suggests that the basher adopts a more directive mediator style than that employed by the trasher. The differences between the trasher and the basher in this regard were perhaps best revealed in their responses to a question we asked concerning the differences between mediation and a judicial settlement conference. The trashers tended to see the settlement conference judge as being much more aggressive than the mediator ("judges can lean on you, mediators I guess can, but they shouldn't"), while the bashers felt just the opposite. Another basher elaborated on his perception of the differences:

> The judge has to be very careful. Because if he expresses an opinion, the next thing he knows he's going to be asked to excuse himself because one side or the other will think he's taking sides. In mediation, you don't have to worry about that. You can say to the plaintiff, "there's no way the defendant is going to pay you that kind of money." You can say things as a mediator that you can't say as a judge.

As soon as the basher has gotten the parties to place settlement offers on the table, as one attorney explained, "there is a mad dash for the middle." One of the retired judges described a case he had mediated that morning:

> [T]he plaintiff wanted $75,000. The defendant told me he would pay $40,000. I went to the plaintiff and said to him, "They're not going to pay $75,000. What will you take?" He said, "I'll take $60,000." I told him I wasn't sure I could get $60,000 and asked if he would take $50,000 if I could get it. He agreed. I then went back to the defendant and told him I couldn't settle for $40,000, but "you might get the plaintiff to take $50,000" and asked if he would pay it. The answer was yes. Neither of them were bidding against themselves. I was the guy who was doing it, and that's the role of the mediator.

A defense attorney found this bidding process to be the most objectionable aspect of circuit mediation. He explained that it discouraged the responsible attorney from carefully evaluating her case beforehand and making an initial settlement offer that was both reasonable and realistic:

> [T]his is one of my real complaints about mediation . . . mediation is a game . . . . What mediation has done has said, "Look, if you do what you should do as a responsible attorney, what you do is establish a floor and when you get to the mediation, the mediator is going to expect you to move up." Otherwise, his position is going to be "wait a minute, you didn't come here with an open mind. You didn't come in a position to negotiate in good faith."

Another attorney found the bashing methodology totally inappropriate for complex, multiparty cases. The attorney offered as an example a groundwater contamination case in which he was involved. He said that the case involved a number of individual parties, insurance companies, and third party complaints against real estate companies. The mediation took place in a courtroom with a retired judge as the mediator. The mediator sat in the front of the courtroom and the attorneys and their clients sat together, theater style:

> We weren't even looking at one another. The mediator didn't have a clue as to what the case was all about. You'd think he would at least try to figure out who should meet with who and whether collateral issues could be dealt with. Just kind of organize the procedure. But he didn't even do that. The mediator was absolutely worthless. It is the fact that the parties were forced to get together to talk that may force some settlements. It's hard to believe that it would be because of anything the mediator did.

Although the basher style is the most directive of the three circuit mediation styles, it apparently is preferred by some attorneys in circuits where it is the predominant style. A mediation program director in one of these circuits explained that she has received complaints from attorneys who felt that the mediator assigned to their case was "not pushy enough." They said that the attorneys had come to expect mediators who would "hammer some sense" into the other side.

### 3. Hashing It Out

The third circuit mediation style can best be described as one involving a hashing out of a settlement agreement because it places greater reliance on direct communication between the opposing attorneys and their clients. The hashers tend to take a much more flexible approach to the mediation process, varying their styles and using techniques such as caucusing selectively, depending on their assessment of the individual case and the needs and interests of the parties. When asked to describe the mediator's role in one sentence, a hasher responded, "Facilitator, orchestrator, referee, sounding board, scapegoat."

The hasher generally adopts a much less directive posture than the trashers and bashers, preferring that the parties speak directly with one another and hash out an agreement. However, if direct communication appears counterproductive, the hasher acts as a communication link. One explained,

If the parties are at war, they communicate through me. If the lawyers are not crazy, they communicate with each other through me. If the lawyers are crazy, and the parties can talk with each other, they talk with each other. If nobody can talk, they communicate through me. My preference is that they communicate with each other.

When asked how he gets the parties to communicate, the mediator elaborated:

I may caucus with them to find out if they can . . . . If they don't want to, I don't force them. If they want to communicate, I put them together and say, "OK, tell them what you told me, if you want to." Or if it's a really complex thing like a long list of demands, I don't want to have to memorize it because I'm liable to misstate something. I simply say, "you tell them." . . . I may warn the other side not to respond, just to hear what they have to say, maybe ask questions, but don't get defensive. Then I'll take them out. Then I'll get with the other side and say, "How do you want to respond to this? Do you want me to bring them in?"

In addition to this more flexible orchestration of the process, the hasher is also unwilling to keep the parties at the mediation session if they express a desire to leave, unlike the trashers and bashers. When asked what he would do if the parties expressed a desire to leave the mediation session prematurely, a hasher responded, "Mediation is essentially a voluntary process even though they're ordered to show up . . . . If they don't want to go through the process or negotiate, they're basically free to walk out." None of the bashers and trashers was willing to give the parties this much latitude. They all expressed the view that it was the mediator's prerogative to decide when the mediation session was over. As one basher explained, "It's my decision to either declare it an impasse and have everybody go home or to continue. It's not their decision. You have to reassert control."

The hashers also differed from the trashers and bashers in reporting a willingness to caucus separately with the attorneys or the clients if they believed it might facilitate settlement. One hasher explained:

Sometimes, I talk to the parties and say, "Do you mind if I talk to your lawyers alone? I want to go through some procedural matters so that this thing will go a little smoother and a little faster." I ask the lawyers, "What do you want to do? How do you guys want to handle it?" Sometimes they say to me, "I really want you to talk to my clients.

They're really unrealistic." I say OK and then figure out how to do it. I don't do it in an opening. I'll do it in a caucus. I'll get some tipoffs and leads by asking some questions of the counsel that leads me to do what I think he needs done. If his assessment is accurate.

Flexibility apparently is the hallmark of the hasher style of mediation. Although hashers prefer to adopt a style that encourages direct party communication to hash out an agreement, they are willing to employ trasher or basher methodologies if they believe it to be appropriate in a particular case.

# NOTES AND QUESTIONS

(1)   Does the identification of these various styles have relevance in the practice world? Consider the following from Thomas J. Stipanowich, *The Multi-Door Contract and Other Possibilities*, 13 Ohio St. J. on Disp. Resol. 303, 371–72 (1998):

> An example involving a leading architectural-engineering (A/E) firm illustrates the downside of indiscriminate emphasis on a hard-driven dollar settlement. . . . The mediator quickly summarized the parties' respective positions and, having apparently reached his own conclusions about the bona fides, separated the disputants and spent the rest of the day "beating on the parties" to achieve a settlement. To the client's horror, no opportunity existed to enter into a mutual discussion or seek a consensus of any kind — only a "shuttlecock dickering" over dollars. Despite a dollar settlement, the client emerged with no intention to repeat the mediation experience.

> If a leading A/E firm represented by sophisticated counsel has this kind of experience in mediation, one wonders what is happening in the great run of cases. Clearly, users and their attorneys need a good deal more education about the range of mediator styles and strategies, permitting meaningful inquiries of prospective neutrals.

Stipanowich's suggestion about educating the parties and their lawyers about mediator styles is a practical one, because it would allow them to ask prospective mediators meaningful questions about their styles prior to retaining the mediator's services. How might this suggestion be put into operation? Would this be best accomplished through mediation classes in law school? Through continuing legal education programs?

(2)   Is one mediator style more effective than another if one measures effectiveness by either the percentage of mediations resulting in settlements or the parties' satisfaction with the mediation process? A few studies have attempted to correlate mediator style with effectiveness. In a study of labor mediators, Brett, Drieghe and Shapiro identified two basic styles — *dealmaking* and *shuttle diplomacy*. Jeanne M. Brett, Rita Drieghe & Debra L. Shapiro, *Mediator Style and Mediation Effectiveness*, 1986 Negotiation J. 277 (1986). Although they found that there were no significant differences in terms of the percentage of settlements associated with each style, they did find a correlation between styles and *types* of settlement. Settlement types ranged from compromise settlements to having the company grant the grievance. They concluded that the five labor mediators they studied "choose behaviors that they believe will facilitate the type of outcome they seek to achieve in a particular grievance." *Id.* at 281. In *The Settlement-Orientation vs. the Problem-Solving Style in Custody Mediation*, 50 J. Soc. Issues 67 (1994), Kenneth Kressel, Edward Frontera, Samuel Forlenza, Frances Butler, and Linda Fish analyzed mediator styles in 32 custody mediation cases and identified two contrasting styles, a *settlement-oriented* style and a *problem-solving* style. They concluded that although the *settlement-oriented* style was used in the majority of cases, the *problem-solving* style "produced a more structured and vigorous approach to conflict resolution during mediation, more frequent and durable settlements, and a generally more favorable attitude toward the mediation experi-

ence." *Id.* at 68. Professor Susan Nauss Exon considers the effect of mediator style on the core value of impartiality in *The Effects That Mediator Styles Impose on Neutrality and Impartiality Requirements of Mediation*, 42 U.S.F. L. Rev. 577 (2008).

(3)   How influential is the type of dispute over the choice of mediator styles or strategies? One group of experienced mediators developed a settlement strategy model that located mediator strategies "along a continuum between two polar positions — neutrality and intervention." Sydney E. Bernard, Joseph P. Folger, Helen R. Weingarten & Zena R. Zumeta, *The Neutral Mediator: Value Dilemmas in Divorce Mediation*, 4 Mediation Q. 61, 62 (1984). They then contrasted labor mediators and divorce mediators, arguing that labor mediators are much less likely than divorce mediators to adopt an interventionist settlement strategy. Is there a difference between mediator styles and mediator strategies? Does the word strategy suggest more of a conscious choice on the part of the mediator, while a mediator's style is more of an unconscious product of the mediator's background, personality, and training?

# Chapter 5

# CONFIDENTIALITY

## A.  INTRODUCTION

Confidentiality is generally considered to be an essential ingredient in mediation. Policy concerns and legal issues arise, however, over the means that may be used to insure that the confidentiality of a mediation session is maintained, as well as the scope of the protection. For example, some jurisdictions extend the confidentiality of mediation communications to the entire world, while others limit the protection to subsequent proceedings. The materials in this chapter represent the various approaches to maintaining the confidentiality of mediation communications and explore legal issues arising in cases challenging confidentiality provisions, invoking a statutory privilege, or compelling a mediator to testify. Excerpts from these cases and provisions of the Uniform Mediation Act are reproduced in this chapter to illuminate salient legal issues.

A popular way to address the interests in providing confidentiality in mediation is through the adoption of a mediation privilege. In 2001, the National Conference of Commissioners on Uniform State Laws approved the Uniform Mediation Act (UMA) (Appendix F). The UMA establishes an evidentiary privilege to assure confidentiality for all the parties involved in a mediation and has been very influential with regard to mediation confidentiality in recent years. It has been welcomed in states that did not have a strong pre-existing framework for establishing the confidentiality of mediation communications.

This chapter presents several approaches to establishing confidentiality in mediation. In Section B, the policy rationales supporting mediation confidentiality are discussed. Section C provides a sample contract that mediators may use to establish confidentiality, followed by a discussion of the enforceability of such contracts. Section D contains material regarding evidentiary exclusions of settlement discussions. Section E discusses the use of a mediation privilege created by statute, particularly the Uniform Mediation Act, and Section F covers exceptions to confidentiality and the implications of those exceptions. Finally, Section G discusses alternatives to the UMA.

## B. POLICY

### TOWARD CANDOR OR CHAOS: THE CASE OF CONFIDENTIALITY IN MEDIATION
12 Seton Hall Legis. J. 1, 1–3 (1988)[*]
By Michael L. Prigoff

Confidentiality is vital to mediation for a number of reasons

#### Effective mediation requires candor

A mediator, not having coercive power, helps parties reach agreement by identifying issues, exploring possible bases for agreement, encouraging parties to accommodate each others' interests, and uncovering the underlying causes of conflict. Mediators must be able to draw out baseline positions and interests, a task which would become impossible if the parties were constantly looking over their shoulders. Mediation often reveals deep-seated feelings on sensitive issues. Compromise negotiations often require the admission of facts which disputants would never otherwise concede. Confidentiality ensures that parties will fully participate.

#### Fairness to the disputants requires confidentiality

The safeguards present in legal proceedings — qualified counsel and specific rules of evidence and procedure — are absent in mediation. In mediation, unlike the traditional justice system, parties often make communications without the expectation that they will later be bound by them. Subsequent use of information generated at these proceedings could be unfairly prejudicial, particularly if the parties' level of sophistication is unequal. Mediation could be used as a discovery device if mediation communications were admissible in subsequent judicial actions. This is especially true where a mediation program is affiliated with an entity of the legal system, such as a prosecutor's office.

#### The mediator must remain neutral in fact and in perception

The mediator's potential to be an adversary in subsequent legal proceedings would curtail the disputants' willingness to confide during mediation. Court testimony by a mediator, no matter how carefully presented, will inevitably be characterized so as to favor one side or the other. This would destroy a mediator's efficacy as an impartial broker.

#### Privacy is an incentive for many to choose mediation

Whether it be protection of trade secrets or simply a disinclination to "air one's dirty laundry in the neighborhood," the option presented by the mediator to settle

---

disputes quietly and informally is often a primary motivator for parties choosing this process.

> Mediators, and mediation programs, need protection against distraction
> and harassment

Fledgling community programs need all of their limited resources for the "business at hand." Frequent subpoenas can encumber staff time, and dissuade volunteers from participating as mediators. Proper evaluation of programs requires adequate recordkeeping. Many programs, uncertain as to whether records would be protected absent statutory protection, routinely destroy them as a confidentiality device.

## NATIONAL LABOR RELATIONS BOARD v. MACALUSO
### United States Court of Appeals for the Ninth Circuit
### 618 F.2d 51 (1980)

WALLACE, CIRCUIT JUDGE:

The single issue presented in this National Labor Relations Board (NLRB) enforcement proceeding is whether the NLRB erred in disallowing the testimony of a Federal Mediation and Conciliation Service (FMCS) mediator as to a crucial fact occurring in his presence. We enforce the order.

### I.

In early 1976 Retail Store Employees Union Local 1001 (Union) waged a successful campaign to organize the employees of Joseph Macaluso, Inc. (Company) . . . Several months of bargaining between Company and Union negotiators failed to produce an agreement, and the parties decided to enlist the assistance of a mediator from the FMCS. Mediator Douglas Hammond consequently attended the three meetings between the Company and Union from which arises the issue before us . . . .

During the spring and summer of 1976 the Company engaged in conduct which led the NLRB to charge it with unfair labor practices. At this unfair labor practice proceeding the NLRB also found that the Company and Union had finalized a collective bargaining agreement at the three meetings with Hammond, and that the Company had violated NLRA sections 8(a)(5) and (1) by failing to execute the written contract incorporating the final agreement negotiated with the Union. The NLRB ordered the Company to execute the contract and pay back-compensation with interest, and seeks enforcement of that order in this court. In response, the Company contends that the parties have never reached agreement, and certainly did not do so at the meetings with Hammond.

The testimony of the Union before the NLRB directly contradicted that of the Company. The two Union negotiators testified that during the first meeting with Hammond the parties succeeded in reducing to six the number of disputed issues, and that the second meeting began with Company acceptance of a Union proposal resolving five of those six remaining issues. The Union negotiators further testified that the sixth issue was resolved with the close of the second meeting, and that in response to a Union negotiator's statement "Well, I think that wraps it up," the Company president said, "Yes, I guess it does." The third meeting with Hammond, according to the Union, was held only hours before the Company's employees ratified the agreement, was called solely for the purpose of explaining the agreement to the Company accountant who had not attended the first two meetings, and was an amicable discussion involving no negotiation.

The Company testimony did not dispute that the first meeting reduced the number of unsettled issues to six, but its version of the last two meetings contrasts sharply with the Union's account. The Company representatives testified that the second meeting closed without the parties having reached any semblance of an agreement, and that the third meeting was not only inconclusive but stridently divisive. While the Union representatives testified that the third meeting was an amicable explanatory discussion, the Company negotiators both asserted that their refusal to give in to Union demands caused the Union negotiators to burst into anger, threaten lawsuits, and leave the room at the suggestion of Hammond. According to the Company, Hammond was thereafter unable to bring the parties together and the Union negotiators left the third meeting in anger.

In an effort to support its version of the facts, the Company requested that the administrative law judge (ALJ) subpoena Hammond and obtain his testimonial description of the last two bargaining sessions. The subpoena was granted, but was later revoked upon motion of the FMCS. Absent Hammond's tie-breaking testimony, the ALJ decided that the Union witnesses were more credible and ruled that an agreement had been reached. The Company's sole contention in response to this request for enforcement of the resulting order to execute the contract is that the ALJ and NLRB erred in revoking the subpoena of Hammond, the one person whose testimony could have resolved the factual dispute.

## II.

Revocation of the subpoena was based upon a long-standing policy that mediators, if they are to maintain the appearance of neutrality essential to successful performance of their task, may not testify about the bargaining sessions they attend. Both the NLRB and the FMCS (as amicus curiae) defend that policy before us. We are thus presented with a question of first impression before our court: can the NLRB revoke the subpoena of a mediator capable of providing information crucial to resolution of a factual dispute solely for the purpose of preserving mediator effectiveness? . . . We must determine . . . whether preservation of mediator effectiveness by protection of mediator neutrality is a ground for revocation consistent with the power and duties of the NLRB under the NLRA.

The NLRB's revocation of Hammond's subpoena conflicts with the fundamental principle of Anglo-American law that the public is entitled to every person's evidence . . . . The facts before us present a classic illustration of the need for every person's evidence: the trier of fact is faced with directly conflicting testimony from two adverse sources, and a third objective source is capable of presenting evidence that would, in all probability, resolve the dispute by revealing the truth. Under such circumstances, the NLRB's revocation of Hammond's subpoena can be permitted only if denial of his testimony "has a public good transcending the normally predominant principle of utilizing all rational means for ascertaining truth." The public interest protected by revocation must be substantial if it is to cause us to "concede that the evidence in question has all the probative value that can be required, and yet exclude it because its admission would injure some other cause more than it would help the cause of truth, and because the avoidance of that injury is considered of more consequence than the possible harm to the cause of truth." 1 Wigmore, Evidence 296 (1940). We thus are required to balance two important interests, both critical in their own setting.

We conclude that the public interest in maintaining the perceived and actual impartiality of federal mediators does outweigh the benefits derivable from Hammond's testimony. This public interest was clearly stated by Congress when it created the FMCS: "It is the policy of the United States that (a) sound and stable industrial peace and the advancement of the general welfare, health, and safety of the Nation and of the best interests of employers and employees can most satisfactorily be secured by the settlement of issues between employers and employees through the processes of conference and collective bargaining between employers and the representatives of their employees; (b) the settlement of issues between employers and employees through collective bargaining may be advanced by making available full and adequate governmental facilities for conciliation, mediation, and voluntary arbitration to aid and encourage employers and the representatives of their employees to reach and maintain agreements concerning rates of pay, hours, and working conditions, and to make all reasonable efforts to settle their differences by mutual agreement reached through conferences and collective bargaining or by such methods as may be provided for in any applicable agreement for the settlement of disputes . . . ." 29 U.S.C. § 171. [F]ederal mediation has become a substantial contributor to industrial peace in the United States. The FMCS, as amicus curiae, has informed us that it participated in mediation of 23,450 labor disputes in fiscal year 1977, with approximately 325 federal mediators stationed in 80 field offices around the country. Any activity that would significantly decrease the effectiveness of this mediation service could threaten the industrial stability of the nation. The importance of Hammond's testimony in this case is not so great as to justify such a threat. Moreover, the loss of that testimony did not cripple the fact-finding process. The ALJ resolved the dispute by making a credibility determination, a function routinely entrusted to triers of fact throughout our judicial system.

. . . .

Public policy and the successful effectuation of the Federal Mediation and Conciliation Service's mission require that commissioners and employees maintain a reputation for impartiality and integrity. Labor and management or other interested parties participating in mediation efforts must have the assurance and confidence that information disclosed to commissioners and other employees of the Service will not subsequently be divulged, voluntarily or because of compulsion, unless authorized by the Director of the Service. No officer, employee, or other person officially connected in any capacity with the Service, currently or formerly shall . . . produce any material contained in the files of the Service, disclose any information acquired as part of the performance of his official duties or because of his official status, or testify on behalf of any party to any matter pending in any judicial, arbitral or administrative proceeding, without the prior approval of the Director. 29 C.F.R. § 1401.2(a), (b) (1979) . . . . To execute successfully their function of assisting in the settlement of labor disputes, the conciliators must maintain a reputation for impartiality, and the parties to conciliation conferences must feel free to talk without any fear that the conciliator may subsequently make disclosures as a witness in some other proceeding, to the possible disadvantage of a party to the conference. If conciliators were permitted or required to testify about their activities, or if the production of notes or reports of their activities could be required, not even the strictest adherence to purely factual matters would prevent the evidence from favoring or seeming to favor one side or the other. The inevitable result would be that the usefulness of the (FMCS) in the settlement of future disputes would be seriously impaired, if not destroyed. The resultant injury to the public interest would clearly outweigh the benefit to be derived from making their testimony available in particular cases.

During oral argument the suggestion was made that we permit the mediator to testify, but limit his testimony to "objective facts." . . . We do not believe, however, that such a limitation would dispel the perception of partiality created by mediator testimony. In addition to the line-drawing problem of attempting to define what is and is not an "objective fact," a recitation of even the most objective type of facts would impair perceived neutrality, "for the party standing condemned by the thrust of such a statement would or at least might conclude that the (FMCS) was being unfair."

We conclude, therefore, that the complete exclusion of mediator testimony is necessary to the preservation of an effective system of labor mediation, and that labor mediation is essential to continued industrial stability, a public interest sufficiently great to outweigh the interest in obtaining every person's evidence. No party is required to use the FMCS; once having voluntarily agreed to do so, however, that party must be charged with acceptance of the restriction on the subsequent testimonial use of the mediator. We thus answer the question presented by this case in the affirmative: the NLRB can revoke the subpoena of a mediator capable of providing information crucial to resolution of a factual dispute solely for the purpose of preserving mediator effectiveness. Such revocation is consonant with the overall powers and duties of the NLRB, a body created to implement the NLRA goals of "promot(ing) the flow of commerce by removing certain recognized sources of industrial strife and unrest" and "encouraging practices fundamental to the friendly adjustment of industrial disputes . . . ." 29 U.S.C. § 151.

## NOTES AND QUESTIONS

(1) The Prigoff article and the *Macaluso* case focus on the policy reasons for protecting confidentiality in mediation. Are the policy reasons mentioned in the *Macaluso* opinion consistent with those enumerated by Prigoff?

(2) Consider the policy reasons offered by the ABA Ad Hoc Committee on Federal Government ADR Confidentiality in its *Guide to Confidentiality Under the Federal Administrative Dispute Resolution Act* (2005):

> Confidentiality enables parties in [mediation] to focus on their interests, as opposed to positions. It assures parties that they may raise sensitive issues and discuss creative ideas and solutions that they would be unwilling to discuss publicly. A party may be willing to accept something less or different than he is advocating formally, but could fear that revealing that willingness in an assisted negotiation would be used to his harm in the event that negotiations do not succeed completely. Without assurance that their confidences will not be disclosed, the parties would be far less willing to discuss freely their interests and possible settlements.

Does this suggest that mediation adds value to the negotiation process? How?

(3)   Would the court's decision in *Macaluso* have been easier if the parties had contracted for confidentiality through an agreement such as the one reprinted in the next section below?

(4)   Note that *Macaluso* holds only that the *mediator* cannot be compelled to testify and does not impose a broader confidentiality restriction (the parties did testify). Does it make sense to prohibit the mediator from testifying but allow the parties to do so? Policy reasons?

(5)   In the following excerpt from *Cassel v. Superior Court*, 244 P.3d 1080 (Cal. 2011), the Supreme Court of California adopts a very strict reading of California's mediation confidentiality statute. As you read the case, consider whether there are any policy arguments for a more flexible interpretation.

## CASSEL v. SUPERIOR COURT
### Supreme Court of California
### 244 P.3d 1080 (2011)

BAXTER, J.

In order to encourage the candor necessary to a successful mediation, the Legislature has broadly provided for the confidentiality of things spoken or written in connection with a mediation proceeding. With specified statutory exceptions, neither "evidence of anything said," nor any "writing," is discoverable or admissible "in any arbitration, administrative adjudication, civil action, or other noncriminal proceeding in which . . . testimony can be compelled to be given," if the statement was made, or the writing was prepared, "for the purpose of, in the course of, or pursuant to, a mediation . . . ." (Evid. Code, § 1119, subds. (a), (b).) "All communications, negotiations, or settlement discussions by and between participants in the course of a mediation . . . shall remain confidential." (*Id.*, subd. (c).) We have repeatedly said that these confidentiality provisions are clear and absolute. Except in rare circumstances, they must be strictly applied and do not permit judicially crafted exceptions or limitations, even where competing public policies may be affected. (*Simmons v. Ghaderi* (2008) 44 Cal.4th 570, 580, 80 Cal.Rptr.3d 83, 187 P.3d 934 (*Simmons*); *Fair v. Bakhtiari* (2006) 40 Cal.4th 189, 194, 51 Cal.Rptr.3d 871, 147 P.3d 653 (*Fair*); *Rojas v. Superior Court* (2004) 33 Cal.4th 407, 415–416, 15 Cal.Rptr.3d 643, 93 P.3d 260 (*Rojas*); *Foxgate Homeowners' Assn. v. Bramalea*

*California, Inc.* (2001) 26 Cal.4th 1, 13–14, 17, 108 Cal.Rptr.2d 642, 25 P.3d 1117 (*Foxgate*).)

The issue here is the effect of the mediation confidentiality statutes on private discussions between a mediating client and attorneys who represented him in the mediation. Petitioner Michael Cassel agreed in mediation to the settlement of business litigation to which he was a party. He then sued his attorneys for malpractice, breach of fiduciary duty, fraud, and breach of contract. His complaint alleged that by bad advice, deception, and coercion, the attorneys, who had a conflict of interest, induced him to settle for a lower amount than he had told them he would accept, and for less than the case was worth.

Prior to trial, the defendant attorneys moved, under the statutes governing mediation confidentiality, to exclude all evidence of private attorney-client discussions immediately preceding, and during, the mediation concerning mediation settlement strategies and defendants' efforts to persuade petitioner to reach a settlement in the mediation. The trial court granted the motion, but the Court of Appeal vacated the trial court's order.

The appellate court majority reasoned that the mediation confidentiality statutes are intended to prevent the damaging use *against a mediation disputant* of tactics employed, positions taken, or confidences exchanged in the mediation, not to protect attorneys from the malpractice claims of their own clients. Thus, the majority concluded, when a mediation disputant sues his own counsel for malpractice in connection with the mediation, the attorneys — already freed, by reason of the malpractice suit, from the attorney-client privilege — cannot use mediation confidentiality as a shield to exclude damaging evidence of their own entirely private conversations with the client. The dissenting justice urged that the majority had crafted an unwarranted judicial exception to the clear and absolute provisions of the mediation confidentiality statutes.

Though we understand the policy concerns advanced by the Court of Appeal majority, the plain language of the statutes compels us to agree with the dissent. As we will explain, the result reached by the majority below contravenes the Legislature's explicit command that, unless the confidentiality of a particular communication is expressly waived, under statutory procedures, by all mediation "participants," or at least by all those "participants" by or for whom it was prepared (§ 1122, subd. (a)(1), (2)), things said or written "for the purpose of" and "pursuant to" a mediation shall be inadmissible in "any . . . civil action." (§ 1119, subds. (a), (b).) As the statutes make clear, confidentiality, unless so waived, extends beyond utterances or writings "in the course of" a mediation (*ibid.*), and thus is not confined to communications that occur *between mediation disputants* during the mediation proceeding itself.

We must apply the plain terms of the mediation confidentiality statutes to the facts of this case unless such a result would violate due process, or would lead to absurd results that clearly undermine the statutory purpose. No situation that extreme arises here. Hence, the statutes' terms must govern, even though they may compromise petitioner's ability to prove his claim of legal malpractice.

. . .

A pretrial mediation of the VDO suit began at 10:00 a.m. on August 4, 2004. Petitioner attended the mediation, accompanied by his assistant, Michael Paradise, and by WCCP lawyers Steve Wasserman, David Casselman, and Thomas Speiss. Petitioner and his attorneys had previously agreed he would take no less than $2 million to resolve the VDO suit by assigning his GML rights to VDO. However, after hours of mediation negotiations, petitioner was finally told VDO would pay no more than $1.25 million. Though he felt increasingly tired, hungry, and ill, his attorneys insisted he remain until the mediation was concluded, and they pressed him to accept the offer, telling him he was "greedy" to insist on more. At one point, petitioner left to eat, rest, and consult with his family, but Speiss called and told petitioner he had to come back. Upon his return, his lawyers continued to harass and coerce him to accept a $1.25 million settlement. They threatened to abandon him at the imminently pending trial, misrepresented certain significant terms of the proposed settlement, and falsely assured him they could and would negotiate a side deal that would recoup deficits in the VDO settlement itself. They also falsely said they would waive or discount a large portion of his $188,000 legal bill if he accepted VDO's offer. They even insisted on accompanying him to the bathroom, where they continued to "hammer" him to settle. Finally, at midnight, after 14 hours of mediation, when he was exhausted and unable to think clearly, the attorneys presented a written draft settlement agreement and evaded his questions about its complicated terms. Seeing no way to find new counsel before trial, and believing he had no other choice, he signed the agreement

. . .

Pursuant to recommendations of the California Law Revision Commission, the Legislature adopted the current version of the mediation confidentiality statutes in 1997. The statutory purpose is to encourage the use of mediation by promoting " ' "a candid and informal exchange regarding events in the past . . . . This frank exchange is achieved only if the participants know that what is said in the mediation will not be used to their detriment through later court proceedings and other adjudicatory processes."

. . .

Judicial construction, and judicially crafted exceptions, are permitted only where due process is implicated, or where literal construction would produce absurd results, thus clearly violating the Legislature's presumed intent. Otherwise, the mediation confidentiality statutes must be applied in strict accordance with their plain terms. Where competing policy concerns are present, it is for the Legislature to resolve them . . . . [I]n *Foxgate*, we concluded that under the confidentiality provisions of section 1119, and under section 1121, which strictly limits the content of mediators' reports, a mediator may not submit to the court, and the court may not consider, a report of communications or conduct by a party which the mediator believes constituted a failure to comply with an order of the mediator and to participate in good faith in the mediation process.

. . .

In *Rojas*, we confirmed that under the plain language of the mediation confidentiality statutes, all "writings" " 'prepared for the purpose of, in the course of, or pursuant to, a mediation,' " are confidential and protected from discovery. We explained that the broad definition of "writings" set forth in section 250, and incorporated by express reference into section 1119, subdivision (b), encompasses such materials as charts, diagrams, information compilations, expert reports, photographs of physical conditions, recordings or transcriptions of witness statements, and written or recorded analyses of physical evidence.

. . .

In *Fair*, we construed subdivision (b) of section 1123, which permits disclosure of a written settlement agreement reached in mediation *if*, among other things, " '[t]he agreement provides that it is enforceable or binding *or words to that effect.*' " (Italics added.) "In order to preserve the confidentiality required to protect the mediation process and provide clear drafting guidelines," we held that, to satisfy section 1123, subdivision (b), the written agreement "must *directly express* the parties' agreement to be bound by the document they sign."

. . .

Most recently, in *Simmons*, we held that the judicial doctrines of equitable estoppel and implied waiver are not valid exceptions to the strict technical requirements set forth in the mediation confidentiality statutes for the disclosure and admissibility of oral settlement agreements reached in mediation. (§§ 1118, 1122, subd. (a), 1124.) Thus, we determined, when the plaintiffs sued to enforce an oral mediation agreement the defendant had refused to sign, the plaintiffs could not claim the defendant's pretrial disclosure of the agreement for litigation purposes estopped her from invoking the mediation confidentiality statutes, or constituted a waiver of their requirements.

. . .

Here, as in *Foxgate, Rojas, Fair*, and *Simmons*, the plain language of the mediation confidentiality statutes controls our result. Section 1119, subdivision (a) clearly provides that "[n]o evidence of anything said or any admission made for the purpose of, in the course of, or pursuant to, a mediation . . . is admissible or subject to discovery . . . ." As we noted in *Simmons*, section 1119, adopted in 1997, "is more expansive than its predecessor, former section 1152.5. Section 1119, subdivision (a), extends to oral communications made *for the purpose of* or *pursuant to* a mediation, not just to oral communications made *in the course of* the mediation. . . . The obvious purpose of the expanded language is to ensure that the statutory protection extends beyond discussions carried out directly between the opposing parties to the dispute, or with the mediator, during the mediation proceedings themselves. All oral or written communications are covered, if they are made "for the purpose of" or "pursuant to" a mediation. (§ 1119, subds.(a), (b).) It follows that, absent an express statutory exception, all discussions conducted in preparation for a mediation, as well as all mediation-related communications that take place during the mediation itself, are protected from disclosure. Plainly, such communications include those between a mediation disputant and his or her own counsel, even if these do not occur in the presence of the mediator or other disputants.

. . .

Neither the language nor the purpose of the mediation confidentiality statutes supports a conclusion that they are subject to an exception, similar to that provided for the attorney-client privilege, for lawsuits between attorney and client. The instant Court of Appeal's contrary conclusion is nothing more or less than a judicially crafted exception to the unambiguous language of the mediation confidentiality statutes in order to accommodate a competing policy concern — here, protection of a client's right to sue his or her attorney. We and the Courts of Appeal have consistently disallowed such exceptions, even where the equities appeared to favor them.

. . .

A United States District Court case, *Benesch v. Green* (N.D.Cal.2009) 2009 U.S. Dist. LEXIS 117641 (*Benesch*), more recent than the Court of Appeal decision in this case, supports our analysis . . . In *Benesch*, a mediation disputant sued her attorney, claiming counsel committed malpractice by inducing her, in the mediation, to sign an enforceable "Term Sheet" that failed to meet her aim of ensuring her daughter's inheritance rights. Defendant attorney sought summary judgment, asserting that the client had no case without introducing evidence protected by the mediation confidentiality statutes, including "the legal advice that [counsel] gave to [the client], and the circumstances in which the Term Sheet was executed." (*Id.*, at p. *5.)

The district court denied summary judgment, ruling that it was not absolutely clear the mediation confidentiality statutes left the client without evidence sufficient to prove her case. Nonetheless, the court agreed that the multiple California cases construing the mediation confidentiality statutes, . . . "generally support Defendant's position" that mediation-related communications, including those only between client and counsel, are not subject to disclosure, even when this may inhibit a client's claim that her lawyer committed malpractice.

. . .

As pertinent here, the *Benesch* court declared, "Communications between counsel and client that are materially related to the mediation, even if they are not made to another party or the mediator, are 'for the purpose of' or 'pursuant to' mediation." Indeed, the court noted, if protected communications did not include those *outside* the mediation proceedings, it would be unnecessary and useless for section 1122, subdivision (a)(2) to provide that communications by and between fewer than all participants in a mediation may be disclosed if all such participants agree and " 'the communication . . . does not disclose anything said or done . . . in the course of mediation.' "

We agree with this analysis. We further emphasize that application of the mediation confidentiality statutes to legal malpractice actions does not implicate due process concerns so fundamental that they might warrant an exception on constitutional grounds. Implicit in our decisions in *Foxgate, Rojas, Fair,* and *Simmons* is the premise that the mere loss of evidence pertinent to the prosecution of a lawsuit for civil damages does not implicate such a fundamental interest.

. . .

We therefore conclude that the evidence the trial court ruled nondiscoverable and inadmissible by reason of the mediation confidentiality statutes was not, as a matter of law, excluded from coverage by those statutes on the mere ground that they were private attorney-client communications which occurred outside the presence or hearing of the mediator or any other mediation participant. Instead, such attorney-client communications, like any other communications, were confidential, and therefore were neither discoverable nor admissible — even for purposes of proving a claim of legal malpractice — insofar as they were "for the purpose of, in the course of, or pursuant to, a mediation . . . ." (§ 1119, subd. (a).) By holding otherwise, and thus overturning the trial court's exclusionary order, the Court of Appeal erred. We must therefore reverse the Court of Appeal's judgment.

## CONCLUSION

The Court of Appeal's judgment is reversed.

WE CONCUR: Kennard, Acting C.J., Werdegar, Moreno, Corrigan, JJ., and George, J.


Chin, J.

I concur in the result, but reluctantly.

The court holds today that private communications between an attorney and a client related to mediation remain confidential even in a lawsuit between the two. This holding will effectively shield an attorney's actions during mediation, including advising the client, from a malpractice action even if those actions are incompetent or even deceptive . . . . This is a high price to pay to preserve total confidentiality in the mediation process.

I greatly sympathize with the Court of Appeal majority's attempt to interpret the statutory language as not mandating confidentiality in this situation. But, for the reasons the present majority gives, I do not believe the attempt quite succeeds.

. . .

. . . I agree with the majority that we have to give effect to the literal statutory language. But I am not completely satisfied that the Legislature has fully considered whether attorneys should be shielded from accountability in this way. There may be better ways to balance the competing interests than simply providing that an attorney's statements during mediation may never be disclosed. For example, it may be appropriate to provide that communications during mediation may be used in a malpractice action between an attorney and a client to the extent they are relevant to that action, but they may not be used by anyone for any other purpose. Such a provision might sufficiently protect other participants in the mediation and also make attorneys accountable for their actions. But this court cannot so hold in the guise of interpreting statutes that contain no such provision. As the majority notes, the Legislature remains free to reconsider this question. It may well wish to do so.

This case does not present the question of what happens if every participant in the mediation *except the attorney* waives confidentiality. Could the attorney even then prevent disclosure so as to be immune from a malpractice action? I can imagine no valid policy reason for the Legislature to shield attorneys even in that situation. I doubt greatly that one of the Legislature's purposes in mandating confidentiality was to permit attorneys to commit malpractice without accountability. Interpreting the statute to require confidentiality even when everyone but the attorney has waived it might well result in absurd consequences that the Legislature did not intend. That question will have to await another case. But the Legislature might also want to consider this point.

## NOTES AND QUESTIONS

(1) This excerpt from the *Cassel* decision, and the other cases referenced in *Cassel* (*Foxgate*, *Rojas*, *Fair*, and *Simmons*), demonstrate that the Supreme Court of California has been very strict in interpreting California's statutory framework for protecting mediation confidentiality. However, as Justice Chin points out in the concurrence to *Cassel*, there are policy arguments for a less strict interpretation of a mediation confidentiality statute. One of those, as this case demonstrates, is legal malpractice. Are there any other situations where confidentiality in mediation may compromise a party's interests?

(2) In her article, *Musings on Mediation, Kleenex, and (Smudged) White Hats*, 33 U. La Verne L. Rev. 5 (2011), Professor Nancy A. Welsh warns that a stringent approach to confidentiality in mediation can lead to exploitation of the non-discoverability and inadmissibility of mediation communications to keep disputants from reaching resolutions or accessing the courts if something goes awry:

> I cannot help but notice the emergence of a line of cases involving allegations of misbehavior in mediation — particularly misbehavior by lawyers. Further, I cannot help but notice the defendant-lawyers asserting the mediation privilege against their own clients, in order to keep them from introducing evidence that might help to prove claims of legal malpractice. In other words, these lawyers are using mediation to prevent potential litigants from accessing the very forum that lawyers are supposed to hold most dear — the public courtroom . . .

> [I]t seems indisputable that mediation is sometimes being used inappropriately: to shield lawyers from potential claims of malpractice; to force parties to settle when they would rather go to trial; and even to find a back door means to fund the staff that courts can no longer afford to hire themselves. . . . We are inviting scandal — and then "reform" by those who may not be friends of our process.

Are Professor Welsh's concerns well founded?

## C. CONTRACT

Many mediators seek to establish confidentiality by having the parties sign a confidentiality agreement prior to the mediation session. A sample agreement is reproduced below. Beyond the potential legal benefits of having contracted for confidentiality, are there other advantages to having the parties sign an agreement? Does it assist in educating the parties about the importance of keeping mediation communications confidential?

### CONFIDENTIALITY AGREEMENT OF RODNEY MAX
Reprinted in ADR Personalities and Practice Tips (1998) at 236*
By James J. Alfini & Eric Galton

This is an agreement by the parties to submit to mediation concerning _____. We understand that mediation is a voluntary process, which we may terminate at any time.

In order to promote communication among the parties, counsel and the mediator, and to facilitate settlement of the dispute, each of the undersigned agrees that all statements made during the course of the mediation are privileged settlement discussions, are made without prejudice to any party's legal position, and are inadmissible for any purpose in any legal proceeding. Any information disclosed by a party, or by a witness on behalf of a party, is confidential.

Each party agrees to make no attempt to compel the mediator's testimony, nor to compel the mediator to produce any documents provided by the other party to the mediator. In no event will the mediator disclose confidential information provided during the course of mediation, testify voluntarily on behalf of either party, or submit any type of report to any court in connection with this case. The mediator may find it helpful to meet with each party separately; in this event, the mediator will not reveal what is said by one participant to the other(s) without permission.

The parties and, if they desire, their representatives, are invited to attend mediation sessions. No one else may attend without the permission of the parties and the consent of the mediator.

We agree to pay fees at the rate of $_____ per hour for all time spent on this matter, plus any out-of-pocket costs. We have agreed to divide this fee equally between the parties.

We agree that the mediator has the discretion to terminate mediation at any time if mediator believes that the case is inappropriate for mediation or that an impasse has been reached.

Signature:
Representing: Signature: Representing:

---

* Copyright © 1998 by American Bar Association. Reprinted with permission.

## NOTE

Although many mediators have the parties sign confidentiality agreements, the courts may be somewhat timid if asked to enforce a confidentiality agreement. Enforcement is generally sought to preserve the confidentiality of a mediation communication, thus preventing the introduction of evidence that may be seen as crucial to deciding a particular case. However, such a result would go against the general policy that frowns on agreements to exclude evidence. Consider how this policy intersects with Rule 408 of the Federal Rules of Evidence, discussed in the next section.

## D.   EVIDENTIARY EXCLUSIONS

### 1.   Introduction

As the court points out in *Macaluso, supra*, the mediator was "the one person whose testimony could have resolved the factual dispute." Yet, the court upheld the revocation of the subpoena of the mediator because "the complete exclusion of the mediator testimony is necessary to the preservation of an effective system of labor mediation." Thus, the court found that the strong policy reasons for preserving mediation confidentiality overrode the similarly strong policy that one is entitled to "every person's evidence." Similarly, Rule 408 of the Federal Rules of Evidence, as reproduced in the *Denture Cream* case, *infra*, excludes from evidence certain communications made during settlement negotiations, reflecting a strong policy of encouraging the settlement of court cases. Most states have similar provisions in their evidence codes. As you read the materials below, consider how far Rule 408 protections extend. For example, would the testimony excluded by the *Macaluso* or *Cassel* courts have been excluded by Rule 408?

### 2.   Federal Rules of Evidence, Rule 408. Compromise Offers and Negotiation

**(a) Prohibited Uses.** Evidence of the following is not admissible — on behalf of any party — either to prove or disprove the validity or amount of a disputed claim or to impeach by a prior inconsistent statement or a contraction:

(1) furnishing, promising, or offering — or accepting, promising to accept, or offering to accept — a valuable consideration in compromising or attempting to compromise the claim; and

(2) conduct or a statement made during compromise negotiations about the claim — except when offered in a criminal case and when the negotiations related to a claim by a public office in the exercise of its regulatory, investigative, or enforcement authority.

**(b) Exceptions.** The court may admit this evidence for another purpose, such as proving a witness's bias or prejudice, negating a contention of undue delay, or proving an effort to obstruct a criminal investigation or prosecution.

## CONFIDENTIALITY, PRIVILEGE AND RULE 408: THE PROTECTION OF MEDIATION PROCEEDINGS IN FEDERAL COURT
60 La. L. Rev. 91, 102–08 (1999)*
By Charles W. Ehrhardt

The policy of fostering free and frank discussions in negotiations which lead to settlement and compromise of actions prior to trial is recognized in Federal Rule of Evidence 408.

. . .

Many jurisdictions at common law limited the protection of the exclusionary rule only to the offers of settlement themselves and not to statements of fact or admissions of fault which were made during the settlement negotiations. However, the drafters of the Federal Rules rejected this distinction on the basis that such a limitation in Rule 408 would hamper "free communication between parties." There would be "an unjustifiable restraint upon efforts to negotiate settlements" and that continuing to recognize this distinction would be "a preference for the sophisticated, and a trap for the unwary."[40]

Two theories have provided a rationale for the rule that offers of settlement and compromise are inadmissible on the issue of liability for the underlying claim. Wigmore's view is that an offer of compromise is not motivated from a belief that the adversary's claim is well-founded but rather a desire for peace. Therefore, he argues that the offer of compromise is not relevant because it does not signify an admission. There is no express or implied concession by a party when a offer is made.

Most modern commentators argue that the justification for the rule excluding offers of compromise is not relevance, but one of evidentiary privilege. This rationale recognizes the strong public policy favoring negotiated dispute resolution requires that offers of compromise be made without fear the offer will be used against the offeror.

. . .

No specific statute or court-rule is necessary for Rule 408 to be applicable in mediation proceedings, regardless of whether the mediation is voluntary or court-ordered. Mediations involve statements made during attempts to settle or compromise a claim. However, some district court local rules as well as some states have specifically adopted a provision which applies Rule 408 to mediation proceedings, probably as a reminder to counsel and the parties.

### B. Inapplicability

Rule 408 precludes the admission at trial of evidence of settlement negotiations which are offered to prove liability for the underlying claim. The second sentence of

---

[40] S. Rep. No. 93-1277 at 10 (1974).

Rule 408 cautions that documents presented during settlement negotiations are not protected simply because they were so presented. In other words, the rule is not a shield behind which one can divulge pre-existing documents during settlement discussions or negotiations and have them protected from admissibility during trial.

The rule does not prohibit discovery of matters pertaining to the settlement negotiations. However, because a party is aware of the statements made by the opponent during the negotiations or the joint sessions, the availability of discovery is not as significant as it is when the party is unaware of the evidence. Although Rule 408 does not prohibit discovery of an opponent's communications regarding negotiation strategies, Rule 26(c) of the Rules of Civil Procedure as well as the attorney-client privilege and the work product doctrine may be applicable to protect these discussions.

Rule 408 is only applicable when the offer of compromise is offered to prove liability. The final sentence of Rule 408 provides that the rule does not require the exclusion of evidence relating to settlement offers when it is offered for another purpose, "such as proving bias or prejudice of a witness, negativing a contention of undue delay, or proving an effort to obstruct a criminal investigation or prosecution." This sentence illustrates some of the purposes for which the rule would not exclude evidence; it is not an exclusive listing.

## 1. Bias or Prejudice

If a witness testifies during a trial, the cross-examining counsel may attack the credibility by showing a relevant bias, prejudice or interest. Evidence of a settlement agreement involving the witness is admissible when it is relevant to show the bias of the witness when testifying in the instant case. The language of Rule 408 does not prohibit admission of the evidence since it is not offered to show the validity or invalidity of the underlying claim. The second sentence of Rule 408 specifically recognizes that evidence of the prior settlement may be admitted to show bias. The details of the settlement agreement are subject to a Rule 403 balancing, as are the details of other evidence being offered to attack credibility by showing bias.

## 2. Act or Wrong Committed During Settlement Negotiations

When the question is not the validity or invalidity of the underlying claim, but rather a material issue of an act which occurred during the negotiations, Rule 408 does not prohibit the admission of evidence. For example, when an alleged wrong is committed during the negotiations; e.g., libel, assault, breach of contract, or unfair labor practice, the evidence of statements made during negotiations is not being offered to prove the liability for the underlying claim and is not prohibited. Wrongful acts are not protected simply because they occurred during settlement discussion. The rule excluding settlement offers and discussions was not intended to be a shield for the commission of independent wrongs. So too, if a suit alleging that an insurance company failed to make a reasonable settlement within the policy limits, either the insured or the insurance company can offer evidence of the settlement offers that were made during the negotiations.

### 3. Impeachment

If a party testifies during the trial, a statement of fact made by the party during settlement negotiations may be offered as a prior inconsistent statement to impeach credibility. Applying the literal language of Rule 408, the evidence is not barred because the evidence of the prior statement is not offered to prove the validity or invalidity of its claim. This interpretation is bolstered by the policy that the rules of evidence should not be a shield to commit perjury. On the other hand, if a party's statements made during settlement negotiations are admissible to impeach whenever they are inconsistent with the party's trial testimony, the freedom of discussion in settlement negotiations will be inhibited. The few cases facing this issue are not in agreement. Most commentators assume that there are, at least, some cases where the interests of justice compel the introduction of prior inconsistent statements made during settlement discussions.

. . . In at least a few cases, statements made during a mediation may be admissible as prior inconsistent statements to impeach a witness who testifies during a trial to material facts which are inconsistent with what the party stated during the mediation. Even though Rule 408 does not protect certain statements made during mediation, a district court's local rule may protect confidentiality.

## IN RE DENTURE CREAM PRODUCTS LIABILITY LITIGATION
United States District Court for the Southern District of Florida
2011 U.S. Dist. LEXIS 59202 (May 20, 2011)

Andrea M. Simonton, United States Magistrate Judge.

This Multi-District Litigation involves claims by numerous Plaintiffs alleging primarily neurological injuries purportedly caused by the ingestion and/or use of denture cream products manufactured, labeled or distributed by various Defendants including The Procter & Gamble Distributing LLC's and The Procter & Gamble Manufacturing Company (collectively "Procter & Gamble"). While the claims raised by the individual Plaintiffs vary, generally, Plaintiffs assert causes of action sounding in strict products liability, negligence, intentional and negligent misrepresentation, breach of warranty and failure to warn.

At issue in the current Motion is whether a subpoena to produce documents issued by Plaintiffs to Carlile Craig, LLP, a Texas based law firm, should be quashed. The Carlile Craig firm previously represented Laura Day, a Plaintiff in an action similar to the one at bar against Defendants Procter & Gamble. By all accounts, the action between Ms. Day and Procter & Gamble was settled after mediation occurred between those parties. That settlement yielded a Settlement Agreement and General Release which contained a confidentiality provision between Ms. Day and Procter & Gamble.

The Carlile subpoena at issue, herein, sought the following documents related to that litigation:

1. Any and all non-privileged and non-attorney work product documents or

communications maintained, received, created, or sent by Carlile Craig, LLP whether to, from, or among Defendants or any third party, or maintained internally by Carlile Craig, LLP relating to:

　　a. Any Deposition in *Day v. Procter & Gamble Distributing LLC*, Case No: 5:07-cv-00120-DF (E.D.Tex.2007) ("Day");

　　b. The identity of any and all court reporters or transcription services used during any and all depositions in Day;

　　c. Laura Day's medical condition relayed to the P & G Defendants, or any other defendant, in Day;

　　d. Any information provided to or received from the P & G Defendants including but not limited to, pre-litigation demands made in Day.

Defendants have now moved to quash the subpoena issued to the Carlile firm ("Carlile subpoena") asserting that any documents relating to the settlement and mediation in the *Day* case are not discoverable. Specifically, Defendants cite to Federal Rule of Evidence 804 for support of its contention that mediation and settlement materials, as well as the confidential Settlement Agreement between the Parties are not discoverable because they are not admissible at trial and are not likely to lead to the discovery of admissible evidence as contemplated by Rule of Civil Procedure 26.

In the written Response to the Motion, Plaintiffs asserted that the information requested is relevant to prove Defendants' prior notice of the allegations raised in this litigation. Specifically, Plaintiffs contended that the *Day* materials likely would show that by at least August 2007, Defendants knew or had reason to know that consumers were using excessive amounts of one of the denture-related products manufactured by Defendants which could lead to neurological injuries. Thus, Plaintiffs asserted they were entitled to the subpoenaed materials pursuant to Fed.R.Civ. Pro. 26 and Fed.R.Evid. 401, 403 and 408(a) because Plaintiffs sought to use the documents to prove notice by the Defendants rather than proving liability, which rendered the document admissible under Federal Rule of Evidence 408(a) and Florida Statute 90.408.

Also, Plaintiffs argued that the confidentiality agreement between the Parties in the *Day* matter did not prevent the discovery of the Settlement Agreement in this case. Further, Plaintiffs contended that the Case Management and Protective Orders in this case place significant limitations on the disclosure and usage of materials and thus address the confidentiality concerns raised by Defendants. In addition, Plaintiffs have agreed to have the dollar amount of the settlement redacted.

At the hearing on the Motion to Quash, Plaintiffs' Counsel clarified that he was not seeking the production of work product materials. Rather, Counsel asserted that Plaintiffs were seeking to discover mediation documents demonstrating Proctor & Gamble's response to the medical literature that discussed the toxicity of the denture product at issue. Counsel thus asserted that such documents were relevant for establishing Defendant's knowledge of scientific literature regarding the products at that time. Similarly, Plaintiffs' Counsel argued that the Settlement

Agreement and mediation materials from the *Day* litigation would demonstrate that the Defendant was on notice of the claims being made related to the denture products. Finally, Plaintiffs made clear that although they were not seeking production of any offers of settlement made by Procter & Gamble in the *Day* matter, that they were seeking to discover settlement demands and damage calculations made by the Plaintiff in that case on the theory that this could demonstrate Defendants' knowledge of the severity of the claims and put them on notice of the need for further investigation.

In response, at the hearing, Defendants asserted that the Settlement Agreement has no probative value because it only sets forth the terms of the settlement between the Parties, and thus would not lead to the discovery of admissible evidence related to the claim. In addition, Defendant argued that the amount of the damages requested and/or set forth in mediation materials by the Plaintiff in the *Day* matter was not relevant because those amounts merely represented claims made by the *Day* Plaintiff and did not necessarily reflect the value of the case. Finally, Defendant argued that Plaintiffs did not need any of the mediation materials because those materials had already been produced to the extent that they bore on the merits of their claims.

Mr. Carlile of Carlile Craig, LLP attended the hearing on the Motion to Quash and explained that the materials in his possession from the mediation held in the *Day* matter consisted of a binder that he had created, containing various mediation related documents, including a demand letter which set forth the damages and the calculations of those damages sought by Ms. Day related to the litigation. Mr. Carlile further indicated that neither he nor Ms. Day objected to the production of any of the mediation materials, other than their need to comply with the confidentiality requirement of their Settlement Agreement.

Finally, the hearing also addressed the discovery request for Procter & Gamble to produce the copy of the mediation materials received by it in the *Day* matter. In this regard, the same arguments were made by the Parties. Plaintiffs asserted that they wanted the materials to avoid any dispute regarding whether Procter & Gamble received the materials which the Plaintiff in *Day* claimed to have produced.

. . .

As stated above, in their Motion and at the hearing, Defendants contended that the mediation and settlement materials from the *Day* matter should not be discoverable in this action because those documents are not admissible under Federal Rule of Evident 408(a). However, Plaintiffs countered that the documents were sought, not for purposes of establishing Defendants' liability, but to demonstrate Defendants' notice of both potential claims regarding the products at issue, as well as, Defendants' knowledge of the state of scientific, medical literature regarding the toxicity of certain products.

At the hearing, the undersigned concluded that the Plaintiffs sufficiently demonstrated that the mediation documents and the Settlement Agreement could be relevant or lead to the discovery of relevant evidence. As such, as ruled at the hearing, pursuant to Federal Rule of Civil Procedure 26, Plaintiffs are entitled to discover those materials. Also, it bears noting that Carlile Craig, LLP, the entity subpoenaed, has no objection to producing the documents and there has been no showing of undue hardship or burdensomeness related to the production of those materials. In fact, they are contained, in substantial part, in a single binder.

In addition, Federal Rule of Evidence 408 clearly only limits the use of such evidence at trial when it is offered to prove liability. While the undersigned makes no determination regarding whether the mediation and settlement materials sought by Plaintiffs will be admissible at the trial of any of the MDL cases, there has been no showing that the Settlement Agreement and mediation materials are irrelevant to other issues in this case, beyond establishing Defendants' liability.

. . .

[A]s ruled at the hearing by the undersigned, Rule 408 does not bar the discovery of the mediation and settlement materials at issue. . . . [The court] concludes that the Confidentiality Agreement in the *Day* matter does not preclude discovery of the Settlement Agreement herein, particularly because there is a thorough and comprehensive Confidentiality and Protective Order in place in this case.

Therefore, for the reasons stated above and based upon the Parties' submissions, the arguments of counsel at the hearing on the Motion, and a review of the record as a whole, and as ruled at the hearing on the Motion to Quash, it is

**ORDERED AND ADJUDGED** that The Procter & Gamble Distributing LLC's and The Procter & Gamble Manufacturing Company's Motion to Quash Subpoena is **DENIED**, to the extent Defendants seek to quash that portion of the subpoena related to the production of mediation and settlement materials, including the Settlement Agreement, from the *Laura Day v. The Procter & Gamble Manufacturing Company and Procter & Gamble Distributing Company*, Case No. 5:07-cv-00120 (E.D.Tex.) matter. Accordingly, Carlile Craig, LLP shall produce the mediation binder and other materials used in the *Day* matter, including the Settlement Agreement, with the settlement amounts redacted, as well as any other materials received from Procter & Gamble related to the mediation, on or before the close of business on Tuesday, May 24, 2011.

In addition, as ruled at the hearing, the Procter & Gamble Defendants shall produce any non-privileged, mediation materials provided to those Defendants by the firm of Carlile Craig, LLP related to the mediation and settlement in the matter of *Laura Day v. The Procter & Gamble Manufacturing Company and Procter & Gamble Distributing Company*, Case No. 5:07-cv-00120 (E.D.Tex.) matter, with settlement amounts redacted, on or before Tuesday, May 24, 2011.

## NOTES AND QUESTIONS

(1) Professor Ehrhardt points out that Rule 408 is only applicable to communications that are offered to prove liability and discusses some of the other evidentiary purposes for which a particular communication would not be shielded by Rule 408. Professor Alan Kirtley describes these limitations as a "weakness" of Rule 408: "Since mediation discussions tend to be free flowing and often unguarded, revelations later serving as impeachment, bias or 'another purpose' evidence are likely. The 'another purpose' clause in the hands of creative counsel leaves little in

mediation definitely exempt from disclosure." Kirtley also points out that Rule 408 offers no protection against *discovery* of mediation discussions or against their admission in proceedings that are not governed by the rules of evidence such as administrative hearings and criminal cases. He thus concludes that Rule 408 is no substitute for a mediation privilege: "A mediation privilege should be of broad unambiguous scope, bar discovery, and exclude evidence in all types of proceedings." Alan Kirtley, *The Mediation Privilege's Transition from Theory to Implementation: Designing a Mediation Privilege Standard to Protect Mediation Participants, the Process and the Public Interest*, 1995 J. Disp. Resol. 1, 11–14.

(2)   The federal court's reasoning in refusing to grant the motion to quash the subpoena in the *Denture Cream* case also demonstrates the limitations of Rule 408. Although the court's interpretation of Rule 408 and the related federal rules seems clear, why did the court refuse to give effect to the confidentiality agreement? Does it reflect a judicial bias against agreements to exclude evidence? If so, does this reinforce the argument for the kind of mediation privilege presented in the next section?

## E.  PRIVILEGE

While the federal government and many states have enacted numerous laws to protect the confidentiality of mediation communications from use in subsequent proceedings, this legislative activity has resulted in a hodgepodge of statutory formulations. To insure that confidentiality will be handled uniformly across all U.S. jurisdictions, the National Conference of Commissioners on Uniform State Laws (NCCUSL) and the American Bar Association (ABA) undertook the drafting of a Uniform Mediation Act. The drafting committee of the NCCUSL/ABA Uniform Mediation Act chose an *evidentiary privilege* as the means of assuring confidentiality. The relevant UMA provisions are reprinted below, preceded by Professor Alan Kirtley's article outlining the contours of an effective mediation privilege.

The cases excerpted following the UMA provisions illustrate that the federal cases seeking to determine whether there is a federal mediation privilege have been inconsistent at best. Similarly, the cases interpreting mediation privilege statutes have not always been in accord with regard to the scope of the privilege.

# THE MEDIATION PRIVILEGE'S TRANSITION FROM THEORY TO IMPLEMENTATION: DESIGNING A MEDIATION PRIVILEGE STANDARD TO PROTECT MEDIATION PARTICIPANTS, THE PROCESS, AND THE PUBLIC INTEREST

1995 J. Disp. Resol. 1, 20, 24–35[*]

By Alan Kirtley

With mediation so widely practiced in varying forms, the initial challenge is crafting a mediation privilege which is neither over-inclusive nor under-inclusive. The ideal statute would cover mediations where confidentiality is intended by the participants, the mediation is conducted by a qualified mediator and the privilege is justified as a matter of public policy.

. . .

Once a mediation falls within the privilege, care must be taken to ensure that the entire process receives the privilege's protection (from the first intake call to the exit interview). Protection is especially needed for the sensitive information that is often disclosed by prospective mediation clients to program staff during intake interviews. Many statutes are vulnerable to narrow interpretation because they do not define the mediation process, define it vaguely with terms like "mediation," "resolution process," or limit the protection to information disclosed "during" or "in the course of" mediation or only when the mediator is present. Such statutes put into question the confidentiality of intake, inter-session and exit interview communications.

The Washington statute contains the phrase "any communication made or materials submitted in, or in connection with, the mediation proceeding."[170] The word "proceeding" encompasses the whole of the mediation process, similar to the word "case" in the litigation context. To add clarity some statutes specifically state that the mediation process commences with initial intake discussions, spans multiple sessions and ends only with resolution or termination.

## B. Persons Covered by the Privilege

Mediators, mediation parties, the parties' lawyers and the staff of mediation organizations are involved in mediation. Others may be present during a mediation session: a party's family members or "support persons," staff members and outside consultants of an organizational party, "witnesses," mediator trainees and other observers. Once a mediation falls within the privilege there is no policy justification for allowing disclosure of information acquired during mediation by anyone. Everyone with access to mediation information should be "burdened" by the privilege.

Statutes vary in their effectiveness on this issue. Those that name no one risk an

---

[170] Wash. Rev. Code 5.60.070(1) (Supp. 1994).

interpretation that the mediation privilege is limited to those in the "professional relationship," the parties and the mediator, leaving others present free to disclose or subject to subpoena. Other statutes which name only the parties, the mediator or both may limit the reach of the privilege to those named. The same result could occur with statutes that use the word "participants." Several statutes extend to all persons present. For example, the Washington statute places the burden of the privilege on "the mediator, a mediation organization, a party or any person present." By specifically listing all who may have access to information arising out of a mediation proceeding, the Washington statute ensures comprehensive protection against disclosure. It also eliminates the argument that confidentiality is waived by the presence of persons other than the mediator and the parties.

### C. Later Proceedings in Which the Privilege Will Be Effective

Crafting a mediation privilege statute also involves considering the subsequent proceedings in which the privilege will apply. Traditionally, confidential information protected by a privilege is exempt from discovery and barred from evidence in civil and criminal actions. Mediation privilege provisions have taken differing approaches. Many are silent or list only "civil" cases. Other statutes extend the privilege to "civil and criminal," "any proceeding," "any subsequent legal proceeding," "judicial or administrative proceeding" or other proceedings.

Statutes referencing "civil and criminal" are consistent with existing privilege law and will undoubtedly be interpreted to extend to such actions. Judicial treatment is less certain for silent statutes and those using vague phrases: "any proceeding" and "any subsequent proceeding." However, if the state involved has a counterpart to Federal Evidence Rule 1101(c), then the rule of privilege will apply to "all stages of all actions, cases, and proceedings." Statutes limiting the privilege to civil cases may reflect a policy judgment that the criminal justice system's need for access to mediation information out-weighs the benefit of preserving mediation confidentiality. A narrower policy consideration may be to protect the safety of those involved in mediation or threatened third parties. The latter concern is better addressed through specific exceptions to the mediation privilege. Mediation privileges which do not apply to criminal cases are inconsistent with traditional privileges and produce a chilling effect upon mediation discussions. Such statutes are particularly onerous in jurisdictions with programs for mediating criminal complaints. Such programs cannot operate unless the accused is assured mediation communications will be barred from the criminal trial. This reality was recognized by the Georgia Court of Appeals in *Byrd v. State*,[200] which, in the absence of a privilege statute, held that a mediation settlement agreement from a criminal diversion program was not admissible in the accused's subsequent criminal prosecution as an admission of guilt. In reaching this result, the Georgia Court of Appeals stated:

> By allowing this alternative dispute resolution effort to be evidenced in the subsequent criminal trial, the trial court's ruling eliminates its usefulness. For no criminal defendant will agree to "work things out" and compromise

---

[200] 367 S.E.2d 300 (Ga. App. Ct. 1988).

his position if he knows that any inference of responsibility arising from what he says and does in the mediation process will be admissible as an admission of guilt in the criminal proceeding which will eventualize if mediation fails.

Even in mediations not directly involving a criminal complaint — family matters, neighborhood disputes and business situations — mediation discussions will be restricted if the parties learn that what they say or submit may be used later in a criminal courtroom.

Statutes, such as Washington's, which extend the privilege to "any judicial or administrative proceeding" properly protect mediation communications from use in criminal cases. They also recognize the prevalence of administrative justice in our contemporary legal system and the need to exclude privileged mediation communications from administrative hearings.

## D. Holders of the Privilege

A critical task of any mediation privilege law is establishing who holds the right to assert or waive the privilege (i.e., a "holder" of the privilege). Holder status varies in the traditional privileges. With the attorney-client and physician-patient privileges the protection of the client/patient disclosure is paramount. Therefore, only the client/patient holds the privilege. In contrast, under the traditional rule husbands and wives are joint holders of the spousal privilege. Each spouse retains control over disclosures by the other.

With respect to the cleric-penitent privilege, statutes vary as to whether the penitent, the cleric, or both are holders of the privilege. In some jurisdictions the cleric may refuse to testify even if the penitent has waived the privilege in deference to the cleric's religious obligation not to discuss confidential communications.

The mediation process presents a unique context for the operation of an evidentiary privilege. Rather than the usual bilateral relationship in traditional privileges, mediation always involves at least three persons: the mediator and two parties. Additionally, two distinct relationships are at work simultaneously in a mediation: a professional relationship between the mediator and each of the parties, and a confidential relationship between the parties. Both relationships generate distinct interests in preserving confidentiality.

Generally, the parties and the mediator share a common interest in maintaining the confidentiality of mediation communications. However, after a failed mediation, interests may diverge as to whether mediation communications ought to be disclosed. Each of the participants — the mediator or either of the parties — in different circumstances may wish to maintain confidentiality, or discover or introduce mediation information in a later proceeding. A mediation privilege must rationally reconcile these potentially competing interests in an unambiguous fashion.

Special care must be taken to protect the role of the mediator. Preserving confidences in order to maintain neutrality is elemental for mediators. As a result, mediators regularly refuse to be the "tie-breaking" witness in a subsequent proceeding, even when the parties so desire. Mediator testimony inevitably leads to one of the parties viewing the mediator as biased. Moreover, if mediator testimony becomes commonplace, the public is likely to form the undesirable perception that the particular mediator or the mediation process does not protect confidences. These important policy considerations were recognized by the Ninth Circuit Court of Appeals in *NLRB v. Macaluso, Inc.* The court stated:

> However useful the testimony of a conciliator might be . . . in any given case, . . . the conciliators must maintain a reputation for impartiality, and the parties to conciliation conferences must feel free to talk without any fear that the conciliator may subsequently make disclosures as a witness in some other proceeding, to the possible disadvantage of a party to the conference. If conciliators were permitted or required to testify about their activities, or if the production of notes or reports of their activities could be required, not even the strictest adherence to purely factual matters would prevent the evidence from favoring or seeming to favor one side or the other.[214]

Subjecting mediators and mediation organization records to subpoena disrupts the delivery of mediation services. This is particularly true for community dispute resolution centers which rely heavily on volunteers. Fighting off subpoenas, the usual response in these cases, is time-consuming, costly and anxiety-provoking. The limited situations in which a mediator may feel compelled to breach confidentiality irrespective of party preferences, such as to protect a vulnerable person or to prevent an injustice, can be accommodated through exceptions to the privilege. For these reasons, a mediation privilege statute should give the mediator holder status which is independent from that of the parties.

As with other aspects of the mediation privilege, statutes vary vastly as to their treatment of this important issue. Some statutes are silent as to who holds the privilege. Others assign the rights to assert and/or waive the privilege to the parties only, the mediator only, or the parties and the mediator as joint holders. A small group of statutes bifurcates the "holder" status by assigning separate rights to the parties and the mediator.

*Silent Statutes:* A silent statute can be expected to generate confusion in the tripartite setting of mediation. In one case, a silent statute has been interpreted to be non-waivable by the mediation parties.

*Party-Holder Statutes:* Statutes making parties exclusive holders of the mediation privilege are in accordance with traditional privilege law. Mediation parties as clients of the mediation professional exercise the privilege rights, as do clients and patients of attorneys and physicians under those privileges. Also, mediation parties exercise holder rights jointly because their special confidential relationship is analogous to the marital privilege. Party-holder statutes are also consistent with mediation ideology that lodges decision-making power with the parties. While the joint party-holder approach is appropriate with respect to *party* disclosures, the mediator is afforded no means to resist compelled testimony. Such statutes undervalue

---

[214] 618 F.2d 51, 55 (9th Cir. 1980).

the critical interest of preserving perceptions of mediator neutrality for all parties in individual cases and the public at large.

*Mediator-Only-Holder Statutes:* Statutes vesting "holder" rights exclusively in the mediator are consistent with the cleric-penitent privilege in a few jurisdictions, but an inversion of traditional privilege rights as to other privileges based on a professional relationship. The mediator is given sole authority to assert or waive the privilege. Mediation clients lose all control over disclosure decisions, even when all are agreeable to disclosure. Party preferences become legally irrelevant as to communications involving their privacy interests. Also, this type of statute invites undesirable lobbying of the mediator by a party wanting to disclose mediation communications. The mediator will make an enemy of one of the parties no matter what she does. The limited benefit of such statutes is that the parties cannot force *mediator* disclosures. Less restrictive alternatives exist to accomplish that result.

*Joint-Holder Statutes:* Statutes making the mediator and the parties joint holders of the privilege ostensibly balance the power to assert or waive the privilege. Mediators have the means to avoid compelled testimony; parties may assert the privilege against a mediator who has decided to disclose mediation information. However, joint-holder provisions have the potential for causing stalemate. While the mediator no longer holds absolute power under a joint-holder statute, she effectively has veto power over parties' disclosures. A mediator is unlikely to join in a waiver of the privilege to permit party disclosures if the result is that she may be called to testify. This statutory scheme also encourages parties to lobby the mediator. One party may seek a mediator's vote for disclosure as a means of convincing the other party to agree to waive confidentiality. Joint-holder provisions represent little improvement over other statutes examined to this point.

*Bifurcated-Holder Statutes:* Another approach to addressing the differing interests of the mediator and mediation parties with respect to disclosure of mediation information has been to bifurcate holder rights. Such statutes recognize that party disclosures should be solely within party control, free of mediator interference. Equally important, mediators are given the means to avoid compelled testimony. A few states have enacted statutes with bifurcated holder rights.

The Washington statute is an example of the bifurcated model. The privilege is waived as to *party* disclosures if all the parties agree in writing. The mediator has no control over *party* disclosures. *Mediator* disclosures, however, require the joint consent of the parties *and* the mediator. The effect of the statute is that a mediator may not disclose confidential mediation information without party approval, nor may the parties compel mediator testimony.

Bifurcated statutes fulfill the critically important function of protecting the mediator from being the forced "tie-breaker" witness. While parties may not compel mediator testimony under a bifurcated statute, their loss is limited. Parties who agree to disclosure may themselves testify freely as to what was said and done at the mediation. At the same time, each party as an independent holder of the privilege may block both *party* and *mediator* testimony. Bifurcated provisions properly balance the interests of preserving mediator neutrality and providing parties with significant control over the disclosure of mediation information.

## UNIFORM MEDIATION ACT
National Conference of Commissioners on Uniform State Laws and the American Bar Association*

**SECTION 2.  DEFINITIONS.** In this [Act]:

(1) "Mediation" means a process in which a mediator facilitates communication and negotiation between parties to assist them in reaching a voluntary agreement regarding their dispute.

(2) "Mediation communication" means a statement, whether oral or in a record or verbal or nonverbal, that occurs during a mediation or is made for purposes of considering, conducting, participating in, initiating, continuing, or reconvening a mediation or retaining a mediator.

(3) "Mediator" means an individual who conducts a mediation.

. . . .

(7) "Proceeding" means:

(A) a judicial, administrative, arbitral, or other adjudicative process, including related pre-hearing and post-hearing motions, conferences, and discovery; or

(B) a legislative hearing or similar process.

(8) "Record" means information that is inscribed on a tangible medium or that is stored in an electronic or other medium and is retrievable in perceivable form.

## SECTION 3.  SCOPE.

(a) Except as otherwise provided in subsection (b) or (c), this [Act] applies to a mediation in which:

(1) the mediation parties are required to mediate by statute or court or administrative agency rule or referred to mediation by a court, administrative agency, or arbitrator;

(2) the mediation parties and the mediator agree to mediate in a record that demonstrates an expectation that mediation communications will be privileged against disclosure; or

(3) the mediation parties use as a mediator an individual who holds himself or

---

* Copyright © 2001 by National Conference of Commissioners on Uniform State Laws. Reprinted with permission. Drafted by the National Conference of Commissioners on Uniform State Laws and by it approved and recommended for enactment in all states at its annual conference meeting in its one-hundred-and-tenth year, White Sulphur Springs, West Virginia, August 10-17 2001. Approved by the American Bar Association House of Delegates, Philadelphia, Pennsylvania, February 4, 2002. Reprinted with notes and official comments at 2003 Journal of Dispute Resolution 1-60.

herself out as a mediator or the mediation is provided by a person that holds itself out as providing mediation.

(b) The [Act] does not apply to a mediation:

(1) relating to the establishment, negotiation, administration, or termination of a collective bargaining relationship;

(2) relating to a dispute that is pending under or is part of the processes established by a collective bargaining agreement, except that the [Act] applies to a mediation arising out of a dispute that has been filed with an administrative agency or court;

(3) conducted by a judge who might make a ruling on the case; or

(4) conducted under the auspices of:

(A) a primary or secondary school if all the parties are students or

(B) a correctional institution for youths if all the parties are residents of that institution.

(c) If the parties agree in advance in a signed record, or a record of proceeding reflects agreement by the parties, that all or part of a mediation is not privileged, the privileges under Sections 4 through 6 do not apply to the mediation or part agreed upon. However, Sections 4 through 6 apply to a mediation communication made by a person that has not received actual notice of the agreement before the communication is made.

*Legislative Note: To the extent that the Act applies to mediations conducted under the authority of a State's courts, State judiciaries should consider enacting conforming court rules.*

## SECTION 4. PRIVILEGE AGAINST DISCLOSURE; ADMISSIBILITY; DISCOVERY.

(a) Except as otherwise provided in Section 6, a mediation communication is privileged as provided in subsection (b) and is not subject to discovery or admissible in evidence in a proceeding unless waived or precluded as provided by Section 5.

(b) In a proceeding, the following privileges apply:

(1) A mediation party may refuse to disclose, and may prevent any other person from disclosing, a mediation communication.

(2) A mediator may refuse to disclose a mediation communication, and may prevent any other person from disclosing a mediation communication of the mediator.

(3) A nonparty participant may refuse to disclose, and may prevent any other person from disclosing, a mediation communication of the nonparty participant.

(c) Evidence or information that is otherwise admissible or subject to discovery does not become inadmissible or protected from discovery solely by reason of its disclosure or use in a mediation.

*Legislative Note: The Act does not supersede existing state statutes that make mediators incompetent to testify, or that provide for costs and attorney fees to mediators who are wrongfully subpoenaed. See, e.g., Cal. Evid. Code Section 703.5 (West 1994).*

## SECTION 5. WAIVER AND PRECLUSION OF PRIVILEGE.

(a) A privilege under Section 4 may be waived in a record or orally during a proceeding if it is expressly waived by all parties to the mediation and:

(1) in the case of the privilege of a mediator, it is expressly waived by the mediator; and

(2) in the case of the privilege of a nonparty participant, it is expressly waived by the nonparty participant.

(b) A person that discloses or makes a representation about a mediation communication which prejudices another person in a proceeding is precluded from asserting a privilege under Section 4, but only to the extent necessary for the person prejudiced to respond to the representation or disclosure.

(c) A person that intentionally uses a mediation to plan, attempt to commit or commit a crime, or to conceal an ongoing crime or ongoing criminal activity is precluded from asserting a privilege under Section 4.

## SECTION 7. PROHIBITED MEDIATOR REPORTS.

(a) Except as required in subsection (b), a mediator may not make a report, assessment, evaluation, recommendation, finding, or other communication regarding a mediation to a court, administrative agency, or other authority that may make a ruling on the dispute that is the subject of the mediation.

(b) A mediator may disclose:

(1) whether the mediation occurred or has terminated, whether a settlement was reached, and attendance;

(2) a mediation communication as permitted under Section 6; or

(3) a mediation communication evidencing abuse, neglect, abandonment, or exploitation of an individual to a public agency responsible for protecting individuals against such mistreatment.

(c) A communication made in violation of subsection (a) may not be considered by a court, administrative agency, or arbitrator.

**SECTION 8. CONFIDENTIALITY.** Unless subject to the [insert statutory references to open meetings act and open records act], mediation communications are confidential to the extent agreed by the parties or provided by other law or rule of this State.

# NOTES AND QUESTIONS

(1)   Does the Uniform Mediation Act (UMA) definition of mediation satisfy Professor Kirtley's over-inclusive/under-inclusive concern? Do the UMA confidentiality provisions extend to a broad range of subsequent proceedings? Are the right persons identified as the holders of the privilege? Are the waiver provisions sensible?

(2)   Does the UMA privilege extend confidentiality protection to all the areas discussed by Professor Ehrhardt as not shielded by Rule 408?

(3)   Although there currently is no federal statute recognizing a general mediation privilege, a number of federal acts provide for a mediation privilege in specific types of proceedings. Most prominently, Congress created a mediation privilege in the Administrative ADR Act that prohibits the disclosure of communications made during mediations under the Administrative Procedure Act. Even then, it is not clear that the federal courts will interpret these congressional acts as providing broad confidentiality protection. In *In re Grand Jury Subpoena*, 148 F.3d 487 (5th Cir. 1998), the federal appeals court refused to uphold the district court's ruling that a federal mediation privilege protected against a federal grand jury subpoena for records of a mediation conducted under a state agricultural loan program. Although the relevant federal act (the Agricultural Credit Act) requires mediations to be "confidential," the Fifth Circuit ruled that it was not clear that Congress had intended to create a privilege that was so broad that it would protect mediation communications from a federal grand jury. In the following cases, compare Magistrate Judge Kaplan's rationale for refusing to find that Congress had provided for a "mediator privilege" in the Alternative Dispute Resolution Act of 1998 that would extend to the mediation communications at issue with that of Magistrate Judge Caiazza in *Sheldone v. Pennsylvania Turnpike Commission*, holding that there is a federal mediation privilege.

(4)   Although widely considered a "confidentiality act," note that the bulk of the UMA focuses on creating a privilege, defining who holds the privilege, and exceptions to the privilege (*see* Section F). *Compare* UMA Section 8 *with* Florida Statutes 44.405(1):

> (1) Except as provided in this section, all mediation communications shall be confidential. A mediation participant shall not disclose a mediation communication to a person other than another mediation participant or a participant's counsel. A violation of this section can be remedied as provided by s. 44.406. If the mediation is court ordered, a violation of this section may also subject the mediation participant to sanctions by the court, including but not limited to, costs, attorney's fees, and mediator's fees.

> 44.406 (1) Any mediation participant who knowingly and willfully discloses a mediation communication in violation of s. 44.405 shall, upon application by any party to a court of competent jurisdiction, be subject to remedies, including:

> (a) equitable relief.

> (b) compensatory damages.

(c) attorney's fees, mediator's fees, and costs incurred in the mediation proceeding.

(d) reasonable attorney's fees and costs incurred in the application for remedies under this section.

What do you think were the reasons that the drafters would adopt a broader statement of confidentiality? Do you think the Florida statute strikes the correct balance to provide protection while also limiting frivolous suits?

## FEDERAL DEPOSIT INSURANCE CORPORATION v. WHITE
### United States District Court for the Northern District of Texas
### 76 F. Supp. 2d 736 (1999)

JEFF KAPLAN, UNITED STATES MAGISTRATE JUDGE.

### MEMORANDUM OPINION AND ORDER

Plaintiff Federal Deposit Insurance Corporation has filed a motion to enforce a settlement agreement entered into between the parties to this litigation at the conclusion of a post-trial mediation. Defendants John A. White and Donna A. White have filed a cross-motion to set aside the settlement agreement. For the reasons stated herein, plaintiff's motion is granted and defendants' motion is denied.

### I.

The FDIC sued the Whites for violations of the Texas Uniform Fraudulent Transfer Act and civil conspiracy. Following a five-day trial, the jury returned a verdict in favor of the FDIC and against the Whites. The Court then ordered the case to mediation. Hesha Abrams was appointed to serve as the mediator. All parties and their attorneys were ordered to attend the mediation "and proceed in good faith in an effort to settle this case." The mediation was held on September 29, 1999. After a full day of negotiations, a settlement was reached and memorialized in a written agreement. The Court subsequently ordered the parties to submit the settlement papers and an agreed judgment by October 29, 1999.

One day before these documents were due, the Whites repudiated the settlement agreement. The Whites allege that "throughout the mediation, they were threatened with criminal prosecution by the FDIC by and through its representative, Andrew Emerson." As a result, the Whites contend that the settlement agreement was coerced and should be set aside. The FDIC maintains the agreement should be enforced according to its terms. Both parties were given an opportunity to brief the issues and present additional evidence and argument at a hearing on December 3, 1999. This matter is now ripe for determination.

### II.

The Whites rely on their own affidavits and the testimony of their former attorneys in order to prove that the settlement agreement was coerced. These affidavits purport to detail the substance of certain comments made by the mediator and FDIC representatives during the mediation. The FDIC argues that this evidence is inadmissible because "mediation communications are privileged." (Plf. Motion to Strike P 4).

The applicability of evidentiary privileges in federal court is governed by Rule 501 of the Federal Rules of Evidence. This rule provides, in relevant part:

> Except as otherwise required by the Constitution of the United States or provided by Act of Congress or in rules prescribed by the Supreme Court pursuant to statutory authority, the privilege of a witness, person, government, State, or political subdivision thereof shall be governed by the principles of the common law as they may be interpreted by the courts of the United States in light of reason and experience.

Fed. R. Evid. 501. The FDIC contends that Congress created a "mediator privilege" as part of the Alternative Dispute Resolution Act of 1998 ("ADRA"), Pub. L. No. 105-315, 112 Stat. 2993. The ADRA directs federal district courts to enact local rules requiring litigants in civil cases to "consider the use of an alternative dispute resolution process at an appropriate stage in the litigation." *Id.*, 112 Stat. 2994, § 4(a), codified at 28 U.S.C. § 652(a). Such local rules must "provide for the confidentiality of the alternative dispute resolution processes and prohibit disclosure of confidential dispute resolution communications." *Id.*, 112 Stat. 2995, § 4(d), codified at 28 U.S.C. § 652(d). In furtherance of this mandate, the Civil Justice Expense and Delay Reduction Plan for the Northern District of Texas has been amended to provide for the confidentiality of ADR procedures. The Plan now provides that:

> all communications made during ADR procedures are confidential and protected from disclosure and do not constitute a waiver of any existing privileges and immunities.

It is obvious that Congress sought to protect communications made during the course of mediation from unwarranted disclosure. "Confidentiality is critical to the mediation process because it promotes the free flow of information that may result in the settlement of a dispute." *In re Grand Jury Subpoena*, 148 F.3d 487, 492 (5th Cir. 1998), *cert. denied*, 119 S. Ct. 1336 (1999), *citing* K. Feinberg, *Mediation — A Preferred Method of Dispute Resolution*, 16 Pepp. L. Rev. S5, S28-29 (1989). However, "confidential" does not necessarily mean "privileged." *Id., citing Nguyen Dan Yen v. Kissinger*, 528 F.2d 1194, 1205 (9th Cir. 1975). Privileges are not lightly created and cannot be inferred absent a clear manifestation of Congressional intent. *United States v. Nixon*, 418 U.S. 683, 710, 94 S. Ct. 3090, 3108, 41 L. Ed. 2d 1039 (1974). The Court does not read the ADRA or its sparse legislative history as creating an evidentiary privilege that would preclude a litigant from challenging the validity of a settlement agreement based on events that transpired at a mediation. Indeed, such a privilege would effectively bar a party from raising well-established common law defenses such as fraud, duress, coercion, and mutual mistake. It is unlikely that Congress intended such a draconian result under the guise of preserving the integrity of the mediation process. Certainly, the Court did not intend such a result by its order. *See also Fields-D'Arpino v. Restaurant Associ-*

*ates, Inc.*, 39 F. Supp. 2d 412, 418 (S.D.N.Y. 1999) (ADRA does not make mediation communications privileged).

For these reasons, the FDIC's motion to strike is denied. The Court will allow the Whites and their former attorneys to testify about statements made at the mediation.

### III.

John A. White and Donna A. White allege that they were threatened with criminal prosecution throughout the mediation. According to John White:

> On the date of the mediation, Attorney for the FDIC, Andrew Emerson, began the session with statements of not-so-subtle innuendos that I was in dire jeopardy of losing my freedom; however, if I would agree and pay the certain "agreed upon" amounts on time; that, while he could not promise me immunity, he would advise the Justice Department that the FDIC was only interested in the money being paid and not in me going to jail. Throughout the entire proceedings and particularly on the date of the mediation, I felt that it was being communicated to me by the representative of the FDIC that if I did not agree to the settlement, the FDIC would take further action through the Justice Department in the form of criminal prosecution.

Donna White testified that she was frightened and intimidated by the prospect of going to jail. She stated that "time and time again, the mention of criminal prosecution was brought up" at the mediation. On one occasion, the mediator told Donna that "one of the worse case scenarios could be that I might be put into a position where I might be offered immunity from jail if I would testify against my husband." Donna said that she "felt coerced into signing the Settlement Agreement just to keep from going to jail." Rosa Orenstein, counsel for John White, confirmed that the issue of criminal prosecution was discussed at the mediation.

### A.

The threat of criminal prosecution may constitute duress whether or not the threatened party is actually guilty of a crime. As one court stated:

> It was never contemplated in the law that either the actual or threatened use or misuse of criminal process, legal or illegal, should be resorted to for the purpose of compelling the payment of a mere debt, although it may be justly owing and due, or to coerce the making of contracts or agreements from which advantage is to be derived by the party employing such threats. Ample civil remedies are afforded in the law to enforce the payment of debts and the performance of contracts, but the criminal law and the machinery for its enforcement have a wholly different purpose, and cannot be employed to interfere with that wise and just policy of the law that all contracts and agreements shall be founded upon the exercise of the free will of the parties, which is the real essence of all contracts.

*Greene v. Bates*, 424 S.W.2d 5, 9 (Tex. Civ. App. — Houston [1st Dist.] 1968, no writ), *quoting Hartford Fire Insurance Co. v. Kirkpatrick*, 111 Ala. 456, 20 So. 651, 654 (1896). *See also* RESTATEMENT (FIRST) OF CONTRACTS § 493, cmt. c (1932). Of course, duress is an affirmative defense that must be proved by the party seeking to avoid an otherwise valid contract. *Greene*, 424 S.W.2d at 8. The critical inquiry is whether the party was induced to enter into the contract by the threat of criminal prosecution. *Id.*

## B.

The evidence shows that the Whites were concerned about their potential criminal exposure long before mediation. And for good reason. David Groveman, in-house counsel for the FDIC, testified that a criminal referral had already been made before the case proceeded to trial in August 1999. Groveman told the Whites, though their attorneys, that "said referral once made is the province of the FBI and U.S. Attorney, not the FDIC." He reiterated this point several times both prior to and during the mediation. Still, Groveman maintained that the FDIC was only interested in getting paid. It was in this context that the mediator raised the issue of criminal liability. Although this subject was fully and openly discussed by the parties throughout the mediation, no overt or subtle threats were ever made by the FDIC or the mediator. In fact, it was *the Whites* who asked for a non-prosecution agreement during the course of settlement negotiations. They agreed to the settlement even after their request was rejected by the FDIC.

The Court finds that the settlement agreement between the FDIC and the Whites was not the result of duress or coercion. Accordingly, the agreement will be enforced as written. *See Bell v. Schexnayder*, 36 F.3d 447, 449 (5th Cir. 1994).

## IV.

The written agreement signed by the parties at the conclusion of the mediation requires the Whites to execute certain documents in furtherance of the settlement. These include: (1) an agreed final judgment in this case; (2) an agreed judgment in John White's pending bankruptcy; and (3) a promissory note in the principal sum of $1 million with a graduated payment schedule. Copies of these documents are attached to the FDIC's motion to enforce the settlement agreement. John A. White and Donna A. White are hereby ordered to sign each document where indicated and return them to counsel for the FDIC by *December 30, 1999*. An agreed final judgment, signed by the parties and their attorneys, must be hand-delivered to the chambers of Magistrate Judge Kaplan by January 7, 2000.

The failure to comply with this order will subject the offending party to monetary sanctions and a possible contempt citation.

# SHELDONE v. PENNSYLVANIA TURNPIKE COMMISSION
United States District Court for the Western District of Pennsylvania
104 F. Supp. 2d 511 (2000)

CAIAZZA, UNITED STATES MAGISTRATE JUDGE.

. . .

The Plaintiffs, members of International Brotherhood of Teamsters, Local 30 ("Local 30") who are employed by the Commission (hereinafter "the Plaintiffs"), filed this lawsuit on October 7, 1999 alleging that the Defendant violated the Fair Labor Standards Act, 29 U.S.C. § 201, *et seq.* ("the FLSA"), by "imposing a fluctuating hours method of compensation on the Plaintiffs." On approximately May 24, 2000, Plaintiffs' counsel noticed the deposition of an authorized agent of the Commission pursuant to Federal Rule of Civil Procedure 30(b)(6). Among other things, the Plaintiffs seek to conduct an examination regarding "[t]he mediation [of] the grievance filed by Roger Haas [ ("Mr.Haas") ] and Michael Pandolfo heard on May 21, 1999, before Mediator Michael W. Krchnar, Jr." ("the Mediation").

The Defendant's motion seeks to preclude the discovery "through any method . . . , including [the] Plaintiffs' noticed deposition," of "[a]ll mediation communications and mediation documents . . . ." As the basis for its request, the Commission urges this Court to recognize a federal "mediation privilege" precluding discovery of such communications and documents.

The Plaintiffs explain that the Mediation constituted the "third step of a grievance procedure under" a "Memorandum of Understanding" between the Commission and Local 30 that "applie[d] to the terms and conditions of" the Plaintiffs' employment. Their opposition brief alleges Mr. Haas testified at his deposition that one of the Commission's attorneys stated that it "settled out of court" another lawsuit brought by many of the same Plaintiffs here because the Commission "found out it was illegal to pay [them] . . . straight time for overtime."

The Plaintiffs argue that this purported admission is "extremely significant to [their] claims of retaliation" and to the Commission's affirmative defense that it acted with a good faith belief it was not violating the law. They also assert the purported admission is highly relevant to their claim that the fluctuating hours method of compensation actually results in "less compensation for overtime hours than under the 'straight time' method" allegedly referenced during the Mediation.

. . .

The parties agree that the four factors annunciated by the Supreme Court in *Jaffee v. Redmond*, 518 U.S. 1, 116 S. Ct. 1923, 135 L. Ed. 2d 337 (1996) provide the standards for determining whether a potential federal evidentiary privilege should be recognized, and this Court joins the other federal courts that have focused on these same standards. The four relevant factors are:

(1) whether the asserted privilege is "rooted in the imperative need for confidence and trust";

(2) whether the privilege would serve public ends;

(3)   whether the evidentiary detriment caused by an exercise of the privilege is modest; and

(4)   whether denial of the federal privilege would frustrate a parallel privilege adopted by the states.

*See Jaffee*, 518 U.S. at 9–13, 116 S. Ct. 1923.

. . .

Both federal and state courts have recognized that confidentiality is essential to the mediation process. The federal circuit court in *Lake Utopia Paper Ltd. v. Connelly Containers, Inc.*, 608 F.2d 928 (2d Cir.1979) succinctly articulated why confidentiality is necessary:

> If participants cannot rely on the confidential treatment of everything that transpires during [mediation] sessions *then counsel of necessity will feel constrained to conduct themselves in a cautious, tightlipped, non-committal manner more suitable to poker players in a high-stakes game than to adversaries attempting to arrive at a just resolution of a civil dispute. This atmosphere* if allowed to exist *would surely destroy the effectiveness of a program which has led to settlements . . . , thereby expediting cases at a time when . . . judicial resources . . . are sorely taxed.*

*Id.* at 930 (emphasis added), *cert. denied*, 444 U.S. 1076, 100 S. Ct. 1023, 62 L. Ed. 2d 758 (1980).

The need for confidence and trust in the mediation process is further evidenced by federal statute, the local rules of federal district courts in Pennsylvania and other states, and state statutes from across the country. The Alternative Dispute Resolution Act of 1998, which requires each federal district court to "provide litigants in all civil cases with at least one alternative dispute resolution process, including . . . mediation," expressly directs the courts to adopt local rules "provid-[ing] for the confidentiality of the alternative dispute resolution processes and to prohibit disclosure of confidential dispute resolution communications." *See* 28 U.S.C. § 652(d).

As directed by Congress, the District Courts of Pennsylvania have adopted provisions addressing the confidentiality of mediation communications and documents.

. . .

[T]his Court concludes that all of the factors in *Jaffee* counsel in favor of recognizing a federal mediation privilege here. Like the psychotherapy-patient privilege adopted in that case, the mediation privilege creates a "public good transcending the normally predominant principle of utilizing all rational means for ascertaining truth." Nothing in the Plaintiffs' opposition brief demonstrates the contrary. First, for reasons articulated above, their suggestion that "[n]o private interest is furthered" by adopting the privilege is entirely without merit. Plaintiffs' counsel apparently attempts to distinguish the Mediation from the "normal mediation process," stating that Local 30 "had no recourse" once mediation did not result in a settlement. Aside from the obvious fact that the *Plaintiffs* have enjoyed the recourse of filing a federal lawsuit, Counsel provides no legal authority for the proposition that Local 30's potential rights are in any way relevant to the privilege issue.

Nor can the Plaintiffs support their suggestion that the Mediation was "essentially meaningless" because the Commission was not bound by any findings of the mediator. By definition, mediation is a non-binding dispute resolution technique through which "a neutral third party . . . *facilitates the resolution of a dispute* by assisting parties *in reaching a voluntary agreement.*" The very nature of this process mandates a need for confidence and trust so that the parties can honestly and openly discuss the strengths and weaknesses of their positions in an attempt to reach a voluntarily settlement. The Plaintiffs' "private interest" arguments are of no avail.

So too are their arguments regarding "public interest." Under this prong, the Plaintiffs merely reiterate their claim that the mediation process here was meaningless and they state that the privilege "would only give the [Commission] a license to lie and encourage disingenuity." The Plaintiffs' sentiments notwithstanding, Congress, the legislatures of nearly every state, and this and other District Courts have recognized the valuable role that mediation plays in our judicial system. Additionally, this Court fails to see how an adoption of the mediation privilege creates a license for litigants to lie or to be disingenuous. To the contrary, the privilege fosters mediation participants' candor and honesty regarding the validity of their positions by alleviating their "fear[s that] an unsuccessful mediation attempt will come back to haunt them in a court of law."

Regarding the third prong in *Jaffee*, the Plaintiffs suggest that the Commission's purported admission "would have been spoken with or without a privilege because" the Defendant agreed to participate in the Mediation. This argument turn's the reasoning in *Jaffee* on its head. The *Jaffee* Court concluded that, if the privilege at issue there "*were rejected*, confidential conversations . . . would surely be chilled," thereby making it unlikely for "admissions against interest by a party" like the purported one here "to come into being." This is the appropriate analysis, and it demonstrates precisely why the Plaintiffs should not be afforded the benefit of the purported admission.

Regarding the fourth prong in *Jaffee*, the Plaintiffs' arguments simply cannot explain away the nearly unanimous voices of state legislatures from across the country adopting mediation privileges.

The only other argument the Plaintiffs present in opposing an application of the mediation privilege is their contention that the Commission "waived the privilege by putting" mediation communications and documents "at issue" in this case. A review of the record, however, reveals the contrary. The mediation issue arose only after Mr. Haas and an agent of Local 30 referenced it in their depositions. The Plaintiffs have not and cannot support their assertion that discussions in depositions of the Mediation by them or agents of Local 30 somehow effectuated a waiver of the privilege on behalf of the Commission.

Having concluded that the federal mediation privilege will be adopted and applied in this case the Court must, to the extent possible, define the contours of the privilege. Because this District's Local Rule 16.3 addresses standards regarding the appropriate scope of confidentiality in the mediation process (albeit, within the context of court-annexed mediation), the Court concludes that the Rule is an appropriate starting point for defining the privilege. Accordingly, the mediation privilege recognized herein shall comport with the following standards:

- The privilege protects from disclosure "all written and oral communications made in connection with or during" a mediation conducted before a "neutral" mediator. *See* W. Dist. Local R. 16.3.5(E), 16.3.1.

- No such written or oral communication may be "used for any purpose (including impeachment) in the civil action or in any other proceedings." *See id.*, R. 16.3.5(E).

- "Except for a written settlement agreement or any written stipulations executed by the parties or their counsel, no party or counsel shall be bound by anything done or said" during the mediation process. *See id.*

In addition, this Court has already concluded that the most compelling reason for recognizing the mediation privilege is the Plaintiffs' lack of entitlement to any admission of the Defendant that, but for the mediation process, would not have come into being. If the Plaintiff is able to elicit any admissions (or facts underlying them) outside the scope of the mediation process, however, the rationale for the privilege would no longer apply. Accordingly, this Court concludes and therefore holds that the mediation privilege does not protect from disclosure "any evidence otherwise" and independently "discoverable merely because it [wa]s presented in the course of" the Mediation. *See generally* Fed.R.Evid. 408; . . . Accordingly, the Plaintiffs remain free to conduct discovery independent of, and unrelated to, the mediation process.

Finally, the Court notes that the elements listed above are by no means intended to be an exhaustive recitation of the standards governing the mediation privilege. Numerous court and legislatures have recognized exceptions and/or limitations to the privilege not implicated in this case. These issues must be saved for another day.

. . .

For the foregoing reasons, the Defendants' motion for a protective order is granted consistent with the reasoning in this Order.

## NOTES AND QUESTIONS

(1) Are the mediation privilege standards outlined in *Sheldone* consistent with those described by Professor Kirtley?

(2) The federal appellate courts have thus far been reluctant to find a federal mediation privilege when presented with the opportunity. For an excellent discussion and analysis of the caselaw relating to the recognition of a mediation privilege in the federal trial and appellate courts, see SARAH R. COLE ET AL., MEDIATION: LAW, POLICY & PRACTICE 306–11 (2011–2012 ed.). The authors conclude that, "[f]ew areas of mediation law are as uncertain as the existence and applicability of a federal

mediation privilege." Accordingly, Professor Ellen Deason has recommended that Congress adopt a federal mediation privilege similar to the UMA. Ellen Deason, *Predictable Mediation Confidentiality in the U.S. Federal System*, 17 Ohio St. J. on Disp. Resol. 239 (2002).

(3)   In states where a mediation privilege has been recognized, questions remain about the nature and scope of the privilege, even in UMA states. Consider the issues raised in the *Society of Lloyds* case excerpted below.

## SOCIETY OF LLOYD'S v. MOORE
United States District Court for the Southern District of Ohio
2006 U.S. Dist. LEXIS 80963

Susan J. Dlott, District Judge.

This matter is before the Court on Defendants' Motion to Strike February 20, 2006 Email from Lawrence A. Glassmann. For the reasons that follow, the Court **GRANTS** Defendants' motion.

The events setting in motion the current dispute date back decades, beginning in the late 1980s when Defendant Lea Ward became an underwriter in the English insurance market. In connection with that position, Ward incurred certain liabilities. On March 11, 1998, The Society of Lloyd's ("Lloyd's") obtained a judgment against Ward in an English court in the amount of £224,138.15 ("English Judgment"). Subsequently, Lloyd's commenced an action in this Court to domesticate the English Judgement ("Collection Action"). The Court ultimately entered summary judgment for Lloyd's in that suit.

Meanwhile, Lloyd's learned that Ward had transferred approximately $2,000,000 in assets to two separate trusts of which she is a beneficiary. Accordingly, Lloyd's sued Ward, Defendants Alfred and Betty Moore, and other parties, alleging claims for common law fraud and fraudulent transfer ("Fraud Action"). On January 3, 2006, the Court granted summary judgment for the Defendants on Lloyd's common law fraud claim, but denied summary judgment on the fraudulent transfer claim.

After the Court issued its summary judgment opinion in the Fraud Action, the parties agreed to submit the remaining matters to arbitration and mediation. The parties executed an Arbitration and Mediation Agreement ("the Agreement"), under which the parties agreed to a procedure known as arb-med. The parties chose a single panelist, Lawrence A. Glassmann, to arbitrate and mediate the dispute. Pursuant to the procedure set forth in the Agreement, the arbitration occurred first. At the close of the arbitration, Glassmann rendered a decision, but did not reveal it to the parties. Instead, the parties attempted to mediate the dispute. During the course of the mediation, on February 20, 2006, Glassmann sent Society of Lloyds an email communicating his opinions about the strengths and weaknesses of Lloyd's case and urging Lloyd's to reach a settlement with Defendants.

Having become clear to all involved that further mediation would not yield a settlement, the parties agreed to the revealing of the arbitrator's decision. On February 21, 2006, Glassmann revealed his decision, wherein he found for the

Defendants and ordered Lloyd's to pay the cost of arbitration.

The following day, Defendants sent Lloyd's a proposed order dismissing with prejudice the remaining claims in the Fraud Action, pursuant to a clause in the Agreement stating that "upon the Arbitrator making known his decision in the event the parties cannot agree in Mediation . . . Lloyd's and Respondents will dismiss the Case with prejudice and execute a full release and hold harmless of all Claims against the other." Lloyd's agreed to the proposed order and on February 24, 2006, the Court entered an order dismissing the Fraud Action with prejudice and allotting the parties 60 days to reopen the action, upon good cause shown, if settlement was not consummated.

Nearly three months later, Lloyd's filed the instant action seeking to vacate the arbitration award on the basis that Glassmann based the award on matters outside the scope of the Agreement. In support of its Motion to Vacate the Arbitration Award (doc. 1), Lloyd's relies almost entirely on the comments Glassmann included in his February 20, 2006 email. Defendants move the Court to strike this email, arguing that it constitutes a confidential mediation communication under the Uniform Mediation Act, Ohio Rev.Code §§ 2710.01 *et seq.* ("the Act"). Lloyd's responds that the Act does not shield Glassmann's communication because: (1) the email discussed matters outside the scope of the Agreement; (2) the Act applies only to mediation rather than to hybrid arb-med procedures; (3) the parties waived any confidentiality or privilege that might otherwise apply; and (4) the parties agreed in advance that such communications would not be privileged.

Ohio Rev.Code § 2710.03 provides, in relevant part, as follows:

(A) Except as otherwise provided in section 2710.05 of the Revised Code, *a mediation communication is privileged* as provided in division (B) of this section *and is not subject to discovery or admissible in evidence in a proceeding* unless waived or precluded as provided in section 2710.04 of the Revised Code.

(B) In a proceeding, the following privileges apply:

(1) A mediation party may refuse to disclose, and may prevent any other person from disclosing, a mediation communication.

(emphasis added). The Act defines "mediation communication" to include "a statement, whether oral, in a record, verbal or nonverbal, that occurs during a mediation or is made for purposes of considering, conducting, participating in, initiating, continuing, or reconvening a mediation or retaining a mediator." Ohio Rev.Code § 2710.01(B). This broad definition encompasses communications such as that at issue in this case. Glassmann's email was sent during the mediation and included comments aimed at fostering a settlement between the parties. Such comments fall squarely within the scope of § 2710.01(B) and are therefore privileged under § 2710.03. Accordingly, the party seeking admission of the comments will prevail only if it can show that: (1) the Act does not apply to the mediation the parties engaged in; (2) the comments are not subject to the privilege, but rather fall within one of the exceptions enumerated under § 2710.05; or (3) the parties have waived the privilege in accordance with § 2710.04. Lloyd's makes all of these arguments but, for the reasons set forth below, fails to demonstrate that Glassmann's email is not a privileged mediation communication.

Lloyd's first contends that Ohio Rev.Code § 2710.03 does not apply to Glassmann's email communication because the email contained comments about matters outside the scope of the Agreement — namely the issue of laches and the resolution of a separate claim against one of the defendants. Lloyd's cites § 2710.02, which provides that:

Except as otherwise provided in division (B) or (C) of this section, sections 2710.01 to 2710. 10 of the Revised Code apply to a mediation under any of the following circumstances:

> (1) The mediation parties are required to mediate by statute or court or administrative agency rule or referred to mediation by a court, administrative agency, or arbitrator.

> (2) The mediation parties and the mediator agree to mediate in a record that demonstrates an expectation that mediation communications will be privileged against disclosure.

> (3) The mediation parties use as a mediator an individual who holds himself or herself out as a mediator, or the mediation is provided by a person that holds itself out as providing mediation.

Lloyd's argues that, pursuant to this section, the Act does not apply to Glassmann's email because it relates to matters that the parties never agreed to mediate. However, § 2710.02 does not indicate that when parties agree to enter mediation, the Act will shield only those communications relating to matters the parties specifically and expressly agreed to mediate. Instead, it speaks generally of certain types of mediation to which the Act applies.

Moreover, even if the Court were to read § 2710.02 as Lloyd's suggests, it finds that the parties did not limit the scope of the mediation in the manner that Lloyd's asserts. The portion of the Agreement that limits the "[i]ssue to be decided" applies only to the arbitration procedure as opposed to both the arbitration and the mediation. As described above, the Agreement describes the arbitration and mediation as separate and distinct proceedings. The parties submitted the dispute to arbitration and did not engage in mediation until after the arbitration was complete and Glassmann had made his decision. The Agreement limits only "the issue to be decided by the Arbitrator" and sets forth the specific issues that the arbitrator is to decide following the Arbitration. As the Agreement required the arbitrator to render his decision at the close of the arbitration and prior to the commencement of mediation, the limiting clause necessarily applies only to the arbitration. It states nothing in regards to limiting the issues the parties may address during the mediation. Nor does any other portion of the Agreement indicate an intent to limit the scope of the parties' mediation.

The very nature of mediation calls for an uninhibited process wherein parties may explore various solutions to their disputes. It is neither uncommon nor unforeseeable that in trying to reach a settlement as to specific claims, parties may engage in a discussion of other related claims. To hold that Ohio Rev.Code § 2710.03 shields only communications regarding matters specifically contemplated and set forth by parties prior to entering mediation would unduly hinder the ability of parties to freely and openly discuss settlement options. It is precisely for this reason that courts have traditionally recognized a broad privilege surrounding mediation and other settlement communications. *See Goodyear Tire & Rubber Co. v. Chiles Power Supply, Inc.*, 332 F. 3d 976, 980 (6th Cir.2003) ("The ability to negotiate and settle a case without trial fosters a more efficient, more cost-effective, and significantly less burdened judicial system. In order for settlement talks to be effective, parties must feel uninhibited in their communications. Parties are unlikely to propose the types of compromises that most effectively lead to settlement unless they are confident that their proposed solutions cannot be used on cross examination, under the ruse of "impeachment evidence," by some future third party. Parties must be able to abandon their adversarial tendencies to some degree. They must be able to make hypothetical concessions, offer creative quid pro quos, and generally make statements that would otherwise belie their litigation efforts. Without a privilege, parties would more often forego negotiations for the relative formality of trial. Then, the entire negotiation process collapses upon itself, and the judicial efficiency it fosters is lost.") . . .

Lloyd's next argues that § 2710.03 applies only to mediation as opposed to a hybrid arbitration and mediation, as occurred in this case. Lloyd's contends that the dual role of an arbitrator/mediator under these circumstances distinguishes Glassmann's email from that of a simple mediation communication. Along the same line, Lloyd's argues that the Court should apply by analogy § 2710.02(B)(3), which provides that § 2710.03 is inapplicable in cases where the "mediation is conducted by a judge or magistrate who might make a ruling on the case." According to Lloyd's, the same concern is present here in that the mediator was also the person vested with authority to render a binding decision upon the parties.

Lloyd's argument fails for several reasons. First, when Glassmann sent the February 20 email, he had already rendered his decision as an arbitrator and was acting solely in the role of a mediator. Second, Lloyd's offers no caselaw suggesting the Court should read and apply § 2710.02(B)(3) as broadly as Lloyd's requests. To the contrary, the Court finds that had the Ohio legislature intended to exclude from the scope of § 2710.03 those cases in which the same individual serves as an arbitrator and a mediator, it would have specifically stated as such. Finally, courts have previously applied this privilege to situations such as that in the instant case in which one person serves as both the mediator and the arbitrator. *See Bowden v. Weickert*, 2003 Ohio App. LEXIS 2871, 2003 WL 21419175, at *6 (Ohio App. 6th Dist. June 20, 2003) (holding that even though the parties had engaged in a hybrid med-arb proceeding, where the same individual served as mediator and arbitrator, the parties' confidential mediation communications remained privileged).

Lloyd's additionally argues that Glassmann's comments would otherwise be discoverable and admissible in the Court's consideration of Lloyd's Motion to Vacate and should not be stricken merely because Glassmann made the comments in the context of a mediation. Lloyd's relies on § 2710.03(C), which provides that "[e]vidence or information that is otherwise admissible or subject to discovery does not become inadmissible or protected from discovery solely by reason of its disclosure or use in a mediation." As stated above, § 2710.03(A) creates a privilege for "mediation communication[s]," defined broadly as "*a statement*, whether oral, in a record, verbal or nonverbal, *that occurs during a mediation.*" Ohio Rev.Code § 2710.01(B) (emphasis added). In contrast, § 2710.03(C) pertains to evidence or information exchanged between the parties and possibly referenced by the parties during mediation, clarifying that the mere fact that the parties might reference that evidence in a mediation communication does not render that evidence inadmissible.

. . . Ohio Rev.Code § 2710.03(C) serves only to prevent parties from immunizing from admissibility documents or other evidence by utilizing this evidence during the mediation. The exception does not apply to the mediator's own comments, made in furtherance of the mediation, regarding his opinion of the strengths and weaknesses of the parties' respective cases.

Defendants finally argue that in the event the Court determines that Glassmann's email falls within the scope and applicability of § 2710.03(C), the parties waived any confidentiality by agreeing to the disclosure of the arbitrator's decision process. As evidence of this alleged agreement, Lloyd's cites to paragraph 4 of the Agreement, in which the parties agree that "[d]uring [the mediation] process, the Arbitrator may, without revealing his verdict, discuss what he perceives to be the weaknesses and strengths of each party's respective case." Lloyd's interpretation of this clause is entirely unsupported. The language Lloyd's cites has nothing to do with the confidentiality of the parties' discussions, but rather authorizes the mediator to disclose his opinions regarding the disputed issues *to the parties, during the course of the mediation.* It in no way authorizes further disclosure of the mediator's comments to outside parties or in the context of separate proceedings such as the instant suit.

Lloyd's additionally argues that the email itself indicates Defendant's intention to waive confidentiality because Glassmann indicates that both parties gave him oral authorization during the course of the proceeding to disclose his thoughts regarding the strengths and weaknesses of each party's position. This alleged oral authorization merely reiterates the language in paragraph 4 of the Agreement and for the same reasons discussed above does not constitute a waiver of confidentiality. Accordingly, Lloyd's fails to demonstrate any basis for this Court to hold that Ohio Rev.Code § 2710.03(C) does not shield Glassmann's email. To the contrary, the Court finds that the email constitutes a confidential mediation communication and is inadmissible in the instant proceeding.

For the foregoing reasons, the Court **GRANTS** Defendants' Motion to Strike Glassman's February 20, 2006 email. The Court will not consider this communication when ruling on Plaintiff's Motion to Vacate the Arbitration Award.

## NOTES AND QUESTIONS

(1) In *Society of Lloyd's v. Moore*, the federal district judge carefully considers various provisions of the Ohio Uniform Mediation Act in holding that the mediator's email was a privileged mediation communication and therefore not admissible in a subsequent proceeding. Note how she also considers legislative intent in ruling that the UMA provision that would exclude the mediation privilege in cases where the "mediation is conducted by a judge or magistrate who might make a ruling on the

case", does not apply in this case, and therefore the mediation privilege does extend to a hybrid process such as arb-med.

(2)  Some courts have been more limited in their thinking when asked to consider how far the mediation privilege extends. In *Mutual of Enumclaw v. Cornhusker*, 2008 U.S. Dist. LEXIS 80266 (Sept. 16, 2008), for example, a federal district judge interpreted provisions of the Washington UMA to allow discovery of evidence of alleged bad faith conduct by an insurer during the mediation. The judge reasoned that the privilege only extends to communications narrowly related to the underlying dispute, and thus does not protect communications related to insurance coverage. Also, in *Hopes v. Barry*, 2011 Ohio App. LEXIS 5523 (Dec. 27, 2011), an Ohio appellate court held that the Ohio mediation privilege did not extend to an email sent by one of the attorneys several weeks after the mediation.

## F.  EXCEPTIONS

Recall that in the *Macaluso* case, *supra*, the mediator was "the one person whose testimony could have resolved the factual dispute." Yet, the court upheld the revocation of the subpoena of the mediator because "the complete exclusion of the mediator testimony is necessary to the preservation of an effective system of labor mediation." Should the court have carved out an exception to confidentiality and considered the mediator's testimony for the limited purpose of determining whether the Company and the Union had reached an agreement? Similarly, as noted in the *Cassel* decision, the Supreme Court of California has consistently refused to carve out exceptions to the mediation confidentiality statute. As you read the Uniform Mediation Act provision dealing with exceptions to confidentiality and the related materials below, consider the policies that are served by each confidentiality exception and whether they are consistent with, or erode, the policies that protect the confidentiality of mediation communications.

### THE MEDIATION PRIVILEGE'S TRANSITION FROM THEORY TO IMPLEMENTATION: DESIGNING A MEDIATION PRIVILEGE STANDARD TO PROTECT MEDIATION PARTICIPANTS, THE PROCESS AND THE PUBLIC INTEREST
1995 J. Disp. Resol. 1, 39–52[*]
By Alan Kirtley

Mediation occurs after the events precipitating a dispute. During mediation preexisting facts, statements, documents and tangible objects are often presented. The availability of such information to the mediation process is critically important. A privilege rule covering such preexisting information encourages party candor. However, other policy considerations weigh in favor of not extending the privilege to otherwise discoverable facts and documents.

While the mediation process needs privilege protection to function effectively, the privilege should not permit mediation to become a black hole into which parties can purposefully bury unhelpful evidence. For example, a party's admission during mediation that he falsified accounting records would be privileged, but his placing the records on the mediation table should not make the records privileged. Allowing discovery of preexisting facts and documents that are presented in mediation is consistent with traditional privilege and evidence law. The Washington statute contains a representative example of an exception for "otherwise discoverable" evidence found in several state privileges. These statutes follow the correct course by leaving the litigation discovery process undisturbed.

This approach, however, causes concern for unwary parties who tell or show "it all" during mediation. Such persons are unlikely to understand the distinction between privileged communications and the later discoverability of disclosed facts and preexisting documents. The concern is that unscrupulous parties will use mediation, where candor is urged and confidentiality promised, as an informal discovery devise. But barring discovery based on clues obtained during mediation would entwine former mediation parties in litigation to determine whether the source of the discovery lead came from or was independent of the mediation. The benefit is not worth the cost. Moreover, such a policy would be inconsistent with other privileges that do not protect facts, but only confidential communications. By carefully explaining the nuances of confidentiality, mediators can reduce the chances that mediation will become an informal discovery devise for unscrupulous parties. Nonetheless, mediation disputants and their counsel need to be aware of the consequences before divulging discovery tips during mediation discussions.

One form of otherwise discoverable mediation information merits privilege protection. In anticipation of mediation, parties may solicit preliminary appraisals, financial statements or expert opinions. This material is obtained to provide "ballpark" information for mediation negotiations. Washington and a few states maintain the privileged status for materials "prepared specifically for use in mediation and actually used in the mediation proceeding." Such statutes are consistent with the attorney-client privilege and the work-product doctrine. Only on very narrow grounds does the work-product doctrine allow discovery of the facts and opinions of consulting experts. Mediation's goals of encouraging informal, prompt and cost-effective settlement are served if parties are not yoked with these preliminary estimates in later litigation.

### b. Party Agreements and the Privilege

Parties usually begin a mediation by entering into a written agreement to mediate. Among other things, an agreement to mediate outlines the process, describes the mediator's role and sets forth the participants' understanding regarding confidentiality. Without an exemption to the privilege, such agreements remain confidential communications. This is despite the fact that mediation participants may need access to the agreement to mediate in order to demonstrate that the privilege was triggered, to evidence participation in a mandated mediation, to establish the terms of the mediator's undertaking or to prove a prior agreement to disclose otherwise privileged material. The Washington statute and a few other statutes have an exception for the agreement to mediate.

Settlement agreements present special considerations. Some parties are attracted to mediation out of the desire to preserve the privacy of their settlements. Yet, in certain cases, such as product liability and environmental cases, secret settlement agreements may do harm to third parties or the public at large. Also, parties may need access to their settlement agreement for enforcement purposes.

. . . .

### c. Subject Matter Exceptions

Among the most difficult policy choices in crafting the mediation privilege is deciding what particular classes of information should be excepted from the privilege in all instances. The process mirrors the analysis involved as to whether a mediation privilege is warranted. As to each type of information, the cost of the loss of evidence to the justice system must be weighted against the benefit of a broad-based mediation privilege.

A "laundry list" of subject matter exceptions has been enacted in various states or suggested. Examples include: (1) admission of threats to commit child abuse, a crime, a felony, physical/bodily harm, and damage to property; (2) information pertinent to a crime, an action claiming fraud or suits against the mediator; (3) information relating to the commission of a crime during mediation, and (4) use of mediation information for research purposes or non-identifiable reporting. In addition, some privilege statutes permit disclosure when mandated by another statute or a court. For purposes of the analysis that follows, the various exceptions have been organized in the categories of past criminal activity, ongoing or future crimes and threats of harm, and breakdowns in the mediation process and enforcement of mediated agreements.

### i. Past Criminal Activity

[I have] argued that the mediation privilege ought to apply in all criminal cases. For the same reasons, admissions of past criminal activity made during mediation should not be excepted from the privilege . . . . [E]xcepting admissions of past criminal activity would eliminate programs mediating criminal cases and stifle mediation communications in other types of disputes.

Admissions of past criminal activity do not necessarily present current or future risks of harm. Such an approach is consistent with the treatment of confidential disclosure of past criminal activity under traditional privileges. Undoubtedly, because of that body of law, most mediation privilege statutes do not exclude disclosures regarding past criminal activity. Mediation disclosures involving ongoing or future plans to do crime and threats of harm require separate analysis.

### ii. Ongoing and Future Crime; Threats of Harm

The few mediation statutes providing for disclosure of criminal activity generally limit the exception to ongoing or future crime. Such exclusions are consistent with some views of the attorney-client privilege; society does not wish to allow individuals to seek out the assistance of a lawyer in planning or carrying out a crime. However, the other privileges generally do not have an exception for ongoing or future crimes. In mediation, where the context is a meeting of persons in conflict, there is substantial risk of retaliatory reporting of mediation information. For example, an exception that allows a party to report, and the mediator to be compelled to testify to, the other party's use of drugs, illegal gambling, welfare misreporting or not paying income taxes is not warranted. The risks such offenses present to individuals or society do not justify penalizing mediation candor. On the other hand, an exclusion aimed at "serious physical harm" is a justified policy choice.

Public policy favoring disclosure of otherwise privileged information is nowhere stronger than in the area of abuse of vulnerable persons such as children, the aged and persons with a disability. In most states statutes exist requiring the reporting of knowledge of abuse or neglect of vulnerable persons to a designated governmental agency, even if learned during a confidential interview. That position is consistent with the law governing traditional privileges where the risk of injury is serious. The interests of mediation confidentiality are not so unique as to justify a different result. It is not surprising that the most common exclusion in mediation privilege statutes is for information relating to child abuse. The same result is reached in states, including Washington, with an exception allowing for disclosure of information "when mandated by statute."

Few mediation privilege statutes allow for disclosure of threats of physical harm made during mediation. Most of these statutes limit the exception to credible threats of serious bodily harm or violence. Such exceptions allow a mediation participant who is so threatened to take protective measures. A more troublesome question arises when the threat is directed toward a nonparticipant of the mediation. Does the mediator have a duty to warn the third party or notify the police of the threat?

Applying the reasoning of *Tarasoff v. Regents of the University of California*[351] to the mediation process, mediators may have an independent duty to report threats against third persons. In that case, a psychologist and others were sued for failing to inform a third person of death threats made by the psychologist's client during confidential treatment sessions. The client killed the threatened person. The court held the risk of serious physical injury or death to an identifiable person created a duty for the professional to warn the intended victim. Important to the case was the fact that both the applicable psychotherapist-patient privilege and professional ethics standards permitted disclosure by the psychologist under the circumstances presented.

In response to *Tarasoff*-like risks in mediation, several mediation privilege statutes have an exception eliminating confidentiality for threats of serious physical harm. The absence of such an exception is a weakness of most mediation privilege statutes, including Washington's. A *Tarasoff* exception for mediation would eliminate the privilege "when the mediator or a party reasonably believes that disclosing the mediation communications or materials is necessary to prevent a mediation party from committing a crime likely to result in imminent death or substantial bodily injury to an identifiable person." Adding a *Tarasoff* exception would implicate

---

[351] 551 P.2d 334 ([Cal.] 1976).

few mediations, resolve the *Tarasoff* dilemma for mediators and potentially save lives.

### iii. Breakdowns in the Mediation Process; Enforcement of Mediation Agreements

As with any dispute resolution mechanism, there will be breakdowns in the mediation process. Mediators may commit malpractice. Parties may fail to bargain in good faith. Mediation agreements may be tainted with fraud, or may be ambiguous or unfair. The mediation privilege should not provide a safe haven for participant wrongdoing or injustice. However, in allowing for disclosure of mediation information to deal with serious process breakdowns, care must be taken not to eviscerate the mediation privilege with exceptions that are too easily called upon.

A party claiming mediator misconduct must have access to mediation information and the mediator's testimony. A privilege that bars access to such information results in de facto immunity for malpracticing mediators. For that reason, and because the few claims of malpractice likely to arise will not greatly impact the operation of the privilege, a clear-cut exception to the privilege for mediator malpractice is appropriate. The Washington statute and a few other statutes address this obvious need. The Washington statute provides an exception to the privilege "in a subsequent action between the mediator and a party to the mediation arising out of the mediation." Exceptions for malpractice by mediators would be improved by explicit language permitting disclosure to mediator licensing authorities as well. Mediators also need access to mediation information to defend themselves against claims and charges, and to bring suit against parties, usually to collect agreed upon fees. Several exceptions accommodate such mediator needs for disclosure.

Good faith bargaining is the pathway to mediated settlements. However, providing an exception to the mediation privilege based on a claim of bad faith bargaining, short of fraud, is problematic. Most parties undertake mediation voluntarily. While such parties often negotiate under a mediator's entreaty to bargain in good faith, they may discontinue negotiations at will. When parties mediate voluntarily, mediation discussions should not be revealed based on a claim of bad faith negotiations. Negotiating in bad faith is often in the eyes of the beholder. Stonewalling or moving in small increments may be justified in particular mediations. Parties who become frustrated by their opponents' bargaining tactics have the option of withdrawing from the mediation and pursuing other means of resolving the dispute.

A different approach is justified when mediation parties come to the table involuntarily and under a statutory obligation to bargain in good faith, such as in labor mediation, farmer/creditor mediation and mandatory child custody mediation. In such cases, mediation communications are essential evidence to prove or defend against a claim of bad faith bargaining. Mediation communications should be available in contexts when parties have a statutory obligation to bargain in good faith, established standards of good faith bargaining exist and bargaining in bad faith is actionable. For example, in a school district/teachers' union mediation, if one side bargains in bad faith, mediation communications must be revealable to an administrative judge or court in order to obtain or oppose the requested relief. For that reason, some mediation privilege statutes eliminate confidentiality for claims of bad faith bargaining in mandatory mediations or simply exclude mediations in which negotiating in good faith is a legal obligation. While in this context parties should be free to introduce mediation communications to enforce good faith bargaining laws, the mediator should not be compelled to testify. It was on precisely that issue that the *Macaluso* and other court decisions provided the genesis of the mediation privilege.

Most would agree that mediation settlements tainted by fraud, obtained through duress or deemed unconscionable should not be enforceable. Yet relatively few mediation privilege statutes address these issues, and those that do mostly contain only fraud exceptions. This deviation from what might be expected may reflect the conclusion that fraud, duress and unconscionability are present in few mediations, and may reflect the concern that exceptions dealing with those ills will open the mediation privilege to wide-spread misuse by parties suffering from "bargainer's remorse." For example, a stated fraud exception to the privilege could be cited by those unwilling to abide by their mediation agreements, whether justified or not. Undoubtedly, states without fraud, duress or unconscionability exemptions, such as Washington, recognize that courts are likely to be willing to set aside the privilege when presented with viable contract defenses to the enforcement of a mediation settlement agreement. Once in court, mediation participants who wish to make out a case of fraud, for example, could seek *a priori* approval from the judge to present mediation information. By hearing the competing claims *in camera*, the court could preserve confidentiality unless disclosure was held to be necessary and appropriate. Since the parties will be able to present evidence related to fraud, duress or unconscionability, mediators should not be compelled to testify as the "tie-breaking" witness. A similar approach is appropriate when interpretive issues arise regarding the meaning of a settlement agreement.

## UNIFORM MEDIATION ACT

National Conference of Commissioners on Uniform State Laws and the American Bar Association*

### SECTION 6.   EXCEPTIONS TO PRIVILEGE.

(a) There is no privilege under Section 4 for a mediation communication that is:

(1) in an agreement evidenced by a record signed by all parties to the agreement;

(2) available to the public under [insert statutory reference to open records act] or made during a session of a mediation which is open, or is required by law to be open, to the public;

---

(3) a threat or statement of a plan to inflict bodily injury or commit a crime of violence;

(4) intentionally used to plan a crime, attempt to commit or commit a crime, or to conceal an ongoing crime or ongoing criminal activity;

(5) sought or offered to prove or disprove a claim or complaint of professional misconduct or malpractice filed against a mediator;

(6) except as otherwise provided in subsection (c), sought or offered to prove or disprove a claim or complaint of professional misconduct or malpractice filed against a mediation party, nonparty participant, or representative of a party based on conduct occurring during a mediation; or

(7) sought or offered to prove or disprove abuse, neglect, abandonment, or exploitation in a proceeding in which a child or adult protective services agency is a party, unless the

[Alternative A: [State to insert, for example, child or adult protection] case is referred by a court to mediation and a public agency participates.]

[Alternative B: public agency participates in the [State to insert, for example, child or adult protection] mediation].

(b) There is no privilege under Section 4 if a court, administrative agency, or arbitrator finds, after a hearing *in camera*, that the party seeking discovery or the proponent of the evidence has shown that the evidence is not otherwise available, that there is a need for the evidence that substantially outweighs the interest in protecting confidentiality, and that the mediation communication is sought or offered in:

(1) a court proceeding involving a felony [or misdemeanor]; or

(2) except as otherwise provided in subsection (c), a proceeding to prove a claim to rescind or reform or a defense to avoid liability on a contract arising out of the mediation.

(c) A mediator may not be compelled to provide evidence of a mediation communication referred to in subsection (a)(6) or (b)(2).

(d) If a mediation communication is not privileged under subsection (a) or (b), only the portion of the communication necessary for the application of the exception from nondisclosure may be admitted. Admission of evidence under subsection (a) or (b) does not render the evidence, or any other mediation communication, discoverable or admissible for any other purpose.

*Legislative Note: If the enacting state does not have an open records act, the following language in paragraph (2) of subsection (a) needs to be deleted: "available to the public under [insert statutory reference to open records act] or."*

## NOTES AND QUESTIONS

(1)   Does the Uniform Mediation Act section dealing with exceptions to a mediation privilege provide for all of the exceptions delineated by Professor Kirtley? Would Kirtley agree with the wording of the UMA exception "a threat to

inflict bodily injury"?

(2)  Considering what you now know about confidentiality and its exceptions, reexamine your mediator's opening statement. How would you describe confidentiality to the parties so that they would feel comfortable sharing information while also ensuring that you are accurate about the degree to which that information might not be confidential. Consider how you might change what you say if the parties are pro se, or if they are represented and their lawyers are present.

(3)  In the following cases, courts wrestle with the application of mediation privilege exceptions. As you read these cases, consider how well each court considers the policy concerns raised by Professor Kirtley and the UMA provision.

# OHIO EX REL. SCHNEIDER v. KREINER
## Supreme Court of Ohio
### 699 N.E.2d 83 (1998)

In 1988, relator, Tom Schneider ("Schneider"), married Theresa Schneider. They had two children. In 1994, the Schneiders divorced and entered into a shared parenting agreement. Subsequently, criminal charges were filed against Schneider for violating the agreement. The criminal case was referred to the Private Complaint Mediation Service ("Mediation Service"). The Mediation Service, established by the Hamilton County Municipal Court, mediates disputes between parties in certain municipal court cases.

During a mediation of this type, the mediator listens to the positions of both parties and then asks each party to agree on the issues and to recommend possible solutions. If an agreement is reached, the mediation concludes, but the parties do not sign a written agreement. However, the mediator may suggest that each party take notes regarding the requirements of the agreement. At the conclusion of the mediation, a "Statement of Voluntary Settlement" is signed by the parties and filed with the court. In addition, the mediator completes a "Preliminary Complaint Form." On the form, the mediator describes the allegations made by the plaintiff, denotes the relationship between the parties, and compiles information relating to the parties and the status of the dispute. The mediator also describes the disposition of the dispute under a section entitled "Hearing Disposition." Under another section, the mediator states what future action may be taken if the agreement is broken and, under a "Comments" section, may make personal observations about the mediation and the dispute. This form is not shown to the parties and, unlike the Statement of Voluntary Settlement, is not signed by them.

In December 1996, the Mediation Service mediated the case. Schneider and his former spouse agreed to perform and refrain from performing certain acts in exchange for the dismissal of the criminal charges against Schneider. The parties signed the Statement of Voluntary Settlement form indicating their agreement.

Subsequently, Schneider requested access to the entire mediation file from respondent, Cathleen Kreiner, director of the Mediation Service. Included in the file was a copy of the complaint form prepared by the mediator. Kreiner denied access to the file. Kreiner later offered to provide Schneider a copy of the Statement of Voluntary Settlement and a disposition report of the mediation service, both of which were filed in the office of the clerk of courts.

Schneider then filed a complaint requesting a writ of mandamus to compel Kreiner to provide him access to the complaint form. Schneider also requested attorney fees. This court granted an alternative writ and issued a schedule for the presentation of evidence and briefs.

This cause is now before the court for a consideration of Schneider's request for oral argument as well as the merits.

MOYER, C.J.

For the reasons that follow, we deny relator's request for oral argument and his request for a writ of mandamus.

. . . .

## II.

Relator contends that he is entitled to a writ of mandamus under R.C. 149.43. We have construed R.C. 149.43 " 'to ensure that governmental records be open and made available to the public * * * subject to only a few very limited and narrow exceptions.' " *State ex rel. The Plain Dealer v. Ohio Dept. of Ins.* (1997), 80 Ohio St. 3d 513, 518, 687 N.E.2d 661, 668, quoting *State ex rel. Williams v. Cleveland* (1992), 64 Ohio St. 3d 544, 549, 597 N.E.2d 147, 151.

Among those exceptions in effect at the time of relator's request was former R.C. 149.43(A)(1)(k), 146 Ohio Laws, Part III, 4661, which provided that public records do not include "records the release of which is prohibited by state or federal law." Respondent asserts that R.C. 2317.023 exempts the requested complaint form from disclosure as a confidential mediation communication. We agree with the respondent.

R.C. 2317.023 provides:

"(A) As used in this section:

"(1) 'Mediation' means a nonbinding process for the resolution of a dispute in which both of the following apply:

"(a) A person who is not a party to the dispute serves as mediator to assist the parties to the dispute in negotiating contested issues.

"(b) A court, administrative agency, not-for-profit community mediation provider, or other public body appoints the mediator or refers the dispute to the mediator, or the parties, engage the mediator.

"(2) 'Mediation communication' means a communication made in the course of and relating to the subject matter of a mediation.

"(B) *A mediation communication is confidential. Except as provided in division (C) of this section, no person shall disclose a mediation communication in a civil proceeding or in an administrative proceeding.*" (Emphasis added.)

Pursuant to the statute, the initial question is whether the complaint form sought by Schneider is a "mediation communication" as defined by the statute. R.C. 2317.023(A)(2) defines a mediation communication as "a communication made in the course of and relating to the subject matter of the mediation." The document sought here is a complaint form completed by the mediator. The mediator, in completing the form, describes information relating to the parties and the nature of the dispute. Significantly, the mediator also describes the disposition of the dispute under a section entitled "Hearing Disposition," and may make personal observations about the dispute under a separate section.

Under the statutory definition, it is clear that this form is a mediation communication. It is made in the course of the mediation by the mediator. The mediator compiles information on the form and then describes the outcome. The form is also related to the subject matter of the mediation. The form contains information about the dispute between the parties. It also reflects the thoughts and impressions of the mediator as to the outcome of the mediation, whether and what action shall be taken in the event of breach of the agreement, and the mediator's own observations about the mediation.

R.C. 2317.023(B) states that "[a] mediation communication is confidential." The words of this statute are clear. Mediation communications are confidential and may not be disclosed. "An unambiguous statute means what it says." *Hakim v. Kosydar* (1977), 49 Ohio St. 2d 161, 164, 3 Ohio Op. 3d 211, 213, 359 N.E.2d 1371, 1373. We give words in statutes their plain and ordinary meaning unless otherwise defined. *Coventry Towers, Inc. v. Strongsville* (1985), 18 Ohio St. 3d 120, 122, 480 N.E.2d 412, 414, 18 Ohio B. Rep. 151, 152. Accordingly, having determined that the document sought by relator is a mediation communication, we are compelled by the words of the statute to conclude that the form is confidential and may not be disclosed, unless one of the exceptions enumerated in R.C. 2317.023(C) applies to the relator's cause.

Relator contends that the confidentiality requirement of R.C. 2317.023(B) does not apply because R.C. 2317.023(C)(1) and (4) preclude the application of R.C. 2317.023(B). We disagree.

R.C. 2317.023(C) provides:

"Division (B) of this section does not apply in the following circumstances:

"(1) * * * To the disclosure by any person of a mediation communication made by a mediator if all parties to the mediation and the mediator consent to the disclosure;

"* * *

"(4) To the disclosure of a mediation communication if a court, after a hearing, determines that the disclosure does not circumvent Evidence Rule 408, that the disclosure is necessary in the particular case to prevent a manifest injustice, and that the necessity for disclosure is of sufficient magnitude to outweigh the importance of protecting the general requirement of confidentiality in mediation proceedings."

R.C. 2317.023(C)(1) does not prevent the application of R.C. 2317.023(B) to this cause. There is no evidence that either relator's former spouse or the mediator has consented to disclosure of the complaint form.

Similarly, R.C. 2317.023(C)(4) does not apply to allow disclosure of the complaint form compiled by the mediator. The plain language of R.C. 2317.023 (C)(4) requires a hearing to determine whether this exception to confidentiality is applicable. The presence of a hearing requirement presupposes that the parties will argue the applicability of the exception at a hearing conducted solely for that purpose. There has been no such hearing or request for such a hearing in this cause.

Even applying the substantive provisions of this provision, the relator's arguments lack merit. Disclosure of the complaint form compiled by the mediator is not necessary to prevent a manifest injustice, nor is the necessity for disclosure of sufficient magnitude to outweigh the importance of protecting the general requirement of confidentiality. Relator's sole assertion for requesting the document is that he may face potential criminal charges if he does not comply with the agreement reached in mediation. However, the mere possibility that the relator may be involved in future litigation cannot possibly establish the presence of a manifest injustice, as required by the statutory exception. Such a conclusion does not comport with the common meaning of "manifest injustice," which is defined as a clear or openly unjust act. *See Webster's Third New International Dictionary* (1986) 1164, 1375. The plain meaning of the words of the statute requires more than a possibility of future litigation.

Likewise, the possibility of future litigation does not create a necessity for disclosure of a magnitude sufficient to outweigh the general requirement of confidentiality. Every agreement in mediation may be breached. Such a breach could result in future litigation. However, this possibility cannot outweigh the plain words of R.C. 2317.023(B), which establish a requirement of confidentiality. By those words, the General Assembly has determined that confidentiality is a means to encourage the use of mediation and frankness within mediation sessions. Were we to agree with the relator's argument, we would severely undermine that determination by the General Assembly, as reflected in the clear words of the statute. Accordingly, R.C. 2317.023(C)(4) does not apply to relator's request.

Finally, relator asserts that R.C. 2317.023(B) does not apply to this cause because the statute was not effective at the time that the record was created, *i.e.*, when the mediation session occurred. R.C. 2317.023 became effective on January 27, 1997, which was after the record was created but before relator requested the form and filed this mandamus action. 146 Ohio Laws, Part II, 4033.

This contention also is meritless. R.C. 2317.023 was effective at the time of the request for the form. The date the form was created is not relevant for the purposes of R.C. 149.43. "Since the statute merely deals with record disclosure, not record keeping, only a prospective duty is imposed upon those maintaining public records." *State ex rel. Beacon Journal Publishing Co. v. Univ. of Akron* (1980), 64 Ohio St. 2d 392, 396, 18 Ohio Op. 3d 534, 537, 415 N.E.2d 310, 313.

Accordingly, there is no authority to overcome the confidentiality requirement of R.C. 2317.023(B). The complaint form sought by the relator is a mediation communication which is not subject to disclosure under R.C. 149.43 because R.C. 2317.023(B) clearly provides for its confidentiality. Therefore, we deny the relator's request for a writ of mandamus, and his request for attorney fees is also denied.

*Writ denied.*

# OLAM v. CONGRESS MORTGAGE COMPANY
United States District Court for the Northern District of California
68 F. Supp. 2d 1110 (1999)

WAYNE D. BRAZIL, UNITED STATES MAGISTRATE JUDGE.

The court addresses in this opinion several difficult issues about the relationship between a court-sponsored voluntary mediation and subsequent proceedings whose purpose is to determine whether the parties entered an enforceable agreement at the close of the mediation session.

As we explain below, the parties participated in a lengthy mediation that was hosted by this court's ADR Program Counsel — an employee of the court who is both a lawyer and an ADR professional. At the end of the mediation (after midnight), the parties signed a "Memorandum of Understanding" (MOU) that states that it is "intended as a binding document itself . . . ."

Contending that the consent she apparently gave was not legally valid, plaintiff has taken the position that the MOU is not enforceable. She has not complied with its terms. Defendants have filed a motion to enforce the MOU as a binding contract.

One of the principal issues with which the court wrestles, below, is whether evidence about what occurred during the mediation proceedings, including testimony from the mediator, may be used to help resolve this dispute. Before we address the merits of these issues, we must decide whose law to apply (state or federal).

[The court discussed the factors surrounding the choice of federal or state (California) law, ultimately deciding to follow California law on the issue of mediator testimony.]

Having decided, for reasons set forth below, that fairness required the court to take evidence from the mediator in this case, I elected to call the mediator to the witness stand after the other principal participants in the September 10, 1998, mediation had testified. But, importantly, I also decided to take the testimony from the mediator in closed proceedings, under seal. After hearing his testimony in this protected setting, and after considering all the other evidence adduced during the hearing, I was positioned to determine much more reliably whether, or to what extent, overriding fairness interests required me to use and publicly disclose testimony from the mediator in making my decision about whether the parties had entered an enforceable settlement contract.

## PERTINENT CALIFORNIA PRIVILEGE LAW

The California legislature has crafted two sets of statutory provisions that must be addressed by courts considering whether they may use in a subsequent civil proceeding any evidence about what occurred or was said during a mediation.

Section 703.5 of the California Evidence Code states, in pertinent part: "No person presiding at any judicial or quasi-judicial proceeding, and no arbitrator or mediator, shall be competent to testify, in any subsequent civil proceeding, as to any statement, conduct, decision, or ruling, occurring at or in conjunction with the prior proceeding, except as to a statement or conduct that could [give rise to contempt, constitute a crime, trigger investigation by the State Bar or the Commission on Judicial Performance, or give rise to disqualification proceedings]."

We note, before proceeding, that by its express terms § 703.5 applies (as pertinent here) only to statements or decisions made, or conduct occurring, in connection with a mediation. Read literally, this statute would not apply to perceptions of participants' appearance, demeanor, or physical condition during a mediation. We also note, however, that compelling mediators to testify or otherwise offer evidence about *anything* that occurred or was perceived during a mediation threatens confidentiality expectations of the participants and imposes burdens on mediators — and that such threats and burdens tend, at least in some measure, to undermine interests that the California legislature likely sought to protect when it enacted this statute. In construing and applying this statute, we endeavor to honor the purposes that drive it.

The other directly pertinent provision from the California Evidence Code is § 1119. It states, in pertinent part: "Except as otherwise provided in this chapter: (a) No evidence of anything said or any admission made . . . in the course of, or pursuant to, a mediation . . . is admissible or subject to discovery, and disclosure of the evidence shall not be compelled, in any . . . noncriminal proceeding . . . (b) No writing . . . prepared in the course of, or pursuant to, a mediation . . . is admissible or subject to discovery, and disclosure of the writing shall not be compelled in any . . . noncriminal proceeding . . . (c) All communications . . . by and between participants in the course of a mediation . . . shall remain confidential."

Of the other provisions that expressly qualify the prohibitions set forth in section 1119, the most important for our purposes is § 1123. It states that "[a] written settlement agreement prepared in the course of, or pursuant to, a mediation, is not made inadmissible, or protected from disclosure . . . if the agreement is signed by the settling parties and . . . (b) The agreement provides that it is enforceable or binding or words to that effect."

As noted above, the "Memorandum of Understanding" that the parties executed at the end of the mediation session in this case states expressly that it "is intended as a binding document itself." No party contends that this MOU is inadmissible.

## WAIVERS BY THE *PARTIES* (BUT *NOT* THE MEDIATOR) OF THEIR MEDIATION PRIVILEGE

As we noted earlier, the plaintiff and the defendants have expressly waived confidentiality protections conferred by the California statutes quoted above. Both the plaintiff and the defendants have indicated, clearly and on advice of counsel, that they want the court to consider evidence about what occurred during the mediation, including testimony directly from the mediator, as the court resolves the issues raised by defendants' motion to enforce the settlement agreement.

Faced with a document that on its face appears to be an enforceable settlement contract, and contending that her apparent consent was not legally valid because of serious temporary impairments in her mental, emotional, and physical condition, plaintiff's waiver reaches not only perceptions by other participants of her appearance, demeanor, condition, and conduct during the mediation, but also their recollections of what she said and what others said in her presence. Her waiver expressly covers testimony about such matters not only by opposing counsel and parties, but also by the mediator and by her then lawyer, Ms. Voisenat. It covers group sessions as well as private caucuses.

While not as complete, defendants' waivers also are substantial. Defendants have not relinquished their right to protect the confidentiality of communications between them and their counsel, or the private communications between the mediator and them or their lawyers. They have stipulated, however, that evidence may be admitted about perceptions and communications made during group sessions — and they have actively sought the testimony of the mediator about his perceptions in and recollections from both the group sessions and his private caucuses with plaintiff or Ms. Voisenat.

The plaintiff and the defendants have made the waivers discussed above on the record, through counsel (plaintiff has directly participated in the hearings in which her waivers have been made). In addition, the court described the waivers with particularity in its Order Re July 21, 1999 Status Conference, filed July 23, 1999. At the beginning of the evidentiary hearing the parties acknowledged and affirmed these waivers in writing by affixing their signatures below the relevant paragraphs on a copy of that July 23rd Order. These waivers are deemed sufficient under § 1122(a)(1) of the California Evidence Code to remove § 1119 as a barrier to admission of the evidence the court accepted during the evidentiary hearing.

## THE MEDIATOR'S PRIVILEGE

California law confers on mediators a privilege that is independent of the privilege conferred on parties to a mediation. By declaring that, subject to exceptions not applicable here, mediators are incompetent to testify "as to any statement, conduct, decision, or ruling, occurring at or in conjunction with [the mediation]," section 703.5 of the Evidence Code has the effect of making a mediator the holder of an independent privilege. Section 1119 of the Evidence Code appears to have the same effect — as it prohibits courts from compelling disclosure of evidence about mediation communications and directs that all such communications "shall remain confidential." As the California Court of Appeal recently pointed out, "the Legislature intended that the confidentiality provision of section 1119 may be asserted by the mediator as well as by the participants in the mediation." It follows that, under California law, a waiver of the mediation privilege by the parties is not a sufficient basis for a court to permit or order a mediator to testify. Rather, an independent determination must be made before testimony from a mediator should be permitted or ordered.

In the case at bar, the mediator (Mr. Herman) was and is an employee of the federal court (a "staff neutral"). He hosted the mediation at the behest of the court and under this court's ADR rules. These facts are not sufficient to justify ordering him to testify about what occurred during the mediation — even when the parties have waived their mediation privilege and want the mediator to testify. Mr. Herman is a member of the California bar — and no doubt feels bound to honor the directives of California law. He also is a professional in mediation — and feels a moral obligation to preserve the essential integrity of the mediation process — an integrity to which he believes the promise of confidentiality is fundamental.

Out of respect for these feelings, the court chose not to put Mr. Herman in an awkward position where he might have felt he had to choose between being a loyal employee of the court, on the one hand, and, on the other, asserting the mediator's privilege under California law. Instead, the court announced that it would proceed on the assumption that Mr. Herman was respectfully and appropriately asserting the mediator's privilege and was formally objecting to being called to testify about anything said or done during the mediation.

Regardless of whether Mr. Herman invoked the mediator's privilege, the wording of section 703.5 can be understood as imposing an independent duty on the courts to determine whether testimony from a mediator should be accepted. Unlike some other privilege statutes, which expressly confer a right on the holder of the privilege to refuse to disclose protected communications, as well as the power to prevent others from disclosing such communications, section 703.5 is framed in terms of competence to testify. In its pertinent part, it declares that (subject to exceptions not applicable here) a mediator is not competent to testify "in any subsequent civil proceeding" about words uttered or conduct occurring during a mediation. This wording appears to have two consequences: it would not empower a mediator to prevent others from disclosing mediation communications, but it would require courts, on their own initiative, to determine whether it would be lawful to compel or permit a mediator to testify about matters occurring within a mediation.

So the issue of whether it was appropriate under California law in these circumstances to compel the mediator to testify was squarely raised both by the court's assuming that Mr. Herman invoked the applicable statutes and by the court's understanding of its independent duty to address this question.

Before turning to other elements of our analysis of this issue, it is important to emphasize one critical and undisputed fact: at the end of the mediation, the parties and their lawyers signed a document, typed clearly by the mediator, which appears on its face to contain the essential terms of an agreement, which expressly states that it "is intended as a binding document itself," and which affirms the parties' agreement that "the court will have continuing jurisdiction over the enforcement of this memorandum of understanding as well as the ultimate settlement agreement and any disputes arising therefrom . . . ."

The fact that the parties and their lawyers signed such a document at the end of the mediation permits California courts to proceed to consider, in a hearing to determine whether the parties entered an enforceable contract, whether to admit evidence about what was said and done during the mediation itself. If there were no signed writing, and the alleged contract was oral, California law would not permit courts to use evidence from the mediation itself to determine whether an enforceable agreement had been reached. *See Ryan v. Garcia*, 27 Cal. App. 4th 1006 (Third Dist. 1994) (applying and interpreting what was then section 1152.5 of the California

Evidence Code, a predecessor to the current version of section 1119 of that Code).

We turn to the issue of whether, under California law, we should compel the mediator to testify — despite the statutory prohibitions set forth in sections 703.5 and 1119 of the Evidence Code. The most important opinion by a California court in this arena is *Rinaker v. Superior Court*, 62 Cal. App. 4th 155 (Third District 1998). In that case the Court of Appeal held that there may be circumstances in which a trial court, over vigorous objection by a party and by the mediator, could compel testimony from the mediator in a juvenile delinquency proceeding (deemed a "civil" matter under California law). The defendant in the delinquency proceeding wanted to call the mediator to try to impeach testimony that was expected from a prosecution witness. That witness and the delinquency defendant had earlier participated in a mediation — and the delinquency defendant believed that the complaining witness had made admissions to the mediator that would substantially undermine the credibility of the complaining witnesses testimony — and thus would materially strengthen the defense. In these circumstances, the *Rinaker* court held that the mediator could be compelled to testify if, after *in camera* consideration of what her testimony would be, the trial judge determined that her testimony might well promote significantly the public interest in preventing perjury and the defendant's fundamental right to a fair judicial process.

In essence, the *Rinaker* court instructs California trial judges to conduct a two-stage balancing analysis. The goal of the first stage balancing is to determine whether to compel the mediator to appear at an *in camera* proceeding to determine precisely what her testimony would be. In this first stage, the judge considers all the circumstances and weighs all the competing rights and interests, including the values that would be threatened not by public disclosure mediation communications, but by ordering the mediator to appear at an *in camera* proceeding to disclose only to the court and counsel, out of public view, what she would say the parties said during the mediation. At this juncture the goal is to determine whether the harm that would be done to the values that underlie the mediation privileges simply by ordering the mediator to participate in the *in camera* proceedings can be justified — by the prospect that her testimony might well make a singular and substantial contribution to protecting or advancing competing interests of comparable or greater magnitude.

The trial judge reaches the second stage of balancing analysis only if the product of the first stage is a decision to order the mediator to detail, *in camera*, what her testimony would be. A court that orders the *in camera* disclosure gains precise and reliable knowledge of what the mediator's testimony would be — and only with that knowledge is the court positioned to launch its second balancing analysis. In this second stage the court is to weigh and comparatively assess (1) the importance of the values and interests that would be harmed if the mediator was compelled to testify (perhaps subject to a sealing or protective order, if appropriate), (2) the magnitude of the harm that compelling the testimony would cause to those values and interests, (3) the importance of the rights or interests that would be jeopardized if the mediator's testimony was not accessible in the specific proceedings in question, and (4) how much the testimony would contribute toward protecting those rights or advancing those interests — an inquiry that includes, among other things, an assessment of whether there are alternative sources of evidence of comparable probative value.

So we turn now to a description of that balancing analysis.

As indicated in an earlier section, the product of the first stage of the analysis was my decision that it was necessary to determine (through sealed proceedings) what Mr. Herman's testimony would be. Reaching that determination involved the following considerations. First, I acknowledge squarely that a decision to require a mediator to give evidence, even *in camera* or under seal, about what occurred during a mediation threatens values underlying the mediation privileges. As the *Rinaker* court suggested, the California legislature adopted these privileges in the belief that without the promise of confidentiality it would be appreciably more difficult to achieve the goals of mediation programs. *Rinaker v. Superior Court, supra*, 62 Cal. App. 4th at 165-166, citing *Ryan v. Garcia*, 27 Cal. App. 4th 1006, 1010 (Third Dist. 1994). Construing an earlier version of the mediation privilege statute, the same court of appeal had opined a few years before that without assurances of confidentiality "some litigants [would be deterred] from participating freely and openly in mediation." That court also quoted approvingly the suggestion from a practice guide that "confidentiality is absolutely essential to mediation," in part because without it "parties would be reluctant to make the kinds of concessions and admission that pave the way to settlement."

While this court has no occasion or power to quarrel with these generally applicable pronouncements of state policy, we observe that they appear to have appreciably less force when, as here, the parties to the mediation have waived confidentiality protections, indeed have asked the court to compel the mediator to testify — so that justice can be done.

If a party to the mediation were objecting to compelling the mediator to testify we would be faced with a substantially more difficult analysis. But the absence of such an objection does not mean that ordering the mediator to disclose, even *in camera*, matters that occurred within the mediation does not pose some threat to values underlying the mediation privileges. As the *Rinaker* court pointed out, ordering mediators to participate in proceedings arising out of mediations imposes economic and psychic burdens that could make some people reluctant to agree to serve as a mediator, especially in programs where that service is pro bono or poorly compensated.

This is not a matter of time and money only. Good mediators are likely to feel violated by being compelled to give evidence that could be used against a party with whom they tried to establish a relationship of trust during a mediation. Good mediators are deeply committed to being and remaining neutral and non-judgmental, and to building and preserving relationships with parties. To force them to give evidence that hurts someone from whom they actively solicited trust (during the mediation) rips the fabric of their work and can threaten their sense of the center of their professional integrity. These are not inconsequential matters.

Like many other variables in this kind of analysis, however, the magnitude of these risks can vary with the circumstances. Here, for instance, all parties to the mediation want the mediator to testify about things that occurred during the mediation — so ordering the testimony would do less harm to the actual relationships developed than it would in a case where one of the parties to the mediation objected to the use of evidence from the mediator.

We acknowledge, however, that the possibility that a mediator might be forced to testify over objection could harm the capacity of mediators in general to create the environment of trust that they feel maximizes the likelihood that constructive communication will occur during the mediation session. But the level of harm to that interest likely varies, at least in some measure, with the perception within the community of mediators and litigants about how likely it is that any given mediation will be followed at some point by an order compelling the neutral to offer evidence about what occurred during the session. I know of no studies or statistics that purport to reflect how often courts or parties seek evidence from mediators — and I suspect that the incidence of this issue arising would not be identical across the broad spectrum of mediation programs and settings. What I can report is that this case represents the first time that I have been called upon to address these kinds of questions in the more than fifteen years that I have been responsible for ADR programs in this court. Nor am I aware of the issue arising before other judges here. Based on that experience, my partially educated guess is that the likelihood that a mediator or the parties in any given case need fear that the mediator would later be constrained to testify is extraordinarily small.

That conviction is reinforced by another consideration. As we pointed out above, under California law, and this court's view of sound public policy, there should be no occasion to consider whether to seek testimony from a mediator for purpose of determining whether the parties entered an enforceable settlement contract unless the mediation produced a writing (or competent record) that appears on its face to constitute an enforceable contract, signed or formally assented to by all the parties. Thus, it is only when there is such a writing or record, and when a party nonetheless seeks to escape its apparent effect, that courts applying California law would even consider calling for evidence from a mediator for purposes of determining whether the parties settled the case. Surely these circumstances will arise after only a tiny fraction of mediations.

The magnitude of the risk to values underlying the mediation privileges that can be created by ordering a mediator to testify also can vary with the nature of the testimony that is sought. Comparing the kind of testimony sought in *Rinaker* with the kind of testimony sought in the case at bar illustrates this point. In *Rinaker*, one party wanted to use the mediator's recollection about what another party said during the mediation to impeach subsequent trial testimony. So the mediator was to serve as a source of evidence about what words a party to the mediation uttered, what statements or admissions that party made.

As the Court of Appeal appeared to recognize, this kind of testimony could be particularly threatening to the spirit and methods that some people believe are important both to the philosophy and the success of some mediation processes. Under one approach to mediation, the primary goal is not to establish "the truth" or to determine reliably what the historical facts actually were. Rather, the goal is to go both deeper than and beyond history — to emphasize feelings, underlying interests, and a search for means for social repair or reorientation. In this kind of mediation, what happened between the parties in the past can be appreciably less important than why, than what needs drove what happened or were exposed or defined by what happened, than how the parties feel about it, and than what they can bring themselves to do to move on.

Moreover, the methods some mediators use to explore underlying interests and feelings and to build settlement bridges are in some instances intentionally distanced from the actual historical facts. In some mediations, the focus is on feelings rather than facts. The neutral may ask the parties to set aside pre-occupations with what happened as she tries to help the parties understand underlying motivations and needs and to remove emotional obstacles through exercises in venting. Some mediators use hypotheticals that are expressly and intentionally not presented as accurate reflections of reality — in order to help the parties explore their situation and the range of solution options that might be available. A mediator might encourage parties to "try on" certain ideas or feelings that the parties would contend have little connection with past conduct, to experiment with the effects on themselves and others of expressions of emotions or of openness to concessions or proposals that, outside the special environment of the mediation, the parties would not entertain or admit. All of this, as mediator Rinaker herself pointed out, can have precious little to do with historical accuracy or "truth."

Given these features of some mediations, it could be both threatening and unfair to hold a participant to the literal meaning of at least some of the words she uttered during the course of a mediation. And testimony from the mediator about what those words were during the mediation might constitute very unreliable (actively misleading) evidence about what the earlier historical facts were.

For these reasons, a court conducting the kind of balancing analysis called for by the *Rinaker* court should try to determine what kind of techniques and processes were used in the particular mediation in issue. The more like the processes just described, the more harm would be done by trying to use evidence about what was said or done during the mediation to help prove what the earlier historical facts really were. On the other hand, if the mediation process was closer to an adjudicate/evaluative model, with a clear focus (understood by all participants) on evidence, law, and traditional analysis of liability, damages, and settlement options, use of evidence from the mediation in subsequent civil proceedings might be less vulnerable to criticism for being unfair and unreliable.

Regardless of which approach or methods the mediator used, however, the kind of testimony sought from the mediator in this case poses less of a threat to fairness and reliability values than the kind of testimony that was sought from the mediator in *Rinaker*. During the first stage balancing analysis in the case at bar, the parties and I assumed that the testimony from the mediator that would be most consequential would focus not primarily on what Ms. Olam said during the mediation, but on how she acted and the mediator's perceptions of her physical, emotional, and mental condition. The purpose would not be to nail down and dissect her specific words, but to assess at a more general and impressionistic level her condition and capacities. That purpose might be achieved with relatively little disclosure of the content of her confidential communications. As conceded above, that does not mean that compelling the testimony by the mediator would pose no threat to values underlying the privileges — but that the degree of harm to those values would not be as great as it would be if the testimony was for the kinds of impeachment purposes that were proffered in *Rinaker*. And in a balancing analysis, probable degree of harm is an important consideration.

What we have been doing in the preceding paragraphs is attempting, as the first component of the first stage balancing analysis, to identify the interests that might be threatened by ordering the mediator, in the specific circumstances presented here, to testify under seal — and to assess the magnitude of the harm that ordering the testimony would likely do to those interests. Having assayed these matters, we turn to the other side of the balance. We will identify the interests that ordering the testimony (under seal, at least initially) might advance, assess the relative importance of those interests, and try to predict the magnitude of the contribution to achieving those interests that ordering the testimony would likely make (or the extent of the harm that we likely would do to those interests if we did not compel the testimony).

The interests that are likely to be advanced by compelling the mediator to testify in this case are of considerable importance. Moreover, as we shall see, some of those interests parallel and reinforce the objectives the legislature sought to advance by providing for confidentiality in mediation.

The first interest we identify is the interest in doing justice. Here is what we mean. For reasons described below, the mediator is positioned in this case to offer what could be crucial, certainly very probative, evidence about the central factual issues in this matter. There is a strong possibility that his testimony will greatly improve the court's ability to determine reliably what the pertinent historical facts actually were. Establishing reliably what the facts were is critical to doing justice (here, justice means this: applying the law correctly to the real historical facts). It is the fundamental duty of a public court in our society to do justice — to resolve disputes in accordance with the law when the parties don't. Confidence in our system of justice as a whole, in our government as a whole, turns in no small measure on confidence in the courts' ability to do justice in individual cases. So doing justice in individual cases is an interest of considerable magnitude.

When we put case-specific flesh on these abstract bones, we see that "doing justice" implicates interests of considerable importance to the parties — all of whom want the mediator to testify. From the plaintiff's perspective, the interests that the defendants' motion threatens could hardly be more fundamental. According to Ms. Olam, the mediation process was fundamentally unfair to her — and resulted in an apparent agreement whose terms are literally unconscionable and whose enforcement would render her homeless and virtually destitute. To her, doing justice in this setting means protecting her from these fundamental wrongs.

From the defendants' perspective, doing justice in this case means, among other things, bringing to a lawful close disputes with Ms. Olam that have been on-going for about seven years — disputes that the defendants believe have cost them, without justification, at least scores of thousands of dollars. The defendants believe that Ms. Olam has breached no fewer than three separate contractual commitments with them (not counting the agreement reached at the end of the mediation) — and that those breaches are the product of a calculated effort not only to avoid meeting legitimate obligations, but also to make unfair use, for years, of the defendants' money.

Defendants also believe that Ms. Olam has abused over the years several of her own counsel — as well as the judicial process and this court's ADR program (for which she has been charged nothing). Through their motion, the defendants ask the court to affirm that they acquired legal rights through the settlement agreement that the mediation produced. They also ask the court to enforce those rights, and thus to enable the defendants to avoid the burdens, expense, delay, and risks of going to trial in this matter. These also are matters of consequence.

And they are not the only interests that could be advanced by compelling the mediator to testify. According to the defendants' pre-hearing proffers, the mediator's testimony would establish clearly that the mediation process was fair and that the plaintiff's consent to the settlement agreement was legally viable. Thus the mediator's testimony, according to the defendants, would reassure the community and the court about the integrity of the mediation process that the court sponsored.

That testimony also would provide the court with the evidentiary confidence it needs to enforce the agreement. A publicly announced decision to enforce the settlement would, in turn, encourage parties who want to try to settle their cases to use the court's mediation program for that purpose. An order appropriately enforcing an agreement reached through the mediation also would encourage parties in the future to take mediations seriously, to understand that they represent real opportunities to reach closure and avoid trial, and to attend carefully to terms of agreements proposed in mediations. In these important ways, taking testimony from the mediator could strengthen the mediation program.

In sharp contrast, refusing to compel the mediator to testify might well deprive the court of the evidence it needs to rule reliably on the plaintiff's contentions — and thus might either cause the court to impose an unjust outcome on the plaintiff or disable the court from enforcing the settlement. In this setting, refusing to compel testimony from the mediator might end up being tantamount to denying the motion to enforce the agreement — because a crucial source of evidence about the plaintiff's condition and capacities would be missing. Following that course, defendants suggest, would do considerable harm not only to the court's mediation program but also to fundamental fairness. If parties believed that courts routinely would refuse to compel mediators to testify, and that the absence of evidence from mediators would enhance the viability of a contention that apparent consent to a settlement contract was not legally viable, cynical parties would be encouraged either to try to escape commitments they made during mediations or to use threats of such escapes to try to re-negotiate, after the mediation, more favorable terms — terms that they never would have been able to secure without this artificial and unfair leverage.

In sum, it is clear that refusing even to determine what the mediator's testimony would be, in the circumstances here presented, threatens values of great significance. But we would miss the main analytical chance if all we did was identify those values and proclaim their Importance. In fact, when the values implicated are obviously of great moment, there is a danger that the process of identifying them will generate unjustified momentum toward a conclusion that exaggerates the weight on this side of the scale. Thus we emphasize that the central question is not which values are implicated, but how much they would be advanced by compelling the testimony or how much they would be harmed by not compelling it.

We concluded, after analysis and before the hearing, that the mediator's testimony was sufficiently likely to make substantial contributions toward achieving the ends described above to justify compelling an exploration, under seal, of what his testimony would be. While we did not assume that there were no pressures or motivations that might affect the reliability of the mediator's testimony, it was obvious that the mediator was the only source of presumptively disinterested, neutral evidence. The only other witnesses with personal knowledge of the plaintiff's condition at the mediation were the parties and their lawyers — none of whom were disinterested. And given the foreseeable testimony about the way the mediation was structured (with lots of caucusing by the mediator with one side at a time), it was likely that the mediator would have had much more exposure to the plaintiff over the course of the lengthy mediation than any other witness save her lawyer.

But it also was foreseeable that substantial questions would be raised about the reliability of the testimony that Ms. Olam's former lawyer, Phyllis Voisenat, would give. We knew, when we conducted this first stage balancing, that Ms. Voisenat no longer represented Ms. Olam. We also knew that strains had developed in that relationship before it had ended, and that lawyer and client had felt that their ability to communicate with one another left a great deal to be desired. Moreover, Ms. Olam had suggested through her new lawyer (the fifth attorney to work with her in connection with her disputes with the defendants) that she might contend during the hearing that Ms. Voisenat, her former lawyer, had been one of the sources of unlawful pressure on her to sign the settlement agreement at the end of the mediation. And there were at least rumblings from the plaintiff's camp about a malpractice suit by Ms. Olam against Ms. Voisenat, who, understandably, expressed concerns about the possible use against her in such litigation of testimony she would give in these proceedings. For all these reasons, there was a substantial likelihood that plaintiff would raise serious questions about the accuracy of Ms. Voisenat's testimony and that, given all the circumstances, the court would not be sure how much it should rely on the evidence Ms. Voisenat would give. We also could foresee that the circumstances in which the mediator would have interacted with Ms. Olam during the mediation held the promise of yielding perceptions of her mental, emotional and physical condition that would be especially well-grounded. Because we know how the court's mediators are trained, we could anticipate that Mr. Herman met with the plaintiff and her lawyer in private, away from the defendants and their counsel — thus freeing plaintiff from the emotional charges, defensiveness, stress, and "pressure to posture" that negotiating in the presence of "the enemy" can inspire. We also could expect (because we know how Mr. Herman trains other people to act as mediators) that in his private meetings with plaintiff and her lawyer Mr. Herman would try to create an environment that was as unthreatening and as comfortable for her as possible. And that environment would likely give him more reliable access to the plaintiff's real condition than any of the witnesses connected with the defense of the case could have had.

In short, there was a substantial likelihood that testimony from the mediator would be the most reliable and probative on the central issues raised by the plaintiff in response to the defendants' motion. And there was no likely alternative source of evidence on these issues that would be of comparable probative utility. So it appeared that testimony from the mediator would be crucial to the court's capacity to do its job — and that refusing to compel that testimony posed a serious threat to every value identified above. In this setting, California courts clearly would conclude the first stage balancing analysis by ordering the mediator to testify *in camera* or under seal — so that the court, aided by inputs from the parties, could make a refined and reliable judgment about whether to use that testimony to help resolve the substantive issues raised by the pending motion.

As noted earlier, we called the mediator to testify (under seal) after all other participants in the mediation had been examined and cross-examined — so that the lawyers (and the court) would be able to identify all the subjects and questions that they should cover with the mediator. With the record thus fully developed, we were well situated to determine whether using (and publicly disclosing) the mediator's testimony would make a contribution of sufficient magnitude to justify the level of harm that using and disclosing the testimony would likely cause, in the circumstances of this case, to the interests that inform the mediation privilege law in California. As our detailed account, later in this opinion, of the evidence from all sources demonstrates, it became clear that the mediator's testimony was essential to doing justice here — so we decided to use it and unseal it.

[The court went on to conclude, based in part on the mediator's in camera testimony, that plaintiff had failed to present adequate evidence that the agreement she entered into was unenforceable.]

## IN RE TELIGENT, INC.
United States Court of Appeals for the Second Circuit
640 F.3d 53 (2011)

[A law firm had moved to lift two protective orders that would have prohibited disclosure of communications made during mediation. The federal bankruptcy judge denied this motion, and a related motion concerning the validity of provisions of the settlement agreement.]

. . .

In this case, the bankruptcy court denied K & L Gates's motion to lift the confidentiality provisions of the Protective Orders based on the court's conclusion that K & L Gates failed to demonstrate a compelling need for the discovery, failed to show that the information was not otherwise available, and failed to establish that the need for the evidence was outweighed by the public interest in maintaining confidentiality. The district court affirmed these conclusions. There was no error in this conclusion.

Confidentiality is an important feature of the mediation and other alternative dispute resolution processes. Promising participants confidentiality in these proceedings "promotes the free flow of information that may result in the settlement of a dispute," and protecting the integrity of alternative dispute resolution generally. We vigorously enforce the confidentiality provisions of our own alternative dispute resolution, the Civil Appeals Management Plan ("CAMP"), because we believe that confidentiality is "essential" to CAMP's vitality and effectiveness.

A party seeking disclosure of confidential mediation communications must demonstrate (1) a special need for the confidential material, (2) resulting unfairness from a lack of discovery, and (3) that the need for the evidence outweighs the interest in maintaining confidentiality.. All three factors are necessary to warrant disclosure of otherwise non-discoverable documents.

We draw this standard from the sources relied upon by the learned bankruptcy court, which include the Uniform Mediation Act ("UMA"), the Administrative Dispute Resolution Act of 1996 ("ADRA 1996"), 5 U.S.C. §§ 571 et seq., and the Administrative Dispute Resolution Act of 1998 ("ADRA 1998"), 28 U.S.C. §§ 651 et seq. Each of these recognizes the importance of maintaining the confidentiality of mediation communications and provides for disclosure in only limited circumstances. For example, ADRA 1996, which applies to federal administrative agency alternative dispute resolution, prohibits disclosure of confidential mediation communications unless the party seeking disclosure demonstrates exceptional circumstances, such as when non-disclosure would result in a manifest injustice, help establish a violation of law, or prevent harm to the public health or safety. Relatedly, under the UMA, the party seeking disclosure of confidential mediation communications must demonstrate that the evidence is not otherwise available and that the need for the communications substantially outweighs the interest in protecting confidentiality. The standards for disclosure under the UMA and the ADRAs are also consistent with the standard governing modification of protective orders entered under Federal Rule of Civil Procedure 26(c). . . .

Here, as the bankruptcy court observed, K & L Gates has sought a blanket lift of the confidentiality provisions in the Protective Orders. However, K & L Gates failed to demonstrate a special or compelling need for *all* mediation communications. Indeed, the law firm failed to submit any evidence to support its argument that there was a special need for disclosure of any specific communication. There was, therefore, no error in the bankruptcy court's conclusion that K & L Gates failed to satisfy prong one of the standard governing disclosure of confidential mediation communications.

Likewise, the bankruptcy court committed no error in holding that K & L Gates failed to satisfy prong two of the test. As the bankruptcy court explained, the law firm failed to demonstrate a resulting unfairness from a lack of discovery, because the evidence sought by K & L Gates was available through other means, including through responses to interrogatories or depositions. Accordingly, the law firm failed to show that "extraordinary circumstances" warrant disclosure.

Finally, because K & L Gates failed to demonstrate a special need for the mediation communications, the law firm did not satisfy prong three of the test, which requires a party seeking disclosure of confidential material to show that its need outweighs the important interest in protecting the confidentiality of the material. As we explained in the context of litigation if "protective orders have no presumptive entitlement to remain in force, parties would resort less often to the judicial system for fear that such orders would be readily set aside in the future." It follows that similar concerns arise in the context of mediation. Were courts to cavalierly set aside confidentiality restrictions on disclosure of communications made in the context of mediation, parties might be less frank and forthcoming during the mediation process or might even limit their use of mediation altogether. These concerns counsel in favor of a presumption against modification of the confidentiality provisions of protective orders entered in the context of mediation. Accordingly, we conclude that there was no error in the denial of K & L Gates's motion to lift the confidentiality provisions of the Protective Orders in this case.

. . .

## CONCLUSION

For the reasons stated herein, we **AFFIRM** the order of the district court.

## NOTES AND QUESTIONS

(1)   Is the Ohio statute cited in *Schneider*, providing for a confidentiality exception "to prevent a manifest injustice," too broad? Does it give too much discretion to the courts in granting an exception? A Wisconsin appellate court admitted into evidence a tape of a mediation session pursuant to a statutorily authorized manifest injustice exception in *In re the Paternity of Emily C.B.*, 677 N.W.2d 732 (Wis. Ct. App. 2004).

(2)   In taking the mediator's testimony "in closed proceedings, under seal" in the *Olam* case, was Judge Brazil, in effect, carving out a "manifest injustice" exception similar to that found in the Ohio statute? Judge Brazil's lengthy commentary on the need for confidentiality displays a sensitivity to important policy concerns. Was his decision to go forward with the mediator's testimony largely influenced by the fact that, as he states, he had been responsible for his court's ADR programs for 15 years and had never before encountered the issue? Was the fact that both parties agreed to waive confidentiality critical to his decision?

(3)   In *Teligent*, the United States Court of Appeals for the Second Circuit takes a firm stand in protecting the confidentiality of mediation communications by establishing a restrictive, three-part test for granting an exception. In *Avocent Redmond Corp. v. Raritan Americas, Inc.*, 2011 U.S. Dist. LEXIS 109596 (S.D.N.Y. Sept. 23, 2011), a federal trial court applied the *Teligent* exceptions in ruling that the party seeking disclosure had "not satisfied any one of the three prongs." Do you think the *Teligent* test is likely to be followed in other federal circuits?

## G.   ALTERNATIVES TO THE UNIFORM MEDIATION ACT

In the first decade following the UMA's approval by the National Conference of Commissioners on Uniform State Laws and the American Bar Association in 2002, the District of Columbia and 10 states (Idaho, Illinois, Iowa, Nebraska, New Jersey, Ohio, South Dakota, Utah, Vermont, and Washington) had enacted UMA statutes. For a current listing of UMA adoptions, visit the Uniform Law Commissioners website at: http://www.uniformlaws.org. Some states have declined to adopt the UMA because they have pre-existing confidentiality legislation that they prefer over the UMA. In particular, the three states (California, Florida, and Texas) that have been the early leaders in the mediation field have clearly stated their preference for their confidentiality provisions over those of the UMA. In the following two articles, Professor Brian D. Shannon makes the case for the superiority of the Texas approach, while Professor Richard Reuben responds to Shannon's concerns.

## DANCING WITH THE ONE THAT "BRUNG US" — WHY THE TEXAS ADR COMMUNITY HAS DECLINED TO EMBRACE THE UMA
2003 J. Disp. Resol. 197, 201–05, 207, 211–15[*]
By Brian D. Shannon

I readily acknowledge that the UMA is a bold and noble project, and it is certainly the result of substantial effort and compromise . . . . That being said, however, much of the Texas mediation community, of which I am a part, has largely opposed enactment of the UMA's framework for our state . . . . The primary concerns . . . relate to two principal areas: (1) the UMA drafters' approach to confidentiality in comparison to the long-established legislative approach set forth in the Texas ADR Act, and (2) the relative complexity of the UMA's provisions.

. . . .

### II. DIFFERING APPROACHES TO CONFIDENTIALITY

The Texas Legislature enacted the Texas ADR Act in 1987. Thus, Texas mediators and courts have over fifteen years of experience in conducting or ordering mediations and other non-binding processes under this statutory scheme. One of the cornerstones of the enactment was the statute's broad confidentiality protection.[6] These confidentiality protections are set forth in two sections of the act. Section 154.073 delineates the primary confidentiality provisions of the law. Apart from certain narrow exceptions set forth in the act, the statute provides that:

> a communication relating to the subject matter of any civil or criminal dispute made by a participant in an alternative dispute resolution procedure, whether before or after the institution of formal judicial proceedings, is confidential, is not subject to disclosure, and may not be used as evidence against the participant in any judicial or administrative proceeding.[8]

In addition,

---

[*] Copyright © 2003. Reprinted with permission of the author and the Journal of Dispute Resolution, University of Missouri-Columbia, Center for the Study of Dispute Resolution, 206 Hulston Hall, Columbia MO 65211.

[6] Dean Ed Sherman has described the Texas ADR Act's confidentiality section as "perhaps the broadest ADR confidentiality provision in the country." Edward F. Sherman, *Confidentiality in ADR Proceedings: Policy Issues Arising From the Texas Experience*, 38 S. Tex. L. Rev. 541, 542 (1997).

[8] Section 154.073(a).

[a]ny record made at an alternative dispute resolution procedure is confidential, and the participants or the third party facilitating the procedure may not be required to testify in any proceedings relating to or arising out of the matter in dispute or be subject to process requiring disclosure of confidential information or data relating to or arising out of the matter in dispute.[9]

. . . .

[S]upplemental to these main confidentiality provisions, Section 154.053 of the Texas ADR Act explicitly places a duty on the mediator to "at all times maintain confidentiality with respect to communications relating to the subject matter of the dispute." Additionally, even if these other provisions are not sufficiently clear, Section 154.053 of the Texas ADR Act provides further that "[u]nless the parties agree otherwise, all matters, including the conduct and demeanor of the parties and their counsel during the settlement process, are confidential and may never be disclosed to anyone, including the appointing court." Hence, taken together these various provisions place limits on future testimony in later adjudications and require confidentiality outside of other legal proceedings.

In contrast to the Texas ADR Act, the UMA approaches confidentiality much differently. As stated by the immediate past chair of the ADR Section Council of the State Bar of Texas, "Whereas the Texas ADR . . . Act's confidentiality provisions start with the general proposition that all ADR communications are confidential, save for several exceptions, the UMA focuses instead on privileges from discovery and admissibility in later proceedings."[12] Indeed, the UMA's drafters declined to include a general requirement of confidentiality. Apparently in response to criticism for this omission, however, the drafters included some coverage of general confidentiality in the final version of the UMA. Section 8 of the UMA provides, "Unless subject to the [insert statutory references to open meetings act and open records act], mediation communications are confidential to the extent agreed by the parties or provided by other law or rule of this State."

The UMA's drafters apparently "were unable to agree on a confidentiality requirement for mediation that would reach beyond the protection of a privilege to govern disclosures in settings other than legal proceedings."[14] Accordingly, the drafters punted on the issue and left the decision-making up to possible agreement by the parties or other state enactments. The drafters observed that they wanted to leave "the disclosure of mediation communications outside of proceedings to the good judgment of the parties to determine in light of the unique characteristics and circumstances of their dispute." Also, and perhaps as a nod to states such as Texas that had raised concerns about the lack of general confidentiality, the drafters

---

[9] *Id.* § 154.073(b).

[12] Letter from Wayne Fagan, Chair, State Bar of Texas ADR Section Council, to Texas members of the ABA House of Delegates, ABA House of Delegates Vote on the Uniform Mediation Act (UMA) 1 (Nov. 14, 2001) www.texasadr.org/umaletter.pdf (accessed March 13, 2003). Mr. Fagan also stated, "The UMA proposal has headed in the wrong direction by not beginning with a wide umbrella of confidentiality protection followed by appropriate exceptions."

[14] Ellen E. Deason, *Uniform Mediation Act — Law Ensures Confidentiality, Neutrality of Process,* Dis. Res. Mag. 7, 9 (Summer 2002).

structured Section 8 to allow states to retain or adopt general confidentiality provisions.

. . . .

One irony of the UMA's approach to general confidentiality of mediation communications in Section 8 is that the drafters have intentionally included a provision that is directly inconsistent with their overall push for uniformity. The goal of uniformity is worthwhile. On the other hand, why should a state such as Texas, with its well-developed ADR statute, shelve that statute for the UMA when there is apparently going to be no uniformity on a central issue of consideration? The drafters have opined that "uniformity is not necessary or even appropriate with regard to the disclosure of mediation communications outside of proceedings." This statement appears incongruous when contrasted with one of the drafters' essential premises — that "[c]andor during mediation is encouraged by maintaining the parties' and mediators' expectations regarding confidentiality of mediation communications." How is such candor enhanced if the parties are advised . . . that the matters to be discussed at the mediation might not be subject to later use as evidence in future adjudicatory proceedings, but may otherwise be freely disclosed? How is uniformity to be achieved if this important issue is left up to the parties or individual states?

Separate from the issue of non-uniformity, the drafters' approach in Section 8 that leaves confidentiality up to the agreement of the parties has dubious merit. Of course, in some situations parties may be willing to engage in a general confidentiality agreement prior to the commencement of a mediation. In addition, certain dispute resolution organizations might require that the parties agree to abide by rules of that organization that call for broad confidentiality. However, the opportunity to secure a pre-mediation agreement will not always be readily achievable. While a dispute is pending and prior to the outset of a mediation, the parties may be well-entrenched in their positions and unwilling to agree to much of anything — particularly with respect to a subject as important as confidentiality that might have far-reaching implications. Similarly, in the case of a court-ordered mediation, the parties may well be entering into the mediation process in a reluctant fashion and not have any strong interest in reaching an agreement at the outset on the issue of confidentiality or anything else. Moreover, . . . once a mediator has attempted to explain the broad array of privileges, waivers, and exceptions that are included in the UMA, it may prove difficult to then explain the distinctions between privileges and confidentiality and whether the parties — particularly unrepresented parties — would also want to enter into a confidentiality agreement.

. . . .

[I]t appears that some courts have effectively engrafted an ad hoc "manifest injustice" exception to broad confidentiality provisions when one is lacking. It is worthy of note that the drafters of the UMA considered the adoption of an exception for "manifest injustice," but discarded the idea during the evolution of the proposal. By way of contrast, the federal Administrative Dispute Resolution Act includes a narrowly tailored exception for situations in which a court determines that the disclosure is necessary to prevent a "manifest injustice."[41]

. . . .

## III. A PROBLEM OF COMPLEXITY

[T]he structure of the proposed UMA is very complex. Instead of providing a broad statement of confidentiality followed by narrow exceptions, the UMA attempts to safeguard confidentiality through a complex, numerous, and dizzying array of privileges, waivers, and exceptions. These provisions are set out in UMA Sections 4-6, and represent the "meat" of the proposed statute. UMA Section 4(a) begins these linked provisions by stating, "[e]xcept as otherwise provided in Section 6, a mediation communication is privileged as provided in subsection (b) and is not subject to discovery or admissible in evidence in a proceeding unless waived or precluded as provided by Section 5." Thus, Section 4 commences with the premise that mediation communications will be privileged from disclosure in later legal proceedings unless there is an exception to privilege under UMA Section 6 or a waiver or a preclusion of privilege under Section 5. However, the language and structure are extremely convoluted and confusing. One short subsection refers the reader to a privilege structure set out in another subsection and lengthy lists of exceptions, waivers, and preclusions in two additional major sections of the proposal. Then, to add to the potential for confusion, Section 4 thereafter provides three differing levels of privilege to a mediation participant depending on whether the person is a party, a mediator, or a nonparty participant. Although the drafters assert that the differentiated tiers of privilege are intended to bring "clarity" to the law, I predict that the distinctions will prove to be difficult for (1) mediators to understand and explain to participants, (2) participants to comprehend and appreciate, and (3) courts to readily comprehend and apply . . . . The complex and highly legalistic nature of the statute may result in effectively eliminating non-attorney mediators and limit the likelihood of parties' participation in mediation absent legal representation by well-trained mediation advocate attorneys.

The three tiers of privilege also will generate confusion with respect to the differing levels of privilege afforded to a party versus that party's attorney. The UMA defines a "mediation party" as a "person that participates in a mediation and whose agreement is necessary to resolve the dispute." Although one would normally expect a party's counsel to be an agent of the party at a mediation session as in other forms of legal representation, this definition appears to be too narrow to include the party's lawyer. Although Section 10 of the UMA specifically allows an attorney to "accompany the party to and participate in a mediation," the drafters' Official Comments state that "counsel for a mediation party would not be a mediation party." Accordingly, the UMA treats the party's attorney as a "nonparty partici-pant" at the mediation. This is both significant and potentially confusing in that Section 4 affords a party a much broader privilege that it confers on a "nonparty participant." The nonparty participant may only refuse to disclose, and prevent others from disclosing, that person's mediation communications, while the party may generally refuse to disclose and block others from disclosing all mediation

---

[41] 5 U.S.C. §§ 574(a)(4)(A), (b)(5)(A) (1996).

communications. Thus, the attorney for the party enjoys a far narrower privilege than does the person the attorney has represented. This dichotomy is potentially troublesome both because of the quizzical concerns it may raise when disclosed either by the attorney or the mediator . . . and its susceptibility to mischief in later legal proceedings.

. . . .

Another bothersome aspect of the UMA's approach to confidentiality relates to the drafters' decision to require *in camera* hearings by a subsequent tribunal for only two of the proposal's many exceptions and waivers to the various privileges. Section 6(b) sets forth exceptions to the act's privileges for mediation communications that are sought or offered in either (1) a later felony court proceeding, or (2) a proceeding in which a contract defense has been asserted to an agreement reached at mediation. If a party seeks discovery or wants to introduce mediation communications for either purpose, the proponent must, in an in camera hearing, demonstrate "that the evidence is not otherwise available" and "that there is a need for the evidence that substantially outweighs the interest in protecting confidentiality." The drafters' formulation of a balancing process for these two exceptions is well-crafted; however, that the drafters opted to require this in camera process prior to disclosure only for these two exceptions speaks volumes about the lack of seriousness with which mediation confidentiality was viewed in general. Why was the *in camera* process not made applicable across the spectrum of exceptions and waivers?

. . . .

The UMA's vast array of exceptions, waivers, and preclusions to privilege, in addition to the differing levels of privilege, will lead inexorably to numerous judicial challenges. Rather than the occasional fight to evade a broad confidentiality statute such as we have experienced in Texas, parties in later legal proceedings in states adopting the UMA will have numerous opportunities to persuade the courts to open the door to mediation communications given the wide-open and labyrinthine structure of the proposal's approach to privilege. Prudent attorneys who represent parties at mediation will either have to provide substantial caution to their clients about the questionable prospects for later success in keeping mediation communications privileged in the event of non-settlement, or advise the client of a strong need to engage in drafting and negotiating a true confidentiality agreement with the opposing counsel prior to the outset of a mediation.

# THE SOUND OF DUST SETTLING: A RESPONSE TO CRITICISMS OF THE UMA
2003 J. Disp. Resol. 99, 111–16, 118[*]
By Richard C. Reuben

[Editor's Note: Professor Reuben served as one of the Reporters to the UMA Drafting Committee.]

### b. A complex problem, not a complex act

In many respects, the UMA is a remarkably clear document as finally drafted, having been washed clean on the rocks of more than a dozen drafts and drafting sessions. For example, the operative provision of the Act says: "(a) Except as otherwise provided in Section 6, a mediation communication is privileged as provided in subsection (b) and is not subject to discovery or admissible in evidence in a proceeding unless waived or precluded as provided by Section 5."[68] This is a fairly straightforward declarative sentence, one that does not even use many big words. It says what the general rule is in a way that is understandable and familiar to both lawyers and non-lawyers, and tells precisely where to find exceptions to this general rule.

Even the Act's most complicated provisions — the blocking rights of mediation participants — are written in plain English.

. . . .

Still, two facts contribute to the appearance of complexity. First, the environment in which this fairly straightforward rule operates is itself complex — complicated by the different types of mediation applications and styles, complicated by the competing and sometimes trumping demands of the justice system for relevant mediation communications evidence, complicated by the unique needs of the mediation process. On the latter point, for example, the mediation privilege is unique among other privileges in that it does not permit waiver by conduct; rather, waiver of the privilege must be express. This was because of concerns about inadvertent waivers by parties or mediators, especially non-lawyers, vitiating the privilege.

The second reason for the appearance of complexity is that the UMA, is more responsible than other "less complex" statutes because it clearly addresses the difficult questions — just what is a mediation, when does it begin and end, what does confidentiality really mean, when should support for mediation confidentiality give way to larger public concerns — rather than leaving them to the courts. This was a deliberate decision, intended to provide clarity and certainty for mediation participants.

---

[*] Copyright © 2003. Reprinted with permission of the author and the Journal of Dispute Resolution, University of Missouri-Columbia, Center for the Study of Dispute Resolution, 206 Hulston Hall, Columbia MO 65211.

[68] Unif. Mediation Act § 4(a) (2001).

### c. Choosing specificity over brevity

In the drafting of any statute, one must make fundamental choices about what matters to address specifically, and what matters, if any, to leave to judicial interpretation. A more specific statute will necessarily be, or will appear to be, more complex, but at the same time it will leave less discretion to the courts and provide parties more certainty. In contrast, a less specific statute will appear to be simpler, but it will be less certain and reliable because it leaves much more room for judicial interpretation.

This is one area in which cultural differences among mediation constituencies made a significant difference. Responding to criticisms of early drafts for complexity, the Drafting Committees adopted the recommendation of the Academic Advisory Faculty for an approach to confidentiality that was very similar to the Texas model: a broad general statement of confidentiality stating that mediation communications would be privileged . . . unless such exclusion would constitute a "manifest injustice."[77] This approach tracked the rule for mediations involving the federal government, and has some precedent in the states, including in Texas.

### 1. Manifest injustice

Lawyers involved in the drafting process were generally willing to trust courts to implement a "manifest injustice" provision narrowly, in accordance with the strong presumption of non-admissibility reflected in the statute's legislative intent. However, a "manifest injustice" exception was patently unacceptable to the mediation community (including many lawyer-mediators). Indeed, while the mediation community rarely spoke with one voice on any given issue, this was the one issue upon which the overwhelming majority of mediators and provider organizations agreed. Articulations varied, but they boiled down to an unwillingness to trust courts to apply the "manifest injustice" standard narrowly. Instead, they feared the "manifest injustice" provision as "an exception that would swallow the rule," one "so big that you could drive a truck through it."[80] The mediators involved in the process lobbied the drafting committees hard to limit judicial discretion at every instance — even at the acknowledged cost of the additional drafting, or "complexity," that would be required to achieve that goal.

The drafters resisted, trying different formulations that would preserve but constrain what they viewed as inevitable judicial interpretation, but the mediators involved in the process made it clear that "manifest injustice" was an issue upon which there would be no compromise. In the end, the drafters relented, deleted the "manifest injustice" provision, and proceeded to draft a more specific — and longer — statute.

Professor Shannon effectively raises this issue again when he holds out the Texas statute, Texas Civ. Prac. & Rem. § 154.073(a), as a better approach to the more

[77] Draft Unif. Mediation Act (June 1999) www.nccusl.org (accessed Apr. 8, 2003).

[80] Letter from Liz O'Brien, president, California Dispute Resolution Council, to Richard C. Reuben, Reporter, ABA UMA Drafting Committee (Aug. 5, 1999) (would create "an impossible environment in which to mediate").

complex privilege structure adopted by the UMA.

. . . .

This statute is somewhat representative of the simple "mediation is confidential" statutes found in some state statutes and court rules. While such statutes are seductive in their simplicity, they are deceptive in that they raise more questions than they answer, promise much more than they deliver, and in the end contribute little to the reliability of mediation confidentiality. At worst, they are downright misleading. In my view, Professor Shannon is correct in contending that the Texas statute provides a good case in point, and therefore is worth a closer look.

### 2. Ambiguity in the Texas statute

As is typical among these "mediation is confidential" statutes, the Texas law conveniently avoids the harder questions that are likely to lead to litigation. For example, while stating that alternative dispute resolution processes are "confidential," the statute does not define what an "alternative dispute resolution proceeding" is for purposes of the act, nor does it define "confidential," nor does it define its express limitation to communications that "relate to the subject matter" of the dispute, nor does it list any exceptions to its general rule of confidentiality.

Professor Shannon and the other members of the ADR Section of the State Bar of Texas interpret this broad language to provide both a categorical rule against the discovery or introduction of mediation communications evidence in subsequent judicial and administrative proceedings (with no exceptions), as well as a categorical rule against disclosure of mediation communications outside of proceedings (with no exceptions).

Maybe. But we all know that wishing does not necessarily make something so — and there are strong judicial pressures against such an interpretation. Rules of evidentiary exclusion are construed narrowly, in keeping with the law's demand for every person's evidence in the pursuit of justice. While it is theoretically possible that a court may view the statute as providing these two bright line rules, it is only a possibility, it is not a rule of law. An equally plausible, and more defensible, judicial reading of the statute's plain language, would seem to compel a more restrictive interpretation — as a relatively narrow evidentiary exclusion for certain statements made during a mediation. In fact, no Texas court to date has construed the statute as being either without exceptions with regard to admissibility of mediation communications in legal proceedings, or as imposing an affirmative duty not to disclose outside of legal proceedings. To the contrary, the relatively extensive case law in Texas makes abundantly clear that the list of unstated judicial exceptions can be extensive.

Texas' own experience with judicially carved exceptions is consistent with that of other states. Courts have generally refused to categorically exclude mediation communications from admissibility. Rather, courts have viewed such "mediation is confidential" statutes as requiring them to balance the mediation confidentiality interests against the parties' interest in the evidence in the case before them — frequently deciding in favor of admissibility. California remains the best example, as its statutory scheme lays out a categorical "mediation is confidential" rule to the use of mediation communications in subsequent civil proceedings. Yet both state and federal courts in California have regularly found exceptions that would permit the admission of mediation communications evidence.

While it is not emphasized in Professor Shannon's analysis, Texas law goes one step further in limiting the scope of mediation confidentiality, providing a broad statutory exception to the broad general rule of confidentiality (whatever it is finally construed to mean). It is found in Subsection (e), and provides:

> If this section conflicts with other legal requirements for disclosure of communications, records, or materials, the issue of confidentiality may be presented to the court having jurisdiction of the proceedings to determine, in camera, whether the facts, circumstances, and context of the communications or materials sought to be disclosed warrant a protective order of the court or whether the communications or materials are subject to disclosure.[93]

On its face, this exception is clearly broader than the proposed "manifest injustice" standard vilified by UMA critics in the early drafting. Indeed, it is difficult to imagine how one might draft a broader exception than Subsection (e). A more accurate description of Texas law might be: "Mediation communications are confidential unless a court wants to hear them." And courts in Texas — arguably more than in other states — have repeatedly shown themselves prone to wanting that information. For this reason, categorical mediation confidentiality statutes have been frequent targets of scholarly criticism, including the Texas statute in particular. For this reason, too, state legislatures have been reluctant to enact such rules, overwhelmingly preferring the privilege structure adopted by the UMA.

. . . .

### 4. The UMA will never be uniform (so why bother?)

[Another] generalized grievance is that the UMA should be rejected because its goal of uniformity will be impossible to achieve. It is probably true that the UMA will not be enacted precisely as written in all fifty states, and by all federal courts through appropriate court rules. But this hardly seems reason to oppose the Act. In fact, no piece of uniform law has ever been adopted uniformly by all fifty states — not even the much-heralded Uniform Commercial Code. Rather, the goal is substantial uniformity among the states that wish to adopt the uniform law.

To be sure, the drafters hope that the Act will be broadly adopted, particularly by the many states that have less developed confidentiality laws. However, most uniform laws require some tinkering to fit within the fabric of existing state law, and the Uniform Mediation Act is no different in this regard. Indeed, as discussed further below, the drafters conceived of the act as a law to complement rather than displace existing state laws, to the extent such laws exist at all, and occasionally use Legislative Notes to underscore this drafting assumption. Again, the goal is substantial uniformity among the states that wish to adopt the UMA. Professor

---

[93] Texas Civ. Prac. & Rem. § 154.073(e).

Shannon's analysis criticizes the UMA for allowing states this flexibility on certain issues, such as the regulation of mediation communications outside of proceedings. More commonly, though, this is viewed as a strength of the UMA, not a weakness, as it permits states to integrate the UMA into their current law with minimal disruption, while at the same time providing a broad framework of uniformity in mediation upon which the public at large can reasonably rely.

## NOTES AND QUESTIONS

(1)   With regard to the confidentiality of mediation communications, Professor Reuben describes Texas law as: "Mediation communications are confidential unless a court wants to hear them." Do the following Texas appellate court decisions support Professor Reuben's description of Texas Law? In *Avary v. Bank of America, N.A.*, 72 S.W.3d 779 (Tex. App. 2002), otherwise confidential information was sought from a party concerning a tort (breach of fiduciary duty) that was allegedly committed during the mediation. The appellate court remanded to the trial court to determine whether disclosure of the information was warranted in light of the "facts, circumstances, and context." The trial court ordered disclosure and the appellate court denied a subsequent request for a protective writ of mandamus. In *Alford v. Bryant*, 137 S.W.3d 916 (Tex. App. 2004), the trial court refused to allow the mediator to testify in an action for attorney malpractice as to disclosures allegedly made by the attorney during mediation. The appellate court reversed and remanded, ruling that the mediator's outcome determinative testimony was erroneously excluded at trial. How would a high court in a state with a UMA statute have decided these cases?

(2)   Is evidence compiled for use in the mediation process subject to the same confidentiality protection as mediation communications? The high courts in two non-UMA states have taken somewhat different approaches in addressing this issue. In *Rojas v. Los Angeles County Superior Court*, 93 P.3d 260 (Cal. 2004), the Supreme Court of California ruled that the state's confidentiality statute not only protects the substance of communications in mediation, but also "raw evidence" exchanged at the mediation, if it was compiled specifically to be used in the mediation. On the other hand, the Supreme Court of Alabama ruled in *Alabama Department of Transportation v. Land Energy Ltd.*, 886 So. 2d 787 (Ala. 2004), that tables prepared by a state agency were not protected and could be admitted in subsequent litigation, because they were not prepared solely for the mediation and were provided after the mediation in response to pre-existing discovery requests.

(3)   Does confidentiality protection extend to matters following the mediation that relate to the substance of the mediation? The Supreme Court of Montana responded in the negative in *In re Estate of Stukey*, 100 P.3d 114 (Mont. 2004). The court ruled that a letter written after the mediation by the estate's attorney to the attorney for the decedent's daughter clarifying the scope of the settlement reached in mediation was not part of the mediation process, and thus not subject to the protection of the state's confidentiality statute.

# Chapter 6

# LEGAL ISSUES IN MEDIATION

## A.  INTRODUCTION

The purpose of this chapter is to present some of the more prominent legal issues, in addition to the confidentiality issues explored in the previous chapter, that have arisen in the mediation process. Chief among these are issues relating to pre-dispute mediation clauses, the power to compel mediation, the requirement of "mediation in good faith," and the enforceability of mediated agreements. While mediation is often touted as a flexible, non-legal process, unfettered by rigid procedures and rules, it is perhaps inevitable that with the more frequent use of mediation by legal professionals attempts would be made to make the mediation process more regularized and uniform. Over the past two decades, we have witnessed rapid growth in the number of statutes and cases dealing with mediation. In addition to the legal issues discussed in this chapter and the previous chapter, other legal issues are covered elsewhere in this course book. For example, legal and ethical issues facing the mediator, such as conflicts of interest and the unauthorized practice of law as well as issues relating to mediator liability and immunity are explored in Chapter 8, *infra*, and legal issues governing a lawyer's participation in mediation, including the lawyer's duty to inform a client of dispute resolution alternatives, are covered in Chapter 10, *infra*.

## B.  AGREEMENTS TO MEDIATE AND STATUTORY REQUIREMENTS TO MEDIATE

What are the consequences of a party's unwillingness to mediate if he or she has a contractual agreement to mediate or is required to mediate pursuant to a federal or state statute? If it were arbitration rather than mediation that was in question, it is now well established that the courts will enforce arbitration provisions. The inclusion in contracts of clauses in which the parties agree to binding arbitration if a dispute among them should arise has become increasingly widespread over the past few decades. The courts have generally been willing to enforce these arbitration clauses unless the party resisting enforcement can show that the arbitration clause was fraudulently induced or otherwise invalid as a matter of contract law. Similarly, courts will enforce statutory requirements to arbitrate unless it can be shown that the statutory scheme places an unconstitutional burden on a party's right to a jury trial.

While contractual agreements to mediate and statutory requirements to mediate are now commonplace as well, their enforceability is seen by some as more problematic than the enforcement of arbitration contracts and statutory mandates.

Some have argued that a court's enforcement of an agreement or requirement to mediate would be futile, because, although parties may be forced to the mediation table, they cannot be forced to settle. Others have argued that public policy now favors mediation as a means of resolving disputes and that courts should further this policy by enforcing mediation requirements. As you read the following cases, consider the policy rationales presented by the courts as they confront issues over whether to enforce mediation agreements or statutory requirements to mediate. Note also the remedies chosen by the courts if they choose to enforce the mediation provision.

## BROSNAN v. DRY CLEANING STATION
United States District Court for the Northern District of California
2008 U.S. Dist. LEXIS 44678 (June 6, 2008)

ELIZABETH D. LAPORTE, UNITED STATES MAGISTRATE JUDGE.

On March 17, 2008, Plaintiffs Timothy Brosnan and Carla Brosnan filed this action in San Mateo County Superior Court alleging state law claims relating to fraud and breach of contract against Defendants Dry Cleaning Station, Inc. and John Campbell. Plaintiffs' claims arise from a Franchise Agreement executed by the parties for operation of a Dry Cleaning Station store. On April 18, 2008, Defendants removed this case to federal court alleging diversity jurisdiction pursuant to 28 U.S.C. § 1332.

On April 23, 2008, Defendants filed a motion to dismiss Plaintiffs' complaint based on Federal Rule of Civil Procedure 12(b) (6) on the grounds that Plaintiffs failed to engage in mediation of this dispute prior to filing their lawsuit as required by the Franchise Agreement. The Franchise Agreement states in relevant part:

Except to the extent that the Company believes it is necessary to seek equitable relief as permitted in Section 20.1, or to recover royalties or other amounts owed to it by the Franchisee, the Company and the Franchisee each agree to enter into mediation of all disputes involving this Agreement or any other aspect of the relationship, for a minimum or four (4) hours, prior to initiating any legal action against the other.

Plaintiffs do not dispute that they failed to engage in mediation prior to filing their lawsuit, but in their opposition seek a stay of this matter rather than dismissal. Because this matter is appropriate for decision without oral argument, the Court vacated the June 3, 2008 hearing.

Failure to mediate a dispute pursuant to a contract that makes mediation a condition precedent to filing a lawsuit warrants dismissal. *See B & O Mfg., Inc. v. Home Depot U.S.A., Inc.*, 2007 U.S. Dist. LEXIS 83998, (N.D.Cal. Nov. 1, 2007) ("A claim that is filed before a mediation requirement, that is a condition precedent to the parties' right to sue as set forth in an agreement, is satisfied shall be dismissed.") (citing *Gould v. Gould*, 240 Ga. App. 481, 482, 523 S.E.2d 106 (1999)). California state law so holds. *See Charles J. Rounds Co. v. Joint Council of Teamsters No. 42*, 4 Cal.3d 888 (1971) (affirming trial court's dismissal of a breach of contract action based on a collective bargaining agreement on the grounds that the dispute was covered by an arbitration clause in the agreement); *see also Johnson v. Seigel*, 84 Cal.App.4th 1087 (2000) (relying on *Rounds* and affirming the trial court's grant of summary judgment on the ground that the plaintiff failed to pursue arbitration as required by the real estate contract prior to filing the lawsuit). The *Rounds* Court provides specific instruction on the effect of a plaintiff's failure to pursue alternative dispute resolution as provided in a contract:

> Specifically, where the only issue litigated is covered by the arbitration clause, and where plaintiff has not first pursued or attempted to pursue his arbitration remedy, it should be held that (1) plaintiff has impliedly waived his right to arbitrate, such that defendant could elect to submit the matter to the jurisdiction of the court; (2) defendant may also elect to demur or move for summary judgment on the ground that the plaintiff has failed to exhaust arbitration remedies; and (3) defendant may also elect to move for a stay of proceedings pending arbitration if defendant also moves to compel arbitration.

*Rounds*, 4 Cal.3d at 899. By contrast, where a plaintiff has "attempted to exhaust its arbitration remedy or raises issues not susceptible to arbitration or not covered by the arbitration agreement," a stay rather than dismissal of the lawsuit is appropriate. *Id.*

Here, there is no dispute that Plaintiffs did not pursue mediation prior filing this lawsuit. Defendants have not elected to submit to the jurisdiction of the Court, nor have they moved to stay this action. Instead, they seek dismissal, to which they are entitled under *Rounds*. Although Plaintiffs prefer a stay, they cite no authority supporting the grant of a stay when Defendants opted for dismissal under these circumstances.

The Franchise Agreement states that if an action is commenced prior to seeking mediation, and if the court dismisses the action, the party against which the lawsuit was brought is entitled to fees and costs "in an amount equal to the attorneys' fees and costs the party seeking dismissal incurred." . . . Because this Court grants Defendants' motion to dismiss, Defendants may be entitled to fees and costs under the Franchise Agreement. However, the Court has dismissed this matter without prejudice, so a fee award may be premature. Further, it appears that Plaintiffs may not have been represented when they entered into the Franchise Agreement, which may raise the question as to whether or not the fees provision is enforceable. *See, e.g., Armendariz v. Foundation Health Psychcare Servs, Inc.*, 24 Cal.4th 83, 113 (2000).

IT IS SO ORDERED.

# KLINGE v. BENTIEN
Supreme Court of Iowa
725 N.W.2d 13 (2006)

STREIT, JUSTICE.

Ambrose Bierce once described litigation as "[a] machine which you go into as a pig and come out of as a sausage." This adage is certainly true in the present case. Two pig farmers attempting to resolve their contract dispute in small claims court, ended up in district court and now our court. Because mediation of farm disputes is mandatory, the decision of the small claims court is void. We reverse and remand for dismissal without prejudice.

John Klinge and Kevin Bentien entered into an oral contract concerning the raising and feeding of pigs. Bentien purchased feeder pigs and placed them at Klinge's farm to be cared for until they reached market weight. Klinge sued Bentien in small claims court for $3000 claiming he was not fully compensated under the terms of the contract. Bentien countersued for $5000 alleging Klinge's negligence killed 100 pigs. Neither party requested mediation under Iowa Code chapter 654B before the commencement of the action or any time thereafter.

The parties appeared before the small claims court for trial. Neither party was represented by counsel. The small claims court ruled in favor of both parties. The court ordered a judgment be entered in favor of Klinge against Bentien in the amount of $3000. Likewise, the court ordered a judgment be entered in favor of Bentien against Klinge in the amount of $5000.

Klinge appealed the judgment against him to the Clayton County District Court. Bentien did not appeal the judgment *15 against him. Again, neither party was represented by counsel. The district court requested "written statements" from both parties. Based upon those statements, the district court found insufficient evidence to support either claim. It found the small claims court "should have dismissed both the claim and the counterclaim." However, since Bentien did not appeal the judgment against him, the district court held the $3000 judgment "must stand." Consequently, the district court only reversed the small claims court with respect to Bentien's claim against Klinge.

Shortly after the ruling, Bentien consulted an attorney for the first time about this case. The next day, Bentien's attorney sent a letter to the district court along with a copy to Klinge. The purpose of the letter was to bring chapter 654B of the Iowa Code to the court's attention. Bentien's attorney represented to the court chapter 654B required the parties in this case to submit to mediation before filing suit. See Iowa Code § 654B.3 (2005). Since neither party requested mediation, the attorney reasoned the court "lacks jurisdiction." "[I]n light of this new information," the attorney requested the court to dismiss the matter "ab initio with respect to both parties."

In response, the district court sent a letter to Bentien's attorney and a copy was sent to Klinge. It first noted neither party raised the issue of mediation in small claims court or on appeal to the district court. The court then refused "to take any further action with regard to this case."

Bentien applied for discretionary review, which this court granted. On appeal, Bentien seeks the reversal of the district court's ruling as well as the dismissal of both Klinge's and Bentien's claims without prejudice on the basis both the small claims court and the district court lacked subject matter jurisdiction and/or authority to hear either claim. Alternatively, Bentien alleges the district court made "several errors in the assessment of the record on appeal and in not allowing the parties to submit additional evidence." Because we hold both courts lacked subject matter jurisdiction, we need not determine whether the district court properly reviewed the evidence.

. . .

The issue before us is whether Klinge's failure to file a request for mediation with the farm mediation service as required by section 654B.3 deprives the small claims court of subject matter jurisdiction. Subject matter jurisdiction is the power " 'of a court to hear and determine cases of the general class to which the proceedings in question belong, not merely the particular case then occupying the court's attention.' " . . . . Subject matter jurisdiction is conferred by constitutional or statutory power. . . . . The parties themselves cannot confer subject matter jurisdiction on a court by an act or procedure. * . . . Unlike personal jurisdiction, a party cannot waive or vest by consent subject matter jurisdiction. . . .

## B. Mandatory Mediation Proceedings Under Section 654B.3

We now turn to section 654B.3. Bentien argues section 654B.3 applies to the present case. He alleges the small claims court did not have subject matter jurisdiction because Klinge failed to satisfy the requirements set forth in section 654B.3(1). Section 654B.3 provides:

A person who is a farm resident, or other party, desiring to initiate a civil proceeding to resolve a dispute, *shall* file a request for mediation with the farm mediation service. The person *shall not* begin the proceeding until the person receives a mediation release . . . .

Iowa Code § 654B.3(1)(*a*) (emphasis added).

. . .

In the present case, it is undisputed both parties are farmers and Bentien's pigs (the subject of the contract) were kept at Klinge's farm. Klinge is a "farm resident" and the contract at issue is a "care and feeding contract." Since the parties' dispute involves a "care and feeding contract," we find section 654B.1 is applicable. Thus, Klinge was required to file a mediation request and receive a mediation release before filing this suit in small claims court.

## C. Consequences for Failing to Request Mandatory Mediation

Bentien argues Klinge's failure to file a mediation request and receive a mediation release deprived the small claims court of subject matter jurisdiction. We treat Bentien's letter to the district court as a motion to dismiss. *Halverson v. Iowa*

*Dist. Ct.*, 532 N.W.2d 794, 799 (Iowa 1995) (noting failure to attach a label to a motion does not determine its legal significance because "we look to the motion's content to determine the motion's real nature"). We must decide whether it was error not to dismiss both claims.

In 1999, a federal district court examined section 654B.3. *Rutter v. Carroll's Foods of the Midwest, Inc.*, 50 F. Supp. 2d 876, 881–82 (N.D.Iowa 1999). Because neither appellate court in Iowa had passed on the question of whether obtaining a mediation release under chapter 654B is a matter of subject matter jurisdiction or authority, the court in *Rutter* predicted how this court would interpret section 654B.3. *Id.* at 882. Instead of using our terminology, the court in *Rutter* used "jurisdictional prerequisite" to refer to subject matter jurisdiction and "condition precedent" to refer to the authority of a court to hear a case. *Id.* The court concluded obtaining a mediation release under chapter 654B is a "condition precedent" to suit, *not a jurisdictional prerequisite.* As such, the defect of failing to obtain such a release does not affect the claimant's standing or the subject matter jurisdiction of the court, but is instead curable after suit has been filed.

*Id.* at 882–83 (emphasis added). As a result, the court stayed the case in order for the plaintiffs to attempt to cure the defect. *Id.* at 883. We see the merit in our learned friend's conclusion, although we would have articulated the issue as a matter of the court's authority to hear the particular case rather than a condition precedent to suit.

However, in 2000 the legislature amended section 654B.3 by stating that filing a mediation request and obtaining a mediation release "are jurisdictional prerequisites to a person filing a civil action . . . to resolve a dispute subject to this chapter." 2000 Iowa Acts ch. 1129, § 2 (codified at Iowa Code § 654B.3(1)(*b*)).

The timing of the amendment, the use of the federal court's term "jurisdictional prerequisites," and the introductory statement to the bill indicate the legislature intended a different result than that of the *Rutter* decision. When interpreting a statute, we are obliged to examine both the language used and the purpose for which the legislation was enacted. *Fjords North, Inc. v. Hahn*, 710 N.W.2d 731, 739 (Iowa 2006) (citing *Albrecht v. Gen. Motors Corp.*, 648 N.W.2d 87, 89 (Iowa 2002) ("We seek to interpret statutes consistently with their language and purpose, and avoid interpretations that are unreasonable.")). The explanation accompanying the introduced version of the amendment sheds light on the legislature's intention. It states:

> This bill amends the mandatory mediation provisions of two Code sections relating to resolution of farm disputes. The bill specifies that the mediation requirements in Code sections 654A.6 and 654B.3 are jurisdictional prerequisites that must be satisfied before a case can be filed under the chapters. A 1999 federal district court ruling held that the current Code language did not prevent the filing of a suit under chapter 654B prior to mediation of the dispute.

H.F. 2521; . . . It is obvious from this explanation the legislature intended to respond to *Rutter. See id.* (citing *Midwest Auto. III, LLC v. Iowa Dep't of Transp.*, 646 N.W.2d 417, 425–26 (Iowa 2002) ("[A]n amendment to a statute raises a presumption that the legislature intended a change in the law.")).

The polestar of statutory interpretation is to give effect to the legislative intent of a statute. We "consider the objects sought to be accomplished and the evils and mischiefs sought to be remedied, seeking a result that will advance, rather than defeat, the statute's purpose."

*State v. Schultz*, 604 N.W.2d 60, 62 (Iowa 1999) (citations omitted). We must conclude the legislature intended obtaining a mediation release from the farm mediation service to be a prerequisite to subject matter jurisdiction. Klinge's failure to file a mediation request and obtain a mediation release before filing his claim deprived the small claims court of subject matter jurisdiction. As a result, both the small claims court order and the district court's decision are void. The district court should have granted Bentien's motion to dismiss.

## IV. Conclusion

Section 654B.3 requires a "farm resident" to file a request for mediation with the farm mediation service and obtain a mediation release before filing suit if the matter involves a livestock "care and feeding contract." Because Klinge failed to satisfy these requirements before filing suit, the small claims court lacked subject matter jurisdiction to hear his claim and Bentien's counterclaim. Consequently, both the decision of the small claims court and the decision of the district court on review are void.

REVERSED AND REMANDED FOR DISMISSAL.

All justices concur except APPEL, J., who takes no part.

# ANNAPOLIS PROFESSIONAL FIREFIGHTERS LOCAL 1926 v. CITY OF ANNAPOLIS
## Maryland Court of Special Appeals
### 642 A.2d 889 (1994)

WILNER, C.J.

The union representing firefighters employed by the City of Annapolis appeals from an order of the Circuit Court for Anne Arundel County declining to enter a preliminary injunction against the City and dismissing the union's complaint. The underlying dispute is whether lieutenants and captains in the fire department are supervisory personnel and, for that reason, ineligible for inclusion within the bargaining unit. The City now claims they are; the union asserts they are not. The issue before us is whether the court erred in refusing to enjoin the City from taking that issue to impasse and then unilaterally removing lieutenants and captains from the unit. Under the circumstances of this case, we hold that the court did not err
. . .

The State Mediation and Conciliation Service is a statutory unit within the State Division of Labor and Industry. The duties of the Service include the mediation of labor disputes and, where the parties agree, establishing arbitration boards to arbitrate such disputes. If mediation fails and a disputant refuses to arbitrate, the Service is authorized to conduct an investigation, decide "which disputant is mainly responsible or blameworthy for continuance of the dispute," and, over the signature of the Commissioner of Labor and Industry or the Chief Mediator, "publish in a daily newspaper a report that assigns responsibility or blame for the continuance of the dispute."

The City has had a collective bargaining agreement with the union for some period of time. During all of that time, the appropriate unit has included captains and lieutenants, notwithstanding the prohibition against mixing supervisory and nonsupervisory personnel in the same unit. Indeed, in the most recent (1990–93) agreement, the City expressly recognized the union as the sole and exclusive bargaining agent for "all eligible employees in the Annapolis Fire Department in the rank of firefighter through captain pursuant to the provisions of . . . Section 3.21.050 of the Annapolis City Code." At least implicit, if not explicit, in this is an historical recognition by the City that captains and lieutenants, despite the common perception of positions so designated, are not supervisory personnel.

The most recent contract between the City and the union became effective July 1, 1990, and was due to expire on June 30, 1993, subject to the provision in art. 27 of the contract that it would "automatically be renewed from year to year hereafter unless a successor to this agreement is executed by the parties hereto." Art. 27 also provided that, should either party desire to modify the agreement, it would have to notify the other party at least 120 days prior to June 30, 1993. Such notice would trigger the duty to negotiate the proposed changes. Article 28 provided:

> "If after a reasonable period of negotiations over the terms of an agreement, a dispute exists between the City and the Union, the parties may mutually agree that an impasse has been reached; except that if such dispute exists as of May 1, 1993 an impasse shall be deemed to have been reached. Whenever an impasse has been reached, the dispute shall be submitted to mediation. If the parties are unable to agree to a mediator the Division of Mediation and Conciliation shall be required to provide a mediator. The parties hereto agree, that should the mediator recommend the process of fact-finding, that process shall be used in an advisory manner."

Negotiations over a new contract began in April, 1993. During the negotiations, the City, for the first time, contended that captains and lieutenants were supervisory personnel and therefore ineligible for inclusion in the same bargaining unit as the rest of the firefighters. The Union rejected that contention but continued to negotiate other matters.

As the expiration date of the agreement approached, the City announced that it would extend the term of the existing agreement for two weeks to allow time for the parties to reach agreement on a new contract. Subsequently, the City made what it termed its "Final Proposal." In that offer, the City proposed that lieutenants could remain in the bargaining unit until October, 1993, while the question of their supervisory status would be referred to a third party for decision; captains, however, would be removed from the unit. The Union rejected that proposal and, subject to the automatic extension provision in art. 27, the collective bargaining agreement expired without a successor agreement having been reached. The City, giving no effect to the automatic extension provision in art. 27, then announced that the collective bargaining agreement had expired, that the parties were at an impasse, and that captains and lieutenants would thereafter be excluded from the bargaining unit. The City also explicitly withdrew its offer to have a third party determine the supervisory status of the lieutenants.

Initially, the Union filed a verified complaint of unfair labor practices with the Division of Labor and Industry. It complained about a number of things, including the City's removal of captains and lieutenants, noting that, of the 80 members of the unit, 22, or more than 25%, were captains or lieutenants. Indeed, the president and secretary of the union, who comprised two-thirds of the union's negotiating committee, were lieutenants. By unilaterally removing such personnel, the union claimed, the City was interfering with the employees' right of self-organization and refusing to negotiate in good faith.

On July 26, 1993, the Commissioner of the Division of Labor and Industry sent appellants a letter stating:

> "As you know, the Mediation and Conciliation Service was once a unit of the Division of Labor and Industry. Due to state budget cuts, the unit was abolished on July 1, 1991, and remains disbanded to date. Accordingly, the entity the City Ordinance authorizes to process the unfair labor practice charge does not exist."

The Commissioner also asserted that the Division would not assert jurisdiction over the charge as the ordinance did not impose an obligation on the State to do so and the Division lacked resources to devote to the matter.

In this appeal, the union raises the single question, "Did the Court below err in failing to grant injunctive relief prohibiting the City of Annapolis from unilaterally excluding Fire Lieutenants and Fire Captains from the collective bargaining unit represented by [the union]?" . . .

In enacting Chapter 3.32, and agreeing to art. 28 of the collective bargaining agreement, the City understood the obvious — that, in the course of collective bargaining, disputes could arise that the parties might not be able to resolve efficiently through unassisted bilateral negotiations. Two areas, or categories, of disputes were particularly recognized — an impasse in negotiating a new agreement and a claim of unfair labor practice. In both instances, a common and sensible way of resolving such disputes was chosen — referral to the State Mediation and Conciliation Service, a unit created by the Legislature for precisely this purpose. The agreement with the union was obviously subject to the ordinance and indeed made several references to it. The impasse provisions of art. 28, dealing with a breakdown in negotiating a new agreement, are entirely consistent with § 3.32.070 of the ordinance, calling for mediation of any dispute over an unfair labor practice charge.

What we have, then, is a legislative direction and a voluntary written agreement to submit the very kind of dispute that arose in this case to mediation, and, failing that, to neutral fact-finding. In *Anne Arundel County v. Fraternal Order*, 313 Md.

98, 543 A.2d 841 (1988), a similar kind of dispute arose between the county and the police union — whether a detention center lieutenant could be included in the bargaining unit with lower level detention center employees. The issue before the Court was whether the county could be required to submit that dispute to arbitration under an arbitration clause in the collective bargaining agreement.

Recognizing that the agreement was not subject to the State Uniform Arbitration Act and assuming that no other statute authorized the arbitration clause, the Court overruled existing common law and held the clause valid under Maryland common law. At 107, it stated the new holding: "We believe that agreements to arbitrate future disputes generally should be enforceable even in the absence of a specific statutory provision." This was consistent with the Court's more general and often-expressed view that "arbitration is a favored method of dispute resolution." *Id.* at 105; also *Bd. of Educ. v. P.G. Co. Educators' Ass'n*, 309 Md. 85, 522 A.2d 931 (1987). More specifically, the Court held that a determination "as to which representation unit is appropriate for a certain group of employees" was a proper subject for arbitration as it "merely permits the Union to bargain with the County on behalf of the employees."

Section 3.32.070 and art. 28 of the agreement are not, strictly, arbitration provisions. They look rather to mediation and, failing that, neutral fact-finding, which are and have long been equally well-recognized and beneficial methods of dispute resolution, especially in labor disputes. As we have observed, the Legislature blessed this mechanism in this very context as early as 1904. For disputes that are susceptible to it, mediation and neutral evaluation have become, throughout the nation and increasingly throughout this State, equally "favored methods of dispute resolution," and we can see no rational basis for not enforcing agreements to utilize such methods in much the same manner as agreements to arbitrate are enforced . . .

We believe that, as a matter of Maryland common law, consistent with the liberal approach now taken to alternative dispute resolution agreements generally, a written agreement to submit either an existing or a future dispute to a form of alternative dispute resolution that is not otherwise against public policy will be enforced at least to the same extent that it would be enforced if the chosen method were arbitration.

What we then have is a dispute for which the parties have chosen a specific, enforceable dispute resolution process. The only "fly in the ointment" is that, because of lack of funding, the agency selected to mediate the dispute or, failing mediation, to engage in neutral fact-finding, has become nonoperational (though still provided for in the State Code) and therefore, as a practical matter, unavailable. The question is whether that unfortunate fact vitiates the chosen process entirely, thereby either leaving the parties without a remedy or requiring the courts to reenter an area from which they have largely, and wisely, been excluded for the past six decades.

There is no reason to vitiate the chosen process, and it makes no sense to do so. The Uniform Arbitration Act (Md. Code Cts. & Jud. Proc. art., § 3-211) requires that, if an arbitration agreement provides a method for the appointment of arbitrators, that method shall be followed, but that a court shall appoint one or more arbitrators if "the agreed method fails or for any reason cannot be followed." The statute further states that a court-appointed arbitrator "has all the powers of an arbitrator specifically named in the agreement."

Although this power, under the Act, is a statutory one, it is not foreign to or inconsistent with the general equitable jurisdiction of a circuit court. Equity courts have long had the power, for example, when specifically enforcing agreements, to appoint trustees to carry out their decrees when a party proves recalcitrant or when otherwise necessary to implement the agreement . . . .

Upon this analysis, it is clear that, had such a remedy been requested by the union, the court could have designated a substitute mediator/neutral fact-finder in light of the parties' inability or unwillingness to agree themselves upon a substitute for the nonfunctional State Mediation and Conciliation Service. Unfortunately, except to the extent included within the union's general prayer for relief, that request was not made. The only specific relief sought was an injunction, the effect of which would have been to retain captains and lieutenants within the bargaining unit until such time, if ever, that the county council, by amendment to the ordinance, declared such positions to be supervisory.

It is, of course, axiomatic that, except in compelling circumstances, the issuance or denial of an injunction rests within the sound discretion of the equity court, and that considerable latitude is afforded to trial judges in exercising that discretion.

In deciding whether the court here abused that discretion, we may take cognizance of both the general policy of the State to avoid injunctions in labor disputes and the fact that a better alternative was available in this particular case. As to the former, whether or not this particular dispute was formally subject to the anti-injunction provisions of Md. Code Labor & Empl. art., title 4, subt. 3, the issuance of such an injunction, given its practical effect, would certainly have been inconsistent with the general policy established by the Legislature in that part of the Code. We note, in that regard, § 4-302(b) expressing the policy of the State that "negotiation of terms and conditions of employment should result from voluntary agreement between employees and employer" and § 4-313 providing that, except where irreparable injury is threatened, a court may not grant injunctive relief in a labor dispute "if the plaintiff has failed to make every reasonable effort to settle the labor dispute . . . with the help of available dispute resolution mechanisms, governmental mediation, or voluntary arbitration."

As to the latter, for the reasons we have explained above, the union, and upon its request, the court, had a viable, less intrusive, and more appropriate alternative to the injunctive relief sought in this case. It is for these reasons that we shall affirm the judgment below, without prejudice to either party seeking further relief in the circuit court consistent with this Opinion.

*Judgment Affirmed.*

# NOTES AND QUESTIONS

(1)  The decision of the federal court in *Brosnan v. Dry Cleaning Station*, dismissing the claims for failure to engage in mediation prior to filing a lawsuit as required by the parties' contract, is consistent with the current tendency of courts nationwide to enforce contractual mediation agreements as a condition precedent to allowing the parties to proceed to litigation. *See, e. g.*, *Santana v. Olguin*, 208 P.3d 328 (Kan. Ct. App. 2009) (mediation clause in a real estate contract created a condition precedent to litigation requiring dismissal of purchaser's lawsuit against vendor); *Cohen v. Cohen*, 2007 N.J. Super. Unpub. LEXIS 271 (July 23, 2007) (child support payments resulting from divorce settlement could not be changed without first attempting negotiation or mediation as required by the contract).

(2)  Note the *Brosnan* court's reliance on the *Rounds* case, which involved an arbitration clause rather than a mediation clause. Does this suggest that the courts will now be giving as much deference to mediation clauses as they have been giving to arbitration clauses? What if the contract clause called for "mediation or arbitration" and the parties disagreed over which process should be used? What if the clause required a "multilayered" (negotiation, mediation, and arbitration) approach to dispute resolution and one of the parties opted to jump forward to arbitration, skipping negotiation and mediation? For an excellent discussion and analysis of the use of mediation clauses in contracts and related caselaw, see COLE, MCEWEN, ROGERS, COBEN & THOMPSON, MEDIATION: LAW, POLICY & PRACTICE (2011).

(3)  In *Klinge v. Bentien*, the Supreme Court of Iowa ruled that the failure to request mediation deprived the small claims court of subject matter jurisdiction. At least two state high courts have refused to view statutory requirements to mediate as absolute. In *Walsh v. Larsen*, 705 N.W.2d 638 (S.D. 2005), the Supreme Court of South Dakota ruled that the statutory mediation requirement was not jurisdictional but more like an affirmative defense that has to be pled and established. Similarly, the Supreme Court of Maine in *Twomey v. Twomey*, 888 A.2d 272 (Me. 2005), ruled that the statutory mediation requirement in child support disputes would be deemed to be waived where a father's motion for a continuance to allow mediation might be viewed as a delaying tactic. How might these decisions be reconciled?

(4)  Note that the court in *Annapolis Professional Firefighters* clearly stated that agreements to mediate should be enforced in the same way as agreements to arbitrate. Why did the court fail to discuss policy arguments against enforcement? Was it because the agreement to mediate had "teeth" in that the state statute required mediation as a precursor to a state investigation to assign blame for the continuation of the dispute? See *DeValk Lincoln Mercury, Inc. v. Ford Motor Co.*, 811 F.2d 326 (7th Cir. 1987), where compliance with a "mediation clause" in a commercial agreement was a condition precedent to pursuing other legal remedies. See also *HIM Portland LLC v. DeVito Builders, Inc.*, 317 F.3d 41 (1st Cir. 2003), where the U.S. Court of Appeals for the First Circuit ruled that a party could not compel arbitration absent a request by either party for mediation where the arbitration clause in the parties' agreement stated that disputes between the parties were subject to mediation as a condition precedent to arbitration. Similarly, in *Tinnerman v. TecStar*, 2012 U.S. Dist. LEXIS 49984 (E.D. Wis. Apr. 10, 2012), the court dismissed the lawsuit over Tinnerman's objection that mediation would be

futile, stating that: "the parties' contract requires that they at least try to work out a compromise through mediation, and until that mediation occurs, Tinnerman cannot proceed with a lawsuit."

## C.  JUDICIAL POWER TO COMPEL MEDIATION

Until recently, some courts had questioned whether they had the power to require parties to participate in ADR processes. In *Strandell v. Jackson County*, 838 F.2d 884 (7th Cir. 1987), for example, the United States Court of Appeals for the Seventh Circuit ruled that a federal district judge did not have the inherent authority to order the parties to participate in a summary jury trial. However, the increasing number of statutes and court rules authorizing judges to manage and control their caseloads by compelling the use of ADR, has established court-ordered mediation as an essential part of the litigation landscape in many jurisdictions. The cases in this section clearly demonstrate that courts have the power to require parties to participate in mediation. In *In re Atlantic Pipe Corp.*, the United States Court of Appeals for the First Circuit traces the sources a federal trial judge's inherent power to compel mediation even in the absence of a specific local rule and over a party's objections.

### IN RE ATLANTIC PIPE CORPORATION
United States Court of Appeals for the First Circuit
304 F.3d 135 (2002)

SELYA, CIRCUIT JUDGE.

This mandamus proceeding requires us to resolve an issue of importance to judges and practitioners alike: Does a district court possess the authority to compel an unwilling party to participate in, and share the costs of, non-binding mediation conducted by a private mediator? We hold that a court may order mandatory mediation pursuant to an explicit statutory provision or local rule. We further hold that where, as here, no such authorizing medium exists, a court nonetheless may order mandatory mediation through the use of its inherent powers as long as the case is an appropriate one and the order contains adequate safeguards. Because the mediation order here at issue lacks such safeguards (although it does not fall far short), we vacate it and remand the matter for further proceedings.

In January 1996, Thames-Dick Superaqueduct Partners (Thames-Dick) entered into a master agreement with the Puerto Rico Aqueduct and Sewer Authority (PRASA) to construct, operate, and maintain the North Coast Superaqueduct Project (the Project). Thames-Dick granted subcontracts for various portions of the work, including a subcontract for construction management to Dick Corp. of Puerto Rico (Dick-PR), a subcontract for the operation and maintenance of the Project to Thames Water International, Ltd. (Thames Water), and a subcontract for the fabrication of pipe to Atlantic Pipe Corp. (APC). After the Project had been built, a segment of the pipeline burst. Thames-Dick incurred significant costs in repairing the damage. Not surprisingly, it sought to recover those costs from other parties. In response, one of PRASA's insurers filed a declaratory judgment action in a local court to determine whether Thames-Dick's claims were covered under its policy. The litigation ballooned, soon involving a number of parties and a myriad of issues above and beyond insurance coverage.

On April 25, 2001, the hostilities spilled over into federal court. . . . Thames-Dick asked that the case be referred to mediation and suggested Professor Eric Green as a suitable mediator. The district court granted the motion over APC's objection and ordered non-binding mediation to proceed before Professor Green. The court pronounced mediation likely to conserve judicial resources; directed all parties to undertake mediation in good faith; stayed discovery pending completion of the mediation; and declared that participation in the mediation would not prejudice the parties' positions vis-à-vis the pending motion or the litigation as a whole. The court also stated that if mediation failed to produce a global settlement, the case would proceed to trial.

After moving unsuccessfully for reconsideration of the mediation order, APC sought relief by way of mandamus. Its petition alleged that the district court did not have the authority to require mediation (especially in light of unresolved questions as to the court's subject-matter jurisdiction) and, in all events, could not force APC to pay a share of the expenses of the mediation.

. . .

There are four potential sources of judicial authority for ordering mandatory non-binding mediation of pending cases, namely, (a) the court's local rules, (b) an applicable statute, (c) the Federal Rules of Civil Procedure, and (d) the court's inherent powers. Because the district court did not identify the basis of its assumed authority, we consider each of these sources.

A district court's local rules may provide an appropriate source of authority for ordering parties to participate in mediation. In Puerto Rico, however, the local rules contain only a single reference to any form of alternative dispute resolution (ADR). . . . The respondents concede that the mediation order in this case falls outside the boundaries of the mediation program envisioned by Rule V. It does so most noticeably because it involves mediation before a private mediator, not a judicial officer. Seizing upon this discrepancy, APC argues that the local rules limit the district court in this respect, and that the court exceeded its authority thereunder by issuing a non-conforming mediation order (i.e., one that contemplates the intervention of a private mediator). The respondents counter by arguing that the rule does not bind the district court because, notwithstanding the unambiguous promise of the CJR Plan (which declares that the district court "shall adopt a method of Alternative Dispute Resolution"), no such program has been adopted to date.

This is a powerful argument. APC does not contradict the respondents' assurance that the relevant portion of the CJR Plan has remained unimplemented, and we take judicial notice that there is no formal, ongoing ADR program in the Puerto Rico federal district court. Because that is so, we conclude that the District of Puerto Rico has no local rule in force that dictates the permissible characteristics of mediation orders. Consequently, APC's argument founders.

There is only one potential source of statutory authority for ordering mandatory non-binding mediation here: the Alternative Dispute Resolution Act of 1998 (ADR Act), 28 U.S.C. §§ 651–658. Congress passed the ADR Act to promote the utilization of alternative dispute resolution methods in the federal courts and to set appropriate guidelines for their use. The Act lists mediation as an appropriate ADR process. *Id.* § 651(a). Moreover, it sanctions the participation of "professional neutrals from the private sector" as mediators. *Id.* § 653(b). Finally, the Act requires district courts to obtain litigants' consent only when they order arbitration, *id.* § 652(a), not when they order the use of other ADR mechanisms (such as non-binding mediation).

Despite the broad sweep of these provisions, the Act is quite clear that some form of the ADR procedures it endorses must be adopted in each judicial district by local rule. *See id.* § 651(b) (directing each district court to "devise and implement its own alternative dispute resolution program, by local rule adopted under [28 U.S.C.] section 2071(a), to encourage and promote the use of alternative dispute resolution in its district"). In the absence of such local rules, the ADR Act itself does not authorize any specific court to use a particular ADR mechanism. Because the District of Puerto Rico has not yet complied with the Act's mandate, the mediation order here at issue cannot be justified under the ADR Act.

. . .

We add, however, that although the respondents cannot use the ADR Act as a justification, neither can APC use it as a nullification.

. . .

The respondents next argue that the district court possessed the authority to require mediation by virtue of the Federal Rules of Civil Procedure. They concentrate their attention on Fed.R.Civ.P. 16, which states in pertinent part that "the court may take appropriate action[ ] with respect to . . . (9) settlement and the use of special procedures to assist in resolving the dispute when authorized by statute or local rule . . . ." Fed.R.Civ.P. 16(c)(9). But the words "when authorized by statute or local rule" are a frank limitation on the district courts' authority to order mediation thereunder, and we must adhere to that circumscription. . . .

Even apart from positive law, district courts have substantial inherent power to manage and control their calendars. This inherent power takes many forms. *See* Fed.R.Civ.P. 83(b) (providing that judges may regulate practice in any manner consistent with federal law and applicable rules). By way of illustration, a district court may use its inherent power to compel represented clients to attend pretrial settlement conferences, even though such a practice is not specifically authorized in the Civil Rules. *See Heileman Brewing Co. v. Joseph Oat Corp.*, 871 F.2d 648, 650 (7th Cir.1989) (en banc).

Of course, a district court's inherent powers are not infinite. There are at least four limiting principles. First, inherent powers must be used in a way reasonably suited to the enhancement of the court's processes, including the orderly and expeditious disposition of pending cases. Second, inherent powers cannot be exercised in a manner that contradicts an applicable statute or rule. Third, the use of inherent powers must comport with procedural fairness. And, finally, inherent powers "must be exercised with restraint and discretion."

. . .

We begin our inquiry by examining the case law. In *Strandell v. Jackson County*, 838 F.2d 884 (7th Cir. 1987), the Seventh Circuit held that a district court does not possess inherent power to compel participation in a summary jury trial. In the court's view, Fed.R.Civ.P. 16 occupied the field and prevented a district court from forcing "an unwilling litigant [to] be sidetracked from the normal course of litigation." *Id.* at 887. But the group that spearheaded the subsequent revision of Rule 16 explicitly rejected that interpretation. *See* Fed.R.Civ.P. 16, advisory committee's note (1993 Amendment) ("The [amended] rule does not attempt to resolve questions as to the extent a court would be authorized to require [ADR] proceedings as an exercise of its inherent powers."). Thus, we do not find *Strandell* persuasive on this point.

The *Strandell* court also expressed concern that summary jury trials would undermine traditional discovery and privilege rules by requiring certain disclosures prior to an actual trial. 838 F.2d at 888. We find this concern unwarranted. Because a summary jury trial (like a non-binding mediation) does not require any disclosures beyond what would be required in the ordinary course of discovery, its principal disadvantage to the litigants is that it may prevent them from saving surprises for the time of trial. Since trial by ambush is no longer in vogue, that interest does not deserve protection. Relying on policy arguments, the Sixth Circuit also has found that district courts do not possess inherent power to compel participation in summary jury trials. *See In re NLO, Inc.*, 5 F.3d 154, 157–58 (6th Cir.1993). The court thought the value of a summary jury trial questionable when parties do not engage in the process voluntarily, and it worried that "too broad an interpretation of the federal courts' inherent power to regulate their procedure . . . encourages judicial high-handedness . . . ."

The concerns articulated by these two respected courts plainly apply to mandatory mediation orders. When mediation is forced upon unwilling litigants, it stands to reason that the likelihood of settlement is diminished. Requiring parties to invest substantial amounts of time and money in mediation under such circumstances may well be inefficient.

The fact remains, however, that none of these considerations establishes that mandatory mediation is always inappropriate. There may well be specific cases in which such a protocol is likely to conserve judicial resources without significantly burdening the objectors' rights to a full, fair, and speedy trial. Much depends on the idiosyncrasies of the particular case and the details of the mediation order.

In some cases, a court may be warranted in believing that compulsory mediation could yield significant benefits even if one or more parties object. After all, a party may resist mediation simply out of unfamiliarity with the process or out of fear that a willingness to submit would be perceived as a lack of confidence in her legal position. In such an instance, the party's initial reservations are likely to evaporate as the mediation progresses, and negotiations could well produce a beneficial outcome, at reduced cost and greater speed, than would a trial. While the possibility that parties will fail to reach agreement remains ever present, the boon of settlement can be worth the risk.

This is particularly true in complex cases involving multiple claims and parties. The fair and expeditious resolution of such cases often is helped along by creative solutions — solutions that simply are not available in the binary framework of traditional adversarial litigation. Mediation with the assistance of a skilled facilitator gives parties an opportunity to explore a much wider range of options, including those that go beyond conventional zero-sum resolutions. Mindful of these potential advantages, we hold that it is within a district court's inherent power to order non-consensual mediation in those cases in which that step seems reasonably likely to serve the interests of justice.

Our determination that the district courts have inherent power to refer cases to non-binding mediation is made with a recognition that any such order must be crafted in a manner that preserves procedural fairness and shields objecting parties from undue burdens. We thus turn to the specifics of the mediation order entered in this case. As with any exercise of a district court's inherent powers, we review the entry of that order for abuse of discretion.

As an initial matter, we agree with the lower court that the complexity of this case militates in favor of ordering mediation. At last count, the suit involves twelve parties, asserting a welter of claims, counterclaims, cross-claims, and third-party claims predicated on a wide variety of theories. The pendency of nearly parallel litigation in the Puerto Rican courts, which features a slightly different cast of characters and claims that are related to but not completely congruent with those asserted here, further complicates the matter. Untangling the intricate web of relationships among the parties, along with the difficult and fact-intensive arguments made by each, will be time-consuming and will impose significant costs on the parties and the court. Against this backdrop, mediation holds out the dual prospect of advantaging the litigants and conserving scarce judicial resources.

In an effort to parry this thrust, APC raises a series of objections. Its threshold claim is that the district court erred in ordering mediation before resolving a pending motion to dismiss for lack of subject-matter jurisdiction (or, alternatively, to abstain). . . . [E]ven if it were error to enter the mediation order before passing upon the motion to dismiss, the error was harmless: it would be an empty exercise to vacate the mediation order on this ground when the lower court has already rejected the challenges to its exercise of jurisdiction..

Next, APC posits that the appointment of a private mediator proposed by one of the parties is per se improper (and, thus, invalidates the order). We do not agree. The district court has inherent power to "appoint persons unconnected with the court to aid judges in the performance of specific judicial duties." In the context of non-binding mediation, the mediator does not decide the merits of the case and has no authority to coerce settlement. Thus, in the absence of a contrary statute or rule, it is perfectly acceptable for the district court to appoint a qualified and neutral private party as a mediator. The mere fact that the mediator was proposed by one of the parties is insufficient to establish bias in favor of that party.

We hasten to add that the litigants are free to challenge the qualifications or neutrality of any suggested mediator (whether or not nominated by a party to the case).

. . .

APC also grouses that it should not be forced to share the costs of an unwanted mediation. We have held, however, that courts have the power under Fed.R.Civ.P. 26(f) to issue pretrial cost-sharing orders in complex litigation. Given the difficulties facing trial courts in cases involving multiple parties and multiple claims, we are hesitant to limit that power to the traditional discovery context. *See id.* This is especially true in complicated cases, where the potential value of mediation lies not only in promoting settlement but also in clarifying the issues remaining for trial.

The short of the matter is that, without default cost-sharing rules, the use of valuable ADR techniques (like mediation) becomes hostage to the parties' ability to agree on the concomitant financial arrangements. This means that the district court's inherent power to order private mediation in appropriate cases would be rendered nugatory absent the corollary power to order the sharing of reasonable mediation costs. To avoid this pitfall, we hold that the district court, in an appropriate case, is empowered to order the sharing of reasonable costs and expenses associated with mandatory non-binding mediation.

The remainder of APC's arguments are not so easily dispatched. Even when generically appropriate, a mediation order must contain procedural and substantive safeguards to ensure fairness to all parties involved. The mediation order in this case does not quite meet that test. In particular, the order does not set limits on the duration of the mediation or the expense associated therewith.

We need not wax longiloquent. As entered, the order simply requires the parties to mediate; it does not set forth either a timetable for the mediation or a cap on the fees that the mediator may charge. The figures that have been bandied about in the briefs — $900 per hour or $9,000 per mediation day — are quite large and should not be left to the mediator's whim. Relatedly, because the mediator is to be paid an hourly rate, the court should have set an outside limit on the number of hours to be devoted to mediation. Equally as important, it is trite but often true that justice delayed is justice denied. An unsuccessful mediation will postpone the ultimate resolution of the case — indeed, the district court has stayed all discovery pending the completion of the mediation — and, thus, prolong the litigation. For these reasons, the district court should have set a definite time frame for the mediation.

The respondents suggest that the district court did not need to articulate any limitations in its mediation order because the mediation process will remain under the district court's ultimate supervision; the court retains the ability to curtail any excessive expenditures of time or money; and a dissatisfied party can easily return to the court at any time. While this might be enough of a safeguard in many instances, the instant litigation is sufficiently complicated and the mediation efforts are likely to be sufficiently expensive that, here, reasonable time limits and fee constraints, set in advance, are appropriate.

A court intent on ordering non-consensual mediation should take other precautions as well. For example, the court should make it clear (as did the able district court in this case) that participation in mediation will not be taken as a waiver of any litigation position. The important point is that the protections we have mentioned are not intended to comprise an exhaustive list, but, rather, to illustrate that when a district court orders a party to participate in mediation, it should take care to assuage legitimate concerns about the possible negative consequences of such an order.

To recapitulate, we rule that a mandatory mediation order issued under the district court's inherent power is valid in an appropriate case. We also rule that this is an appropriate case. We hold, however, that the district court's failure to set reasonable limits on the duration of the mediation and on the mediator's fees dooms the decree.

We admire the district court's pragmatic and innovative approach to this massive litigation. Our core holding — that ordering mandatory mediation is a proper exercise of a district court's inherent power, subject, however, to a variety of terms and conditions — validates that approach. We are mindful that this holding is in tension with the opinions of the Sixth and Seventh Circuits in *NLO* and *Strandell*, respectively, but we believe it is justified by the important goal of promoting flexibility and creative problem-solving in the handling of complex litigation.

That said, the need of the district judge in this case to construct his own mediation regime ad hoc underscores the greater need of the district court as an institution to adopt an ADR program and memorialize it in its local rules. In the ADR Act, Congress directed that "[e]ach United States district court shall authorize, by local rule under section 2071(a), the use of alternative dispute resolution processes in all civil actions . . . ." 28 U.S.C. § 651(b). While Congress did not set a firm deadline for compliance with this directive, the statute was enacted four years ago. This omission having been noted, we are confident that the district court will move expediently to bring the District of Puerto Rico into compliance.

We need go no further. For the reasons set forth above, we vacate the district court's mediation order and remand for further proceedings consistent with this opinion. The district court is free to order mediation if it continues to believe that such a course is advisable or, in the alternative, to proceed with discovery and trial.

*Vacated and remanded.*

## LIANG v. LAI
### Supreme Court of Montana
### 78 P.3d 1212 (2003)

Appellant sued Respondents for damages in the Eleventh Judicial District Court, Flathead County. The District Court later issued an Order on Motion for Change of Venue. Appellant's notice of appeal from that order was filed on August 12, 2003; the notice stated that "this appeal is subject to the mediation process required by Rule 54, M.R.App.P." . . . Appellant filed an Unopposed Motion to Dispense with Mediation. As was the case with the notice of appeal, Appellant's motion concedes that the appeal is subject to Rule 54, because it involves an underlying suit for money damages. *See* Rule 54(a)(3), M.R.App.P. Appellant contends that *Hanley v. Lanier*, 305 Mont. 175, 2001 MT 91, 24 P.3d 206, and *McDonald v. Cosman*, 297 Mont. 108, 1999 MT 294, 995 P.2d 922, support all counsels' position here that mediation may be dispensed with because money damages are not an issue in the appeal and, consequently, mediation will not assist or hasten the resolution of the appeal. *Hanley* and *McDonald* are inapplicable here.

In *Hanley*, we addressed a motion to dismiss for failure to comply with Rule 54, and the issue was whether or not the appeal was subject to Rule 54. We determined that the overall thrust of the underlying action involved easement, real property and injunction issues which are not within the purview of Rule 54 and, consequently, the fact that an incidental issue regarding monetary attorney fees — which was dependent on the trial court's resolution of the primary issues — did not subject the appeal to the mandatory mediation requirements of Rule 54, M.R.App.P. Similarly, the issue before us in *McDonald* was whether an appeal from a judgment for specific performance of a contract, with an attendant award of attorney fees pursuant to the contract, was subject to Rule 54, M.R.App.P. We determined that, because the primary issue in the case involved specific performance of a contract, a type of action not subject to Rule 54's requirements, a contract provision authorizing attorney fees to the prevailing party was insufficient to bring the appeal within the Rule 54(a)(3), M.R.App.P., category of "[a]ppeals in actions seeking monetary damages/recovery." Unlike *Hanley* and *McDonald*, the case underlying this appeal clearly and admittedly falls within the ambit of Rule 54(a)(3), M.R.App.P., as a suit seeking money damages. Neither *Hanley* nor *McDonald* held that mediation could be dispensed with in an appeal in which the underlying action clearly comes within Rule 54.

In *Dobrocke v. City of Columbia Falls*, 300 Mont. 348, . . . [this court concluded] that in deciding whether an appeal is or is not subject to Rule 54, "the determining factor is the relief sought and not the type of order or judgment being appealed."

We reach the same conclusion here. There is no legitimate question here about whether this appeal is or is not subject to Rule 54; Appellant concedes that it is. We reiterate that it is the nature of the underlying action, not the type of order or judgment on appeal, which is determinative of whether the appeal is subject to the mandatory mediation requirements of Rule 54, M.R.App.P. The notions that only a legal issue is on appeal and, therefore, that mediation is not required, were disposed of in *Dobrocke* more than three years ago.

Nor does the Rule contemplate counsel for the parties to an appeal requesting this Court to "dispense with mediation" pursuant to a stipulation or unopposed motion simply because counsel do not believe mediation will resolve the appeal. Rule 54 is mandatory for the categories of cases set forth therein; it contemplates a good faith effort by counsel to resolve the case through mediation. Had the Rule been otherwise, it is unlikely that more than one or two cases would have been mediated on appeal, since the prevailing reaction among legal practitioners at the time the Rule was implemented was that not a single case could or would be resolved through mediation on appeal.

Counsel across the state should be aware by now that this Court intends Rule 54, M.R.App.P., to be self-executing. Neither we, nor clients, can afford the extra resources consumed by motion practice on Rule 54.

THEREFORE,

IT IS ORDERED that Appellant's unopposed motion to dispense with mediation is DENIED; and

IT IS FURTHER ORDERED that the 75-day period for completion of the mediation shall run from the date of this Order.

The Clerk is directed to mail a true copy of this Order to counsel of record.

/s/ Karla M. Gray

Chief Justice

## NOTES AND QUESTIONS

(1) The various sources of judicial authority for federal judges to compel mediation discussed in *Atlantic Pipe* parallel those available to state court judges. Note that while the court ruled that the trial judge had the power to require mediation, it stated that the court should set reasonable limitations on the length of the mediation and the mediator's fees. Do you think it is appropriate for the court to limit the parties' self-determination regarding these issues? If so, do you think the court offered sufficient guidance regarding the parties' ability to choose who will mediate? Some courts have denied motions to compel mediation, often citing futility. *See, e. g., Wells Fargo Bank Minnesota v. Kobernick*, 2009 U.S. Dist. LEXIS 81703 (S.D. Tex. Aug. 26, 2009), where the court reasoned that the parties had already tried to reach agreement but failed.

(2) In *Liang v. Lai*, the Supreme Court of Montana refuses to grant the appellant's motion to dispense with mediation even though it is unopposed. The court insists that the Montana rule requiring mediation by parties to an appeal be followed. Note that the rule requires that the mediation be completed within 75 days. Do you think the arguments for mandatory mediation at the appellate court level are different from those at the trial court level?

## D.   MEDIATION IN "GOOD FAITH"

Although mediation is considered a consensual, voluntary process, is a party in a mediation under some obligation to treat the mediation with a certain degree of seriousness, particularly where the mediation is court-ordered? The preceding section explored the consequences of a party's refusal to participate in mediation when required to do so by contract or statute. What if the party participates in the mediation but does so half-heartedly or strategically — so much so that the party is arguably not making a "good faith" effort to settle the case? This section presents the arguments and policy concerns over imposing a "good faith" participation requirement in mediation.

## PITTS v. FRANCIS

United States District Court for the Northern District of Florida
2007 U.S. Dist. LEXIS 93047 (Dec. 19, 2007)

RICHARD SMOAK, DISTRICT JUDGE.

Plaintiff Brittany Pitts has sued Defendant Joseph R. Francis and Defendant business entities operating under the name "Girls Gone Wild" Pitts alleges that in April 2003, while on her spring break vacation in Panama City Beach, Florida, Francis and another Girls Gone Wild employee approached her on the beach and coerced her into exposing her breasts on film. Pitts contends that she did not consent to be filmed and was sixteen years of age, a sophomore in high school, at the time of the alleged incident. Pitts' image was displayed on the cover of a Girls Gone Wild video and DVD, which were sold and distributed throughout the United States. The five-count First Amended Complaint asserts claims for unjust enrichment; violations of the Florida Deceptive and Unfair Trade Practices Act, unauthorized publication of likeness under *Fla. Stat. § 54.08;* commercial misappropriation of one's likeness; and false light doctrine of invasion of privacy.

The motion requests that I disqualify or recuse myself from this case under *28 U.S.C. § 455(a)*. Defendants contend that my impartiality in this case might be questioned based on the history of civil and criminal proceedings involving Defendants and a former Girls Gone Wild cameraman over which I have presided. As grounds for disqualification and/or recusal Defendants contend that:

1.  I forced Francis to settle the civil lawsuit under the threat of incarceration;

2.  I would not consider "less onerous alternatives" other than incarceration to compel Francis' compliance with my order to mediate the civil lawsuit;

3.  I required that Francis personally attend a criminal sentencing hearing and read aloud a victim impact statement on behalf of his corporation, Mantra Films, Inc., after the corporation pled guilty to committing federal crimes; and

4.  I made various comments to Francis and to Mark Schmitz, a Girls Gone Wild cameraman, at judicial proceedings. Defendants contend that the comments demonstrate bias and prejudice against them. The comments are set forth and addressed in this opinion . . .

. . .

It is noteworthy that Defendants do not contend that they *themselves* interpreted my order as requiring that Joe Francis settle the case. All parties present at the contempt hearing, including counsel for Joe Francis and Girls Gone Wild, *did* understand that my order required that Joe Francis simply mediate in good faith, not settle, the case:

> **THE COURT:** Mr. Francis can cure his contempt and have this sanction of incarceration removed upon his proper participation in mediation. And I direct that the plaintiffs are to cooperate in every possible way in expediting the scheduling of the resumption of the mediation.

Whenever the mediation is due to start, I direct that everybody concerned are to arrive in Bay County no later than the evening before so that there will be no possibility, hopefully, of mediation not getting started on time. . . .

If necessary, this mediation could be conducted here in the courthouse and I will wait to hear from the attorneys about this offer. Regardless, I will be immediately available in the event any further problems arise.

Now, at the mediation, Mr. Francis will be dressed and groomed appropriately as if for the appearance before this court in this courtroom. This means a business suit and a tie, business shoes and socks and he will conduct himself and communicate in a manner during the mediation with the demeanor and courtesy expected in serious business transactions and appearance before this court. . . .

Mr. Francis will be released from incarceration when the mediator certifies in person to me that Mr. Francis has fully complied with this order and has participated in the mediation in good faith.

Now, the further guidance is that there must — while mediation — this obligation to settle, there must be participation by all parties and the attorneys in a discussion — frank and thorough discussion — as stated in Local Rule 16.3. And this is to identify the interests that are at stake, to suggest alternatives, analyze the issue, question existing perceptions, to conduct private caucuses, to stimulate negotiations and to keep this thing under order.

**THE COURT:** We are looking at this point, Mr. Francis, to do without reservation what my order, scheduling mediation order, required in the first instance. His conduct, which I think is not disputed — I don't know if I've been sufficiently articulate, but Mr. Burke, in all of my years of being a trial layer, and a mediator, and then — and as a mediator trying to keep up with the law and the guidance in Florida, the Dispute Resolution Center with the Florida Supreme Court, tried to keep all mediators involved of current issues — I can't think of any worse behavior anytime in my career. If necessary we'll take this a step at a time.

**MR. BURK:** In light of the court's order, *which seems to be to be premised on the fact — on the finding that Mr. Francis did not meaningfully participate, or that the mediation was not conducted pursuant to the court's scheduling order in good faith*, I would like to proffer on behalf of the defendants, under seal, so that the matter may be reviewed by both — either Your Honor or by the court of appeal — the actual offers that were made at the mediation, so that a court may consider whether in fact mediation proceeded in good faith by the defendants and by Mr. Francis in particular.

The quoted statements prove, beyond a reasonable doubt, that defense counsel correctly understood my order as requiring that Joe Francis mediate in good faith, not settle, the case. As specifically articulated on the record and as quoted verbatim above: "[T]his obligation to mediate does not impose an obligation to settle." . . .

. . .

On March 23, 2007, the plaintiffs in *Doe v. Francis* filed a motion requesting sanctions against Joe Francis. The motion alleged that Francis had behaved in a threatening and abusive manner toward the plaintiffs and their attorneys at a court-ordered mediation. Because of the seriousness of those allegations, I held a hearing to determine whether a more formal, evidentiary hearing on the motion was warranted. Francis' attorney, Michael Dickey, was present at the hearing. Mr. Dickey stated that

> I'm not sure under the circumstances, Your Honor, what I could have done, or any of the other attorneys in the room could have done to stop [Francis'] out-burst [at the mediation], short of what transpired, which was the plaintiffs' lawyers got up and left which was appropriate, I would put to you, under the circumstances.

In the other words, Mr. Dickey, Joe Francis' attorney, agreed that the behavior of his *own* client at a court-ordered mediation was so incredibly abusive and inappropriate as to justify plaintiffs and their counsel to simply *leave* the mediation. Relying on Mr. Dickey's representation, I found it appropriate to schedule an evidentiary hearing on the motion for sanctions to afford Francis the opportunity to defend himself. I entered an order that unambiguously stated the purpose of the hearing:

> Defendant Joseph R. Francis is ordered to appear . . . to show cause why he should not be held in contempt for failure to comply with **Paragraph 8** of the Scheduling and Mediation Order and to show cause why Plaintiff's Motion for the imposition of sanctions should not be granted.

Thus, the sole purpose of the hearing, per my written order, was to consider whether Francis had violated my standard order requiring all litigants in this Court to attempt to resolve their cases through mediation.

At the evidentiary hearing, Francis was represented by Michael Burke, general counsel for Girls Gone Wild, and by Mr. Dickey. The testimony and evidence presented at the evidentiary hearing and in the written documents filed on the docket were shocking:

To report that Francis arrived late at the mediation is an understatement. Francis arrived *four hours* late, keeping the out-of-town plaintiffs and their attorneys waiting.

Francis' tardiness did not result from time spent primping; rather, Francis arrived at the mediation wearing sweat shorts, a backwards baseball cap, and was barefoot. He was playing on an electronic devise.

As plaintiff's counsel began his presentation, Francis put his bare, dirty feet on the table, facing plaintiff's counsel. Plaintiff's counsel said four words before Francis interrupted him.

Francis then erupted into a tantrum, yelling repeatedly: "Don't expect to get a fucking dime — not one fucking dime!"

Francis shouted: "I hold the purse strings; I will not settle this case at all. I am only here because the court is making me be here!"

Reasonably concluding that mediation was futile, the plaintiff's attorneys began to leave the room. As if he had not made his point, Francis threatened: "We will bury you and your clients! I'm going to ruin you, your clients, and all of your ambulance-chasing partners!"

As they exited the room, Francis, without provocation, charged plaintiffs' counsel, "got in his face," and appeared as though he was going to physically assault plaintiff's counsel. "I thought he was going to slug me," plaintiffs' counsel testified.

A witness confirmed that

> it was the way — you had to be there, but it was the way that Mr. Francis came around the table in a very rapid motion and got nose to nose with [plaintiffs' counsel], was shouting profanities that you heard testimony about, and it seemed to me that he was trying to provoke a physical confrontation.

Francis' own attorney had to position himself between Francis and plaintiffs' counsel to prevent a brawl.

Francis' goodbye wish to plaintiffs' counsel was "Suck my dick."

. . .

Simply put, Francis' behavior was not mediation. It was not posturing. It was *violent.* Anyone attending that mediation, including Joe Francis himself, could have been injured. I will not permit a litigant in this *federal* court to exploit an order issued by me for the sole purpose of abusing and threatening another party. As judge, it is my responsibility to ensure the orderly administration of justice in the cases over which I preside. *Code of Conduct for United States Judges*, Canon 3A(2) ("A judge . . . should maintain order and decorum in all judicial proceedings.") To Joe Francis, my mediation order was apparently a conduit through which he could threaten and assault the other party and its attorneys under the cloak of confidentiality:

> **THE COURT:** [U]nder no stretch of the imagination can Mr. Francis' comments and his conduct be construed as being part of the mediation process. I think, to the contrary, he made it clear unequivocally and graphically that he was not there to mediate.
>
> I would characterize Mr. Francis' comments not of anything deserving or intended to foster the purposes of mediation, but rather something you might expect from a drunk fight in the parking lot of a bar at 3:00 in the morning.
>
> I find that his conduct and his statements were extreme, they were hostile, they were vulgar, they were obscene, and they are unacceptable, not only in just about every setting of our everyday life, Mr. Francis, but they are unacceptable in this court and in any activity required by this court . . .

If Francis had simply mediated in good faith and an impasse had resulted, he would not have been sanctioned. Indeed, many cases on this Court's dockets do not result in settlement, and parties are not sanctioned. Francis, however, failed to make an attempt at mediation. Worse, he exploited the mediation process for abusive purposes.

It is important to note that neither Francis nor his attorneys filed a motion to dispense with the mediation. Even at the evidentiary hearing on the motion for sanctions, Francis' attorneys expressed hope that settlement was a possibility. Had Francis filed a motion to dispense with mediation, I would have considered the reason stated in the motion, like any other motion filed on the dockets of this court, and rendered an appropriate ruling. Certainly, had Francis moved to dispense with mediation on the grounds that he would threaten and abuse the other party, I would have taken appropriate measures to prevent that. This Francis and his attorneys failed to do. Instead, Francis chose to attend the "mediation" and waste the time and money of his adversaries. He made a mockery of himself and of the alternative dispute resolution process . . .

. . .

In weighing the propriety of each sanction, I determined that financial sanctions alone would not be effective in forcing Francis to obey my order:

> And because of the financial situation of Mr. Francis and his totally controlled enterprises, thoroughly documented before this court, and the related criminal case, financial sanctions alone may not be sufficient and are unlikely to cause Mr. Francis to comply with the order this court . . .

I then concluded that

> Therefore, coercive incarceration is an appropriate sanction for this situation. Mr. Francis can cure his contempt and have this sanction of incarceration removed upon his proper participation in mediation . . .

## GOOD FAITH MEDIATION IN THE FEDERAL COURTS
### 26 Ohio St. J. on Disp. Resol. 363 (2011)*
### By Peter N. Thompson

"We will go where the river takes us" is not what we might expect to hear from the presiding official in today's highly-regulated and tightly-managed federal court litigation process. The Federal Rules of Civil Procedure and a managerial judiciary ensure a predictable process consistent with approved and published rules. Yet, when counsel for Wells Fargo Bank was ordered to mediation in Bankruptcy Court in In re A.T. Reynolds & Sons,[1] and inquired who was attending and what issues would be addressed, the mediator's response was "[w]e will go where the river takes us." Wells Fargo objected to the uncertainty of the process and was decidedly uncooperative. The bankruptcy judge ultimately sanctioned Wells Fargo and its counsel for bad faith mediation conduct. The judge added a twist to the river metaphor, making it clear that the mediator, not the parties involved in the

---

[1] In re A.T. Reynolds & Sons, 424 B.R. 76, 80-82 (Bankr. S.D.N.Y. 2010).

mediation, decides which fork in the river to explore, what will take place at the mediation, and how it will be conducted.

For the most part the "rules" of the mediation process are not written, but are committed to the discretion of the mediator. There are rules of course. Federal Rule of Civil Procedure 16(f) and the local rules sending Wells Fargo to mediation require that the parties participate in good faith. Good faith, however, is not defined. Good faith in this context meant leaving behind adversarial instincts and tactics and cooperating, or at least playing along, with the demands of the mediator.

Wells Fargo and its counsel were sanctioned, in part, because of their attempts to "wrest control" of the mediation from the mediator and their unwillingness to temporarily suspend their adversarial zeal. They refused to listen to positions and arguments with which they disagreed without interrupting, and were unwilling to consider hypothetically that their legal analysis might be wrong. The river ran one direction — downstream toward settlement. Wells Fargo did not want to settle or leave the perceived safe waters provided by the adversary system, and was unwilling to plunge downstream into uncharted waters. They were lost among a conflict of cultures between the rules-based adversarial system and a largely unregulated system of mediation.

. . .

For the most part, the pretrial process works well. Occasionally, however, adversarial zeal, or plain lack of professionalism, causes parties to refuse to follow orders or rules, or otherwise attempt to use the process improperly to obtain an unfair adversarial advantage. Courts respond with an elaborate enforcement system of judicial oversight and sanctions to assure that the rules are followed, parties are protected, and court orders are upheld.

The mediation process, on the other hand, is not designed to be adversarial. Mediation is championed as a private, confidential process centered on party autonomy and self-determination, where a neutral third party "facilitates communication and negotiation between parties to assist them in reaching a voluntary agreement regarding their dispute." Confidentiality, self-determination, and conciliation are lauded as essential features of the traditional mediation session. Superimposing this private, facilitative process in the midst of the public adversarial pretrial process is not an easy matter, and as many commentators have remarked, creates a "process dissonance" or clash of cultures.

This clash of cultures is apparent when assessing the role of the court in supervising or compelling mediation conduct in light of mediation values of confidentiality and self-determination. If self-determination and voluntary agreement are key mediation values, how can a court compel parties to mediate in good faith in circumstances where the parties do not want to settle? If confidentiality is a core value, how can a court police the mediation process and assure good faith participation without breaching the confidentiality of that process? What is required of parties who do not want to settle but are ordered to participate in mediation in good faith?

. . .

What are the expectations of the parties when a party who does not want to settle is ordered to go to mediation? In the context of court-mandated mediation, the substance of any good faith requirement must emanate from the expectations of the judge or from the text of the governing rules. What is it that the judge expects the parties to do when she orders them to mediation? Is this an order to plunge downstream toward settlement?

Courts and court rules repeatedly assure parties that there is no duty to settle a case and forego the right to trial. There also is no obligation to make a settlement offer and forego the right to trial. Yet, some court rules and pronouncements come sufficiently close, so that it may feel to the parties that they are being ordered to settle and forego their right to trial or suffer sanctions. Thus, there is ambiguity in terms of expectations in court-compelled mediation.

. . .

If a party does not want to settle, what are its obligation to mediate in good faith? Any scheme requiring parties to attend mediation should identify the expectations for party behavior and guard against the appearance of compelling parties to give up their right to trial. Although the local rules in nearly two dozen districts require that parties ordered to mediation must mediate in good faith, few of the rules provide a definition. Several commentators have attempted to provide a definition of good faith in the context of mediation. Kimberlee Kovach suggests various factors in a model rule that she proposes, including such requirements as complying with applicable law, court orders, the contract to mediate, and the mediator's rules.[2] In addition, parties should prepare for the mediation, attend the mediation with settlement authority, and participate in meaningful discussions. Included in the obligation is a duty not to affirmatively mislead the mediator or the adverse party. Kovach also includes an obligation not to file any new motions in the proceedings until the mediation is completed.

Carter provides a more generalized standard. He argues bad faith occurs when a participant "uses the mediation process primarily to gain strategic advantage in the litigation process; uses mediation to impose hardship rather than to promote understanding and conflict resolution; or neglects an affirmative material obligation owed to another participant, the mediator, or the court."[3]

Sherman advances a more limited definition that would require meaningful participation or participation that is necessary to prevent frustration of ADR process objectives. This would include a duty for parties and representatives with settlement authority to attend, listen, present positions, and pay for the mediator.[4] Sherman, however, argues against broader "good faith" requirements that focus on the quality of bargaining.

---

[2] Kimberlee K. Kovach, Good Faith in Mediation — Requested, Recommended, or Required? A New Ethic, 38 S. Tex. L. Rev. 575, 616–17, 620–23 (1997)

[3] Roger L. Carter, Oh, Ye of Little (Good) Faith: Questions, Concerns and Commentary on Efforts to Regulate Participant Conduct in Mediations, 2002 J. Disp. Resol. 367.

[4] Edward F. Sherman, Court-Mandated Alternative Dispute Resolution: What Form of Participation Should Be Required?, 46 SMU L. Rev. 2079 (1993).

At the very least, good faith participation in mediation requires that parties prepare for and attend the mediation with settlement authority. Imposing sanctions for these "objective" requirements usually does not involve a deep intrusion into mediation communications and parties' litigation strategies. While even these issues can give rise to some indeterminacy, the more controversial issues surround questions relating to the court's power to police the quality of the bargaining.

. . .

The crux of the dispute over court enforcement of any obligation to participate in good faith centers on questions of whether, consistent with principles of confidentiality, the court can:

(1)    compel the parties to actually listen to and communicate with the adverse party or mediator about the issues in the case.

(2)    require that the parties actually bargain with each other and exchange offers to settle;

(3)    police the mediation process to protect parties from offensive, abusive conduct, or efforts to misuse the mediation process for unfair adversarial advantage.

Several recent federal court decisions shed some light on these questions.

In In re A.T. Reynolds & Sons, introduced at the beginning of this article, Wells Fargo and counsel were sanctioned for, among other things, their disruptive behavior at mediation. Wells Fargo's duty to mediate in good faith came from a local court rule embodied in a standing order that was specifically incorporated in the order sending the party to mediation. The bankruptcy judge had little difficulty addressing the confidentiality rules since the local rules specifically provided that the "mediator shall report any willful failure to attend or participate in good faith." Consequently, the judge concluded that the mediator was free to file a report and provide testimony about the mediator's perceptions of what went on during the mediation. The judge provided no explanation of what justified testimony from both parties about the bargaining communications at the mediationAllowing parties to testify to mediation communications is an anathema to the mediation community. Allowing a mediator to testify is worse.

. . .

The concern with permitting or requiring a mediator report on what transpired at the mediation, however, raises additional issues. There is a concern that this practice may impair the role of the mediator as an impartial, neutral facilitator. Perhaps the leading case expressing this concern is NLRB v. Macaluso, a federal labor case in which the court precluded the mediator's testimony on the issue of whether the parties had reached an agreement in mediation. The court reasoned, "the public interest in maintaining the actual or perceived impartiality of federal mediators outweighs the benefits of relevant and decisive testimony on the issue at hand."

. . .

If the mediator is required to assess whether the parties are bargaining in good faith, however, the mediator may be acting more in an adjudicative role than as a facilitator. It is possible that parties might take a different approach with a mediator who purely facilitates the dispute as opposed to a mediator who has a responsibility or right to judge whether the parties are mediating in good faith. It is also possible that it makes no difference at all to most parties whether they are mediating in a jurisdiction with an obligation to mediate in good faith. The hope, of course, is that parties will be deterred from acting in bad faith if they are accountable to the mediator. Numerous districts allow, or require, a mediator to report bad faith conduct in mediation. This right or duty to report bad faith mediation conduct has been in place in many jurisdictions for many years.

It is possible that the mediator's relationship with the party accused of bad faith may be jeopardized, and in situations involving repeat players and a limited number of neutrals this could cause a problem. Macaluso, a labor dispute, implicated issues of national industrial peace and the need to preserve confidence in the Federal Mediation and Conciliation Service. According to the court, "The complete exclusion of mediator testimony is necessary to the preservation of an effective system of labor mediation, and that labor mediation is essential to continued industrial stability, a public interest sufficiently great to outweigh the interest in obtaining every person's evidence." When Macaluso was decided there were only 325 federal mediators and over twenty thousand disputes. The personal relationship between the mediator and Wells Fargo was strained in A.T. Reynolds, but there is no indication that this impaired personal relationship will harm the bankruptcy or justice system in New York. This mediator, who was threatened by defendants, would not be a good choice to mediate subsequent disputes with these parties even if the mediator had not reported the bad faith conduct.

Resort to mediator evidence should be avoided, unless necessary to resolve the legitimate issue of compliance with court duties. There is a strong interest in preserving mediation confidentiality and easing the burden on mediators. Where mediator testimony is necessary, it should be limited. The concern about neutrality may arise when the courts ask the mediator to go beyond reporting on what the mediator observed and seek the mediator's subjective views about the motivations of the parties. This assessment function is better left to adjudicators and not mediators. To the extent that it is essential to have full input about what transpired at the mediation to enforce court orders, to protect parties from abusive practices and to "preserve the integrity of the judicial process," it is rarely necessary for the court to hear the mediator's opinions about the subjective motivations of the parties.

## NOTES AND QUESTIONS

(1)    The judge in the *Girls Gone Wild* case (*Pitts v. Francis*) pointed out that the defendant (Francis) had not moved to dispense with mediation, but instead, "he exploited the mediation for abusive purposes." If Francis had sought to dispense with mediation, but the judge had denied his motion, would the judge's decision to sanction Francis for his egregious conduct and refusal to mediate in good faith be less justified? Do you think Judge Pitts would have reacted so strongly if Francis was merely "uncooperative" or just unwilling to reach an agreement? It is also worth noting that this was a federal case. The state judges in Florida have

consistently refused to find a "good faith" obligation beyond appearance. The leading state court case on this topic is *Avril v. Civilmar*, 605 So. 2d 988 (Fla. Dist. Ct. App. 1992), in which the court reversed sanctions which were imposed on a party for "failure to negotiate in good faith." The court held:

> the order is a departure from the essential requirements of law . . . Plaintiff does not contend that defendants refused to attend or participate in mediation. Rule 1.720(b) allows sanctions only for failing to appear at a duly noticed mediation conference . . . .Likewise, rule 1.730(c) allows sanctions only for a breach or failure to perform under a mediation agreement . . . .Neither circumstance is present here.

> At bottom, plaintiff's only basis for sanctions is merely that defendants were unwilling to make an offer of settlement satisfactory to him. The mediation statutes, however, do not require that parties actually settle cases. Section 44.1011(2), Florida Statutes (1991), explains that mediation:

>> is an informal and nonadversarial process with the objective of helping the disputing parties reach a mutually acceptable and voluntary agreement. In mediation, decisionmaking authority rests with the parties.

> It is clearly not the intent to force parties to settle cases they want to submit to trial before a jury. There is no requirement that a party even make an offer at mediation, let alone offer what the opposition wants to settle.

(2)   In Professor Thompson's article, he refers to Kimberlee Kovach's proposed statute, which places the responsibility on the court rather than the mediator, in court-annexed mediations, to "make the final determination of whether good faith was present in the mediation." Although placing responsibility on the court may initially overcome concerns over compromising confidentiality and mediator neutrality, how will a court make this determination absent input from the mediator?

(3)   Other commentators have contributed to this debate. Professors Carol L. Izumi and Homer C. La Rue survey the debate and argue that good faith requirements strike at the heart of the mediation process by undermining core mediation values of party self-determination, confidentiality, and third-party neutrality, in *Prohibiting "Good Faith" Reports Under the Uniform Mediation Act: Keeping the Adjudication Camel out of the Mediation Tent*, 2003 J. Disp. Resol. 67. Izumi and La Rue assert that the Uniform Mediation Act (UMA) strikes the correct balance by rejecting arguments in favor of mediator reports to judges and others about the sanctions and statements of parties during the mediation for the purpose of assessing and sanctioning "bad faith" behavior, and that for the rare and extreme case, the UMA provides a mechanism to address egregious party behavior such as lying and fraudulent inducements causing another party to settle. Would imposing a good-faith requirement deter and punish bad faith conduct in a few truly egregious cases at the expense of overall confidence in the system of mediation?

(4)   In *Using Dispute System Design Methods to Promote Good-Faith Participation in Court-Connected Mediation Programs*, 50 UCLA L. Rev. 69 (2002), Professor John Lande argues that enforcing a good-faith requirement would

subject all participants to uncertainty about the impartiality and confidentiality of the process and could heighten adversarial tensions and inappropriate pressures to settle cases. Lande proposes using less risky means to achieve some of the ends being pursued by proponents of imposing a generalized "good-faith" requirement (by proposing the use of system design principles to promote desired conduct). In *Oh Ye of Little Good Faith: Questions, Concerns and Commentary on Efforts to Regulate Participant Conduct in Mediations*, 2002 J. Disp. Resol. 367, Roger L. Carter, as mentioned in the Thompson article, responds to Professor Lande by proposing narrowly tailored rules for mediation participants to reduce bad faith conduct and preserve party autonomy. Carter suggests that mediation's high aspirations will only be met if parties are free to shape outcomes unburdened by the fear of retributive sanctions. Even if courts were to provide litigating parties and their attorneys with clear rules, would the concerns expressed by Professor Sherman in the Thompson article remain? No matter how clear the rules are, might they impose requirements that compromise mediation's core values?

(5)   Consider how the courts made the good faith determination in the following two cases.

## IN RE BOLDEN
### District of Columbia Court of Appeals
### 719 A.2d 1253 (1998)

FARRELL, ASSOCIATE JUDGE:

In the course of a tax appeal, the Superior Court judge imposed a civil penalty — a fine of $200 — on attorney A. Scott Bolden after Bolden, in the judge's words, "unilaterally [aborted]" a mediation session held under the Superior Court's Multi-Door Dispute Resolution ("Multi-Door") system. The judge's authority for the sanction was Super. Ct. Tax R. 13 (b), which states in relevant part:

> If counsel or an unrepresented party . . . fails to appear for *or participate in good faith* in any alternative dispute resolution session, the Court may dismiss the case with or without prejudice, or take such other action, including the award of attorney's fees and reasonable expenses, and the imposition of . . . *such other penalties and sanctions as it deems appropriate.* [Emphasis added.]

*See also* Super. Ct. Civ. R. 16 (l), 16-II.

Underlying the judge's imposition of the fine was her determination that Bolden "did not have the agreement of all the parties when counsel aborted said mediation." We observe, however, that no judge is present at Multi-Door mediation sessions, nor was the record of the meeting in question here transcribed or taped. The District of Columbia, a party to the tax appeal, *was* present at the mediation and has conceded in its brief and oral argument to us that the record as constituted does not support the finding of an unconsented, "unilateral" termination of the mediation by Bolden. The judge apparently relied on statements such as the following in written submissions Bolden filed:

"Petitioners' counsel decided not to go forward"; "Petitioners' counsel advised the respondent's [i.e., the District's] counsel, the mediator, and the [Tax] Division representative of his decision to seek a new mediation schedule."

We agree with Bolden that these are insufficient, without more, to support the finding of a unilateral termination.

Elsewhere Bolden explained to the judge:

"The respondents . . . did not object to rescheduling of the mediation. In fact, although respondents advised petitioners' counsel that they were ready to proceed [with the mediation], they also confirmed that they would not (and did not) take a position or object if petitioners' counsel made the appropriate representations to the Court regarding a *request* for rescheduling of the mediation." (Emphasis in original.)

The District does not dispute this account.

While Tax Rule 13(b) requires counsel to "participate in good faith in any alternative dispute resolution session," nothing in it suggests that there must be a formal, on-the-record consent to an adjournment pending a party's request for rescheduling by the court. That would impose undue formality on a process which, while mandatory when applicable, is meant to be flexible and to preserve the parties' ultimate control over their case. Moreover, Bolden's reason for wanting postponement is clearly relevant to whether he took part in good faith. Bolden represented, and the District has not disputed, that the reason he suggested rescheduling the mediation was the mediator's refusal upon objection by the District to allow his tax expert, who had become physically unavailable on short notice, to participate via telephone conference call. Correct though that ruling may have been, Bolden's consequent unwillingness to go forward until the expert was available is understandable — particularly since, as he also represented, the agreed purpose for this meeting had been to hear the expert's opinion. Although the judge opined that the expert's views and supporting information "could have been made available to counsel, prior to the mediation, for counsel's use during the mediation," the District rightly points out that this entails considerable surmise as to what sort of presentation would have been acceptable to the District and sufficient to make the mediation fruitful.

A trial judge's decision to impose a sanction under Tax Rule 13(b), like similar decisions under Super. Ct. Civ. R. 16(l) and 16-II, will be reviewed only for an abuse of discretion. Informed discretion, however, "requires that the trial court's determination be based upon and drawn from a firm factual foundation." We hold that this foundation is lacking for the judge's conclusion that Bolden acted in bad faith in causing adjournment of the mediation session. Accordingly, we vacate the sanction ordered by the trial judge.

# NICK v. MORGAN'S FOODS, INC.
United States District Court for the Eastern District of Missouri
99 F. Supp. 2d 1056 (2000)

Rodney W. Sippel, J.

Morgan's Foods, Inc. seeks reconsideration of this Court's order sanctioning it for its failure to participate in mediation in good faith.

In contravention of this Court's Order referring this matter to Alternative Dispute Resolution (ADR), Morgan's Foods failed to submit the required mediation memorandum and failed to send a corporate representative with authority to settle the case to the mediation. Not surprisingly, the mediator was unable to mediate a settlement. After being called upon to explain why it ignored the Court's Order regarding ADR, counsel for Morgan's Foods admitted that his client — on his advice — made a calculated decision to disregard some of the provisions of the ADR Referral Order. Based on Morgan's Foods' failure to comply with key provisions of the ADR Referral Order, the Court concluded that Morgan's Foods failed to participate in mediation in good faith and entered sanctions accordingly. Morgan's Foods now asks the Court to reconsider the imposition of sanctions. Because the Court remains convinced that Morgan's Foods and its counsel did not participate in good faith in the ADR process, its motion for reconsideration will be denied. Moreover, the Court will impose additional sanctions for the frivolous nature of this motion and Morgan's Foods' vexatious multiplication of these proceedings.

## Background

Gee Gee Nick filed this lawsuit against Morgan's Foods alleging sexual harassment and retaliation in violation of Title VII of the Civil Rights Act of 1964. A scheduling conference pursuant to Federal Rule of Civil Procedure 16 (Rule 16) was held on May 20, 1999. At that time, the parties were asked if they wished to participate in the ADR process pursuant to E.D.Mo. L.R. 6.01–6.05. The matter was set for referral to ADR on August 1, 1999. The parties were to complete the ADR process and report back to the Court the results of the mediation by September 30, 1999.

The August 2, 1999 Order of Referral required the ADR process to be conducted in compliance with E.D.Mo. L.R. 6.01–6.05. The Order of Referral also specifically required:

(1) **Memoranda:** Not later than seven (7) **days** prior to the initial ADR conference, each party will **provide the neutral with a memorandum** presenting a summary of disputed facts and a narrative discussion of its position relative to both liability and damages. These memoranda shall be treated as **Confidential Communications** and shall not be filed in the public record of the case nor provided to any other party or counsel.

(2) **Identification of Corporate and/or Claims Representatives:** As a part of the written memoranda described in paragraph (1), counsel for corporate parties or insurers shall state the name and general job titles of the

employee(s) or agent(s) of the corporation or insurance company who will attend ADR conferences and participate on behalf of the entity.

(3) **Authority of Neutral:** The neutral shall have authority to consult and conduct conferences and private caucuses with counsel, individual parties, corporate representatives and claims professionals, to suggest alternatives, analyze issues and positions, question perceptions, stimulate negotiations, and keep order.

(4) **Duty to Attend and Participate:** All parties, counsel of record, and corporate representatives or claims professionals **having authority to settle claims** shall attend all mediation conferences and **participate in good faith**. Early neutral evaluation conferences shall be attended by all counsel of record.

(5) **Compliance with Deadlines:** all deadlines must be complied with in a timely fashion and the appropriate forms filed with the Clerk of the District Court. If a deadline cannot be met, the designated lead counsel shall **file a motion requesting an extension of the deadline** prior to the expiration of that deadline. **Noncompliance of any deadline set herein by this Court may result in the imposition of sanctions to the appropriate party or parties.**

(emphasis added)

Prior to the mediation, counsel for Morgan's Foods indicated to Nick's counsel, but not the Court, that he did not feel that the mediation would be fruitful. Morgan's Foods' only request for relief directed to the Court was a request to hold the ADR conference on October 18, 1999. The Court allowed the parties to delay mediation until that date.

The parties appeared before the Court on another matter on October 15, 1999. At that time, the Court inquired into the parties' preparedness for the upcoming mediation. Counsel for Morgan's Foods assured the Court that his client was prepared to discuss settlement in good faith and that he would have a representative present with authority to settle.

The ADR conference was held on October 18, 1999. Present at the conference was Nick, Nick's court-appointed counsel, counsel for Morgan's Foods, the local regional manager of Morgan's Foods, and the neutral.

Nick provided the required memorandum to the neutral and attended the ADR conference with full authority to settle the case.

Morgan's Foods did not provide the memorandum to the neutral as was required by the Court's Order. Morgan's Foods also failed to have a representative attend the conference who had authority to settle. Morgan's Foods' corporate representative who attended the conference did not have any independent knowledge of the case, nor did she have authority to reconsider Morgan's Foods' position regarding settlement. The limit of Morgan's Foods' regional manager's authority was $500. Negotiation of any settlement amount above $500 had to be handled by Morgan's Foods' general counsel, who was not present at the ADR conference.

Not surprisingly, the ADR conference did not result in a settlement. Nick made an offer of settlement which was rejected without a counteroffer by Morgan's Foods. Nick made another offer to settle the case. Again, this offer was rejected without a counteroffer. The ADR conference was terminated shortly thereafter.

The neutral reported back to the Court after the close of the ADR conference. At that time, the neutral informed the Court of the level of Morgan's Foods' participation in the ADR process. On October 22, 1999, the Court issued an Order directing Morgan's Foods to show cause why it should not be sanctioned for its failure to participate in good faith in the Court-ordered ADR process.

Morgan's Foods responded to the Court's Show Cause Order on October 29, 1999. In that response, Morgan's Foods asserted that the August 2, 1999 referral Order was merely a "guideline" provided to parties suggesting a manner in which they might participate in the ADR process. Morgan's Foods admitted that it made a calculated strategic decision not to comply with the "guideline" because Morgan's Foods felt compliance would be a waste of time.

In the meantime, Nick filed a Motion for Sanctions. Nick requested that Morgan's Foods be sanctioned for failing to participate in the ADR process in good faith. Nick requested an award of the costs and fees of her participation in the failed mediation.

The Court held a hearing on its Show Cause Order and Nick's Motion for Sanctions on December 1, 1999. Counsel for Morgan's Foods appeared at the hearing and reasserted the positions taken in Morgan's Foods' response to the Court's Show Cause Order. Counsel confirmed that the Morgan's Foods' corporate representative had only $500 of authority to settle the case. Counsel further confirmed that any decision to change the company's settlement position had to be made by Morgan's Foods' general counsel who was not present at the ADR conference but was available by telephone. Morgan's Foods' counsel also took full responsibility for the decision not to file the memorandum required by the August 2, 1999 referral order. Morgan's Foods continued to advance its argument that filing the required mediation memorandum would have been a waste of time and money.

After hearing argument by both sides, the Court made its ruling on the record. The Court found that Morgan's Foods failed to participate in good faith in the Court-ordered ADR process and sanctioned Morgan's Foods in an amount to include the total cost of the ADR conference fees and Nick's costs in preparing for and attending the conference. The Court also ordered counsel to obtain a copy of the hearing transcript, provide the transcript to his client, and return a letter to the Court confirming that Morgan's Foods had read the transcript.

Morgan's Foods filed a Motion for Reconsideration and Vacation of the Court's

Order Granting Plaintiff's Motion for Sanctions on December 20, 1999. It is that motion for reconsideration which is before the Court.

. . .

The Court understands that ADR conferences and settlement negotiations can fail to achieve the settlement of a case for many reasons. The Federal Rules of Civil Procedure, this court's local rules and the specific court order in this case referring the case to ADR do not mandate settlement. Good faith participation in ADR does not require settlement. In fact, an ADR conference conducted in good faith can be helpful even if settlement is not reached. On the other hand, the rules and orders governing ADR are designed to prevent abuse of the opponent, which can and does occur when one side does not participate in good faith.

When a party agrees to participate in a mediation process in good faith, the Court is entitled to rely on that representation. Implicit in the concept of good faith participation is the assurance that the parties will participate in ADR in accordance with the Court's order. . . .

Morgan's Foods has made it clear that it considered the memorandum requirement a waste of time. Morgan's Foods is right that its failure to prepare the required memorandum wasted valuable time. Unfortunately for Morgan's Foods, it is right for all of the wrong reasons. Morgan's Foods' failure to prepare the memorandum was a waste of plaintiff's time, plaintiff's counsels' time, the neutral's time and the Court's time.

Morgan's Foods' contention that a mediation memorandum is a waste of time is simply wrong. The memorandum would have permitted the neutral to prepare for the ADR conference. At a minimum the memorandum might have alerted the neutral that Morgan's Foods' corporate representative was not an appropriate participant in the ADR conference. It is even possible that Morgan's Foods' memorandum would have compelled the neutral to delay or even cancel the conference.

Morgan's Foods' calculated refusal to prepare a mediation memorandum was a direct violation of the Court's local rules and the Court's ADR Referral Order.

### Good Faith Participation in ADR Requires the Participation of A Corporate Representative With Authority to Settle

Morgan's Foods also violated the Referral Order by failing to have an appropriate corporate representative attend the mediation.

The August 2, 1999 Referral Order specifically required attendance of a "corporate representative . . . having authority to settle claims." Presence of the corporate representative is the cornerstone of good faith participation.

. . .

During the ADR conference, all parties have the opportunity to argue their respective positions. In the Court's experience, this is often the first time that parties, especially corporate representatives, hear about the difficulties they will face at trial. As a practical matter this may also be the first time that firmly held positions may be open to change. For ADR to work, the corporate representative must have the authority and discretion to change her opinion in light of the statements and arguments made by the neutral and opposing party.

Meaningful negotiations cannot occur if the only person with authority to actually change their mind and negotiate is not present. Availability by telephone is insufficient because the absent decision-maker does not have the full benefit of the

ADR proceedings, the opposing party's arguments, and the neutral's input. The absent decision-maker needs to be present and hear first-hand the good facts and the bad facts about their case. Instead, the absent decision-maker learns only what his or her attorney chooses to relate over the phone. . . . . . . Instead of a negotiation session, the mediation becomes a stealth discovery session, to the unfair benefit of the party whose decision-maker is not in attendance. When that happens, the Court's referral to mediation has been callously misused. "Meanwhile, the opposing side has spent money and time preparing for a good-faith, candid discussion toward settlement. If the other party does not reciprocate, most if not all of that money and time has been wasted." *Id.*

In sum, when a corporate representative with the authority to reconsider that party's settlement position is not present, the whole purpose of the mediation is lost, and the result is an even greater expenditure of the parties' resources, both time and money, for nothing.

## Conclusion

Morgan's Foods did not participate in good faith in the ADR process. The absence of good faith is evidenced not by the parties' failure to reach settlement, but by Morgan's Foods' failure to comply with the Court's August 2, 1999 Referral Order. Morgan's Foods' failure to participate in the ADR process in good faith would not be vindicated by a defendant's verdict at trial. Whether the parties participated in good faith in the ADR process is measured by their actual conduct at the mediation, not by the hypothetical result of a subsequent trial.

. . .

If Morgan's Foods did not feel that ADR could be fruitful and had no intention of participating in good faith, it had a duty to report its position to the Court and to request appropriate relief. Morgan's Foods did not do so and sanctions are appropriate to remedy the resulting waste of time and money.

As a final thought, I feel compelled to address Morgan's Foods' suggestion that the sanction order was the result of "understandable frustration that cases like the one Plaintiff foists upon this Court clog the Court's docket." Morgan's Foods suggests that my actions were motivated by frustration stemming from frivolous allegations in Nick's Complaint.

Morgan's Foods is well aware that each United States District Judge takes an oath to "administer justice without respect to persons, and do equal right to the poor and to the rich . . . and [to] faithfully and impartially discharge and perform all duties . . . under the Constitution and laws of the United States." 28 U.S.C. § 453. That knowledge alone should have prevented Morgan's Foods from suggesting that the sanction order was merely the result of some misplaced temper tantrum. It should go without saying that this Court does not believe that allegations of sexual harassment on the job are frivolous.

It is unfortunate that when confronted with its willful violation of the Court's

Order, Morgan's Foods refused to acknowledge the failings of its own behavior and instead attacked the Court. Admittedly the Court felt frustration at the way this case was handled, but that frustration stemmed completely from Morgan's Foods' flagrant and willful disregard of the Court's August 2, 1999 Order referring the matter to ADR.

Many of the arguments advanced by Morgan's Foods' motion are frivolous, accomplishing nothing but increasing the cost of litigation. The Court therefore will impose additional sanctions to reflect the frivolous nature of this motion.

Accordingly,

**IT IS HEREBY ORDERED** that Defendant Morgan's Foods' Motion for Reconsideration [Doc. # 71] is DENIED.

**IT IS FURTHER ORDERED** that Defendant Morgan's Foods shall pay $1,390.63 to counsel for plaintiff as sanctions in this matter. Defendant's counsel shall pay $1,390.62 to counsel for plaintiff as sanctions in this matter. That amount includes $1,045.00 in attorney's fees for preparing and attending the mediation in this case, the $506.25 fee paid to the neutral for the cost of the ADR conference, and $1,230.00 in attorney's fees for preparing and arguing the motion for sanctions regarding Morgan's Foods' participation in the mediation.

**IT IS FURTHER ORDERED** that Defendant Morgan's Foods shall pay $30.00 to Plaintiff Gee Gee Nick for the costs she incurred in attending the mediation of this case. Defendant's counsel shall also pay $30.00 to Plaintiff Gee Gee Nick for the costs she incurred in attending the mediation of this case.

**IT IS FURTHER ORDERED** that Defendant Morgan's Foods shall pay $1,500.00 to the Clerk of the United States District Court, Eastern District of Missouri as sanctions in this matter. That amount reflects the savings realized by Morgan's Foods by virtue of its failure to prepare the required mediation memorandum and its decision not to send Morgan's Foods' general counsel to attend the ADR conference. Defendant Morgan's Foods and its counsel shall each pay $1,250.00 to the Clerk of the United States District Court, Eastern District of Missouri as a sanction for vexatiously increasing the costs of this litigation by filing a frivolous Motion for Reconsideration which further demonstrated the lack of good faith in Morgan's Foods conduct in this case.

## NOTES AND QUESTIONS

(1)   The decision in *Nick v. Morgan's Foods, Inc.*, 270 F.3d 590 (8th Cir. 2001), was upheld by the United States Court of Appeals for the Eighth Circuit . Note that both counsel and the party were subject to monetary sanctions. Why was the *Nick* court more willing to find a violation of the good faith requirement than the *Bolden* court?

(2)   In *Pitman v. Brinker International*, 216 F.R.D. 481 (D. Ariz. 2003), another federal district court arguably went further than the *Nick* court in upholding the imposition of sanctions for failure to "settle" in good faith. The court upheld the imposition of sanctions by a federal magistrate on defendant corporation and its attorney not only for failure to provide a corporate representative with genuine settlement authority at the conference and failure to notify the court ahead of time that the conference would be futile, but also for failure to make meaningful

settlement offers before the conference. However, this was technically a judicial settlement conference conducted by a federal magistrate, rather than a mediation. Should different standards apply? Courts have also sanctioned parties for unintentional disobedience. *See Lucas Automotive Engineering, Inc. v. Bridgestone/Firestone, Inc.*, 275 F.3d 762 (9th Cir. 2001) (upholding sanctions against a representative of the defendant who failed to appear as ordered at a mediation session due to an incapacitating headache even though the failure to appear was not intentional; sanctions were upheld on appeal because of the representative's failure to notify the court that he would not be in attendance).

(3) After many years of relying on an "appearance requirement" rather than a "good faith" requirement for mediation, in 2012 the Florida Supreme Court amended Rule 1.720, Florida Rules of Civil Procedure. The rule still requires that the following "persons are physically present: (1) the party or a party representative having full authority to settle without further consultation; and (2) the party's counsel of record; and (3) a representative of the insurance carrier for any insured party." The amended rule now includes a definition of "party representative having full authority to settle" and establishes a "certification of authority requirement" whereby 10 days prior to appearing at a mediation, each party "shall file with the court and serve all parties a written notice identifying the person or persons who will be attending the mediation conference as a party representative or as an insurance carrier representative, and confirming that those persons have the [required] authority." The rule retains the courts ability to sanction a party for failure to appear without good cause and adds "[t]he failure to file a confirmation of authority . . . or failure of the persons actually identified in the confirmation to appear at the mediation conference, shall create a rebuttable presumption of a failure to appear."

Do you think that this rule balances interests of those who seek participation and those who want to preserve parties rights not to settle in mediation?

(3) The ABA Section of Dispute Resolution issued a policy statement on mediation in good faith; excerpts appear below:

## ABA SECTION OF DISPUTE RESOLUTION ON GOOD FAITH REQUIREMENTS FOR MEDIATORS AND MEDIATION ADVOCATES IN COURT-MANDATED MEDIATION PROGRAMS
### Approved by Section Council, August 7, 2004

The ABA Section of Dispute Resolution ("Section") has noted the wide range of views expressed by scholars, mediators, judges, and regulators concerning the question of whether courts should have the authority to sanction participants in mediation for bad-faith conduct in court-mandated mediation programs. The Section has also noted court rules and statutes that require mediators in court-mandated programs to make reports to court administrators or specific judges concerning alleged bad-faith conduct of participants in mediation. The Section believes that the public interest, court systems, and the practice of mediation would benefit from a re-examination and revision of some of these statutes and rules to preserve the core values of the mediation process, namely, party self-determination, mediator impartiality, and mediation confidentiality. These values are integral to the public's perception of the legitimacy of mediation as a consensual, flexible, creative, party-driven process to resolve disputes.

. . . .

The Section has concluded that, in order for the core values of the mediation process to be honored and preserved, the appropriate approach to be taken by court-mandated mediation programs should address three policy areas: (1) what conduct should be sanctionable; (2) what conduct or other information may mediators be required to report to court administrators or judges; and (3) what actions court-mandated mediation programs should take to promote productive behavior in mediation. The Section emphasizes that all of these elements are needed to create an effective policy.

The rules must comply with statutes and rules protecting the confidentiality of mediation communications, which generally limit reports and disclosures about alleged bad-faith conduct. Rules authorizing sanctions may be necessary but not sufficient to promote productive behavior in mediation and thus additional measures may be needed.

. . . .

## A. Sanctions.

*Sanctions should be imposed only for violations of rules specifying objectively-determinable conduct.*

. . . .

Such rule-proscribed conduct would include but is not limited to: failure of a party, attorney, or insurance representative to attend a court-mandated mediation for a limited and specified period or to provide written memoranda prior to the mediations. These rules should not be labeled as good faith requirements, however, because of the widespread confusion about the meaning of that term. Rules and statutes that permit courts to sanction a wide range of subjective behavior create a grave risk of undermining core values of mediation and creating unintended problems. Such subjective behaviors include but are not limited to: a failure to engage sufficiently in substantive bargaining; failure to have a representative present at the court-mandated mediation with sufficient settlement authority; or failure to make a reasonable offer.

. . . .

## B. Mediator Reports to the Court or Court Administrators.

*The content of mediators' reports to the court or court administrators should be narrowly restricted.*

. . . .

Requiring mediators to report negotiating behaviors or alleged bad-faith conduct to the court imperils the confidentiality of the mediation process and the public's trust in it.

. . . .

Under these statutes and rules, a negative report to a court from a mediator can cause a party to face the wrath of the court in the form of a tarnished reputation, adverse rulings, or the imposition of actual sanctions. In a sanctions hearing on allegations of a party's bad-faith conduct in mediation, the mediator is typically subpoenaed to testify, thereby further breaching the confidentiality of the mediation process. The lack of confidentiality protection creates uncertainty, engenders distrust of the mediation process, and impairs the public's full use of the process.

The Uniform Mediation Act ("UMA") precludes disclosure of mediation communications regarding alleged bad faith . . . . The official Reporter's Notes to Section 7 of the UMA state: "The provisions [of the UMA] would not permit a mediator to communicate, for example, on whether a particular party engaged in 'good faith' negotiation, or to state whether a party had been 'the problem' in reaching a settlement."

The Section believes that protecting mediation communications as provided in the UMA will foster the public's trust in the legitimacy and integrity of mediation as a useful process to resolve disputes. Especially in states adopting the UMA, statutes and rules should not require or permit disclosures about bad-faith conduct unless there is a valid waiver of the privilege. Given the ABA's approval of the UMA, the Section recommends that no states should adopt statutes or rules inconsistent with the UMA.

## E.  ENFORCEABILITY OF MEDIATED AGREEMENTS

Which legal principles should a court apply when being asked to enforce a mediated agreement? In many jurisdictions, the answer to this question is unclear at present. In other jurisdictions, the courts or the state legislatures have decided that mediated agreements should be enforced in the same manner as a contract. Even in these jurisdictions, however, the enforceability issue may be complicated by the fact that there may be other relevant laws that contradict the mediation enforcement provisions. Enforceability may also implicate confidentiality concerns. If the parties are fighting over the interpretation of certain terms in the mediation agreement, relevant evidence over what the parties intended may be excluded because of confidentiality requirements. Indeed, the parties may even be disagreeing over whether an agreement was struck. Recall the *Macaluso* case excerpted in Chapter 5, where the court refused to hear testimony from the mediator even though the court stated that it would be the best evidence of the existence of a mediated agreement.

The cases in this section are illustrative of the range of policy concerns over whether and how to enforce a mediated agreement. In *Fidelity and Guaranty Insurance Co. v. Star Equipment Corp.*, the United States Court of Appeals for the First Circuit applies Massachusetts contract law in a diversity case to enforce a mediated settlement agreement based on mutual assent. In *Guthrie v. Guthrie*, the court elects to apply contract principles to enforce a mediated settlement agreement, and the *Ames* case illustrates problems of statutory interpretation that may confront a court faced with an enforceability issue. While the *Silkey* case also has the court wrestling with an issue of statutory interpretation, there it revolves around the enforceability of an oral mediation agreement. The *Haghighi* litigation suggests that a legislature may create more problems than it solves when it seeks to address the enforcement issue head-on. Finally, traditional defenses to contract enforcement such as duress and impossibility are raised in *DelBosque v. AT&T Adv.* and *Ferguson v. Ferguson.*

# FIDELITY AND GUARANTY INSURANCE CO. v. STAR EQUIPMENT CORP.
United States Court of Appeals for the First Circuit
541 F.3d 1 (2008)

LIPEZ, CIRCUIT JUDGE.

This diversity case arises out of a dispute over a construction contract and an attempt to mediate that dispute through the district court's alternative dispute resolution program. Appellee Fidelity and Guaranty Insurance Company ("Fidelity") executed, as surety, a performance bond on behalf of Appellant Star Equipment Company ("Star") for work on a water main installation project that Star was to perform for Appellee Town of Seekonk, Massachusetts ("Seekonk"). Appellants Charlene and John Foran ("the Forans"), the principals of Star, executed a General Agreement of Indemnity, promising to reimburse Fidelity for any losses, costs, and expenses, including attorney's fees, incurred by Fidelity as a result of the performance bond issued to Star.

After Seekonk declared Star to be in default on its construction contract with the town, Fidelity filed a declaratory judgment action to determine the rights and obligations of the parties under the performance bond. The parties entered mediation and emerged with a Settlement Memorandum of Understanding, signed by all the parties and their attorneys. When Star and the Forans refused to go forward with the settlement, Fidelity and Seekonk filed a motion to enforce the memorandum as a settlement of all claims in the case except the claim of Fidelity against Star and the Forans for indemnification, which had been explicitly reserved in the settlement agreement. The district court granted that motion, and subsequently granted Fidelity's motion for summary judgment on the indemnification claim. After a damage hearing, the court found that Star and the Forans were liable to Fidelity for $111,313.43, plus costs and interest. Star and the Forans appeal the enforcement of the settlement agreement, the summary judgment ruling, and the amount of the damage award. We affirm.

. . .

The mediation took place on April 4, 2006, with all of the parties and their counsel present. At the close of the session, the mediator drafted a hand-written document entitled, "Settlement Memorandum of Understanding." It stated in full:

1. Fidelity and Guaranty Ins. Co. ("Fidelity") will pay to the Seekonk Water District/Town of Seekonk, Mass., the sum of Fifty Thousand dollars ($50,000.00);

2. The parties hereto agree to Release all claims asserted in the action entitled *Fidelity & Guaranty Ins. Co. v. Star Equipment Corp., et al.*, # 1:04-cv-10250-EFH (D.Mass.) except that Star, Charlene Foran & John Foran and Fidelity do not release claims & defenses they have against each other.

3. This settlement is conditioned upon:

(a)    Approval by appropriate municipal authorities; and

(b)    Execution of customary releases and settlement agreement.

The document was signed by each of the parties, their counsel, and the mediator. The mediator reported to the court that "significant progress was made towards full settlement of this matter."

Subsequently, Seekonk obtained the requisite municipal approvals and the releases were drafted and their language approved by Star's counsel. However, the Forans asserted that no binding settlement agreement had been reached and refused to execute the releases, claiming that their agreement to settle with Seekonk was contingent on a satisfactory resolution of the indemnification dispute with Fidelity. Fidelity and Seekonk then filed a Joint Motion to Enforce Settlement Agreement, which the Indemnitors opposed. The court initially denied this motion without explanation or hearing. Fidelity and Seekonk then filed a Joint Motion for Reconsideration. On November 28, 2006, the court held a hearing on the motion for reconsideration. It then entered an order, on November 29, granting the motion and enforcing the "Settlement Memorandum of Understanding" as a settlement agreement. Fidelity paid Seekonk $50,000 pursuant to the terms of the agreement.

On March 5, 2007, Fidelity filed a motion for summary judgment on its indemnification claim against Star and the Forans. The Indemnitors filed an opposition to the motion, asserting bad faith on the part of Fidelity as a defense to the indemnification agreement. On March 26, 2007, the court entered an order granting Fidelity's motion for summary judgment, concluding that "the defendants ha[d] failed to present any material facts which would give rise to a factual dispute as to a 'want of good faith' on the part of [Fidelity]."

The court then held a hearing on damages on April 2, 2007. Fidelity and the Indemnitors stipulated that the amount of loss payments Fidelity had made pursuant to the performance and payment bonds, including Fidelity's attorney's fees, was $111,313.43. The Indemnitors argued, however, that Fidelity's damage award should be reduced by $41,000 to account for the value of the Indemnitors' cross-claim against Seekonk. The district court rejected this argument, explaining that the cross-claim could not be used to offset Fidelity's damages because the Indemnitors had agreed to drop that claim against Seekonk in the Settlement Memorandum of Understanding. Accordingly, on April 10, 2007, the court issued a judgment in favor of Fidelity against the Indemnitors for $111,313.43, plus costs and interest.

The Indemnitors filed this timely appeal, contesting the enforcement of the settlement agreement, the grant of summary judgment, and the refusal to reduce the damage award by the amount of the cross-claim.

In this diversity case, we apply Massachusetts contract law. . . . The district court's determination that an enforceable settlement agreement existed is a mixed question of fact and law, which we review on "a sliding scale standard of review under the label of clear error review." . . . In other words, "[t]he more the district court's conclusions are characterized as factual conclusions, the more our review of those facts is for clear error; the more the district court's conclusions are conclusions of law, the more independent review we give."

Settlement agreements enjoy great favor with the courts "as a preferred alternative to costly, time-consuming litigation." . . . Thus, a party to a settlement agreement may seek to enforce the agreement's terms when the other party refuses to comply . . . . Where, as here, the settlement collapses before the original suit is dismissed, the party seeking to enforce the agreement may file a motion with the trial court. The trial court may summarily enforce the agreement, provided that there is no genuinely disputed question of material fact regarding the existence or terms of that agreement. When a genuinely disputed question of material fact does exist, the court should hold a hearing and resolve the contested factual issues.

On appeal, the Indemnitors argue that they were entitled to an evidentiary hearing as to whether the Settlement Memorandum of Understanding should be enforced as a settlement agreement. They claim that the Settlement Memorandum of Understanding was not binding because it had not settled all of the issues in the case. They explain that they signed the memorandum because of "explicit representations of Fidelity's representative at the mediation that she would 'work with the Forans' to resolve the Fidelity-Foran dispute in a manner that would be palatable to them; and, that their cooperation in the mediation would go a long way toward a favorable outcome in that resolution." However, these assertions are not sufficient to generate a genuine disputed question of material fact, entitling the Indemnitors to an evidentiary hearing. The Forans' subjective belief that the agreement was not "final" does not bar enforcement in the face of their assent — in writing — to the memorandum's unambiguous terms. . . .

The Indemnitors attempt to marshal the terms of the agreement in their favor on appeal, pointing to paragraph 3 of the memorandum, which states that the settlement was conditioned upon "[e]xecution of customary releases and settlement agreement." They argue that this paragraph reflected an understanding that no enforceable agreement would exist until an agreement settling all issues in the case, including the indemnification dispute, had been reached. However, the plain language of the memorandum does not support this interpretation . . . . Paragraph 2 of the memorandum explicitly states that the parties had agreed to settle all the claims in the case except those involving the indemnification agreement. Thus, the agreement reflects that the *other* issues in the case had been definitively settled, subject only to conditions in paragraph 3 — municipal approval and the execution of "customary releases and settlement agreement." A settlement of the indemnification dispute cannot be what is contemplated by those boilerplate conditions, given the language in paragraph 2 expressly excluding the indemnification claim from the scope of the agreement.

Moreover, the fact that the hand-written agreement contemplated execution of a more formal agreement does not preclude enforcement of the hand-written agreement. *Bandera*, 344 F.3d at 52. As we explained in *Bandera*, "[a]n agreement to make a further more detailed agreement could in some instances not be intended as a binding contract, or might be too indefinite; but neither is necessarily or even ordinarily so." *Id.* at 52 n. 2. Here, the language of the memorandum reflects a present intent by all the parties to settle all of the claims except the indemnification dispute. The terms of this settlement are clear and unambiguous. They are not contingent on the successful outcome of further negotiations to resolve the indemnification issue. Indeed, the Indemnitors do not argue that terms of the agreement were ambiguous or indefinite, nor do they claim that they were coerced into signing the agreement or that their counsel settled their claim without authority to do so. Accordingly, we find no error in the district court's order enforcing the Settlement Memorandum of Agreement as a settlement agreement that disposed of all the claims in the case except the indemnification dispute.

. . .

*Affirmed.*

# GUTHRIE v. GUTHRIE
Supreme Court of Georgia
594 S.E.2d 356 (2004)

SEARS, PRESIDING JUSTICE.

. . . Sandra Guthrie, and the decedent, Dallis Guthrie, were married in February, 1998. Ms. Guthrie initiated divorce proceedings in April of 2000, and the parties participated in mediation ordered by the trial court. As a result of the mediation, the Guthries executed a settlement agreement, signed by the parties and their attorneys. Before the divorce court's consideration of the agreement, Dallis obtained new counsel, renounced the agreement, and moved to set it aside. Dallis died before the divorce court had an opportunity to rule on the agreement or enter a decree of divorce. Thereafter, on motion by Dallis' attorney, the unadjudicated divorce proceeding was dismissed . . . .

The executors of Dallis' estate admitted his will to probate in Fulton County. Ms. Guthrie, in turn, brought the instant action in Fulton Superior Court to enforce the mediated settlement agreement. The executors answered, asserting that the agreement was unenforceable due to lack of consideration and thereafter filed a motion for summary judgment. In granting summary judgment to the executors, the trial court pronounced that it was acting in the nature of a divorce court in reviewing the settlement agreement and . . . the trial court exercised its discretion to reject the agreement and to grant summary judgment to the executors. The Court of Appeals disagreed and reversed the trial court, finding that the court was only authorized to treat the matter before it as a contractual dispute, not a divorce case, and that it was error to summarily reject an otherwise valid contract because it arose out of a divorce proceeding . . . .

. . . For the reasons that follow, we affirm.

1. The trial court erroneously determined that even though the divorce proceeding had abated, the settlement agreement was subject to the same review that

applies in a pending divorce action. When a trial court is presented with a settlement agreement in a divorce proceeding, the divorce court may exercise its discretion in deciding whether to make any or part of the settlement agreement between the parties a part of the final decree . . . . This discretionary power can only be exercised at the time the divorce decree is entered or during the term of court at which the decree incorporating the agreement was rendered . . . .

Whereas in pending divorce cases the settlement agreement ultimately becomes the "judgment of the divorce court itself," and is thus subject to a trial court's "discretion to approve or reject the agreement, in whole or in part," the interpretation of a settlement agreement that a party seeks to enforce outside of the parameters of the divorce proceeding is strictly governed by the rules of contract construction . . . . In addition, we have held that the enforceability of a settlement agreement disposing of property upon marital separation does not turn on whether both parties to the contract survive or on whether a final judgment of divorce is entered . . . .

For the foregoing reasons, we agree with the Court of Appeals that the trial court should have evaluated the parties' agreement under the ordinary rules of contract construction and thus erred by evaluating the agreement under the rules that control when a trial court is determining whether to incorporate a settlement agreement into its final judgment of divorce.

2. The executors contend that the agreement was expressly contingent upon a decree of divorce being entered and approval by the court of the agreement. We disagree with this contention. To begin, the question whether the agreement was dependent upon the occurrence of these contingencies is controlled by the intent of the parties. In this regard, "[w]e look first to the language employed in the agreement to determine the intent of the parties. If the language is plain and unambiguous and the intent may be clearly gathered therefrom, we need look no further." . . . .

Examining the language of the agreement in this case, we conclude that the parties clearly did not intend for the agreement to be contingent upon the approval of the agreement by the trial court and the granting of a final judgment of divorce. The agreement was executed on May 31, 2000, and its provisions were to begin taking effect either immediately or shortly after that date. For example, the agreement provided that on July 1, 2000, one month from the date the agreement was executed, the husband had to pay the wife $100,000; that on June 1, 2000, one day after the agreement was executed, the husband had to begin paying the wife $2,000 per month for 24 months; that these payments "[were] not subject to any contingency"; that on or before July 1, 2000, the husband had to pay the wife $5,000 for her attorney fees; and that within 30 days from the date the agreement was executed, the parties had to execute all the numerous documents that were necessary to pay loans, transfer property titles, and "effectuate this agreement." In sum, these provisions demonstrate that the parties intended for the agreement to be effective immediately and not contingent upon the granting of a divorce and the approval of the agreement by the trial court.

For the foregoing reasons, we hold that the Court of Appeals was correct in determining that the agreement could be enforced even where one of the parties died before the entry of a judgment of divorce.

# IN RE MARRIAGE OF AMES
## Texas Court of Civil Appeals
## 860 S.W.2d 590 (1993)

H. BRYAN POFF, JR., J.

Appellant Raymond K. Ames appeals from the trial court's final decree granting him and his wife Nancy Jo Ames a divorce. In four points of error, Raymond contends the trial court erred in (1) not recognizing his repudiation of the mediated settlement agreement; (2) entering the decree of divorce without any evidence to support it; (3) modifying the settlement agreement; and (4) overruling his motion for new trial. We note that Raymond initially argues the settlement agreement is invalid; however, anticipating we might not agree, he alternatively argues that the agreement is inviolable and the court erred in modifying the agreement. His second argument compels us to reverse the judgment and remand the cause to the trial court.

Raymond filed suit to divorce his wife Nancy, appellee. Nancy answered Raymond's petition and filed a counter-petition for divorce. The parties were ordered to mediation which resulted in a community property settlement agreement reached on June 5, 1991. Both parties and their respective attorneys signed the settlement agreement. The record reflects that on June 20, 1991, Raymond attempted to withdraw his consent to the settlement agreement by means of a letter from his attorney to Nancy's attorney. On August 20, 1991, Nancy filed a "Motion For Entry of Decree of Divorce" based on the June 5 settlement agreement. On November 27, 1991, the trial court entered a decree of divorce.

In the first of four points of error, Raymond contends that the trial court erred in entering its decree of divorce on the basis of the settlement agreement because he had repudiated the agreement. We disagree. In its order of mediation, the trial court stated that "this case is appropriate for mediation pursuant to Tex. Civ. Prac. & Rem. Code §§ 154.001 *et seq.*" Chapter 154 of the Texas Civil Practice and Remedies Code is entitled "Alternative Dispute Resolution Procedures." Section 154.071(a) states:

> If the parties reach a settlement and execute a written agreement disposing of the dispute, the agreement is enforceable in the same manner as any other written contract.

Tex. Civ. Prac. & Rem. Code Ann. § 154.071(a) (Vernon Supp. 1993). We interpret this statute to mean, inter alia, that a party who has reached a settlement agreement disposing of a dispute through alternative dispute resolution procedures may not unilaterally repudiate the agreement.

While parties may be compelled by a court to participate in mediation, Tex. Civ. Prac. & Rem. Code §§ 154.021, 154.023 (Vernon Supp. 1993), "[a] mediator may not impose his own judgment on the issues for that of the parties." Tex. Civ. Prac. & Rem. Code § 154.023(b) (Vernon Supp. 1993). Put another way, a court can compel disputants to sit down with each other but it cannot force them to peaceably resolve their differences. *Decker v. Lindsay*, 824 S.W.2d 247, 250 (Tex.App. — Houston [1st Dist.] 1992, no writ). The job of a mediator is simply to facilitate communication between parties and thereby encourage reconciliation, settlement and understanding among them. Tex. Civ. Prac. & Rem. Code Ann. § 154.023(a). Hopefully, mediation will assist the parties in reaching a voluntary agreement that will serve to resolve their dispute and avoid the need for traditional litigation.

If voluntary agreements reached through mediation were nonbinding, many positive efforts to amicably settle differences would be for naught. If parties were free to repudiate their agreements, disputes would not be finally resolved and traditional litigation would recur. In order to effect the purposes of mediation and other alternative dispute resolution mechanisms, settlement agreements must be treated with the same dignity and respect accorded other contracts reached after arm's-length negotiations. Again, no party to a dispute can be forced to settle the conflict outside of court; but if a voluntary agreement that disposes of the dispute is reached, the parties should be required to honor the agreement.

Raymond argues strenuously, however, that section 154.071(a) does not apply in this case. Raymond maintains that section 154.071(a) conflicts with Tex. Fam. Code Ann. § 3.631(a) (Vernon 1993), and that the Family Code provision is controlling. Section 3.631(a) states:

> To promote amicable settlement of disputes on the divorce or annulment of a marriage, the parties may enter into a written agreement concerning the division of all property and liabilities of the parties and maintenance of either of them. The agreement may be revised or repudiated prior to rendition of the divorce or annulment unless it is binding under some other rule of law.

Raymond contends that section 3.613(a) controls over section 154.071(a) of the Texas Civil Practice and Remedies Code because section 3.613(a) deals with an agreement incident to divorce while section 154.071(a) concerns agreements in general. Raymond cites the well-known rule that a specific statute should control over a general statute and thus concludes that section 3.613 (a) is controlling.

We are not convinced, however, that the two statutes are in conflict. Even though section 3.613(a) is the more specific statute in this case, the Family Code provision expressly states that an agreement may be repudiated prior to rendition of the divorce "unless it is binding under some other rule of law." Pursuant to section 154.071(a) of the Practice and Remedies Code, the settlement agreement is binding. Raymond could not unilaterally repudiate the agreement. The trial court was empowered to consider the settlement agreement. Point of error one is overruled.

In his third point of error, Raymond, in the alternative, argues that if the agreement was not repudiated, the trial court erred in dividing the community property because the court's division differed significantly from the settlement agreement. Nancy contends that this argument is not properly before us because Raymond did not prepare and submit a proposed judgment to the court for signature as he was entitled to do under Tex. R. Civ. P. 305. While it is true that Raymond did not submit a proposed judgment, this does not preclude him from challenging the judgment entered by the court.

We agree with Raymond that there are several provisions of the divorce decree that are not found in the settlement agreement. First, while the settlement agreement is silent as to income tax liabilities, the divorce decree requires Raymond to pay all income tax liabilities of the parties through December 31, 1990. Second, the settlement agreement recites that Raymond will execute a $320,000 promissory note to Nancy; the divorce decree orders Raymond to execute the note and also orders him to pay a $320,000 money judgment. Third, the settlement agreement states that the stock of Raymond's company (Ridgmont Construction) is to be pledged as collateral for the promissory note if it will not impair Ridgmont's bonding capacity; the divorce decree contains no such conditional language.

Nancy contends that the divorce decree is "sufficiently representative of the agreement reached by the parties" to be upheld on appeal. We disagree. In *Vineyard v. Wilson*, 597 S.W.2d 21, 23 (Tex.Civ.App. — Dallas 1980, no writ), the court invalidated a judgment that did not embody the exact terms of the agreement on which it was based. "In order for a consent judgment to be valid, the parties must have definitely agreed to all the terms of the agreement. Nothing should be left for the court to provide." *Id.* In a judgment by consent, "the court has no power to supply terms, provisions, or essential details not previously agreed to by the parties." *Matthews v. Looney*, 132 Tex. 313, 317, 123 S.W.2d 871, 872 (1939). In fact, the court must accept the express terms of the agreement as binding "unless it finds that the agreement is not just and right." Tex. Fam. Code Ann. § 3.631(b) (Vernon 1993). The trial court made no such finding in this case. Therefore, the court was bound to accept the agreement. Because the trial court added terms to its decree of divorce that were not in the settlement agreement, the divorce decree cannot be allowed to stand. Point of error three is sustained.

In his second point of error, Raymond contends that the trial court erred in entering the decree of divorce because there is no evidence to support the decree. Clearly, the settlement agreement provides no evidence of the above-mentioned additional provisions of the decree. We also note that, contrary to the recitations in the decree of divorce, the parties never appeared before the trial judge at a hearing. The only evidence before the trial court was the settlement agreement. The record contains no evidence to support the court's modification of the agreement. The judgment and decree are therefore not supported by the evidence. Point of error two is sustained.

In his fourth point of error, Raymond contends that the trial court erred in refusing to grant his motion for new trial. We sustain this point of error. Inasmuch as one of the bases for a new trial was that "there are many provisions in the Decree of Divorce signed by the Court on November 27, 1991, contrary to or beyond the scope of, the agreement signed by the parties at the conclusion of the Mediation," a new trial should have been granted.

The judgment of the trial court is reversed and the cause is remanded to that court for proceedings not inconsistent with this opinion.

# NOTES AND QUESTIONS

(1)  Is the Georgia Supreme Court's decision to apply contract principles in resolving the enforceability issue in *Guthrie v. Guthrie* convincing in light of the fact that the decedent had sought to repudiate the agreement prior to his death? For the application of contract principles to an oral settlement agreement in an environmental case read the decision of the Supreme Court of Iowa in *Sierra Club v. Wayne Weber LLC*, 689 N.W.2d 696 (Iowa 2004).

(2)  Note that the relevant Texas ADR statute in *Ames* makes written settlement agreements "enforceable in the same manner as any other written contract," but a provision of the relevant family law statute provides that a settlement agreement "may be revised or repudiated prior to rendition of the divorce or annulment unless it is binding under some other rule of law." Do you agree with the court's rationale in choosing the ADR provision over the family law provision? Texas appellate courts are split on this issue. *See Alvarez v. Reiser*, 958 S.W.2d 232 (Tex. App. 1997) (holding in accord with *Ames*), and *Cary v. Cary*, 894 S.W.2d 111 (Tex. App. 1995) (holding disagrees with *Ames*).

(3)  The *Ames* divorce case involved a mediated property settlement. Should the law permit mediated agreements to be more open to repudiation if they involve the custody or support of minor children? See *Wayno v. Wayno*, 756 So. 2d 1024 (Fla. Dist. Ct. App. 2000), where a Florida appellate court upheld a trial court's order setting forth different child support and custody arrangements than had been agreed to by the parties in a mediated court-approved, settlement agreement.

(4)  Note that the *Guthrie* and *Ames* cases deal with family law. Are family cases more likely to raise enforceability issues? Why or why not? Consider the following case.

## SILKEY v. INVESTORS DIVERSIFIED SERVICES, INC.
### Indiana Court of Appeals
### 690 N.E.2d 329 (1997)

RILEY, JUDGE.

## STATEMENT OF THE CASE

Appellants, Herschel J. Silkey and Wanda Louise Silkey (Silkeys), appeal from an order granting Appellees', Investors Diversified Services, Inc. (IDS) and Mark Powers' (Powers) (collectively referred to as the Brokers) amended Motion to Enforce Mediation Agreement and Request for Sanctions.

We affirm.

## ISSUES

The Silkeys present two issues for our review which we restate as:

I. Whether the trial court erred in determining that an oral agreement reached during a mediation session was a final and binding agreement.

II. Whether the trial court erred in determining that the verbal agreement reached during a mediation session complied with the Indiana Statute of Frauds, Ind. Code § 32-2-1-1.

## FACTS AND PROCEDURAL HISTORY

In early 1983, the Silkeys received a capital gain of $650,000 from the sale of their farm land to a coal company. They sought investment assistance from Powers, who was a registered representative of IDS and possessed all the necessary securities licenses to qualify for that position. IDS is a securities dealer and brokerage firm with its principal offices located in Minneapolis, Minnesota, with an office located and doing business in Evansville, Indiana, and at other locations throughout the State of Indiana.

As a result of meetings and discussions, Powers recommended, and the Silkeys purchased, several investments, including a $100,000 investment in JMB Carlyle Real Estate Limited Partnership XII. This investment's performance did not meet the Silkeys' expectations, and on June 29, 1994, the Silkeys filed a complaint against IDS and Powers alleging misrepresentation, violations of the Indiana Securities Act, breach of fiduciary duty, and constructive fraud.

On August 16, 1995, the trial court ordered the parties to mediation. Mediation was held in Evansville, Indiana on January 17, 1996, five days before the scheduled trial date, with a mutually agreed-upon mediator. The mediator concluded the mediation with an oral recitation of the terms of the agreement and received verbal assent from all of the parties to the terms. This exchange was recorded on an audio tape. The tape was later transcribed by the mediator, and copies were sent to all parties. On January 18, 1996, the mediator filed with the trial court a Mediation Report which confirmed that a settlement had been reached, and the trial was removed from the court's calendar. On January 22, 1996, a typed transcription was sent to all parties by the mediator. On February 19, 1996, the Brokers forwarded to the Silkeys a Settlement Agreement and Mutual General Release (Agreement) which was prepared by counsel for the Brokers and signed by IDS and Powers. After receiving the Agreement, the Silkeys refused to sign it, and the Silkeys' counsel informed the Brokers of the repudiation. Subsequently, the Silkeys' counsel withdrew their representation, and the Silkeys obtained new counsel.

The Brokers filed a Motion to Enforce Agreement for Settlement on August 23, 1996. The trial court found that this was not a case where the parties were disputing whether the document accurately reflected the agreement, but rather the Silkeys were attempting to repudiate the agreement. The trial court concluded that an enforceable agreement was reached by the parties. The trial court ruled that the audio tape recording was a legally binding form of the agreement which set forth with reasonable certainty the terms and conditions and the parties' agreement to these terms and conditions. The trial court then directed that the terms of the audio tape recording be reduced to writing and that, when the writing fairly and accurately reflected the terms of the agreement, the parties would sign and file the agreement with the court.

## DISCUSSION AND DECISION

### I. Effect of the Oral Agreement

The central question in this case is what effect, if any, should be given to the oral agreement reached by the parties at the conclusion of the mediation. The Silkeys argue that the Rules of Alternative Dispute Resolution control the disposition of this question. The rules provide that:

> (2) If an agreement is reached, it shall be reduced to writing and signed. The agreement shall then be filed with the court. If the agreement is complete on all issues, it shall be accompanied by a joint stipulation of disposition.

> (3) After the agreement becomes an order of the court by joint stipulation, in the event of any breach or failure to perform under the agreement, the court, upon motion, may impose sanctions, including costs, interest, attorney fees, or other appropriate remedies including entry of judgment on the agreement.

A.D.R. 2.7(E) (1996).

The Silkeys acknowledge that an agreement was reached and that it was reduced to writing. Appellant's Brief at 20. They also acknowledge that they have rescinded their verbal assent to the terms of the agreement. *Id.* They argue that because this agreement was neither signed by them nor filed with the court, there was no contract or breach; therefore, they argue neither enforcement nor sanction is appropriate. *Id.* We disagree.

The Silkeys present their appeal as one of statutory interpretation; therefore, we begin with consideration of the A.D.R. rules. The Indiana Supreme Court has noted in the preamble to the A.D.R. rules that the rules were "adopted in order to bring some uniformity into alternative dispute resolution with the view that the interests of the parties can be preserved" in non-traditional settings. A.D.R. Preamble. Mediation is a process to "assist[] the litigants in reaching a mutually acceptable agreement." A.D.R. 2.1. Although a court may order parties to participate in mediation and require that participation be in good faith, it cannot order them to reach agreement. *Id.* The ultimate goal of mediation is to provide a forum in which parties might reach a mutually agreed resolution to their differences. The A.D.R. rules provide a uniform *process* for negotiation, but they do not change the law regarding settlement agreements or their enforcement. Nothing in the text of the A.D.R. rules for mediation suggests the Indiana Supreme Court intended to change the trial court's role in enforcing settlement agreements. Thus, although the *process* of the mediation is controlled by the A.D.R. rules, the enforcement of any valid agreement is within the authority of the trial court under the existing law in Indiana.

"The judicial policy of Indiana strongly favors settlement agreements." *Germania v. Thermasol, Ltd.*, 569 N.E.2d 730, 732 (Ind. Ct. App. 1991). Courts retain the inherent power to enforce agreements entered into in settlement of litigation which is pending before them. *Id.* Settlement is always referable to the action in the court, and the carrying out of the agreement should be controlled by that court.

The Silkeys argue that because no written agreement was ever signed, no joint stipulation was ever entered, and therefore, no breach occurred which could allow the court to enforce the agreement. The Silkeys misunderstand the rule. The text to which the Silkeys refer does, in fact, explain the manner in which the parties will present their agreement to the trial court in order to have it *transformed by the court* into an *order* of joint stipulation. This promotes judicial efficiency by assuring that the parties do not appear before the court in a later dispute over the same issue or action. Thus, the rule provides a uniform procedure by which parties dispose of an action in accordance with the terms of their agreement.

The Silkeys argue that they were never compelled to agree and so should not be held to an agreement about which they have changed their minds. Such a rule would clearly create a disincentive for settlement. Additionally, it would allow mediation to serve not as an aid to litigation, but as a separate and additional impetus for litigation. Neither the A.D.R. rules nor the law support such an interpretation.

The Silkeys are correct that a party has full authority over whether to settle his case or proceed to trial. Having decided to accept a settlement, however, the party is bound to that decision. "In the absence of fraud or mistake a settlement is as binding and conclusive of the parties' rights and obligations as a judgment on the merits." The Silkeys do not allege fraud or mistake in reaching this settlement agreement; in fact, they do not question the terms of the agreement at all. Instead, they assert that they "no longer agree" to the terms of the settlement. This is not a sufficient ground to rescind a contract.

The Silkeys argue that the agreement was not final or binding because it is oral. A settlement agreement is not required to be in writing. Whether a party has consented to particular terms is a factual matter to be determined by the fact-finder.

The trial court found that the terms of the agreement were not in dispute. In reaching this decision, it relied on the parties' affidavits, pleadings, and memoranda of law. At the hearing on the matter, the trial court admitted the tape recording of the recitation of agreement over the Silkeys' objection. It does not appear from the trial court's written findings that it relied on the tape recording of the agreement in reaching its decision, nor was it required to do so because neither the content nor the authenticity of the tape was in question. In fact, as noted, the Silkeys raise the issue that the agreement reached in the mediation was preliminary for the first time on appeal. Having failed to raise this issue before the trial court, it is waived.

The evidence before the trial court clearly supports its finding that the parties entered an agreement at the close of the mediation session. The trial court had available to it a tape and a transcript which clearly indicated the parties had agreed in substance to the terms of the mediation. The Silkeys did not argue to the trial court that there were any changes or defects in the terms as they were reduced to writing by the Brokers. Having found that a settlement agreement had been reached, the trial court acted within its authority under the A.D.R. rules and the case law in Indiana in directing the parties to reduce their agreement to writing and sign and file it with the court.

## II. Statute of Frauds

The second issue raised by the Silkeys is that the verbal agreement is not in compliance with the Statute of Frauds and is, thus, unenforceable. They make three arguments on this issue: first, that the terms did not constitute the entire agreement; second, that the audio tape is insufficient to meet the requirements of a writing in order to take the agreement outside the Statute of Frauds; and third, that the agreement cannot be performed within one year of its making.

The Statute of Frauds provides:

> No action shall be brought in any of the following cases: . . .

> Fifth: Upon any agreement that is not to be performed within one (1) year from the making thereof . . . .

> Unless the promise, contract or agreement upon which such action shall be brought, or some memorandum or note thereof, shall be in writing, and signed by the party to be charged therewith, or by some person thereunto by him lawfully authorized . . . .

Ind. Code § 32-2-1-1. The Silkeys argue that the Statute of Frauds is applicable to this agreement due to the fact that it will not be performed within one year. They argue that this agreement will not be fully performed until January 31, 2001. However, the agreement is not this definite. The terms of the agreement guarantee that the Silkeys would receive an initial payment of cash immediately and a guarantee of a distribution of an additional fixed sum *on or before* January 31, 2001. If the investment pays a dividend equivalent to this additional sum before January 31, 2001, there is no further obligation on the part of the Brokers. The fact that this agreement *may not* be performed within one year is insufficient alone to make it subject to the requirements of the Statute of Frauds:

> It must affirmatively appear by the terms of the contract, that its stipulations are not to be performed within a year after it is made, in order to bring it within the provisions of the statute of frauds. (*sic*) The Statute of Frauds has always been held to apply only to contracts which, *by the express stipulations of the parties*, were not to be performed within a year, and not to those which *might or might not*, upon a contingency, *be* performed within a year. The one year clause of the Statute of Frauds has no application to contracts which are *capable* of *being* performed *within* one year of the making thereof.

It is possible that the agreement could be fully performed within one year of its making if the underlying investment were to pay a distribution equal to or greater than the guarantee amount within the first year. There is no express stipulation between the parties that the agreement would not be performed within one year. Thus, the agreement falls outside the Statute of Frauds. Because the Statue of Frauds is not applicable to this settlement agreement due to the fact that it could be completed within one year, we need not address whether it meets the other requirements of the Statute of Frauds.

## CONCLUSION

The trial court acted within its authority to enforce a settlement agreement in a case pending before it where the parties clearly agreed to the terms, but later attempted to rescind their assent. The oral settlement agreement is enforceable, and the parties may be ordered to reduce their agreement to writing and file it with the court. Additionally, because the oral agreement may be performed within one year and there is no express stipulation between the parties that it will not be performed, it is outside the Statute of Frauds.

*Affirmed.*

# NOTES AND QUESTIONS

(1)   What if one of the brokers in *Silkey* sought to disassociate himself from the agreement the other broker was seeking to enforce? For a discussion of a party's First Amendment right to disassociate himself or herself from a settlement agreement, see *Krystkowiak v. W.O. Brisben Companies, Inc.*, 90 P.3d 859 (Colo. 2004). In *Krystkowiak*, a member of a homeowner's association (Krystkowiak) sought to contest a development even after the homeowner's association (NECSNA) mediated an agreement to discontinue its opposition. The developer sued Krystkowiak for tortious interference with contract, contending that Krystkowiak contracted away his right to continue protesting the development when the homeowner's association president signed the proposed settlement agreement. Moreover, the developer argued that Krystkowiak tortiously interfered with its contract with NECSNA because he knew about the contract and intentionally induced NECSNA not to perform it by continuing to protest. In ruling in favor of Krystkowiak, the court explained that Krystkowiak had the right to disassociate from NECSNA once it no longer represented his individual viewpoint:

> Forced inclusion of a member is no more acceptable when an association's expressive activity becomes inconsistent or incompatible with the member's viewpoint as an individual. If this occurs, the person is free to drop his or her membership and disassociate from the organization . . . . Once NECSNA's and Krystkowiak's viewpoints diverged, he was free to disassociate from the organization and continue to petition against the development in his individual capacity. The fact that Krystkowiak was initially acting in a representative capacity does not subsume his individual rights . . . [W]e conclude that Krystkowiak's continued opposition to [the] development was not prohibited by contract, and that he was free to invoke the First Amendment to defend against [the] suit.

(2)   What if a party to a settlement agreement argues that its enforcement would be unfair in light of subsequent circumstances? In *Walker v. Gribble*, 689 N.W.2d 104 (Iowa 2004), the Iowa Supreme Court affirmed the trial court's enforcement of a mediated settlement between former law partners regarding future division of contingency fee recoveries in overtime pay cases. The court found no violation of public policy based on professional responsibility rules and concluded that the lawyer could not now renegotiate fees simply because she ended up

working more than she anticipated when she finalized the fee agreement in mediation. The court explained:

> The fact that one [(or both)] of the parties was wrong does not provide a basis for overturning a settlement agreement that was entered into as a result of arms-length negotiations by parties who are not only attorneys themselves but who were both also represented throughout the negotiations by other attorneys . . . . Walker must live with the bargain she freely entered into . . . . Even if it was a bad bargain, under general principles of contract law, she lives with that bargain. . . . We will not interfere with their agreement — fully performed with the exception of the payment of fees — simply because one party got the better end of the bargain.

## ALI HAGHIGHI v. RUSSIAN-AMERICAN BROADCASTING CO.
United States District Court for the District of Minnesota
945 F. Supp. 1233 (1996)

This matter was originally before the Court on September 27, 1996, upon plaintiff's motion for an order "declaring the settlement agreement of February 14, 1996, to be valid and enforceable and further declaring defendant to be in breach thereof." The Court treated plaintiff's motion as a motion to enforce a settlement agreement and scheduled an evidentiary hearing for November 25, 1996. *See Beihua Sheng v. Starkey Laboratories, Inc, 53 F.3d 192 (8th Cir. 1995). The Court also requested that the parties submit supplemental briefs addressing whether mediator Gerald Laurie is a competent witness or is privileged from testifying at the evidentiary hearing, and the effect of Minn. Stat. § 572.35, subd. 1 on the enforceability of any settlement.*

Defendant argues the settlement agreement alleged by plaintiff is defective as a matter of law because it fails to state that it is binding as required by Minn. Stat. § 572.35. Minn. Stat. § 572.35, subd. 1 states:

> A mediated settlement agreement is not binding unless it contains a provision stating that it is binding and a provision stating substantially that the parties were advised in writing that (a) the mediator has no duty to protect their interests or provide them with information about their legal rights; (b) signing a mediated settlement agreement may adversely affect their legal rights; and (c) they should consult an attorney before signing a mediated settlement agreement if they are uncertain of their rights.

On its face, the statute appears to preclude settlements unless the settlement document includes the four provisions listed in the statute. Such a reading of the statute, however, creates a trap for both the unwary and the wary. The Court does not believe the Minnesota Legislature intended this result, particularly in mediations where both parties are represented by counsel and are fully aware of the binding effect of a settlement agreement. Accordingly, the Court finds Minn. Stat. § 572.35 does not bar enforcement of the alleged settlement.

In addition, Defendant's then-counsel failed to include this language in a settlement document he drafted, and which he claimed was legally sufficient to settle the parties' dispute. Thus, Defendant has waived any argument that either Minn. Stat. § 572.35, subd. 1 or the parties' Mediation Agreement require the settlement document to state it is binding. The evidentiary hearing scheduled for November 25, 1996 will go forward as scheduled. Plaintiff bears the burden of proving that a settlement agreement was reached.

Defendants also argue that a recent amendment to Minn. Stat. § 595.02 precludes either party from calling the mediator, Mr. Laurie, to testify at the evidentiary hearing. Minn. Stat. § 595.02, subd. 1a provides:

> No person presiding at any alternative dispute resolution proceeding established pursuant to law, court rule, or by an agreement to mediate, shall be competent to testify, in any subsequent civil proceeding or administrative hearing, as to any statement, conduct, decision, or ruling, occurring at or in conjunction with the prior proceeding, except as to any statement or conduct that could: (1) constitute a crime; (2) give rise to disqualification proceedings under the rules of professional conduct for attorneys; or (3) constitute professional misconduct.

Although it is unclear whether the statute creates a privilege or a rule of competency, in either case, the Federal Rules of Evidence require that "in civil actions and proceedings with respect to an element of a claim or defense as to which State law supplies the rule of decision," the competency or privilege of a witness "shall be determined in accordance with State law." *See* Fed. R. Evid. 501 and 601. Although the Court questions the appropriateness of such a limitation on testimony in circumstances where a dispute arises regarding the existence of a mediated settlement, the statute clearly supports Defendant's argument that Mr. Laurie may not testify. Therefore, neither party may call Mr. Laurie at the evidentiary hearing on November 25, 1996.

*It is so ordered.*

## ALI HAGHIGHI v. RUSSIAN-AMERICAN BROADCASTING CO.
### Supreme Court of Minnesota
### 577 N.W.2d 927 (1998)

BLATZ, CHIEF JUSTICE.

This case comes to us on an Order of Certification issued by the United States Court of Appeals for the Eighth Circuit under the Uniform Certification of Questions of Law Act. The certified question asks:

> Whether a hand-written document prepared by the parties' attorneys at the conclusion of a mediation session conducted pursuant to the Minnesota Civil Mediation Act, and signed contemporaneously on each page by the respective parties attending the mediation session but which does not itself provide that the document is to be a binding agreement, is rendered unenforceable as a mediated settlement agreement by virtue of Minn. Stat. § 572.35, subd. 1?

We answer the question in the affirmative.

Defendant Russian-American Broadcasting Company, L.P. (RABC), provides ethnic programming, including Russian language radio and cable programming. Plaintiff Ali Haghighi, d/b/a International Radio Network (IRN), distributes foreign language radio programming on a subscriber basis. On March 23, 1993, RABC and IRN entered into a contract whereby RABC allowed IRN to rebroadcast its Russian language radio programming over IRN's subcarrier signal to subscribers in the Minneapolis/St. Paul area. Shortly thereafter, the contractual relationship between the parties began to deteriorate, and in July 1995, IRN initiated a breach of contract action against RABC. RABC filed an answer denying that it had breached the contract and a counterclaim seeking recovery of overdue payments that RABC alleged were owed by IRN under the contract. The parties agreed to mediate their dispute.

Before the mediation session, both parties signed a Mediation Agreement. Among other provisions, the Mediation Agreement fully incorporates the language of Minn. Stat. § 572.35, subd. 1 (1996). The Mediation Agreement states in pertinent part:

> Minnesota Civil Mediation Act. Pursuant to the requirements of the Minnesota Civil Mediation Act, the mediator hereby advises the parties that: (a) the mediator has no duty to protect the parties' interests or provide them with information about their legal rights; (b) signing a mediated settlement agreement may adversely affect the parties' legal rights; (c) the parties should consult an attorney before signing a mediated settlement agreement if they are uncertain of their rights; and (d) a written mediated settlement agreement is not binding unless it contains a provision that it is binding and a provision stating substantially that the parties were advised in writing of (a) through (c) above.

The mediation session took place on February 14, 1996, and lasted the entire day. RABC was represented by Russell Moro, its Chief of Staff, who had the authority to bind RABC. IRN was represented by its owner, Ali Haghighi. Both parties' attorneys were present as well — Kirk Reilly on behalf of RABC, and Robert Gust on behalf of IRN. The mediation was a typical shuttle format, with both parties in separate rooms while the mediator went back and forth between them, attempting to find common ground. After four or five hours of negotiation, the mediator brought the parties together and recited terms which he believed the parties agreed upon. Both the mediator and RABC's attorney, Kirk Reilly, suggested that the parties write the terms down before Moro left town.

Because Moro had a plane to catch, the parties did not type up a formal document. Instead, Reilly and Gust drafted a handwritten document together, with Reilly drafting the majority of the document. The finished product contained fourteen terms and consisted of three pages. Both attorneys reviewed the document and initialed each of the terms and revisions. Moro and Haghighi then signed each page. The document did not contain a provision stating that it was binding, as required by both the Mediation Agreement and the Minnesota Civil Mediation Act.

On August 28, 1996, IRN filed a summary judgment motion to declare the handwritten document enforceable as a settlement agreement. The district court treated IRN's motion as a motion to enforce a settlement agreement and scheduled an evidentiary hearing. Before the evidentiary hearing, the district court requested that the parties submit supplemental briefs addressing the impact of the Minnesota Civil Mediation Act, Minn. Stat. § 572.35, subd. 1, on the enforceability of any settlement agreement. On November 8, 1996, the district court issued an order stating that, although on its face Minn. Stat. § 572.35, subd. 1 appears to preclude enforcement of the handwritten document, the court did not believe that the legislature intended such a result in mediations "where both parties are represented by counsel and are fully aware of the binding effect of a settlement agreement." Accordingly, the district court concluded that Minn. Stat. § 572.35, subd. 1 did not bar enforcement of the handwritten document.

After holding an evidentiary hearing to determine whether the parties intended the handwritten document to represent a binding settlement agreement, the district court found that the objective words and conduct of the parties both during and after the mediation session demonstrated that both parties intended to be bound by the handwritten document and that the document represented a final and complete settlement of the case and an agreement as to all essential terms. Therefore, the district court concluded that IRN met its burden of proving that a settlement agreement existed and granted IRN's motion to enforce the handwritten document. RABC appealed, and the United States Court of Appeals for the Eighth Circuit certified to this court the question of whether Minn. Stat. § 572.35, subd. 1 renders the handwritten document unenforceable.

"A certified question is a matter of law and this court is free to independently review it on appeal." As a threshold issue, the certified question requires this court to assume the handwritten document was prepared at the conclusion of a mediation session conducted pursuant to the Minnesota Civil Mediation Act. Given these facts, we conclude that the handwritten document is rendered unenforceable by the plain language of Minn. Stat. § 572.35, subd. 1.

Canons of statutory interpretation provide that "when the words of a law in their application to an existing situation are clear and free from all ambiguity, the letter of the law shall not be disregarded under the pretext of pursuing the spirit." In accordance with this principle, this court has consistently stated that when a statute is free from ambiguity, we will not look beyond the express language of the statute.

There is no ambiguous language in the provision at hand. The statute clearly provides that a mediated settlement agreement will not be enforceable unless it contains a provision stating that it is binding. The handwritten document prepared by the parties did not contain such a provision. Given a strict, plain language reading, the statute precludes enforcement of the document.

However, IRN contends that such a reading would accomplish an absurd result in this case. When the literal meaning of the words of a statute produces an absurd result, we have recognized our obligation to look beyond the statutory language to other indicia of legislative intent. IRN argues that the legislature clearly intended to protect parties who are unrepresented at mediation and who might not be aware of the legal consequences of the proceedings. Thus, IRN argues that when parties are represented at mediation by attorneys, there is no need for the requirement that the mediation settlement contain a provision stating that it is binding. We disagree. Requiring that a settlement agreement contain a provision stating that it is binding, even when both parties are represented by attorneys, does not produce an absurd result. While IRN contends that the legislature intended this statute to protect only unrepresented parties, it is just as likely that the legislature intended that a settlement document state that it is binding in order to encourage parties to participate fully in a mediation session without the concern that anything written down could later be used against them. If the literal language of this statute yields an unintended result, it is up to the legislature to correct it. This court "will not supply that which the legislature purposefully omits or inadvertently overlooks."

The plain language of the Minnesota Civil Mediation Act requires that a mediated settlement agreement prepared at the conclusion of a mediation session conducted under this Act contain a provision stating that the settlement agreement is binding. Because the handwritten document does not contain such a provision, it is, therefore, unenforceable.

Certified question answered in the affirmative.

## NOTES AND QUESTIONS

(1)   Note that the federal district court in *Haghighi* ruled that the Minnesota statute prevents the mediator's testimony. However, the court questions the "appropriateness of such a limitation on testimony in circumstances where a dispute arises regarding the existence of a mediated settlement." Why? For an excellent analysis of the dilemma a court has to deal with when attempting to enforce mediated settlement agreements in the face of statutory confidentiality provisions, see Ellen E. Deason, *Enforcing Mediated Settlement Agreements: Contract Law Collides with Confidentiality*, 35 U.C. Davis L. Rev. 33 (2001).

(2)   In response to the decision of the Minnesota Supreme Court, the Eighth Circuit reversed the federal district court's decision and remanded the case for further proceedings in light of the state court's decision on the certified question. *Ali Haghighi v. Russian-American Broadcasting Co.*, 173 F.3d 1086 (8th Cir. 1999). For a trenchant discussion and critique of the *Haghighi* litigation and the relevant Minnesota rule, see James R. Coben & Peter N. Thompson, *The Haghighi Trilogy and the Minnesota Civil Mediation Act: Exposing a Phantom Menace Casting a Pall over the Development of ADR in Minnesota*, 20 Hamline J. Pub. L. & Pol'y 299 (1999).

(3)   In *National Union Fire Ins. Co. of Pittsburgh, PA v. Price*, 78 P.3d 1138 (Colo. Ct. App. 2003), the Court of Appeals of Colorado refused to enforce an alleged oral mediated settlement as contrary to the requirements of Colorado's Dispute Resolution Act which mandates that settlements be reduced to writing, be approved and signed by all parties, and presented to the court for approval.

(4)   In *Caballero v. Wikse*, 92 P.3d 1076 (Idaho 2004), the Supreme Court of Idaho upheld a trial court's order requiring specific performance of an oral settlement agreement in a wrongful discharge case. Moreover, the court enforced the agreement over the plaintiff's objection that his attorney did not have the authority to settle the case in the plaintiff's absence. The plaintiff had walked out

prior to the end of the mediation and arguably authorized his attorney to settle. Clearly, the case would have had a different result if Idaho had a statute similar to that in Minnesota. Is this the mediation party the Minnesota legislature was seeking to protect?

# DEL BOSQUE v. AT & T ADVERTISING
### United States Court of Appeals for the Fifth Circuit
### 2011 U.S. App. LEXIS 19280 (Sept. 16, 2011)

Before GARZA, SOUTHWICK, AND HAYNES, CIRCUIT JUDGES.

PER CURIAM

Sylvia Del Bosque filed suit against AT & T in the United States District Court for the Western District of Texas in May of 2008. Del Bosque's complaint, as amended, alleged that AT & T discriminated against her in her employment on the basis of race and sex and retaliated against her after she formally complained to AT & T's human resources staff, both in violation of Title VII of the Civil Rights Act of 1964.

The parties engaged in settlement discussions throughout the pretrial process, culminating in a mediation on November 18. The case did not settle on the day of mediation, but from November 18, 2010, until November 22, 2010, the parties continued efforts to attempt to resolve the case. Del Bosque was represented by counsel throughout this process. On November 22, 2010, Del Bosque and her attorney signed a settlement agreement after making certain handwritten changes on the face of the agreement that had been proposed by AT & T. On November 29, 2010, AT & T's attorney signed the agreement and initialed the changes Del Bosque had made.

On November 30, 2010, Del Bosque filed a pro se motion to revoke the settlement agreement. AT & T responded by filing motions with supporting affidavits to enforce the settlement agreement and to dismiss the case. Del Bosque filed a response without formal evidence. . . . [T]he district court conducted a hearing on December 13, 2010, at which Del Bosque, the attorney who represented Del Bosque at the mediation, and AT & T's attorney spoke. No witnesses were presented, but it appears that the district court considered the attendees' statements as evidence; the affidavits and exhibits presented with the motion to enforce were also considered as evidence. The district judge carefully and diligently listened to both attorneys and Del Bosque. At the conclusion of the hearing, the district judge advised Del Bosque that he intended to enforce the settlement agreement and to deny her motion to revoke the agreement; the district court entered an order to that effect the same day but deferred dismissal of the case until AT & T had paid Del Bosque according to the terms of the settlement. Del Bosque filed a notice of appeal following the entry of this order. After AT & T satisfied the court that it had paid Del Bosque, the district court entered an order and final judgment dismissing the case with prejudice on December 30, 2010. Del Bosque then filed a second notice of appeal, and the two appeals were consolidated before us.

. . .

We address only the issue of whether the district court erred in enforcing the settlement agreement.

As an initial matter, we conclude that the question of the enforceability of the settlement agreement is, under our precedent, to be determined by reference to federal law, not — as AT & T would have us hold — Texas law. . . . Del Bosque contends that the agreement — including the choice-of-law provision — is the product of incapacity or coercion. . . .

Under federal law, " '[o]ne who attacks a settlement must bear the burden of showing that the contract he has made is tainted with invalidity.'. The burden, therefore, lay with Del Bosque to establish before the district court that there was some basis for holding the agreement invalid. As the district court concluded, she has not met this burden; indeed, she offered virtually no basis for the court to rule in her favor.

First, although Del Bosque initially suggested that she had not in fact signed the settlement agreement that AT & T presented to the district court, she admitted at the hearing that she had, in fact, signed the agreement.

Second, Del Bosque asserted that she had been coerced into signing the settlement agreement. When the court inquired as to how and why Del Bosque felt coerced, she first stated that she had had insufficient time to review the agreement despite having reviewed it over a weekend and having consulted with counsel before signing. On further questioning, Del Bosque asserted only that "everybody wanted it done" and then asked the court for a recess. She offered no other evidence of coercion or even statements that would show coercion. The district court did not clearly err in finding that the facts did not support the defense of coercion. . . .

Third, Del Bosque argues that she lacked capacity to enter into the settlement agreement. Del Bosque gave the district court a signed, unsworn letter from Holli Esteban (the "Esteban Letter"), a nurse at an endocrinology practice, addressed "To Whom It May Concern" and expressing the opinion that "[d]ue to Ms. Delbosque's [sic] recent worsening condition, she may not have been in the best medical condition to enter into a legal agreement." Although the district court reviewed and considered the Esteban Letter, Del Bosque affirmatively refused to allow the court to receive the letter into evidence — nor is it at all clear that the district court could have accepted the letter as evidence even if Del Bosque had offered it. Even assuming arguendo that this Letter constituted medical evidence, it falls far short of proving "incapacity." Other than telling the court that she was "distraught" during the mediation, Del Bosque offered no other purported evidence to support her claim of incapacity. The district court's determination of the facts was not clearly erroneous, and the district court did not abuse its discretion in rejecting the defense of incapacity. . . .

Instead of being a case about incapacity or duress, this seems to be a case where Del Bosque expected the mediation to give her a feeling of closure that she did not get. Del Bosque argued to the district court (and on appeal) that there was no "meeting of the minds" as to the settlement agreement. On further questioning from the district court, Del Bosque explained that the basis for her argument was that the mediation did not resolve, and the settlement agreement was not predicated upon, the full resolution of certain fact questions that Del Bosque had wanted the court to resolve when she filed the lawsuit. For example, it did not resolve whether the circumstances of her departure from AT & T constituted termination, retirement, or a disability release. However, she expressed no misunderstanding or mistake about the terms of the settlement agreement *itself.* Instead, at the hearing, Del Bosque confirmed that she understood the amount of money that she would receive under the agreement but nevertheless argued that the agreement was invalid because it did not explain how the agreement arrived at that amount.

Del Bosque appears to have been under the misimpression that reaching an agreement on stipulated facts was somehow a required precursor to the mediation process. That is not so: as the district court explained, frequently the opposite is the case — a mediated agreement reaches an ultimate disposition that fundamentally avoids the resolution of disputed facts. "[S]ettlement is a process of compromise in which, in exchange for the saving of cost and elimination of risk, the parties each give up something they might have won had they proceeded with the litigation, rather than an attempt to precisely delineate legal rights. Ultimately, it seems that this misapprehension of the process, rather than any misunderstanding as to the terms of the agreement, drove Del Bosque's motion. A misunderstanding that does not "ha[ve] a material effect on the agreed exchange of performances" has no effect on the validity of the contract.

Del Bosque was represented when she negotiated and entered into the agreement. To the extent that Del Bosque's argument is predicated on an alleged misunderstanding of the legal effect of the contract, the fact that she was represented by retained counsel seriously undercuts that position. . . . We therefore perceive no abuse of discretion in the district court's decision to enforce the settlement agreement on this record. The district court acted within its discretion in refusing to set aside a facially valid settlement agreement on the basis of the sparse evidence offered by Del Bosque in support of her motion. The district judge very patiently gave her every opportunity to say whatever she wished at the hearing — even granting her request for a recess to allow her to consider what she wanted to say. The court then issued a ruling well-grounded in the facts (and lack of facts) presented. No more was required.

AFFIRMED. MOTIONS GRANTED in part, DENIED in part.

# FERGUSON v. FERGUSON
District Court of Appeal of Florida, Third District
54 So. 3d 553 (2011)

SHEPHERD, J.

This is an appeal from an order voiding a provision of a mediated marital settlement agreement as a result of changes in the economy. Based upon the bedrock principle of contract law — applicable as well to marital settlement agreements — that bad deals are as enforceable in the law as good deals, we reverse the order under review.

The mediated marital settlement agreement in this case was signed and the final judgment of dissolution entered on August 8, 2008.

. . .

Although not a candidate for a future style manual, the agreement is unambiguous. Subsection (C) obligated the former wife to execute and deposit a quitclaim deed in escrow with the former husband's counsel upon execution of the marital settlement agreement, which she did. Subsection (B) required the former husband to pay the former wife an "equalization payment" of $185,000 (subject to minor adjustments) within sixty days of the date the agreement was executed. Subsection (C) requires the former husband to refinance the home within 120 days of the agreement's execution. The plain language of the agreement establishes that its object was (1) to bring about an unconditional payment of $185,000 to the former wife; (2) achieve an ownership transfer of the property to the former husband; and (3) relieve the former wife of any further financial responsibility for the property contemporaneously with the transfer. Notably, the couple, in paragraph (E) of the agreement, anticipated the possibility of one future circumstance, the failure of the former husband to refinance the property within 120 days of the execution of the agreement. In that circumstance, the parties agreed the property immediately would be placed for sale, with the net proceeds going to the former husband. It cannot be gainsaid that the couple's mutual understanding of the value of the property influenced the negotiation.

Shortly after August 8, 2008, and apparently unanticipated by the former husband, the Florida real estate market entered into one of its periodic downward adjustments, for which it has become famous since the time of the Great Depression. The former husband neither paid his former wife the approximate $185,000 equalization payment nor tried to refinance the house. Instead, he unilaterally sought to list the house for sale with a realtor, but the former wife, who has lived in the home with the parties' minor child, has not cooperated.

Rather, the former wife filed a motion for contempt and enforcement of paragraph eighteen, specifically for the payment of $185,000 and the refinancing of the house. The former husband filed a motion requesting the trial court to order the former wife to cooperate with the sale of the home pursuant to the parties' agreement. In his motion, the former husband stated, "Due to the real estate market conditions, the former husband has not been able to refinance the former marital home solely under his name and thus has not been able to pay the monies owed to the former wife pursuant to the parties' agreement."

After hearing arguments on the motions, the trial court declared paragraph eighteen "to be an impossibility of performance due to changes in the economy and therefore void." The court further ordered the former wife to vacate the home, that the home be appraised, and finally that it immediately be listed for sale with the net proceeds divided between the parties. The former wife appeals.

. . . In this case, we find the trial court reversibly erred by voiding paragraph eighteen of the mediated marital settlement agreement for impossibility of performance due to changes in the economy.

A marital settlement agreement entered into by the parties and ratified by a final judgment is a contract, subject to the laws of contract. Because of the central importance placed upon the enforceability of contracts in our culture, the defense of impossibility (and its cousins, impracticability and frustration of purpose) must therefore be applied with great caution if the contingency was foreseeable at the inception of the agreement.

The important question [in an impossibility inquiry] is whether an unanticipated circumstance has made performance of the promise vitally different from what should reasonably have been within the contemplation of both parties when they entered into the contract. If so, the risk should not fairly be thrown upon the promisor.

In this case, the decline in the real estate market shortly after the Former Husband signed the marital settlement agreement, while marked and unfortunate, was not the sort of unanticipated circumstance that falls within the purview of the doctrine of impossibility. Economic downturns and other market shifts do not truly constitute unanticipated circumstances in a market-based economy. The assignment of this risk before a final closing of the transaction between the parties was therefore among those for which a reasonably prudent person, represented by counsel, might have provided. A trial court is not authorized to intervene to ameliorate a hardship that a promisor, such as the former husband in this case, could have thus avoided. . . .

In addition, the former husband cannot sidestep the consequence of his failure to include such a provision with the argument that the lack of such a provision renders this otherwise unambiguous agreement ambiguous. . . . The former husband is bound to the agreement he struck.

Accordingly, the trial court was obligated to enforce the mediated marital settlement agreement as voluntarily agreed upon by the parties. The former wife is entitled to a judgment against the former husband for the $185,000 equalization payment after any adjustments required by the marital settlement agreement. If the marital residence has a temporary certificate of occupancy, the former wife and child shall be entitled to occupy the house consistent with the terms of the marital settlement agreement until such time as the equalization amount is paid or the house is sold. The marital residence should be listed for sale with a real estate agent chosen by the former husband, who shall be contractually entitled to receive the net proceeds of the sale, as provided in the marital settlement agreement.

Reversed and remanded for further proceedings consistent with this opinion.

## NOTES AND QUESTIONS

(1) In ruling against Ms. Del Bosque's defense of duress, was the Fifth Circuit panel less sympathetic than they would have been if they were considering enforceability of a contract rather than a mediated settlement agreement? For cases reaching similar outcomes to a duress defense, see *In re D. E. H.*, 301 S.W.3d 825 (Tex. App. 2009), where the court ruled that the pressure and anguish caused by the possibility of losing parental rights were not sufficient to deny enforcement of the agreement, and *Thomas v. Sandstrom*, 2012 U.S. App. LEXIS 1497 (3d Cir. Jan. 25, 2012), where a dog owner brought a lawsuit alleging civil rights violations

in connection with confiscation of his dog and claimed he was coerced into signing the agreement "by the broken bond of love for his dog." Although a duress defense is rarely successful, in *Cooper v. Austin*, 750 So. 2d 711 (Fla. Dist. Ct. App. 2000), a party was successful in claiming duress where his wife extracted a favorable settlement in mediation by threatening to deliver incriminating juvenile sex pictures to the prosecutor if he did not agree to her settlement terms.

(2)   Did the Florida appellate court in *Ferguson v. Ferguson* set the bar fairly high in deciding to reverse the lower court and rule against Mr. Ferguson's impossibility defense? Might the court have been more sympathetic if Mr. Ferguson had attempted to abide by the terms of the mediated agreement?

(3)   In *Atlantic Pipe* (Section C, *supra*), the judge refers to mediation as a "non-binding" process. Given the cases in this section, is that an accurate description?

# Chapter 7

# DIVERSITY, POWER, AND JUSTICE

## A. INTRODUCTION

Mediation, when conducted well, promotes individual autonomy in the decision-making process; the result is that each person's values and aspirations assume a dominant role in how people discuss, develop, and shape their mediated outcomes. This raises two significant considerations: first, as a matter of policy, is it desirable to use a dispute resolution process in which individual differences and preferences potentially have more weight in determining settlement terms than do publicly known rules that are impartially applied? Second, how can a mediator simultaneously respect individual differences and facilitate collaborative problem-solving efforts? These basic questions, explored below in reverse order, arise in the following ways.

*First*, individual differences require the mediator to be sensitive to how different backgrounds and values affect each individual's participation in the discussion process; a mediator must deploy her communication skills to ensure that mediated conversations foster maximum participation and understanding by all participants. These issues are discussed in Section B.

*Second*, parties command different resources and skills that affect how they negotiate; the danger is that mediation participants, through the dynamics of the bargaining process, might accept proposed settlement terms that exacerbate pre-existing inequalities, thereby raising the undesirable possibility that participating in mediation undermines rather than advances a person's fundamental interests. We focus on these concerns in Section C.

*Third*, in Section D, we examine three distinct perspectives on how justice principles are used to assess or conduct a mediation. First, since each party decides what priority to attach to various principles and norms to resolve their dispute, the possibility exists that the parties' settlement terms clash with outcomes required by law; this dilemma presents the basic question of how to structure the proper relationship between the mediation process and the rule of law. Second, the manner in which a mediator conducts the process can be praised or criticized on procedural justice principles; process informality, critics observe, must not displace dignified human treatment. Third, it is important — and controversial — to consider whether and how a mediator stimulates discussion of justice principles when promoting dialogue among mediation participants.

As you study the following excerpts, envision yourself in multiple roles: as a party, an advocate, a mediator, or a professional who designs justice systems. Ask yourself: does the process as structured and implemented comport with our fundamental convictions about treating persons with dignity and respect?

## B. DIVERSITY, INDIVIDUAL DIFFERENCES, AND THE RESOLUTION OF DISPUTES

We live in a diverse society. To facilitate effective communication and understanding among persons of differing backgrounds, a mediator must discern the cognitive and affective meanings of the disputing parties' comments and behaviors and make certain that each party understands the other's concerns and proposals. This begins at the very basic level of ensuring that parties comprehend what each mediation participant is saying. If persons speak different languages, then a mediator must secure a language interpreter. Diversity differences, though, penetrate far more subtly.

We value things differently, and that leads to behavioral differences. In some cultures, for example, people show respect by not having direct eye contact with their discussion counterparts; other individuals, however, might interpret a person's not maintaining eye contact as a sign of disrespect. Similarly, in some religious traditions, a married man will not shake hands with a female who is not his wife; a woman raised in a different tradition may view that man's refusal to shake her hand as a deliberate act of disengagement or hostility. People from different cultures develop different habits regarding what constitutes a comfortable physical distance between persons talking to each other; if one person invades the other's space, deliberately or accidentally, discomfort ensues. Similarly, the fact that some individuals speak more loudly or quickly than others sometimes leads persons to conclude that the person speaking loudly is disrespectful, or that the fast-talking individual is being deceptive.

What is the significance of such complexities for a mediator? The mediator must adopt procedural and conversational practices that enable all parties to feel that they are being treated with dignity and respect. The mediator, for instance, would try to place parties at the conference table at a distance comfortable for everyone; the mediator, if female, would not demand to shake the hand of a male party whose culture or religion forbade such conduct. The mediator would schedule meeting times in a manner that respected the participants' desire to celebrate particular holidays or religious events, or serve parties with food and beverages that reflected their differing cultures. By behaving in such a manner, the mediator displays fundamental sensitivity and respect to persons of varying backgrounds, and thereby enables all participants to feel included.

At the same time, a mediator cannot fall into the trap of interacting with disputants based on stereotypes. There is an important difference between one's being conscious of differences based on race, gender, ethnicity, or religion, and one's engaging in stereotyping. While group membership tends to create commonalities among members, each individual adopts particular views, behaviors, and values in their own way. A mediator must be sensitive to blending a respect for group norms with awareness of how each individual embraces or rejects that norm. In this very fundamental way, a mediator takes seriously the belief that every case is different because each person is unique.

Diversity conflicts can reflect clashes not only of behavioral habits but also of fundamental values. Controversies regarding leadership succession in a family-operated business can pit one family member's belief about the priority of family cohesiveness against another person's desire to exercise autonomy by pursuing other life callings. Deep value conflicts emerge when a group's cultural values define gender roles in a manner that is sharply at odds with the dominant culture's public policy, as can occur in controversies surrounding the practice of Female Genital Mutilation. In each of these situations, a mediator can encourage persons to engage in discussions to search for a workable, acceptable resolution; some efforts will succeed and others fail. While no mediator should be deterred from trying to assist parties to such a dispute, the mediator must recognize that more is at stake than simply trying to deploy an effective technique to help parties respect alternative practices; rather, one party may be asking the other to alter a web of fundamental convictions. These controversies, in particular, also raise the question of whether the mediator's own background enables her to act in a neutral fashion, or be perceived and accepted by the parties as so acting.

In sum, there are many types of differences among parties. Minimally, the mediator wants to ensure that parties do not declare impasse by drawing incorrect inferences based on erroneous stereotyping or ignorance of one another's cultural practices. Affirmatively, the mediator, to the extent possible, wants to capitalize on the strengths of parties' differences to assist them design and shape imaginative, acceptable bargaining outcomes. The first excerpt below, from Michelle LaBaron Duryea and J. Bruce Grundison, highlights at a general level how immigrants to a new culture (in this instance, Canada) might perceive and interact with citizens of the dominant culture. It poignantly references how making adjustments to living in a new culture creates challenges both within a family or cultural group unit as well as between that family/group unit and citizens and institutions of the dominant culture. In the Notes and Question that follow it, you are asked to identify strategies and tactics that a mediator from the dominant culture could use to promote party understanding and settlement when these cultural diversity dynamics lace the parties' dispute.

## CONFLICT AND CULTURE: RESEARCH IN FIVE COMMUNITIES IN VANCOUVER, BRITISH COLUMBIA
University of Victoria Institute for Dispute Resolution 28–42 (1993)[*]
By Michelle LeBaron Duryea & J. Bruce Grundison

[Ed. Note: Methodologically, the authors refer to the persons whom they interviewed at this stage of their research as "key informants."]

### "IMMIGRANT SYNDROME"

While immigrant groups are diverse in many ways, they also have much in common. An interesting discussion was presented by a key informant commenting on the Latin American community who identified what he called the "immigrant syndrome." While his comments related to the Latin American community, there were themes that may apply to other immigrant groups.

In his framework, the immigrant syndrome has four components: the linguistic choke, the cultural choke, the social-familial choke, and the loss of identity choke. The linguistic choke occurs when individuals without skills to communicate with the dominant culture turn to their children to help them with their communication. This causes conflicts in the family because children realize that they can gain power in the family through linguistic aptitude. The linguistic choke also affects one's possibilities of gaining employment. Sometimes women are able to get jobs faster than men, not because they acquire the language faster, but because many jobs that women can find do not need sophisticated language skills. Cleaning is an example. Power in the spousal unit changes, and many marriages have broken up because of the independence that immigrant women can achieve in Canada.

The social-familial choke refers to the social and familial changes in the family structure. Many Latin Americans, for example, were well off in their countries of origin and left their countries because of political and civil wars. When they come to Canada many of these refugees are treated as "third-class citizens." This change in status can cause problems in adaptation to Canadian ways.

A more subtle problem is called the cultural choke. When immigrants come to Canada they are faced with a value system different from the one they were accustomed to in their countries of origin. Depression is high among immigrants, many of whom never really overcome the losses they experience: many have lost their families, friends, and homes. In Canada they feel alone and lonely. Values about achievement are very different. Americans and Canadians value an individualistic focus on achievement whereas some cultures value a group focus on achievement.

The fourth component is the loss of identity choke. Latin American individuals, for example, may refer to themselves as Salvadoreans, Colombians, or Guatemalans, but in Canada they are collectively labeled as Hispanics or Latin Americans. Immigrants attempt to build a community by trying to adapt to the new social identity assigned to them by the dominant culture in Canada. Many refugees are in a state of mourning; they grieve the loss of their homes, families, and climate, and require counselling to help them with their feelings of depression and isolation.

## CONFLICT ISSUES INTRODUCTION

When asked about issues in their communities around which there may be conflict, individual key informants focused considerable attention on family conflict even though they were invited to comment on several categories of conflict.

One key informant, commenting on the emphasis on family conflict, said that conflicts within families often arise in immigrant communities in which there are many related people and potential interferers. Family conflict has been studied quite extensively already, said the key informant, with casework on families where ethnicity is the key variable being the most studied area even in analyses focusing on religion, language and education. Given the amount of work already devoted to family conflict, the informant cautioned that the family conflict category should not be allowed to dominate the research agenda.

## FAMILY CONFLICTS

Key informants in all groups discussed conflicts arising from challenges to traditional family structures, such as generational and gender roles, which occur when immigrants adopt Canadian lifestyles. The role of the extended family is important in each community. Family unity is highly valued, and conflict can cause all family members to suffer: spouses, parents, children, teens, young adults, and older generations.

Key informants from the Chinese community indicated that disorder and imbalance in spousal roles may occur when spouses immigrate at different times. The following paraphrase from one key informant's comments describes some of the problems:

> Whoever comes to Canada first will automatically be dominant, because they will know better where to go and what to do. They will know society better and have better language skills. In one case, the woman came first. Then her husband came. He had to rely upon his wife all of the time. He felt lost as a man and as a professional; he did not have the same status here in Canada that he had in China. There were many arguments that came from this experience. If a woman is a professional worker in China and comes here after her husband, she will have problems of a similar nature to those described by this husband.

. . . .

Key informants from the Latin American community also reported shifts in power within the spousal unit as a result of changes in roles within the family. Women often gain authority because they are able to gain employment faster than men. They can get jobs where English language skills are not essential. While divorce is not encouraged in countries of origin, divorce rates are high among Latin Americans who move to Canada because of the independence that Latin American women are able to achieve in Canada.

In Canada, immigrant children gain power by learning to speak the language. Within the Latin American community, children are frequently required to interpret for the family. This role reversal contributes to the parents' sense of loss of status and control, and power struggles between parents and children can result.

Key informants reported that family problems in this community are very serious and need attention. Parent-teen conflict can become so severe that teens run away from home and begin to sell drugs to make money to survive. Key informants reported needing programs on effective parenting and parental rights. Families are highly valued in the Latin American culture, so if the family begins to disintegrate there is profound difficulty and loss for the family members, particularly the elder generations.

Changing parental roles may cause family conflicts within the Polish community, but in ways that differ from some of the other communities. One of our key informants suggested that Poland's egalitarian society prepares women to have careers that may take priority over those of their husbands. In Canada, however, many recent immigrants of Polish descent perceive that men hold most positions of power. Polish men may see their wives, many of whom at one time had professional careers, working as homemakers or in jobs with low social status. Here the men may begin to accept a subordinate social status for women. Other Polish informants suggest that women have better opportunities for advancement in Canada than they did in Poland . . . .

In the Polish community, children may experience their parents' frustration through physical abuse, but key informants indicated that intergenerational violence is less common than differences in values. Rules such as curfews may seem onerous to some children who compare their own parents to those of friends. Although spanking or slapping may have been common in Poland, children soon learn at school that such treatment can be illegal, and they may threaten to telephone the 9-1-1 emergency number if their parents touch them. Children may not openly shun their Polish heritage, but parents have difficulty teaching their children about Polish customs, manners, and language. Also, children usually master a new language rapidly and become more fluent in English than their parents. Combined with the difference in cultural values, this can be a recipe for continuing conflict.

Finally, key informants noted that Polish families sometimes immigrate in phases, with dynamics within the families changing as each member arrives. Prolonged separation causes some of the difficulties as the parents form new attachments and relationships outside their marriage bond. Other problems result from the different stages of adaptation through which family members go; the first to arrive will likely know more English than the later arrivals and will certainly know more about resources and services available in the new country . . . .

Intergenerational conflicts arise from differences in attitude about family values and traditions. Parents try to uphold traditional values; children retaliate. A key informant reported that sons are valued more than daughters, and preferential treatment for boys can cause conflicts among siblings. Domestic help is expected from the daughters, but not from sons. Challenges to traditional work ethics can cause intergenerational disputes within the family. Parents may value hard work, but younger children may not see any reasons for hard work.

Conflicts also occur between older children and grandparents who are accustomed to having decision-making authority within the family. In Canada, grandparents are not given this authority . . . [this] can create tension and divisions in the family. Sometimes grandparents try to strengthen their own position by winning over a certain grandchild as an ally.

Older generations may also be exploited by family members who may ask them to care for the grandchildren or to give their pension to support the family. Stripped of the power and authority they used to have in the extended family structure in Vietnam, seniors may feel ignored and isolated, and there are very few programs aimed at helping them.

## INTERGROUP CONFLICT

A number of the key informants were asked to assess the state of intergroup relations in British Columbia, having particular reference to the Lower Mainland, on a scale of 1 to 10, with 0 representing serenity and 10 an explosive state. While one Chinese key informant mentioned that intergroup relations are better now than when she was a youngster, all key informants said that there is room for improvement. With the exception of the key informants from the Polish community who rated British Columbia between 5 and 6 on the scale, all respondents assessed the volatility of intergroup relations as 7 or higher. Considerable emphasis was placed on the urgency of addressing this issue. Several key informants assessed the situation as potentially explosive . . . .

One key informant stated that while the dominant Canadian culture is polite and respectful, many Canadians hold stereotypical beliefs about different ethnocultural groups. For example, many Canadians do not know the differences that exist between the Latin American peoples and may assume that anyone speaking Spanish must be Mexican. Latin Americans may be stereotyped as lazy, loud, or violent. Misinterpretation of mannerisms or customs may encourage stereotyping. For example, police may think that a Hispanic individual is "shifty" if he does not make eye contact in the same manner as other Canadians.

The issue of stereotyping is illustrated further in the following section on conflict issues.

## CONFLICTS INVOLVING POLICE

Key informants from immigrant communities indicate they have been subject to discrimination and stereotyping by police. For example, Latin American youths may be seen as "gang members" whether or not they actually have such affiliations.[1] Police may go to arrest a Latin American youth on an immigration matter and also arrest ten of his friends, subjecting them to strip searches and questioning.

Key informants from the Polish and Latin American groups reported they are accustomed to seeing the police as corrupt representatives of repression, so there is little room for trust or positive interaction. The process of understanding laws and developing trust of public authorities is hindered for Latin Americans because of negative experiences in their countries of origin and the lack of established community support in Canada. Perceived harassment of community youth perpetuates this distrust. Distrust of police has led in some cases to immigrants taking the law into their own hands, which causes further difficulties.

One key informant suggested there could be major trouble if there is no improvement in relationships between police and minorities. Gang-related and other organized criminal activity has been increasing, but youth gangs are not

---

[1] Use of the term "gang" is problematic because of its connotations with extreme violence, lawlessness, and organized crime. Key informants suggested the use of the word "group," but we have retained "gang" out of fidelity to the original data. It should not be taken from this that gangs are necessarily involved in serious crime, nor that their mention here in any way implies a specific connection between ethnicity and gang membership.

limited to immigrant communities. There is a clear need to train institutional staff in effective ways of resolving conflict and in dealing effectively with a diverse community.

Police departments in Victoria and Vancouver have been doing intercultural awareness training. The issue is sensitive because some training has been found to reinforce negative stereotypes. Recently, the Canadian Centre for Police Race Relations was opened in Ottawa. It will provide information about bias-free standards, policies, and procedures for the selection, recruitment, and performance of police officers. In addition, the centre will provide crosscultural and anti-racism training for police officers, as well as developing effective liaison, consultation and out-reach mechanisms for police to use in dealing with diverse clients and communities.

Liaison between cultural groups and police is one step being taken to address key issues. In Vancouver an identified need is to have storefront police offices for specific groups. A group of British Columbia's Aboriginal people have been involved in creating such a service in Vancouver. They have been particularly concerned about issues of credibility and official recognition and have considered it important that the individual overseeing the project report directly to the government or to the Vancouver Police Department, not to an independent board. A similar centre has been set up for Chinese people to provide translation, referral, and response services that suit victim needs. In another initiative, police representatives have been communicating with their counterparts in Hong Kong to get a better understanding of some of the cultural variables involved in organized crime in the Chinese community . . .

## CONFLICTS INVOLVING ORGANIZATIONS

Because of unpleasant experiences in their countries of origin, many in the Latin American community mistrust authority figures such as police, government officials, and social service workers. Some individuals in the Latin American community have experienced political imprisonment and torture, including some refugee claimants from Guatemala and El Salvador. Many view authority as abusive and oppressive and are suspicious of the police and social service agencies.

Their backgrounds may lead them to mistrust interventions in the family by social workers. One key informant commented that the Ministry of Social Services ("MSS") is perceived as an "agency designed to destroy families." If children do not like the discipline from their parents they may call Social Services. Parents may be afraid. Some do not understand the authority and the role of the social workers. Others challenge social workers, feeding stereotypes that Latin American men are threatening and violent. The key informant said that better communication might be achieved by providing social workers with information about families' cultural values and providing parents with information about how the services can help them, including when and how a social worker can intervene to help with family problems.

Difficulties with communicating in English can hinder interventions. One reported example involved a Latin American woman who was placed in a transition house after deciding to leave her abusive husband. She felt isolated because her inability to speak English prevented her from communicating with others in the transition house. After a few weeks the woman returned to her husband because, despite the abuse, she could at least speak with him in Spanish.

Government organizations and agencies usually do not have workers available who speak Polish or understand the Polish culture. Polish immigrants may not get the services they require because either they cannot communicate their needs or they do not seek out help, fearing the English-speaking institutions. Furthermore, some Poles may be suspicious of volunteer organizations because they expect others to be motivated by the need to make money.

Members of the South Asian community reported conflicts with Workers' Compensation Board ("WCB"), Unemployment Insurance Commission ("UIC"), Insurance Corporation of British Columbia ("ICBC"), and MSS. Key informants said these organizations hold stereotypical beliefs that South Asians take undue advantage of their services. As a result, persons of South Asian descent may be considered "guilty until proven innocent" of "milking the system." South Asian clients of ICBC complain that they are not dealt with fairly and that their word may not have the same weight as that of an accident victim from the dominant culture.

One key informant indicated that immigrants bring with them assumptions about how to proceed with bureaucracies. In many cases they are accustomed to a big shadow economy. Some do not understand the workings of ICBC or WCB. Others may be unwilling to make use of the social assistance system. The key informant said that depending on the context of conflict, one person may attribute difficulties with an organization to racism, others to their understanding of how the bureaucracy works. South Asian immigrants have acquired a real distrust of bureaucracy in their countries of origin, a distrust which they bring to Canada. They may assume there is considerable elasticity regarding discretionary powers and may not realize the constraints placed on individual discretion within bureaucracies. They may search for the right button to press and become confused when this does not work. A person who knows how to deal with a bureaucracy such as ICBC is a valued individual in the community.

Conflicts with UIC often relate to transient workers employed in farm work, in which the South Asian population is disproportionately represented. Workers who move from one location to another may be denied UIC benefits because of government regulations.

In addition, South Asians may not see intervention into families by MSS as helpful. They may view social workers and other social service providers as akin to police. They resist the invasion of their family. One key informant indicated that no matter how specialized or respectful the bureaucracy becomes, South Asian families may still resist outside interference . . . .

## SCHOOL CONFLICT

Different styles of teaching and classroom management are the source of conflicts between teachers and parents from certain cultural backgrounds. For example, Chinese and South Asian parents expect that teachers will use types of classroom discipline different from those techniques usually employed in Canadian schools. Teachers sometimes fail to use their authority correctly, some parents think. South Asian parents typically view any call for participation in parent-teacher conferences as negative because they are unfamiliar with this approach. Parents may be uncomfortable with the consultative model proposed by the British Columbia School Act, preferring to give teachers and the educational system full control.

Aside from the interference in family issues mentioned above, schools may be a source of conflict when the teachers attempt to communicate about problems the children have. One key informant suggested that presenting parents with several choices works much better than criticizing them or telling them outright what to do.

A number of South Asian key informants have reported that their children have not been treated fairly in school. Children have been shunned by their peers as a result of cultural stereotyping. Young boys who wear turbans, for example, have been teased by other children at school. In many cases the schools do not address this problem. This can lead to conflicts between the parents and the school as well as to conflicts between the child and the parents.

Incidents of name-calling discrimination against students of South Asian heritage have been attributed to biased press reports about ethnocultural groups. For instance, after a recent shooting in the South Asian community, the local press described several weapons confiscated by police from "Asian gangs" during the preceding month.[2] The timing and description of these reports did not assist in creating a positive public image of the South Asian community. One key informant questioned whether in other circumstances the press would report that there had been "another Caucasian shooting"; it had labelled the South Asian incident "another Sikh shooting."

## NEIGHBOURHOOD AND HOUSING CONFLICTS

Latin American and South Asian key informants reported neighbourhood and housing conflicts. Landlord/tenant problems can arise from the different style and ingredients of cooking used by South Asians as well as from the number of adults living in single-family dwellings. Community reaction to the extended family traditions of South Asians can lead to and can reinforce prejudices, stereotypes, and racist behavior. Members of the South Asian group also find that because of religious differences, they are not accepted by the dominant society. Many Sikh men feel discriminated against because of their turbans . . . .

## EMPLOYMENT CONFLICTS

Conflicts relating to employment were mentioned particularly by key informants from the Latin American community. This issue is particularly important to adult immigrants who have been trained in specific careers in their home countries. Doctors and lawyers find it hard to have their credentials accepted. Loss of one's

[2] *See* footnote 1, *supra.*

status and one's career is difficult to bear. As well, the lack of Latin American lawyers, doctors, psychologists, and other professionals is a disadvantage for community members who need these services and may not be fluent in English.

Immigrants from Poland experience many conflicts about employment as well. Employment counsellors may advise some to lower their expectations and to accept jobs which require far less training than the often highly-educated immigrants have. Canadian officials in Poland who warmly accept immigration applications from professionals and assure the new immigrants that there will be jobs may raise people's expectations about life in Canada. The situation is further aggravated by lack of opportunities for advanced training in English, job retraining, and gradual integration into their chosen professions.

# NOTES AND QUESTIONS

(1)    Assume that the perspectives of the key informants reported in the Duryea/Grundison study accurately portray similar experiences for immigrant persons living in the United States and that you are mediating a case in the United States in which one party is claiming unlawful termination from his/her employment. The defendant is a member of the majority culture. What discussion dynamics might the mediator anticipate if the plaintiff is (a) a male member of the majority culture? (b) a female immigrant from a Latin American country whose husband is unemployed? (c) a male son living with his parents and sister who recently emigrated from Poland? What might the mediator do to avoid engaging in inappropriate assumptions or stereotypes? What type of interparty dynamics due to cultural interactions might a mediator anticipate?

(2)    You are mediating a case involving a schoolteacher, guidance counselor, and a seventh-grade student and his parents. The student has been reported as habitually tardy, if not truant, from school. Under state law, the school district must file charges in juvenile court against the student and parents if his unexcused absences continue. During the mediation conference, you learn that: the student and parents immigrated to this country 12 months ago; the parents rely on their son to take a school-bus to and from school each day; the student's mother is employed and leaves for work daily at 6:00 a.m.; the father, a trained engineer who was gainfully employed before coming to the United States, has been unemployed since his arrival; the father believes that it is a mother's responsibility to raise the child, including providing the child with a healthy breakfast each day; the father, often depressed by his not having found work in the United States, frequently socializes with male companions until the early morning hours and is often asleep when his wife leaves for work. School district participants state that both parents have a responsibility for making certain that their son attends school. What "diversity" challenges confront the mediator and parties? What options might exist for constructively addressing the situation?

(3)    If a party's background makes her skeptical of persons who are authority figures, how can a mediator explain and execute her role in the dispute resolution process to engender trust? Does it make a difference if a mediator adopts an evaluative rather than facilitative orientation (*see* Chapter 4, *supra*)? Conversely, if a party's background leads her to rely on authority figures for establishing and

enforcing basic norms, would it make a difference if a mediator adopts a facilitative rather than evaluative orientation?

(4)   As noted in Chapter 1, *supra*, mediation's use during its foundational years was highly valued because it provided a forum for participants to discuss their interests and concerns that significantly affected the way in which they interacted with one another. This was especially important for addressing such matters as police-community relations, where the topics to be discussed did not constitute legal causes of action. (For an account of a recent, extensive intervention dealing with this topic, see Improving Police-Community Relations in Cincinnati: A Collaborative Approach (2002), written and compiled by Jay Rothman, Collaborative Director and Special Master for this litigation.) This capacity for participants to address multiple matters, not just litigation topics, assumes added urgency when matters of diversity are involved, for persons can experience being harmed or aggrieved whether or not the legal system recognizes a cause of action.

One striking example is the phenomenon of "hate speech." There is a significant tension in weighing the competing interests of free speech and the harm experienced by those individuals who are the objects of racist speech. For a compelling account of these tensions, see Mari J. Matsuda, *Public Response to Racist Speech: Considering the Victim's Story*, 87 Mich. L. Rev. 2320 (1989). Professor Matsuda's proposal for combating this type of speech is to develop both civil and criminal legal interventions to prohibit it, thereby providing incentives for persons to change their behavior. But, is making the undesired conduct illegal the only, or best, way to minimize its presence? Universities have tried to combat racist speech on campus by students toward one another by developing speech codes. Some of these codes have been declared unconstitutional. *See Doe v. University of Michigan*, 721 F. Supp. 852 (E.D. Mich. 1989). Could various university stakeholders, with a mediator's assistance, develop a workable set of protocols that effectively address these matters? For a probing analysis of the deeper issues raised by this topic, see Catherine A. MacKinnon, *Only Words* (1993).

(5)   For a perspective on how the mediator's own cultural background influences the manner in which he or she conducts a conversation, see Mary E. Pena-Gratereaux & Maria I. Jessop, Mediation and Culture: Conversations with New York Mediators from Around the World, Washington Heights Inwood Coalition Mediation Program (2000). Adapting a different analytical approach to examine the related question of mediator neutrality, Professor Carol Izumi cites recent social science evidence labeled "behavioral realism" that reveals the significant distorting impact of an individual's implicit biases on her aspiration to behave in a non-discriminatory manner. Izumi, *Implicit Bias and the Illusion of Mediator Neutrality*, 34 Wash. U. J.L. & Pol'y 71 (2010). For further discussion of Professor Izumi's analysis, see Section C, *infra*, Notes and Questions (6).

If the mediator's own values and individual characteristics prompt her to act in a way that undermines respect for the values and aspirations of the mediation parties, should she disqualify herself from service? *See* Standard IV of The Model Standards of Conduct for Mediators (Appendix A, *infra*).

The following excerpt by Professors Kolb and Coolidge raises each of the basic questions noted at the outset: first, their insights suggest that a mediator must be sensitive to how individual differences based on gender influence the manner in which persons participate in consensual decision-making process; in that sense, the lessons are similar to those raised above by Duryea and Grundison. Second, a possible implication of Kolb's analysis is that participating in mediation may systematically disadvantage persons of a particular gender; that theme is picked up in the Grillo article appearing on page 359. Although this Kolb/Coolidge article was written more than two decades ago, it reflects, better than other negotiation theory articles, how insights regarding reported gender differences toward ethical questions — an ethic of justice or an ethic of caring — first articulated by Carol Gilligan in her path-breaking book, *In a Different Voice* (1982), might connect to negotiating styles embraced respectively by men and women. Today, many persons challenge the accuracy of Kolb/Coolidge's reported account of gender differences but the Kolb/Coolidge insights continue to point to fundamental questions relevant to justice dynamics.

# HER PLACE AT THE TABLE: A CONSIDERATION OF GENDER ISSUES IN NEGOTIATION[*]

*In* Negotiation Theory and Practice 261–71 (William Breslin & Jeffrey Z. Rubin, Eds.) (The Harvard Program on Negotiation Books, 1991)
By Deborah M. Kolb & Gloria C. Coolidge

Our purpose here is to explore the ramifications of feminist theories of development and social organization to the exercise of power and the resolution of conflict in negotiated settings . . . [W]e suggest that there are four themes that are most relevant to an understanding of some of the ways that women frame and conduct negotiations. These are:

— a relational view of others;

— an embedded view of agency;

— an understanding of control through empowerment; and

— problem-solving through dialogue.

## HER VOICE IN NEGOTIATION

There are at least three reasons why the subject of an alternative voice in negotiation is not closed. First, our experience and those of others suggest that there are significant differences in the ways men and women are likely to approach negotiation and the styles they use in a search for agreement.

[A]t least some women experience their gender as a factor in negotiation. The fact that research may not capture this experience may derive from the settings of the research (usually the laboratory) and the questions the research poses (which are usually aggregate behavioral indicators). Second, there is evidence that in real negotiations (as opposed to simulations), women do not fare that well . . . . If negotiation is a woman's place, we would expect women to excel, not be disadvantaged. There is a third reason . . . [T]he prescriptions to get to win-win outcomes in negotiation offer ambiguous advice to the negotiator, whether male or female. The advice to focus on interests, not positions, and invent options for mutual gain emphasizes the relational dimension of negotiation . . . .

On the other hand, advice to separate people from problems and focus on objective criteria gives a rationalized and objective cast to negotiation that may be quite different from the subjective and embedded forms of feminine understanding . . . [I]n the press to provide prescription, it is the technical and rationalized analysis that increasingly dominates. Integrative bargaining, or joint-gain negotiation, while acknowledging the importance of empathetic relationships, suggests that the critical skills necessary to implement win-win outcomes are primarily technical and analytic.

[T]he prescriptive voice of principled or joint gain negotiation, while there is much to applaud in its perspective, has a tendency to drown out alternative ways of seeing and doing things. We need to consider the structures and contexts in more nuanced ways. From our perspective we begin with gender and the themes that might comprise an alternative voice.

## HER PLACE AT THE TABLE

### Styles of Talk

The essence of negotiation is strategic communication. Parties want to learn about the alternatives available and the priority of interests of the other. At the same time, they want to communicate in ways that further their own aims, whether it is to elucidate their interests or obfuscate them, depending on strategy. Research on gender in communications suggests that women's distinctive communication style, which serves them well in other contexts, may be a liability in negotiation.

Women speak differently. Their assertions are qualified through the use of tag questions and modifiers . . . [T]he female pattern of communication involves deference, relational thinking in argument, and indirection. The male pattern typically involves linear or legalistic argument, depersonalization and a more directional style. While women speak with many qualifiers to show flexibility and an opportunity for discussion, men use confident, self-enhancing terms. In negotiation, these forms of communication may be read as weakness or lack of clarity and may get in the way of focusing on the real issues in conflict . . . .

Similarly, women's modes of discourse do not signal influence. Women's speech is more conforming and less powerful. Women talk less and are easily interrupted while they, in turn, are less likely to interrupt. In mixed groups, they adopt a deferential posture and are less likely to openly advocate their positions. At the same time, there is a proclivity to be too revealing — to talk too much about their attitudes, beliefs, and concerns.

Given that the process of negotiation as it is customarily enacted calls for parties to be clear and communicate directly and authoritatively about their goals, feelings, interests, and problems, a deferential, self-effacing, and qualified style may be a significant detriment. It is also possible that such a stance can also be an asset in projecting a caring and understanding posture. The choice for women is to learn to become more conversant with negotiation skills but also adept in an alternative style of communication at the negotiating table, one that is more congruent with the task.

## Expectations at the Table

[E]vidence from research on women in organizations, particularly in management, suggests that it is not so easy for women to act forcefully and competitively without inviting criticism and questions about both her femininity and ability and threatening something of the accustomed social order. When performance in decision-making and negotiating tasks is judged equivalent by objective measures, men and women are rated differently by those involved, to the detriment of women. They are seen as less influential and receive less credit for what influence they may have exerted. As mediators they are judged less effective, even when the outcomes they achieved are superior.

At the same time, women are expected to do the emotional work in a group. In negotiation contexts, they often carry the burden for attending to relationships and the emotional needs of those involved. While such a burden might be consistent with a voice she might like to speak in, a woman who has trained herself to negotiate from a different premise might find that these expectations frequently constrain her ability to maneuver for herself or those she represents. Learning how to use their strengths and manage the dual impressions of femininity and strategic resolve are important aspects of negotiating tactics for women.

## Relational View of Others

There seem to be two major ways that a relational view of self is potentially manifest in negotiation. The first is the conception a woman has of herself as a party negotiating. She conceives of her interests within a constellation of responsibilities and commitments already made. That is, she is always aware of how her actions in one context impact on other parts of her life and on other people significant to her.

The second implication is that relational ordering in negotiation may be a prerequisite for interaction. Relational ordering means creating a climate in which people can come to know each other, share (or do not share) values, and learn of each other's modes of interacting. Expressions of emotion and feeling and learning how the other experiences the situation are as important, if not more important, than the substance of the discourse. In other words, separating the people from the problem is the problem. Negotiation conducted in a woman's voice would, we predict, start from a different point and run a different course than either a purely principled or purely positional model.

## Embedded View of Agency

Women understand events contextually both in terms of their impact on important ongoing relationships and as passing frames in evolving situations which grow out of a past and are still to be shaped in the future. The male imagination stereotypically focuses on individual achievement and is sparked by opportunities for distinctive activity that are bounded by task and structure. This exemplifies a self-contained concept of agency. An embedded form of agency emphasizes the fluidity between the boundaries of self and others. Thus, women are energized by their connections and so interpret and locate activities in a spatial and temporal context in which boundaries between self and others and between the task and its surroundings are overlapping and blurred.

If one operates from an embedded view of agency, any negotiation must be understood against the background from which it emerges. That means that there is the expectation that people in negotiation will act in a way that is consistent with their past and future behavior in other contexts. Negotiation is not, therefore, experienced as a separate game with its own set of rules but as part of the extended organization context in which it occurs.

## Control Through Empowerment

Power is often conceived as the exertion of control over others through the use of strength, authority or expertise. It is usually defined as the ability to exert influence in order to obtain an outcome on one's own terms. Conceiving of power in this way leads to a dichotomous division between those who are powerful and those who are powerless. A model in which power is accrued for oneself at the expense of others may feel alien to some women and/or be seen by others as somehow incongruent with female roles. Anticipating that assertiveness may lead away from connection, women tend to emphasize the needs of the other person so as to allow that other to feel powerful. Her behavior may thus appear to be passive, inactive or depressed.

. . . An empowerment view which allows all parties to speak their interests and incorporates these into agreements that transcend the individualized and personalized notion of acquiring, using, and benefiting from the exercise of power is often dismissed as hopelessly naïve. However, it is clear that there are situations (particularly those that involve ongoing and valued relationships) in which mutual empowerment is a much desired end.

## Problem Solving Through Dialogue

Dialogue is central to a woman's model of problem solving. It is through communication and interaction with others that problems are framed, considered, and resolved. This kind of communication has specific characteristics that differentiate it from persuasion, argument, and debate . . . .

Problem solving through dialogue in negotiation suggests a special kind of joining and openness in negotiation. In place of a strategic planning model of negotiation, in which considerable effort is devoted to analyzing and second-guessing the possible interests and positions of the other, problem solving through dialogue involves the weaving of collective narratives that reflect newly-emerging understanding. There exists through this kind of interaction the potential for transformed understanding and outcomes. It is a stance of learning about the problem together and is built on the premise that you have a high regard for the other's interest and she has a high regard for yours. Such a framework suggests a rather different structure of negotiation than the "dance" of positions.

It also suggests a different process from that which is often described as the essence of joint gain negotiation. The essence of negotiating for joint gains involves a search for those sets of agreements that satisfy interests which the parties are seen to value differently. The tactics entail the logical identification of these differences and the creative exploration of options which will satisfy them. Implied in this model is a view that goals and interests are relatively fixed and potentially known by the parties. The secret to making agreement lies in designing a process where goals and interests can be discovered and incorporated into an agreement. In problem solving through dialogue, the process is less structured and becomes the vehicle through which goals can emerge from mutual inquiry. The stance of those involved is one of flexibility and adaptiveness (distinguished from control) in response to potential uncertainty. This kind of sensing may lead to transformed understandings of problems and possible solutions.

## NOTES AND QUESTIONS

(1)   If Kolb and others are correct in describing communication patterns among men and women as being significantly different, what impact, if any, should that have on the procedural guidelines by which mediators conduct conversation? For example, is the standard guideline of "no interruptions and only one person speak at a time" a rule that systematically favors one gender? Professor Deborah Tannen uses discourse analysis to examine gender differences in her popular books, *You Just Don't Understand* (1990) and *Talking 9 to 5: Women and Men at Work* (1995). For the impact of storytelling on mediation dynamics, see Sara Cobb & Janet Rifkin, *Practice and Paradox: Deconstructing Neutrality in Mediation*, American Bar Foundation, 1991.

(2)   In *Shadow Negotiation* (2004), with Judith Williams, Professor Kolb suggests that persons — women in particular — must pay attention to a variety of considerations that surround a particular negotiation interaction, not just the tactics or behaviors deployed within that negotiation. Linda Babcock & Sara Laschever, in *Women Don't Ask: Negotiation and the Gender Divide* (2003), examine related themes, particularly how women negotiate workplace benefits that impact their career development and earning power.

(3)   The salience of a party's individual characteristics arises in a mediation session most frequently as challenges posed to the mediator. The following hypothetical situations have been used when training new mediators:

## COMMUNITY DISPUTE RESOLUTION TRAINING MANUAL, REVISED EDITION
### Michigan Supreme Court, 1996
### By Joseph B. Stulberg & Lela P. Love

1. You are Caucasian or Hispanic and mediating a case between an African American male and female. Before you can complete your opening, the male gets up to leave, saying, "You can't help us because this involves heterosexual issues." How

would you respond: if you are heterosexual? if you are homosexual? Assuming you give a response to the first challenge that the parties find acceptable for your continued service as a mediator, what if the challenge becomes, "You can't help us because you're white"? What should you do?

2. You are co-mediating a case with a co-mediator of the opposite gender. The parties are 2 men from Latin America, who direct all their comments and eye contact to the male co-mediator. What should you do?

3. You are mediating a case which involves parties from the Caribbean. One of the issues involves an incident in which the respondent stepped over the complainant's baby while the baby was playing in a narrow hallway. The baby was not touched, but the complainant became so angry at the respondent's conduct that she bashed in the hood of the respondent's car with a bat. The complainant keeps saying, "he stepped over my baby's legs." You do not understand what concerns the complainant and she will not explain why stepping over the baby is such a serious matter. What should you do?

4. You are mediating a case in which racial or gender epithets are being flung across the table. A party (a) who is female is called a "w," (b) who is Asian-American is called "slant," or (c) who is African-American is called "n." What should you do?

5. You are mediating a case in which the complainant talks about fires being started in the apartment below her and illnesses and afflictions happening to occupants of the complainant's apartment. You suspect that the complainant may be accusing the respondent of practicing some sort of black magic. What should you do?

## C.  POWER AND THE RESOLUTION OF CONFLICT

People and organizations possess power, and some have more than others. When persons or groups interact with one another, they start from different initial positions with respect to their capacity to influence what the other can or will do.

Power inequalities can arise at an interpersonal level or institutional level. Whereas mediation advocates identify process informality as one of mediation's distinctive strengths, critics assert that mediation's informality permits bargaining behavior to reinforce or exacerbate power disparities. To prevent or minimize such inequities, critics suggest adopting one of two strategies: reshape the mediation process to incorporate rules and procedures that reduce inequalities, or impose obligations on the mediator to ensure fair outcomes.

# FAIRNESS AND FORMALITY: MINIMIZING THE RISK OF PREJUDICE IN ALTERNATIVE DISPUTE RESOLUTION
1985 Wis. L. Rev. 1359, 1360–01, 1367–74, 1387–91, 1402–04[*]
By Richard Delgado, Chris Dunn, Pamela Brown,
Helena Lee & David Hubbert

[W]e [raise] a concern that has seemingly been overlooked in the rush to deformalize — the concern that deformalization may increase the risk of class-based prejudice. ADR has been promoted, in large part, with the rhetoric of egalitarianism. Moreover, it is aimed at serving many groups whose members are particularly vulnerable to prejudice. Thus, if our criticism is correct — if rhetoric is untrue or if ADR injures some of those it is designed to help — society should proceed cautiously in channeling disputes to alternative mechanisms . . . .

## II. PROCEDURAL SAFEGUARDS IN FORMAL ADJUDICATION

Virtually absent from previous discussions of ADR is consideration of the possibility that ADR might foster racial or ethnic bias in dispute resolution. Before turning . . . to that question, [we survey] the main elements of formal adjudication that operate to reduce prejudice at trials . . . .

The American legal system strives to provide litigants a fair trial: to this end, it has developed an array of rules. To secure their intended purpose, however, the rules must be applied even-handedly. That task falls, in the first instance, to the trial judge.

Both internal and external constraints are designed to keep a judge from exhibiting bias or prejudice. Internal constraints stem from a judge's professional position. Many judges are appointed for lengthy terms, in some cases for life, and are to that extent freed from having to be politically responsive in their decisions. Moreover, when a judge is appointed he or she agrees to apply an existing system of rules. The simple act of applying rules reduces bias. Furthermore, the repetitive nature of their caseloads disposes judges to perceive a case not in terms of the parties in dispute, but of the legal and factual issues presented — for example, as a pedestrian-intersection accident case, rather than one of a black victim suing a white driver. The doctrine of *stare decisis* is intended to produce consistent results in similar cases, and anomalous results can be subjected to appellate review.

External constraints also operate to control bias. The Code of Judicial Conduct requires judges to disqualify themselves from cases in which their impartiality is in question; it specifically requires disqualification if a judge feels any animus or prejudice towards a party. If a judge should disqualify himself or herself, but does not do so, recusal statutes enable parties to request a new judge . . . .

In addition to rules that limit prejudice by circumscribing the role of judge or jury, modern procedural systems contain rules that limit prejudice by prescribing the events that occur in the course of litigation. Some of these rules promote fairness and discourage prejudice more or less directly. Others promote fairness

---

indirectly by equalizing the parties' knowledge or by requiring public trials . . . .

One group of rules lessens the scope for bias in adjudication by requiring notice of the suit to all parties and timely filing of pleadings, motions, and responses. Early notice enables defendants to move to eliminate duplicative lawsuits, possibly filed to harass, or suits that have no foundation in fact. The rules requiring pleadings and motions to be filed with the court and opposing counsel enable parties to learn about and respond promptly to significant events in the action . . . .

Other rules specify that pleadings need only give a brief, plain statement indicating the basis of a claim or defense and provide for liberal amendment. These rules encourage resolution of lawsuits on their merits, rather than on the basis of the traditional complex pleading rules that benefited wealthy or experienced parties. The rules require that the complaint state the basis of the claim. That disclosure may warn a party and the court that the claim is groundless and motivated by prejudice, enabling appropriate action to be taken.

Another rule requires counsel to sign all papers filed in a case. The signature certifies that the attorney, after reasonable inquiry, believes that the paper is grounded in fact and either warranted by existing law or by a good faith argument for modification of current law. The attorney's signature also certifies that the paper is not filed for an improper purpose such as bias or prejudice.

. . . If scandalous or indecent matter, a possible indication of prejudice, appears in any paper filed, the rules provide for sanctions against the attorney who filed it, and that portion of the paper may be stricken. These provisions confine pleadings and other papers to material issues and punish those who inject matter for the purpose of embarrassing or harassing the adversary.

The use of pretrial orders also serves to reduce prejudice. A federal rule requires the parties to consider and define the issues for trial. Once agreement is reached, a pretrial order is entered which guides the course of trial. This order may only be modified to prevent manifest injustice . . . . If an extraneous issue, motivated by bias or prejudice, arises later it may be excluded based on the pretrial order.

The requirement that the court state its findings and opinions further limits bias. It puts judges' reasoning into the public record, allows for appellate review, and encourages judges to find the facts in an unbiased manner. Finally, the rules provide for a new trial if it can be shown that the proceedings were affected by prejudice, bias or improper influence of the jury.

Rules of evidence also serve to reduce prejudice. These rules are intended to facilitate introduction of all relevant evidence . . . . Evidence which is not relevant but rather is offered to induce prejudice should be excluded. Even when relevant, evidence may be excluded if its probative value is outweighed by the danger of prejudice, confusion of the issues, or misleading the jury.

. . . [M]odern rules of procedure and evidence contain numerous provisions that are intended to reduce prejudice in the trial system by defining the scope of the action, formalizing the presentation of evidence, and reducing strategic options for litigants and counsel. ADR, to date, has very few such safeguards; indeed, the absence of formal rules of procedure and evidence is often touted as an advantage

— it enables ADR to be speedy, inexpensive, and flexible. ADR decisionmakers or other third parties are rarely professional, and there is rarely a decision-making body similar to a jury. Rules of evidence are absent or open-ended; the inquiry is wide-ranging, probing, "therapeutic." The proceedings are often conducted out of the view of the public; in an intimate setting; and with little, if any, provision for review.

## III. THEORIES OF PREJUDICE AND ADR

The selection of one mode or another or dispute resolution can do little, at least in the short run, to counter prejudice that stems from authoritarian personalities or historical currents. Prejudice that results from social-psychological factors is, however, relatively controllable. Much prejudice is environmental — people express it because the setting encourages or tolerates it. In some settings people feel free to vent hostile or denigrating attitudes towards members of minority groups; in others they do not.

Our review of social-psychological theories of prejudice indicates that prejudiced persons are least likely to act on their beliefs if the immediate environment confronts them with the discrepancy between their professed ideals and their personal hostilities against out-groups. According to social psychologists, once most persons realize that their attitudes and behavior deviate from what is expected, they will change or suppress them.

Given this human tendency to conform, American institutions have structured and defined situations to encourage appropriate behavior. Our judicial system, in particular, has incorporated societal norms of fairness and even-handedness into institutional expectations and rules of procedure at many points. These norms create a "public conscience and a standard for expected behavior that check *overt* signs of prejudice." They do this in a variety of ways. First, the formalities of a court trial — the flag, the black robes, the ritual — remind those present that the occasion calls for the higher, "public" values, rather than the lesser values embraced during moments of informality and intimacy. In a courtroom trial the American Creed, with its emphasis on fairness, equality, and respect for personhood, governs. Equality of status, or something approaching it, is preserved — each party is represented by an attorney and has a prescribed time and manner for speaking, putting on evidence, and questioning the other side. Equally important, formal adjudication avoids the unstructured, intimate interactions that, according to social scientists, foster prejudice. The rules of procedure maintain distance between the parties. Counsel for the parties do not address one another, but present the issue to the trier of fact. The rules preserve the formality of the setting by dictating in detail how this confrontation is to be conducted.

. . . .

## V. PREJUDICE IN ADR — ASSESSING AND BALANCING THE RISKS

. . . [We] showed that the risk of prejudice is greatest when a member of an in-group confronts a member of an out-group; when that confrontation is direct, rather than through intermediaries; when there are few rules to constrain conduct;

when the setting is closed and does not make clear that "public" values are to preponderate; and when the controversy concerns an intimate, personal matter rather than some impersonal question . . .

It follows that ADR is most apt to incorporate prejudice when a person of low status and power confronts a person or institution of high status and power. In such situations, the party of high status is more likely than in other situations to attempt to call up prejudiced responses; at the same time, the individual of low status is less likely to press his or her claim energetically. The dangers increase when the mediator or other third party is a member of the superior group or class . . .

ADR also poses heightened risks of prejudice when the issue to be adjudicated touches a sensitive or intimate area of life, for example, housing or culture-based conduct. Thus, many landlord-tenant, interneighbor, and intra-familial disputes are poor candidates for ADR. When the parties are of unequal status and the question litigated concerns a sensitive, intimate area, the risks of an outcome colored by prejudice are especially great. If for reasons of economy or efficiency ADR must be resorted to in these situations, the likelihood of bias can be reduced by providing rules that clearly specify the scope of the proceedings and forbid irrelevant or intrusive inquiries, by requiring open proceedings, and by providing some form of higher review. The third-party facilitator or decisionmaker should be a professional and be acceptable to both parties. Any party desiring one should be provided with an advocate, ideally an attorney, experienced with representation before the forum in question. To avoid atomization and lost opportunities to aggregate claims and inject public values into dispute resolution, ADR mechanisms should not be used in cases that have a broad societal dimension, but forward them to court for appropriate treatment.

Would measures like these destroy the very advantages of economy, simplicity, speed, and flexibility that make ADR attractive? Would such measures render ADR proceedings as expensive, time-consuming, formalistic, and inflexible as trials? These measures do increase the costs; but, on balance, those costs seem worth incurring. The ideal of equality before the law is too insistent a value to be compromised in the name of more mundane advantages. Continued growth of ADR consistent with goals of basic fairness will require two essential adjustments: (1) It will be necessary to identify those areas and types of ADR in which the dangers of prejudice are greatest and to direct those grievances to formal court adjudication; (2) In those areas in which the risk of prejudice exists, but is not so great as to require an absolute ban, checks and formalities must be built into ADR to ameliorate these risks as much as possible.

# THE MEDIATION ALTERNATIVE:
# PROCESS DANGERS FOR WOMEN
### 100 Yale L.J. 1545, 1547–51, 1555–59, 1563–79, 1581–2, 1610 (1990)[*]
### By Trina Grillo

The western concept of law is based on a patriarchal paradigm characterized by hierarchy, linear reasoning, the resolution of disputes through the application of abstract principles, and the ideal of the reasonable person. Its fundamental aspiration is objectivity, and to that end it separates public from private, form from substance, and process from policy. This objectivist paradigm is problematic in many circumstances, but never more so than in connection with a marital dissolution in which the custody of children is at issue, where the essential question for the court is what is to happen next in the family. The family court system, aspiring to the ideal of objectivity and operating as an adversary system, can be relied on neither to produce just results nor to treat those subject to it respectfully and humanely.

There is little doubt that divorce procedure needs to be reformed, but reformed how? Presumably, any alternative should be at least as just, and at least as humane, as the current system, particularly for those who are least powerful in society. Mediation has been put forward, with much fanfare, as such an alternative. The impetus of the mediation movement has been so strong that in some states couples disputing custody are required by statute or local rule to undergo a mandatory mediation process if they are unable to reach an agreement on their own. Mediation has been embraced for a number of reasons. First, it rejects an objectivist approach to conflict resolution, and promises to consider disputes in terms of relationships and responsibility. Second, the mediation process is, at least in theory, cooperative and voluntary, not coercive. The mediator does not make a decision; rather, each party speaks for himself. Together they reach an agreement that meets the parties' mutual needs. In this manner, the process is said to enable the parties to exercise self-determination and eliminate the hierarchy of dominance that characterizes the judge/litigant and lawyer/client relationships. Third, since in mediation there are no rules of evidence or legalistic notions of relevancy, decisions supposedly may be informed by context rather than by abstract principle. Finally, in theory at least, emotions are recognized and incorporated into the mediation process. This conception of mediation has led some commentators to characterize it as a feminist alternative to the patriarchally inspired adversary system . . . .

[I] conclude that mandatory mediation provides neither a more just nor a more humane alternative to the adversarial system of adjudication of custody, and, therefore, does not fulfill its promises. In particular, quite apart from whether an acceptable result is reached, mandatory mediation can be destructive to many women and some men because it requires them to speak in a setting they have not chosen and often imposes a rigid orthodoxy as to how they should speak, make decisions, and be.

This orthodoxy is imposed through subtle and not-so-subtle messages about appropriate conduct and about what may be said in mediation. It is an orthodoxy that often excludes the possibility of the parties' speaking with their authentic voices.

Moreover, people vary greatly in the extent to which their sense of self is "relational" — that is, defined in terms of connection to others. If two parties are forced to engage with one another, and one has a more relational sense of self than the other, that party may feel compelled to maintain her connection with the other, even to her own detriment. For this reason, the party with the more relational sense of self will be at a disadvantage in a mediated negotiation. Several prominent researchers have suggested that, as a general rule, women have a more relational sense of self than do men, although there is little agreement on what the origin of this difference might be. Thus, rather than being a feminist alternative to the adversary system, mediation has the potential actively to harm women.

Some of the dangers of mandatory mediation apply to voluntary mediation as well. Voluntary mediation should not be abandoned, but should be recognized as a powerful process which should be used carefully and thoughtfully. Entering into such a process with one who has known you intimately and who now seems to threaten your whole life and being has great creative, but also enormous destructive, power. Nonetheless, it should be recognized that when two people themselves decide to mediate and then physically appear at the mediation sessions, that decision and their continued presence serve as a rough indication that it is not too painful or too dangerous for one or both of them to go on . . . .

. . . .

## II. THE BETRAYAL OF MEDIATION'S PROMISES

. . . .

Persons in the midst of a divorce often experience what seems to them a threat to their very survival. Their self-concepts, financial well-being, moral values, confidence in their parenting abilities, and feelings of being worthy of love are all at risk. They are profoundly concerned about whether they are meeting their obligations and continuing to be seen as virtuous persons and respectable members of society. They are especially vulnerable to the responses they receive from any professional with whom they must deal. Against this backdrop, mediation must be seen as a relatively high-risk process. To begin with, for most people it is a new setting. Its norms are generally not understood by the parties in advance, with the result that the parties are extremely sensitive to cues as to how they are supposed to act; they will look to the mediator to provide these cues. Mediators are often quite willing to give such cues, to establish the normative components of the mediation, and to sanction departures from the unwritten rules. The informal sanctions applied by a mediator can be especially powerful, quite apart from whatever actual authority he might have. These sanctions might be as simple as criticizing the client for not putting the children's needs first, or instructing her not to talk about a particular issue. That these informal sanctions might appear trivial does not mean they will not be as influential in changing behavior as sanctions that might on their face appear more severe; "the microsanctions of microlegal systems to which we are actually susceptible may be much more significant determinants of our behavior than conventional macrosanctions which loom portentously, but in all likelihood will never be applied to us."[41]

. . . .

Traditional western adjudication is often criticized for its reliance on abstract principles and rules rather than on subjective, contextualized experience . . . .

Of course, under the common law some context, in the form of the facts of an individual case, is also to be considered. The concern for the particular facts of a dispute has been characterized as a feminine search for context, while the pursuit of applicable legal principles has been viewed as a masculine search for certainty and abstract rules. To the extent that its issues are framed merely as questions of law, simply involving precedents and rights, the result in a case may be insensitive to the particular facts of the dispute. The invocation of *stare decisis* to establish the broad rules of a decision also serves to minimize the importance of the factual context to the resolution of a particular case. Finally, a primary focus on questions of law masks many underlying social and political questions.

Where child custody is being determined, a system that ostensibly brings context — *this* mother, *this* father, *these* children — into the process of dispute resolution, and renders a decision based on the lives of those actually involved in the dispute rather than on the basis of a general rule, has much to offer. There is, however, a cost to this change in emphasis; for although the language of legal rights may divert public consciousness away from the real roots of anger, the assertion of rights may also clarify and elucidate those roots. The process of claiming rights, by itself, can be empowering for people who have not shared societal power. Thus the risk of mediation is that if principles are abandoned, and context is not effectively introduced, we end up with the worst of both worlds . . . .

A series of attempts has been made to make the court system more responsive to the actual situation of persons undergoing a divorce and to their children by deemphasizing claims of right and principle. The first of these attempts consisted of reduced reliance on the notion of fault. Before this change, the principles shaping the legal process of divorce were not difficult to discern. In the absence of flagrant misconduct on the part of the spouse, one was to stay in one's marriage. One was not to engage in adultery. A man was to support his wife and children. A mother was to be the primary caretaker of her children.

. . . .

With the advent of "no-fault" divorce, these rules changed, signaling an as yet undefined departure from the principles upon which they had been based. It is now typical for states to allow divorce on grounds that do not require fault by either spouse. For the most part, one spouse need only show that the marital relationship is irreparable. These changes have increased the individual autonomy of married persons and given husbands and wives freedom to extricate themselves from unhappy relationships. They have reduced the oppressiveness of principles which,

---

[41] Reisman, *Looking, Staring and Glaring: Microlegal Systems and Public Order*, 12 Den. J. Int. L. & Pol'y 165, 177 (1983).

although written into the law, did not fit the manner in which many persons choose to lead their lives.

But there have been other consequences of these changes. For example, results were once much more predictable than they are now, both in terms of the availability of support and the likelihood of the father's being able to obtain custody of the children. This lack of predictability generally harms the party who has the lesser amount of power in the relationship, or who is most risk-averse . . . .

The chief means by which mediators eliminate the discussion of principles and fault is by making certain types of discussion "off-limits" in the mediation. Mediation experts Jay Folberg and Alison Taylor propose the following as one of the "shared propositions" upon which nearly all mediators agree:

> *Proposition 5.* In mediation the past history of the participants is only important in relation to the present or as a basis for predicting future needs, intentions, abilities, and reactions to decisions.[74]

It is typical for mediators to insist that parties waste no time complaining about past conduct of their spouse, eschew blaming each other, and focus only on the future. For example, one of the two essential ground rules mediator Donald Saposnek suggests a mediator give to the parties is the following:

> There is little value in talking about the past, since it only leads to fighting and arguing, as I'm sure you both know . . . . Our focus will be on your children's needs for the future and on how you two can satisfy those needs . . . . [U]nless I specifically request it, we will talk about plans for the future.[75]

Thus, while one of the principal justifications for introducing mediation into the divorce process is that context will be substituted for abstract principles, in fact, by eliminating discussion of the past, context — in the sense of the relationship's history — is removed. The result is that we are left with neither principles nor context as a basis for decision making.

. . . .

Felstiner, Abel and Sarat note that some people are apparently able to tolerate substantial amounts of distress and injustice.[77] This "tolerance," they posit, comes from a failure to perceive that they have been injured. They describe a three-step process by which (1) injurious experiences are perceived (naming), (2) are transformed into grievances (blaming), and, (3) ultimately, become disputes (claiming). "Naming" involves saying to oneself that a particular experience has been injurious. [An] acquaintance who called me could barely go this far. "Blaming" occurs when a person attributes fault to another (rather than to an impersonal force, such as luck or the weather). One cannot arrive at "claiming," that is, the assertion of rights, without passing through "blaming." By making blaming off-limits, the process by

---

[74] J. FOLBERG & A. TAYLOR, MEDIATION 14 (1984).

[75] D. SAPOSNEK, MEDIATING CHILD CUSTODY DISPUTES 70 (1983).

[77] *See* Felstiner, Abel & Sarat, *The Emergence and Transformation of Disputes: Naming, Blaming, Claiming . . .* , 15 L. & SOC'Y REV. 631, 633 (1980–81).

which a dispute is fully developed — and rights are asserted — cannot be completed. Short-circuiting the blaming process may fall most heavily on those who are already at a disadvantage in society. Whether people "perceive an experience as an injury, blame someone else, claim redress, or get their claims accepted . . . [is a function of] their *social position* as well as their individual characteristics."[81]

The cultural commitment to access to justice has focused on the last stage of disputing — claiming. The more critical place at which inequality is manifested, however, is before experiences are transformed into disputes, that is, at the naming and blaming stages. One adverse consequence of deemphasizing discussion of principle and fault is that some persons may be discouraged from asserting their rights when they have been injured. Even more troubling, some persons may cease to perceive injuries when they have been injured, or will perceive injuries but those injuries will remain inarticulable, because the language to name them will not be easily available. My acquaintance whose husband had an affair and left her did not trust her sense that she had been injured, treated in a way that human beings ought not to deal with each other. She did not have the support of a clear set of legal principles to help her define her injury; rather, she had been exposed to a discourse in which faultfinding was impermissible, so that she ended up unable to hold her husband responsible for his actions, and instead felt compelled to share his fault. To the extent that there is something to be gained by the assertion of rights, especially for women and minorities, this is unacceptable.

. . . .

Rights assertion cannot take place in a context in which discussion of fault and the past are not permitted, for recognition and assertion of rights are ordinarily based on some perceived past grievance, as well as on some notion of right and wrong. From the point of view of the courts, minimizing conflict is always a good thing: less litigation means less expenditure of court time and resources. From the point of view of the individual, however, conflict sometimes must occur. Conflict may mean that the individual has realized he has been injured, and that he is appropriately resisting the continuation of that injury. The perception of injury arises from a sense of entitlement, which in turn is "a function of the prevailing ideology, of which law is simply a component."[95] If mediation creates a sense of disentitlement, it will interfere with the perception and redress of injuries in cases where they have in fact occurred . . . .

Context is also destroyed by a commitment to formal equality, that is, to the notion that members of mediating couples are, to the extent possible, to be treated exactly alike, without regard for general social patterns and with limited attention to even the history of the particular couples. Thus, it becomes close to irrelevant in determining custody that the mother may have been home doing virtually all the caretaking of the children for years; she is to move into the labor market as quickly as possible. It is assumed that the father is equally competent to care for the children. In fact, it frequently is said that one cannot assume that a father will not

---

[81] Felstiner, Abel & Sarat, *supra* note 77, at 636.

[95] Felstiner, Abel & Sarat, *supra* note 77, at 643.

be as competent a caretaker as the mother just because he has not shown any interest previously:

Many women have told me, "He never did anything with the children. If he is given even part-time responsibility for them, he'll ignore them, he won't know what to do."

Research has shown, however, that little correlation exists between men's involvement with the children before and after divorce . . . . When they gain independent responsibility for the children, many men who were relatively uninvolved during the marriage become loving and responsive parents after divorce.[98]

In mediation, insistence on this sort of formal equality results in a dismissal of the legitimate concerns of the parent who is, or considers herself to be, the more responsible parent. Such concerns are often minimized by characterizing them as evidence of some pathology on the part of the parent holding them. The insistence of a mother that a young child not be permitted to stay overnight with an alcoholic father who smokes in bed might be characterized as the mother needing to stay in control. Or the mediator might suggest that it is not legitimate for one party to assume that the other party will renege on her obligations, simply because she has done so in the past . . . . The point is not that mothers never inappropriately desire to stay in control, or that people who have not fulfilled their obligations once will continue to fail to do so, but rather that by defining the process as one in which both parties are situated equally, deep, heartfelt, and often accurate concerns either are not permitted to be expressed or are discounted.

Equating fairness in mediation with formal equality results in, at most, a crabbed and distorted fairness on a microlevel; it considers only the mediation context itself. There is no room in such an approach for a discussion of the fairness of institutionalized societal inequality. For example, women do not have the earning power that men have, and therefore are not in an economically equal position in the world. All too often mediators stress the need for women to become economically independent without taking into account the very real dollar differences between the male and female experience in the labor market. While gaining independence might appear to be desirable, most jobs available for women, especially those who have been out of the labor market, are low-paying, repetitious, and demeaning. Studies show that women in such dead-end jobs do not experience the glories of independence, but rather show increased depression . . . .

The notion of equality, used so effectively to remove control of children from women by treating men as equally entitled to custody regardless of their prior childcare responsibilities, is not nearly so effective when it comes to requiring men to assume responsibility for their children should they choose not to. One rarely hears of joint custody's being used to mandate that a father participate in the raising of his child although many women might desire that help. But fathers who wish to participate even marginally in childrearing are given full rights, and even special privileges to enable them to do so. These privileges are paid for by the mother in terms of inconvenience and instability in her own life. Fathers who do not want to be concerned with raising their children need only pay support, and many

---

[98] R. ADLER, SHARING THE CHILDREN 33 (1988).

do not even do that. Despite the presumption in favor of joint custody, it is assumed, by and large, that the mother will be available to care physically and emotionally for the children for as much or as little time as she is granted.

Western wage labor is based on the availability of an "ideal" worker with no childcare responsibilities. Joan Williams has written that in this system men are raised to believe they have the right and responsibility to perform as ideal workers. Women are raised to believe that they should be able to spend some time with their small children and, upon return to outside employment, must shape their work around the reality that they have continuing childcare responsibilities.

The laws governing custody are now, in theory, gender neutral. Mediators, however, are as likely as others in society to assume that women's work commitments are secondary to those of men, and to give more credence to the work obligations and ambitions of fathers. Women may be encouraged in mediation not to think of themselves as ideal workers so that they will be able to take on primary responsibility for the children.

The result of assuming that one parent will make herself available in this way is that disproportionately more attention is paid to ensuring the access of the parent without physical custody (usually the father) to his children than to meeting the needs of the parent who, in all likelihood, will bear the primary responsibility for these children.

Custody decrees frequently specify joint legal or physical custody, or both, when in fact the children are with one parent — generally the mother — as much or more than children who are living under a sole custody arrangement. The result of such a discrepancy under a joint custody arrangement is that the caretaking parent may be subject to the control of the noncaretaking parent without being relieved of any sizable amount of day-to-day responsibility for the children . . . .

        . . . .

Another criticism of the traditional adversary method of dispute resolution is that it does not provide a role for emotion. Decisions by adversarial parties are posited as rational, devoid of emotion, self-interested, and instrumental (result-oriented). Some proponents of mediation and other methods of alternative dispute resolution believe these characteristics should be retained in mediation to the extent they permit parties to serve their self-interests efficiently. Others have argued that mediation and other forms of alternative dispute resolution provide an opportunity to bring intuition and emotion into the legal process.[117] This latter group of proponents points out that family conflicts in particular often involve a combination of emotional and legal complaints, so that the "real" issues are often obscured in the adversarial setting. Thus, "there may be a great need for an open-ended, unstructured process that permits the disputants to air their true sentiments."

Although mediation is claimed to be a setting in which feelings can be expressed, certain sentiments are often simply not welcome. In particular, expressions of anger

---

[117] *See, e.g.*, S. GOLDBERG, E. GREEN & F. SANDER, DISPUTE RESOLUTION 313 (1985) ("Family disputes are also well suited to alternative forums because the conflicts often involve a complex interplay of emotional and legal complaints.").

are frequently overtly discouraged. This discouragement of anger sends a message that anger is unacceptable, terrifying and dangerous. For a person who has only recently found her anger, this can be a perilous message indeed. This suppression of anger poses a stark contrast to the image of mediation as a process which allows participants to express their emotions.

Women undergoing a divorce, especially ones from non-dominant cultural groups, are particularly likely to be harmed by having their anger actively discouraged during the dissolution process. Women have been socialized not to express anger, and have often had their anger labeled "bad." A woman in the throes of divorce may for the first time in her life have found a voice for her anger. As her early, undifferentiated, and sometimes inchoate expressions of anger emerge, the anger may seem as overwhelming to her as to persons outside of it. And yet this anger may turn out to be the source of her energy, strength, and growth in the months and years ahead. An injunction from a person in power to suppress that anger because it is not sufficiently modulated may amount to nothing less that an act of violence . . . .

People are necessarily angry at divorce, in two senses. First of all, anger is inevitable in ending a marriage; almost everyone who obtains a divorce becomes angry sooner or later. This anger may have many different causes: it may be a result of anticipated losses, wrongful treatment, or the myriad compromises of self that may have been made along the way to the marriage's end. Second, some anger is necessary for the disengagement which is essential to the completion of the divorce. It is thus critical that any system of marital dissolution take anger into consideration and establish a means by which it is permitted to enter into the divorce process . . . .

Some mediation literature suggests that mediators should proceed by discouraging the expression of anger. This literature evinces a profound lack of respect for the anger that divorcing spouses feel. For example, Donald Saposnek suggests that "[i]n many ways, the mediator must act as a parent figure to the parents, since their struggles are often not unlike those of siblings squabbling over joint possessions."[129] Saposnek's depiction of divorcing parents suggests that their struggles are devoid of content. He characterizes their anger and conflict as "squabbling" rather than as arising from substantively important conflicts or as a necessary and important step in the divorce process.

Saposnek suggests that the mediator ask questions of the parties that will imply to them that elaboration of their feelings during conflicts with each other is "irrelevant and counterproductive" and that the mediator is "interested in . . . ideas for solutions to these problems." Saposnek thus views the expression of feelings as antithetical to problem-solving; a mediator must choose one or the other . . . .

Even when mediation literature does approve of bringing anger into the process, it often recommends doing so in a way that subtly undercuts the legitimacy of the anger. Mediators are encouraged, where necessary, to permit parties to "vent" their anger, after which the parties can move on to discuss settlement. This view does not

---

[129] D. Saposnek, Mediating Child Custody Ddisputes 176 (1983).

take anger seriously enough. Because it treats expressed anger as having no long-range impact on the party who is exposed to it, it is not necessarily seen as objectionable to require one party to be present and endure the other party's "venting" — even where the party enduring the venting has been the subject of abuse in the marriage. The effects of exposure to anger in such a case can be devastating. If the privilege of expressing anger has not been distributed equally in the relationship prior to mediation, then the mediator should not grant that privilege equally during the mediation.

Second, and equally critically, the view of anger as something to be "vented" does not take anger seriously as a path to clarity and strength. Anger that is merely vented has lost its potential to teach, heal, and energize; it is ineffective anger, anger that "maintains rather than challenges" the status quo.

Not all writers suggest that anger be suppressed or vented in the service of eventual suppression. Some mediators, however, especially those in mandatory settings, do advocate that parties suppress their anger. The mediator's personal antagonism toward anger and conflict may lead her to urge clients to keep their angry feelings to themselves.

At the same time, there are other forces which may intensify this dynamic of suppression. Mediators working under time pressures recognize that it takes time to express anger, and its full expression might, indeed, jeopardize a quick settlement. More significantly, there are substantial societal taboos against the expression of anger by women, taboos which have particular force when the disputant is a woman of color. For a woman who has just found her anger, anger which has enabled her to free herself from an oppressive relationship and involve herself and her family in a divorce proceeding, the suppression of the very force that has driven her forward is a devastating message.

. . . .

## CONCLUSION

Although mediation can be useful and empowering, it presents some serious process dangers that need to be addressed, rather than ignored. When mediation is imposed rather than voluntarily engaged in, its virtues are lost. More than lost: mediation becomes a wolf in sheep's clothing. It relies on force and disregards the context of the dispute, while masquerading as a gentler, more empowering alternative to adversarial litigation. Sadly, when mediation is mandatory it becomes like the patriarchal paradigm of law it is supposed to supplant. Seen in this light, mandatory mediation is especially harmful: its messages disproportionately affect those who are already subordinated in our society, those to whom society has already given the message, in far too many ways, that they are not leading proper lives.

Of course, subordinated people can go to court and lose; in fact, they usually do. But if mediation is to be introduced into the court system, it should provide a better alternative. It is not enough to say that the adversary system is so flawed that even a misguided, intrusive, and disempowering system of mediation should be embraced. If mediation as currently instituted constitutes a fundamentally flawed process in the way I have described, it is more, not less, disempowering than the adversary system — for it is then a process in which people are told they are being empowered, but in fact are being forced to acquiesce in their own oppression.

## NOTES AND QUESTIONS

(1) Professor Delgado concludes that the risk of mediated outcomes being influenced by prejudice is especially great in many landlord-tenant, inter-neighbor, and intra-familial disputes. Yet, since mediation's foundational years, these types of cases have constituted the typical caseload in many mediation programs, and those program advocates believe mediation is particularly well suited to handle those matters. Is Delgado's concern misplaced? Are mediation advocates ignoring a fundamental problem? Another concern that Delgado's thesis references is whether persons participating in mediation are being accorded "second class" justice; the literature refers to this topic as "access to justice." For a thoughtful analysis of these issues as they relate to mediation's use, see Craig A. McEwen & Laura Williams, *Legal Policy and Access to Justice Through Courts and Mediation*, 13 Ohio St. J. on Disp. Resol. 865 (1998).

(2) If Delgado's concerns are well placed, what are their implications for the structure and practice of mediation? If one introduces into the mediation process the types of formalities that Delgado proposes, would that advance or undermine mediation's core values? What capacities or protections, if any, does the mediation process afford to minimize the adverse impact of prejudice influencing the dialogue and outcome? These themes are referenced in the excerpts on justice in mediation, appearing in Section D, below.

(3) The late Trina Grillo was herself an active mediator. The concerns she discusses arise, she believed, with particular urgency when parties are mandated to use mediation. Do you agree that the impact of mediation on women would be substantially different depending on whether the process was mandatory or voluntary? Others believe that the force of Grillo's critique stems not from its conceptual account but rather from identifying, and properly criticizing, multiple examples of poor mediating. For a thoughtful response to Grillo's article, see Joshua D. Rosenberg, *In Defense of Mediation*, 33 Ariz. L. Rev. 467 (1991).

(4) Concerns about power imbalance are especially sharp when mediation is used in family cases in which there is a history of spousal or child abuse. *See, e.g.,* Andree G. Gagnon, *Ending Mandatory Divorce Mediation for Battered Women*, 15 Harv. Women's L.J. 272 (1992). For a list and discussion of the criticisms leveled at mediation when used in this context, see Kathleen O'Connell Corcoran & James C. Melamed, *From Coercion to Empowerment: Spousal Abuse and Mediation*, 7 Mediation Q. 303 (1990). There are many persons who support using mediation in this context, but with appropriate safeguards. See, for example, Rene Rimelspach, *Mediating Family Disputes in a World with Domestic Violence: How to Devise a Safe and Effective Court-Connected Mediation Program*, 17 Ohio St. J. of Disp. Resol. 95 (2001). For a thoughtful review of the multiple elements relevant to mediating these cases in a manner consistent with fairness concerns, see Susan Landrum, *The On-Going Debate About Mediation in the Context of Domestic*

*Violence: A Call for Empirical Studies of Mediation's Effectiveness*, 12 Cardozo J. Conflict Resol. 425 (2011).

(5)   Other authors have conducted studies to determine whether females who are parties to a divorce proceeding do worse in mediation than in adjudication. Their results suggest that outcomes generated in a mediation session are perceived by both female and male participants to be as equitable and fair as those outcomes developed through the adversarial process. *See* Joan B. Kelly, *Mediated and Adversarial Divorce: Respondents' Perception of Their Processes and Outcomes*, 24 Mediation Q. 71, 71–88 (1989); and Jessica Pearson, *The Equity of Mediated Divorce Agreements*, 9 Mediation Q. 179 (1991). The Herman et al. study, excerpted below, reports mixed results as to gender and ethnicity, though in a different substantive setting.

# AN EMPIRICAL STUDY OF THE EFFECTS OF RACE AND GENDER ON SMALL CLAIMS ADJUDICATION AND MEDIATION
Institute of Public Law, University of New Mexico,
xiii–xxxii (Jan. 1993)*
By Michelle Hermann, Gary LaFree, Christine Rack &
Mary Beth West

## I. INTRODUCTION

A basic tenet of conflict theory is that socio-cultural factors influence decision-making processes. Applying this theory to the judicial system, scholars have asked whether informal processes, such as alternative dispute resolution, are more susceptible than adjudication to bias. In theoretical work and studies involving controlled experimental conditions, several authors have studied the differences between courts and alternative dispute resolution mechanisms in this context. The basic conclusions from these studies have been that the adversarial procedure of adjudication counteracts decision-maker bias, and that the risks of prejudice are greatest in informal settings involving direct confrontation where few rules exist to constrain conduct.

In addition, studies during the past 10 to 15 years have described the composition of parties, cases and outcomes in small claims courts and have tested the hypotheses that mediation is superior to adjudication in generating positive attitudes among litigants of small claims, that mediation is superior in altering post-dispute behavior (i.e., in achieving compliance), and that the two types of dispute resolution lead to significantly different case outcomes.

We proposed empirically to test the conclusions of some of these studies in actual mediations and adjudications in the Bernalillo County Metropolitan Court in Albuquerque, New Mexico.[1] Our research hypotheses were as follows:

---

* Copyright © 1993. Reprinted with permission.

[1] [Ed. Note: The final study sample consisted of 603 cases, 323 of which were adjudicated and 280 mediated.]

That women and minorities achieve less in both mediated and adjudicated small claims settlements than males and nonminorities achieve in similar cases.

That the disparity between outcomes achieved by women and minorities and the outcomes achieved by males and nonminorities is greater in mediated small claims settlements than in adjudicated decisions.

That disputes involving inherent power imbalances, such as landlord-tenant or creditor-lender disputes, are more subject to the effects of bias in small claims mediation.

That the participation of women or minority mediators or adjudicators in small claims disputes involving minority disputants reduces the effects of bias.

. . .

## IV. RESULTS

### 1. Ethnicity

. . . [W]e sought to test the hypothesis that both minority and female claimants would do more poorly in the study cases. Moreover, because mediation is a less formal, less visible, and less controlled forum than adjudication, we hypothesized that effects of ethnicity and gender would be greater for mediated than adjudicated cases. Looking at objective monetary outcomes, our results confirmed our hypothesis for ethnicity, but not for gender. Measures of subjective satisfaction, however, were more complex and showed different patterns.

As measured by the objective Vidmar outcome ratio, minority claimants consistently received less money than nonminorities in our study cases, while minority respondents consistently paid more. These effects were stronger for mediated than adjudicated cases. When case characteristics were added to the model, claimant and respondent ethnicity was no longer statistically significant in the adjudicated cases. It is notable, however, that the most influential case character factors (being represented by a lawyer and being involved in a collection case) were both ethnically and sociologically related. For example, monetary outcomes were higher for collection cases involving individual respondents in which the claimant was either a lawyer or was represented by a lawyer. Whites were more likely to be claimants in collection cases, as well as to be lawyers or be represented by lawyers. Thus, monetary outcomes in adjudicated cases were due primarily to case characteristics and, secondarily, to the ethnicity of participants, with strong interrelationships between the two. In contrast, ethnicity remained significantly more important for predicting outcomes of mediated cases, even with the addition of the case characteristic variables. Case characteristics (such as whether the case was a collection case, whether a counterclaim was involved, the size of the dispute, whether claimants and respondents were individuals or businesses and whether lawyers were involved) had relatively little effect on outcomes in mediation. The one exception to these results occurred when the mediated agreement created a payment plan. Payment plans did help to explain the differences between white and minority outcomes. White claimants were more likely to enter into payment plans than minority claimants and minority respondents were more likely to enter into payment plans than white respondents. Because payment plans typically exchange a long time to pay smaller incremental amounts for a larger total amount paid, they become a significant factor in increasing the amounts paid by minority respondents. The only additional characteristic of claimants and respondents which had a significant effect on monetary outcomes in either mediation or adjudication was education. Higher education worked to the disadvantage of the respondent in adjudicated cases and to the advantage of the claimant in mediated cases.

Having found that minority claimants received less and minority respondents paid more in mediation cases, we sought to explore whether these effects might be counteracted by the ethnicity of the mediators. Our results were quite startling, showing that having two minority mediators eliminated the negative impact on the size of monetary outcomes for minority claimants in mediation. The combination of one minority mediator and one white mediator, however, did not produce a similar result.

Our analysis of subjective outcome and procedural satisfaction by ethnicity produced interesting contrasts. In general, claimants were no more or less satisfied in mediation than in adjudication with regard to procedure, outcome or long-term outcome. Compared to claimants in adjudication, however, mediation claimants reported the outcome as being fairer and less biased. In contrast, respondents in mediation were far more satisfied with the procedure, outcome and long-term outcome, as well as with fairness. The tendency for claimant and respondent satisfaction to be inversely related in adjudication was not found in mediation.

Despite their tendency to achieve lower monetary awards as claimants and to pay more as respondents in mediation, minority claimants taken together were more likely than nonminority claimants to express satisfaction with mediation. Minority claimants and respondents were consistently more positive about mediation than they were about adjudication on all satisfaction and fairness measures. They also reported process satisfaction significantly more often than nonminorities in mediation.

Minority claimants were more likely to be satisfied with the procedure when the two mediators were also minorities.[2] In fact, white as well as minority claimants were more likely to report procedural satisfaction when the mediation involved a minority respondent and two minority mediators . . . .

## 2. Gender

The effects found for minority participants were generally not replicated when the data were analyzed for gender. Gender of claimant and respondent had no direct effect on monetary outcomes for either adjudicated or mediated cases. The only statistically reliable tendency we found was for female respondents to pay lower monetary outcomes in mediation than adjudication.

Looking at measures of satisfaction, we found that as claimants and respondents,

---

[2] [Ed. Note: The mediation format used in the New Mexico program assigned two persons to act as co-mediators for each case.]

compared to all other ethnic/gender groups, white women report relatively greater satisfaction with adjudicated outcomes. While white female respondents achieved significantly better (i.e., lower) monetary outcomes than the other three groups in mediation, they also reported the lowest rates of satisfaction. Furthermore, compared to other mediation respondents, white women were less likely to see the mediation process as fair and unbiased. Minority women, on the other hand, reported higher satisfaction with mediation, despite their tendency to receive less as claimants and to pay more as respondents.

Female mediators had a significantly greater likelihood of having their disputants reach agreement in mediation. Mediations with two male mediators had the lowest agreement rate. Mediations with mixed gender pairs fell in the middle. Testing for disputant/mediator gender interactions, we found that female claimants were less likely to express procedural satisfaction and reported a lack of fairness more often in cases where the two mediators were women. Conversely, respondents in those cases with a female claimant and two female mediators were somewhat more likely to report satisfaction with the outcome.

Both claimant and respondent groups in mediation were more likely to respond favorably to the procedure with a mixed gender pair of mediators.

### 3. Long-term Satisfaction and Compliance

The higher frequency of respondent satisfaction in mediation remained unchanged over time. Approximately six months after initial interviews, mediation respondents still reported higher levels of satisfaction than adjudication respondents . . .

Although we found few effects by ethnicity or gender, minority claimants tended to report higher long-term satisfaction levels in mediation than nonminority claimants. Women respondents in general, and minority women in particular, were more likely to comply with mediated agreements and non-monetary obligations. In contrast, white men were most likely to comply with court rulings.

### V. DISCUSSION

It is apparent that among the rich variety of data we gathered about mediation and adjudication of small claims cases in Albuquerque, New Mexico, two findings are especially provocative. One is the finding that white women tend to do as well or better than others in mediation, yet are less satisfied with the outcome. The other is the finding that ethnic minorities achieve relatively poorer monetary outcomes than do whites, especially in mediation, yet are more satisfied with the outcome.

The findings for women are interesting from at least two perspectives. First, many scholars have argued that mediation is unfair to women because they are likely to achieve poorer outcomes in the process. Our study shows this fear to be unfounded, at least in the types of small claims dispute that we have examined here . . . .

Second, the gender findings are interesting because they show that white women are relatively less satisfied with the outcome of mediation and perceive it to be less fair, even though they achieve objectively more positive results. An examination of the open-ended responses of women in mediation shows a significant number who expressed anger. A number of white women also reported that they thought that the mediation process was unfair or biased. Surprisingly, unfairness was reported by female claimants and respondents most frequently when there were two female mediators . . . .

The data involving minorities raise substantial concerns about the fairness of the mediation process. This study demonstrates that the fears of scholars who have postulated that the invisible, informal, nonreviewable forum of mediation produces worse results for minority disputants may be well founded. What is particularly telling is that the presence of two minority mediators largely erases the disadvantage, so that the outcomes of minority disputants in mediation becomes nearly equal to those achieved by white disputants.

What is far less clear about these unequal results is what causes them and what their implications are for mediation.

## NOTES AND QUESTIONS

(1)   One research challenge in this area is definitional: what is meant by a "successful" outcome in mediation and can each element be quantitatively measured? In the Herman study, outcome comparisons relate to elements of legally defined issues and remedies. But if a Respondent apologized to a Claimant for improper or insensitive behavior and that apology led the Claimant to agree to a lower financial settlement, does that mean that the Claimant did "worse" than someone who received more money but no apology? How would an evaluator capture that sense of "fairness" that was so important to a party?

(2)   Does the Herman finding regarding white women reporting greater satisfaction with adjudicated outcomes than mediated outcomes constitute contrary evidence to Kolb's gender-orientation claim that a female prefers a relational ethic while a male prefers a rule-governed system?

(3)   Does the Herman finding regarding the favorable impact of a minority mediator team on mediated outcomes constitute evidence to support Delgado's claim that parties alter their behavior to conform to what is expected of them in the social context? If so, does that suggest, contrary to Delgado's conclusion, that nonminority claimants might behave constructively when participating in a mediation with parties of differing ethnicities, races, or religions?

(4)   Some authors argue that it is the mediator's responsibility to address and rectify power imbalances. *See, e.g.,* Jacqueline M. Nolan-Haley, *Informed Cosent in Mediation: A Guiding Principle for Truly Educated Decision Making,* 74 Notre Dame L. Rev. 775 (1999). One California statute converts this sentiment into a statutory duty for a mediator: "Mediation of cases involving custody and visitation concerning children shall be governed by uniform standards of practice adopted by the Judicial Council. The standards of practice shall include, but not be limited to, all of the following . . . *the conducting of negotiations in such a way as to equalize power relationships between the parties."* Cal. Fam. Code § 3162(b)(3) (Supp. 1998) (emphasis added). Scott Hughes, in his article entitled *Elizabeth's Story,* 8 Geo. J.

Legal Ethics 553 (1995), combines a superb narrative of his client's divorce mediation experience with a penetrating analysis of the dangers of using mediation in a matrimonial dissolution setting when there are both explicit and subtle power disparities among the divorcing partners.

(5)   In the Test Design Project, referenced in Chapter 3, *supra*, experienced mediators, arbitrators, and other third-party neutrals created a list of basic competencies and skills required of a mediator. Would a person so qualified reduce the critic's fear concerning the adverse impact of the mediation process or persons who have been denied equal treatment because of race, ethnicity, gender, or historical origin, or is the source of their concern exclusively structural?

(6)   As noted in Section B, *supra*, Professor Izumi examines the phenomenon of prejudice and its impact on mediator conduct from the perspective of social science research that examines the concept of "implicit bias." C. Izumi, *Implicit Bias and the Illusion of Mediator Neutrality*, 34 Wash. U. J.L. & Pol'y 71 (2010). Professor Izumi reports that this research suggests "actors do not always have conscious, intentional control over the processes of social perception, impression formation, and judgment that motivate their actions." Izumi's conclusion is not that one's implicit biases make it impossible for there to be a meaningful concept of mediator neutrality. Instead, she invites us to consider neutrality as consisting of an external dimension and an internal dimension, and that for each dimension, there are precise practices a mediator can adopt to minimize the dissociation between her explicit and implicit attitudes. Izumi elaborates as follows:

> External neutrality consists of conduct and statements to show freedom from bias or favoritism in the way mediation is conducted. Internal neutrality is the state of being aware of the operation of biases toward the disputants and working to minimize it . . . .
>
> . . . [M]ediators can attend to external neutrality concerns by: being sensitive to language usage; valuing individual party narratives; ensuring that disputants 'tell their stories' in their own words and style; self-policing for essentialist assumptions; monitoring for biased party interventions . . . ; adopting a reflexive approach that is deliberatively self-conscious; using co-mediator teams that leverage differences and similarities; and employing instructional methods that require mediators to grapple with racial and other difficult issues [that] further reduce the potential for mediator partiality and bias . . . .
>
> . . . [M]ediators have the ability to enhance internal neutrality by adopting explicit plans to reduce the application of stereotypes activated through encounters with parties and by replacing biased thoughts and reactions with non-prejudiced ones. Mediators must be aware of and acknowledge unconscious biases in order to garner the motivation to self-correct . . . Practices that sharpen a mediator's awareness, listening skills, and concentration . . . may help mediators attain freedom from bias and prejudice.

Students can complete a demonstration test at https://implicit.harvard.edu/implicit/demo/

# D.  JUSTICE: MEDIATION AND THE RULE OF LAW

Mediation advocates thoughtfully argue that mediation's primary strength is that it empowers participants to decide for themselves what priority to accord to conflicting legal, business, prudential, and personal principles. For many individuals, knowing the answer to the question: "what am I legally entitled or obligated to do?" does not conclusively answer the question: "what should I do to resolve this dispute?" The dialogue over what role public rules play in the dispute resolution process raises fundamental jurisprudential and policy questions.

To justify the use of mediation philosophically requires an account of how the rule of law is compatible with supporting mediation's commitment to promoting participant decision-making. Legal Positivists, most eloquently through the writings of H.L.A. Hart, offer a simple, compelling distinction: what the law is can differ from what the law ought to be. So, if mediation participants develop settlement terms that constitute, from their perspective, their shared vision of what ought to be, should their resolution be supported if it conflicts with what the law requires? Does it matter if the disputants have equal power and resources? Probing such questions requires one to examine complex theories of legal obligation, legal legitimacy, and the concept of change in a democratic society.

Although investigating these more abstract philosophical concepts significantly enriches policy analysis, important practical questions about mediation's use, regrettably, often cannot await their answers. So persons examine these matters by analyzing concrete practices. Professor Fiss, in his celebrated article, maintains that privatizing justice by using a structured, facilitated negotiated settlement process — i.e., mediation — erodes important public values; he argues that having parties approve settlement terms should not be the decisive standard for determining if the controversy has been resolved. Professor Menkel-Meadow takes issue with Fiss by highlighting competing considerations between those who advocate settlement and those supporting adjudication. Embedded in each of their accounts are assumptions about the relationship, if any, between the mediation process and considerations of justice. In the Hyman/Love excerpt, the authors delineate the varying dimensions that justice principles address. The Alfini/Waldman exchange displays how one uses principles of procedural justice to assess mediator orientation and conduct. And the final excerpt by Hyman thoughtfully explores whether and how a mediator, at the most practical of levels, should trigger conversation about justice among mediation participants to facilitate problem-solving.

## AGAINST SETTLEMENT
### 93 Yale L.J. 1073, 1075–80, 1082–83, 1085–87 (1984)[*]
### By Owen Fiss

[I]n my view . . . the case for settlement rests on questionable premises. I do not believe that settlement as a generic practice is preferable to judgment. [I]t should be treated instead as a highly problematic technique for streamlining dockets. Settlement is for me the civil analogue of plea bargaining: Consent is often coerced; the bargain may be struck by someone without authority; the absence of a trial and judgment renders subsequent judicial involvement troublesome; and although dockets are trimmed, justice may not be done.

## THE IMBALANCE OF POWER.

. . . [S]ettlement is . . . a function of the resources available to each party to finance the litigation, and those resources are frequently distributed unequally . . .

The disparities in resources between the parties can influence the settlement in three ways. First, the poorer party may be less able to amass and analyze the information needed to predict the outcome of the litigation, and thus be disadvantaged in the bargaining process. Second, he may need the damages he seeks immediately and thus be induced to settle as a way of accelerating payment, even though he realizes he would get less now than he might if he awaited judgment. All plaintiffs want their damages immediately, but an indigent plaintiff may be exploited by a rich defendant because his need is so great that the defendant can force him to accept a sum that is less than the ordinary present value of the judgment. Third, the poorer party might be forced to settle because he does not have the resources to finance the litigation, to cover either his own projected expenses, such as his lawyer's time, or the expenses his opponent can impose through the manipulation of procedural mechanisms such as discovery. It might seem that settlement benefits the plaintiff by allowing him to avoid the costs of litigation, but this is not so. The defendant can anticipate the plaintiff's costs if the case were to be tried fully and decrease his offer by that amount. The indigent plaintiff is a victim of the costs of litigation even if he settles.

. . . [O]f course, imbalances of power can distort judgment as well: Resources influence the quality of presentation, which in turn has an important bearing on who wins and the terms of victory. We count, however, on the guiding presence of the judge, who can employ a number of measures to lessen the impact of distributional inequalities. He can, for example, supplement the parties' presentations by asking questions, calling his own witnesses, and inviting other persons and institutions to participate as amici. These measures are likely to make only a small contribution toward moderating the influence of distributional inequalities, but should not be ignored for that reason. Not even these small steps are possible with settlement. There is, moreover, a critical difference between a process like settlement, which is based on bargaining and accepts inequalities of wealth as an integral and legitimate component of the process, and a process like judgment, which knowingly struggles against those inequalities. Judgment aspires to an autonomy from distributional inequalities, and it gathers much of its appeal from this aspiration.

## THE ABSENCE OF AUTHORITATIVE CONSENT

The argument for settlement presupposes that the contestants are individuals. These individuals speak for themselves and should be bound by the rules they generate. In many situations, however, individuals are ensnared in contractual relationships that impair their autonomy. Lawyers or insurance companies might, for example, agree to settlements that are in their interests but are not in the best interests of their clients, and to which their clients would not agree if the choice were still theirs. But a deeper and more intractable problem arises from the fact that many parties are not individuals but rather organizations or groups. We do not know who is entitled to speak for these entities and to give the consent upon which so much of the appeal of settlement depends.

Some organizations, such as corporations or unions, have formal procedures for identifying the persons who are authorized to speak for them. But these procedures are imperfect. They are designed to facilitate transactions between the organization and outsiders, rather than to insure that the members of the organization in fact agree with a particular decision. Nor do they eliminate conflicts of interests. The chief executive officer of a corporation may settle a suit to prevent embarrassing disclosures about his managerial policies, but such disclosures might well be in the interest of the shareholders. The president of a union may agree to a settlement as a way of preserving his power within the organization; for that very reason, he may not risk the dangers entailed in consulting the rank and file or in subjecting the settlement to ratification by the membership.

[T]hese problems become even more pronounced when we turn from organizations and consider the fact that much contemporary litigation involves even more nebulous social entities, namely, groups. Some of these groups, such as ethnic or racial minorities, inmates of prisons, or residents of institutions for mentally retarded people, may have an identity or existence that transcends the lawsuit, but they do not have any formal organizational structure and therefore lack any procedures for generating authoritative consent . . .

Going to judgment does not altogether eliminate the risk of unauthorized action, any more than it eliminates the distortions arising from disparities in resources. The case presented by the representative of a group or an organization admittedly will influence the outcome of the suit, and that outcome will bind those who might also be bound by a settlement. On the other hand, judgment does not ask as much from the so-called representatives. There is a conceptual and normative distance between what the representatives do and say and what the court eventually decides, because the judge tests those statements and actions against independent procedural and substantive standards. The authority of judgment arises from the law, not from the statements or actions of the putative representatives, and thus we allow judgment to bind persons not directly involved in the litigation even when we are reluctant to have settlement do so.

## THE LACK OF FOUNDATION FOR CONTINUING JUDICIAL INVOLVEMENT

. . . [D]ispute-resolution . . . trivializes the remedial dimensions of lawsuits and mistakenly assumes judgment to be the end of the process. It supposes that the judge's duty is to declare which neighbor is right and which wrong, and that this declaration will end the judge's involvement . . . . Often, however, judgment is not the end of a lawsuit but only the beginning. The involvement of the court may continue almost indefinitely. In these cases, settlement cannot provide an adequate basis for that necessary continuing involvement, and thus is no substitute for judgment.

The parties may sometimes be locked in combat with one another and view the lawsuit as only one phase in a long continuing struggle. The entry of judgment will then not end the struggle, but rather change its terms and the balance of power. One of the parties will invariably return to the court and again ask for its assistance, not so much because conditions have changed, but because the conditions that preceded the lawsuit have unfortunately not changed. This often occurs in domestic-relations case, where the divorce decree represents only the opening salvo in an endless series of skirmishes over custody and support.

The structural reform cases that play such a prominent role on the federal docket provide another occasion for continuing judicial involvement. In these cases, courts seek to safeguard public values by restructuring large-scale bureaucratic organizations. The task is enormous, and our knowledge of how to restructure on-going bureaucratic organizations is limited. As a consequence, courts must oversee and manage the remedial process for a long-time — maybe forever. This, I fear, is true of most school desegregation cases, some of which have been pending for twenty or thirty years. It is also true of antitrust cases that seek divestiture or reorganization of an industry.

The drive for settlement knows no bounds and can result in a consent decree even in the kinds of cases I have just mentioned, that is, even when a court finds itself embroiled in a continuing struggle between the parties or must reform a bureaucratic organization. The parties may be ignorant of the difficulties ahead or optimistic about the future, or they may simply believe that they can get more favorable terms through a bargained-for agreement. Soon, however, the inevitable happens: One party returns to court and asks the judge to modify the decree, either to make it more effective or less stringent. But the judge is at a loss: He has no basis for assessing the request. He cannot, to use Cardozo's somewhat melodramatic formula, easily decide whether the "dangers, once substantial, have become attenuated to a shadow," because, by definition, he never knew the dangers.

## JUSTICE RATHER THAN PEACE

The dispute resolution story makes settlement appear as a perfect substitute for judgment . . . by trivializing the remedial dimensions of a lawsuit, and also by reducing the social function of the lawsuit to one of resolving private disputes. In that story, settlement appears to achieve exactly the same purpose as judgment — peace between the parties — but at considerably less expense to society . . . .

In my view, however, the purpose of adjudication should be understood in broader terms. Adjudication uses public resources, and employs not strangers chosen by the parties but public officials chosen by a process in which the public participates. These officials, like members of the legislative and executive branches, possess a power that has been defined and conferred by public law, not private agreement. Their job is not to maximize the ends of private parties, nor simply to secure the peace, but to explicate and give force to the values embodied in authoritative texts such as the Constitution and statutes: to interpret those values and to bring reality into accord with them. This duty is not discharged when the parties settle.

In our political system, courts are reactive institutions. They do not search out interpretive occasions, but instead wait for others to bring matters to their attention. They also rely for the most part on others to investigate and present the law and facts. A settlement will thereby deprive a court of the occasion, and perhaps even the ability, to render an interpretation. A court cannot proceed (or not proceed very far) in the face of a settlement. To be against settlement is not to urge that parties be "forced" to litigate, since that would interfere with their autonomy and distort the adjudicative process; the parties will be inclined to make the court believe that their bargain is justice. To be against settlement is only to suggest that when the parties settle, society gets less than what appears, and for a price it does not know it is paying. Parties might settle while leaving justice undone. The settlement of a school suit might secure the peace, but not racial equality. Although the parties are prepared to live under the terms they bargained for, and although such peaceful coexistence may be a necessary precondition for justice, and itself a state of affairs to be valued, it is not justice itself. To settle for something means to accept less than some ideal . . .

## THE REAL DIVIDE

To all this, one can readily imagine a simple response by way of confession and avoidance: We are not talking about those lawsuits. Advocates of ADR might insist that my account of adjudication, in contrast to the one implied by the dispute-resolution story, focuses on a rather narrow category of lawsuits. They could argue that while settlement may have only the most limited appeal with respect to those cases, I have not spoken to the "typical" case. My response is twofold.

First, even as a purely quantitative matter, I doubt that the number of cases I am referring to is trivial. My universe includes those cases in which there are significant distributional inequalities; those in which it is difficult to generate authoritative consent because organizations of social groups are parties or because the power to settle is vested in autonomous agents; those in which the court must continue to supervise the parties after judgment; and those in which justice needs to be done, or to put it more modestly, where there is a genuine social need for an authoritative interpretation of law. I imagine that the number of cases that satisfy one of these four criteria is considerable; in contrast to the kind of case portrayed in the dispute-resolution story, they probably dominate the docket of a modern court system.

Second, it demands a certain kind of myopia to be concerned only with the number of cases, as though all cases are equal simply because the clerk of the court assigns each a single docket number. All cases are not equal. The Los Angeles desegregation case, to take one example, is not equal to the allegedly more typical suit involving a property dispute or an automobile accident. The desegregation suit consumes more resources, affects more people, and provokes far greater challenges to the judicial power. The settlement movement must introduce a qualitative perspective; it must speak to these more "significant" cases, and demonstrate the propriety of settling them. Otherwise it will soon be seen as an irrelevance, dealing with trivia rather than responding to the very conditions that give the movement its greatest sway and saliency.

## NOTES AND QUESTIONS

(1)   Do commentators such as Professors Fiss and Delgado make the mistake that Legal Positivists accuse lawyers of making — *viz.*, assuming that whatever is legal is also morally desirable? Is Fiss accurate when he states, as his final challenge, that the mediation process might be irrelevant because it deals with "trivial" rather than "significant" cases? Revisit Chapter 1's account of mediation's use in its foundational years and examine the types of controversies in which it was used.

(2)   Professor Fiss observes that persons with power may have no incentive to talk to others if they believe their interests are secure. In such settings, the use of the legal system by parties who seek to challenge existing arrangements constitutes a crucial resource for triggering change in a non-violent manner. For example, without the Ohio Supreme Court declaring that the state's system for funding public elementary and secondary education was unconstitutional, there appears to be no compelling incentive for residents of wealthier school districts to support reallocating their tax dollars to financially poorer districts. *See DeRolph v. Ohio*, 728 N.E.2d 993 (Ohio 2000). Yet, once parties are in litigation, participating in mediated negotiations might create opportunities for creative problem-solving. The simultaneous interplay of multiple dispute resolution processes, which is the realistic context for most dispute resolution efforts, creates significant challenges. For a more thorough discussion of the interrelationship between law and mediation, see Chapter 9, *infra*.

(3)   During the course of a mediation conference involving a claim by the landlord for rent arrears, the mediator learns that the landlord is renting the basement area of his home in violation of the zoning ordinance governing single-family-home-use in that neighborhood; the mediator also learns that the tenant is an immigrant who is not lawfully in the U.S. Both parties develop mutually acceptable settlement terms to pay the rent arrears and continue the tenancy. What should the mediator do? For a discussion of similar dilemmas, see the portion of Chapter 8, *infra*, dealing with Mediator Ethics.

## WHOSE DISPUTE IS IT ANYWAY? A PHILOSOPHICAL AND DEMOCRATIC DEFENSE OF SETTLEMENT (IN SOME CASES)
83 Geo. L.J. 2663, 2663–71, 2692 (1995)*
By Carrie Menkel-Meadow

In the last decade or so, a polarized debate about how disputes should be resolved has demonstrated to me once again the difficulties of simplistic and adversarial arguments. Owen Fiss has argued "Against Settlement"; Trina Grillo and others have argued against mediation (in divorce cases and other family matters involving women); Richard Delgado and others have questioned whether informal processes are unfair to disempowered and subordinated groups; Judith Resnik has criticized the (federal) courts' unwillingness to do their basic job of adjudication; Stephen Yeazell has suggested that too much settlement localizes, decentralizes, and delegalizes dispute resolution and the making of public law; Kevin C. McMunigal has argued that too much settlement will make bad advocates; and David Luban and Jules Coleman, among other philosophers, have criticized the moral value of the compromises that are thought to constitute legal settlements. On the other side, vigorous proponents of alternative dispute resolution, including negotiation, mediation, and various hybrids of these forms of preadjudication settlement, criticize the economic and emotional waste of adversarial processes and the cost, inefficiency, and political difficulties of adjudication, as well as its draconian unfairness in some cases.

In my view, this debate, while useful for explicitly framing the underlying values that support our legal system, has not effectively dealt with the realities of modern legal, political, and personal disputes. For me, the question is not "for or against" settlement (since settlement has become the "norm" for our system), but *when, how, and under what circumstances* should cases be settled? When do our legal system, our citizenry, and the parties in particular disputes need formal legal adjudication, and when are their respective interests served by settlement, *whether public or private?*

As several recent commentators have noted, the role of settlement in our legal system has increased: some think because it is actively promoted by such developments as the Civil Justice Reform Act; others by simple caseload pressures, and still others because of the desirability of party-initiated or consented-to agreements to resolve disputes. While court administrators, judges, and some lawyers suggest that we must continue to mine the advantages of settlement for caseload reduction, or equity among claimants, especially in mass torts or class action settings, many legal scholars continue to express concern with the use of settlement as a device for resolving our legal disputes.

The difficulty with the debate about settlement vs. adjudication is that there are many more than two processes, as well as other variables that affect the processes, to consider. The diverse interests of the participants in the dispute, the legal system, and society may not be the same. Issues of fairness, legitimacy, economic efficiency, privacy, publicity, emotional catharsis or empathy, access, equity among disputants, and lawmaking may differ in importance for different actors in the system, and they may vary by case — this is the strength of our common law system.

. . . David Luban argues that settlement is problematic because it reduces public participation in the business of dispute resolution and, consequently, reduces production of rules and precedents — in short, settlement leads to an "erosion of the public realm." Settlement works in favor of "private peace" and in opposition to "public justice." Luban, like other critics of settlement, suggests that the legal system is designed to engage us (and our judges, lawyers, and litigants) in the public discourse of lawmaking and policy debate that concerns itself with justice and self-defined societal values — in our case, democratic deliberation. By judging and enunciating rules, judges set baselines for political endowments and entitlements and alternately close and open debates by reviewing facts and articulating the rules and values that underlie particular legal positions. Settlements, on the other hand, represent cruder "compromises" of raw bargaining skill and extrajudicial power imbalances (economics, legal skill, and repeat play experience). Luban acknowledges that we can no longer imagine a "world without settlement." We need it simply to muddle through the hundreds of thousands of disputes our modern society produces. Unlike Fiss, he acknowledges that not all disputes are occasions for "structural transformation" or public elucidation of basic values. And, as he suggests realistically, "too many cases will make bad law." With an increase of cases, and trial and appeals courts making more and more law, there are likely to be irreconcilable inconsistencies in decisional law, producing a virtual "tower of Babel" of legal precedents.

Thus Luban shifts the focus to a consideration of *when and how* settlements should take place. His ultimate focus is on the need to keep settlements public and to decry the loss to democratic discourse when too many settlements are kept secret. Luban argues that secret settlements deprive us not only of "result" information, but the "facts" of discovery, necessarily "privatizing" information to which a democratic society should have access. He suggests that those who continue to favor secret settlements prefer the "problem-solving" (dispute resolution) conception of our legal system to "public production of rules and precedents" or the "public goods and discourse" function. Thus Luban is willing to tolerate settlement, but only if it is open to the "sunshine" laws and serves "at least some of the public values of adjudication," by keeping the settlement process and its information open to the public.

In this essay, I hope to explore some of the same questions that Professor Luban has framed for us — how can we decide which settlements to be for and which to be against? In other words, how can we tell good settlements from bad ones, and when should we prefer adjudication to settlement? . . . . In the words of current academic cachet, much depends on the context — of disputes, of disputants, and of the system being considered.

Those who criticize settlement suffer from what I have called, in other contexts, "litigation romanticism," with empirically unverified assumptions about what courts can or will do. More important, those who privilege adjudication focus almost exclusively on structural and institutional values and often give short shrift to those who are actually involved in the litigation. I fear, but am not sure, that this debate can be reduced to those who care more about the people actually engaged in disputes versus those who care more about institutional and structural arrangements. I prefer to think that we need both adjudication and settlement. These processes can affect each other in positive, as well as negative ways, but in my view, settlement should not be seen as "second best" or "worst case" when adjudication fails. Settlement can be justified on its own moral grounds — there are important values, consistent with the fundamental values of our legal and political systems, that support the legitimacy of settlements of some, if not most, legal disputes. Those values include consent, participation, empowerment, dignity, respect, empathy and emotional catharsis, privacy, efficiency, quality solutions, equity, access, and yes, even justice.

Though some have argued that compromise itself can be morally justified, I . . . argue . . . that compromise is not always necessary for settlement and that in fact, some settlements, by not requiring compromise, may produce better solutions than litigation.

[I]t seems to me that the key questions implicated in the ongoing debate about settlement vs. adjudication are:

1. In a party-initiated legal system, when is it legitimate for the parties to settle their dispute themselves, or with what assistance from a court in which they have sought some legal-system support or service?

2. When is "consent" to a settlement legitimate and "real," and by what standards should we (courts and academic critics) judge and permit such consent?

3. When, in a party-initiated legal system, should party consent be "trumped" by other values — in other words, when should public, institutional, and structural needs and values override parties' desire to settle or courts' incentives to promote settlement? In short, when is the need for "public adjudication" or as Luban suggests, "public settlement" more important (to whom?) than what the parties may themselves desire?

I have here tried to make the following arguments on behalf of the "best" aspects of settlement:

1. Settlements that are in fact consensual represent the goals of democratic and party-initiated legal regimes by allowing the parties themselves to choose processes and outcomes for dispute resolution.

2. Settlements permit a broader range of possible solutions that may be more responsive to both party and system needs.

3. What some consider to be the worst of settlement, that is, compromise, may actually represent a moral commitment to equality, precision in justice, accommodation, and peaceful coexistence of conflicting interests.

4. Settlements may be based on important nonlegal principles or interests, which may, in any given case, be as important or more important to the parties than "legal" considerations. Laws made in the aggregate may not always be appropriate in particular cases, and thus settlement can be seen as yet another "principled" supplement to our common law system.

5. Settlement processes may be more humanely "real," democratic, participatory, and cathartic than more formalized processes, permitting in their best moments, transformative and educational opportunities for parties in dispute as well as for others.

6. Some settlement processes may be better adapted for the multiplex, multiparty issues that require solutions in our modern society than the binary form of plaintiff-defendant adjudication.

7. Despite the continuing and important debates about discovery and information exchange in the litigation process, some settlement processes (mediation and some forms of neutral case evaluation and scheduling) may

actually provide both more and better (not just legally relevant) information for problem-solving, as well as "education" of the litigants.

8. When used appropriately, settlement may actually increase access to justice, not only by allowing more disputants to claim in different ways, but also by allowing greater varieties of case resolutions.

# NOTES AND QUESTIONS

(1) Professor Menkel-Meadow criticizes Fiss and others for maintaining a romanticized vision of the adjudication process; she believes that party-facilitated settlements (mediation) can often secure more desirable outcomes than those obtained through adjudication. Do you agree? By contrast, can one criticize Menkel-Meadow for offering a romanticized vision of mediation? Lela P. Love and Cheryl B. McDonald's *A Tale of Two Cities: Day Labor and Conflict Resolution for Communities in Crisis*, provides a concrete setting in which competing visions of fairness collide.

(2) Commentators observe that many mediated negotiations are conducted "in the shadow of the law," so that failure to reach settlement might result in one party continuing to pursue her litigation options. Do the benefits of settlement dissipate if the negotiating context is divorced from this litigation fallback?

(3) Menkel-Meadow asserts that encouraging party settlement reflects one goal of democratic legal regimes. Do you agree? Does her account of the "best" aspects of settlement satisfactorily meet the concerns raised by commentators such as Delgado and Grillo that power inequities are reinforced through mediated negotiations rather than rectified?

(4) Since its foundational years, disputing parties have turned to mediation as an important tool to resolve controversies involving significant social issues. Recently, mediation has been used extensively to help resolve environmental controversies involving multiple stakeholders. Many such initiatives are reported in *Consensus*, a regular publication focusing on what professionals refer to as "policy disputes."

(5) Empirical research on the question of how party perceptions concerning outcome fairness affect compliance with the mediated outcome has yielded somewhat mixed results. *See* Craig A. McEwen & Richard M. Maiman, *Mediation in Small Claims Court: Achieving Compliance Through Consent*, 18 Law & Soc'y Rev. 11 (1984); Neil Vidmar, *The Small Claims Court: A Reconceptualization of Disputes and an Empirical Investigation*, 18 Law & Soc'y Rev. 515 (1984); Craig A. McEwen & Richard M. Maiman, *The Relative Significance of Disputing Forum and Dispute Characteristics for Outcome and Compliance*, 20 Law & Soc'y Rev. 439 (1986); Neil Vidmar, *Assessing the Effects of Case Characteristics and Settlement Forum on Dispute Outcomes and Compliance*, 21 Law & Soc'y Rev. 155 (1987); Roselle Wissler, *Mediation and Adjudication in the Small Claims Court: The Effects of Process and Case Characteristics*, 29 Law & Soc'y Rev. 323 (1995).

# IF PORTIA WERE A MEDIATOR: AN INQUIRY INTO JUSTICE IN MEDIATION

9 Clinical L. Rev. 157, 159–62, 166–70, 172–73 (2002)*

By Jonathan M. Hyman & Lela P. Love

## INTRODUCTION

Using mediation rather than adjudication to resolve disputes carries important implications for justice. How can an agreed-upon solution, crafted by disputing parties rather than by duly appointed arbiters, judges or juries, comport with ideals of justice? Critics claim that mediation and settlement sacrifice a just result . . . for mere efficiency or expedience. Such critiques neglect the multi-faceted nature of justice . . . [We examine] how a justice rationale undergirds the consensual resolution of disputes, while another justice rationale undergirds adjudication. Justice-seeking is a central component of all dispute resolution processes, and one that mediators, like judges and arbitrators, must attend to. Rather than abandoning justice, the unique attributes of mediation enable mediators to help those who ultimately have the most intimate understanding of the complexities of their situation achieve a resolution they find "just."

Justice in adjudicative systems comes from above, from the application by a judge, jury or arbitrator of properly created standards or rules to "facts" as determined by the adjudicator. Justice inheres in two aspects of that system — in the standards or rules that are applied, and in the process that is used to apply them. Mediation has parallel, but very different, aspects. The rules, standards, principles and beliefs that guide the resolution of the dispute in mediation are those held by the parties. The guiding norms in mediation may be legal, moral, religious or practical. In mediation, parties are free to use whatever standards they wish, not limited to standards that have been adopted by the legislature or articulated by the courts. Consequently, justice in mediation comes from below, from the parties.

## I. WHAT WE MEAN WHEN WE TALK ABOUT JUSTICE

When parties talk about fairness and justice, without the overlay of the elaborate system of adjudicatory justice, they will most likely find themselves talking about the well-known Aristotelean categories of reparative justice, distributive justice, and procedural justice.

A.     *Reparative Justice.* Parties in mediation may use claims of justice to seek repair of what they see as a wrongful deprivation or harm imposed on them by the other. They need not limit their claims of injustice to acts that may have violated the law. A party who has taken more than is "fair" from the complaining party might have arguably committed an injustice that needs to be corrected, even if the law does not prohibit the taking. Treating someone disrespectfully, taking or diminishing their dignity, for example, might become part of a claim that an injustice was done even though there

---

may be no cognizable "cause of action" for such a wrong . . . .

B. *Retribution and Revenge.* What if a party to a mediation seeks revenge for the wrong claimed to have been done? The notion of "an eye for an eye" is an ancient form of balancing that some experience as both just and "reparative." Frequently, mediated discussions result in the parties' recognition that the wrong they experienced may be counter-balanced by a wrong they sponsored. Or, the proverbial "eye" they wish to extract can be given in a more meaningful (and less costly) way than blinding the other side. In other words, mediated discussions of justice can be responsive to desires for revenge even though revenge, as it is normally conceived, is not usually the product of mediation . . . .

C. *Distributive Justice.* . . . The well-known concepts by which we can measure the justice of distributions are equality, equity, and need.

*"Splitting the difference" between settlement demands, a common last step in a negotiated distribution, is a claim to equality, and has a powerful attraction to people's sense of fairness and common sense justice.* Similarly, siblings, employees, or victims who must share resources in a common fund may be guided by understandable principles of equal treatment.

Equity, as distinct from equality, can support distributions other than an even split. A victim's feelings or a perpetrator's ability to pay can be more important for determining a just distribution than simply splitting the difference or precisely measuring actual losses. The concept of *Pareto efficiency* also carries implications for justice. That concept asks us to consider, for any given or proposed distribution of resources, whether there is another possible distribution that would make at least one party better off without making any other party worse off . . . .

The relative needs of the parties also play into questions of distributive justice. Such considerations make it acceptable for disparate treatment such as the rich being taxed at a higher rate than the poor. The precept *from each according to his ability, to each according to his need* can fuel claims of justice and lead to responsive settlement terms and sometimes acts of generosity which restore families and communities . . . .

E. *Procedural justice.* While mediation lacks the formality and elaborate rules of litigation, it nonetheless provides a rich opportunity to implement procedural justice. From a disputant's perspective, the perception of fairness is linked to having a meaningful opportunity to tell one's story, to feeling that the mediator considers the story, and to being treated with dignity and in an even-handed manner. Adherence to principles of procedural justice influences the parties' perceptions about the fairness of the process, as well as their perceptions of substantive justice and their willingness to comply with the outcome of the dispute resolution process.

# NOTE AND QUESTION

(1)   The Model Standards of Conduct for Mediators (*see* Appendix A) are designed to provide guidance for the ethical conduct of mediators. In that sense, "ethical" is a term of broad meaning and captures guiding conduct across multiple topics. Standard IV, for example, imposes a duty on the mediator to be qualified to perform the service. That is an ethical norm, but would not fall under the regime of "justice elements" that are cited by Hyman and Love. When analyzing the Model Standards, consider which Standards relate to justice principles and which do not.

## THE WORLD OF CONFLICT RESOLUTION: A MOSAIC OF POSSIBILITIES

Association for Conflict Resolution Annual Conference 2003, Session on
*Justice in Mediation*
5 Cardozo J. Conflict Resol. 190–200 (2004)*

*Professor (Lela P.) Love:* The first question goes to Dean Alfini. Jim, you have talked about mediators "trashing" and "bashing" parties . . . . Are trashing and bashing compatible with "justice"? If there is no justice rationale for activities like "trashing" and "bashing," should we house those activities under the roof of a courthouse?

*Dean [James J.] Alfini:* Good question. Lela's references are to an article that I wrote . . . entitled *Trashing, Bashing and Hashing It Out: Is This The End of "Good Mediation?"* [Editor's note: See more complete excerpt from this article above at pages 200–05]. The inspiration for this article came from a workshop that we conducted in 1988 in Tallahassee at the dawn of the court-sponsored mediation movement in Florida. During the workshop, Albie Davis commented, "This is the end of good mediation" when referring to lawyers being brought into the mediation process as both representatives of the parties in mediations and as the mediators themselves. So again, at the dawn of the court-sponsored movement, like Don Quixote, I set off on this quest to find out if this was the end of good mediation by looking first for the mediation setting where lawyers are most prevalent in Florida. That happened to be, of course, in the circuit court programs. Circuit court mediation in Florida handles high-stakes civil cases for the most part, cases where lawyers are almost always present, where lawyers play a big part in the mediation process and where lawyer-mediators under the Florida rules are almost always used in those cases. So what I did was interview, with the help of Sharon Press and others, mediation participants to inquire whether court-annexed mediation marked the end of "good" mediation. I am going to change it a bit, and I think Albie would be willing to allow me to do this. Is this the end of "just" mediation? What I think this means is that mediation is no longer just, or perhaps unjust. Instead, does it fail to adhere to the core values of mediation or does it fail, as Lela suggests, to give the parties a voice in mediation, to yield an impartial mediator, or to permit parties' self-determination during the course of the mediation? Here, I owe a debt of gratitude to . . . people like Nancy Welsh who . . . has analyzed current court practices in courtsponsored programs in a procedural justice context.

---

One of the practices . . . found most problematic in the present court-sponsored mediation context was the tendency toward the abandonment of the joint session. That is, the tendency towards, early in the mediation process, putting parties in separate rooms and keeping them there sometimes for the entire mediation. Going back to the Florida study and the "trashing" style of mediation, let me . . . read . . . a brief except . . . that describes the style:

> The mediators who employ a trashing methodology spend much of the time "tearing apart" the cases of the parties. Indeed, one of these mediators suggested the "trasher" characterization: "I trash their cases. By tearing them apart and then building their cases back up, I try to get them to the point where they will put realistic settlement figures on the table." To facilitate uninhibited trashing of the parties' cases, the overall strategy employed by these mediators discourages direct party communication. Following the mediator's orientation and short (five to ten minutes) opening statements by each party's attorney, the mediator puts the parties in different rooms. The mediator then normally caucuses with the plaintiff's attorney and her client in an effort to get them to take a hard look at the strengths and weaknesses of their case.

The problem from a procedural justice standpoint and from a party satisfaction standpoint — and they be roughly the same — is that it tends to minimize party participation in the process. Parties are deprived of the opportunity to meet and discuss face-to-face. There is a tendency for attorneys to take over and the process then becomes much less "party-centric" and much more "lawyer-centric."

The "bashing" methodology was described in the article as:

> Unlike the trashers, the mediators who use a bashing technique tend to spend little or no time engaging in the kind of case evaluation that is aimed at getting the parties to put "realistic" settlement figures on the table. Rather, they tend to focus initially on the settlement offers that the parties bring to mediation and spend most of the session bashing away at those initial offers in an attempt to get the parties to agree to a figure somewhere in between. The mediation sessions thus tend to be shorter than those of the trashers, and they tend to prefer a longer initial joint session, permitting direct communication between the parties. Most of the bashers interviewed were retired judges who draw on their judicial experience and use the prestige of their past judicial service to bash out an agreement.

To the extent that this style erodes party self-determination, I would think in most cases it does because this is a highly evaluative technique. The mediator is substituting the mediator's judgment in many cases for that of the parties. This, I think, is problematic from a procedural justice standpoint. The mediator has a tendency to limit a party's decision-making.

Finally, the "hashing it out" style was described as:

> The hashers tend to take a much more flexible approach to the mediation process, varying their styles and using techniques such as caucusing selectively, depending on their assessment of the individual case and the needs and interests of the parties. When asked to describe the mediator's

role in one sentence, a hasher responded, "facilitator, orchestrator, referee, sounding board, scapegoat." The hasher generally adopts a much less directive posture than the trashers and bashers, preferring that the parties speak directly with one another and hash out an agreement.

From the procedural justice standpoint, I would think that the "hashing it out" style is much more consistent with our notions of procedural justice or what we might expect from a mediation setting. To summarize, "trashing" and "bashing" erodes certain norms or core values, if you will, or has a tendency to do that. It has a tendency to pull the parties apart physically, and in the course of doing that, allows the parties less of a voice in the mediation setting, at least the "trashing" style does, and the "bashing" tends again to limit a party's decision-making . . . .

*Professor Love:* Thank you, Jim. I am going to ask Ellen Waldman to respond . . . .

*Professor [Ellen] Waldman:* I . . . do not look at all amiss at "trashing." I see that as really part of all our spectrum of mediation behaviors. I share Jim's concern for the erosion of procedural justice in mediation and I think that we should be vigilant in preserving the aspects of the process that enhance party participation and voice. On the other hand, at least with regard to the "trashing" *modus operandi*, case evaluation or bringing in norms from the legal system have always been a part of at least certain mediations as they occur in certain contexts. Therefore, I do not think that aspect of "trashing" *per se* is contrary to the mediation process. The "bashing" approach, in my view, is much more problematic because it is entirely unprincipled. When a mediator does a case evaluation, at least the mediator is assessing the parties' viewpoints according to reigning norms. When the mediator simply sees that it is his or her role to chip away at the parties' bottom lines in an effort to somehow "split the baby" and meet in the middle, there is no principle involved. There is no effort to ascertain whether an important norm has in fact been enforced. Therefore, "bashing" is actually the model that I find most disturbing . . . . I am not sure that I would ban the "trashing" model. I would simply make a space in the "trashing" model for greater party participation and I do not see this as an either/or proposition. Case evaluation can occur in conjunction with traditional party ventilation and negotiation.

## NOTES AND QUESTIONS

(1)   Do you agree with Professor Waldman that a mediator could conduct a mediation in the *trashing* style described by Dean Alfini in a way that embraces meaningful party participation? Would the mediator be *trashing* the legal or non-legal arguments? If the former, how would the client meaningfully participate? Similarly, do you agree that "chipping away" at the parties' bottom lines by the mediator who is a *basher* has no "norms" to ground it (i.e., it is, in Professor Waldman's terms, without principle)? In a given case, might one such norm grounding the *basher's* discussion be what Hyman and Love refer to as a principle of equity?

(2)   For probing accounts of the relationship between questions of procedural justice and mediation, see Nancy A. Welsh, *Disputant's Decision Control in*

*Court-Connected Mediation: A Hollow Promise Without Procedural Justice*, 2002 J. Disp. Resol. 179. *See also* Welsh, *The Place of Court-Connected Mediation in a Democratic Justice System* in Chapter 9, *infra*. For a contrary perspective on these matters, see Deborah R. Hensler, *Suppose It's Not True: Challenging Mediation Ideology*, 2002 J. Disp. Resol. 81.

# SWIMMING IN THE DEEP END:
## DEALING WITH JUSTICE IN MEDIATION
6 Cardozo J. Conflict Resol. 19, 19–20, 21–22, 32–41 (2004)*
### By Jonathan M. Hyman

## I. INTRODUCTION

Justice is a troublesome issue for mediators. It is not their role to decide who was right and who was wrong. Mediators have no authority to determine if a resolution is fair or just. That role and that authority are reserved for judges, juries, and arbitrators. But if mediators should not decide what is fair and just, why should they even think about those matters? Even learning only what the parties deem fair or unfair about past actions, or what is just or unjust about pending settlement proposals, without trying to impose any "correct" outcome would leave the mediator with useless knowledge. How could it help the parties reach an agreement? And it would leave the mediator frustrated. If mediators were to allow themselves to develop their own sense of what is fair and just, they would either have to squelch that opinion or try to get the parties to act in accordance with it. Burying their opinions would lead to frustration and a nagging sense of internal discord. But if they try to get the parties to adopt their view, the resulting agreement would become that of the mediator, rather than the parties.

While some version of the foregoing aversion to justice is common among mediators, it is not my view . . . . [I] think mediators should be more willing to pay attention to justice in mediation. They should develop their skill at using justice, just as they develop their other mediation skills. Such a skill is important to improve the profession of mediation, as well as to protect the independence and autonomy of the parties . . . . . . Common sense ideas of fairness are never far from our thoughts. Such ideas may form a prominent part of our conscious reactions when we assess a person's past actions or future plans. These common sense ideas may lie dormant, as potential ideas helping to make sense of other things that we discuss. While, sometimes, an explicit invocation of fairness seems appropriate, at other times it seems overdone. Of course, ideas of fairness often surface in conflict situations. Each party is conscious of the perceived unfairness of the other party's past actions and future plans, and conversely aware of the fairness of its own actions and decisions. Even when a mediator does not have an opinion about the fairness of the parties' actions and proposals, the large moral vocabulary of fairness is easily accessible to any mediator who wants to discuss the issue . . . .

Once we clarify that "justice" includes common sense ideas of fairness, it

---

becomes easier to see why we should pay attention to how mediators deal with it. Fairness is part of the ordinary backdrop of concepts against which we conduct many of our charged or contentious debates. Thoughts about fairness are always available to become part of the discussion. This inevitably leads us to a meta-fairness question: When should we include fairness in our attempts to resolve conflicts and in what circumstances? A decision to exclude certain fairness questions from a mediation session is itself a question of fairness and must be justified as such.

This article addresses . . . how and why the mediator should permit or encourage ideas of fairness and justice in the mediation conversation.

. . . [I] will address the various ways a mediator could deal [with questions of fairness and justice]. A mediator has many options. He or she could exclude them from discussion by saying, for example, "we're here to compromise and settle this dispute in an expeditious manner, not to debate fairness and justice." Or, he or she could permit the parties to explore issues of fairness and justice if the parties chose to do so, on their own, saying, for example, "you've brought up the issue of fairness. Does each of you want to talk some more about that?" The mediator might also suggest that the parties consider fairness, saying for, example, "I think it might be useful for each of you to talk more about fairness." Furthermore, a mediator could even offer his or her own opinion about the fairness and justice regarding the dispute or about possible resolutions, saying, "that demand seems much too big for the harm you said you have suffered."

Discussions of justice may threaten the parties' autonomy. The mediator may lead the discussion in such a way that the solution becomes the mediator's view of what is fair and just, regardless of what the parties think. I will conclude by suggesting that this danger, though real, is exaggerated and not inevitable. Protection of the parties' autonomy lies in the kind of moral reasoning the mediator uses, and the extent to which the mediator frames discussions about fairness more as dialogue than as logical command. Mediators who use a form of moral reasoning that relies on richly textured descriptions of particular situations, replete with analogies and factual distinctions, reduce the risk of imposing a result that the parties do not desire or are not willing to adopt. Mediators are not judges. Their own positions on justice and fairness are not privileged over those of the parties. Mediators may only facilitate communication. On questions of fairness and justice, they have no more authority to command the parties than the parties have over each other. Differences about what is fair stem from different perceptions about the facts, different expectations for the future, and different experiences and assumptions about what people are like . . . . Considerations of fairness and justice can be appropriate in mediation when the discussion of those matters becomes a triangular one between three equally independent parties, the mediator being one voice among equals . . . .

### III. WHY MEDIATORS SHOULD NOT TALK ABOUT FAIRNESS

I think mediators should be willing to engage in a non-directive discussion of fairness. But before describing how and why that can be done, I would like to review what I take to be the key arguments against such mediation work.

## A. Imposing the Mediator's Views

The most apparent objection to asking the parties about their views of fairness and justice is implied: Asking about these issues may be the precursor for the mediator to inject his or her own views about fairness and justice. If the mediator starts voicing his or her own views, the inevitable next step would seem to be abandoning neutrality and taking sides, preferring the disputant whose views are most like that of the mediator. This slippery slope could fall even lower, with the mediator trying to force, or at least strongly influence, the parties to abandon their own views and act in accordance with those of the mediator. Such an intervention by the mediator would add insult — and disrespect for the parties' autonomy — to injury by implicitly taking sides.

## B. A Waste of Time

The second objection is that inquiry into fairness and justice would be fruitless, and a waste of time. This objection rests on the idea that questions of substantive fairness and justice are purely personal and subjective. Because they are personal and subjective, they cannot be changed any more than one's tastes about ice cream or alternative rock music. If they cannot be changed, spending time on them would produce no results and would take time away from the kinds of discussions and mediator interventions that could increase the likelihood of agreement, or a better agreement. Even worse, spending time on something that seems so fruitless could become no more than mediator voyeurism.

Under this view, the parties' ideas of fairness and justice differ qualitatively from the other kinds of ideas and perceptions they bring to mediation. The other kinds can be changed. As a result of mediation, for instance, the parties may change their predictions of what would happen in court if the matter were not voluntarily resolved, what tangible benefits would flow their way from a proposed settlement, or what additional negotiating concessions the other side is likely to make. Such changes can result from learning additional facts about the objective world, such as the evidence supporting the claims, the latest law, or the parties' financial circumstances. They can result from learning facts about the parties themselves, such as their taste for conflict and the degree to which they can tolerate risk. But, unlike this kind of factual and predictive information, it is assumed that personal, subjective views of justice and fairness cannot be modified by additional facts.

Similarly, a mediator can help resolve a matter by identifying and counter-acting various distortions in the parties' thinking processes, for example, from expectations that are "anchored" to some inaccurate perception, or arise from examples that arbitrarily happen to be salient and available, from reactive devaluation of settlement proposals made by the other side, or from the tendency to refuse an offer if it is seen as a "loss," even if one would take the same offer if it were seen as a "gain." These thinking processes are labeled "distortions," they presume that there is a different, more objective state of understanding that a clear-thinking party could appreciate if the distortions were to be wiped away.

Intervening to clear up "distortions," however, is useless for questions of fairness and justice. A person's personal and subjective views of fairness and justice are by definition completely "true." There are no cognitive distortions for the mediator to try to correct. Any attempt at "correction" threatens to impose the mediator's "personal" views of fairness and justice on the parties.

## C. Throwing Fuel on the Fire

Inquiring about fairness and justice might also be thought to be bad mediation because it might intensify the conflict between the parties. Claims of unfairness and injustice are often part of the vocabulary of conflict. Each side clearly sees the fairness of its actions and its own proposals, and sees just as clearly the unfairness of the other side's actions and proposals . . . [C]laims and defenses about fairness are often linked with anger, or at least strong feelings, so a discussion of competing claims of fairness and unfairness can distract the parties from discussing other aspects of their dispute, and can elicit feelings that interfere with reasonable problem solving.

## D. Intruding on the Parties' Privacy

Even if a mediator does not try to force a party to accept his or her idea of what is fair and just, simply raising the question might be seen as an improper intrusion on that party's autonomy: Personal moral views about what is fair and just lie at the heart of our sense of personhood. Suggesting that those views are open to question or reconsideration might be seen as an effort to change something that is very basic to a person's identity. Under this objection, such suggestions would be off limits to a mediator.

Typically, mediators make suggestions for discussion topics; advise further negotiation steps; ensure that the parties understand each other; suggest, or help the parties develop, new, mutually beneficial ideas for resolution; and offer advice about possible time, expense, risks and outcome of pending litigation or continuing the dispute. These matters are largely fact-based, and not automatically value-laden. Unlike questions of justice and fairness, those matters refer to the kinds of knowledge we share with each other. Asking someone to consider new facts, and/or take action on the basis of that consideration does not challenge one's personhood or autonomy. On the contrary, consideration of such matters is part of enhancing the parties' rational thought . . . . As with the foregoing objections, this one also rests on the assumption that questions of justice and fairness are categorically different from more "factual" matters, and discussion threatens the parties' autonomy in a way that discussion of factual matters does not.

## IV. WHY MEDIATORS SHOULD TALK ABOUT FAIRNESS

The foregoing objections are overdrawn. First, mere talk about fairness does not necessarily create undue mediator influence. Second, even if talk of justice and fairness does not help pave the road to agreement or lead the parties to change their minds, it can be valuable regardless of any effect on the outcome. Third, mediators should be able to handle any tension or strong feeling elicited by a discussion of fairness and justice. And fourth, discussion of fairness and justice, even if it involves the personal views of the mediator, is not necessarily a threat to the parties' autonomy. The key question is not *whether* matters of justice and fairness become part of the mediation discussion, but *how*.

. . . [I] will consider . . . why it might be important for these issues to be part of mediation.

. . . Assume that a mediator has successfully arrived at two settlement proposals. Each side sees *both* proposals as equally acceptable; both of them provide a better outcome to each side than the alternative of continuing the dispute and seeking an alternative way to resolve it. The two proposals could differ in a variety of respects. One might provide for payment over time, while the other provides for a larger cash payment right away. One might provide for continuing relationship between the parties, which both parties value, while the other provides more resources to help one of the parties develop different opportunities. When all the pros and cons of each are considered, there is nothing to make one preferable to the other. How should the parties decide between them?

The mediator might ask a variety of questions to help articulate the parties' needs, perceptions, and wishes, and thus help make a sound choice. These might include the following: "Which will provide you more income?" "Which will give you more ability to go into the future in the direction you want?" "Which will be better for your relationship with X and how important is that to you?" "Which will allow you to sleep better at night?" All of these relate to both material and to affective benefits, to material things of value the parties might gain, and to emotional satisfaction they might achieve. None, however, deal with the parties' sense of fairness or justice.

Let us assume further, that, after this inquiry, the two proposals still seem equally valuable; there is no obvious way to choose. What if one of the proposals seems fairer to one party than it does to the other? That would be a good reason to prefer that proposal. By adopting that proposal, the party obtains more fairness (and justice). Further, the other party is no worse off, since both proposals were equally valuable. The argument for choosing the "fairer" proposal would be even stronger if *both* parties see it as more fair and just.

This possibility tells us the next question for the mediator to ask: "Does one of these proposals seem fairer and more just to you?" The mediator has now put his or her toe in fairness waters. This question could lead to deeper inquiry into the question. If the party says one solution seems fairer, the mediator might want to know what makes it seem fairer. Once that is understood, there may be ways to increase its fairness. If the party says that both seem equally fair — or more likely, seem equally unfair — the mediator could try to learn more about what the party is thinking. Perhaps one of the proposals could be modified, at no loss to the other side, to make it fairer for the first party. The mediator's entire foot is now in fairness waters.

So far, these questions have been limited to determining what the parties think is fair and just. But the mediator cannot effectively talk about these matters and learn what the parties think of them without drawing on his or her own sense of fairness and justice. Our concepts of fairness and justice, whatever else they are, are part of our ordinary moral discourse, and operate in a complex web of shared and differing views. We only recognize the moral claims of others, whether we agree with them or not, by thinking about them in terms of our own moral frameworks. Mediators need to draw on their own concepts of fairness and justice to understand the parties' views and to help the parties use their own views more productively. Now the mediator seems to be into the fairness waters at least up to his or her knees.

Invoking the mediator's sense of fairness might seem to be going too far, but consider the alternative; if we say that mediators should *refuse* to attend to the parties' views of fairness and justice, we will be giving material interests and feelings a privileged position over a sense of fairness and justice. Put this way, the distinction seems rather odd. The mediator has made a unilateral decision to deal with only some things that are of material and perhaps emotional interest to the parties and not with others. This creates a kind of paradox for mediators. We saw above that respect for the parties' autonomy is an overriding value in mediation, and the fear of intruding on that autonomy makes mediators reluctant to inquire into the parties' views of fairness and justice. But not paying attention to the parties' sense of fairness and justice can equally constitute a disregard for the parties. If their sense of fairness and justice is important to them, it would enhance their autonomy to weave those concerns into mediation work rather than exclude them. The task seems to be determining how to provide room for the parties sense of fairness and justice as part of mediation work, but, in so doing, not to detract from the parties' independence and free choice.

The conclusion is that mediators should put the parties' sense of fairness and justice on equal footing with the various interests and concerns attended to by mediators . . .

Of course, my thought experiment is quite artificial. It is unusual to find parties indifferent to two settlement proposals. Usually, they would find one proposal better than another for a variety of reasons, with or without regard to fairness. It also seems counterintuitive to imagine seeking out fairness late in a negotiation to break a tie between various proposals. A party's sense that he or she has been treated unfairly is often one of the first perceptions to arise in a dispute, not the last, and continually intrudes on and directs his or her thinking throughout the mediation. A party's other interests, such as finances, future security, and relationship, can seem more or less important or compelling depending on how consistent they are with his or her sense of fairness.

But these differences do not change the conclusion about the proper place of fairness and justice in mediation. If fairness and justice are relevant factors to break ties, they are just as relevant early on in the mediation when they are one among a number of interests that need to be satisfied. Attending to them is just as important a recognition of the party's autonomy early in the mediation as it is at the end. And the institution of mediation will be strengthened to the extent it can incorporate a consideration of fairness and justice, while remaining true to its dedication to the parties' mutual power to control the outcome for themselves.

## NOTE AND QUESTION

Hyman proposed that the drafters of the Model Standards of Conduct for Mediators include a specific standard requiring a mediator, as part of her ethical obligation, to discuss questions of justice with parties in a mediation conference. *See* Hyman, Association for Conflict Resolution Annual Conference 2003, *The World of Conflict Resolution: A Mosaic of Possibilities*, 5 Cardozo J. Conflict Resol. 205–06 (2004). Do you believe that such a provision would be desirable? Workable?

# Chapter 8

# ETHICAL ISSUES FOR MEDIATORS

## A.  INTRODUCTION

This chapter explores ethical issues for mediators, including the special concerns that arise when the mediator is also licensed as an attorney. Section B presents the components of typical mediator codes of conduct and the challenges associated with defining mediator behavior in the context of ethical standards. Section C examines enforcement options for breaches of ethical and professional standards, including civil suits and disciplinary procedures. Section D analyzes the intersection between the legal community and mediation, focusing specifically on the regulation of attorneys serving as mediators and the potential for allegations of the "unauthorized practice of law" for non-attorney mediators. As you read this chapter, consider the impact that the mediator roles, styles and orientations covered in Chapter 4, *supra*, have on what is considered to be ethical behavior.

## B.  MEDIATOR STANDARDS OF CONDUCT

As the use of mediation has expanded, there has been increased interest in developing and codifying standards of conduct for mediators and disciplinary procedures. In 1986, Hawaii became the first state to adopt such a code, entitled "Standards for Private and Public Mediators in the State of Hawaii." In the years that followed, several states have followed suit; some, such as Florida, Georgia, and North Carolina, are in their second or third incarnation of such standards. In addition, several professional associations have adopted standards of conduct for their members, including the development of "joint Model Standards" by the American Arbitration Association, the American Bar Association, and the Association for Conflict Resolution, which is now in its second iteration.

In theory, mediator standards of conduct should address the ethical issues that arise for mediators. In 1992, Professor Robert A. Baruch Bush published a study of ethical dilemmas, *The Dilemmas of Mediation Practice: A Study of Ethical Dilemmas and Policy Implications*. Drawing on extensive interviews he conducted with practicing community, divorce and civil mediators, he identified two major problems with mediator standards that existed as of that date, specifically,

> First, the codes and standards promulgated thus far almost always suffer from internal inconsistency. That is, where the mediator is confronted in a dilemma with the need to choose between two values, like fairness and self-determination, the codes typically contain provisions that, read together, tell her *to choose both*. For example, they tell her to protect and to leave alone, when she can't possibly do both . . .

> The second problem . . . is, the codes and standards are framed at a level of generality that is not responsive to the mediator's need to know how to apply the principles in specific situations. They lack concreteness . . . [y]et clearly, given the kinds of problems mediators encounter, specific guidance is what they most need.

Mediator standards of conduct vary in the language used to describe behavior that is condoned and sanctioned, but there is general agreement as to the topics that should be included. In this section, we identify these consensus topics and then describe recurring practice dilemmas that help clarify a standard's purposes and application. Because the 2005 Model Standards of Conduct for Mediators have been adopted by many jurisdictions, its language is cited to provide a discussion context for the mediation dilemmas that are posed. In the Appendix, the complete version of the 2005 Model Standards of Conduct for Mediators (Appendix A) and its Reporter's Notes (Appendix B) appear, as do two additional examples of ethical standards, The Model Standards of Practice for Family and Divorce Mediation (Appendix C), and the Florida Standards of Professional Conduct and Disciplinary Procedures found in the Florida Rules for Certified and Court-Appointed Mediators (Appendix E).

When analyzing the dilemmas set out below, recall Professor Bush's insight that something rises to the level of being an ethical dilemma when there are two (or more) mediation values that govern the situation but offer competing guidance, so the mediator must choose which value take precedence. So, while the examples are raised in the context of a single standard, examine how other standards may also relate to the issues that are raised. For additional examples of ethical issues, see The American Bar Association Section of Dispute Resolution's searchable National Clearing House for Mediator Ethics Opinions which can be found on line at http://www.americanbar.org/directories/mediator_ethics_opinion.html. Finally, as you read this section, consider Professor Bush's critique. Are the standards internally consistent? Are they written with a sufficient degree of specificity?

## 1. Self-Determination

This includes the ethical responsibility of a mediator not to interfere with the parties' right of self-determination both in terms of substance and process. Interference with party self-determination often implicates other standards such as impartiality and professional advice or opinions.

### a. Model Standards of Conduct for Mediators

#### STANDARD I. SELF-DETERMINATION

**A.** A mediator shall conduct a mediation based on the principle of party self-determination. Self-determination is the act of coming to a voluntary, uncoerced decision in which each party makes free and informed choices as to process and outcome. Parties may exercise self-determination at any stage of a mediation, including mediator selection, process design, participation in or withdrawal from the process, and outcomes.

     **1.** Although party self-determination for process design is a fundamental principle of mediation practice, a mediator may need to balance such party self-determination with a mediator's duty to conduct a quality process in accordance with these Standards.

2. A mediator cannot personally ensure that each party has made free and informed choices to reach particular decisions, but, where appropriate, a mediator should make the parties aware of the importance of consulting other professionals to help them make informed choices.

B. A mediator shall not undermine party self-determination by any party for reasons such as higher settlement rates, egos, increased fees, or outside pressures from court personnel, program administrators, provider organizations, the media or others.

## b.  Mediation Dilemmas for Discussion

1.  The parties to a dissolution of marriage mediation are set to make an agreement regarding a parenting plan which would, in the mediator's opinion, be detrimental to the young children; or, one parent is ready to agree to an amount of child support which is significantly below the guidelines. Neither party is represented. What are the competing values? How should the mediator handle this situation?

2.  Party B appears to be emotionally intimidated by Party A. Party A, in a firm, authoritative tone, proposes a financial settlement that requires Party B to make a substantial monetary payment within a short period of time. Doing so will severely restrict her ability to meet other financial obligations, but she agrees to pay. What are the mediator's ethical obligations? What if Party A threatens Party B with bodily harm?

3.  You are mediating a case that involves a high degree of animosity between the parties, so you are making extensive use of caucuses. After meeting with each party once, you return to the plaintiffs who appear to be entirely different in demeanor from the initial joint session and your first caucus with them. They now are willing to resolve the dispute for a fraction of the proposal which they had adamantly stated earlier. No one has said what has caused this significant change but you suspect that their attorney has pressured them by implying that since mediation was court-ordered, they are unable to leave the mediation without resolving the case. What should you do?

4.  Is a mediator's obligation regarding self-determination any different depending on whether the parties are represented by legal counsel or not?

5.  After a lengthy mediation in which both parties are represented by competent counsel, everyone agrees that they have reached impasse. Given the time that the parties have invested in the mediation, and the high esteem to which they hold the mediator, the lawyers ask the mediator to become the arbitrator and render a binding decision. Can the mediator ethically do so? Does it make a difference if the request is made by the parties (not their attorneys)? How should a mediator balance ethical obligations to honor self-determination and a quality process (see below)?

# NOTES AND QUESTIONS

(1)   Should there be a maximum time limit on the length of a particular mediation session? Can individuals make good decisions if they are physically and mentally exhausted? In Florida, a party filed a grievance after a 10-hour mediation. The party alleged that by the ninth hour, the party was emotionally and physically exhausted and reported just wanting to get out of the session. The party alleged that she was unable to exercise self-determination due to her exhausted state. Another example of a similar grievance included the allegation that a party was hypoglycemic and had not been given sufficient opportunity to eat prior to signing a mediation agreement.

(2)   What does party "informed decision-making" mean in terms of the mediator's obligation? Imagine mediating a personal injury case where both parties are represented by counsel. A very experienced PI attorney represents the defendant while a family friend who is a transactional lawyer represents the plaintiff. During the course of the mediation, it becomes clear that the plaintiff is receiving bad advice from his/her attorney who does not know the law in this subject area. How does this ethical obligation relate to the obligation for a mediator to maintain impartiality (see below)?

(3)   Standard I (regarding self-determination) in the Model Standards of Practice for Family and Divorce Mediation (*see* Appendix C) includes the following affirmative ethical obligation for mediators. "A family mediator shall inform the participants that they may withdraw from family mediation at any time and are not required to reach an agreement in mediation." Do you believe that a similar provision should be in the Model Standards for Mediators? Why or why not?

(4)   Professor Nancy Welsh, in *The Thinning Vision of Self-Determination in Court-Connected Mediation: The Inevitable Price of Institutionalization?*, 6 Harv. Negot. L. Rev. 1 (2001), explores the way courts are modifying the meaning of self-determination and analyzes their implications for mediation in the court context. She concludes her article by suggesting that the best way to protect party self-determination is by modifying the presumption that a mediated settlement agreement is immediately binding:

> . . . and the standards currently used to determine whether parties exercised their "free will" in reaching a negotiated agreement are likely to fall short in protecting the fundamental principle of self-determination. Therefore, we may be *required to embrace and advocate for* a protection that holds court-connected mediation to a higher standard than traditional negotiation. The [most effective] protection [would be] the imposition of a three-day non-waivable cooling off period before mediated settlement agreements (whether oral or written) become binding. . . .

> . . . .

> . . . [T]he benefits provided by this cooling-off proposal clearly outweigh the possible risks. First, a cooling-off period . . . is relatively straight forward, easily-administrable, and unlikely to invite litigation and/or intrusions upon the confidentiality of mediation.

. . . [T]his option would [importantly] reward mediators who view their role as primarily facilitative and penalize mediators who use techniques designed to force an agreement.

What do you think of Professor Welsh's proposal?

(5)   Drawing the line between ethical mediator behavior that supports party self-determination and inappropriate manipulation of party conduct is sometimes difficult. As you analyze the suggestions offered by Professors Coben and Love, in *Trick or Treat, The Ethics of Mediator Manipulation*, Dispute Resol. Mag. 18–19 (Fall 2010),* below, consider whether their proposal would help you to determine the appropriateness of intervening in the dilemmas presented above.

> [M]uch of what good mediators do can be characterized as "helpful interventions" that assist the parties toward legitimate goals such as a better understanding, a platform for developing options, and (where the parties choose) an agreement or settlement. In those senses . . . failure to make certain interventions would be poor practice.

> The problem, of course, is that all such "helpful interventions" are inevitably manipulative, in the sense that the mediator is, often unilaterally, making "moves" with profound impact on the parties' bargaining.

> . . . To evaluate the ethics of any individual move we propose asking two questions.

> First, to be "OK," a move should further or *help* a legitimate party or process goal and be in keeping with the Model Standards of Conduct for Mediators that advance party self-determination in decision making . . . In other words, does the move support self-determination?

> Second, a move should not be manipulative in such a way that it disadvantages one side or undermines the integrity of the mediator or the mediation process. . . . Moves that, if discovered, would be considered "tricky" and underhanded would not pass the test we propose. Following this logic, we would ask of the move: Is it consistent with mediator and mediation process integrity (i.e., not "tricky" or devious)?

> If we can respond "yes" to the two questions, then the mediator move is more likely to be ethically sound.

> Of course, different mediator goals will drive different practices . . . Despite differences in strategies, we believe all mediation interventions should be both helpful to a legitimate party goal and to party self-determination. Interventions should also be nondevious so that mediators and mediation integrity remains intact.

(6)   The Florida ethical standards (*see* Appendix E) highlight the connection between self-determination and competence in Rule 10.310(d) by requiring a mediator to cancel or postpone a mediation in the event that a party is "unable to exercise self-determination." The committee note to this standard suggests that a

---

mediator should be mindful of such things as "the threat of domestic violence, existences of substance abuse, physical threat or undue psychological dominance" which might "impair any party's ability to freely and willingly enter into an informed agreement."

## 2.   Impartiality/Conflicts of Interest

Mediation is universally defined as involving an "impartial" or "neutral" individual who serves as the mediator. Standards of conduct typically track this requirement that mediators maintain impartiality throughout the mediation process and that they do not mediate matters that present clear or undisclosed conflicts of interest.

## a.   Model Standards of Conduct for Mediators

### STANDARD II. IMPARTIALITY

**A.** A mediator shall decline a mediation if the mediator cannot conduct it in an impartial manner. Impartiality means freedom from favoritism, bias or prejudice.

**B.** A mediator shall conduct a mediation in an impartial manner and avoid conduct that gives the appearance of partiality.

    **1.** A mediator should not act with partiality or prejudice based on any participant's personal characteristics, background, values and beliefs, or performance at a mediation, or any other reason.

    **2.** A mediator should neither give nor accept a gift, favor, loan or other item of value that raises a question as to the mediator's actual or perceived impartiality.

    **3.** A mediator may accept or give *de minimis* gifts or incidental items or services that are provided to facilitate a mediation or respect cultural norms so long as such practices do not raise questions as to a mediator's actual or perceived impartiality.

**C.** If at any time a mediator is unable to conduct a mediation in an impartial manner, the mediator shall withdraw.

### STANDARD III. CONFLICTS OF INTEREST

**A.** A mediator shall avoid a conflict of interest or the appearance of a conflict of interest during and after a mediation. A conflict of interest can arise from involvement by a mediator with the subject matter of the dispute or from any relationship between a mediator and any mediation participant, whether past or present, personal or professional, that reasonably raises a question of a mediator's impartiality.

**B.** A mediator shall make a reasonable inquiry to determine whether there are any facts that a reasonable individual would consider likely to create a potential or actual conflict of interest for a mediator. A mediator's actions necessary to accomplish a reasonable inquiry into potential conflicts of interest may vary based on practice context.

**C.** A mediator shall disclose, as soon as practicable, all actual and potential conflicts of interest that are reasonably known to the mediator and could reasonably be seen as raising a question about the mediator's impartiality. After disclosure, if all parties agree, the mediator may proceed with the mediation.

**D.** If a mediator learns any fact after accepting a mediation that raises a question with respect to that mediator's service creating a potential or actual conflict of interest, the mediator shall disclose it as quickly as practicable. After disclosure, if all parties agree, the mediator may proceed with the mediation.

**E.** If a mediator's conflict of interest might reasonably be viewed as undermining the integrity of the mediation, a mediator shall withdraw from or decline to proceed with the mediation regardless of the expressed desire or agreement of the parties to the contrary.

**F.** Subsequent to a mediation, a mediator shall not establish another relationship with any of the participants in any matter that would raise questions about the integrity of the mediation. When a mediator develops personal or professional relationships with parties, other individuals or organizations following a mediation in which they were involved, the mediator should consider factors such as time elapsed following the mediation, the nature of the relationships established, and services offered when determining whether the relationships might create a perceived or actual conflict of interest.

## b. Mediation Dilemmas for Discussion

1. An insurance company maintains a short list of mediators who it feels comfortable utilizing when a case is referred to mediation. These mediators have mediated hundreds of times for this company and are familiar with the insurance representatives and their attorneys. The plaintiffs typically are one time players. Should the mediators have any ethical concerns?

2. A mediator who lives in a relatively small town is the only trained mediator in the area. A couple who knows the mediator very well is getting a divorce. They call the mediator to request a mediation. They tell the mediator that they do not wish to engage in an adversarial process and that they are "not worried about any conflicts of interest or inappropriate dual roles" that the mediator might experience in taking on their case. May the mediator accept this mediation? What constitutes the type of conflict of interest that "might reasonably be viewed as undermining the integrity of the mediation"? Given the importance of self-determination, should a mediator be obligated to withdraw "regardless of the expressed desire or agreement of the parties to the contrary"?

3. The mediator has a niece by marriage who is currently working as a paralegal for a large multi-office law firm. Is it a conflict of interest for the mediator to mediate cases with the law firm? What if the niece is an attorney (not a paralegal)? What if she is the mediator's daughter?

4. If a mediator discovers a conflict of interest or issue related to her impartiality once the parties have arrived at mediation, can the mediator effectively obtain a waiver or will parties feel obligated to go forward since they already have taken the time to attend the mediation. How can a

mediator protect herself that a waiver is legitimate? Can an attorney effectively waive the conflict for his client?

5.  What are the allowable limits of a mediator's marketing efforts? May a mediator take "prospective" attorney mediation participants to lunch at the mediator's expense? Host a luncheon for prospective attorney mediation participants or judges who will make referrals? May the mediator give or accept football tickets for the purpose of expanding his/her mediation practice?

6.  What's the appropriate balance for building rapport and maintaining impartiality? For example, prior to mediation, should the mediator "google" the parties and their lawyers to find possible connections? What if the mediator did so not for the purpose of building rapport but to determine if there were any potential conflicts of interest? If the mediator discovers a connection, such as the mediator and one party grew up in the same town or attended the same undergraduate university, must the mediator disclose the connection? If disclosure is not ethically required, should the mediator, as a matter of best practice, disclose it anyway?

## NOTES AND QUESTIONS

(1)  How do a mediator's obligations related to conflict of interest compare to those of an attorney?

(2)  There are critics who suggest that "impartiality" is not only impossible but it is also undesirable. *See* Leah Wing & Janet Rifkin, *Racial Identity Development and the Mediation of Conflicts, in* New Perspectives on Racial Identity Development (Charmaine L. Wijeyesinghe & Bailey W. Jackson III, eds., New York University Press 2001). Does the definition of impartiality in the standards of conduct address this sufficiently? Does a standard that requires a mediator to be impartial favor preserving the status quo, thereby putting individuals with low power at risk during mediation? *See* Chapter 7.

(3)  Failure to maintain impartiality is the most common grievance filed against mediators. Examples of grievances filed include: (a) the mediator did not allow one of the parties to present information the party believed critical to the mediation; and (b) during a mediation caucus, the mediator first learned that his law partners had a business relationship with one of the parties to the mediation, an architect; and the subject of the mediation was the alleged misrepresentation of the architect's credentials.

## 3.  Mediator Competence

This requirement takes many different forms, including ethical provisions that require a mediator to acquire and maintain professional competence or that require a mediator, in a particular case, to withdraw if the facts or circumstances of that mediation are beyond that mediator's competence.

## a. Model Standards of Conduct for Mediators

### STANDARD IV. COMPETENCE

**A.** A mediator shall mediate only when the mediator has the necessary competence to satisfy the reasonable expectations of the parties.

    **1.** Any person may be selected as a mediator, provided that the parties are satisfied with the mediator's competence and qualifications. Training, experience in mediation, skills, cultural understandings and other qualities are often necessary for mediator competence. A person who offers to serve as a mediator creates the expectation that the person is competent to mediate effectively.

    **2.** A mediator should attend educational programs and related activities to maintain and enhance the mediator's knowledge and skills related to mediation.

    **3.** A mediator should have available for the parties' information relevant to the mediator's training, education, experience and approach to conducting a mediation.

**B.** If a mediator, during the course of a mediation determines that the mediator cannot conduct the mediation competently, the mediator shall discuss that determination with the parties as soon as is practicable and take appropriate steps to address the situation, including, but not limited to, withdrawing or requesting appropriate assistance.

**C.** If a mediator's ability to conduct a mediation is impaired by drugs, alcohol, medication or otherwise, the mediator shall not conduct the mediation.

## b. Mediation Dilemmas for Discussion

1. Having completed your mediation class, you are eligible to add your name to the court's roster (or to become certified) which you do. Amazingly, you are contacted by a party requesting that you serve as a mediator. From what you learn by reviewing the parties' statements, the case is complicated and neither party is represented by counsel. What are your ethical obligations?

2. You are an attorney who has served for many years as in-house counsel for a major corporation. You completed family mediation training a few years ago, but have not actually conducted any mediation. Today, you are contacted by a divorcing couple to mediate the matters involved in the dissolution of their marriage. What are your ethical obligations?

3. You are hired to conduct a mediation involving a dissolution of marriage which you feel competent to handle. The parties to the mediation reach a full agreement only after the woman makes some significant concessions. Following the mediation, the woman retains counsel and files a grievance against you (the mediator) for failure to identify that the woman was intimidated during the mediation by her now ex-husband due to long standing domestic violence issues. Pursuant to Standard IV, did you have an ethical obligation to screen participant capacity in advance of this mediation? . . . Or to have special training or expertise in identifying

domestic violence dynamics? Does the mediator's ethical duty in this situation differ if the woman were represented by counsel at the mediation?

## NOTES AND QUESTIONS

(1)   How does mediator competence relate to mediator style? Should there be a different standard of competence depending on the style of mediation offered by a mediator? For example, if one is an evaluative mediator, must she have some particular expertise or be licensed to practice law?

(2)   If a mediator finds that he is not competent to proceed with a mediation, what are the mediator's ethical obligations with regard to fees?

### 4.   Confidentiality

Confidentiality parameters can be established by legal rules or developed through contractual commitments. Thus, the mediator's ethical obligations typically focus on the mediator's duty to ensure that the parties are aware of the extent to which a mediation communication would be considered confidential and address the mediator's obligations governing his use or disclosure of such information when executing his mediating tasks.

### a.   Model Standards of Conduct for Mediators

#### STANDARD V. CONFIDENTIALITY

**A.** A mediator shall maintain the confidentiality of all information obtained by the mediator in mediation, unless otherwise agreed to by the parties or required by applicable law.

**1.** If the parties to a mediation agree that the mediator may disclose information obtained during the mediation, the mediator may do so.

**2.** A mediator should not communicate to any non-participant information about how the parties acted in the mediation. A mediator may report, if required, whether parties appeared at a scheduled mediation and whether or not the parties reached a resolution.

**3.** If a mediator participates in teaching, research or evaluation of mediation, the mediator should protect the anonymity of the parties and abide by their reasonable expectations regarding confidentiality.

**B.** A mediator who meets with any persons in private session during a mediation shall not convey directly or indirectly to any other person, any information that was obtained during that private session without the consent of the disclosing person.

**C.** A mediator shall promote understanding among the parties of the extent to which the parties will maintain confidentiality of information they obtain in a mediation.

**D.** Depending on the circumstance of a mediation, the parties may have varying expectations regarding confidentiality that a mediator should address. The parties may make their own rules with respect to confidentiality, or the accepted practice of an individual mediator or institution may dictate a particular set of expectations.

### b.  Mediation Dilemmas for Discussion

1.  A party files a complaint against her attorney alleging that the attorney failed to advise her of her rights relative to the mediated settlement of her case. The client in her complaint to the bar association alleges that the attorney spent too much time reminiscing with the mediator about "old times." Does the filing of the attorney complaint with specific references to what was said in the mediation remove the mediator's obligation to keep confidential personal knowledge about the mediation which would vindicate the attorney?

2.  In a court-ordered foreclosure mediation, the borrower is unrepresented and the lender is represented by counsel who is physically at the mediation and by a representative "with full settlement authority" who is not physically present but is participating in the mediation by speaker phone. Before the mediator completes her opening statement, the representative of the lender who is on speaker phone announces that the telephone conversation is being recorded for "compliance purposes." Should the mediator continue? What if the borrower objects?

3.  In the mediator's opening statement, she states that while everyone may take notes, at the conclusion of the mediation, she will collect the notes and dispose of them. One party states that he intends to keep his notes. How should the mediator respond?

4.  Imagine you are the mediator in the *Girls Gone Wild* case excerpted in Chapter 6. In that case, the judge issued an order for the parties to try mediation to resolve their case that included a specific requirement that the parties "participate in good faith." Following the mediation, the judge asks you to describe to him the participation level of each party. How should you respond?

5.  During the course of a mediation, one party discloses to you in caucus that he is severely depressed over the lawsuit and is seriously contemplating suicide. He describes to you in detail his plans to end his life and you believe that he intends to follow through with those plans. What should you do?

6.  You are serving as a mentor for a new mediator by observing that person conduct a mediation. During caucus, a party shares sensitive information with the mediator trainee in confidence. When the mediator trainee meets with the other side, he discloses this information and asks them not to let the other party know that they know this information. What are your ethical obligations?

7.  If there is an applicable confidentiality statute in the jurisdiction in which the mediator is conducting her case and she violates that statutory

provision, is that act, by definition, also a breach of the mediator's ethical duty?

## 5.  Quality of Process

Standards relating to quality of process include such matters as delivering appropriate opening statements, knowing when to terminate or postpone a mediation, mediating only when the mediator has sufficient time to commit to the mediation, and promoting honesty and candor between and among all participants. For purposes of exposition and clarity, the analysis below divides these elements into four categories, with notes and comments for each category.

### a.  Timeliness

### i.  Model Standards of Conduct for Mediators

#### STANDARD VI. QUALITY OF THE PROCESS

**A.** A mediator shall conduct a mediation in accordance with these Standards and in a manner that promotes diligence, timeliness, safety, presence of the appropriate participants, party participation, procedural fairness, party competency and mutual respect among all participants.

**1.** A mediator should agree to mediate only when the mediator is prepared to commit the attention essential to an effective mediation.

**2.** A mediator should only accept cases when the mediator can satisfy the reasonable expectation of the parties concerning the timing of a mediation.

### ii.  Mediation Dilemmas for Discussion

1.  The day before a scheduled mediation, the mediator's 84-year-old mother falls and breaks her hip and wrist and has emergency surgery. The mediator is the primary caregiver and patient advocate for his mother. The mediation has been scheduled for several weeks and the court hearing date for the parties is shortly after the scheduled mediation. Both parties are represented by counsel. The mediator believes that he can spare approximately three hours for mediation before going to see his mother. What should the mediator do?

2.  You are a very popular mediator and your calendar fills quickly. You are contacted by an attorney to schedule a one-day mediation. Your first available date is one month away but you are only available for a half day; in your mediation experience, a certain number of cases settle prior to the scheduled mediation so you are confident that you will be able to provide the full-day for mediation. May you accept the case?

3.  Before you begin a court-ordered mediation, one of the parties announces that she has no intention of participating in the mediation and requests that the mediator report an impasse to the court. What are your ethical obligations?

# NOTES AND QUESTIONS

(1) The Florida Rules for Certified and Court-Appointed Mediators (*see* Appendix E) include the following provisions: "A mediator shall schedule a mediation in a manner that provides adequate time for the parties to fully exercise their right of self-determination" (Rule 10.430) and "A mediator shall . . . (2) adjourn or terminate any mediation which, if continued, would result in unreasonable emotional or monetary costs to the parties; (3) adjourn or terminate the mediation if the mediator believes the case is unsuitable for mediation or any party is unable or unwilling to participate meaningfully in the process." (Rule 10.420(b)). What are the challenges for a mediator in adhering to both of these provisions?

## b.   Participation and Candor

### i.   Model Standards of Conduct for Mediators

#### STANDARD VI. QUALITY OF THE PROCESS

**3.** The presence or absence of persons at a mediation depends on the agreement of the parties and the mediator. The parties and mediator may agree that others may be excluded from particular sessions or from all sessions.

**4.** A mediator should promote honesty and candor between and among all participants, and a mediator shall not knowingly misrepresent any material fact or circumstance in the course of a mediation.

### ii.   Mediation Dilemmas for Discussion

1.   An unrepresented party asks to have a friend join her in the mediation. May the mediator deny this request? If the other side does not object? If the other side objects? *Note the interplay with self-determination requirements.*

2.   In a mediation of a dissolution of a business partnership, the mediator learns in caucus with one party that that individual has been cheating the business by funneling money to an off-shore bank account that the other partners know nothing about. The mediator does not have permission to share this information. What should the mediator do? *Note the interplay with confidentiality requirements.*

# NOTES AND QUESTIONS

(1)   The Model Standards of Practice for Family and Divorce Mediation (*see* Appendix C) Standard III states that before family mediation begins, a mediator ". . . should provide the participants with an overview of the process and its purposes, including: . . . informing the participants that the presence or absence of other persons at a mediation, including attorneys, counselors or advocates, depends on the agreement of the participants and the mediator, unless a statute or regulation otherwise requires or the mediator believes that the presence of another person is required or may be beneficial because of a history or threat of violence or other serious coercive activity by a participant." How would a mediator implement

this ethical obligation if there was no statute or regulation in place, but the mediator believed that the participation of a support person for one of the parties was necessary? What if that party wanted to go forward without the support person?

(2)   According to the Reporter's Notes to the Model Standards (Appendix B), Standard VI(A)(4) was intended to reflect "the nuanced environment in which mediation occurs" by prohibiting a mediator from knowingly misrepresenting a material fact or circumstance to a mediation participant while acknowledging that resolving matters in mediation is not always predicated on there having been complete honesty and candor among those present. Is this balance consistent with or supported by other Standards? *Note the interplay with Standard I regarding self-determination.*

(3)   How, if at all, does an attorney's ethical obligations regarding truthfulness in negotiations (*see* Chapter 2) support or undermine the mediator's ethical obligation set forth in Standard VI(A)(4)?

(4)   Note that the language of the standard is "promote" rather than "ensure" honesty and candor. In what ways does a mediator "promote honesty and candor between and among all participants"? Does it matter if one or more of the parties are unrepresented?

## c.   Advice, Opinions, Information

### i.   Model Standards of Conduct for Mediators
#### STANDARD VI. QUALITY OF THE PROCESS

**5.** The role of a mediator differs substantially from other professional roles. Mixing the role of a mediator and the role of another profession is problematic and thus, a mediator should distinguish between the roles. A mediator may provide information that the mediator is qualified by training or experience to provide, only if the mediator can do so consistent with these Standards.

**6.** A mediator shall not conduct a dispute resolution procedure other than mediation but label it mediation in an effort to gain the protection of rules, statutes, or other governing authorities pertaining to mediation.

**7.** A mediator may recommend, when appropriate, that parties consider resolving their dispute through arbitration, counseling, neutral evaluation or other processes.

**8.** A mediator shall not undertake an additional dispute resolution role in the same matter without the consent of the parties. Before providing such service, a mediator shall inform the parties of the implications of the change in process and obtain their consent to the change. A mediator who undertakes such role assumes different duties and responsibilities that may be governed by other standards.

### ii.   Mediation Dilemmas for Discussion

1.   If the mediator concludes that the parties are at impasse, may the mediator, consistent with these standards, propose the following: if both sides are willing, each will privately reveal to the mediator their "bottom

line." With this information, the mediator will determine if the bottom line numbers overlap; if they do, the mediator will split the difference and inform the parties of the number and the case will settle at that number. If the numbers are close but do not overlap, the mediator will tell the parties "you are close and I suggest that we continue to mediate." If the mediator determines that the parties are "too far apart," the mediator will inform them that they are at impasse.

2. An authorized agent for a financing company brings an action in small claims court against a party, alleging failure to make monthly payments pursuant to a legally executed contract and note. Both the contract and the note are standard documents used by the consumer lending company. The claim is for $1,250. At a pre-trial session, the defendant admits to owing the money. The judge asks the defendant if there is a reason why she should not award a judgment to the plaintiff. The defendant states that she would like to work out a payment schedule, so the judge orders a session of mediation. At the mediation session, the mediator scans the agreements and notices a provision that obligates the defendant to pay interest at the rate of 29.5% per year if her payments are in arrears. In the mediation conversation, the mediator learns that the company representative had told the defendant in the hallway before the court session that she should avoid a judgment because it would hurt her credit. The mediator is not an attorney but she knows that interest on judgments accrue at the rate of 8% per year. With this context, the defendant proposes a payment schedule of $110 per month until the entire debt, including interest charges, is paid; the plaintiff quickly accepts the offer and requests that the agreement is written to reflect the contractual interest rate of 29.5% per year. Would it be permissible for the mediator to ask the defendant, "Are you aware that if a judgment were entered against you, the interest would be reduced from 29.5% to 8%?" Does your answer depend on whether the mediator is an attorney?

3. After mediating for a significant period of time, the parties are showing fatigue and frustration that they have been unable to arrive at a settlement. They turn to the mediator and request that you render a decision that resolves each of the contested issues. Can you do so ethically? Does it depend on whether your "decision" will be binding on the parties or just advisory? What if only one party makes the request?

## NOTES AND QUESTIONS

(1)   The Reporter's Notes to the Model Standards (*see* Appendix B) suggest that the language of Standard VI (A)(5) "recognizes the differing roles that a mediator as an individual assumes in his or her life and then supports the mediator sharing information that he or she is qualified by training or experience to provide only if it is done in a manner consistent with other Standards, most notably promoting party self-determination and sustaining mediator impartiality." As a practical matter, how does a mediator share information, which presumably favors one side, while "sustaining mediator impartiality?"

(2)    Dilemma 2, *supra*, (regarding the finance company in mediation) is based on a request for an ethical opinion in Florida. The Mediator Ethics Advisory Committee (MEAC) responded:

> It is improper for a mediator to provide legal advice by any method within the scope of a mediation, whether such advice be by statement, question or any other form of communication. The mediator, while fulfilling the role of reality tester, must be aware of, and consciously avoid, crossing the line between partiality and impartiality, neutrality and non-neutrality. The mediator may, however, often obtain the desired information if the question is framed more generally. It appears to the panel that the mediator wishes to be certain that the party is aware of the alternatives available for satisfaction of the debt-fulfillment of the contracted payments or payment through a judgment. It is the opinion of the panel that the mediator can obtain that information by asking the following: "Is interest levied on a judgment? Does either of you know?" These two questions set the stage for the parties to provide information to the mediator and to each other without placing the mediator in the position of providing that information. In so doing, the mediator assists in maximizing the exploration of alterna-tives, and adheres to the principles of fairness, full disclosure, self-determination, and the needs and interests of the participants while honoring the commitment to all parties to move toward an agreement.

Professor Jeffrey W. Stempel took issue with the MEAC's opinion in *Beyond Formalism and False Dichotomies: The Need for Institutionalizing a Flexible Concept of the Mediator's Role*, 24 Fla. St. U. L. Rev. 949 (1997). [*] Specifically, he stated:

> Although the issues of interpreting the law and the Rules are reasonably close, I believe the [Committee] opinion was in error and took an excessively restrictive view of mediator discretion under Florida law. The [rule] prohibits a mediator's giving of "legal advice," an admittedly mal-leable term, but hardly one that requires the expansive definition placed upon it by the [Committee]. As a law professor, like most lawyers, I am frequently asked about legal problems by students and friends. Although I have yet to agree to represent any of them (and could not do so in Florida without obtaining pro hac vice admission because I am a member of the Minnesota bar), I feel compelled as a teacher or friend to at least alert them to the apparent legal issues and to inform them of sources of information, potential counsel, and so on. Am I practicing law? Not at all (although some older vintage lawyers might assert it). Am I giving legal advice? Only in the broadest sense.

Do you agree with Professor Stempel?

(3)    Do these standards suggest that one style of mediation is preferable? Can one mediate in an evaluative manner and still adhere to the ethical guidelines?

(4)    Should an attorney mediator be accountable for the outcome? Professor

---

[*] Copyright © 1997 by the Florida State University Law Review. Reprinted with permission

Judith Maute argues: "when mediated settlement supplants public adjudication, the mediator is accountable for procedurally fair process and minimally fair substantive outcome. Procedural intervention to insure access to relevant information and independent advice is consistent with neutrality . . . . As to substantive fairness, the probable litigated outcome should serve as a reference point; the parties are free to find a solution that better serves their personal values and concerns. The mediator, however, should refuse to finalize an agreement when one party takes undue advantage of the other, when the agreement is so unfair that it would be a miscarriage of justice, or when the mediator believes it would not receive court approval. Completed agreements failing this standard should be vulnerable to rescission for a limited period of time on request of a party or during public review. If rescission is not possible, the disadvantaged party should have recourse against a mediator for malpractice." Judith Maute, *Public Values and Private Justice: A Case for Mediator Accountability*, 4 Geo. J. Legal Ethics 503 (1991). How does Maute's position compare to the Susskind/Stulberg debate which you read in Chapter 4? You should consider these mediator ethical standards when reviewing the question "Is Mediation the Practice of Law?" section later in this chapter.

## d.   Adjournment or Termination

### i.   Model Standards of Conduct

#### STANDARD VI. QUALITY OF THE PROCESS

**9.** If a mediation is being used to further criminal conduct, a mediator should take appropriate steps including, if necessary, postponing, withdrawing from or terminating the mediation.

**10.** If a party appears to have difficulty comprehending the process, issues, or settlement options, or difficulty participating in a mediation, the mediator should explore the circum stances and potential accommodations, modifications or adjustments that would make possible the party's capacity to comprehend, participate and exercise self-determination.

**B.** If a mediator is made aware of domestic abuse or violence among the parties, the mediator shall take appropriate steps including, if necessary, postponing, withdrawing from or terminating the mediation.

**C.** If a mediator believes that participant conduct, including that of the mediator, jeopardizes conducting a mediation consistent with these Standards, a mediator shall take appropriate steps including, if necessary, postponing, withdrawing from or terminating the mediation.

### ii.   Mediation Dilemmas for Discussion

1.  What is the mediator's ethical obligation if all of the parties want to continue with the mediation but the mediator is concerned with regard to one party's capacity to participate for any of the reasons detailed above? If the mediator decides to terminate a mediation, as a practice matter, how should she do it?

2.  You are the mediator for a community mediation. The dispute is between two neighbors; the complainant alleges that members of Respondent's

family damaged the roof on the Complainant's home. One proposed settlement option they identify is for the Respondent to perform the required repair work; this would result in considerable financial savings for the Complainant because the Respondent is not a licensed contractor. Do you have any ethical obligations to intervene?

3.  Party A, a former employee of Party B, files a claim seeking severance pay; the matter is referred to mediation. During the course of the discussion, Party B offers a cash settlement that is "off the books" so that various federal, state, and city taxes will not have to be paid. Party A immediately accepts the offer and they both ask that you, the mediator, assist them in drafting the agreement for their signature. Assuming that neither party is represented by counsel, how should you respond? Does it matter if you are licensed as a lawyer?

4.  As you escort the parties to the room for mediation, the attorney for Party A informs you that her client will not sit in the same room as Party B and she requests that the mediation be conducted exclusively by means of caucus. Party B adamantly rejects that proposed approach, asserting that he will not participate unless he gets to confront the lies that Party A is spreading. What are your ethical obligations? How should you respond? Does it depend on whether Party B is represented by an attorney at the mediation?

5.  You are the mediator who has been hired for this case. When you greet the parties and their attorneys, you detect a strong odor of alcohol on one of the parties. What should you do? What if the parties are unrepresented? What if you are fairly certain it is not the party but his attorney? What if you did not detect anything at the start of the mediation, but as the mediation has continued, you note that one of the parties appears to be under the influence of drugs or alcohol and does not appear to be tracking the conversation. Would your response differ if the party was unrepresented?

## NOTES AND QUESTIONS

(1)  The Reporter's Notes to the Model Standards (Appendix B) explain that there were public comments that suggested that the mediator's duty in situations where mediation is "being used to further criminal conduct" should be to affirmatively report such conduct to appropriate legal authorities. "The Joint Committee rejected that suggestion for two reasons. First, the subtly of such matters — including there being multi-issue cases in which only one issue raised a specter of criminal conduct — requires that a mediator be firm but flexible in addressing such a situation; second, confidentiality laws or agreements may prevent it, such that unless there were an exception in the confidentiality agreement for this situation or a mediator had a duty to report such conduct, a mediator might expose himself or herself to liability by reporting such conduct." Do you believe that the standard was appropriately crafted? Does an attorney who is an officer of the court have a higher duty?

(2)   Guardianship cases are sometimes mediated. If the presenting issue in the case is the capacity of one of the parties, can mediation be ethically offered? If so, how?

(3)   The Model Standards of Practice for Family and Divorce Mediation contain standards specifically devoted to situations involving child abuse and neglect (Standard IX) and domestic abuse (Standard X). Standard X(D) states that "the mediator shall consider taking measures to insure the safety of participants and the mediator." Does "shall consider" provide sufficient guidance to a mediator? Should a similar provision be included in the Model Standards of Conduct for Mediators?

## 6.   Advertising/Solicitation

In general, mediators are not restricted from advertising. They must, however, ensure that their advertising is truthful and not misleading. Given the confusing status regarding certification, qualification and licensure of mediators, the requirement accurately represent one's qualifications can pose subtle, but significant challenges.

### a.   Model Standards of Conduct for Mediators

#### STANDARD VII. ADVERTISING AND SOLICITATION

**A.** A mediator shall be truthful and not misleading when advertising, soliciting or otherwise communicating the mediator's qualifications, experience, services and fees.

     **1.** A mediator should not include any promises as to outcome in communications, including business cards, stationery, or computer-based communications.

     **2.** A mediator should only claim to meet the mediator qualifications of a governmental entity or private organization if that entity or organization has a recognized procedure for qualifying mediators and it grants such status to the mediator.

     **B.** A mediator shall not solicit in a manner that gives an appearance of partiality for or against a party or otherwise undermines the integrity of the process.

     **C.** A mediator shall not communicate to others, in promotional materials or through other forms of communication, the names of persons served without their permission.

### b.   Mediation Dilemmas for Discussion

1.   Is the following advertisement ethically permissible: *Want Your Case Settled? Hire Larry Settle, Certified Mediator — 95% settlement rate.* What if there was no mediator certification scheme in the locale in which the advertisement ran?

2.   May a mediator describe mediation as "a dispassionate evaluation by a neutral third party?"

# NOTES AND QUESTIONS

(1) In 2010, the Florida Supreme Court revised the mediator standard of conduct relating to advertising. The basic provision is "A mediator shall not engage in any marketing practice, including advertising, which contains false or misleading information." In addition to re-titling the standard from "Advertising" to "Marketing Practices," the court added the following provisions:

> (c) Other Certifications. Any marketing publication that generally refers to a mediator being "certified" is misleading unless the advertising mediator has successfully completed an established process for certifying mediators that involves actual instruction rather than the mere payment of a fee. Use of the term "certified" in advertising is also misleading unless the mediator identifies the entity issuing the referenced certification and the area or field of certification earned, if applicable.

> (d) Prior Adjudicative Experience. Any marketing practice is misleading if the mediator states or implies that prior adjudicative experience, including, but not limited to, service as a judge, magistrate, or administrative hearing officer, makes one a better or more qualified mediator.

> . . .

> (f) Additional Prohibited Marketing Practices. A mediator shall not engage in any marketing practice that diminishes the importance of a party's right to self-determination or the impartiality of the mediator, or that demeans the dignity of the mediation process or the judicial system.

### Commentary

2010 Revision. . . . The roles of a mediator and an adjudicator are fundamentally distinct. The integrity of the judicial system may be impugned when the prestige of the judicial office is used for commercial purposes. When engaging in any mediation marketing practice, a former adjudicative officer should not lend the prestige of the judicial office to advance private interests in a manner inconsistent with this rule. For example, the depiction of a mediator in judicial robes or use of the word "judge" with or without modifiers to the mediator's name would be inappropriate. However, an accurate representation of the mediator's judicial experience would not be inappropriate.

## 7. Fees and Expenses

Most standards contain provisions regarding fees that a mediator may charge for services. Minimally, they require that a mediator disclose the basis of fees to be charged.

### a. Model Standards of Conduct

#### STANDARD VIII. FEES AND OTHER CHARGES

**A.** A mediator shall provide each party or each party's representative true and complete information about mediation fees, expenses and any other actual or potential charges that may be incurred in connection with a mediation.

     **1.** If a mediator charges fees, the mediator should develop them in light of all relevant factors, including the type and complexity of the matter, the qualifications of the mediator, the time required and the rates customary for such mediation services.

     **2.** A mediator's fee arrangement should be in writing unless the parties request otherwise.

     **B.** A mediator shall not charge fees in a manner that impairs a mediator's impartiality.

     **1.** A mediator should not enter into a fee agreement which is contingent upon the result of the mediation or amount of the settlement.

     **2.** While a mediator may accept unequal fee payments from the parties, a mediator should not use fee arrangements that adversely impact the mediator's ability to conduct a mediation in an impartial manner.

## b.  Mediation Dilemmas for Discussion

1. Presume that there is a highly publicized dispute in a community. The parties have not been willing to pay for a mediator because they do not think "more talking" will help to resolve it. Can a mediator encourage the parties to use mediation by offering to mediate pro bono?

2. A large employer has found using mediation to be useful and cost-effective in handling employment disputes. In order to encourage employees to use mediation rather than pursue litigation, the employer offers to pay the costs for these mediations. May a mediator ethically work under such an arrangement?

3. An insurance company maintains a short list of two or three mediators whom it will agree to utilize in the event that one of their cases is referred to mediation. As a result of the volume of work this insurance company generates, these mediators earn most of their annual income from this one insurance company. Does this arrangement raise any concerns about the mediator's impartiality as required by Standard VIII(B)?

4. The mediation unexpectedly extends through the dinner hour. In order to maintain momentum, the mediator orders food for the participants and the attorneys to be delivered to the mediation office. If the mediator's initial fee statement did not include any information about meals, must the mediator cover the costs?

5. Your normal fee for mediation is $100/hour. You are contacted by a large company to handle a mediation. You know that it would be no problem for the company to pay a mediator's fee of $500/hour or more. Is it ethically permissible for you to charge more for the large company case?

## NOTES AND QUESTIONS

(1)  The propriety of the use of contingency fees in mediation received spirited attention during the Model Standards revision process. Some argued that any contingent fee puts the mediator in the position of having a vested interest in the outcome of the mediation, and therefore it is inherently wrong because it compromises a mediator's impartiality. Others suggested that mediators should be entitled to a "success fee" or a "bonus" — especially in very large cases in which all of the parties are represented by counsel and are very sophisticated. For a more detailed discussion of contingency fees in the context of mediation, see Scott Peppet, *Contractarian Economics and Mediation Ethics: The Case for Customizing Neutrality Through Contingency Fee Mediation*, 82 Tex. L. Rev. 227, 239 (2003). Proponents of such arrangements contend that the mediator should be working for a settlement, so there is no conflict regarding a mediator's impartiality — such an arrangement simply enables the mediator to share in the value created by a settlement. Do you believe mediators should be restricted from all contingent fee arrangements?

## 8.   Obligations to the Profession

Many standards include aspirational provisions, in addition to ethical duties that resolve particular practice dilemmas. These provisions encourage a mediator to help to mentor/train less experienced mediators, support research, foster diversity within the field, and strive to make mediation accessible to all.

### a.   Model Standards of Conduct

#### STANDARD IX. ADVANCEMENT OF MEDIATION PRACTICE

**A.** A mediator should act in a manner that advances the practice of mediation. A mediator promotes this Standard by engaging in some or all of the following:

**1.** Fostering diversity within the field of mediation.

**2.** Striving to make mediation accessible to those who elect to use it, including providing services at a reduced rate or on a pro bono basis as appropriate.

**3.** Participating in research when given the opportunity, including obtaining participant feedback when appropriate.

**4.** Participating in outreach and education efforts to assist the public in developing an improved understanding of, and appreciation for, mediation.

**5.** Assisting newer mediators through training, mentoring and networking.

**B.** A mediator should demonstrate respect for differing points of view within the field, seek to learn from other mediators and work together with other mediators to improve the profession and better serve people in conflict.

## NOTES AND QUESTIONS

(1)   What is the relationship of standards of conduct to "best practices"?

(2)   If a mediator never provides pro bono mediation services or assists new mediators as a mentor, should that mediator be subject to sanctions, such as removal from the court's roster of mediators? Does it matter if the mediator has never been asked to do so? Should the mediator only be subject to sanctions if someone files a complaint?

## C.  ENFORCEMENT OF ETHICAL STANDARDS

Once standards of conduct are adopted, the next phase to consider is enforcement. In the following excerpts, Michael Moffitt reviews the most common ways a mediator can be susceptible to a civil suit for malpractice, a disciplinary action for misconduct, a criminal proceeding, or sanction by a professional association, and Mel Rubin suggests actions a mediator may pursue to prevent being subject to a malpractice claim. As you read these excerpts, consider if the standards of conduct referenced above are written in a manner that would enable one to successfully sustain a misconduct or malpractice claim against a mediator.

### TEN WAYS TO GET SUED:
### A GUIDE FOR MEDIATORS
8 Harv. Negot. L. Rev. 81, 81–86, 89–90, 92–98,
102–05, 107–31 (2003)*
By Michael Moffitt

Mediators have practiced for decades without significant exposure to legal actions stemming from their mediation conduct. Despite the thousands, if not millions, of disputants who have received mediation services, instances of legal complaints against mediators are extraordinarily rare. Several factors likely contribute to the historical lack of litigation against mediators. Many parties are happy with mediators' services, making lawsuits irrelevant. In some practice contexts, mediators enjoy qualified or quasi-judicial immunity from lawsuits. Confidentiality protections and privileges often prevent public and, sometimes, even private examination of mediators' behaviors. Mediators and former mediation parties may also be inclined to settle post-mediation disputes out of court. Perhaps most significantly, the legal requirements of likely causes of action present considerable obstacles to any plaintiff seeking to recover from a former mediator.

. . . .

Mediators confronted with complaints regarding their mediation services face sanctions from four basic sources. First, some mediator misconduct may create personal, civil liability under which the mediator would owe compensation to the complaining party for injuries caused by mediator misconduct. Most of the examples outlined in this article create at least a risk of private civil lawsuits alleging either contractual or tort-based liability. Second, certain mediator misconduct may constitute criminal behavior, subjecting the media-tor to sanctions ranging from fines to imprisonment. Only a few of the behaviors listed below rise even to the level of criminal misdemeanors.

---

Third, mediators operating within formal referral programs risk exposure to the complaint mechanisms of the programs in which they serve. Not all mediators operate within the structure of a formal program. However, mediators who operate within referral structures such as court-annexed pro-grams or community pro-grams are almost always subject to a set of standards of conduct. In many circumstances, mediators operating in affiliation with a court-sponsored or court-annexed mediation program do not face civil liability because they will qualify for either quasi-judicial or qualified immunity. A mediator who fails to uphold the standards of most referral programs risks sanctions that could range from reprimands to disqualification from future service in the program to the imposition of the costs of the proceeding in which the misconduct took place.

Fourth, many mediators maintain membership in voluntary associations, most of which require their members to uphold certain principles or standards of conduct. A party complaining of mediator misconduct can seek sanctions within the voluntary association by demonstrating a violation of those standards. Many voluntary organizations have developed complaint or grievance procedures. A mediator who violates the terms of an organization's standards of conduct risks sanctions ranging from required apologies and additional training to suspension or revocation of membership. Some voluntary associations may even publish the names of mediators found to have engaged in improper behavior. In most circumstances, violations of voluntary association standards of conduct would not directly create the basis for legal action. If, however, the mediator's contract made reference to membership in the voluntary association, then the terms of the association's standards of conduct may be implied into the agreement to mediate, possibly creating a basis for legal action.

Technically, perhaps, the term "getting sued" applies only to sanctions creating personal civil liability through a contract or tort-based claim. Nevertheless, actions within each of these four categories may be significant to a mediator seeking to avoid sanction for misconduct.

I. Fail to Disclose a Conflict of Interest

Melissa Mediator is a member of a small consulting firm specializing in corporate dispute resolution. One of the firm's clients is a large, multi-national conglomerate. Unlike most of her colleagues, Melissa has never done work for the conglomerate. A dispute arises between one of the subsidiaries of the conglomerate and a local business. Melissa agrees to mediate the dispute and discloses nothing about the relationship between the conglomerate and her firm.

A mediator who holds an interest in opposition to one or more of the parties, and who fails to disclose that interest to the parties, opens the door to the prospect of legal action . . . .

Beyond the prospect of programmatic or organizational sanctions, a media-tor faces the possibility of civil liability if he or she fails to disclose a conflict of interest. In some circumstances, failure to disclose a potential conflict of interest could amount to a breach of an express contractual term . . . .

Even in contracts lacking such express promises, impartiality may be implied as a term of the mediation contract . . . . No court has yet implied impartiality into a mediation contract, but the legal foundations of implied impartiality are sufficient to make such a ruling a genuine possibility. Mediators, therefore, may not necessarily avoid all potential legal consequences of conflicting interests merely by remaining contractually silent on the question.

A mediator faces significant liability for failure to disclose a conflict of interest only if the mediator's bias led him or her to take actions that resulted in injury to a mediation party . . . .

A mediator's obligations regarding conflicts of interest are not extinguished by initial disclosures . . . .

Perhaps even more significantly, a mediator's duty to avoid acquiring interests in conflict with parties may extend beyond the life of the mediation. For example, in *Poly Software International v. Su*,[34] a lawyer-mediator conducted a mediation involving a dispute between a corporation and two former employees. Following the mediation, a dispute arose between the former employees, one of whom sought to retain the mediator as legal counsel. Citing Utah's Rules of Professional Conduct, the court disqualified the mediator from representing one former mediation party against another former mediation party in the new lawsuit. The court drew on language in Model Rule 1.9 in concluding that the ban against subsequent adverse representations in a "substantially related matter" applied to this case because of the "confidential relationship" between mediators and mediation parties. Many voluntary associational standards of conduct have codified this result with provisions that require mediators to guard against subsequent professional relationships that may give rise to the appearance of partiality. No theory bars, in perpetuity, a mediator from acquiring any interests in conflict with a former mediation party. Nevertheless, a mediator's obligation to avoid conflicts of interests does not extinguish at the moment when a mediation concludes.

II. Breach a Specific Contractual Promise Regarding Structure or Outcome

Marijke Mediator has the disputants sign her standard Agreement to Mediate. The agreement says, "In addition to talking together as a group, each party will have a chance to meet with the mediator privately." Marijke's standard agreement also states, "At the conclusion of the mediation, the mediator will assist the parties in writing up the terms of an agreement." The parties sign the agreement, and Marijke conducts the mediation. After several hours of joint session discussions, Marijke concludes that the mediation is unlikely to produce a useful result and terminates the mediation . . . .

One relatively common set of contractual promises that create exposure to liability involves pre-commitments regarding the mediation structure . . . For example, in the hypothetical contract described at the outset of this section, Marijke promises to meet with each of the parties separately . . . [A] party might complain that Marijke failed to implement a specifically described step in the process and in so doing breached the mediation contract. Damages in such a claim would be

---

[34] 880 F. Supp. 1487 (D. Utah 1995)

difficult to establish, given the parties' voluntary participation in the mediation and the extraordinary degree of speculation required to determine what would have occurred if the mediator had undertaken the step in question. However, a mediator who describes a mediation process with specificity and then fails to implement that process risks civil liability for breach of contract.

A second potential risk in the structure of some mediation agreements comes from express, or even implied, promises of particular outcomes . . . As a general matter, a mediator is at no liability risk merely because he or she presides over a mediation that produces no settlement. If, however, a mediator promises a particular result, he or she risks civil liability if the mediation fails to produce that outcome . . . .

Similarly, liability may result from contractual guarantees about the nature of any settlement . . . [A] mediator is responsible only to assure that the parties' participation in the mediation is voluntary, and that any outcome is the product of an autonomous and informed decision. However, a mediator who contractually undertakes to assure the equity or efficiency of mediated settlement terms disrupts that baseline assumption in a way that may create subsequent liability. A mediator who promises to help the parties to reach, for example, a "fair outcome," risks a subsequent allegation that he or she failed to assure that a particular outcome was substantively and distributively fair.

## III. Engage in the Practice of Law

After considerable efforts to facilitate an agreement, and at the request of the disputants, Marjorie Mediator examines the evidence each side has compiled and develops her best assessment of a court's likely disposition of the case. The parties then quickly agree to basic settlement terms. Again at the parties' request, Marjorie drafts a formal contract to capture the terms of the parties' agreement . . .

In some states, a mediator who predicts the outcome of a disputed legal issue engages in the practice of law . . . . The practice of law is often defined as including drafting settlement documents whose terms go beyond those specified by the disputants. A mediator who advances one settlement option as more favorable than another may also be engaging in the practice of law. However, as the North Carolina Bar has admitted in their treatment of the topic, "there are no bright lines" in defining the practice of law.

## IV. Engage in the Practice of Law Badly

Mortimer Mediator facilitates an agreement between disputing former business partners. The agreement includes a voluntary dismissal of certain pieces of litigation, a new licensing agreement on the partnership's intellectual property, and a division of the partnership's assets. Based on Mortimer's advice about a "tax smart" way to craft the deal, the parties agree to a novel agreement structure proposed and drafted by Mortimer. Later, a dispute arises over the interpretation of a poorly drafted clause in the agreement, and both parties find themselves stuck with substantial tax burdens that could have been avoided with a more standard agreement.

A mediator who negligently engages in the practice of law faces not only the kinds of complaints described in the section immediately above, but also the prospect of a professional negligence or legal malpractice suit . . . . The threat of legal malpractice applies equally to attorney-mediators and non-attorney-mediators whose behavior constitutes the practice of law . . . .

Any legal malpractice claim requires a demonstration that the attorney owed a duty to the plaintiff and caused injury to the plaintiff by breaching that duty . . . . Without answering, therefore, the question of whether a mediator owes a duty of loyalty to a particular client, the mediator owes at least a duty not to provide negligent legal services to the parties. A mediator who refuses to render legal services to a mediation party may be at no risk of subsequent legal action, but if he or she chooses to render legal services, the services must be at least minimally competent . . . .

[M]ediators who choose to pursue activities constituting the practice of law will be held responsible for conducting legal research to supplement their legal understanding . . . .

## V. Breach Confidentiality Externally

To the surprise of the disputants, Marcus Mediator calls a press conference during a break in the mediation. At the press conference, Marcus reveals that the plaintiffs have indicated an intention not to pursue at least certain parts of their original lawsuit against the City. Marcus further says to the press, "Now, with a little flexibility from the City, we should be able to get the whole thing settled."

. . . .

A mediator who breaches confidentiality externally . . . faces the prospect of civil liability for damages resulting from that breach . . . . A mediator who shares mediation information with non-participants in violation of those terms will be liable to a mediation party who can demonstrate an injury stemming from that breach of confidentiality . . . .

Under certain circumstances, a mediator could even be liable for breaches of confidentiality under the tort theory of privacy . . . . Public disclosure of private information may create tort-based liability if a person of ordinary sensibilities would find the information disclosed to be "highly offensive" and "objectionable." . . .

A mediator's duties regarding confidentiality do not extinguish at the termination of a mediation . . . . Most programs requiring [post-mediation] reports now strictly limit the information to be included in those reports. A mediator who supplements these reports with other information stands at risk of program sanction and civil liability.

## VI. Breach Confidentiality Internally

Plaintiffs brought suit seeking injunctive relief to force a change in a particular policy at the defendant corporation and seeking modest monetary damages. During a private caucus, Marsha Mediator learns that the defendant has already decided to change the policies in question, in a way the plaintiffs will embrace. When Marsha asks defense counsel why they have not told the plaintiffs about the corporation's plans, they indicate that they hope to use the change in policies as a "trade-off concession" in order to minimize or eliminate any financial payment. In a subsequent private meeting with the plaintiffs, without the consent of the defendant, Marsha says, "Look, the defendants have already told me that they're going to make the policy change. The only issue is money."

. . . A mediator who receives private information faces considerable strategic and ethical decisions about how to handle the information. In some circumstances, a mediator who takes information privately shared by one party and improperly discloses it to other parties may face the prospect of sanction or civil liability . . . .

[A] mediator who makes explicit oral statements regarding confidentiality at the outset of a private caucus with a party creates at least the possibility of contract-based obligations regarding internal confidentiality.

Mediators violating internal confidentiality also face the possibility of tort liability under the theory of interference with prospective advantage . . . . A party whose information was leaked may reasonably believe that he or she is placed at a comparative disadvantage because of the breach of internal confidentiality . . . .

## VII. Maintain Confidentiality Inappropriately

Maurice Mediator learns during a conversation with a divorcing couple that the children are regularly subjected to living arrangements tantamount to abuse or neglect. Maurice mentions his concern, but both of the parents swear that the circumstances will change once they can finalize the divorce. Maurice says nothing to anyone outside of the mediation and proceeds to assist the parties in finalizing the terms of the divorce.

. . . .

The most obvious illustrations of conditions in which a mediator risks sanction for improperly maintaining confidentiality arise with so-called "mandatory reporting." Mandatory reporter laws hold certain individuals responsible for informing state authorities of incidences of misconduct such as child abuse, elder abuse, and abandonment . . . .

Mediators who fail to uphold the requirements of mandatory reporting face a range of sanctions . . . .

Failure to report in a mandatory reporting situation can also create grounds for civil liability. As with criminal prosecutions, actions in tort against persons who improperly fail to report abuse are rare. Nevertheless, mediators stand some risk of civil liability for failing to report instances of abuse.

Referral sources and voluntary associations typically provide standards of conduct either permitting or demanding a breach of confidentiality in conditions such as those under consideration here . . . .

Beyond the circumstance of mandatory reporting requirements, so-called *Tara-*

*soff*[139] conditions may also create an obligation for mediators to breach confidentiality. The *Tarasoff* case involved a psychologist who learned that one of his patients intended to kill a woman in whom the patient had an unrequited romantic interest. The psychologist maintained confidentiality, and his patient murdered the woman. The woman's family brought a wrongful death action against the psychologist. The California Supreme Court ultimately ruled that the psychiatrist had a duty to prevent harm to the victim, even if that meant breaching patient confidentiality. States vary broadly regarding the existence or scope of *Tarasoff* disclosure obligations, with most retreating from any duty to warn . . . . Fortunately, *Tarasoff* conditions are extremely rare, but they create a second set of circumstances in which a mediator may be exposed to complaints for upholding confidentiality inappropriately.

## VIII. Advertise Falsely

Mitchell Mediator's website touts his mediation services as "expert." In part, it says, "Over 1,000 cases of experience. Certified and sanctioned by the State and by prominent national mediation organizations." Mitchell is a former judge who presided over more than a thousand civil cases during his years on the bench. He has formally mediated, however, only a few dozen cases. Furthermore, neither the state nor the national mediation organizations to which Mitchell belongs certifies or sanctions mediators. Mitchell is simply a member of the mediation rosters each body maintains.

. . . .

The risk of civil liability for advertising falsely stems principally from a theory of fraudulent inducement. In order to prevail in a complaint against a mediator on this theory, a plaintiff needs to demonstrate that the mediator knowingly made a false representation about a material issue, that the plaintiff reasonably relied upon the representation, and that the plaintiff's reliance produced injury . . . .

In addition to facing private civil lawsuits for compensatory damages, a mediator who improperly advertises his or her credentials or services may also face the prospect of private actions under consumer protection laws . . . .

A mediator making false public statements about his or her credentials may also be subject to criminal charges . . . .

## IX. Inflict Emotional Distress on a Disputant

During the mediation, Muriel Mediator adopts an aggressive approach to creating settlement. As always, she had told the parties, a divorcing couple, "Bring your toothbrushes when you show up to my mediation." The divorcing wife, unrepresented by counsel, is visibly worn down by Muriel's relentless efforts at "persuasion." When the wife protests and indicates a desire to leave, Muriel threatens to report to the judge that the wife did not participate in the mediation in good faith. Muriel further indicates that such a report would "all but guarantee

---

[139] *See* Tarasoff v. Regents of the University of California, 551 P.2d 334 (Cal. 1976)

that you'll lose your claim for custody of the children."

While mediators have no obligation to guarantee the comfort and happiness of mediation parties, mediators do not operate with carte blanche regarding their treatment of parties . . . [I]f a mediator's conduct rises to the level of tortious infliction of emotional distress, the mediator is exposed to a threat of civil liability.

All jurisdictions provide for common law, tort-based claims against people who inflict emotional distress on others under certain circumstances. The most common construction of the tort of intentional infliction of emotional distress requires a plaintiff to demonstrate that the mediator intentionally or recklessly engaged in extreme or outrageous conduct, causing emotional distress in the plaintiff. Jurisdictions vary in the evidence required to demonstrate emotional distress. Some jurisdictions also recognize claims sounding in negligence rather than intentional tort. In most circumstances, however, a plaintiff must demonstrate that the mediator intentionally or recklessly inflicted the distress. Fortunately, few imaginable mediator behaviors are sufficiently outrageous to satisfy the elements of the tort of infliction of emotional distress . . . .

Disputants can enter mediations in fragile emotional states. Mediators' practices often encourage the parties to develop trust in the mediator, and some practices even encourage a degree of deference. In such a context, a mediator who recklessly disregards the psychological impacts of his or her mediation conduct risks creating actionable emotional distress.

## X. Commit Fraud

In a private caucus, the plaintiffs tell Manuel Mediator that they would be able to break this case wide open if only they could get some cooperation from a few important executives in the defendant corporation. They admit, how-ever, that they have had no luck so far in their efforts. Manuel then sits down privately with the general counsel for the defendant and says, "Look, I spoke with the plaintiffs. They have just lined up some key insider witnesses, including a couple members of your management team. It's time for you to end this." The general counsel looks surprised but increases the defendant's offer considerably. The mediator takes the new offer to the plaintiffs, who quickly agree to it.

. . . . A mediator commits fraud if the mediator knowingly misrepresents a material fact and a mediation party reasonably relies on that misrepresentation to his or her detriment . . . .

A mediator's misrepresentation creates a risk of fraud only if the subject of the misrepresentation is material to the topic of the mediation . . . . In all but the most extraordinary cases, statements of opinion cannot constitute fraud . . . For example, a mediator who merely tells one party, "I think this is a fair settlement offer" runs little risk of a subsequent complaint in which the party later accuses the mediator of fraud for having shared the opinion. On the other hand, a mediator who knowingly misrepresents the existence of witnesses and says, "I know that they have just secured cooperation from members of your management team and have uncovered a smoking gun memo," and then adds, "so I think this is a fair settlement offer" exposes himself or herself to a fraud claim . . . . A bright line does not always exist between what constitutes an opinion (not material) as opposed to a statement of fact (potentially material), leaving mediators who employ misrepresentations as part of their mediation practice exposed to liability.

. . . .

Honorable Mention: Mediate Poorly

Michael Mediator misses an opportunity to improve the parties' understanding of each other and of the relevant issues. Michael creates an unhelpful agenda and refuses to adapt his approach. Michael misreads the parties' primary concerns. He makes inappropriate suggestions. Michael is unprepared.

He listens horribly. Michael oversees a lengthy process that produces no agreement and worsens the parties' relationship.

. . . While mediators face a theoretical risk of a malpractice or negligencebased suit, the nature of mediation practice makes negligence an unlikely source of liability exposure.

. . . To establish negligence, a plaintiff must demonstrate that the mediator breached his or her duty of care toward the plaintiff. A successful negligence-based claim would also require a demonstration of causation and injury . . . .

The difficulty of defining a standard or customary set of practices against which to measure a mediator's performance creates a significant challenge to any plaintiff pursuing a negligence-based action against a mediator . . . For better or worse (and I largely think it is for the better), the diversity of mediation renders the articulation of an identifiable customary practice difficult.

The nearly ubiquitous principle of mediation confidentiality further complicates the issue of identifying customary mediation practice . . . . [T]he cumulative effect of confidentiality prevents outsiders from generating a clear picture of what actually takes place in an "ordinary" mediation. This generalized secrecy presents an extraordinary barrier for a plaintiff trying to demonstrate a customary mediation practice . . . .

Even if a plaintiff successfully establishes a breach of duty by the mediator, causation and damages pose additional hurdles . . . . Unless a party can demonstrate that his or her capacity to exercise autonomy was impaired in some way, it would be difficult to lay blame for the terms of the agreement at the feet of the mediator.

The complex question of establishing damages further clouds a negligence-based claim . . . . Proving what would have happened in settlement discussions but for the interventions of a mediator or any other party demands extraordinary speculation . . . .

In the second circumstance, involving allegedly improper non-settlement, a plaintiff will have similar difficulty proving that the disputants would have reached a settlement but for the mediator's negligence. Many mediation cases fail to settle for reasons entirely separate from the mediator's competence . . . .

Establishing damages further complicates the claim in a non-settlement circumstance. Mediation parties have no general obligation to remain in mediation, even in so-called mandatory mediation contexts . . . . The fact that parties can vote with their feet makes negligence claims in non-settlement circumstances even more difficult to sustain . . . .

. . . Complaints against mediators are unlike natural disasters in that they are neither random nor entirely beyond mediators' control. An understanding of the possible foundations of liability, coupled with some care in describing and dispensing mediation services will help a mediator avoid getting sued.

## MEDIATOR MALPRACTICE: A PROPOSED DEFENSIVE PATH THROUGH THE MINEFIELD
Disp. Resol. Magazine, Vol. 17, No. 23, 24–25 (Fall 2010)[*]
By Melvin Rubin

So what are we to do to ensure that the process of mediation, the parties, and the mediator are protected? Below are some of the preventative as well as the curative measures. First the preventative acts:

1. One of the most important things that a mediator can do is define, distinguish, and clarify their role, preferably both in writing and in their opening statement. To accomplish this, mediator would have a thoughtful and well-worded opening statement and a letter to the participants in the mediation. The role of the mediator should be clearly stated, especially in contrast to any other roles that the mediator could be misconstrued as performing. This is especially true if the mediator comes from, or practices, another profession. . . . This role distinction is important enough to warrant repetitive comments during the course of the mediation and again, certainly, at the conclusion of the mediation when an agreement is being executed.

2. Any actions or behaviors that could be possibly construed as creating liability should be immediately addressed by the mediator. As an example, references to the mediator as "judge," "lawyer," "therapist," or any other professional designation should be clearly and immediately corrected . . . .

3. This corrective language can be made either in joint session or in caucus. However, from a preemptive strike perspective, the more witnesses to the statement, the better.

4. Marathon mediation should be carefully watched, and the "pulse" of the participants, especially the clients, be taken regularly. "We have been here now for more than five hours: is everybody willing to continue?" or a variation of this question should be asked by the mediator on a regular basis during marathon mediations. Equally important, those questions should be asked either in a joint session or with as many other parties/lawyers witnessing the question and the answer to verify everyone's consent to the continuation.

5.  The execution of the agreement should be conducted in such a manner as to dissuade any would-be later objector from filing any motions to challenge the agreement. This can take a variety of forms. This author has practiced a procedure of an oral voir dire in combination with the execution of the settlement agreement. Assuming the parties have reached an agreement and can be in the same room together for the execution of the agreement, a joint session should be called at which time the mediator asks the following series of questions of each client as they sign:

    a.  Have you read the agreement?

    b.  Do you understand the agreement?

    c.  Do you understand by signing such an agreement you are entering into a fully enforceable contract?

    d.  Are you signing this agreement voluntarily?

    e.  Have you asked your attorney any and all questions you might have and has she answered those satisfactorily?

    f.  Is there anything physical, psychological, or emotional that would have prevented you from understanding what we did here today? And finally,

    g.  Do you understand that I have performed the function of a mediator solely and exclusively and no other role and that you have made your own decision?

    . . . .

    From both a confidentiality and evidentiary standpoint, the voir dire has been allowed by the courts on the basis that they are conducted by the mediator as a regular course of conduct in all of their mediations.

6.  Undertake pro se cases with care and caution. Legal representation provides a buffer for the mediator. Without attorneys (or worse, with only one attorney) present, the dynamics and burdens change dramatically . . . clarification and repetition of one's role is essential.

7.  Be extremely careful in reference to confidentiality in multiparty cases,

From a curative nature, certain defenses would be fundamental should a mediator be faced with a malpractice suit or motion to set aside agreement.

1.  Assert any immunity provisions of your state or court.

2.  Mediator, as professionals, should carry professional malpractice insurance.
    . . .

3.  Whether to keep copious notes is a debate within the professions. . . . That decision must be made on an individual basis by the mediator . . . .

# NOTES AND QUESTIONS

(1)   Should Rubin's recommendation to include a "voir dire" before any mediation agreement is signed be standard practice for a mediator? Why or why not?

(2)   For an overview of mediator regulatory schemes, and an in-depth analysis of mediator grievance programs for court-connected mediation pro-grams in Florida, Georgia, Maine, Minnesota, and Virginia, see Paula Young, *Take It or Leave It, Lump It or Grieve It: Designing Mediator Complaint Systems That Protect Mediators, Unhappy Parties, Attorneys, Courts, the Process, and the Field*, 21 Ohio St. J. on Disp. Resol. 721 (2006).

(3)   Attorney mediators often can obtain riders to their legal malpractice coverage for their mediation activities. It is also possible for attorney and non-attorney mediators to obtain separate mediator malpractice insurance coverage. For a critical review of insurance coverage for mediators, see Paula Young's article, *Insurance Coverage for Mediators: You May as Well Be "Going Bare," or "There's No There There"* (unpublished).

(4)   In conjunction with the adoption of its standards of conduct in 1992, Florida adopted a disciplinary procedure to enforce the standards. In contrast, the AAA/ABA/ACR standards were not drafted with an enforcement scheme, although ACR utilizes the standards as part of the requirements for membership. Further, in the Standards themselves, the introduction states that "the fact that these Standards have been adopted by the respective sponsoring entities, should alert mediators to the fact that the Standards might be viewed as establishing a standard of care for mediators." What influence does the presence or absence of an enforcement scheme have on the standards? What would you expect to be some of the difficulties in attempting to enforce standards of conduct for mediators?

(5)   In Florida, the standards as originally adopted contained the following provision: "A mediator shall withdraw from mediation if the mediator believes the mediator can no longer be impartial." In 2000, the provision was revised to read: "A mediator shall withdraw from mediation if the mediator is no longer impartial." Is the 2000 language more enforceable? If so, how? Review the Model Standards with a view toward enforcement. Are the standards objective? Are they clear?

## D.   MEDIATION AND THE LEGAL SYSTEM

In the first portion of this section we examine the relationship between the mediation process and the mediator to legal practice. Is mediation the practice of law? Should it be?

The second section focuses on the special ethical and practical issues facing the lawyer mediator. When attorneys choose to work as mediators, they encounter special ethical constraints. In 1996, a Pennsylvania attorney mediator asked the local Bar Association whether, assuming compliance with the Model Standards of Conduct for Mediators, the attorney would also be deemed to have complied with the obligations under the Rules of Professional Conduct. The bar committee stated that the Rules of Professional Conduct may often impose additional burdens beyond the Model Standards. (Pa. Bar Ass'n Comm. on Legal Ethics and Prof. Resp.

Informal Op. No. 96-167, December 30, 1996.) The ethical burdens are especially complex for those lawyer-mediators who attempt to offer a mediation practice while maintaining their traditional law practice. For some lawyers in this situation, continuing their law practice may be a short-term financial necessity as they build their mediation business into a full-time endeavor. Other lawyer-mediators, however, enjoy pursuing both practices simultaneously, and believe that they are supportive of one another. "Aside from representing clients in dispute-resolution processes, lawyers often serve as third-party neutrals." (ABA Model Rules of Prof. Resp. Rule 2.4, cmt. 1.)

One author has stated: "Nowhere is cross-professionalism as problematic as it is for lawyer-mediators." Maureen E. Laflin, *Preserving the Integrity of Mediation Through the Adoption of Ethical Rules for Lawyer-Mediators*, 14 Notre Dame J.L. Ethics & Pub. Pol'y 479, 479 (2000). The ABA Model Rules focus on two ethical problems that are relevant to lawyer mediators. First, disputants in a mediation may experience "role confusion" if they are unsure whether a lawyer-mediator is acting only as a neutral or also has a duty to represent and protect their interests. Second, the ABA Model Rules recognize that lawyer mediators must deal with distinctive conflict of interest issues. For example, if a lawyer mediator mediates a dispute for a large company, has he created a conflict of interest which would prevent his representation of anyone having a dispute with that company? The law in this area is still developing and significant differences often exist between various jurisdictions. The lawyer-mediator must research the extant law and operative ethical opinions in to ensure that her conduct is in compliance with the duties imposed by the multiple professional standards. Finally, the combination of advocate and neutral practices also raises challenging business concerns including such issues as how to handle advertisement and solicitation materials. In addition, if the lawyer-mediator wishes to establish a mediation practice with non-attorneys, the lawyer will need to confront restrictions related to profit sharing between attorneys and non-attorneys.

## 1.   Is Mediation the Practice of Law?

## MEDIATION AND THE LEGAL SYSTEM, IS MEDIATION THE PRACTICE OF LAW?
14 Alternatives 57 (May 1996)*
By Carrie Menkel-Meadow

One of the hottest questions in ADR ethics is whether mediating a case is the "practice of law."

. . . . .

---

How we answer the question . . . will determine the standards by which we judge the work — whether we rely on legal ethics codes, or those of "coordinate" professions . . . .

If mediation is the practice of law (or as Geoffrey Hazard has argued, it is the "ancillary" practice of law), we must refer to lawyers' ethics codes. Trouble is, they provide little, if any, guidance about issues like: confidentiality (among parties and with mediators), conflicts of interests, fees, and unauthorized practice (in co-mediating, for example, with a non-lawyer).

. . . .

The risk, as with many ethical issues, is that the desired solution to one problem determines the conclusion. Most of us in the field are concerned about access to mediation — expanding the pool of capable mediators, and the choices for consumers of mediation services. Therefore, we would like to define mediation broadly, so that it doesn't involve the practice of law. To that end, we argue that mediation in its "pure" form of facilitation does not involve law, but communication and other skills.

One example of this approach is a proposal by the District of Columbia Bar to clarify and revise the local ethics rule dealing with the unauthorized practice of law. The proposed amendment expressly exempts mediation because "ADR services are not given in circumstances where there is a client relationship of trust and reliance and it is common practice for providers of ADR services explicitly to advise participants that they are not providing the services of legal counsel," Proposed Clarification and Revision of District of Columbia Court of Appeals Rule 49 Concerning the Unauthorized Practice of Law, Rule 49 Committee of the District of Columbia Bar.

## Lawyer-Client Relationship

This approach to the issue, one of the more popular ones, treats the absence of a lawyer-client relationship as the governing test. It allows a broad range of individuals to mediate, including non-lawyers and lawyers who are not members of the local or state bar.

Another route to the same result is to simply define away the problem. A report two years ago to the Tennessee Supreme Court Commission on Dispute Resolution by the state Board of Professional Responsibility illustrates this approach. It recommends a rule of professional responsibility that says: "A neutral shall give legal opinions to a party only in the presence of all parties, providing, however, that a prediction of litigation outcomes by a lawyer acting as a dispute resolution neutral shall not for purposes of this section constitute the provision of a legal opinion."

. . . .

For people concerned about standards and quality control in mediation, here's the problem: to the extent that mediators, especially those who work within court programs or by court referral, "predict" court results or "evaluate" the merits of the case (on either factual or legal grounds), they are giving legal advice.

Mediators, courts and rules may disclaim responsibility for any information mediators give out, or treat it as not given by an agent, fiduciary, or "counsel." But as a practical matter, parties and others may rely on what the mediator tells them, in assessing their alternatives, suggesting other options, and agreeing to settlements.

### Reliance on the Mediator

. . . .

The current trend . . . is to grant quasi-judicial immunity to at least court-based third-party neutrals . . . . However, that means parties have virtually no recourse against a third-party neutral when they rely on a mediator's information or advice that is unfair, unjust, or just plain wrong . . .

Ideally, we should analyze the work of third-party neutrals to see what they do, and then attempt to develop the appropriate regulatory models. I disagree with the argument that mediators can give neutral, unbiased "legal information" that is not the practice of law . . .

. . . .

While some ADR experts pin their analysis on "client representation," I prefer to look at reliance . . . .

When mediators engage in some prediction or application of legal standards to concrete facts — and especially when they draft settlement agreements, I think they are "practicing" law. That means neutrals who are not trained as lawyers need to be wary of evaluative mediation. They still have other options as mediators: they can limit their role to facilitation, co-mediate with lawyers, or ask the parties to release them from liability for bad legal advice. Non-lawyer mediators might still be subject to the . . . regulation against unauthorized practice of law . . . .

Giving legal predictions and evaluations is law work, whether or not there is a lawyer-client relationship. Within these boundaries, we need rules that permit qualified people without legal training to mediate . . .

Still there's clearly a quality control problem. Just because a mediator has a law degree — or even an up-to-date license to practice — does not mean that he or she will give accurate legal advice, prediction or evaluation.

## LAWYERS WHO MEDIATE ARE NOT PRACTICING LAW
14 Alternatives 74 (June 1996)*
By Bruce Meyerson

Generally speaking, to practice law, one must have a client. Assuming that mediators clarify with parties that no attorney-client relationship exists, engaging in a legal discussion would not be the practice of law. Specifically, in order for a mediator's conduct in advising parties about the legal aspects of a particular dispute to be considered the practice of law, the party to the mediation must view the

---

mediator as her lawyer and therefore assume that she is receiving legal advice for her personal benefit. If the parties are represented by counsel, or if the mediator has carefully clarified that the unrepresented parties do not view the mediator as their lawyer, I cannot imagine a situation where parties to the mediation will be confused about the mediator's role and mistakenly assume that the mediator is functioning as a lawyer . . . .

If . . . mediators are practicing law any time they give evaluations or predict outcomes, a number of undesirable consequences will follow. First, lawyer-mediators would be subject to all of the duties and obligations under the Model Rules, and presumably would owe these duties to the parties in the mediation. Although it is possible that a lawyer can function as a neutral mediator on behalf of clients in certain limited circumstances, Ethics Rule 2.2, in most instances the role of a mediator is fundamentally incompatible with an attorney's role in representing a client. For example, a mediator is supposed to be impartial and evenhanded during the mediation. On the other hand, a lawyer representing a client owes that client a duty of undivided loyalty. Most certainly, this obligation is inconsistent with the neutral duties owed to all of the parties in mediation . . . .

Second, a conclusion that mediation is the practice of law would raise the specter that thousands of professionals in other disciplines are engaged in the unauthorized practice of law. Surely, this is casting the "practice of law" net too widely.

Third, if mediation is the practice of law, judges presiding over settlement conferences would be breaking ethical rules in many jurisdictions. That could happen in states that prohibit judges from practicing law while they serve on the bench. Under these rules, judges would be practicing law when, in an attempt to settle a case, they discuss the legal merits of a case with disputing parties. A judge engaged in this common settlement technique would be engaged in unethical conduct . . . .

Clearly, we need a framework for regulating mediation. But we can develop that framework without labeling mediation as the practice of law.

## NOTES AND QUESTIONS

(1)   The Department of Dispute Resolution Services of the Supreme Court of Virginia adopted Guidelines on Mediation and the Unauthorized Practice of Law (UPL) in response to a UPL case filed in Virginia as an effort to "provide guidance and protection" particularly to the non-attorney mediator population. The Guidelines have sparked considerable debate on both sides of the issue. Concerns raised include that the guidelines are overly restrictive and "rob mediation of its fluidity and flexibility." In the June 2000 edition of *Alternatives*, Geetha Ravindra, then-director of the Department of Dispute Resolution Services explained the committee's actions in the following excerpt:[*]

---

[*]   Geetha Ravindra, *The Response: The Goal Is to Inform, Not Impede ADR*, Alternatives to the High Cost of Litigation, Vol. 18 No. 6, pp. 124–25 (June 2000). Copyright © 2000. All rights reserved. Reprinted with permission.

[The UPL committee] recognized by definition, the mediation process is not the practice of law. There are activities, however, that mediators engage in during the mediation process, that may constitute the practice of law. The committee aspired to identify a test by which activities could be measured to assess whether they fall within the definition of the practice of law . . . .

As a result, the guidelines try to identify the extent to which evaluation may be provided in mediation without UPL concerns and when evaluation more clearly falls into the category of the practice of law. The guidelines . . . allow mediators to offer evaluation of, for example, strengths and weaknesses of a case, assess the value and cost of settlement alternatives, or barriers to settlement.

The committee believed that mediators should not predict the specific resolution of legal issues because such activity is part of a lawyer's function as advisor and counselor and could give rise to an implicit lawyer/client relationship . . . [however] neutrals may be able to provide a range of possible outcomes under this definition.

Is this proposal consistent with the Model Standards of Conduct for Mediators?

(2)  In 2002, the American Bar Association Section of Dispute Resolution adopted a resolution on Mediation and the Unauthorized Practice of Law which contained the following principles: mediation is not the practice of law; mediators' discussions of legal issues do not constitute legal advice, whether or not the mediator is an attorney; the preparation of a memorandum of understanding or settlement agreement by a mediator, incorporating the terms of settlement specified by the parties, does not constitute the practice of law (but, if the mediator drafts an agreement that goes beyond the terms specified by the parties, he or she may be engaged in the practice of law); and the mediator should inform parties that the mediator is not providing them with legal advice, that a settlement agreement may affect the parties' legal rights, and that each of the parties has the right to seek advice of independent legal counsel throughout the mediation process.

(3)  The Association for Conflict Resolution addressed this issue by adopting the following resolution in 2006:

ACR affirms that mediation is a distinct practice with its own body of knowledge, foundational principles, values and standards of practice. While ACR recognizes that the definition of and penalties associated with the unauthorized practice of law are matters of state law, ACR affirms that mediators who practice mediation consistent with standards of conduct approved by ACR should not be considered to have engaged in the unauthorized practice of law. If an ACR member is charged with unauthorized practice of law, ACR will provide assistance and/or support as may be appropriate.

What are the differences in the approaches taken by the ABA and ACR?

(4)  What are the arguments supporting and opposing the statement that mediation is the practice of law? Is there a relationship between style of practice

and the validity of such a statement?

(5)   See Paula Young, *A Connecticut Mediator in a Kangaroo Court?: Successfully Communicating the "Authorized Practice of Mediation" Paradigm to "Unauthorized Practice of Law" Disciplinary Bodies*, 49 S. Tex. L. Rev. 1047 (2008), for an interesting discussion of what happened when a non-attorney mediator was charged with the unauthorized practice of law.

## 2.   Confusing the Role of Lawyer and Mediator

While recognizing that both lawyers and non-lawyers may serve as mediators, the ABA Model Rules of Professional Conduct explain that lawyer-mediators face a unique problem in that unrepresented parties may be confused as to the lawyer-neutral's role and responsibilities. Thus, the Model Rule requires lawyer-mediators to clarify their role to unrepresented clients.

Rule 2.4(b), and its accompanying comments, make clear that the nature and extent of disclosure required will depend on the factual context of the situation, including the subject matter at issue, who the parties are, and the nature of the dispute resolution process. Lawyer-mediators are responsible for deciding precisely how and when to make the required disclosure, and may in some cases choose to make the disclosure in writing. Lawyer-mediators would be well advised to include a statement describing their role in an agreement to mediate that is signed by the disputants.

Concerns about possible role confusion may also limit the tasks in which the lawyer-mediator may engage. The Utah State Bar opined that it is improper for a lawyer-mediator to draft a settlement agreement and necessary court pleadings on behalf of divorcing disputants, after having successfully mediated their issues. Ethics Adv. Op. Comm. Op. No. 05-03, May 6, 2005 explains that drafting such documents is "the practice of law" and that it is improper in Utah to represent two adverse parties. However, the Opinion recognizes that a number of jurisdictions have reached contrary conclusions, and several committee members also dissented.

---

## RULE 2.4   LAWYER SERVING AS THIRD-PARTY NEUTRAL

(a) A lawyer serves as a third-party neutral when the lawyer assists two or more persons who are not clients of the lawyer to reach a resolution of a dispute or other matter that has arisen between them. Service as a third-party neutral may include service as an arbitrator, a mediator or in such other capacity as will enable the lawyer to assist the parties to resolve the matter.

(b) A lawyer serving as a third-party neutral shall inform unrepresented parties that the lawyer is not representing them. When the lawyer knows or reasonably should know that a party does not understand the lawyer's role in the matter, the lawyer shall explain the difference between the lawyer's role as a third-party neutral and a lawyer's role as one who represents a client.

### Comments

[1] Alternative dispute resolution has become a substantial part of the civil justice system. Aside from representing clients in dispute-resolution processes, lawyers often serve as third-party neutrals. A third-party neutral is a person, such as a mediator, arbitrator, conciliator or evaluator, who assists the parties, represented or unrepresented, in the resolution of a dispute or in the arrangement of a transaction. Whether a third-party neutral serves primarily as a facilitator, evaluator or decisionmaker depends on the particular process that is either selected by the parties or mandated by a court.

[2] The role of a third-party neutral is not unique to lawyers, although, in some court-connected contexts, only lawyers are allowed to serve in this role or to handle certain types of cases. In performing this role, the lawyer may be subject to court rules or other law that apply either to third-party neutrals generally or to lawyers serving as third-party neutrals. Lawyer-neutrals may also be subject to various codes of ethics, such as the Code of Ethics for Arbitration in Commercial Disputes prepared by a joint committee of the American Bar Association and the American Arbitration Association or the Model Standards of Conduct for Mediators jointly prepared by the American Bar Association, the American Arbitration Association and the Society of Professionals in Dispute Resolution.

[3] Unlike non-lawyers who serve as third-party neutrals, lawyers serving in this role may experience unique problems as a result of differences between the role of a third-party neutral and a lawyer's service as a client representative. The potential for confusion is significant when the parties are unrepresented in the process. Thus, paragraph (b) requires a lawyer-neutral to inform unrepresented par-ties that the lawyer is not representing them. For some parties, particularly parties who frequently use dispute-resolution processes, this information will be sufficient. For others, particularly those who are using the process for the first time, more information will be required. Where appropriate, the lawyer should inform unrepresented parties of the important differences between the lawyer's role as third-party neutral and a lawyer's role as a client representative, including the inapplicability of the attorney-client evidentiary privilege. The extent of disclosure required under this paragraph will depend on the particular parties involved and the subject matter of the proceeding, as well as the particular features of the dispute-resolution process selected.

[4] A lawyer who serves as a third-party neutral subsequently may be asked to serve as a lawyer representing a client in the same matter. The conflicts of interest that arise for both the individual lawyer and the lawyer's law firm are addressed in Rule 1.12.

[5] Lawyers who represent clients in alternative dispute-resolution processes are governed by the Rules of Professional Conduct. When the dispute-resolution process takes place before a tribunal, as in binding arbitration (*see* Rule 1.0(m)), the lawyer's duty of candor is governed by Rule 3.3. Otherwise, the lawyer's duty of candor toward both the third-party neutral and other parties is governed by Rule 4.1.

## NOTES AND QUESTIONS

(1)  Does Rule 2.4 adequately address all of the concerns raised by potential role confusion?

(2)  Another approach was highlighted in the *Ali Haghighi v. Russian-American Broadcasting Co.* cases included in Chapter 6. The Minnesota Civil Mediation Act includes a provision (Minn. Stat. § 572.35, subd. 1(1999)) that a mediated settlement agreement is not binding unless: "(1) it contains a provision stating that it is binding and a provision stating substantially that the parties were advised in writing that (a) the mediator has no duty to protect their interests or provide them with information about their legal rights; (b) signing a mediated settlement agreement may adversely affect their legal rights; (c) they should consult an attorney before signing a mediated settlement agreement if they are uncertain of their rights; or (2) the parties were otherwise advised of the conditions in clause (1)."

## 3.  Conflict of Interest Issues Facing the Lawyer-Mediator

Lawyer-mediators must worry about the possibility of conflicts of interest stemming from their dual practice. May an attorney attempt to mediate a dispute between two parties if she has, in the past, represented one or both parties? Is an attorney barred from mediating or litigating due to past representation by other members of her firm? Is the firm barred from litigating all disputes involving a particular company because a member of the firm mediated a dispute involving that company? Alternatively, once an attorney has served as a mediator in a dispute involving two clients, is the attorney forever precluded from representing either client as an advocate? The ABA Model Rules of Professional Conduct address many of these issues and are examined below. In addition, an article that examines the experiences of the Florida firm Cobb Cole & Bell illustrates how these problematic issues forced a firm that previously included both litigators and lawyer-mediators to break up into multiple entities.

## RULE 1.12  FORMER JUDGE, ARBITRATOR, MEDIATOR, OR OTHER THIRD-PARTY NEUTRAL

(A) Except as stated in paragraph (d), a lawyer shall not represent anyone in connection with a matter in which the lawyer participated personally and substantially as a . . . mediator . . . unless all parties to the proceeding give informed consent, confirmed in writing.

(b) A lawyer shall not negotiate for employment with any person who is involved as a party or as lawyer for a party in a matter in which the lawyer is participating personally and substantially as a . . . mediator . . .

(c) If a lawyer is disqualified by paragraph (a), no lawyer in a firm with which that lawyer is associated may knowingly undertake or continue representation in the matter unless:

(1) the disqualified lawyer is timely screened from any participation in the matter and is apportioned no part of the fee therefrom; and

(2) written notice is promptly given to the parties and any appropriate tribunal to enable them to ascertain compliance with the provisions of this rule.

# NOTES AND QUESTIONS

(1) Several aspects of this Rule should be highlighted. First, as a general matter a lawyer-mediator is foreclosed from representing a party for whom she earlier mediated a dispute. This prohibition can be waived by the parties, but only in writing. Second, the firm at which the lawyer works is *also* disqualified, but that disqualification can be overridden when the individual lawyer-mediator is "screened" from actual or financial participation in the new matter. Comment 4 to Rule 1.12 explains that while the screened lawyer may continue to receive her regular salary or partnership share established "by prior independent agreement," she may not be provided compensation "directly related to the matter in which the lawyer is disqualified."

(2) It is important to take note of two important situations that are not covered by Rule 1.12. First, the Rule only covers a situation where the lawyer-mediator first mediates, and then seeks to represent a disputant. It does not govern the situation where a lawyer who initially represented a disputant as an advocate is now called upon to mediate that dispute. Lawyer-mediators should look to the mediation ethical rules and standards that would govern this question. Second, Rule 1.12 makes clear that it sets a floor rather than a ceiling for the ethics of lawyer-mediators. Comment 2 notes that "[o]ther law or codes of ethics governing third-party neutrals may impose more stringent standards."

(3) In addition to ethical concerns, the attempt to integrate mediation and litigation practices has raised practical concerns for some attorneys, particularly when they are part of a larger firm that provides substantial litigation services. For many reasons, lawyers acting as mediators often bring less money into the firm than lawyers acting as litigators. First, lawyer-mediators often charge a lower hourly rate when operating in their mediator capacity than when performing traditional litigation functions. Moreover, lawyer-mediators typically do not need the assistance of associate attorneys or paralegals, thereby eliminating the firm's ability to bill for work performed by these additional personnel. Further, mediators use only a fraction of the overhead services that is often required by litigators. While they made need greater than normal time for conference room bookings, they rarely require messenger assistance and typically need little, if any, secretarial support. The business reality is that it may be difficult for attorneys who decide they want to spend substantial time as mediators to work out an equitable financial arrangement with their own firms. These sorts of pressures, as well as others, may sometimes lead lawyer-mediators to leave their firms to establish an independent mediation practice.

(4) The reading below explains the travails of one firm that initially sought to combine litigation and mediation practices. Consider whether you believe that the steps taken by the Florida firm were consistent with the ABA Model Rules that were adopted well after the events described in the article.

# WITH CONFLICTS AT ISSUE, FLORIDA FIRM AND ITS FORMER PARTNERS RESTRUCTURE ADR — AGAIN
15 Alternatives to the High Cost of Litig. 131, 137 (Oct. 1997)*

A Florida law firm that spun off an alternative dispute resolution practice into three separate companies early this year to avoid conflicts apparently didn't go far enough. In the face of a court challenge putting the setup at issue — which the firm ultimately won — the three companies have been reorganized. In addition, the principal ADR company's name has been changed to eliminate a lingering perception of its affiliation to the law firm.

Daytona Beach, Fla.-based Cobb Cole & Bell on Jan. 1 established the three corporations to provide ADR and administrative services . . .

. . . .

The novel setup didn't last long. In June, CCB Mediation officially changed its name to Upchurch Watson White & Fraxedas, after its top mediators. A second company focusing on ADR training established in the original transaction was folded into Upchurch Watson. And, at press time, the third company, CC&B Enterprises, Inc., which provided administrative services to the law firm and the two ADR firms, and was intended to service other clients, was being reabsorbed by Cobb Cole.

The problem with the original structure arose from the exact source that the setup was intended to address, the appearance of conflicts between mediators and litigators. Soon after the spinoff, attorneys for the city of Vero Beach, Fla., asked that Cobb Cole be disqualified from representing Vero Beach's adversary in a litigation matter. The city had not used the firm as its counsel, but it had hired two of its attorneys as mediators in three cases, before the reorganization.

When a suit against Vero Beach was filed early this year in a Sunshine Laws case, the city moved to have Cobb Cole, which was representing the plaintiff, disqualified from the case. In July, Cobb Cole defeated the motion. The decision was upheld by a Florida appellate court on Aug. 28, and the firm retained representation in the matter

But Cobb Cole, as well as CCB Mediation and the other companies, began the second restructuring soon after Vero Beach filed the disqualification motion late last winter. "The primary reason for the spinoff was to avoid downstream conflicts," says John J. Upchurch, a former Cobb Cole partner and former president of CCB Mediation, explaining that "the use of CCB Mediation Inc. simply didn't convey to the legal community that we were a distinct organization." Upchurch is now president of Upchurch Watson.

After Vero Beach's disqualification motion, Upchurch says that the law firm partners and the ADR firms' officers "decided it would be more effective and cause less strain if we were each responsible for our own administration and management." He adds that "in the glare of an actual case or controversy, we realized that

---

to an independent finder of fact that it might not appear to be as sharp a separation" as the original transaction intended . . .

Cobb Cole partner Jonathan D. Kaney says that the firm is satisfied that it wasn't disqualified in the litigation matter, and that the original arrangement withstood the court's scrutiny, even if it didn't last. The court "found for us and concluded as a matter of law there was no attorney-client relationship" created by the mediations, says Kaney, adding that the court also found that the firm and ADR companies "perfected the division."

Adds Cobb Cole managing partner Samuel P. Bell III, the case "merely confirmed the thinking that brought about the initial separation . . . . The basic issue is this need for separation. I think it has been confirmed and I believe it will be the future for everyone. I don't think there is any way people will be able to [have] an ADR operation inside a law firm."

In his July 17 opinion, Indian River County Circuit Judge Charles E. Smith found that the former Cobb Cole "mediation counsel," John S. Neely, Jr., had followed Florida's professional conduct standard rule 10.80 on mediator confidentiality with regard to the Vero Beach cases he had handled. Smith also concluded that Neely and C. Welborn Daniel, another former Cobb Cole mediation counsel, were not a part of Cobb Cole after the Jan.1 reorganization.

Furthermore, Smith concluded that even if it was assumed that Vero Beach was a Cobb Cole client, there was no violation of conduct rules because the new litigation matter wasn't the same or substantially related to the mediation cases, and no lawyer remained in Cobb Cole that had material information from those matters. *Zorc v. City of Vero Beach*, Case No. 95-0250 CA 16 (Indian River County Ct. July 17, 1997). On Aug. 28, Florida's Fourth District Court of Appeals affirmed Smith's ruling without an opinion. *Zorc v. City of Vero Beach*, Case No. 97-00465 (Fla. 4th Dist. Ct. App. Aug. 28, 1997).

## NOTES AND QUESTIONS

(1)   Do you believe the ABA Model Rules pertaining to lawyer-mediators are adequate? Do they need to be more stringent? Less stringent? Would you revise them in any respect?

(2)   What rationale might be offered for preventing a person who had previously mediated a dispute involving a particular client from representing that client in future litigation in an unrelated matter?

(3)   What rationale might be offered for preventing a person who had previously represented a particular client in litigation from subsequently serving as mediator in a dispute involving that client in an unrelated matter?

(4)   The Virginia legal ethics committee considered a request for an opinion related to the following challenge. A lawyer who owned a mediation company was also "of counsel" to a law firm in which his/her spouse was a partner. After a mediation was terminated, having failed to resolve all the issues, one of the parties to the mediation asked an associate in the law firm to file a divorce on his/her behalf. The Committee, consistent with rationales discussed above, found that the indi-

vidual lawyer-mediator could not represent that disputant even if both clients consented. But, the Committee further explained that, while associates in the firm were not entirely disqualified, due to confidentiality concerns, an associate in the firm nonetheless could represent that client only with the consent of both parties. Va. Leg. Ethics Op. 1759 (Feb. 18, 2002).

(5) In *McEnany v. West Del. County Community School Dist.*, 844 F. Supp. 523, 533 (N.D. Iowa 1994), the court refused to void a settlement reached in mediation on grounds of bias, even though the mediator was an attorney with a firm that had done various kinds of legal work for one of the parties for more than 10 years. The court emphasized that the mediator himself had neither performed any of that legal work nor had particular knowledge of it, and that he had disclosed the relationship prior to commencing the mediation. Do you agree with the result? Is it consistent with the current ABA Model Rules that are currently in effect?

(6) If an individual or a firm seeking to combine mediation and litigation practices solicited your advice, what steps would you suggest to them to avoid potential conflicts of interest?

(7) Conflict-of-interest rules that are developed to govern lawyer-mediators may also have an impact on other legal practices. In *Fields-D'Arpino v. Restaurant Assocs., Inc.*, 39 F. Supp. 2d 412 (S.D.N.Y. 1999), the court examined a situation in which the firm representing the defendant designated an attorney at the firm to meet with the plaintiff and try to settle the case. Calling this process "mediation," the court held that the defense firm must be disqualified from further representation, given a New York ethical rule stating that "[a] lawyer who has undertaken to act as an impartial . . . mediator should not thereafter represent in the dispute any of the parties involved." *Id.* at 414 (citing N.Y. Code of Prof. Resp. EC 5-20).

(8) For a discussion of potential legal malpractice issues facing lawyer-mediators, see David Plimpton, Liability Pitfalls May Be Waiting for Lawyer-Neutrals, 18 *Alternatives to High Cost of Litigation* 65 (Apr. 2000).

## 4. Fee Sharing Issues Facing the Lawyer-Mediator

The traditional rule barring lawyers from sharing fees with non-lawyers poses some issues for mediation practices that seek to include both lawyers and non-lawyers. The ABA's Model Rule of Professional Conduct 5.4 is quite explicit in barring lawyers from sharing legal fees with non-lawyers. That rule also prohibits lawyers from practicing in the form of a professional corporation or association authorized to practice law for a profit if any non-lawyer owns an interest in that firm or has the right to control activities of the firm. Citing these rules, several jurisdictions have wrestled with the question of whether or how lawyers and non-lawyers may join together in a practice to offer mediation services. A Florida Opinion provides that "any non-lawyer mediators employed by the inquirer's law firm may not have an ownership interest in either the law firm or the mediation department. To do so would implicate rules prohibiting sharing fees with non-lawyers, partnership with non-lawyers, and assisting in the unauthorized practice of law." (Fla. Ethics Op. 94-6, Apr. 30, 1995.) A Rhode Island Opinion also seems to preclude such an arrangement, emphasizing that a lawyer who provides mediation services will nonetheless be perceived as an attorney, and stating that the rule "avoids the possibility of a non-lawyer's interference with a lawyer's independent professional judgment and avoids encouraging non-lawyers from engaging in the unauthorized practice of law." (RI Op. 95-1, Rep. No. 558, Mar. 6, 1995.) On the other hand, a Vermont Opinion states that so long as the partnership between lawyer and non-lawyer does not include the "practice of law," in that legal advice will not be offered by the attorney or any members of the attorney's firm, lawyer and non-lawyer mediators may join together to form a business (Vt. Ethics Op. No. 93-5, *undated*).

Another fee-sharing issue is raised when lawyer-mediators seek to provide referral fees to others who provide them with mediation clients. An Illinois ethics opinion addressing this issue found that lawyer mediators were precluded from paying a 20% referral fee to an accounting firm that sent them mediation business, even though the lawyers sought to establish a separate mediation firm that, while containing some members of the law firm, would only provide mediation services. The Opinion found this "mediation firm" to be a "sham" that did not excuse lawyers from the usual rules barring sharing of fees with non-lawyers (Ill. St. Bar Assoc. Adv. Op. on Prof. Cond. No. 01-05, Jan. 2002).

## NOTES AND QUESTIONS

(1)   Why do ethical rules generally prohibit fee-sharing between lawyers and non-lawyers?

(2)   Given the purpose of the rule prohibiting fee-sharing between lawyers and non-lawyers, does it make sense to prohibit lawyers and non-lawyers from sharing fees in a mediation practice? Does the distinction drawn in the Vermont opinion above make sense?

## 5.   Advertising and Solicitation Issues Facing the Lawyer-Mediator

Lawyers face very strict rules on advertisement and solicitation. (*See, e.g.*, ABA Model Rules of Professional Conduct 7.1–7.5.) Do these same rules apply to lawyers who choose to practice mediation exclusively or in combination with their advocacy practice? Opinions differ. Most jurisdictions provide that lawyers who mediate are nonetheless governed by the strict rules relating to attorney advertising. Thus, a Kansas Opinion states that the same restrictive advertising rules apply, even though "mediation may be a new addition to the 'forms' of practice." (Kan. Formal and Informal Op. No. 95-02, May 26, 1995.) A New York opinion similarly states that even if mediation is not technically considered the "practice of law," a "lawyer's role as a neutral mediator may include rendering advice about legal questions or preparing a separation agreement." It further notes that even where a mediator "serves as a mediator outside of the law office, gives no legal advice or opinions, and does not draw up an agreement," participants would be aware of the fact that the mediator was an attorney. Therefore, opined the committee, lawyer-mediators should be proscribed from participating in a referral service that might mistakenly be thought by clients to be a disinterested agency.

(N.Y. St. Bar Ass'n Comm. on Prof. Ethics, Op. 678, (42–95) Jan. 10, 1996.) By contrast, an Illinois Opinion states that "[i]f the advertising and promotional material for the mediation business does not amount to advertising for the lawyer's law practice, it is not subject to the rules on lawyer advertising." (Ill. Op. No. 92-05, 10/92.)

On the other hand, most jurisdictions are permissive in letting lawyers tout their mediation background in promotional materials. Thus, Kansas, South Carolina, and Tennessee have each stated that lawyers may indicate they are certified mediators on their letterhead, so long as the statement is truthful. (Kan. Op. 95-02, May 26, 1995; SC Bar Advisory Op. 96-29; Tenn. Ethics Op. 98-F-142(a), Dec. 11, 1998.) However, several jurisdictions have carefully examined precisely how the mediator's status may be defined, so as to avoid misleading the public. In Tennessee, a lawyer-mediator may state that she is a "Rule 31 Listed Mediator" but not an "Approved Rule 31 Mediator," because the latter does not indicate what body issued the approval. (Tenn. Ethics Op. 98-F-142(a), Dec. 11, 1998.) Similarly, in Minnesota lawyer mediators may state that they are a "qualified neutral under Rule 114" but may not simply identify themselves as a "certified" mediator. (Minn. Gen. Rule of Practice 114 (Appendix Rule VI), 2005.) A Florida ethics opinion, in a related matter, proscribes the mediation department of a law firm from using the trade name "Sunshine Mediation," as it would be misleading unless applied to the entire law practice. (Fla. Ethics Op. 94-6, Apr. 30, 1995.)

A Vermont ethics panel faced an unusual issue. According to the practice of the Vermont Environmental Court, litigants are asked in a pretrial conference whether they would be willing to use mediation. If the litigants are undecided, a mediator from a court list may contact the party to discuss the benefits of mediation. The panel ruled that even when the mediators who make such contacts are attorneys, their conduct does not violate anti-solicitation rules in that "service as a mediator does not involve an attorney client relationship, and consequently does not implicate the ethical rules directed to such a relationship." (Vt. Bar Assoc. Adv. Ethics Op. 2001-08.)

## NOTES AND QUESTIONS

(1) What are the rationales for restricting advertising and solicitation by attorneys?

(2) Do these rationales apply when a lawyer offers services as a mediator?

(3) Note that even where non-lawyer mediators are not governed by ethical rules restricting advertising, they do potentially face the risk of a civil lawsuit or even criminal liability if they advertise falsely. *See* Michael Moffitt, *Ten Ways to Get Sued: A Guide to Mediators*, 8 Harv. Negot. L. Rev. 81, 116–20 (2003) (excerpted above).

(4) Restrictions on advertisements or solicitation by mediators (regardless whether they are attorneys) may sometimes be more stringent than those applied to non-mediator attorneys. Consider how the following rulings in opinions issued by the Florida Mediator Ethics Advisory Committee compare to constraints on attorney-advocate activity:

(1) 95-007 (precluding a mediator from advertising that the mediator would provide "a dispassionate evaluation by a neutral party," reasoning that this activity was not consistent with Florida's definition of mediation);

(2) 99-013 (prohibiting a law firm from listing Circuit Court Mediation as a specialty, where only one member of the two-person firm was a certified mediator); and

(3) 2001-006 (prohibiting mediators from giving away items of value such as embossed golf shirts, and also prohibiting mediators from treating prospective clients to lunches or golf outings).

# Chapter 9

# THE INSTITUTIONALIZATION OF MEDIATION IN THE COURTS

## A. INTRODUCTION

This chapter will focus on the institutionalization of mediation. Although, as discussed in Chapter 1, *supra*, mediation can trace its roots to community programs, today mediation is closely tied to numerous major societal institutions. Mediation is now established as part of many federal and state court programs, is employed by many federal and state agencies, is embraced by many corporations, and is used in schools, prisons, and other settings. By 1994, every state, plus the District of Columbia and Puerto Rico, had enacted at least one statute relating to the use of mediation.

Not surprisingly, courts have provided the most intense institutional use of mediation. In some jurisdictions, judges are required to order mediation in certain types of cases (*e.g.*, divorce actions in which children are involved). Judges in many other state and federal courts have the discretion to refer (or order) parties to mediation in many or all civil cases. In other courts, the judge may suggest or recommend mediation or conduct a judicial settlement conference using mediation techniques. Because of this intense use, the focus of this chapter will be a close examination of the development of mediation within the court context. It should be noted that many of the implications raised by the institutionalization of mediation in the courts are also evident in other institutional settings. While reading the chapter, consider what similarities and differences there may be between institutionalization of mediation within the courts and in other arenas.

While such institutionalization has certainly helped to increase the use of mediation dramatically, there may also be some drawbacks to this trend. As you read this chapter, consider the positive outcomes achieved through institutionalization, as well as the potential negative consequences of what happens when a flexible process is placed in a structured environment. Certainly, institutionalization raises some new issues that require substantial thought.

Section B will highlight the development of mediation as an institution. Section C will explore the policy choices to be made in institutionalization including those related to certification of mediators. Section D examines the results from empirical research on mediation in the court context. Section E presents critiques of institutionalization. Finally, Section F explores the issues raised by active judges serving as mediators in cases assigned to them for adjudication.

## B.  DEVELOPMENT OF INSTITUTIONALIZATION

As described in Chapter 1, the modern movement towards institutionalization of ADR in general and mediation in particular traces its roots to experimental court-related mediation programs in the 1960s and 1970s. A seminal event in the institutionalization of these programs was the Pound Conference in 1976 in which judges, court administrators, and legal scholars gathered together to discuss the public's pervasive dissatisfaction with the administration of justice. At that conference, Professor Frank E.A. Sander delivered a paper in which he described a courthouse of the future where parties could go for a variety of services to assist them in resolving their disputes. His vision, which was subsequently coined the "multi-door" courthouse, was premised on the state providing the necessary financial support not only for judges but also for intake specialists, mediators, arbitrators, and other dispute resolvers.

For a variety of reasons, however, mediation as an institution has not grown in that direction. In fact, the Pound Conference "Follow-Up" Committee did not endorse the "multi-door courthouse" and instead recommended that "the American Bar Association, in cooperation with local courts and state and local associations, invite the development of models of Neighborhood Justice Centers, suitable for implementation as pilot projects." The primary reason why the multi-door courthouse has not been implemented is that the concept is very expensive for the sponsoring institution. Even as mediation has become more integrated into the court, many courts continue to rely on volunteers and private providers to serve mediation programs rather than court staff. A secondary reason is that while the concept of an intake specialist is reasonable in the abstract, in reality, sorting cases has proven to be very difficult and complex. Despite a number of studies that have been conducted, researchers have not conclusively identified objective criteria that can be used to reliably determine which cases are most likely to benefit from each process. The individuals and the attorneys involved in the case, the amount in controversy, the status of negotiations, and the state of the law all will have an impact on the case dynamics. Thus, courts have shied away from the multi-door concept in part because the analysis needed to sort cases is extremely subtle.

In the following excerpt, Professor Frank E.A. Sander reflects on the history of the mediation movement and speculates on the future of mediation in light of institutionalization.

### THE FUTURE OF ADR
2000 J. Disp. Resol. 3, 3–8[*]
By Frank E.A. Sander

Because I've been fortunate to observe the ADR scene for much of its recent development, I'm often asked my views of where we stand now. My somewhat flip answer is, "On Monday, Wednesday and Friday, I think we've made amazing progress. On Tuesday, Thursday and Saturday, ADR seems more like a grain of

---

[*] Copyright © 2000 by the Journal of Dispute Resolution. Reprinted with permission of the Journal of Dispute Resolution. University of Missouri-Columbia, Center for the Study of Dispute Resolution, 206 Hulston Hall, Columbia, MO 65211.

sand on the adversary system beach." . . .

What are some of the signs that the glass is half full? What are the things that give me optimism . . . ? First, in 1998, the Congress of the United States enacted the Dispute Resolution Act, which directs each federal district to establish an ADR program by local rule [28 U.S.C. sections 651-658 (Supp. IV 1998)]. There is also comparable state legislation in a large number of states, sometimes mandating referral of specific cases to ADR or authorizing judges to do so in their discretion.

Second, dispute resolution clauses, sometimes quite sophisticated, are increasingly being used in contracts of all kinds.

Third, some businesses and law firms systematically canvass cases for ADR potential . . . .

Fourth, the CPR Institute for Dispute Resolution, an impressive New York organization of representatives from 800 leading businesses and law firms, is dedicated to the goal of educating its members and others concerning better ways of resolving disputes. Its CPR pledge commits signers to explore ADR before resorting to court . . . .

Fifth, a number of states now require that lawyers discuss ADR options with clients or to certify on the pleadings that they have done so . . . .

Sixth, for disputes in the public sector, the Administrative Dispute Resolution Act of 1996 requires federal agencies to consider the use of ADR and to appoint an ADR specialist. And there have been some Executive Orders issued by the President to stimulate similar action in the U.S. Department of Justice.

Seventh, about half the states now have state offices of dispute resolution that seek to facilitate the resolution of public disputes by providing technical assistance or recommending competent dispute resolvers.

Eighth, virtually every law school as well as many schools of business and planning now offer one or more ADR courses . . . .

So those are a few of the positive indicators. What are the downsides and remaining challenges?

Let me pause briefly for a little historic summary. I think there have been three periods in the approximately twenty-five years of the modern ADR development. Obviously, we didn't invent mediation . . . . But, by common agreement, it was about 1975 that the current interest in ADR began. The first period . . . was about 1975 to 1982. I call it, "Let a thousand flowers bloom." There were many experiments . . . .

The second period, about 1982 to 1990 . . . I call "Cautions and caveats": Concerns about where we're heading, attempts to sort out the wheat from the chaff. . . .

The third period, starting about 1990, is what I call "Institutionalization." The question there is: How do we weave ADR into the dispute resolution fabric so that ADR options are systematically considered at various points along the life of a dispute rather than putting the onus on the party who wants to use ADR, which will often be construed as a sign of weakness? . . .

What are the present obstacles and impediments to institutionalization, and what are some of the hopeful signs? When you look at the situation from the disputant's perspective there is often a lack of knowledge of ADR . . . [T]he prevailing assumption that the court is the place to resolve disputes is a major part of the problem.

Second, there is a lack of readily available public dispute resolution options — the absence of a public facility like a comprehensive justice center where someone can go to have access to mediation or arbitration — a place where the sign over the door says, "This is where disputes get handled. The experts here will help you decide which is the best process for your case." . . .

What if we look at the situation from the perspective of lawyers? What are the impediments there? . . .

The fact is that in ADR [lawyers] lose control, particularly in flexible procedures like mediation . . . . So lawyers are sometimes reluctant to get involved with an unfamiliar, threatening procedure.

There are also economic incentives for lawyers to stay with litigation . . . There are also other perverse incentives. For example, in some companies a settlement is charged to the budget of that division, but litigation costs are not charged to a department. So in that company there's an incentive to litigate rather than settle a case. Attorney compensation also sometimes takes account of successful wins but not of money-saving settlements.

Finally, there is a public policy impediment, and that is the lack of adequate cost-benefit studies . . . [I]t's very difficult to document the specific money savings of pursuing a case through mediation rather than court adjudication. We have some anecdotal data, but when you think about it, that kind of research is incredibly difficult to do. For example, one claim for mediation is that in cases of continuing relationships, it's often a more lasting solution. That is, it prevents future disputes because you get at the underlying concerns and it teaches the parties how to resolve disputes more effectively by themselves in the future. That means you have to have a longitudinal study, spanning over many years in order to document that kind of thing, quite aside from the difficult questions of how you measure the peace of mind that comes from an absence of future lawsuits . . . .

. . . .

Let me end up with some promising future directions for overcoming these impediments and advancing the cause of institutionalization. In the short run, we need to strengthen some of the institutionalization devices such as . . . the duty of a lawyer to apprize a client about ADR options as part of professional consultation, coupled with early court consideration of ADR possibilities, and judicial power to refer cases to appropriate ADR processes. All these institutionalization devices have an important indirect effect. They not only teach clients about these possibilities, but they also get lawyers up to par . . . .

. . . This is also why I favor mandatory mediation at the present time. There are some hot arguments in the literature with some people saying, "Mediation means voluntarily agreeing to a result. How can you force somebody to voluntarily agree to a result?" I think that confuses coercion *into* mediation with coercion *in* mediation. If you have coercion *in* mediation, it is not mediation . . . [W]e have evidence that the process is very powerful, that it works for people who use it, but for some of the reasons I mentioned earlier, people don't seem to be using the process sufficiently voluntarily. So my view about mandatory mediation is about the same as affirmative action — that is, it's not the right permanent answer, but it is a useful temporary expedient to make up for inadequate past practices.

My basic view is that it is for the court, not the parties, to allocate the precious public resource that is the court. The courts and the legislature should decide how much use you should make of courts and in what kind of cases, not the parties or their lawyers . . . .

In the long run we need more education of lawyers and clients . . . .

Second, I am concerned about the long-term professional issues that are raised by ADR. At the moment we have a lot of people who have been trained in ADR, but there is insufficient paying work for them . . . . There are many places where ADR is done by volunteers, and that's a good thing . . . . But I get concerned about developing career paths by which talented graduates of law schools can become self-purporting ADR professionals . . . Increasingly over this period of twenty-five years, more and more people have made careers out of ADR, but it's still extremely difficult and there's no simple way to do it . . . . That's not a good way of developing a new profession.

## NOTES

In 2012, after serving as chair for 18 years, Professor Frank Sander assumed the role of chair-emeritus of the editorial board of the American Bar Association's Dispute Resolution Magazine. In appreciation of Professor Sander's work, the Fall 2012 edition of the magazine featured several articles reflecting on his leadership including "The Pound Conference Remembered" by Earl Johnson.

## C.    INSTITUTIONALIZATION OF MEDIATION IN THE COURT CONTEXT: POLICY DEVELOPMENT

The following section presents excerpts regarding the policy considerations for the development of court-connected mediation. In the first excerpt, Professor Baruch Bush details an imaginary conversation with a judge who has been given an opportunity to order cases to mediation. Through this conversation, Professor Bush highlights the underlying philosophical decisionmaking which must take place before one embarks on institutional use of mediation. In the second excerpt, Professor John McCrory explores policy considerations through the eyes of the litigants. Finally, Donald Weckstein discusses mediator qualifications in the context of certification and licensing schemes.

## MEDIATION AND ADJUDICATION, DISPUTE RESOLUTION AND IDEOLOGY: AN IMAGINARY CONVERSATION
3 J. Contemp. Legal Issues 1, 1–10, 14–15, 18–21, 23–24 (1989)*
By Robert A. Baruch Bush

This essay started out as an informal talk to a number of dispute resolution colleagues concerning what I believe is a neglected and important perspective on our field. My goal here is to bring some attention to that perspective, at two levels. First, I want to show that there is an underlying ideological dimension to the ongoing controversy over adjudication and mediation that accounts for a lot of the heat, if not the light, that goes on in the discussion of these and other dispute resolution processes. Second, I want to dig a bit deeper than I think most of us have dug so far to try to say what that ideological dimension is . . . .

Instead of approaching these goals through a formal or abstract analysis, however, I intend to pursue them through imagining a story or conversation which, as it were, gives voices to the different positions taken in the controversy over mediation and adjudication. I invite the reader to listen and respond to this conversation . . . .

The setting for the conversation is as follows. A judge has been empowered by a state statute to refer cases from his civil docket to mediation. The statute says that he can, in his discretion, refer any and all cases; the decision is his, and the parties cannot refuse mediation without showing good cause. The judge can send all his cases to mediation on a blanket basis, or certain categories of cases, or individual cases on a case-by-case basis, whichever he decides . . . . The problem is that the judge is uncertain how to exercise this new power . . . .

So he picks six representative cases from his civil docket: a divorce case with a custody question, a complex commercial litigation, a landlord-tenant case, a discrimination suit, a consumer case, and a personal injury litigation. He sends copies of the case files, with names deleted, to four individuals who are friends or associates: his law clerk, his court administrator, his former law professor, and a practicing mediator . . . . The judge asks each of them for their advice . . . .

He is a bit startled when he gets back the results of this survey, because he gets four completely different recommendations. From the law professor, he gets the recommendation that he should send no cases to mediation; all the cases should stay in court. The law clerk . . . says that the discrimination case, the consumer case, and the personal injury case should be kept in court, but the divorce, the landlord-tenant, and the commercial cases should go to mediation. The court administrator says he should send them all to mediation, unless both parties to the dispute object; if both parties object, he shouldn't refer them to mediation, whatever the type of case. Finally, the mediator tells him that he should send all the cases to mediation, whether or not the parties object.

The judge is puzzled by this set of responses . . . .

[So] he calls all four advisors and says, "I'd like you to argue this out in front of

---

me. I want to hear what you have to say in the presence of one another.."

So the four advisors come together with the judge . . . . The court administrator goes first. ". . . As far as I'm concerned, the most important goal we have here is saving time and money . . . . The courts are heavily backlogged, delay is epidemic, and adding new judges and courtrooms appears fiscally — and politically — impossible. Settlements are the only solution . . . [S]ince all cases have some potential to settle," she continues, "and we don't know which ones will and which ones won't, it makes sense to refer them all to mediation, unless we have a clear indication in advance that there's no real settlement possibility . . . . That's the reason for my recommendation. Refer to mediation, unless it's clear that there's opposition on both sides to settlement."

> The law clerk then is called upon. He says, ". . . In my view, the main goal
> is not saving time and money, regardless of what the legislature may have
> had in mind. There are goals of dispute resolution that are much more
> important."

". . . [P]rotecting individual rights and ensuring some kind of substantive fairness to both sides in the resolution of the dispute are the most important goals. And where rights and substantive fairness are most important, adjudication in court is the best tool we have to accomplish those goals. However, there are cases where rights and fairness are not the only or the most important goals. For example, if there is an ongoing relationship between the parties, preserving that relationship may be very important both to the parties and to the public. In that case, mediation would be desirable, because preserving relationships is something that mediation does better than the adjudication process. Therefore, I think that you can distinguish between cases on the basis of the ongoing relationship factor. When you have such a relationship, refer to mediation; otherwise, keep the case in court . . . ."

Next is the mediator's turn. "I both agree and disagree with the administrator and the law clerk . . . . Sometimes the best solution will be one that saves the parties time and money; sometimes it will be one that preserves the relationship. Sometimes it will be one that does neither of these. That will all depend on many details of the case."

"But whatever the details, there is plenty of evidence that in terms of achieving the best results for the individual case in question, mediation is a process that has tremendous advantages over adjudication. The process is flexible, issues can be framed more effectively and discussed more fully, a greater variety of possible solutions can be considered, and unique, innovative and integrative solutions are possible, even likely. Therefore, mediation ought to be tried first in all cases because the potential to arrive at superior substantive results is always greater in mediation than in adjudication. If mediation doesn't work . . . then the parties can go back to court . . . ."

Finally the law professor speaks. "Your Honor," he begins, "I'm sorry I have to disagree. But all of your other friends have missed the point . . . . A court is a public institution, and the goal of a court as a public institution is not to save time and money; nor is it to help private parties secure private benefits in individual cases. Your goal as a public institution is to promote important public values. That ought to be your primary concern: the promotion and the securing of important public values through the dispute resolution process . . . ."

"I submit to you, your Honor, that the most important public values at stake in dispute resolution are basically four . . . .[T]he public values a court must concern itself with are: protection of fundamental individual rights, provision of social justice, promotion of economic welfare, and creation of social solidarity."

". . . [T]he rule-based, public adjudication process is an excellent — an unparalleled — instrument for accomplishing these values. Mediation, on the other hand, weakens and undermines every single one of these values . . . ."

"This brings me to the heart of my argument . . . [f]irst, we can't sacrifice public values of this statute solely to save time and money . . . [T]o adopt a public policy saying that values like rights protection and social justice are less important than saving money and judicial economy would be inexcusable. Second, there's no way of neatly dividing up cases on the basis that some involve these public values and others do not . . . . All six of the kinds of cases that you submitted to us involve one or more of these public values . . . Therefore . . . 'channeling' of different cases to different processes is undesirable."

"Finally, you cannot, as the mediator suggested, consider the value of better results for the parties in the individual case superior to these public values.. As a matter of public policy, we cannot put private benefit over the public good. Therefore, your Honor, I say all of these cases should remain in court, unless perhaps a petition is submitted by both parties to adjourn pending voluntarily initiated settlement discussions or mediation."

. . . .

Before the judge has a chance to adjourn and consider the arguments more thoroughly, however, the mediator asks the judge for one more minute . . . "When I say mediation ought to be used in all these cases, my reason is also based on promoting public values, public values which are important to all of the cases you sent us, public values different from and more important than the ones that the professor mentioned. In other words, like the professor's argument for adjudication, my argument for mediation is also a public values argument, but it is based on a different view of public values than the view he presented."

"Now my problem is that it is hard to articulate clearly what these different public values are. I think they're evoked or implied by concepts like reconciliation, social harmony, community, interconnection, relationship, and the like. Mediation does produce superior results, as I argued earlier. But it also involves a non-adversarial process that is less traumatic, more humane, and far more capable of healing and reconciliation than adjudication. Those are the kinds of concerns that make me feel that these cases ought to be handled in mediation, not for private benefit reasons and not for expediency reasons, but because of these reconciliatory public values promoted by mediation."

. . . .

Let us pause for a minute from this story. The conversation to this point should be familiar to many readers as a parallel to the state of the adjudication/mediation debate today . . . .

Given the state of the debate right now, what are the prospects for the immediate future in the use of adjudication and mediation? What are judges like the one in the story likely to do? I think there are three possible scenarios. First — and most likely, despite the good intentions of the judge in our story — expediency and private interest may rule. Mediation will be used widely, and perhaps indiscriminately, to reduce court caseload and to satisfy private disputants' individual needs. Second, and less likely . . . the public values argument could lead to rejection of mediation generally and retrenchment back to adjudication in court as the primary way of resolving disputes . . . Third, and least likely, if a clear and persuasive public value argument can be articulated on behalf of mediation, then in all likelihood mediation will spread more widely — but perhaps in a different form than the private-benefit/ expediency version.

The present debate over adjudication and mediation therefore has two dimensions. One is the public-value versus private-benefit/expediency dimension . . . [I]t is a clash over whether the public good matters, not what the public good is . . . . The second dimension is the public-value versus public-value dimension, and it is reflected in the conflict . . . here, between the professor and the mediator . . . . In this dimension, both adjudication and mediation represent public values, and the question is which public values are more important. This is a clash over what the public good is, a clash of social vision or ideology . . . . This is the dimension of the debate . . . to which the conversation above is about to proceed.

. . . .

The judge repeats his question to the mediator: "What exactly is this public value underlying mediation . . . ?"

. . . .

". . . Simply put, it is the value of providing a moral and political education for citizens, in responsibility for themselves and respect for others. In a democracy, your Honor, that must be considered a crucial public value and it must be considered a public function . . . . It cannot be accomplished in adjudication . . . . In my view, this civic education value is more important than the values the professor is concerned about . . . . And . . . even if the parties had reached no agreement in mediation, that education could still have occurred anyway. The case could then have gone back to court where those other values could have been dealt with as secondary matters."

"Finally, I just want to clarify an important connection between my argument here and our earlier discussion. On reflection, I've realized that the 'superior results' argument . . . is also based, at least in part, on the public value I'm talking about here . . . [T]he 'superiority' of results we speak of is not only, or primarily, that the results better serve the individual interests of the parties — a private benefit — but that they express each individual's considered choice to respect and accommodate the other to some degree — a democratic public value . . . ."

. . . .

Let us take another pause. What we have now in the story is a parallel of yet another debate that we see in a much larger field . . . .

Once the public-value argument for mediation is fully stated and set against the public-value argument for adjudication, it becomes clear that the adjudication/ mediation debate derives from a much deeper debate between the liberal/ individualist and the communitarian/relationalist visions of society . . .

. . . .

To return to and conclude our conversation . . . what additional advice does this reading suggest we might want to offer the judge in our story? In answer to this question, I want to exercise a little poetic license and jump into the conversation myself, to speak directly to this judge.

Based on what we have heard from the others so far, I would say, "Judge, you're asking what kind of choice you should make, as between keeping cases in court and referring them to mediation. But it's clear to me and I hope it's clear to you that you have a deeper choice to make here: a choice between different social visions. If you accept the prevailing individualist vision, Judge, then you should reject mediation completely, or limit it very severely, to en-sure that public values like those advocated by the professor are not under-mined . . . . On the other hand, if you accept the relational vision, then you should not merely use mediation; you should expand it to ensure the accomplishment of the most important public values under that vision . . . ."

"But whatever you do . . . as a public servant you should not use mediation at all, if you're going to use it simply as a tool for saving time and satisfying private litigants' individual interests. Because this will undermine both of the contending visions . . . ."

". . . [M]ediation — as the mediator presented it to you — is either being co-opted or rejected entirely. No real attention has been given to the relational vision, and the potential of mediation as a transformative instrument, a means of civic education."

. . . .

"This sort of approach . . . — preference for mediation over adjudication across the board — means changing completely the terms of reference in this discussion. It means regarding mediation as a primary dispute resolution process, not an 'alternative' dispute resolution process . . . ."

"Finally . . . if you are going to explore this vision of mediation, it means making sure that mediation as practiced is in fact an opportunity for self-determination and self-transcendence on the part of the parties, and not simply a tool of expediency . . . ."

". . . Am I suggesting mandatory mediation for every case, absent good cause for exemption . . . ? . . . [Y]es, I advise you to use your mandatory mediation power fully; but in any event, do whatever you consider appropriate to encourage mediation in every case."

". . . If you're not prepared . . . to make sure mediation really provides an opportunity for self-determination and self-transcendence — then my advice to you is very different. Forget mediation . . . . Salvage what you can of the individualist vision. Improve the courts . . . ."

"Some people may ask: If I support mediation, then why should I care what the reasons are for expanding it? . . . Let's expand it first, and worry later about clarifying the reasons . . . . I disagree . . . I am afraid that publicly sponsored, court-connected mediation oriented towards efficiency and private benefits alone would crowd out other versions and reduce the chance for the educational vision to develop."

. . . .

That is what I would say to the judge — for now, at least. And that is where I close this installment of the conversation. And I throw it open to you, reader. For other voices are surely needed to continue this conversation. After all this, what would you say?

## MANDATED MEDIATION OF CIVIL CASES IN STATE COURTS: A LITIGANT'S PERSPECTIVE ON PROGRAM MODEL CHOICES
14 Ohio St. J. on Disp. Resol. 813, 825–36, 842–43, 847, 849–51 (1999)[*]
By John P. McCrory

Identifying the interests of litigants in civil case mediation programs to facilitate an inquiry as to how those interests can best be addressed is the central theme of this Article . . . . Litigants . . . may be most concerned with the quality of mediation services provided, to ensure that the time and money spent participating in mandated mediation will maximize chances for fair and efficient settlement.

. . . .

When courts mandate mediation, one of the first questions asked is: Who will pay the cost of administering the program and the cost of the mediation services? One view is that courts should not mandate an ADR process and then require that the litigants pay the cost of providing the services. The SPIDR Law and Policy Committee recommended that: "Funding for mandatory dispute resolution programs should be provided on a basis comparable to funding for trials." While arguments that courts or legislatures should provide funding to cover the cost of mandated mediation services has an obvious justification and appeal, as a practical matter, there are more important concerns for civil case litigants.

The cost of mediation services is likely to be only a fraction of the total costs to litigants participating in mandated mediation . . . .

Assuming that the user fee for court-mandated mediation is reasonable, a more important consideration for litigants is the quality of the program and the services provided . . . . For many courts, there is tension between providing quality mediation services and finding resources that can be devoted to a mediation program. In many states, it is unlikely that legislatures will be willing to, or courts will be able to, fully fund high-quality court-mandated programs . . . .

Preoccupation with demands for providing mediation services without a user fee may be unproductive and may divert attention from the more important question of how a high-quality program can be established with reasonable and affordable user fees. As a practical matter, planners may be left to decide which of the various program models has the greatest potential for providing a high-quality program with the least possible burden on the litigants who are mandated to mediation . . . . From a consumer standpoint, quality should be a paramount program planning objective.

. . . .

When planning a court-based civil mediation program, several things should be remembered. First, the parties will normally have attorneys and litigation will have been started. To some extent, positions and expectations will be fixed. Second, commencement of litigation places a dispute in an arena that is the domain of lawyers who are likely to employ traditional litigation tools and strategies. Finally, the types of cases referred to mediation will vary and the needs of the parties, in terms of the assistance they need from a mediator to resolve their differences, will also vary.

There is concern in some quarters that the institutionalization of mediation in the courts will diminish party self-determination, result in mediation that is evaluative, and cause coerced settlements . . . . A flexible approach to the role of mediators in civil mediation will best serve the interests of litigants.

. . . .

The focus should . . . be on early settlement. The longer a case remains in the litigation process, the less likely the chances of achieving the time-and cost-saving goals of the mediation program. Delay may also inhibit the settlement efforts because of the parties' financial and psychological investment in a case. Early settlement does not mean uninformed settlement. The appropriate time for mediation will vary on a case-by-case basis and, for that reason, rigid approaches to scheduling mediation have been criticized. There must be a thoughtful balance between the parties' legitimate need for information and scheduling mediation at sessions at times when settlement efficiency can be maximized . . . .

The parties' need for information is often equated to the need for discovery.. Some cases will not require discovery, which may mean that mediation can be scheduled very early in the life of the case. In cases in which the need for discovery is modest, that need may be satisfied by an information exchange during mediation. In more complex cases, in which discovery is a significant factor, there is evidence that lawyers who are experienced in mediation are comfortable participating with limited discovery. The foregoing suggests possibilities for scheduling mediation at an early date without prejudicing the parties' need for information that is required for an informed and fair settlement.

The SPIDR Law and Policy Committee recommended that mandatory mediation should be used only when high-quality programs permit party participation. Many courts require that parties be present at the mediation sessions, but attendance alone does not ensure effective participation. Providing parties with an opportunity to speak and be key participants n a relaxed and informal atmosphere should be a program objective.

. . . .

Mediation program planners should be concerned about the "ADR literacy" of the attorneys who will represent litigants that are referred to mediation and should take steps to ensure that the clients are adequately prepared for and involved in the process . . . .

[I]f the objectives of mediation are to be realized, planners should focus on the nature and quality of party participation . . . . Realistically, lawyers will have primary responsibility for the level and quality of their clients' participation. This does not diminish the role of courts and mediators to monitor the quality of party involvement . . . .

Mediation is not a quick fix. Time is required for a mediator to gain a sufficient understanding of a dispute to be helpful to the parties. Time is needed for the parties to fully air their perspectives in an unhurried atmosphere. Finally, time is required to develop and explore acceptable options for settlement. If insufficient time is allotted, parties may believe they were not heard and understood, that settlement options were not clear, or that they were required to mediate in a coercive atmosphere.

. . . Planning should recognize the need for adequate time in mediation for all referred cases, including flexibility to accommodate complex cases that have extraordinary time requirements.

A key factor in the quality and success of a court-based program is the panel of mediators that is selected to provide mediation services. Where mediation is mandated, the court has a special responsibility to ensure that the mediators to whom cases are referred are competent. In addition, it is important that the mediator panel is the following:

- diverse in gender, race, and ethnicity;

- diverse with respect to mediation styles;

- diverse with respect to subject matter familiarity;

- of sufficient size to provide equal access to all referred or eligible cases; and

- experienced.

. . . .

Some commentators contend that the opportunity for party choice in selecting the mediator should be maximized . . . . It permits parties to select a mediator whom they believe to be right for their particular dispute and it gives them a greater stake and degree of confidence in the mediation process. While these concerns are important, there are competing considerations. Experience has shown that when litigants are free to choose any mediator from a court panel, a relatively small number of panel members do most of the work . . . .

From a consumer perspective, the following two competing factors must be balanced: the opportunity for party choice in the assignment of mediators and the overall experience and competence of the mediator panel . . . .

In some states there is concern and uncertainty regarding the relationship, and perhaps tension, between court-based mediation and private sector mediation providers . . . . From the litigants' standpoint, program planners should define the relationship to the public sector in a way that will maximize access to qualified mediators . . . .

. . . [F]rom a consumer's perspective, when mandatory court-based programs are put in place, the sponsors have an obligation to ensure that the litigants' time, money, and efforts are not wasted . . . .

The philosophy of a mediation program and its image in the eyes of litigants and their lawyers will be an important factor in determining its success. Fundamentally, there is an option between two models, diversion and integration. A diversion model might resemble small claims mediation in which the court says, go to mediation and do not return unless you cannot settle . . . .

The second model, integration, envisions incorporating mediation into case management and coordinating its use with other events, such as discovery.. Mediation should have a clear relationship to other procedures and be timed to maximize its effectiveness . . . .

The major distinguishing features in comparing program models are the source of mediators and their relationship to the court. The options are the following: court employees, referral to community mediation centers, volunteer court panels, court panels of private practitioners who work for a fixed fee, and private practitioners selected and paid by the parties. Planners should consider how the selection of a particular model will influence a court's ability to effectively do the following:

- integrate mediation into case handling procedures and

- monitor the quality and consistency of mediation services . . . .

## MEDIATOR CERTIFICATION: WHY AND HOW
### 30 U.S.F. L. Rev. 757, 760–62, 767–73 (1996)*
### By Donald T. Weckstein

### I. Is There a Need for Certification of Mediators?

#### A. Certification vs. Licensing

. . . . .

What purposes . . . are served by certification which would not be more effectively served by licensing? Both licensing and certification offer protection to consumers by seeking to identify those who have met standards relevant to the

---

* Copyright © 1996 University of San Francisco Law Review. Reprinted with permission.

practice of the profession or other occupation. Licensing, however, is anti-competitive. It creates a practice monopoly which tends to artificially limit the availability of services and foster high prices for services rendered. Licensing is also elitist. It imposes barriers to entry which may exclude potentially competent persons who happen to be poor, non-conforming, or unable to obtain the requisite training due to lack of time, financial resources, or proximity to a training facility.

Accordingly, licensing is best reserved for those occupations which cannot be competently practiced without extensive education and/or skills, and where the consumer is unlikely to be able to detect incompetent or unethical services until after serious or irreparable damage has been inflicted . . . . The case has not been, and probably cannot be, convincingly made for mediators. As stated in the SPIDR Qualification Commission's 1995 report:

> it is inappropriate for a government entity to formally license dispute resolution practitioners [because] licensure risks establishing arbitrary standards that could unnecessarily limit party choice of practitioners and limit access to the field by competent individuals . . . could work toward domination of the field by an exclusive group . . . [and] could inappropriately "freeze" the standards in a fluid field . . . .

. . . .

SB 1428 [California legislation which was introduced in 1995] expressly disclaimed any intent to provide for the licensure of mediators in California. Accordingly, under legislation similar to SB 1428, a mediator could choose to make the necessary investments to obtain certification, or forego that marketing advantage and rely upon existing reputation, contacts, or other characteristics to maintain a mediation practice. Parties also would be free to choose a person who had never mediated but in whom they had confidence due to personal contacts or a reputation earned in another occupation such as government service, law, clergy, or counseling.

Nevertheless, aspects of licensing could conceivably result from mediator certification legislation. For example, a court may determine that it will refer cases only to a certified mediator, thus essentially licensing only certified mediators to mediate the rich source of judicially referred matters. Any regulatory scheme should take account of these potential uses of mediator certification and seek to guard against anti-competitiveness and elitism not justified by compelling public interests.

. . . .

## C. The Case for Certifying Mediators

Potential public interests supporting state regulation of mediation include:

(1) the protection of the public from the consequences of incompetent or unethical mediation services; (2) the prevention of existing professions from monopolizing the practice of mediation; (3) the reduction in court congestion through the encouragement of judges to refer legal actions to presumably qualified mediators; and (4) the promotion of mediation by (a) discouraging its practice by

those who would besmirch its reputation, (b) channeling mediation business to those who have met established standards of training and practice, and (c) enhancing the credibility of the practice of mediation by facilitating its claim to professional status.

# NOTES AND QUESTIONS

(1)    Professor Bush intentionally presents the ideological debate as an either/or choice over which set of public values one adopts. Might they be integrated? If so, how?

(2)    Do you agree with Professor Bush that a person who adopts an individualist vision should reject mediation completely or limit it severely?

(3)    Professor McCrory asserts that the general civil docket is the most complex environment for implementing a mediation program. Do you agree? Why or why not? Are the policy considerations he raises the same or different than they are for other types of cases?

(4)    For another view on the policy decisions involved in institutionalizing a mediation program, see Sharon Press, *Building and Maintaining a Statewide Mediation Program: A View from the Field*, 81 Ken. L.J. 1029 (1992–93).

(5)    Professor McCrory highlights the competency of the mediators to whom cases are referred as a key factor in the quality and success of a court-based program. A seminal report on this subject was produced by the Society of Professionals in Dispute Resolution (now the Association for Conflict Resolution) Commission on Qualifications in 1989. A brief excerpt follows:

> The most commonly discussed purposes of setting criteria for individuals to practice as neutrals are (1) to protect the consumer and (2) to protect the integrity of various dispute resolution processes. Concerns also have been raised, particularly about mandatory standards or certification, including: (1) creating inappropriate barriers to entry into the field, thus, (2) hampering the innovative quality of the profession, and (3) limiting the broad dissemination of peacemaking skills in society. . . .
>
> In determining how best to promote competence and quality in the practice of dispute resolution, the Commission considered several policy options. These included reliance on the free market, disclosure requirements, public and consumer education, "after-the-fact" controls such as malpractice actions, rosters, ethical codes, mandatory standards for neutrals and for programs, and improvements in training, including enhanced opportunities for apprenticeships.
>
> After weighing these options, the Commission adopted three central principles, which recognize the need to strike an appropriate balance between competing concerns:
>
> • that no single entity (rather, a variety of organizations) should establish qualifications for neutrals;
>
> • that the greater the degree of choice the parties have over the dispute resolution process, program or neutral, the less mandatory

the qualification requirements should be; and

- that qualification criteria should be based on performance, rather than paper credentials.

In 2006, the Florida Supreme Court revised the qualification requirements for certified mediators from one based on professional education to a "point system" which recognized the variety of ways individuals may obtain competence. *See* Rules 10.100–10.105, Florida Rules for Certified and Court-Appointed Mediators in Appendix E. Does the certification scheme in Florida fulfill the principles in the Commission on Qualifications Report? Do you believe that the requirements will result in a roster of competent mediators?

(6)   The voluntary certification bills addressed in Weckstein's article were not adopted but did provide opportunity for additional commentary on the topic of certification. An additional challenge engendered by a certification process is how to ensure mediator competence while preserving diversity. Ellen Waldman's article, *The Challenge of Certification: How to Ensure Mediator Competence While Preserving Diversity*, addresses this knotty issue in the context of S.B. 1428. 30 U.S.F. L. Rev. 723, 724–25 (1996). In this article, she raised the following criticism of the proposed legislation:

> [T]he proposed Bill's overall sensitivity to the diverse professional mix which mediators bring to their work was laudable. However, the Bill displayed less sensitivity to the variety of mediator approaches prevalent in the field. SB 1428 failed to make clear that mediator training and performance evaluations must be implemented in ways that encourage the full panoply of regnant mediator styles. In so doing, the Bill threatened to establish credentialing machinery which constricted rather than enriched mediation practice.

You should reflect back on the materials in Chapter 4, Mediator Roles, Styles and Orientations, *supra*, when considering the operationalization of a credentialing scheme. Is there a risk that mediators preferring a particular mediator style or orientation will dominate the certification process, leading to an undesirable homogenization of the mediation field? Or, if written too broadly, is there a risk that there will be a lack of clarity as to what qualifies as appropriate mediator practice? Waldman framed her criticism of the legislation in terms of diversity of style. Is there a similar concern regarding cultural, ethnic, and racial diversity? Consider how the empirical findings in the New Mexico study described in Chapter 7, Diversity, Power, and Justice, *supra*, relate to the issues of qualifications, certification, and licensure of mediators.

(7)   In addition to different operational models utilized by the court mediation programs, Joseph P. Folger, Dorothy J. Della Noce, and James R. Antes found that court programs exhibit different ways of connecting to the court, namely assimilative, autonomous, and synergistic. "Assimilative" programs are marked by practices that imbue mediation with the authority and formality of the courts, the mapping of legal language onto mediation, and an emphasis on case processing; the "autonomous" approach call for program operation with a separate identity from the court that are resistant to assimilation of the values and norms of the judicial system. The

characteristics of the "synergistic" approach are program leadership with a synergistic vision; partnering with community members; and practices that show an emphasis on the mediation process itself. *See* A Benchmarking Study of Family, Civil and Citizen Dispute Mediation Programs in Florida at http://www. transformativemediation.org/cart/proddetail.php?prod=Benchmark.

Which approach is best for the courts? For the parties? For the programs? In this excerpt, Sharon Press highlights the positive aspects of institutionalization, if managed appropriately.

## INSTITUTIONALIZATION: SAVIOR OR SABOTEUR OF MEDIATION?
### 24 Fla. St. U. L. Rev. 903, 904–13, 917 (1997)*
### By Sharon Press

[O]ne of the most exciting and challenging developments for practitioners in the past ten years has been the increased institutionalization of ADR particularly in relation to mediation within the court system. Spreading ADR processes has been a goal many who are committed to the field have pursued with great vigor. As the old cliché reminds us, however, "be careful what you wish for." The growth and development of mediation and other dispute resolution processes in institutional settings, while certainly producing more exposure and interest in these processes, has also brought with it a host of concerns I believe worthy of thought and discussion . . . .

. . . For purposes of this article, I use the term "institutionalization" to refer to any entity (governmental or otherwise) which, as an entity, adopts ADR procedures as a part of doing business. Some examples include schools that develop peer mediation programs, courts that establish rules to govern referral to ADR procedures, and government agencies that incorporate ADR processes in developing rules and regulations. My discussion will focus primarily on the institutionalization of court mediation programs, with examples drawn from Florida's experience because that is what I know best; however, I believe that many of the same opportunities and concerns raised are readily transferable to other institutions. To me, Florida's experience with court-connected mediation can serve as a case study for how and why bureaucracies develop.

Institutionally, Florida entered the ADR movement in the mid-1970s with the establishment of "citizen dispute settlement" (CDS) centers. The CDS centers are similar to the neighborhood justice centers of other jurisdictions and handle disputes (mostly minor criminal, neighborhood-type disputes) that are voluntarily brought by the individuals involved in the disputes. The model pursued for the Florida CDS centers, after the initial ones came into being, centered around local development with strong support from the Office of the State Courts Administrator (OSCA) and the Chief Justice of the Florida Supreme Court . . . .

Some argued that this development was not in keeping with the primary goal of the CDS movement, which was to empower those in the local community to resolve

---

issues for themselves. On the other hand, these programs would not have spread as quickly or completely had it not been for the Florida Supreme Court's support. The research conducted by OSCA provided the data to show that the programs worked, the organizational manuals provided the step-by-step information on how to establish programs, and the training manuals and guidelines provided some measure of consistency and quality control that led to confidence in the program. Looking around the nation, one finds that programs have flourished primarily in those states in which the courts provided an institutional home, established institutional frameworks, and promoted the use of these processes. I believe there is a direct correlation. In Florida, the CDS programs thrived when the supreme court focused attention on the program. When attention shifted from the CDS programs toward the court programs, no new programs were established and many of those that were in existence expanded to include court cases. Within a few years, the bulk of the CDS centers' cases had shifted away from communities and towards courts. This shift is not surprising, based upon the difficulty CDS or neighborhood justice centers have in generating cases. Because the number of cases that a community center actually mediates is significantly lower than the number of cases that are scheduled (due to the inherent difficulty in getting both parties to attend a completely voluntary process), the centers face a continuing challenge, resulting in disappointingly low caseloads.

. . . .

If we start from the premise that mediation and other alternative processes provide a positive means of resolving disputes, then it seems to follow that providing for the more rapid spread and more comprehensive use of these processes would also be a positive step. As practitioners, we have longed for more cases to be referred to mediation so more disputants can benefit from the empowerment possibilities of mediated disputes (and also so there is enough work for us to pursue our chosen field). Institutionalization certainly focuses attention on the processes, and it can be very instrumental in promoting its uses; yet increased institutional-ization is not without its downside . . . .

Since 1987, Florida has experienced tremendous growth in the number of rules and laws surrounding the mediation program. From an administrative perspective, each additional rule has been necessary and important in the maturation of the program. Overall, however, I remain concerned about the ultimate effect that additional rules will have on the mediation process, i.e., what will happen when a flexible process, like mediation, is incorporated into the traditional court process. Which process changes?

A description of some of the recent revisions and additions to the Florida Statutes and the Florida Rules of Civil Procedure serves as an ideal way to illustrate this dilemma. In 1988, the Florida Supreme Court adopted qualifications for court mediators. To promote use of the qualifications and add to the comfort level of the judges and lawyers who would ultimately be the users of the process, the court relied heavily on previous experience and "paper credentials." The national mediation community was outraged by the development of mediator qualification requirements by an institution. Nevertheless, if an institution takes the step to order parties who file in court to participate in mediation prior to (or hopefully instead of) obtaining a trial before a judge, doesn't it logically follow that the court has an affirmative obligation to ensure that the individual to whom the case is referred has some expertise? To take it a step further, wouldn't it be irresponsible, if not negligent, for the courts not to develop some method of determining who should mediate for the courts and who should not? I do not see easy answers to these questions. While I am sympathetic to the view that the qualifications originally established by the Florida Supreme Court are not perfect, I do believe that the establishment of mediation as an alternative within the court system brought with it the obligation to provide some means for individuals ordered to mediation to have confidence in their mediator. I also believe, based on discussions I have had over the years with judges and attorneys, that mediation would not have succeeded in the court system if the early mediators in large cases were not attorneys.

This is not to say that the obligation of the court or institution that establishes the program ends with its initial rules and its ability to gain acceptance for the program. On the contrary, I am a strong proponent of the notion that if a court undertakes to institutionalize mediation, it has an ongoing obligation to routinely and systematically review the governing policies, rules, and procedures with an eye toward continual revision. To me, this is a crucial step in preventing the ossification of a flexible process.

. . . .

[T]he Florida Legislature has revised the statute governing mediation and arbitration several times since its adoption in 1987.

One of the legislative changes adopted provides for "judicial immunity in the same manner and to the same extent as a judge." . . . The passage of this legislation created a situation that led to the need for the next major set of rules, namely, the Florida Rules for Certified and Court-Appointed Mediators, which contain the standards of conduct and rules of discipline for supreme court-certified and court-appointed mediators.

The original legislation establishing the comprehensive mediation program contained a provision that the Florida Supreme Court would establish mini-mum standards and procedures for professional conduct and discipline. However, the adoption of the immunity for mediators provided the real impetus to adopt standards and a disciplinary procedure. Absent such adoption, parties to court-ordered mediation had no redress for inappropriate mediator behavior . . .

With such a backdrop, one can readily appreciate the need for the development of standards of conduct. In 1992, the Florida Supreme Court adopted such a code of conduct and a means for enforcing the standards . . . . I remain concerned about the impact that these standards will have on the process. I come back again to the overriding concern that mediation is a flexible process and that adoption of a code of conduct will somehow rigidify the process. If the standards are written broadly to allow for the subtle nuances of an individual situation, might they then offer no real guidance to mediators in discharging their duties? If they are written very specifically, might they then inhibit a mediator's ability to handle each situation creatively?

A concrete example of how the standards might change the practice of mediation in an unintended manner is in the simple practice relating to the retention of notes. Because communication in court-connected mediation is privileged and cannot be disclosed absent a waiver of the privilege by all parties to the mediation, mediators typically do not retain notes from concluded mediation sessions. In fact, in the past, most trainers recommended to student mediators that they not retain notes. Will the adoption of a standard of conduct and the potential for a grievance being filed cause mediators not only to keep notes of their sessions, but also to request that parties sign off on statements that say they were fully capable of participating or that they were aware of their legal rights and were still desirous of pursing this mediated agreement? I wonder whether changes in these procedures will cause a greater underlying change in the way mediation is conducted. Will it lead to more party refusals to mediate? If so, maybe those were cases that should not have been mediated in any event.

After more than four years of experience under the mediator code of conduct and grievance system, we are starting to see some trends . . . [A]n analysis of the grievances filed shows common concerns, namely the failure of the mediator either to allow the parties to exercise self determination, to act impartially, or to refrain from providing professional advice. A summary of the grievances that have been filed is published in the DRC newsletter . . . for educational purposes. The hope is that this formal (institutional) process of handling grievances will enable mediators to better understand their role in the process and prevent inadvertent inappropriate behavior.

. . . .

. . . I believe that the institutionalization of mediation programs has served a worthwhile purpose. It is only with institutionalization that we are able to achieve the increased attention and high level of debate around these issues. I have seen firsthand . . . how helpful — and transforming — these programs can be. I know that most people are still not very sophisticated in thinking through their options for resolving disputes. In the school setting, students frequently view their options as limited to ignoring the situation, telling a teacher or other authority, or fighting it out. For adults, the choices are surprisingly similar: ignoring the conflict, appealing to the authority of the courts, or fighting it out . . . . Institutionalization provides necessary legitimacy and widespread utilization to a process that is only useful if one knows about it. One can only make informed decisions about whether to use mediation if one is aware that the process exists.

## NOTES AND QUESTIONS

(1)   For a more recent critique of the Florida program by Sharon Press, see *Institutionalization of Mediation in Florida: At the Crossroads*, 108 Penn St. L. Rev. 43 (2003).

(2)   While the courts have been in the forefront of the move to institutionalize mediation, they are not unique. Federal and state agencies have also been using mediation and creating institutional mediation opportunities. In 1990, Congress passed the first Administrative Dispute Resolution Act ("ADRA" Public Law

101-552, 104 Stat. 2736, 5 U.S.C. § 581 *et seq.* (1990)). This statute required each federal agency to "adopt a policy that addresses the use of alternative means of dispute resolution," "designate a senior official to be the dispute resolution specialist of the agency," and "review each of its standard agreements for contracts, grants . . . [to] encourage the use of alternative means of dispute resolution." In 1996, the ADRA was reenacted and was made a permanent law without an expiration date. According to the EEOC, "[i]n 1998, EEOC's Federal Sector ADR Study reported that more than half of the federal agencies surveyed had active ADR programs. Thereafter, in 2000, EEOC required all federal agencies to establish or make available an ADR program during the pre-complaint and formal complaint stages of the EEO process. *See,* 29 C.F.R. § 1614.603. This regulation requires agencies to make reasonable efforts to voluntarily settle EEO discrimination complaints as early as possible throughout the administrative process." ADR Report: ADR in the Federal Sector EEO Process for FY 2006.

The employee grievance arena has proven to be particularly conducive to mediation. Here, the conflict is often between individuals who have an ongoing relationship which will often benefit from a private, informal process of resolution. For a complete description of the U.S. Equal Employment Opportunity Commission's mediation program, see http://www.eeoc.gov/eeoc/mediation/index.cfm.

In 1994, the United States Postal Service established a mediation program for employment issues which operates within the transformative framework. *See* Chapters 3 and 4, *supra.* For a review of the initial evaluation of this program, see *Mediating Employment Disputes: Perception of Redress at the United States Postal Service,* 17 Rev. Pub. Personnel Admin. 20 (1997).

What similarities and differences are there between the institutionalization of legal disputes through the court system and through government agencies or private companies?

(3)   Institutional uses of mediation can also be found in schools — from primary and pre-school through high school and universities — as peer mediation programs or for resolution of school related conflicts such as truancy or for alleged breaches of the student code of conduct. See the Education Section of the Association for Conflict Resolution for resources and additional information on programs.

(4)   One of the most recent institutional uses of mediation was in response to the mortgage foreclosure crisis. As part of a Symposium on Conflict Resolution and the Economic Crisis organized by the University of Nevada, Las Vegas, William S. Boyd School of Law University Saltman Center, Sharon Press, Andrea Schneider, and Natalie Fleury published articles in the Nevada Law Journal (Spring 2011) examining mortgage foreclosure mediation programs in Florida and Wisconsin respectively. As you read the following excerpts, consider mediation programs' ability to respond to future crises.

In *Mortgage Foreclosure Mediation in Florida — Implementation Challenges for an Institutionalized Program,* 11 Nev. L.J. 306 at 307 (2011), Press observed:

> Given Florida's extensive experience with court-connected mediation, one would have expected that Florida would have been the first state to pursue mediation of mortgage foreclosure cases. Further, given the extensive

infrastructure in place, Florida would have easily accomplished the task. Instead, the degree to which mediation has been institutionalized added a layer of complexity and created additional obstacles to Florida's attempt to establish mortgage foreclosure mediation.

After detailing some of the obstacles which included a presumption that mortgage foreclosure cases should not be mediated and that state resources could not be used for these cases, Press discussed the responses which included revisions to the procedural rules and concluded:

> . . . the field should closely monitor the procedural revisions to mediation which may impact mediation in general in order to judge their efficacy. In particular, the mortgage foreclosure procedures codify for the first time that someone other than the mediator "take attendance," plaintiffs are permitted . . . to appear electronically, and plaintiffs are required to disclose in advance of the mediation who will appear at the mediation "with full authority." What impact will these decisions have on perceptions of procedural justice, confidentiality, and self-determination?

> . . . the mortgage foreclosure crisis highlighted the difficulties an established mediation program had in responding quickly . . . .

> While I have . . . expressed concerns about the dark side of institution-alization, on balance, I believe that ultimately, the Florida mortgage foreclosure program was designed better and offered greater protection to the parties by virtue of the extensive infrastructure that existed. While flexibility must remain the hallmark of mediation, there are limits. Flexibility does not mean that one sacrifices core values . . . in the interests of expediency.

In *There's No Place Like Home: Applying Dispute Systems Design Theory to Create a Foreclosure Mediation System*, 11 Nev. L.J. 368 (2011), Schneider and Fleury describe the development of the Milwaukee, Wisconsin mortgage foreclosure mediation program which operates out of Marquette University Law School. The mediation program was designed by a working group consisting of representatives from Legal Aid, the law school, the lenders' counsel, housing counselors, consumer groups, bankruptcy attorneys, the mayor's office, and the courts. Schneider and Fleury conclude their article by summarizing the lessons learned in the design process (at 395–96).

> A first key lesson . . . is that stakeholders really matter . . . . Having the stakeholders at the table from the outset provided two crucial items. We were able to learn from each of the stakeholders so that the *content* of the process itself was better than it would have been without them. Additionally, the *buy-in*, and therefore the participation in the program would also not have been so high without all stakeholders at the table . . . .

> A second lesson is in the fluidity and flexibility of whatever dispute system is designed . . . . Stakeholders and funders need to be prepared for the inevitable contingencies and delays that occur . . . .

Another lesson is in the recognition that comparatively huge financial problems . . . need analogous resources devoted toward alleviating these problems. Both the limited funding through grants and the traditionally lean staffing model often used at academic institutions means programmatic trade-offs . . . .

The final lesson . . . we have witnessed the putting of theory into practice in a wonderful way.

## D.    EMPIRICAL EVALUATIONS

In the previous section, the focus was on the policy implications of institutionalization, and the positive impact, from an impressionistic vantage point. In this section, we turn to empirical evaluations.

## EFFICIENCY: MEDIATION IN COURTS CAN BRING GAINS, BUT UNDER WHAT CONDITIONS?
Disp. Resol. Magazine, Vol. 9, No. 11 (Winter 2003)[*]
By Jennifer Shack

Does mediation save courts and litigants time and money? Does it increase the satisfaction of those using the court system?

These are the questions that have most interested courts when considering the implementation or continuation of mediation programs. But these questions will invariably lead to ambiguous conclusions because they are based on the assumption that all mediation programs are the same. The questions "Can mediation save time and money? Can it increase the satisfaction of those using the court system?" are more productive and change the answer from "We don't know" to the resounding "Yes!" that mediation practitioners have long desired.

To fully understand the answer to those questions, however, the focus of research regarding the effectiveness of mediation should shift from whether mediation saves time, reduces cost, and increases satisfaction to a more constructive examination of under what circumstances it is most likely to do so.

A survey of 62 studies that evaluate the effectiveness of more than 100 court mediation programs has underlined the importance of making this shift . . . Some find that mediation does save time, reduce costs, and increase satisfaction, while others find that it does not, and still others find that it has a negative effect on time and money.

These results do not provide an answer to the usual question of what the impact of mediation is on time, cost and satisfaction, but point instead to the importance of variances in program, case and process characteristics in determining the effectiveness of mediation . . .

The studies indicate that litigants like mediation and its outcome, and that they like it more when they settle the case than when they do not. Combined, they show that more than 70 percent are satisfied with the mediation process and that a similar percentage is satisfied with its outcome . . . .

A high percentage of parties were also convinced of the fairness of the mediation process and any agreement that resulted from it . . . .

Not all studies included in the survey make comparisons between programs or cases . . . . Upon evaluation of the comparative studies, 17 studies were retained for analysis. The findings of these studies differ as to the effectiveness of the mediation programs they examined. The studies do not agree, for example, as to whether the programs increased satisfaction and perception of fairness for parties who participated in mediation as compared to those who did not . . . .

Now that researchers know that programs vary in both structure and effectiveness, the next step in the research should be to examine these differences . . . .The following are four recommendations on how to achieve these goals.

If we are to understand better how program characteristics are implicated in the varying outcomes of mediation, studies need to focus more on how programs are designed and function. The first step in doing so is to describe the characteristics of the mediation program, such as when referrals are made, who the mediators are, how voluntary the program is, and especially what is meant by "mediation," since the term is now used for a variety of processes, some of which place decision-making responsibility on the neutrals or do not include the litigants in the sessions.

The second step is to determine whether the program is functioning as designed. . . .

Equally important is understanding the design and functioning of the traditional program to which mediation is being compared. . . .

. . . [R]esearchers need to pay more attention to the role that specific cases characteristics may play in the effectiveness of mediation. The impact of mediation on a particular case can be different depending on the characteristics of the participants, the case type and complexity, and the manner in which each case arrives at the mediation table . . . . More consistent comparisons made on such variables as when in the life of the case it went to mediation, the attributes of the mediator, the complexity of the case, and the issues involved would provide courts and attorneys with valuable information to assist them in making decisions about which cases to send to mediation, when to send them, and whom to select as mediator . . . [K]nowing which cases are most likely to benefit from mediation will enhance the effectiveness of mediation programs and litigants experience of the courts system.

. . . Whatever the goals of a specific program are knowing what happens within the mediation process is essential to assessing the strength of the program.

As difficult as these changes may be, they will also have to be accompanied by sound research design. . . .

Sound research design does not end with the decision regarding what data to collect. Care must be taken as well to ensure that the results of the evaluation are reliable and valid. . . .

## NOTES AND QUESTIONS

(1)   In a 2003 article entitled *Institutionalization: What Do Empirical Studies Tell Us About Court Mediation?*, 9 Disp. Resol. Magazine 8 (2003), Bobbi McAdoo, Nancy Welsh, and Roselle Wissler developed a list of program design options which enhance one or more of the following without diminishing any of the others: institutionalization, settlement, and perceptions of justice. They made the following recommendations:

To maximize the use of court-connected civil mediation programs:

- Enlist the bench and bar in developing a program that fits the local legal culture.

- Obtain ongoing judicial support for referring cases to the program.

- Make mediation use compulsory if one side requests it, or require attorneys to consider mediation early in the litigation process.

To increase the likelihood of settlement in mediation:

- Schedule sessions fairly early in the life of the case.

- Require that critical motions be decided before the session.

- Adopt a system that ensures that the mediators get enough cases to keep their mediation skills sharp.

To heighten litigants' perceptions that the program provides procedural justice:

- Require litigants to attend the session and invite them, along with their attorneys, to participate.

- Urge lawyers to adopt a cooperative approach and prepare their clients for mediation.

- Restrict more extreme evaluative interventions such as recommending a specific settlement.

Which of the recommendations do you think will be most difficult to implement? Why?

(2)   The 2004 Fall-Winter Issue of Conflict Resolution Quarterly was devoted to the topic, *Conflict Resolution in the Field: Assessing the Past, Charting the Future* (Vol. 22, No. 1–2). In that issue, Roselle L. Wissler reviewed the empirical research on mediation in small claims, general jurisdiction trial cases, and appellate cases. *See The Effectiveness of Court-Connected Dispute Resolution in Civil Cases*, 22 Conflict Resol. Q. 55 (2004).* She concluded:

In small claims cases, a majority of studies find that compared to trial, mediation receives more favorable assessments from litigants, reduces the rate of noncompliance, and at least in cases that settle, has more positive effects on the parties' relationship. In general civil jurisdiction cases, a

---

* Copyright © 2004. Reprinted with permission of John Wiley & Sons, Inc.

majority of studies find no differences between mediation cases and non-mediation cases in participants' assessments, transaction costs, the amount of discovery, and the number of motions filed. The findings are mixed with regard to whether mediation does or does not increase the rate of settlement or reduce the trial rate, reduce the time to disposition, and enhance compliance compared to the traditional litigation process . . . . In appellate cases, a majority of studies find that mediation reduces the rate of cases that go to oral argument and reduces the time to disposition compared to cases that are not assigned to mediation. Mediation does not, however, appear to reduce transactional costs in appellate cases.

. . . The mode of referral to mediation does not affect the likelihood of settlement or participants' assessments in some studies, but in others the voluntary use of mediation has positive effects. Earlier sessions reduce the time to disposition and the number of motions filed, and in some studies also increase the likelihood of settlement; but in other studies, timing has no impact on settlement. With regard to mediator qualifications, a majority of studies find that more mediation experience is associated with more settlement, but mediation training and subject matter expertise do not affect settlement rates . . . . The impact of the neutral's approach on participants' assessments seems to vary depending on what the mediators do, when they do it, and what approach was expected. A majority of studies find that neither the general case type category nor the litigants' relationship is related to settlement, but some studies suggest that other case characteristics might play a role.

. . . . Our ability to draw clear conclusions about the relative effectiveness and efficiency of court-connected mediation, neutral evaluation, and traditional litigation is limited by the small, number of studies with reliable comparative data based on the random assignment of cases to dispute resolution processes and the use of statistical significance tests. The variation in findings across studies and across court levels also might reflect the use of different measures in different studies or differences in program design or the court context in which different programs operate . . . . Future studies need to address these gaps in the research.

(3)   In the same issue of Conflict Resolution Quarterly, psychologist Joan Kelly who has researched children's adjustment to divorce, custody and access issues, and divorce mediation, analyzed family mediation research, *Family Mediation Research: Is There Empirical Support for the Field?*, 22 Conflict Resol. Q. 3 (2004).[*] She concluded:

In public and private sectors, in voluntary and mandatory services, and when provided both early and late in the natural course of these disputes, family mediation has been consistently successfully in resolving custody and access disputes, comprehensive divorce disputes, and child protection disputes. Mediation has given evidence of its power to settle complex,

---

highly emotional disputes and reach agreements that are generally durable. . . .

Client satisfaction has been surprisingly high in all studies and settings on a large number of process and outcome measures. . . .

. . . . When contrasted to parents in adversarial processes, parents using a more extended mediation process experience a decrease in conflict during divorce, and in the first year or two following a divorce, they are more cooperative and supportive of each other as parents and communicate more regarding their children, after controlling for any preintervention group differences. One astonishing result has been that twelve years following divorce, fathers in mediation remained more involved with their children compared to the litigation fathers.

Cautions as well emerge from the literature. Consistently, 15 to 20 percent of parents of both sexes are dissatisfied with aspects of mediation process and outcomes. Although this represents half the rate of dissatisfaction of adversarial clients, it is important to know if this reflects a more rushed or coercive mediation process, untrained or inept mediators, or parents who are angry and dissatisfied with any divorce process and outcome that does not produce what they expected or wanted. With the trend to limit court custody mediation to one session, more difficult cases with multiple serious issues most likely will not be given sufficient opportunity to settle, and settlement rates may decline.

. . . To date . . . this research has not led to more complex second generation research, in part due to chronic lack of research funding for mediation, the complexity of what is required, and an apparent diminishing interest in research questions in the field.

(4)    One of the most significant institutional implementations of mediation in the courts occurred as part of the Civil Justice Reform Act (CJRA) of 1990. Importantly, the implementation included an evaluation conducted by the prestigious RAND Institute for Civil Justice which was published in 1996. The study's objectives were to assess implementation, costs, and effects of mediation and neutral evaluation programs in six pilot and comparison federal district courts. The Report concluded that there was "no strong statistical evidence that the mediation or neutral evaluation programs, as implemented in the six districts studied, significantly affected time to disposition, litigation costs, or attorney views of fairness or satisfaction with case management . . . [the] only statistically significant finding is that the ADR programs appear to increase the likelihood of a monetary settlement."

The dispute resolution community was very disappointed by the results of the study and a series of responses followed its release. Most significantly, mediation proponents pointed out that there were significant quality issues in terms of education and training of the neutrals in the programs which were studied. In addition, the programs which were studied were examined early in their development and some experienced substantial revisions to correct design flaws after the data were collected. Specifically, "one of the four mediation programs violated most of what is known about building successful court ADR programs. The court required no training for its lawyer-mediators, excluded settlement empowered clients and insurers from the mediations, and held short and often perfunctory mediation sessions." *Concerns and Recommendations*, 15 Alternatives 6, 72 (May 1997).

(5)    See John Lande, *Getting the Faith: Why Business Lawyers and Executives Believe in Mediation*, 5 Harv. Negot. L. Rev. 137, 216–17 (2000),* for another view on the institutionalization of mediation via the corporate legal community. Lande based his article on interviews conducted with "inside counsel, outside counsel, and non-lawyer executives." One of the outcomes of his survey was this understanding regarding institutionalization:

> Observations and accounts of the process of "getting the faith" in mediation also support the explanation of an institutionalization process. There seems to be a general pattern in which attorneys initially resist new mediation programs, and then, in relatively short order, become some of the biggest proponents for mediation use. Indeed, it has become something of a ritual at continuing legal education programs for "converts" to mediation to give testimonials about how they initially balked at using mediation, but how they are now satisfied believers who use it as often as possible and appropriate. Clearly, these "conversions" are based on experience, which presumably provides opportunities for comparison of litigation with and without mediation. However, the sharp shifts in avowed belief from skeptic to strong proponent suggest that the conversions are more a function of a change in perceived legitimacy of dispute resolution procedures than careful calculation of advantages and disadvantages. Obviously, the purpose of such public testimonials at professional gatherings is to legitimize mediation in order that others may make similar conversions in belief and practice.
>
> Over time, repeated exposure to public and private testimonials, as well as the mediation process itself, transforms mediation from an innovation into a routine part of the disputing practice that becomes taken for granted as the (currently) normal way of doing things. After the mediation innovation has become institutionalized for a time, it becomes difficult to conceive of alternative arrangements, and even those who initially resisted the innovation are likely to resist changing a new status quo.

(6)    In 1994, the National Center for State Courts conducted a National Symposium on Court Connected Dispute Resolution Research under a cooperative agreement with the State Justice Institute (SJI). SJI had a history of funding such research for a number of years and was desirous of determining what was now known as a result of the research and even more importantly, determining where further evaluation and research were still needed. The research that had been conducted to date was collected and published in the *National Symposium on Court-Connected Dispute Resolution Research: A Report on Current Research Findings — Implications for Courts and Future Research Needs* (NCSC Publica-

---

tion No. R-152). The National Center for State Courts reported that the following themes emerged, which highlight the challenges of this type of research:

- . . . courts need to know more about the dynamics of the litigation process and attorneys' expectations about how ADR fits into that scheme. . . .

- courts need more reliable findings on the benefits of ADR . . . . Future studies should use more consistent sets of measures in order to develop more comparable sets of findings across jurisdictions.

- . . . courts need significantly greater knowledge about the most effective methods for training, qualifying, and selecting ADR providers.

- innovative measures of participant satisfaction should be developed because most individual litigants are one-time users of the justice system and thus have no reference for comparing the dispute resolution process they experienced with other processes. In addition, research on satisfaction should address a broader array of factors and identify those that contribute to greater satisfaction with the dispute resolution process and its outcomes.

- courts need better access not only to research findings, but also to practical guides for implementing, operating and evaluating ADR programs.

What type of studies or research do you think are needed?

## E.  CRITIQUES OF INSTITUTIONALIZATION

The trend toward institutionalization of mediation has not been accepted universally or without criticism. In the following section, various authors highlight the potential "dark side" to institutionalization. Professor Carrie Menkel-Meadow raises questions about the potential co-option of the flexible mediation process when it becomes institutionalized in the rule-bound legal system; Dean James Alfini moderates a panel discussion regarding the impact institutionalization has on the parties, the attorneys, and the court; and U.S. Magistrate Judge (Northern District of California) Wayne Brazil shares his perspective on Court ADR, 25 years after the Pound Conference. Finally, Professor Nancy Welsh analyzes court-connected mediation programs in relation to procedural justice.

# PURSUING SETTLEMENT IN AN ADVERSARY CULTURE: A TALE OF INNOVATION CO-OPTED OR "THE LAW OF ADR"

19 Fla. St. U. L. Rev. 1, 1–2, 5, 7, 11, 25, 30–33, 36–44 (1991)*
By Carrie Menkel-Meadow

In this Article I tell a tale of legal innovation co-opted. Put another way, this is a story of the persistence and strength of our adversary system in the face of attempts to change and reform some legal institutions and practices. In sociological terms, it is an ironic tale of the unintended consequences of social change and legal reform. A field that was developed, in part, to release us from some — if not all — of the limitations and rigidities of law and formal legal institutions has now developed a law of its own. With burgeoning developments in the use of non-adjudicative methods of dispute resolution in the courts and elsewhere, issues about alternative dispute resolution (ADR) increasingly have been "taken to court." As a result, we are beginning to see the development of case and statutory law and, dare I say, a "common law" or "jurisprudence" of ADR.

. . . .

. . . In this Article, I explore the larger institutional issues presented when lawyers, judges, and parties to a conflict come together to resolve disputes using new forms within old structures. As a proponent of a particular version of ADR — the pursuit of "quality" solution — I am somewhat troubled by how a critical challenge to the status quo has been blunted, indeed co-opted, by the very forces I had hoped would be changed by some ADR forms and practices. In short, courts try to use various forms of ADR to reduce caseloads and increase court efficiency at the possible cost of realizing better justice. Lawyers may use ADR not for the accomplishment of a "better" result, but as another weapon in the adversarial arsenal to manipulate time, methods of discovery, and rules of procedure for perceived client advantage. Legal challenges cause ADR "issues" to be decided by courts. An important question that must be confronted is whether forcing ADR to adapt to a legal culture or environment may be counterproductive to the transformations proponents of ADR would like to see in our disputing practices.

. . . .

. . . The major question I wish to explore here is whether, in a more likely scenario, the power of our adversarial system will co-opt and transform the innovations designed to redress some, if not all, of our legal ills. Can legal institutions be changed if lawyers and judges persist in acting from traditional and conventional conceptions of their roles and values?

. . . .

. . . . [O]utcomes derived from our adversarial judicial system or the negotiation that occurs in its shadows are inadequate for solving many human problems. Our legal system produces binary win-lose results in adjudication. It also produces

---

unreflective compromise — "split the difference" results in negotiated settlements that may not satisfy the underlying needs or interests of the parties. Human problems become stylized and simplified because they must take a particular legal form for the stating of a claim. Furthermore, the "limited remedial imagination" of courts in providing outcomes restricts what possible solutions the parties could develop. Some of us have argued that alternative forms of dispute resolution, or new conceptualizations of old processes, could lead to outcomes that were efficient in the Pareto-optimal sense of making both parties better off without worsening the position of the other. In addition, the processes themselves would be better because they would provide a greater opportunity for party participation and recognition of party goals. Thus, the "quality" school includes both elements of process and substantive justice claims. Some of the arguments here have been supported by the jurisprudential and anthropological work of those studying the different structures that human beings have developed in response to different disputing functions.

. . . .

Partly because of the institutionalization of ADR, some of its earlier proponents, including anthropologist Laura Nader, now oppose ADR because it does not foster communitarian and self-determination goals. Instead, it is used to restrict access to the courts for some groups, just at the time when these less powerful groups have achieved some legal rights. Indeed, some critics have argued that ADR actually hurts those who are less powerful in our society — like women or racial and ethnic minorities — by leaving them unprotected by formal rules and procedures in situations where informality permits the expression of power and domination that is unmediated by legal restraints. In other criticisms, proceduralists have argued that various forms of ADR compromise our legal system by privatizing law making, shifting judicial roles, compromising important legal and political rights and principles, and failing to grant parties the benefits of hundreds of years of procedural protections afforded by our civil and criminal justice rules.

From another quarter, where the claims are usually brought by non-parties to the litigation, one of the major critiques of the development of ADR techniques has been that ADR privatizes disputing. To the extent that mandatory settlement conferences, mediation, and summary jury trials result in settlements before a full public trial, they may rob the public of important information. Some critics charge that with so much private settlement there will not be enough public debate, or enough cases going through the traditional adversary system, to produce good law.

. . . .

Public access and first amendment issues are only a few of the constitutional challenges that have been leveled against ADR. Invoking a first amendment claim, both litigants and the public may seek to open settlement processes that were designed to permit confidential and open exploration of options and possibilities for settlement.

I will not pursue in great detail the claims about the constitutionality of ADR because they have been well canvassed by others. As ADR proceeds in its various forms through the courts, advocates have raised issues about violations of the right to jury trial, due process, equal protection, and separation of powers. Most of these claims have failed, and it is clear that with certain protections like nonbinding results, rights to *de novo* hearings, and limited penalties, ADR can constitutionally be conducted in the courts. Thus, in the constitutional arena the key issue is how the particular ADR programs are structured. Nonbinding settlement devices have virtually all been sustained against constitutional challenges. Binding procedures, or those that tax too greatly the choice of process (such as cost or fee shifting penalties), are likely to be more problematic. Constitutional challenges are not likely to eliminate or abolish ADR in the courts, though they may have some role in shaping the particular forms that are used.

. . . .

The use of settlement activity in the courts should be understood as the clash of two cultures. To the extent that settlement activity seeks to promote consensual agreement through the analysis of the point of view of the other side, it requires some different skills and a very different mind-set from those litigators usually employ. Thus, the issue is whether judges and lawyers in the courts can learn to reorient their cultures and behaviors when trying to settle cases or whether those seeking settlement continue to do so from an adversarial perspective. To the extent that we cannot identify different behaviors in each sphere, we may see the corruption of both processes. If one of the purposes of the legal system is to specify legal entitlements from which settlements may be measured, or from which the parties may depart if they so choose, then having the adjudicators engage in too much mediative conduct may compromise the ability of judges to engage in both fact-finding and rule-making. If courts fail to provide sufficient baselines in their judgments, we will have difficulties determining if particular settlements are wise or truly consensual. There is danger in the possibility that good settlement practice will be marred by over-zealous advocacy or by over-zealous desire to close cases that may require either full adjudication or a public hearing.

. . . .

In an important sense, the ADR movement represents a case study in the difficulties of legal reform when undertaken by different groups within the legal system. At the beginning were the *conceptualizers* — academics and judicial activists who developed both the critique of the adversary system and, in some cases, the design of alternative systems of dispute resolution. The implementers developed the concrete forms these innovations took when they moved into the legal system. Some of the *conceptualizers* — Frank Sander and several of the judges — were also *implementers*. In addition, other judges and judicial administrators principally concerned about case load management, and about the quality of solutions or decisions, became *implementers*. Support for the implementation of these ADR programs came from the principal foundation and government funding sources, as well as from groups of change-oriented practicing lawyers who have played an important catalytic role in supporting and using some of the first alternative procedures.

Finally, the *constituents* of these ADR systems — lawyers and their clients as consumers — were "acted upon," sometimes somewhat consensually, by the force of court rules or judicial encouragement. We are just beginning to see some of their reactions in the litigation developing from ADR innovation and in evaluation research.

Each of these groups of actors within the ADR legal reform movement inhabit different cultural worlds — academia, the judiciary, law practice, the business world, and everyday life. Each group uses, transforms, and "colonizes" the work of the others. The research of academics is ignored or simplified; judges move cases along and adopt the language of case management rather than justice; lawyers "infect" clients with a desire for adversarial advantage, or in other cases clients do the same to lawyers; and professionals argue about credentialing and standards for the new profession.

Each of these actors in the dispute resolution arena may be serving different masters. As the ideas are institutionalized, they develop into new and different forms of dealing with problems. Those who work in the field have attempted to create environments for dialogues among and between these constituencies. Some of these meetings have been productive and have fostered "cross-class" understanding. Just as often, however, such meetings leave people confirmed in their views that their particular paradigm is most accurate. Others do not understand the particular reality that some may face — whether it be the crush of caseloads or the lack of "justice" in settlements.

In my view, productive discourse about ADR will have to transcend the language of these cultural differences. Academics, and particularly those who theorize about jurisprudential concerns, need to root their views in the practicalities of our empirical world. Occasionally, judges and legal practitioners need to step back and review the larger jurisprudential and policy issues implicated in "quick-fix" reforms. Practitioners and clients need to consider new forms of practice and process while diminishing their adversarial ways of thinking. A professional life should be one of re-examination, growth, and change. If we are really looking for new ways to process disputes — both to increase case-processing efficiency and to promote better-quality solutions — then we have to be willing to look critically at the innovations and their effects from all quarters. I believe that social innovation and transformation are possible here — the issues are whether conventional mind-sets will "infect" these innovations on the one hand, or whether the "cure" will be worse than the disease on the other.

In a sense, we are at a second stage in the development of alternative dispute resolution innovations. The bloom on the rose has faded as some experiments have been tried and now present their own problems or dilemmas. Some of us still aim for consciousness transformation and institutionalized forms of ADR and what can be done to make them work. Many of the issues raised by these developments require policy judgments for which we have an inadequate empirical data base; others require us to make normative choices based on what we value in a procedural system. If ADR is to meet the basic levels of fairness, then the following questions must be collected to prevent ADR from becoming totally swallowed by the adversarial system:

1. To what extent will courts lose their legitimacy as courts if too many other forms of case-processing are performed within their walls? If the "other" processes are not considered legitimate within public institutions,

they will be legally challenged and transformed so that they will no longer be "alternatives," but only watered-down versions of court adjudication. These watered-down versions may be violative of the legal rights and rules our courts are intended to safeguard. Are theorists, practitioners, and citizens capable of changing our views of what courts should do?

2. Should some case types be excluded from alternative treatment?

3. What are the purposes for using particular forms of alternative dispute resolution? . . . If the goals and purposes of particular ADR institutions are clarified now, future problems based on overly abstract goals may be avoided.

4. What forms of ADR should be institutionalized? Not all ADR devices are the same. There is a tendency in the literature and in the rhetoric to homogenize widely different approaches to dispute resolution. A more thorough and careful consideration of each of the devices might lead to different conclusions about the utility and legitimacy of these devices . . .

5. What are the politics of ADR? Does ADR serve the interests of particular groups? This is not an easy question to answer. Many have argued that "minor" disputes have been siphoned out of the public legal system, while "major" disputes have continued to receive the benefits of the traditional court system. Large corporations are also removing their cases from the court system. Through the increased use of private ADR, the economics of dispute resolution are more subtle. Some may be "forced" out while others choose to opt out. What will this mean for payment and subsidies of dispute resolution? Will "free market" forces decide the fate of ADR? Who will control decision-making about ADR — judges, lawyers, clients, or legislators? If those with the largest stake in the system exit, who will supply the impetus and resources for court and rule reform? At the level of institutional decision-making, are these issues for individual judges, for the Congress, or for the United States Supreme Court to decide?

6. What are the cultural forces producing these legal changes at these particular times? Has the larger culture around us changed since particular legal innovations were adopted? If attempts to incorporate party participation in disputing were made in the "participatory" 1960s and 1970s, then does the 1980s era of privatization of public services dictate other considerations in the use of ADR? How has the rhetoric of quality justice been transformed into a rhetoric of quantity and case processing?

7. How are different forms of ADR actually functioning? . . .

. . . In order for ADR to develop in a way that enhances our trust in the American legal system, several important reforms should accompany our experimentation.

First, some forms of ADR should remain mandatory, but not binding . . . Second, if some settlement processes are to be made mandatory, certain essential legal protections may have to flow from those processes. If they do not, then processes may have to be chosen consensually or voluntarily . . . .

Third, if settlement processes are to be conducted within the courts, they should be facilitated by those who will not be the ultimate triers of fact. Because I believe that good settlement practice frequently depends on the revelation of facts that would be inadmissible in court, the facilitator of settlement cannot be the same person who will ultimately find facts or decide the outcome of the case . . .

Fourth, settlement facilitators must be trained to conduct settlement proceedings, particularly those that depart from conventional adjudication models . . .

Fifth, we must provide the evidence for systematic evaluation of alternative dispute resolution devices. To accomplish this goal, I recommend the recording of proceedings, as well as more sophisticated data collection at the court level.

. . . .

Sixth, different forms of ADR should be unbundled and separately evaluated . . .

Finally, categorical judgments about particular processes are likely to be unhelpful. Mediation or summary jury trials *per se* do not violate our procedural rules or jurisprudential norms. More often, the issue is whether a particular process is carried out sensitively or "coercively."

# WHAT HAPPENS WHEN MEDIATION IS INSTITUTIONALIZED?: TO THE PARTIES, PRACTITIONERS, AND HOST INSTITUTIONS
9 Ohio St. J. on Disp. Resol. 307, 307–14, 316–19, 321–24, 327–29, 331–32 (1994)*
By James Alfini, John Barkai, Robert Baruch Bush, Michele Hermann, Jonathan Hyman, Kimberlee Kovach, Carol Liebman, Sharon Press & Leonard Riskin

. . . .

**Dean James Alfini:** . . . The general question we'll be addressing today is: What are the real and potential effects of this institutionalization of mediation? In particular, we'll concern ourselves with the impact of institutionalization on: First, the mediation process. Second, the parties to the dispute, or the case in court. Third, the lawyers and the legal profession generally. Fourth will be the courts. . . .

Let's put the discussion in a hypothetical context. . . .

The Chief Justice of the State of Fiss . . . is very interested in bringing mediation into the court system, particularly into the trial court system . . . Our panel is a consulting team that has been brought into the State of Fiss with the purpose of advising these policy makers on these important matters.

. . . .

Let's start with the concerns of the professional mediator in the State of Fiss. As you can imagine, their general concern is whether, once the court system —

---

* Copyright © 1994. Reprinted with permission of Ohio State Journal on Dispute Resolution and the authors.

particularly lawyers and judges — get their mitts on this new process, mediation as they know it — good mediation — will come to an end. Whether lawyers and judges will, in fact, bastardize the process.

. . . .

**Professor Baruch Bush:** . . . The thing to be concerned about as mediation becomes institutionalized — not just through connections with the courts . . . — is that what tends to happen is the hardening of mediation practice into . . . the technocratic face rather than the humanistic face.

Let me be a little more specific, because there are a number of different things we can consider institutionalization. Courts' and lawyers' involvement is one. This tends to mean that the advancement of settlement and agreement is set up as an all important goal of mediation because disposition of cases matters very much to courts. Also, legal standards become imported into the definition of what constitutes a good agreement in mediation, as opposed to purely the parties' preferences. . . .

. . . A growing body of research on practice suggests, that despite the image of mediation as reflecting self-determination and a more humanistic face, actual practice follows more of a problem-solving or technocratic approach, a directive approach to the process . . . [T]hat kind of directive model of practice seems to be quite predominate, as opposed to an approach that focuses more on self-determination, choice-making, communication, perspective-taking — concepts that originated the field of mediation. . . . [T]his dimension has tended to get less emphasis the more the process crystallizes.

. . . Mediation had, and has, the potential to offer something truly different, something truly alternative. However, if that's going to happen, this trend towards crystallization into the technocratic model must be avoided.

. . . I think mediators themselves are the best source of control on this trend. . . .

**Professor Carol Liebman:** . . . The California and New York experiences teach critical lessons about institutionalizing ADR. The higher the volume, the more routinized and de-humanized the process is likely to become, the more important the doorkeeper to the multi-door courthouse becomes and the harder that door keeping job is . . .

It is difficult to maintain quality when you get mediators — sometimes paid, sometimes getting expenses, sometimes volunteers — who are doing a number of these every day, with little or no supervision . . . . If what you want is a quick fix, faster/cheaper mediation and that's all you want, mediation can be a very serious problem in terms of cutting off peoples' rights and pushing them out of the system without their getting a fair process — whether it's a fair hearing or a fair mediation.

. . . .

**Professor Michele Hermann:** . . . [M]y first thought is that the impact of institutionalization is going to be driven by the motivation of the courts that institutionalize.

. . . .

**Dean Alfini:** . . . What's going to be the impact of institutionalized mediation on the parties themselves? . . .

**Professor Hermann:** . . . In the mediation literature, women have been predicted to do worse in mediation . . . . [O]ur study [in the small claims court in Albuquerque, New Mexico] in mediation found that women did better in mediation than they did in adjudication. And women did better than men. The flip side in terms of satisfaction was that women liked mediation less than they liked adjudication and were most likely to describe the mediation process as being unfair when their case was co-mediated by two women . . .

In terms of disputants of color, who in our sample were eighty seven percent self-described Hispanic, the minority disputants did somewhat worse in adjudication than did white disputants, but not enough to be really statistically significant. In mediation, they did dramatically worse than did white disputants . . . . But if both of the mediators were mediators of color then the outcome was no longer distinguishable from the outcome of white disputants. [I]n terms of satisfaction, both claimants and respondents of color were more enthusiastic about mediation than they were about adjudication, and were more enthusiastic . . . than were white people in mediation.

. . . .

**Ms. Sharon Press:** . . . [I]n Florida . . . what we knew before we got started was that approximately ninety-six percent of all cases settled and did not go on to trial . . . . What we've seen is a difference in how those cases settle. Traditionally the way cases settled — those ninety-six percent — is that the two or more lawyers who are representing the parties get together outside their clients and discuss settlement, and they come up with a settlement and that settlement is then presented to the clients. The clients don't have as much input or as much understanding as to why the case is settled the way it is settled. The difference in an institutionalized system like Florida is that the parties are mandated to participate in those settlement discussions . . . . I think that helps people to understand what's going on and I think it leads to better settlements as well.

We also know that people didn't choose to go to mediation, at least initially, when they didn't understand what the process was about . . . . Now that we have five or six years of institutionalized mediation experience, the courts need to mandate mediation in fewer cases. In more and more cases, the parties are saying to their lawyers they would like to use mediation . . . . So in that way, having an institutionalized system — at least initially in mandating it — you educate the parties and spread mediation in a way that is much faster than if you went through a slow learning curve of just letting people seep through the system.

. . . .

The final point that I have is slightly outside of the court system . . . . By participating in a mediation — whether it is mandated or not — I think that there is a spillover effect to people involved in it, that they learn that there are ways to resolve disputes. This was dramatically shown to me when I worked in a high school mediation program — a different kind of institution but an institution nonetheless. The students that came in as the disputants learned a process, learned a way of thinking about disputes that they may not have thought about before. And what we saw was that many of them wanted to become mediators . . . . [U]nless you have widespread institutionalization or the placing of this process in institutions, you don't have that kind of spillover. . . .

. . . .

**Professor John Barkai:** . . . Michele's impressive and useful research raises the question, "What is 'culturally appropriate' mediation?" . . . My experience is that different cultures use different forms of mediation. In Asia, mediation is often referred to as "conciliation." Asian conciliation, in either a business or personal setting, typically includes the seeking of an opinion from a wise and respected person within the community whom Westerners might call a mediator . . . . [Asians] do not seek or expect something that looks like American community mediation which seeks to enhance communication, empower the parties, and uncover underlying interests . . . . All of this leads me to the conclusion that if a mediator is working with disputants from other cultures, the mediator might want to ask, "What kind of mediation assistance would you like to have?"

. . . .

**Professor Bush:** . . . One possible explanation for some of the sort of paradoxical results that Michele got . . . is that perhaps people don't care mostly about money. . . .

. . . .

. . . It could be that the reason why women liked mediation less was that it wasn't outcome that mattered to them most, it was how the process worked, how they were treated. So even though they got favorable outcomes, they disliked mediation because something else mattered more to them. And for the disputants of color, it was the same thing. Even though they got unfavorable outcomes, they liked mediation because something else mattered more.

. . . .

**Dean Alfini:** . . . Professor Hyman, you've been doing research on settlement conferences recently. Does that research suggest how mediation or its institution-alization might have an impact on lawyers and the legal profession generally?

**Professor Jonathan Hyman:** . . . I think the key to a lot of these questions is the depth and sophistication of the understanding of lawyers, themselves, about the mediation process. If they see mediation in a kind of mechanical light — trying to speed up a series of offers and demands and exchange of concessions — if they see mediation as the way to advance that kind of dispute resolution process, which is the one they're mostly familiar with, then I don't think that institutionalizing mediation is going to have much effect for things other than small claims. . . .

. . . When we did a survey of civil litigators in New Jersey — these are non-matrimonial civil cases claiming over $5,000 — we asked them about two kinds of settlement practices. . . . We received five hundred responses to our question-naire, and surveyed most of the lawyers who were on the trial lists over a period of time throughout New Jersey. They reported to us that at least seventy percent of the cases that they knew about in their experience were settled by the positional method, not by the problem-solving method. But sixty percent of the respondents wanted more of the problem-solving method. And almost half wanted less of the positional method.

. . . This would tie in closely with what mediation can do; it's this kind of situation in which a mediator can be very helpful.

. . . .

[T]here's a substantial risk that the lawyers are going to swallow whatever system you adopt. They're going to keep replicating the same things they do now, and they'll take control of it. But there's an opportunity for letting lawyers participate in expanding the use of problem-solving methods and finding ways that they can do that . . .

. . . .

**Dean Alfini:** . . . Texas, again, has been introducing more and more court-sponsored programs into their judicial system. The final set of concerns that we have, have to do with the impact on the courts. . . . What's the likelihood of the impact on the courts?

**Professor Kovach:** . . . It depends on what I think the state is willing to do on the front end. I think it also depends on identifying the specific goals, which was brought out earlier . . . [T]he courts that did not take the time at the front end to become educated about the mediation process, educated about referral, and things like that, ended up spending more time on a case because of objections on the referral process, on the selection of the mediator, or fee issues, etc. . . . And it also then depends . . . if you have the resources. . . . What has turned out in the latest round of plans is that once the resources dried up, ADR plans and mediation plans have been the first to be dropped out of those plans.

. . . .

**Professor Barkai:** As we try to forecast the future of mediation in the courts, I think that we are failing to look at the incentives and disincentives ADR holds for lawyers. The practice of law is a business, and lawyers are trying to figure out how ADR will impact their practice. The fee structure significantly impacts incentives for using ADR. There is not much economic incentive for a lawyer on an hourly-fee to engage in mediation, court-annexed arbitration, or any form of ADR before almost all pretrial discovery is complete. Although ADR may mean reducing costs for clients, it also means reducing income for lawyers. There is an obvious conflict of interest there.

. . . .

**Professor Bush:** . . . [A]s "institutionalization" proceeds, I would argue for not placing transformation off the end of the spectrum. Instead, I think that we need to de-mystify that term, and talk about the possibility, and value, of change on a much more incremental, much more "micro" level. It's too soon to rigidify things and say, "this is possible and this is not," even when we're talking about courts, lawyers and "purely monetary disputes." It is certainly true, there are cases where people don't want to have somebody assist them in approaching conflict as a sort of change process. If so, then that shouldn't happen; that should be clearly a choice of the parties. On the other hand, if this kind of approach in not even available, because institutionalization has made it difficult or impossible for this to occur in mediation, then that's a limitation of choice of a different kind. And I don't think that's a wise idea to do that at this stage of our development.

. . . .

**Professor Hyman:** Well, it seems from what we've been talking about here that you shouldn't rely on any institutions to make changes; that changes have to come from the bottom up — from the people on a more micro level. The proper role of the courts seems to be more in making those kinds of changes possible, understanding them, welcoming them, providing room for them, encouraging them, but not trying to institutionalize them.

# COURT ADR 25 YEARS AFTER POUND: HAVE WE FOUND A BETTER WAY?
18 Ohio St. J. on Disp. Resol. 93, 98–100, 104, 107–09, 111, 114–16, 120–21, 124–25, 128, 130, 132–33, 135, 141–48 (2002)*
By Wayne D. Brazil

. . . .

"Has the addition of ADR to pretrial processes improved the administration of justice?"

Before responding to this . . . question, we must try to identify the criteria we should use to identify "improvements" in the "administration of justice." Hopefully, as we work through the issues, we will remain more concerned about justice than administration. It is simple-minded, however, to suggest that justice and administration are not related. So it is fair to ask, when we try to identify the criteria for identifying "improvements," whether we should focus primarily on efficiency values. If so, efficiency for whom? For the courts? For lawyers? For parties? Is efficiency for one necessarily efficiency for all? Or, when we determine what constitutes an improvement in the administration of justice, should we also look to a broader range of values: (1) party and lawyer feelings about fairness and about the utility of the process (taking into account the full range of parties' values), (2) the extent to which the process permits or encourages participation by parties (reducing levels of alienation from the system), (3) what the process contributes to the clarity of the parties' understanding of their situation and their options, and (4) the parties' feelings about the system of justice and our judicial institutions.

With respect to the last mentioned criterion, we should take into account the impact the ADR process or program has on the inferences parties draw about what values and concerns animate the courts as institutions. We also should consider what effect the ADR programs have on how well served the parties feel by the system of justice and on whether their experience in the court system enhances or

---

reduces their respect for and feeling of connection with their government. Because how people feel about their governmental institutions is so important in a democracy, when we ask whether the addition of ADR to the pretrial menu has improved the administration of justice, we need to give full and fair consideration to both objective and subjective measures.

. . . .

We should take heart from the fact that in studies of the programs that I know best, the subjective data support, often strongly, a conclusion that the addition of ADR to court services has improved (in the all-important eyes of users) the administration of justice — regardless of the criteria we use to define improvement.

. . . .

So one way to conceptualize our court now is as an institution that offers three kinds of processes: (1) traditional litigation, (2) ADR processes (arbitration, ENE, and some versions of evaluative mediation) that proceed within the context of traditional litigation but help parties combat some of its limitations and problems, and (3) ADR processes (variations of facilitative mediation) that enable and encourage parties to pursue goals and to behave in ways that are quite different from those associated with traditional adversarial litigation.

. . . .

. . . I must acknowledge that despite the considerable progress and the many achievements described in the preceding sections, we have not realized many ambitions. A great deal remains to be done. There are many challenges and dangers on the road ahead for court ADR, and we disserve ourselves and the values we hold dear if we do not try to identify them accurately and face them squarely.

. . . My guess is that appreciably less than half of the civil cases filed in this country have real access to court-sponsored ADR services. In many courts, there are entire categories of civil matters that receive no ADR services at all. Perhaps the most disturbing and challenging example is pro se cases.

Moreover, in many jurisdictions no parties can secure ADR services unless they pay full market rates for a private neutral whose connection with the court often is tenuous, at best (and over whom the court, realistically, exercises virtually no "quality control"). The requirement of paying the neutral a substantial fee serves as a real barrier for some litigants and triggers difficult policy questions about why the courts offer litigation services for free, but ADR services only at a substantial price.

. . . .

. . . We also have discovered occasions in which neutrals have misunderstood, sometimes fundamentally, the role they were to play or the specific characteristics of the process they were to host. We work hard to try to control what is being done by our neutrals under the auspices of our program, but we need to do more. We also worry about what happens in programs where the courts do less. Because of serious shortfalls in means to assure quality control in many programs there likely is considerable variability in the quality of the neutral services received in different cases.

There also is a distressing level of unevenness in ADR offerings between different jurisdictions. . . .

. . . In sum, there are great inequalities both in access to and in the character of court ADR products.

. . . .

. . . I will close by identifying some internal sources of peril — matters about ourselves and our program design decisions that could become sources of danger for court ADR.

A. Sources of Peril in Our Relationships with Legislatures

. . . .

There is a risk that perceived abuses . . . in the private sector would unfairly contaminate the standing of all ADR in the minds of influential lawmakers and the public. The risk of contamination is particularly great in courts that "outsource" some or all of the ADR services they sanction or that fail to adopt stringent conflict of interest requirements and quality control mechanisms. The more a court depends on professional service providers from the private sector, the greater the risk that legislators will paint court and corporate ADR programs with the same broad brush of suspicion.

. . . .

Ironically, a second peril in our relationships with legislatures is animated by policy concerns that cut in the opposite direction. Legislatures can generate program-distorting pressures by insisting on using only efficiency criteria to assess the value of court ADR . . .

. . . Those who would insist on using only efficiency criteria to assess the value of ADR programs jeopardize the courts' most precious and only necessary assets: public confidence in the integrity of the processes the courts sponsor and public faith in the motives that underlie the courts' actions. We must take great care not to make program design decisions that invite parties to infer that the courts care less about doing justice and offering valued service than about looking out for themselves as institutions (e.g., by reducing their workload, or off-loading kinds of cases that are especially taxing or emotionally difficult or that are deemed "unimportant").

B. Sources of Peril From Our Relationship with Judges

. . . .

The first of the concerns that can fuel judicial inhospitality to court ADR is fear that ADR threatens the vitality of the jury system as a critical tool of democracy — as an essential weapon to discourage and to discipline abuse of public or private power. There are judges who believe passionately that one of the most powerful and essential deterrents to misbehavior in our society is fear of the jury trial, the public exposure and humiliation it can generate, the great transaction costs it can impose, and the huge damage awards to which it can lead . . .

. . . [A second] concern is about money, more specifically, budgets for courts. The financial resources available to the courts to perform their traditional core functions are already strained in many jurisdictions, and some judges and court administrators fear that supporting good ADR programs consumes resources that the courts simply cannot afford to divert. . . .

A very different source of judicial skepticism about the place of ADR in courts is concern that ADR processes, especially facilitative mediation, tend to be analytically sloppy. Some judges worry that there is considerable risk that decisions made by lawyers and clients in these settings will be based on unreliable data or inaccurate legal premises, or on a blurring of thinking and emoting about matters relevant under the law and matters irrelevant under the law. They fear all of this will increase the risk that important rights will not be protected and legal norms will not be followed.

. . . .

An independent judicial concern at a very different level is that ADR threatens delay or disruption of traditional litigation — that it jeopardizes timeliness of dispositions by eroding the pressure that derives from early and firm trial dates. . . .

. . . .

C. Sources of Peril From Our Relationships with Practicing Lawyers

. . . Lawyers could undermine or sabotage court ADR programs by failing to inform clients that they have ADR options, failing to accurately consider the pros and cons of those options with their clients, or by actively discouraging their clients from trying to use ADR or from participating in good faith in ADR events. Lawyers also may undermine ADR programs, more subtly but no less significantly, by failing to take full advantage of the potential in an ADR proceeding when they prepare for and attend it. Sometimes failings of these kinds are attributable to ignorance, sometimes to inertia, sometimes to fear of unfamiliar processes and fora, of loss of control over inputs to and from the client, and sometimes to greed.

. . . .

D. Sources of Peril in Our Relationships with the Fourth Estate

. . . .

There is one additional policy arena of potential tension between court ADR programs and the private ADR provider community that warrants mention here: compensation for neutrals. Some courts and parties will want neutrals to work at economy rates, or pro bono, while organizations of neutrals are likely to press for payment at professionals' market rates (agreeing to perform only limited work for free as a public service). While lobbying for higher levels of compensation may be vulnerable to cynical inferences about self-interest, organized mediators would contend that their real purpose is to protect against compromising the quality of mediator services. They would argue that if neutrals are not paid at market rates, the quality of neutrals will suffer, or the quality of the effort that neutrals are willing to commit to individual cases will suffer, thus harming the integrity and viability of mediation generally.

. . . .

E. Perils with Sources in Ourselves

. . . .

The first such peril arises from the temptation to impose on parties and their lawyers a generalized requirement to participate in "good faith" in our ADR processes . . . [S]uch a requirement could do considerable damage without yielding sufficient offsetting benefits.

. . . .

Like the imposition of a generalized good faith requirement, the devolution of court ADR programs into one hybrid but largely evaluative process could have several dangerous consequences . . . .

. . . If we fail to maintain clear differences between processes and permit all court ADR to become some blur of evaluative mediation and a settlement conference we will needlessly compromise our ability to be responsive to the full range of values and needs that litigants bring to our courts. We will reduce the occasions on which parties perceive the court as reaching out to them, trying to help them pursue the goals that are most important to them. Offering only an evaluative form of ADR also could increase the risk of parties inferring that the courts' only real interest in the program is getting cases settled, thus reducing occasions for parties to feel grateful to the court for providing a party-oriented service. Moreover, the more that "evaluation" pervades an ADR process, the greater the risk of the "litigization" of that process, which in turn, reduces the capacity of ADR to contribute in unique ways to problem solving.

. . . .

The more like a smorgasbord an ADR process becomes, the greater the risk that the neutral will make poor judgments about which process route to follow or which techniques are appropriate. As these risks increase, so does the likelihood that neutrals in the same court program, hosting what is nominally the same kind of ADR process, would use different procedures in similar circumstances. If neutrals in the same program use different procedures and techniques in parallel settings, it becomes appreciably more difficult for parties and lawyers to predict what will occur in any particular ADR event.

As predictability of process declines, so does the parties' ability to prepare adequately, which not only jeopardizes the usefulness of the ADR event but also increases the risk that parties will feel that the program is unfair. Parties are more likely to be resentful when they encounter turns in the process which they did not anticipate. Turns in process that parties do not anticipate are more likely to be viewed as inconsistent with the court's rules and of dubious propriety, or as offending deeply rooted feelings about what the appropriate roles of lawyers, clients, and the court are. An ADR program that spawned resentment toward the court, instead of gratitude, could hardly be considered an improvement in the administration of justice.

The prospect of ADR program rigidification raises two primary concerns. The first is the possibility that the way we institutionalize ADR programs could encourage, both in parties and counsel, dependency, complacency, and passivity about ADR (in particular) and settlement (in general). We need to design into our systems incentives and prods that will discourage litigants from simply sitting back and waiting for the ADR service that the court offers or compels. We must look for ways to encourage litigants to take the initiative to pursue settlement earlier and on their own.

The second, related concern is to avoid kinds of program rigidity in which routine referrals to ADR discourage or replace case-specific dialogue about ADR with a judge or a staff professional. There is a growth curve in the history of ADR in most jurisdictions. Early in that history, before the local bar and litigant groups have developed a substantial appreciation for the benefits that ADR has to offer, courts may need to push litigants into ADR experiences. At some point, the angle of that learning curve will decline substantially and it is at that point that we need to be sure that our systems do not thoughtlessly force parties into ADR when it would likely not be productive for them. To do so discredits the court and makes its motives look institutionally selfish. In contrast, by engaging in real, open minded dialogue with litigants to determine what they need and whether there is a real prospect that they would benefit from a referral to ADR the court encourages respect for itself and a perception that it understands itself as fundamentally a service institution.

Moreover, if our rules and practices make ADR easier (and less expensive) to fake than to escape, we risk corrupting and de-valuing ADR. Parties who feel forced into ADR when it has little to offer them are more likely just to go through the motions and to be perceived by the neutrals and other parties as so doing. Such rituals without real prospect of reward can erode the public's confidence in both the court and in ADR, and foreseeable bad experiences with ADR are not likely to encourage parties to consider its use when it really could deliver value.

Another peril with an internal source is that we will assess ADR program value with myopic self-congratulation or through ideological filters rather than with an accurate understanding of what our programs really are delivering and a square acknowledgment of their limitations. One source of this concern is a pattern I have noticed in responses to some surveys that ask parties, lawyers, and neutrals to report what occurred at an ADR session and to assess the contributions the ADR process made. In this pattern . . . the reports from the neutrals are consistently much more favorable than the reports from the lawyers or the parties. The lawyers usually are at least a little more positive than the parties, but often the gap is greater between the neutrals and the other participants.

. . . [W]e also must take great care to avoid the perils that we would create if we were to promise our constituencies or ourselves that our ADR programs will deliver more than they can. Creating unrealistic expectations would unnecessarily invite judgments under inappropriate standards, thus both jeopardizing appreciation for what the programs are in fact accomplishing and generating falsely premised disappointment and disaffection. We increase the risk that both our constituents and we will turn away from this work if we succumb to the temptation to claim too much.

As important, inflated expectations or promises could tempt us to cut process or program design corners that could compromise values that are essential to public confidence both in ADR and in the court system. If we promise "results" as measured by specified effects on the courts' dockets, for example, we will feel pressure to increase settlement rates — and that pressure could lead us to pressure our neutrals to elevate ends over means or to insist on using only one assertively evaluative approach even when parties would be comfortable only with a purely facilitative process. Or if we strain our resources to try to serve the greatest possible number of cases, we take serious risks with quality control and thus with the character of the work done in the courts' name. So we must discipline ourselves to abjure the temptations that beset unbridled enthusiasts. Ours is not a movement rooted in unconditional faith, but simply an effort to better serve.

The temptation to over-promise, however, may not be the greatest peril with an internal source. Ironically, that peril could well be underestimating the importance of what we are trying to do.

# THE PLACE OF COURT-CONNECTED MEDIATION IN A DEMOCRATIC JUSTICE SYSTEM
5 Cardozo J. Conflict Resol. 117, 121–23, 134–43 (2004)[*]
By Nancy A. Welsh

A justice system, and the processes located within it, ought to deliver justice. That seems simple enough. But, of course, delivering justice is never so simple. Justice and the systems that serve it are the creatures of context . . .

• For the past several decades, nearly every democratic institution has come under increasingly injurious attack as inefficient, unable to fulfill its mission, and often inept. The public justice system has been no exception . . .

• Professor Judith Resnik has written extensively about the federal courts' evolving composition and self-understanding, concluding that "the federal judiciary has adopted an anti-adjudication and pro-settlement agenda," which includes a diminution in the role of traditional judges and the embrace of a variety of "new" quasi-judges or judicial adjuncts. In the process, the "markers of difference [between traditional judges and other fact-finders] have diminished, while enthusiasm for delegation has grown."

This evolution may, as Professor Resnik suggests, represent the judicial system's inventive (or desperate) response to the nation's growing demand for adjudicative services accompanied by politicians' refusal to allocate the funds needed for a significantly expanded judiciary. The judicial system's evolution may even be anticipated by organizational theories that predict that over-whelmed organizations

---

will react by "increasing the numbers and kinds of providers, delegating duties, routinizing processes, and reconfiguring the work." Indeed, social psychological theories may have predicted the judicial system's recent tendency to mirror the growth and bureaucratization of the other two branches of government and to spawn more tiers of hierarchy.

. . . .

A few observations are now in order. First, as the courts have approved the delegation of adjudication to administrative judges and arbitrators, they have permitted state-sanctioned decision-making to migrate from a public and impartial body to third parties often selected by one of the disputing parties — usually the institutional, repeat players with greater economic strength. Second, as the courts have come to rely on these adjuncts, they have facilitated a shift from decision-makers whose legitimacy rests in being representatives of a democratic people to those who are more likely to espouse the legal/ technical norms preferred by the institutional parties. To a lesser, but nonetheless significant degree, the courts are affecting a similar shift as they abandon reliance on civil juries and instead dispose of cases based on sterile "paper trial[s] on the merits." Ultimately, though perhaps unconsciously, the courts seem to be distancing state-sanctioned decision-making from the messiness of democracy and placing greater faith in the predictability and efficiency of decision-making by organizational technocrats.

III. The Current Place of Mediation in the Evolution of the Judicial System

. . . .

There can be little doubt that the "contemporary mediation movement" of the late 1970s and early 1980s was inspired by the principles of democracy. Mediation proponents emphasized the central role to be played by citizens in disputes. Citizens — not judges or attorneys or other professionals — would communicate and negotiate directly with each other, identify the issues to be discussed, determine the substantive norms that were legitimate and relevant (including the pursuit of harmony and reconciliation if they wished), create the options for settlement, and control the final decision regarding whether or not to settle and on what terms. The mediator's role was to facilitate and to help these disputing parties find their own voices and solutions. Ultimately, mediation "seemed to embody both a faith in the dignity and autonomy of individual citizens and a skepticism regarding the legitimacy of government authorities and professionals."

Certainly, there are ways in which court-connected mediation has stayed true to this democratic spirit. Consistent with the values of self-determination and account-ability, there is no binding outcome in mediation unless the parties agree to it. Attorneys, who generally attend these mediation sessions, report that their understanding of their clients' goals and potential solutions are influenced by the clients' presence. No doubt, some mediation sessions result in creative resolutions that reflect the particular needs, abilities, and preferences of parties. Court-connected mediation also offers citizens at least some degree of participation. At most mediation sessions, the parties attend and contribute to the discussion either directly or through their attorneys. The parties thus are not forced to rely blindly on their attorneys to conduct separate, bilateral settlement negotiations.

But substantial data also suggests that mediation is not infusing the courts with a new manifestation of democracy. Instead, as the courts have come to rely on mediators as the next set of judging adjuncts, the mediation process and the roles of both mediators and parties have changed. When parties failed to make significant voluntary use of mediation, courts made the process mandatory. Thus, citizens lost the ability to decide for themselves whether or not to try mediation. As attorneys have become more frequent participants in mediation sessions and have assumed responsibility for selecting mediators, the process has become less focused on empowering citizens and more focused on forcing these citizens to confront and become reconciled to the legal, bargaining and transactional norms of the court-house. Attorneys select fellow attorneys as mediators and especially value those who possess substantive expertise and the ability to value cases and conduct "reality testing" with the parties. Many of these mediators maximize their own influence by minimizing the time spent by the parties in joint session. These mediators quickly separate the parties and become their sole channel of communication and negotiation, shuttling back and forth with the information and descriptions of offers and counter-offers that will facilitate settlement. Attorneys also now dominate the discussion and negotiation in mediation sessions. Indeed, in many personal injury and medical malpractice cases, the defendants are not expected to attend mediation sessions, and in some courts, parties generally are discouraged from attending. These changes in the implementation of mediation, though often understandable, generally have the effect of constrict-ing, not celebrating, citizens' ability to engage in self-governance and demand accountability from the mediators, the mediation process and mediated outcomes. In sum, court-connected mediation has evolved from a process that focused on enhancing individual citizens' voice, control and assurance of accountability into a mechanism that resolves cases by reconciling these citizens to the institutional reality (or at least mediators' and attorneys' perception of the reality) of the courts and litigation.

In addition, and consistent with the courts' minimal oversight of administrative law judges and arbitrators, most courts do very little to assure the accountability of the mediation process, individual mediators, or mediated outcomes. The mediators on many courts' rosters are private providers who are selected by attorneys and paid by the parties, not the courts. This structure permits court-connected mediation programs to operate quite self-sufficiently and, from the courts' perspective, quite cost-effectively. Indeed, in many states, mediation is now a business, with a small group of insurers as repeat players and a select group of mediators handling a large number of the cases. Though courts generally require mediation skills training in order to qualify for service on a roster of court-connected mediators, few courts have designated a staff member to monitor the mediators' performance, regularly observe mediation sessions, or gather and evaluate feedback from parties and attorneys . . .

Courts might also exercise quality control by carefully scrutinizing mediated settlement agreements, particularly when one of the parties objects to enforcement of the agreement or seeks to set it aside. Increasingly, courts are hearing these sorts of arguments, often accompanied by allegations that mediators engaged in coercive and/or biased behaviors. Courts, however, are rarely sympathetic to these parties who seek to undo settlement agreements. Mediators' evaluative interventions, even when they are quite aggressive, are unlikely to qualify as "coercive enough" to merit returning cases to the courts' trial dockets. Indeed, some courts seem to view unhappy parties' attempts to undo their mediated settlement agreements as nothing less than an affront to the judicial system itself.

Thus, courts' delegation of the settlement function to mediators is marred by the same coupling of deference and lack of real accountability that characterizes the courts' delegation of adjudicative functions to administrative and arbitral forums.

. . . .

. . . The remainder of the Article will consider the program design decisions that can and should be made in order to reassure citizens that the courts and their adjuncts — at least mediators as settlement adjuncts — remain accountable to "the people" and thus can be trusted to deliver justice.

The first program design choice actually involves ADR advocates more than it does courts . . . . Mediation advocates need to help our courts overcome their current problems and regain an appropriate measure of self-respect for their unique role in enabling a democratic people to govern themselves. This means, of course, becoming advocates for sufficient funding for courts, the appointment of sufficient numbers of judges and the protection of judges' independence from inappropriate economic or political influence. ADR experts who have traveled to other countries to teach or consult regarding ADR have realized that healthy ADR programs require healthy judicial systems. The same mutually symbiotic relationship should exist in the United States.

The second program design choice is likely to appear painful, but may be less so than it first seems. Courts should end their reliance on mandatory mediation. The courts are lending their legitimacy to mediation in requiring its use. The combination of mandatory programs and a lack of significant accountability measures, however, invite abuse and a potential deterioration of the courts' legitimacy. If mediation is truly a valuable process that responds to citizens' desires for an alternative means to resolve disputes, the process should be able to stand on its own, freely selected by parties as their disputes arise. At the very least, the courts' authority to mandate mediation should sunset within two to three years after a court-connected mediation program has been introduced. During this initial phase, attorneys will become educated about the process. Research indicates that once attorneys use mediation, they become advocates for its future use. If attorneys have not become advocates, there is probably something wrong with the program, and it deserves to end.

Finally, and especially while the use of mediation is mandatory or strongly encouraged by judges, the courts should view mediators as their agents — and provide for meaningful oversight that assures just resolution. Courts can accomplish such oversight by establishing expectations beyond settlement for their mediators. The procedural justice literature provides a rich set of measures of those behaviors that are likely to be perceived as just. Courts also should assign staff to monitor mediators' performance through periodic observations, distribution and assessment of meaningful post-mediation surveys and interviewing of attorneys and parties. Such monitoring exists in good court-connected programs. It should be common in all programs.

Though procedural justice often results in perceptions of substantive justice, courts also need to do more to ensure that mediated outcomes are fair according to some principled set of norms . . . . [C]ourts could provide a short cooling-off period for mediated settlement agreements, during which the parties themselves could evaluate the fairness of the outcome — using whatever norms they deem legitimate — and choose to accept or rescind their agreements without penalty. Such cooling-off periods are relatively common in divorce and child custody mediation and are relatively straightforward mechanisms to ensure that parties perceive their agreements as sufficiently just. From the courts' perspective, the adoption of cooling-off periods for mediated agreements would signal mediators' ultimate accountability to the citizens involved in this court-connected process. A cooling-off period would reward productive mediator behaviors that build parties' commitment to and investment in their agreements and create a negative consequence for those mediators who employ aggressive tactics that endanger courts' legitimacy as the domain in which citizens will experience justice.

## NOTES AND QUESTIONS

(1)   Professor Menkel-Meadow uses the term "ADR" in her article. Are the concerns she raised generic to alternative processes? Are mediation and arbitration equally susceptible to the concerns?

(2)   In 1991, Professor Menkel-Meadow raised the question of whether the adversarial system would co-opt ADR. Ten years later, James J. Alfini and Catherine G. McCabe analyzed the emerging case law related to the requirement to mediate in good faith and the enforcement of mediation agreements. In particular, the authors focus on the tension between mediation's core values and principles and the general principles favoring settlement. *See* James J. Alfini & Catherine G. McCabe, *Mediating in the Shadow of the Courts: A Survey of the Emerging Case Law*, 54 Ark. L. Rev. 171, 173 (2001). The authors conclude with this caution:

> In general, the courts have demonstrated an understanding of the mediation process, a sensitivity to the core values and principles of mediation, and a clear desire to further the general policy favoring settlement in deciding cases involving mediation process issues. . . .

> On the other hand, the general policy favoring settlement, while advancing the goal of judicial economy, may not always be consistent with mediation principles and values. In particular, allegations of settlement coercion raise troubling issues relating to mediation's core values of party self-determination, voluntariness, and mediator impartiality that may not be easily discerned or correctable through the judge process.

How do these concerns compare with the "sources of peril" raised by Wayne Brazil?

(3)   Professor Menkel-Meadow refers to the 1960s and 1970s as "participatory" and the 1980s as the era of "privatization." How would you describe the current era?

(4)  Given the concerns surrounding the mandatory use of mediation, do you believe that mandatory (court-ordered) mediation should be utilized only for a brief period of time to promote understanding of the process and then transition to being available only on a voluntary basis?

(5)  Professor Welsh suggests three program design decisions to "reassure citizens that the courts and their adjuncts . . . . remain accountable . . . and thus can be trusted." Can you identify additional options which could be implemented to address these concerns?

## F.  JUDICIAL MEDIATION

As the courts have begun to refer cases to mediation, making it an essential part of the litigation landscape, it is perhaps inevitable that many judges would take on the dual role of judge and mediator. In this section, we explore issues related to active judges serving as mediators. Questions related to retired judges serving as mediators are raised in Chapter 8, *supra*.

Some have argued that judges qua judges are particularly well-qualified to serve as mediators insofar as they possess legal knowledge, are intimately familiar with the litigation process, are highly respected by the parties and their attorneys, and have the authority to ensure that the parties will attend the mediation and take it seriously. Others raise concerns that parties will be unable to fully exercise self-determination when confronted with a judge serving as mediator, and there is a significant risk of coercion.

Either way, judicial service in the context of mediation raises important policy and ethical issues. For example, may judges mediate cases that have been assigned to them for trial, and then try those cases where mediation failed? In the following excerpts, the Court of Appeals of Kentucky and the District Court of Appeal of Florida, express very different opinions on this issue.

### HOME DEPOT, U.S.A., INC. v. SAUL SUBSIDIARY I LTD. PARTNERSHIP
Court of Appeals of Kentucky
159 S.W.3d 339 (2004), *discretionary rev. den'd*,
2005 Ky. LEXIS 147 (Apr. 13, 2005)

DYCHE, JUDGE.

The parties to this appeal own adjoining tracts of real estate upon which Lexington Mall was developed in the 1970s. The mall prospered for several years but eventually fell upon hard times in the mid-1990s. The dispute herein centers upon the mutual covenants contained in the original agreement that the parties' predecessors in title entered into which permitted the development of the mall (the 1969 agreement), and the enforcement of those covenants. The Fayette Circuit Court, on remand from this court in an earlier appeal, adjudged that Home Depot breached those covenants and ordered the demolition of Home Depot's store on the mall property . . . .

The original trial judge was recused on remand, and the new judge conducted extensive mediation sessions in an effort to resolve the matter. The parties came close to an agreement, but the negotiations ultimately failed, and the trial court issued an opinion holding that no evidentiary hearing was required, and that Home Depot had made a deliberate business decision to proceed with its project while the original appeal was pending, knowing the "risk involved yet making a deliberate choice to proceed." The court further found that Saul's monetary damages could not be reasonably calculated, that its discretion was extremely narrow, and that Kentucky appellate decisions compelled the enforcement of the covenants. The court issued a mandatory injunction for removal of the offending structure and replacement of the original structure, allowed one year for compliance, but granted Home Depot ninety days within which to make a proposal as to how it could conform without demolition. No acceptable plan was presented, and final judgment was entered. This appeal followed.

Home Depot first argues that the trial judge should have recused herself, on its motion, after having conducted mediation sessions in an attempt to resolve this matter by settlement. Home Depot maintains that it was deprived of due process in that "the decision the Court entered was all based on information outside the record, shared in confidence, and without any evidentiary hearing . . ."; that "[m]ediation predisposes the decision-maker to the result"; and that "[t]he judicial code and other authorities forbid what the judge did here."

We disagree that the trial judge was compelled to recuse herself after having conducted mediation in this matter. Our Code of Judicial Conduct specifically provides for such action. Canon 3(B)(7)(d) provides, "A judge may, with the consent of the parties, confer separately with the parties and their lawyers in an effort to mediate or settle matters pending before the judge." Home Depot suggested or acquiesced in the trial court's mediation efforts. Home Depot has made no showing of bias or partiality, and we can find none. Absent such showing, the trial court's hint that it might pass this case to another judge if mediation happened to be unsuccessful is insufficient ground to require recusal.

## EVANS v. STATE
District Court of Appeal of Florida, Fifth District
603 So. 2d 15 (1992)

DIAMANTIS, JUDGE.

. . . .

This matter arose out of a lawsuit instituted by Ted Williams (the former baseball player) against Vincent Antonucci. Appellant is an attorney representing Antonucci in the lawsuit. On May 15, 1991 the trial judge conducted a case management conference at which all parties were present with their attorneys. During the conference the trial judge offered to attempt to mediate the case, provided that all of the parties and their attorneys agreed that they would not use the trial judge's attempt to mediate the case as a basis for disqualification. The parties agreed and the judge attempted to mediate the case; however, no settlement was reached.

On May 31, 1991, appellant filed on behalf of Antonucci a motion to disqualify the trial judge pursuant to rule 1.432 of the Florida Rules of Civil Procedure. The motion to disqualify was based upon statements that the trial judge made to Antonucci during the mediation process.

Upon receipt of this motion the trial judge cited appellant for direct criminal contempt. After a hearing on the contempt citation, the trial judge adjudicated appellant guilty of direct criminal contempt, finding that appellant had lied when, in agreeing to permit the judge to mediate the case, he assured the judge that said procedure would not be later used as grounds to seek recusal.

The unrefuted and unimpeached testimony of both appellant and Antonucci at the contempt hearing was that appellant filed the motion for recusal upon Antonucci's insistence, based upon comments made by the trial judge to Antonucci during the mediation conference. Antonucci testified that he was enraged by the trial judge's statement that "there'll always be people like [you] around, but let's face it, there's only one Ted Williams." Both Antonucci and appellant testified that Antonucci felt that the trial judge considered Ted Williams to be superior to Antonucci and that the trial judge was prejudiced against Antonucci. Appellant further testified that Antonucci insisted that he file the motion for recusal and that before doing so he researched this matter and spoke to other attorneys before concluding that there was a legal basis for the motion based on Antonucci's genuine fear that the trial judge was prejudiced against him. Other comments which Antonucci considered improper include the judge's advice to Antonucci to "get real" when Antonucci provided him with a settlement figure, and comments regarding the costs of protracted litigation and likelihood of prevailing on his claim for relief.

We conclude that this uncontroverted and unimpeached testimony regarding the reason for filing the motion to disqualify must be accepted. Consequently, we find that the evidence does not support the trial judge's finding that appellant lied when he agreed not to move to disqualify the trial judge for acting as a mediator. The motion for disqualification was based upon the comments made by the trial judge to Antonucci during the mediation conference. Antonucci had a subjective fear that the trial judge placed Ted Williams on a higher level and that this would prejudice his case. Antonucci's fear was real to him and appellant had a duty to advocate his client's position consistent with any agreements that were made concerning mediation. The agreement not to seek recusal was limited to the trial judge acting as a mediator and not to the nature of any comments that the trial judge would make during the mediation proceedings. To construe the agreement as encompassing any and all comments that the trial judge could conceivably make as a mediator would not be reasonable, and such a construction is not supported by the record. It is highly doubtful that all the parties and their attorneys would enter into such an agreement.

. . . .

The trial judge, the parties, and the attorneys in good faith agreed to mediate the underlying civil dispute with the explicit understanding that this would not result in the trial judge being recused. However, regardless of the good faith of all concerned, this case more than points out the basic fallacy in such an agreement — that a judge can act as both mediator and judge. The function of a mediator and a judge are conceptually different. The function of a mediator is to encourage settlement of a dispute and a mediator uses various techniques in an attempt to achieve this result. A mediator may separate the parties and conduct ex parte proceedings in which the mediator may either subtly or candidly point out weaknesses in a particular party's factual or legal position. A mediator, through training and experience, approaches different parties in different ways. Because a mediator will not be deciding the case, both the mediator and the parties are free to discuss without fear of any consequence the ramifications of settling a particular dispute as opposed to litigating it. This is one of the reasons that a mediator must generally preserve and maintain the confidentiality of all mediation proceedings. . . .

In contrast, the judge's role is to decide the controversy fairly and impartially, consistent with established rules of law. In this regard, to paraphrase Socrates: Four things belong to a judge; to hear courteously; to consider soberly; to decide impartially; and to answer wisely.

As a caveat, we suggest that mediation should be left to the mediators and judging to the judges. If a judge decides to mediate a case with the consent of all concerned parties, the judge should act only as a settlement judge for another judge who will hear and try the matter in the event mediation fails, such as in the situation where a retired judge mediates a case but does not try the case. If this had been done in the instant matter, an unnecessary, unproductive and unrewarding confrontation between a member of the bar and a member of the bench would have been avoided.

We reverse appellant's conviction of direct criminal contempt and remand this cause to the trial court with directions that the judgment of guilt be vacated and a judgment of not guilty be entered.

Reversed and remanded.

## NOTES AND QUESTIONS

(1)   Did the Kentucky appellate court in *Home Depot v. Saul Subsidiary I Ltd. Partnership* explain adequately its decision that the trial judge was not required to recuse herself? Was the fact that the Kentucky Code of Judicial Conduct permitted *ex parte* communications in judicial mediations enough support to allow the mediating judge to resolve the matter on the merits following a failed mediation?

(2)   Consider the following excerpt from the article by Judge Cratsley. Do you agree that judicial involvement in settlement should be regulated and how it should be regulated?

# JUDICIAL ETHICS AND JUDICIAL SETTLEMENT PRACTICES: TIME FOR TWO STRANGERS TO MEET
21 Ohio St. J. on Disp. Resol. 569, 570–76, 581, 583–87 (2006)*
By Honorable John C. Cratsley

. . . .

Our American legal tradition promises the public an impartial trial judge detached from the work of the attorneys and free to render judgment or guide a jury under settled principles of law. In fact, our adversary system of trial rests on the assurance of the truly neutral magistrate who emerges from his or her chambers, without preconceptions, to moderate the battles of counsel.

Over the past twenty years, however, a consensus has emerged among the bench and bar that judicial participation in the settlement of civil cases is a wise and useful activity. Only a few have questioned the appropriate boundaries for this judicial intervention into what was once the exclusive domain of attorneys who were free to negotiate their own settlements.

Currently the ethical limits of such activity have been left to the judge and counsel. The judge may disqualify himself or herself and pass the case along to a colleague if he or she felt their settlement efforts raised an issue of impartiality. In the absence of judicial self-appraisal, one of the attorneys could seek disqualification of the judge. The growth of alternative dispute resolution (ADR) during these same twenty years has only worked to stimulate judicial participation in the settlement of civil cases. Untrained trial judges have mimicked mediators with techniques loosely borrowed from private mediation, but unfamiliar in the halls of justice.

All of this novel settlement activity engaged in by judges who are assigned to try these matters confuses the public, undermines the traditional judicial role and, in the end, can lead to coerced settlements. The time has arrived, this author believes, for the enactment of explicit ethical rules in the Model Code of Judicial Conduct governing judicial settlement activity in civil cases. This article proposes one simple ethical rule — a bar on any judge who undertakes settlement activity from ultimately trying the case if settlement fails — as well as other more detailed ethical rules such as written consent of the parties to participate in judicial settlement activities, disclosure of the settlement technique to be used by the judge, and mandatory training for any judge undertaking mediation or any other form of settlement activity.

. . . .

While the emergence of ADR techniques is only the latest variation in the methods of settlement used by judges, the fundamental issue remains the same over the last quarter century-what price in terms of the public perception of the judicial role is paid for all these accomplishments, all these settled cases? No one can dispute that thousands of hours of trial time and thousands of dollars of client expense are saved by these judicial interventions. And no one can dispute that a judge has the greatest standing and resources to promote settlement. However, one

---

can legitimately ask whether the lawyers and clients are truly participating voluntarily in these judicially run settlement efforts, and whether an atmosphere of fairness and neutrality is fostered, particularly when more and more disclosures are requested and opinions given in what are essentially ex-parte sessions with the same judge who is assigned to try the case.

One can also legitimately ask whether clients who have a laypersons understanding of the neutrality and independence of the judiciary, as well as of the workings of the adversary process, can comprehend how judges committed to these ideals can informally, in the privacy of their offices, discuss likely outcomes of both legal and financial issues. In fact, counsel from several state judicial conduct organizations have reported receiving complaints of judicial coercion and intimidation in settlement conferences. Regardless of whether these are ultimately found to be about real or perceived judicial behavior, the fact that they have been filed is cause for concern.

A related and equally legitimate concern when judges attempt to settle cases using ADR approaches like mediation is their competency. While this issue is not one implicating judicial ethics like bias and coercion, nor one which strikes at the heart of the judicial process like the promise of a fair trial before a neutral magistrate, it has a direct bearing on choosing the best practice, the best policy, for judicial settlement activity. In fact, the lack of training impacts on both the timing and method by which a judge will offer a final evaluation and, thus, a potentially coercive opinion on the value of the case.

. . . .

What then is the urgency or even the necessity for increased regulation of judicial settlement activity? First and foremost, the rapid expansion of these efforts, fueled by ADR techniques, has created an ever expanding range of settlement practices which have been questioned by academics, practicing attorneys and a few judges. Second, the reality of a number of complaints to state judicial conduct organizations suggests an issue of national concern. Third, the lack of training in the techniques of informal dispute resolution, i.e. mediation, on the part of those judges who choose to actively settle civil cases means their efforts are unskilled and open to misunderstanding, thereby reducing public confidence in our courts. And fourth, the inescapable human tendency, even by members of the judiciary, to develop opinions about the legal and factual issues developed during settlement discussions creates the likelihood of real or perceived bias on the part of the judge assigned to continue with the case and conduct the trial.

. . . .

Other approaches to this problem are not as likely to provide the same impact on judicial conduct as the directive language of the Model Code [of Judicial Conduct]. Appellate decisions about disqualification due to judicial settlement activity are few and very fact-specific, and thus offer little guidance to the trial judge on a daily basis. Advisory opinions, such as that issued to federal judges in 1999, usually repeat the balance found in the existing ethical provisions between the usefulness of judicial settlement conferences on one hand and the twin considerations of avoiding coercive behavior and promoting judicial objectivity on the other. The

ABA's 1993 formal advisory opinion on this subject concluded with a ringing endorsement of the judge's role in facilitating settlement. Local rules, particularly for federal judges, often differ across the nation. Educational activities, usually favored as the solution to complex issues of judicial behavior, also repeat the competing considerations in the prevailing code and ask those judges who attend to address hypothetical situations.

. . . .

The simplest and most straightforward change to the Model Code of Judicial Conduct addressing the issue of judicial involvement in the settlement of civil cases is the enactment of language prohibiting any trial judge who conducts settlement activity from proceeding to conduct the trial of the case when his or her settlement efforts fail. While this approach is mentioned in the literature, no writer to date has actually proposed explicit language to accomplish this result. This may well be because the barriers to implementation of such a rule are real, including what to do in geographic areas where another judge is hard to obtain or actually unavailable and how to measure just how much judicial involvement would be enough to trigger this rule.

Another straightforward ethical rule, entirely consistent with the first, would require the judge who undertakes settlement activity to first obtain the written consent of all the parties to the litigation before proceeding with such an informal, off-the-record approach. This consent would follow delivery by the court to all counsel and their clients of a written description of the settlement process including any ADR technique, such as mediation, which would be employed by the judge and how it differs from trial. The document would also include the assurance that the judge doing the settlement activity would not be the trial judge should there be no settlement. Obviously, each jurisdiction adding this rule to their Code of Judicial Conduct could prescribe the precise content of the written acknowledgment.

A third and more complex change in the Model Code of Judicial Conduct would be a requirement that any judge who undertakes settlement activity follow the ethical standards for dispute resolution conduct imposed by rule or statute in that state for neutrals who do mediation and other types of dispute resolution in the trial courts. This would insure that issues like adequate preparation, disclosure of conflicts of interest, coercion, and voluntariness of any settlement were addressed by the judge, with counsel and the parties, before and during any settlement conference judicial mediation. It would also give counsel and parties detailed assurance of the expected conduct from the settlement judge.

Finally, the Model Code of Judicial Conduct should contain a provision that any judge, who undertakes settlement activity in civil cases, whether using mediation or another ADR technique, have the same training that court rules or statutes require a third-party neutral to have when undertaking that same type of dispute resolution activity in connection with a pending court case. Most states now have court rules or statutes specifying the type of training non-judicial neutrals must have to do court-connected mediation, arbitration, conciliation, etc. A judge doing the same type of dispute resolution in his or her pending civil cases should have the same training.

In fact, there is no reason that all four of these changes to the Model Code of Judicial Conduct could not be enacted. Each works to insure that judges who undertake settlement activity in cases pending before them for trial do so with the consent and full knowledge of the parties, following the same ethics as neutrals who do this work for the court, with the same training as neutrals who do this work for the court, and with the assurance that should their efforts be unsuccessful they will not try the case.

## NOTES AND QUESTIONS

(1)   Is there a difference between a judge conducting a settlement conference and a judge serving as mediator? In a series of articles, Professor Peter Robinson has explored the various techniques that judges use to effect settlement and analyzed empirical data on judicial practices and attitudes during settlement conferences. In his fourth article, *Opening Pandora's Box: An Empirical Exploration of Judicial Settlement Ethics and Techniques*, 27 Ohio St. J. on Disp. Resol. 53, 107–108 (2012),* Professor Robinson concludes:

> There are legitimate concerns about judges facilitating settlement, especially when they are doing so for cases assigned to them for trial. The concerns are amplified if the case will be decided by the judge in a bench trial. The data reveals that most judges are not being discouraged from attempting to settle cases assigned to them for trial. Some have no systemic alternative; the result is that most judges actively participate in assisting settlement, for many including the cases assigned to them for trial.

> . . . many of the nitty-gritty questions about judicial settlement techniques and ethics are being largely resolved on an individual basis. These issues can be clarified by case law when parties ask for appellate review of the behavior of settlement judges. The question is whether there should be uniformity in some of the practices reported in this article. Should judges be required to make a finding of essential/approximate fairness or unconscionability when they supervise a settlement? If not, should judges be required to clearly explain their function as a neutral facilitator when they are assisting with settlement?

> Although most settlement judges report being less directive when serving as the trial judge, a significant minority report being more directive. Should this variation in these practices be accepted as a matter of personal preference and professional deference to judges? . . . The data begs many questions for the best practices by individual judges and institutions providing advisory and mandatory guidance for judges.

(2)   Consider whether Advisory Opinion No. 95, issued by the Committee on Codes of Conduct of the Judicial Conference of the United States, for federal judges, and the Rule 2.06 of the 2007 version of the ABA Model Code of Judicial Conduct, fully address Judge Cratsley's and Professor Robinson's concerns.

---

## COMMITTEE ON CODES OF CONDUCT ADVISORY OPINION NO. 95
### Approved by the Judicial Conference of the United States
### January 14, 1999

Judges Acting in a Settlement Capacity.

Concerns have recently been articulated about the practice of judges acting in a settlement capacity in a case. The following questions have been submitted to the Committee on Codes of Conduct for consideration:

(1) may a judge presiding over a trial properly participate directly in settlement discussions with the parties?

(2) would it make any difference if the trial is to be before a jury rather than the judge?

(3) would the existence of an established local rule permitting the practice have any bearing on the propriety of the judge's action?

### Code Provisions

The Code of Conduct for United States Judges contains two provisions bearing on the subject of judges' involvement in settlement discussions. First, Canon 3A(4) advises that judges should not engage in ex parte communications on the merits. As an exception to this general advice, the canon further provides that a "judge may, with consent of the parties, confer separately with the parties and their counsel in an effort to mediate or settle pending matters." Second, Canon 3C(1) sets out the standard for impartiality that judges must meet in the performance of their judicial duties, including participation in settlement discussions. Canon 3C(1) provides that "[a] judge shall disqualify himself or herself in a proceeding in which the judge's impartiality might reasonably be questioned."

Nothing in the Code expressly addresses the practice of judges discussing settlement with all parties simultaneously or presiding over joint settlement conferences. Since the drafters of the Code believed it was necessary to expressly permit ex parte settlement discussions between judges and parties with their consent, it is reasonable to infer that joint settlement discussions do not contravene the Code. We read the Code of Conduct to acknowledge that judges may engage in a range of permissible settlement activities, and that recusal follows from those activities only where a judge's impartiality might reasonably be questioned because of what occurred during the course of those discussions.

### Federal and Local Rules on Settlement

Discussion of the possibility of settlement is a common practice at pretrial and status conferences and is expressly sanctioned in general terms by the Federal Rules of Civil Procedure. Rule 16(a)(5) allows judges to convene pretrial conferences for the purposes of "facilitating the settlement of the case" and Rule 16(c)(9) indicates that settlement is a proper subject for "consideration" and "appropriate action" at pretrial conferences. The clear implication in Rule 16 is that judges will be involved in facilitating settlement. Rule 16 does not prevent a judge who engaged in settlement discussions from presiding over a trial.

Many district courts have local rules comparable to Rule 16 of the Federal Rules; that is, rules that generally permit settlement activities but do not specifically address the extent or manner of judges' participation in settlement discussions. Other local rules contain more specific provisions, including: (1) local rules indicating judges have some direct role to play in settlement discussions but not restricting the judge from subsequently handling the trial of the case or serving as the finder of fact (*see* E.D. Pa. Rule 16.1(d)(3); D.N.H. Rule 16.3); and (2) local rules restricting judges who participate in settlement discussions from handling a subsequent trial of the case, including one that prohibits this (*see* S.D. Ill. Rule 11(d)), one that prohibits discussion of settlement amounts in nonjury cases absent consent of the parties (*see* N.D. Tex. Rule 16.3(b)), and one that permits the parties to consent to trial by the settlement judge (*see* S.D. Cal. Rule 16.3(c)).

## Ethical Standards

A trial judge's participation in settlement efforts is not inherently improper under the Code of Conduct for United States Judges. As with any aspect of a judge's conduct of a case, particular actions by a judge may raise ethical concerns in some cases, but there is no per se impropriety in a judge's participation in settlement discussions or in a judge's conduct of a trial following participation in settlement talks. The existence of local rules explicitly permitting judges to preside over settlement discussions lends support to the propriety of a judge's actions in this respect. On the other hand, the existence of local rules prohibiting judges from handling successive settlement and trial responsibilities forecloses judges in some jurisdictions from exercising certain combinations of settlement and trial responsibilities (or from doing so without consent). Whether ethical concerns arise in a particular proceeding, in the absence of a local rule prohibiting the judge's participation, is a fact-specific determination that depends on the nature of the judge's actions and whether the judge's impartiality might reasonably be questioned. Judges should evaluate their actions under the standards discussed herein.

Ethical concerns are less likely to arise when a judge handles settlement negotiations and then presides over a jury trial, or when the parties consent to the judge's handling of successive settlement and trial phases. Concerns are more likely to arise in nonjury trials, when a judge may be involved in settlement discussions, probe the parties' assessments of the value of the case, review the parties' settlement offers (and perhaps suggest to them specific settlement amounts), and then, when settlement talks fail, try the case and award damages. In the latter circumstances, it may be reasonable to question whether the trial judge can be an objective trier of fact, or whether the case should instead be tried by another judge unfamiliar with settlement discussions.

The Code's ethical standards are not violated every time a judge in a nonjury case learns of inadmissible information as a result of settlement discussions and then tries the case. Judges (and juries as well) periodically receive information that is not admissible and exclude it from their deliberations before rendering judgment. It is not inherently unreasonable to credit their ability to be impartial in these circumstances. Nor does it necessarily offend Canon 3C(1) for a trial judge to comment on the strengths and weaknesses of the parties' case before trial. On the other hand, comments a judge makes in the course of settlement discussions may create an appearance of bias. Similarly, a trial judge's awareness of information obtained during settlement discussions that is otherwise unlikely to be made known to the judge during the trial may undermine the judge's objectivity as a fact finder and give rise to questions about impartiality. When a judge's impartiality might reasonably be questioned, Canon 3C(1) advises that the judge "shall disqualify." *See also* 28 U.S.C. § 455(a). One useful test for these purposes is "whether the conduct would create in reasonable minds, with knowledge of all the relevant circum-stances that a reasonable inquiry would disclose, a perception that the judge's ability to carry out judicial responsibilities with integrity, impartiality, and competence is impaired." *See* Code of Conduct for United States Judges, Commentary to Canon 2A.

Settlement practices must be examined on a case-by-case basis to determine their ethical propriety. Factored into this calculus should be a consideration of whether the case will be tried by judge or jury, whether the parties themselves or only counsel will be involved in the discussion, and whether the parties have consented to the discussions or to a subsequent trial by the settlement judge. Judges must be mindful of the effect settlement discussions can have not only on their own objectivity and impartiality but also on the appearance of their objectivity and impartiality. Despite a judge's best efforts there may be instances where information obtained during settlement discussions could influence a judge's decision-making during trial. Parties who have confronted deficiencies in their cases, or who have negotiated candidly as to the value of their claims, may question whether the judge can set aside this knowledge in a case tried to the judge, whereas in a case tried to a jury, there may be less reason to question the judge's impartiality. The extent to which a judge's impartiality may be compromised, in either reality or appearance, will depend in part on the nature and degree of the judge's participation in settlement discussions and the extent to which the judge has become privy to information that relates directly to the issues the judge will be called upon to decide in cases tried to the judge (for example, evaluations of the merits and damages) or issues which the judge may be called to rule upon during the course of a trial by jury. In the end, a judge's recusal decision following involvement in settlement discussions will be fact specific and should be informed by an appropriate sensitivity to the requirements of impartiality and the appearance of impartiality.

In 2007, the American Bar Association promulgated a revised MODEL CODE OF JUDICIAL CONDUCT that contains the following rule and related commentary:

### RULE 2.6    *Ensuring the Right to Be Heard*

. . .

**(B) A judge may encourage parties to a proceeding and their lawyers to settle matters in dispute but shall not act in a manner that coerces any party into settlement.**

**COMMENT**

. . .

[2] The judge plays an important role in overseeing the settlement of disputes, but should be careful that efforts to further settlement do not undermine any party's right to be heard according to law. The judge should keep in mind the effect that the judge's participation in settlement discussions may have, not only on the judge's own views of the case, but also on the perceptions of the lawyers and the parties if the case remains with the judge after settlement efforts are unsuccessful. Among the factors that a judge should consider when deciding upon an appropriate settlement practice for a case are (1) whether the parties have requested or voluntarily consented to a certain level of participation by the judge in settlement discussions, (2) whether the parties and their counsel are relatively sophisticated in legal matters, (3) whether the case will be tried by the judge or a jury, (4) whether the parties participate with their counsel in settlement discussions, (5) whether any parties are unrepresented by counsel, and (6) whether the matter is civil or criminal.

[3] Judges must be mindful of the effect settlement discussions can have, not only on their objectivity and impartiality, but also on the appearance of their objectivity and impartiality. Despite a judge's best efforts, there may be instances when information obtained during settlement discussions could influence a judge's decision making during trial, and, in such instances, the judge should consider whether disqualification may be appropriate. See Rule 2.11(A)(1).

## NOTES AND QUESTIONS

(1)   Note how Commentary [2] to the ABA Rule, which is primarily intended for state judges, tracks the language of the federal judges Advisory Opinion No. 95.

(2)   Consider the statements of the federal magistrate judges in the following two case excerpts in light of this advisory opinion.

### BLACK v. KENDIG
United States District Court for the District of Columbia
227 F. Supp. 2d 153 (2002)

FACCIOLA, UNITED STATES MAGISTRATE JUDGE.

Currently pending and ready for resolution is *Defendant's Motion for Recusal and Memorandum in Support*. After careful consideration and for the reasons articulated below, defendant's motion will be granted, albeit for different reasons than the defendant offers.

### BACKGROUND

On January 21, 2000, Judge Sullivan referred this case to me for settlement. I spoke with and met with the parties on numerous occasions during which we had frank discussions about this case. On June 26, 2001, I flew to Augusta, Georgia and met with plaintiff personally in the prison in which she was confined to discuss her case and finalize the details of the settlement. On July 23, 2001, Judge Sullivan accepted the settlement agreement and my referral ended.

On May 21, 2002, almost one full year after the parties had ostensibly reached a settlement, plaintiff moved for reinstatement of his complaint, expedited discovery, leave to file a second amended complaint, a preliminary injunction, and a temporary restraining order. On May 22, 2002, Judge Sullivan re-referred the case to me for a Report and Recommendation on the pending motions. The parties are now bitterly divided over the meaning of one provision of the settlement agreement.

The agreement allowed the Bureau of Prisons a three month period during which it was obliged to create and propose a treatment plan for plaintiff. Dr. Frederick S. Berlin was also to prepare a treatment plan. Once both proposals were prepared, paragraph 5 of the agreement provided:

The BOP's Medical Director, Dr. Newton E. Kendig, will review the BOP's assessment and treatment plan, together with the assessment(s) and treatment plan(s) prepared by Dr. Berlin and the BOP's consulting doctor if any. Dr. Kendig will then decide which plan, or combination of plans, will be offered to plaintiff.

As plaintiff reads this provision, Kendig is obliged to adopt a treatment plan and order that plaintiff be given estrogen therapy if the plans recommended it. Defendant denies that this provision imposes any such obligation on Kendig. As defendant sees it, he can refuse to give plaintiff estrogen therapy even though, for example, both Dr. Berlin and the BOP treatment plan recommend it.

Defendant now seeks my recusal.

The pertinent sections of the recusal statute provide:

§ 455. Disqualification of justice, judge, or magistrate judge

(a) Any justice, judge, or magistrate of the United States shall disqualify himself in any proceeding in which his impartiality might reasonably be questioned.

(b) He shall also disqualify himself in the following circumstances:

(1) Where he has a personal bias or prejudice concerning a party, or personal knowledge of disputed evidentiary facts concerning the proceeding;

28 U.S.C.A. § 455(a) & (b) (1993).

To resolve the government's motion, it is first helpful to clear some brush away. First, while it is not clear that the government still relies upon the point, I do not have any disqualifying "personal knowledge of disputed evidentiary facts concerning the proceeding.". Obviously, presiding over the settlement discussions is within my judicial responsibilities and I gained no knowledge of any facts pertaining to this dispute in any other way. Recusal on this ground is, therefore, unavailable. *U.S. v. Pollard*, 959 F.2d 1011, 1031 (D.C.Cir.1992)(only personal knowledge of disputed facts gained other than by presiding requires reversal).

Second, I have no intention whatsoever of permitting either party or myself to breach the confidentiality of the settlement discussions. As the government points out, I yield to no one in my insistence that settlement discussions remain confidential. I will not permit either party to refer in any way to anything anyone, including me, said during settlement discussions. My issuing a Report and Recommendation in this case will, therefore, not threaten either a violation of Fed.R.Evid. 408, of the wise policy that animates it, or of the Court's own Mediation Program.

Third, it is certainly not true that presiding over settlement discussions requires the recusal of a judge who then must preside over the case that was not settled. The converse seems to be true.. Any such absolute rule would be silly. Some settlement discussions begin with the defendant offering "nuisance value" and the plaintiff walking out five minutes later in a huff. To preclude the magistrate judge who presides over such theatrics from then doing anything else in that case is to waste a judicial resource as badly as cutting one's throat on a good rug.

What I think the government is grasping for but cannot reach, is the real question presented: whether, having presided over the settlement discussions, I should then resolve what the parties meant during those very settlement discussions because they so utterly disagree over what the agreement means.

Judges are presumed to be able to compartmentalize information upon which they can predicate their decisions, and information of which they are otherwise aware, but cannot use as a basis for their decisions. It is also said that whether or not the appearance of impartiality is offended is to be determined objectively, not subjectively. The question is not whether I think that I can be objective and fair but whether a reasonable, objective person has reason to doubt my impartiality no matter how fair I think I can be. To put this all together, the question is whether a reasonable person would find that the appearance of fairness would be offended by a magistrate judge resolving the interpretation of a contract that the parties negotiated under that judge's intensive supervision. While the question is a close one, I believe that I must recuse myself.

No matter how much I am presumed to be able to compartmentalize information I learned while presiding over the settlement discussions from any evidence the parties may tender at any hearing, I would be obliged to engage in remarkable mental gymnastics. I would have to consider what the parties said occurred during their settlement discussions while mentally suppressing my own recollection of what they said. I would have to segregate what they claimed they intended from what I perceived they intended based on what I heard them say during the settlement discussions.

Indeed, there is one view of the matter that suggests that it is not too far fetched to imagine that I could become a witness in this case if the parties differ bitterly as to what occurred at the settlement discussions and Judge Sullivan, in his wisdom, decided that one party or the other could call me as a witness. While I cannot predict with certainty that any of this will occur, the possibility that I might have to be a witness gives me pause. If, in the interim, I provide Judge Sullivan with a Report and Recommendation that speaks to the very issue about which I might have to testify, I would be acting as witness and judge in the same case. I cannot imagine how any one could possibly defend such a curious mixing of roles. I surely believe that any reasonable person would find that co-mingling highly offensive to the appearance of impartiality.

Finally, there is an institutional interest that has to be factored into the calculus. As the government correctly points out, presiding over settlement conferences has become an important responsibility of magistrate judges. At the same time, their responsibilities over the substantive aspects of cases have grown as well. For example, more parties express their consent to magistrate judges' presiding over trials. I have held enough settlement conferences to know that my success is a direct function of the parties' certainty that what they tell me will remain confidential and their perception of my utter objectivity. I can easily understand why a party would be less than frank if that party could foresee the possibility that what they said to me during settlement discussions would influence how I would ultimately rule on a substantive matter in the same case. The impact that fear would have on the success I might otherwise achieve in settling that case compels me to conclude that the line between the magistrate judge as mediator and the magistrate judge as presiding judge must be kept straight and true.

I, therefore, have decided to recuse myself from issuing the Report and Recommendation. On the other hand, I note my continued desire to help the parties finally settle this matter if they believe I can assist them.

An Order accompanies this Memorandum Opinion.

## NOVAK v. FARNEMAN
United States District Court for the Southern District of Ohio
2011 U.S. Dist. LEXIS 114398 (Sept. 30, 2011)

ALGENON L. MARBLEY, DISTRICT JUDGE.

This matter is before the Court on Plaintiffs' Motion to Recuse and for an Evidentiary Hearing. For the reasons set forth below, the Court hereby recuses itself from presiding over this matter any further. Plaintiffs' Motion to Recuse and for an Evidentiary Hearing is GRANTED. All further matters related to this action will be set for immediate referral to a different court.

Plaintiff John F. Novak, who owns a small green technology company, Enviro-Wave Energy, LLC ("EnviroWave") in Frederkicktown, Ohio, developed an environmental technology ("the Technology") that converts scrap tires to diesel fuel and carbon dust without the use of heat. Novak filed a patent application regarding the Technology in February 2006. Novak contends that Defendants Keith L. Welch, who worked as a sales representative for EnviroWave beginning in 2000, and John O. Farneman, an "investor" who expressed interest in potentially acquiring the Technology in 2004, signed non-disclosure agreements ("NDAs") under which they were provided confidential trade secret information about the Technology. Plaintiffs further contend that because Novak repeatedly refused to sell Defendants the Technology, the Defendants then misappropriated trade secrets and confidential information pertaining to the Technology for incorporation into their own system in violation of the NDAs.

In May 2010, Plaintiffs learned that Defendants filed their own patent application in December 2006. Plaintiffs allege that Defendants' patent application contains trade secrets and confidential information provided to Defendants under the NDAs they signed. Defendants' patent application discloses confidential information that was not revealed in Plaintiffs' patent application. Plaintiffs now fear that Defendants are trying to sell the Technology.

. . . .

On June 27, 2011, at the request of the parties, this Court presided as the mediator over the parties' first settlement conference in chambers. At this first settlement conference, a settlement was reached by the parties, and the material terms of the agreement were placed on the record. The parties were then ordered to work together to memorialize the settlement agreement in writing and prepare the appropriate dismissal papers.

Among the individuals present on behalf of the Defendants at the settlement conference was Mr. Edward Bacome, who holds a financial interest in Defendants' company. This Court disclosed to all parties that he is an acquaintance of Mr. Bacome and that his wife was an associate at the Vorys firm at which this Judge was a partner. Although this judge expressed a firm belief in his ability to remain fair and impartial as mediator, parties were given the option of ceasing the settlement conference or seeking the assistance of another mediator. Both parties elected to proceed, with neither party raising any objections to the mediation going forward, or to the Court's participation in the mediation.

Following the June 27, 2011 settlement conference, however, the parties could not agree on the scope of certain terms of the agreement, and a further status conference was held with the Court on August 25, 2011, to attempt to resolve the outstanding disputed details. This second settlement conference, too, was unsuccessful. At the conclusion of the second settlement conference, the Court indicated that it would entertain the Defendants' proposed motion to enforce the original settlement. Only then did Plaintiffs announce their intention to move for the Court's recusal. Plaintiffs' instant motion followed in the form of a cross motion to Defendants' motion to enforce the original settlement reached in June.

Plaintiffs' request for the Court's recusal is predicated on two bases, both of which are lacking in merit, and the second of which rests on a fabricated account of the Court's statements during settlement proceedings. First, Plaintiffs argue that the Court should recuse itself from making a determination on whether to enforce a settlement agreement that it was actively involved in facilitating. Second, Plaintiffs assert that the Court's relationship with the Bacome family prevents it from maintaining impartiality. Plaintiffs claim that this Court expressed "sympathy" for Mr. Bacome during the settlement conference because Mr. Bacome was facing a potential financial loss in the event of an unfavorable outcome for the Defendants. The Court now takes this opportunity to address these arguments and factual contentions.

The district judge has an initial and abiding responsibility to recuse himself from a case. Under the 28 U.S.C. § 455(a), a judge must recuse himself in circumstances that give rise to a reasonable inference of impropriety or lack of impartiality. This broad and objective standard "is designed to promote public confidence in the impartiality of the judicial process by saying, in effect, if there is a reasonable factual basis for doubting the judge's impartiality, he should disqualify himself and let another judge preside over the case." The Court first treats Plaintiffs' argument that the Court cannot fairly and impartially continue to preside over the breakdown of a settlement which it had assisted in brokering. Plaintiffs rely on a District of Columbia case, *Black v. Kendig*, 227 F. Supp. 2d 153 (D.D.C. 2002), where the magistrate judge felt compelled to recuse himself (although he reported it was a "close call") from being called on to interpret the terms of a contract he had mediated, and where he could have conceivably been called as a witness. The more appropriate controlling authority, however, comes from the Sixth Circuit's opinion in *Bosley v. 21 WFMJ TV., Inc.*, 245 F. App'x. 445 (6th Cir. 2007), which expressly distinguished *Black* in upholding the district court's decision not to recuse itself in a strikingly similar situation to the one presented here.

In *Bosley*, as here, the defendants argued that the district judge should have recused himself from continuing to preside over the case, which included ruling on a motion to enforce the prior settlement, because the district judge "was responsible for helping facilitate the agreement that resulted in the settlement of that case" and therefore had "somehow become invested" in "vindicating" the outcome of the prior settlement. The Circuit Court explained that, absent any display of "deep-seated favoritism or antagonism," the parties were by no means necessarily denied an impartial hearing simply because the district court chose to preside over the case in which it had mediated a prior settlement that now required review. *See Bosley*, 245 F.App'x at 455 ("[T]he Supreme Court has recognized that judges may properly form opinions 'on the basis of facts introduced or events occurring in the course of the current proceedings.' ") (quoting *Liteky*, 520 U.S. at 555).

The argument that a Court cannot impartially determine whether to enforce a settlement it helped to mediate was wrong in *Bosley* and it is wrong here. This Court is perfectly capable of impartially ruling on the issues and terms surrounding the parties' settlement despite having acted as mediator, for judges "are often called upon to compartmentalize their knowledge of information surrounding a case." *United States v. Glick*, 946 F.2d 335, 337 (4th Cir. 1991); . . . And, *Bosley* makes it clear that recusal is certainly not "required" under 28 U.S.C. § 455, as Plaintiffs assert.

Next, Plaintiffs seize upon the Court's acquaintance with Mr. Bacome and his wife as a second supporting factor in their argument for recusal. Of course, the existence of a "personal bias or prejudice" on the part of the presiding judge concerning one of the parties will trigger the judge's duty to recuse himself. *See* 28 U.S.C. § 455(b). However, common sense, as well as Supreme Court precedent, instructs that "the pejorative connotation of the terms 'bias' and 'prejudice' demands that they be applied only to judicial predispositions that go beyond what is normal and acceptable." *Liteky*, 510 U.S. at 552.

This Judge disclosed his prior acquaintance with Mr. Bacome at the outset of settlement proceedings, and assured parties that he was confident in the Court's ability to remain fair and impartial nonetheless. . . .

Perhaps out of an understanding that "mere acquaintance is typically not sufficient to warrant recusal," counsel for Plaintiffs attests in his declaration that the Court made additional comments during settlement negotiations revealing a clear bias in favor of Defendants. Specifically, Mr. Wagner claims that this Judge identified Mr. Bacome's wife as a former mentor of his during his time as a partner at the Vorys, Sater, Seymour & Pease law firm, and that he was troubled that Mr. Bacome would have to pay for mistakes of the past. At best, counsel was apparently too hurried in preparing a self-serving sworn declaration to correct for demonstrably false representations. At worst, Mr. Wagner made intentional misrepresentations.

First, with respect to the mentor relationship Mr. Wagner claims, the facts belie his declaration. This Judge was on the hiring committee which hired Mrs. Bacome, and it was she who worked with him on occasion as she was an associate in the litigation group in which this Judge was a partner. Mrs. Bacome is significantly this Judge's junior, and during the short time they worked together at the firm, Vorys was not in the practice of having junior associates mentor partners. Indeed, Mrs. Bacome never mentored this Judge.

The contention that this Judge expressed his "sadness" at Mr. Bacome's having to pay for mistakes made by Defendants is equally untrue, and absurd. This Court remarked that if the case did not settle, then the parties would have to pay mounting legal fees for ongoing discovery, trial preparation, the trial itself, and any appeal. At no time did the Court single out Mr. Bacome. As with Mr. Wagner's contention regarding Mrs. Bacome's mentor relationship to this Judge, Mr. Wagner is once again incorrect on the facts.

. . . [T]he Court's statements in the presence of parties during settlement were . . . benign. The Court merely commented on the obvious fact that a failure to settle would only create more legal costs for all parties. That Mr. Wagner would make such reckless and patently incredible mischaracterizations of the Court's statements in a sworn declaration strains this Court's credulity.

There being no objective threat to impartiality raised by the Court continuing to preside over the disputes regarding the settlement that it oversaw as mediator, and likewise no objectively inappropriate bias arising from this Judge's acquaintance with the Bacome family, recusal in this case is most certainly not required. Nevertheless, while the Court's belief in its ability to be fair and impartial in this case remains unshaken by Plaintiffs' arguments and Plaintiffs' counsel Wagner's factual inaccuracies, it is the public's trust and perception of this Court with which the Court must concern itself. The Court therefore hereby recuses itself in this matter, strictly to avoid even the remote possibility that the further proceedings might be tainted with a suggestion of bias or impropriety.

## NOTES AND QUESTIONS

(1) Although both of the federal judges in these two cases decided to recuse themselves, each appeared to have a different philosophy concerning the ability to maintain his impartiality in a subsequent proceeding if the judge has served in the dual role of mediator. Indeed, the magistrate judge in *Black v. Kendig* expresses skepticism over judges' ability to "compartmentalize their knowledge of information

surrounding a case," while the district judge in *Novak v. Farneman* appears to accept this notion as an article of faith. Do you think that a judge can "compartmentalize" his or her knowledge in this way?

(2)    There have now been numerous state and federal court opinions dealing with issues arising from judges serving in the dual role of mediator and judge. For an excellent discussion of this confusing case-law, see Sarah R. Cole et al., *Mediation: Law, Policy & Practice* 548–54 (2012) (3d ed. 2011).

(3)    Should judges be required to adhere to ethical standards for mediators while conducting settlement conferences?

# Chapter 10

## MEDIATION AND THE LAWYER AS ADVOCATE

## A. INTRODUCTION

To this point, we have analyzed mediation from the perspective of the mediator and the parties. This chapter shifts the focus to the special role that lawyers play as advisors and advocates in mediation. Although litigation and mediation are distinct processes, they are significantly related to one another. Even if no case has been filed with the court, parties evaluate their dispute with a consideration of their legal rights and obligations and the likely court outcome. For many cases, lawyers file pleadings and are then encouraged by both clients and court personnel to consider or participate in mediation. The challenge in these circumstances becomes how to manage their participation in distinct, simultaneous processes in a way that does not operate at cross purposes with one another. These advocate challenges were aptly characterized by Mnookin and Kornhauser when they observed, in discussing negotiator conduct, that negotiations often take place in the "shadow of the law." *See* Robert H. Mnookin & Lewis Kornhauser, *Bargaining in the Shadow of the Law: The Case of Divorce*, 88 Yale L.J. 950 (1979). In addition, for those disputes which are filed, many are both litigated and mediated, sometimes virtually simultaneously.

This mixing of processes affects the work of lawyers as they must consider their obligations in new ways. What responsibility does a lawyer have to advise his client about the use of mediation? Should a lawyer participate in mediation? If so, how? How does a lawyer effectively protect her client in a non-adversarial process? Are advocacy skills in mediation comparable to or distinct from trial skills?

This chapter explores these questions. Section B examines the interrelationship between litigation and mediation and the "evolution of the new lawyer." Section C focuses on the role attorneys do and should play as their client's representative prior to and during the mediation process, including consideration of relevant ethical issues.

## B. THE RELATIONSHIP BETWEEN MEDIATION AND LITIGATION

Mediation and litigation are often intertwined. When parties and their counsel file pleadings to advance a case, a court might order the participants to try to resolve some or all matters in mediation, or the parties themselves might voluntarily opt to try mediation to avoid the need for a trial. In such circumstances, all participants must skillfully navigate their conduct to insure that their participation in one process supports or does not harm their effectiveness in the other. As lawyers and their clients engage in mediation, they will consider settlement proposals advanced in mediation as compared to their likely success in litigation. But there are many tactical and strategic matters to consider long before that BATNA question, such as: What disclosures should or should not be made during the mediation in light of the pending litigation? If an agreement *is* reached in mediation, what is gained or lost in terms of the litigation? Is the privacy of the mediation process — and potentially a confidential agreement — the most constructive environment for raising one's client's concerns? Simultaneously, while lawyers proceed with the litigation process both pre-mediation and post-mediation, they and their clients must consider the implications of their moves for the mediation. For example, what discovery should or should not be sought prior to a pending mediation? At what stage of the litigation does it make most sense to mediate? Should the attorney file certain motions in order to further the chances of resolving the dispute in mediation, or is it better to delay filing such motions, for fear of wasting time or angering the opposition?

Of course, parties and their counsel need not have filed formal pleadings in order for them to experience the interplay of mediation and litigation. For example, lawyers and their clients may recognize that pursuing litigation is a distinct possibility if their efforts to resolve their dispute through mediation are not successful, so their preparation for and conduct in the mediation process itself is shaped by their assessment of necessary discovery procedures, information that is or is not appropriately shared in mediated conversations, and the likely court outcome.

Attorneys have responded in diverse ways to the rapid growth of mediation over the last 40 years. As Professor Len Riskin observed in 1982, the "standard philosophical map" of lawyers can sometimes vary radically from the premises on which mediation is founded. Leonard L. Riskin, *Mediation and Lawyers*, 43 Ohio St. L.J. 29, 43 (1982). Building on Riskin's thoughts, Professor Chris Guthrie has argued that even in a world mandating facilitative mediation, mediation with lawyer-mediators is unlikely to be a purely facilitative process because of the lawyer's philosophical map and the disputant's perceptual map. Chris Guthrie, *The Lawyer's Philosophical Map and the Disputant's Perceptual Map: Impediments to Facilitative Mediation and Lawyering*, 6 Harv. Negot. L. Rev. 145, 148–50 (2001). Although some litigators assume that one party's gain is inevitably the other party's loss, you have seen that mediation is dependent on creative problem solving that searches for mutual gains. Professor Robert Rubinson has similarly observed that mediation and litigation are dependent on very different "narratives," explaining that whereas litigation attempts to convince a decision maker as to what really happened and who was right, mediation seeks to reframe or expand negotiating issues thereby transforming conflict through collaboration. Robert Rubinson, *Client Counseling, Mediation, and Alternative Narratives of Dispute Resolution*, 10 Clinical L. Rev. 833 (2004). Despite these potential philosophical differences, many lawyers have embraced mediation, recognizing that it offers a better solution for their clients in many situations.

In the following excerpt, Professor Julie Macfarlane describes how the changes in legal practice have led to a movement away from adversarial advocacy and toward the development of conflict resolution advocacy. Based on her empirical research, she asserts that a new professional identity for lawyers has emerged in response to a changing climate for disputes. These changes include the "vanishing trial" phenomenon, a dramatically altered business model, and an increase in institutional uses of mediation, see *supra* Chapter 9.

As you read the excerpt, consider how mediation and litigation might blur into one another as fewer cases are resolved through trials. Is it desirable or possible to retain the uniqueness of each process?

## THE EVOLUTION OF THE NEW LAWYER: HOW LAWYERS ARE RESHAPING THE PRACTICE OF LAW
2008 J. Disp. Resol. 61, 62–70, 73–75, 77–80[*]
By Dr. Julie Macfarlane

### I. TIMES OF CHANGE

There have been seismic changes in the legal profession — especially in its internal structures and in legal disputing procedures — over the last thirty years. The "vanishing trial" phenomenon is just one aspect of this, but it is a vital one. A 98% civil settlement rate and the increasing use of negotiation, mediation, and collaboration in resolving lawsuits have dramatically altered the role of the lawyer. The traditional conception of the lawyer as "rights warrior" no longer satisfies client expectations, which center on value for money and practical problem solving rather than on expensive legal argument and arcane procedures.

At the same time, the business model of the profession has altered dramatically. . . . Both corporate and personal customers appear increasingly unwilling to passively foot the bill for a traditional, litigation-centered approach to legal services, preferring a more pragmatic, cost-conscious, and time-efficient approach to resolving legal problems.

. . .

Changes in procedure, voluntary initiatives, and changing client expectations are coming together to create a new role for counsel and a new model of client service. This role is moving away from the provision of narrow technical advice and strategies that center on litigation and fighting (i.e. the "warrior lawyer") towards a more holistic, practical, and efficient approach to conflict resolution. The result is a new model of lawyering practice that builds on the skills and knowledge of traditional legal practice but is different in critical ways. The new lawyer is not completely unrelated or dissimilar to the warrior lawyer but an evolved, contemporary version. . . .

Both the emerging and the traditional models of lawyering place legal intelligence at their center as the primary and unique skill of the lawyer. Both approaches require excellent client communication skills, good writing skills, and, sometimes, persuasive oral advocacy skills. Both approaches require effective negotiation. However, the new lawyer realizes that she needs to utilize these skills in different ways and in new and different processes, designed to facilitate earlier settlement. The goals of these processes are almost always information exchange and the exploration of options. Sometimes they include the settlement of some peripheral issues, sometimes full resolution. The warrior lawyer is more familiar with processes that rehearse and replay rights-based arguments, look for holes in the other side's case, and give up as little information as possible. The new lawyer bases her practice on the undisputed fact that almost every contentious matter she handles will settle without a full trial, and some will settle without a judicial hearing of any kind. She assumes that negotiation, often directly involving her clients, is feasible in all but the most exceptional cases and that in this capacity she is an important role model and coach for her clients. The new lawyer understands that not every conflict is really about rights and entitlements and that these are conventional disguises for anger, hurt feelings, and struggles over scarce resources. The new lawyer recognizes that part of her role is to assist her clients to identify what they really need, while constantly assessing the likely risks and rewards as well as what they believe they "deserve" in some abstract sense. She also understands the purpose and potential of information in settlement processes. In adversarial processes, information is used to gain an advantage over the other side (information as "power over"); in settlement meetings, information is used as a valuable shared resource to broaden the range of possible solutions (information as "power with"). The new lawyer must develop the best possible outcome — often in the form of a settlement — for her client, using communication, persuasion, and relationship building. This is a different role than making positional arguments and "puffing" up the case. It moves beyond the narrow articulation of partisan interests to the practical realization of a conflict specialist role for counsel.

. . .

## III. CONFLICT RESOLUTION ADVOCACY

. . .

The new lawyer will conceive of her advocacy role more deeply and broadly than simply fighting on her clients' behalf. This role comprehends both a different relationship with the client — closer to a working partnership — and a different orientation towards conflict. The new lawyer must help her client engage with the conflict, confronting the strategic and practical realities as well as making a game plan for victory. The new lawyer can offer her client skills and tools for conflict analysis, an understanding of how conflict develops and evolves over time, and the experience of working continuously with disputants on (perhaps similar) disputes. Conflict resolution advocacy means working with clients to anticipate, raise, strategize, and negotiate over conflict and, if possible, to implement jointly agreed outcomes . . . .

. . . Conflict resolution advocacy understands rights-based strategies as important and useful but rarely exclusive tools for engaging with conflict and seeking solutions. As a result of broadening discussions to include non-legal issues and potential solutions, the role of the client in conflict resolution advocacy becomes more significant in both planning and decision making, modifying the simple notion of the lawyer as the expert who is "in charge." . . . Finally, conflict resolution advocacy does not deny or contradict justice as process, but it takes what lawyers already know about the importance of integrity in the processes and procedures of conflict resolution and applies this awareness to private ordering outside the legal system. As a consequence the new lawyer will be deeply involved in, and knowledgeable about, the design of processes and procedures of negotiation, mediation, and other Collaborative processes . . .

## IV. CONFLICT RESOLUTION ADVOCACY AND CLIENT LOYALTY

There is no lessening of the lawyer's responsibility to achieve the best possible outcome for his client in client resolution advocacy. In fact, advocacy as conflict resolution places the constructive and creative promotion of partisan outcomes at the center of the advocate's role and sees this goal as entirely compatible with working with the other side. In fact, this goal can *only* be achieved by working with the other side. The new lawyer remains just as dedicated to achieving her clients' goals as the warrior or adversarial advocate. What changes is that her primary skill becomes her effectiveness and ability to achieve the best possible negotiated settlement, while she remains prepared to litigate if necessary. . . .

Counsel's loyalty and focus should be on achieving the client's best possible outcome(s). . . . A contradiction between client loyalty and creative consensus building only exists if counsel is convinced that the only effective way to advance the client's wishes is by using rights-based processes. Aside from these fairly exceptional cases, the goal of the conflict resolution advocate is to persuade the other side to settle — on her client's best possible terms.

Adversarial advocacy offers no frameworks to counsel to resolve classic dilemmas such as when and how to settle, or how to balance their own judgment with the clients' aspirations. Admitting a need to compromise in any way undermines the core of zealous advocacy. Conflict resolution advocacy both anticipates these dilemmas and makes them resolvable on a principled basis. Whereas adversarial advocacy tends to view settlement as capitulation, conflict resolution advocacy is committed to evaluating the pros, cons, and alternatives of any settlement option, which includes an evaluation of the legal, cognitive, and emotional dimensions because all of these are part of how clients appraise settlement.

## V. FACT GATHERING AND INFORMATION IN CONFLICT RESOLUTION ADVOCACY

The dominant epistemology of litigation is that knowledge and information have the sole purpose of advancing the client's legal case. This approach means that only information that fits the legal argument is either sought or utilized, and ignores other information that may be important to realizing the client's goals. The adversarial advocate approaches fact-gathering and information as a competitive process, with information withheld from the other side even where it may be of little or no consequence, and often where it would be beneficial in clarifying the relative goals and expectations of each.

In a conflict resolution model the purpose and uses of information are understood differently. First, the type of information that may be important is expanded. . . .

If counsel takes seriously her responsibility to engage the client in the resolution of the conflict, she will seek out information that could be key to understanding how to advance the client's interests and needs, as well as his legal entitlements.

Second, conflict resolution advocacy regards information as a shared resource that may advance all party interests. This approach to information sharing requires significant reorientation, both conceptual and collegial. For a less aggressive and more collaborative approach to information sharing to work, lawyers need to be able to build trusting relationships with other counsel and other professionals. There is an obvious need for norms of reciprocity. . . .

## VI. RE-ENVISIONING OUTCOMES IN CONFLICT RESOLUTION ADVOCACY

. . .

In envisioning and evaluating potential outcomes, conflict resolution advocacy will certainly include proximity to an "ideal" (i.e., successful) legal outcome, but many other factors will also be important. For example, responsible counsel will always consider the issue of costs in planning a conflict resolution strategy. Conflict resolution advocates should consider how far any one outcome will meet client interests. Aside from "winning," these might include, for example, recognition and acknowledgment, business expansion or solvency, future relationships both domestic and commercial, vindication and justice, emotional closure, and reputation. These interests have both short-term and long-term elements. They reflect not only outcome goals but also the importance of procedural justice — feeling listened to, being taken seriously, and being fairly treated. In a conflict resolution model of advocacy, it is not only the final deal that matters but also how the client feels about how it was reached, which includes a sense that the outcome is fair and wise . . . .

Conflict resolution advocacy . . . does not mean abandoning rights-based advocacy and even trial work in appropriate cases. In fact, conflict resolution advocacy builds on some traditional skills and knowledge, notably information assimilation, legal research, effective oral communication, strategic planning, and insider knowledge, which are core elements of effective trial advocacy. Conflict resolution advocacy takes these familiar tools and applies them to a newly articulated and more realistic goal: the pursuit of acceptable, reasonable, and durable settlements that meet client interests.

## VII. PLACING NEGOTIATION AT THE CENTER OF LEGAL PRACTICE

. . . [C]onflict resolution advocacy demands that negotiation planning be addressed even in the earliest stages of file development as a part of the process of canvassing goals, priorities, and alternatives with the client. An early and explicit focus on the potential for negotiated settlement requires the holistic framing of the problem rather than the selective use of information in a way that narrows the case to its generic legal issues. . . .

[Conflict resolution advocates] have a sense not only of when to be accommodating but also of when to be tough in order to protect their clients' interests, working incrementally to create trust and enhanced solutions. They understand and develop norms of reciprocity with the other side, beginning with establishing comfort and rapport. This process requires good interpersonal and communication skills, including the ability to put the other side at ease, demonstrate respect and perhaps even empathy, and, most challengingly, create a shared sense of trust. . . .

Lawyers who are experienced in settlement advocacy settings identify a number of discrete negotiation skills — implicating both cognitive and emotional abilities and qualities — which enable them to be most effective. These include preparing an effective opening statement . . . which adopts a firm yet not overly positional tone; matching the appropriate informal process to the case; displaying confidence and openness; and thinking outside the "box" of conventional, legal solutions in developing creative problem-solving skills. . . . Critical to being able to persuade the other side to settle on your client's best terms is an understanding of what the other side needs in order to be able to settle. . . .

## X. DECISION MAKING AND CONTROL

. . . Reframing the lawyer-client relationship as a working partnership has profound implications for the balance of power in lawyer-client relationships. A partnership gives the client far greater power not only to review and critique decisions but also to participate in making them.. . . .

In anticipation of early mediation, there are many questions that the lawyer now needs to ask at the planning stage — questions that only the client can answer and that are not necessarily related to making the legal case. . . .

Expanding the number of issues that will be considered is a natural consequence of engaging the client more completely in the development of the case and in the dispute resolution strategy. If he is directly involved in planning for mediation, for example, a business client is likely to provide additional information on business needs and goals, both long-term and short-term, which can be effectively incorporated into planning a strategy for negotiation. Issues that would not be apparent otherwise may surface. Instead of removing emotional and psychological issues from the negotiation, the inclusion of clients in planning may mean that important and otherwise unspoken barriers to settlement can be raised and discussed.

. . . Reconceiving lawyer-client relations in this way means that much of the weight of both moral and practical responsibility shifts from the lawyer to her client. Depending on the extent to which counsel embraces a working partnership with her client, this shift may be a significant one or it may be more marginal — but it will occur in some way. . . .

. . .

## XI. CLIENT PARTICIPATION

. . . In informal settlement procedures, lawyers have far less control over the proceedings and need to be able to understand how their client will behave and how to relate to him throughout the process. The new lawyer needs to not only be able to minimize any negative consequences of the client being present but also to maximize the benefits.

. . . Instead of the lawyer bringing a proposal back to the client from the other side and presenting it to the client with her own overlay of analysis and recommendations, decisions in mediation may be made on the spot as new offers emerge or solutions develop . . . .

Counsel experienced in mediation and other convened settlement processes have learned that bringing a client with them who is not prepared and has not agreed in advance on how to present the issues (for example, how much and what information to disclose, or what options to canvass) may be a recipe for disaster. . . .

. . . Unless both lawyer and client embrace a new partnership model, new processes that are inclusive of clients will actually look and function in a very similar manner to traditional ones. Some clients complain that their lawyers often fail to prepare them fully, or to consult them on how to use the process effectively. There is also some evidence that some clients are extremely dissatisfied with being excluded or silenced by their lawyers in mediation. . . .

. . . A working partnership between lawyer and client aims to produce superior solutions — that is, superior to those solutions negotiated privately by lawyers or imposed by a judge. Involving clients in negotiation and mediation processes can significantly advance this goal. Face-to-face interaction allows parties in both domestic and commercial disputes to explore their understanding of what feels fair and realistic and to refine details that might otherwise follow a standard or assumed path. . . . There is the potential for value-added outcomes that include creative substantive dimensions . . . as well as secondary benefits such as enhanced communication and relationships.

## NOTES AND QUESTIONS

(1)   Do you agree that mediation and litigation rely on different philosophical mindsets or narratives? To the extent you agree, do you think it is possible for a single person to be a competent advocate in the worlds of both litigation and mediation? Professor Rubinson's article, *Client Counseling, Mediation, and Alternative Narratives of Dispute Resolution*, 10 Clinical L. Rev. 833 (2004), provides advice to lawyers on how to properly counsel their clients regarding mediation. *See also* Jacqueline M. Nolan-Haley, *Lawyers, Clients, and Mediation*, 73 Notre Dame L. Rev. 1369, 1370–71 (1998) (arguing that "[m]ediation offers enormous potential for lawyers to recognize and honor the missing human dignity dimension in current versions of adversarial lawyering," and offering suggestions to lawyers on how to be good counselors with respect to mediation).

(2)   In 1997, John Lande published, *How Will Lawyering and Mediation Transform Each Other?*, 24 Fla. St. U. L. Rev. 839 (1997) in which he coined the term "litimediation" to refer to the phenomenon that mediation would be the normal way to end litigation. At the time he wrote his article, he was to some degree predicting what the impact would be of blending litigation and mediation cultures. From what you know of the legal culture in your own area, how accurate were Professor Lande's predictions? What is your own prediction for how the relationship

between mediation and litigation will continue to evolve?

(3)   Several studies have examined the attitudes of litigators toward ADR, including mediation. As might be expected, their findings reflect diverging attitudes among attorneys, and also show that some cultural differences exist among jurisdictions. *See* Dr. Julie Macfarlane & Michaela Keet, *Civil Justice Reform and Mandatory Civil Mediation in Saskatchewan: Lessons from a Maturing Program*, 42 Alberta L. Rev. 677 (2005); Roselle L. Wissler, *Barriers to Attorneys' Discussion and Use of ADR*, 19 Ohio St. J. on Disp. Resol. 459 (2004) (focusing on Arizona); Bobbi McAdoo & Art Hinshaw, *The Challenge of Institutionalizing Alternative Dispute Resolution: Attorney Perspectives on the Effect of Rule 17 on Civil Litigation in Missouri*, 67 Mo. L. Rev. 473 (2002); Bobbi McAdoo, *A Report to the Minnesota Supreme Court: The Impact of Rule 114 on Civil Litigation Practice in Minnesota*, 25 Hamline L. Rev. 401 (2002).

(4)   The changes in the legal system have implications for the teaching of law school classes. The authors of *It's Time to Get It Right: Problem-Solving in the First-Year Curriculum*, 39 Wash. U. J. L. & Pol'y 39 (2012) (Bobbi McAdoo, Sharon Press, and Chelsea Griffin) and *Separate and Not Equal: Integrating Civil Procedure and ADR in Legal Academia*, 80 Notre Dame L. Rev. 681 (2005) (Jean Sternlight), argue that given the interrelatedness of ADR and litigation (Sternlight) and the importance to all lawyers of the skills taught in ADR courses (McAdoo, Press, and Griffin), law schools err to the extent that they segregate the teaching of litigation/lawyering and ADR into totally separate courses. Do you agree?

(5)   Would it be desirable to keep mediation more distinct from litigation? Would it be possible?

(6)   Note that mediation is not the only dispute resolution process that challenges some lawyers' adoption of a purely adversarial mindset. For example, in 2009 (amended 2010), the National Conference of Commissioners on Uniform Laws promulgated a Uniform Collaborative Law Rules/Act. In a collaborative law practice, lawyers contract in advance to try to resolve their clients' issues in a cooperative way, including a commitment to terminate their legal services to their clients if parties opt to pursue some or all matters in a traditional court process. The Uniform Law attempts to standardize the most important features of a collaborative law practice. *See* http://www.uniformlaws.org/Act.aspx?title=Collaborative%20Law%20Act. For debate regarding some of the ethical issues surrounding this approach, see James K.L. Lawrence, *Collaborative Lawyering: A New Development in Conflict Resolution*, 17 Ohio St. J. on Disp. Resol. 431 (2002); Sandra S. Beckwith & Sherri Goren Slovin, *The Collaborative Lawyer as Advocate: A Response*, 18 Ohio St. J. on Disp. Resol. 497 (2003); and Christopher M. Fairman, *Ethics and Collaborative Lawyering: Why Put Old Hats on New Heads?*, 18 Ohio St. J. on Disp. Resol. 505 (2003).

## C.  LAWYERS' ROLE IN MEDIATION

It is well recognized that lawyers do and should perform many roles for their clients in addition or as an alternative to representing them in litigation. For example, the Preamble to the ABA Model Rules of Professional Conduct states:

As a representative of clients, a lawyer performs various functions. As advisor, a lawyer provides a client with an informed understanding of the client's legal rights and obligations and explains their practical implications. As advocate, a lawyer zealously asserts the client's position under the rules of the adversary system. As negotiator, a lawyer seeks a result advantageous to the client but consistent with requirements of honest dealing with others. As an evaluator, a lawyer acts by examining a client's legal affairs and reporting about them to the client or to others.

Model Rule 2.1 explains that "In rendering advice, a lawyer may refer not only to law but to other considerations such as moral, economic, social and political factors, that may be relevant to the client's situation." Nonetheless, in part because the Model Rules do not expressly address the lawyer's role as a representative in mediation, some issues remain as to lawyers' responsibilities in this context.

In 1990 Professor Frank Sander and Attorney Michael Prigoff engaged in a debate in the pages of the *A.B.A. Journal* (Nov. 1990) regarding whether attorneys do or should have a duty to advise their clients about mediation or other forms of ADR. Professor Sander argued that the duty may already exist, and, if not, should be imposed. Mr. Prigoff agreed that it is often desirable, as a matter of good lawyering, to inform clients of ADR options, but suggested that it would be unwise to create an ethical duty requiring such conversations. Today, a number of jurisdictions *explicitly* impose such a requirement by court rule. *E.g.*, Minn. Gen. R. Prac. 114.03 (noting that courts shall provide parties and attorneys with ADR information and stating that "[a]ttorneys shall provide clients with the ADR information"); Mo. Sup. Ct. R. 17.02(b) (requiring attorneys to advise their clients of the availability of ADR programs). Alternatively, some jurisdictions have used their ethical codes or lawyers' creeds to impose such a duty. *E.g.*, S.D. Tex. L.R. 16.4.B ("Before the initial conference in a case, counsel are required to discuss with their clients and with opposing counsel the appropriateness of ADR in the case."). It is important to note that some jurisdictions *require* consultation while others merely *encourage* attorneys to advise clients about ADR. The hard rule would at least theoretically be enforceable, whereas the precatory rule or statute is not. Furthermore, some rules require attorneys merely to describe existing programs, whereas others require a more general discussion of all dispute resolution approaches. Finally, some rules and statutes prescribe a duty to inform clients, whereas others focus on a duty to discuss ADR with opposing counsel. For a 50-state survey of whether attorneys have a duty to advise clients of ADR options, see Marshall J. Breger, *Should an Attorney Be Required to Advise a Client of ADR Options?*, 13 Geo. J. Legal Ethics 427 (2000) (Appendix I). As a practical matter, because increasing number of courts now mandate mediation in some or all cases (*see* Chapter 9), attorneys are increasingly finding it essential to discuss mediation with their clients.

Once it has been decided that a particular dispute will be mediated, various issues arise regarding the appropriate role of the lawyer-representative in the mediation. Section 1 below examines what role a lawyer should play in selecting a mediator. Section 2 addresses the question whether lawyers ought to participate in mediation. Section 3 looks at how lawyers should conduct themselves in order to provide effective representation of their clients in mediation. Finally, Section 4 examines ethical constraints on lawyers in mediation.

# NOTES AND QUESTIONS

(1)    There are many articles in addition to Professor Sander's article referenced above in which the author examines the question of whether attorneys already have an implicit duty to inform their clients of the benefits of mediation. For example, see Suzanne J. Schmitz, *Giving Meaning to the Second Generation of ADR Education: Attorneys' Duty to Learn About ADR and What They Must Learn*, 1999 J. Disp. Resol. 29 (arguing that they do have such a duty); Monica L. Warmbrod, *Could an Attorney Face Disciplinary Actions or Even Legal Malpractice Liability for Failure to Inform Clients of Alternative Dispute Resolution?*, 27 Cumb. L. Rev. 791, 809 (1996–97) (concluding that they could); and Stuart M. Widman, *Attorneys' Ethical Duties to Know and Advise Clients About Alternative Dispute Resolution*, The Professional Lawyer 18 (1993 symposium issue) (arguing that attorneys have a duty to inform their clients about mediation where it might save them money). Do you believe attorneys have an implicit duty to inform their clients about mediation under the ABA Model Rules of Professional Conduct? For an article discussing lawyers' duty to discuss ADR in the family law context, see Nicole Pedone, *Lawyer's Duty to Discuss Alternative Dispute Resolution in the Best Interest of the Children*, 36 Fam. & Conciliation Cts. Rev. 65 (1998).

(2)    Presumably, the point of a duty to inform clients about mediation is to foster the use of mediation. Yet, empirical questions exist as to whether imposing such a duty really will enhance the use of mediation, and as to whether it matters how or where such a duty is imposed. For example, if an attorney who does not believe using mediation will be beneficial is required to discuss its possible use with his client, the likelihood that his client will find it an attractive option is low. One article notes that corporate lawyers who were instructed to consider using mediation in their cases did not do so regularly until they had received more education on mediation and until other relevant incentives were changed. Nancy H. Rogers & Craig A. McEwen, *Employing the Law to Increase the Use of Mediation and to Encourage Direct and Early Negotiations*, 13 Ohio St. J. on Disp. Resol. 831, 862–63 (1998). However, a study of Arizona attorneys concluded that "[b]ased on the limited empirical evidence available to date, requiring attorneys to both assess ADR options with clients and confer about using ADR with opposing counsel seems to hold promise as a means to increase voluntary ADR use." Roselle L. Wissler, *Barriers to Attorneys' Discussion and Use of ADR*, 19 Ohio St. J. on Disp. Resol. 459, 506 (2004). *See also* Roselle L. Wissler, *When Does Familiarity Breed Content? A Study of the Role of Different Forms of ADR Education and Experience in Attorneys' ADR Recommendations*, 2 Pepp. Disp. Resol. L.J. 199, 237 (2002) (merely taking a CLE course or law school course on ADR has little or no correlation with attorneys' likelihood to recommend ADR to their clients).

(3)    In your view, if there *should* be a duty for attorneys to inform their clients of the availability of mediation as an alternative to negotiation or litigation, when should such a duty arise? Only if the opposing party is or might be amenable to mediation? Only if a court program has been provided? Only if the case is a "reasonable" candidate for mediation, in the attorney's opinion? In what body of law

should such a duty be contained? (Court rule? Statute? Code of Ethics?) What, if any, sanction can be applied against attorneys who fail to fulfill such a duty? For an argument that "[t]he ABA should amend the Model Rules to require lawyers to present the option of pursuing ADR to the client," see Robert F. Cochran Jr., *ADR, the ABA, and Client Control: A Proposal That the Model Rules Require Lawyers to Present ADR Options to Clients*, 41 S. Tex. L. Rev. 183, 200 (1999). *See also* Marshall J. Breger, *Should an Attorney Be Required to Advise a Client of ADR Options?*, 13 Geo. J. Legal Ethics 427, 460 (2000) (arguing that the ABA should adopt a rule providing that "[a] lawyer has a duty to inform his client about the availability and applicability of alternative dispute resolution procedures that are reasonably appropriate under the circumstances").

(4)   In your view, do attorneys currently have a duty to *learn* about mediation or other forms of ADR? If they have such a duty, where is it currently enunciated? Do you believe attorneys *should* have a duty to inform themselves about mediation?

## 1.   Lawyers' Role in Selecting a Mediator

Even when mediation is court-ordered, many jurisdictions allow disputants to choose their own mediator rather than simply accepting the individual who has been assigned by the court from its staff or a roster of certified mediators. When mediation is conducted pre-suit or voluntarily, the disputants have complete discretion to select a mediator. *See* Mo. Sup. Ct. R. 17.03 (allowing court to appoint neutral when parties cannot agree); Fla. R. Civ. P. 1.720(j)(1) (providing parties with 10-day period in which to appoint mediator of own choosing).

The reality, for better or for worse, is that attorneys rather than their clients typically make the selection of a mediator when this discretion is left to the disputant. Some attorneys may make a selection without consulting their clients. When clients are consulted, they often elect to leave the selection of the mediator to their attorneys. Clients may believe that their attorneys are likely to be more qualified than clients in identifying both the traits that are desirable in a mediator and those individuals that possess such traits.

The fact that attorneys, not clients, are typically responsible for selecting the mediator has a significant impact on which persons are chosen most frequently to be mediators. For example, because attorneys tend to focus on the legal aspects of disputes they are likely to believe that it is important that a mediator be knowledgeable regarding the relevant law, so they often select only an attorney or a retired judge to serve as a mediator. Further, attorneys typically pick someone they know, such as an attorney, with or against whom they have litigated, who is now a practicing mediator. Perhaps if clients held more responsibility for selecting mediators, they would be more likely to select persons knowledgeable in areas such as psychology, communications, science, or accounting, but who were not necessarily attorneys. Greater client participation in selecting mediators might also increase the diversity among mediators in terms of race, gender, and ethnicity. Today, most mediators who handle large civil cases are white male attorneys.

The following reading by David Geronemus outlines factors attorneys ought to consider when they select a mediator. In his account, Mr. Geronemus relies significantly on Professor Riskin's four-quadrant grid, which divides mediators along the dimensions of evaluative to facilitative and broad to narrow. *See* Chapter 4, Section C.1., *supra*. Emphasizing that the "grid" is a good starting point for selecting a mediator, Mr. Geronemus suggests that attorneys should also consider a variety of other factors relating to expertise, style, and philosophy. He argues that attorneys should think through their decision carefully in each case, based on their perceptions of what barriers are precluding that case from settling. A mediator who is suitable for assisting parties in resolving one dispute could be a poor match for helping in another.

The second reading, by Professor Jean Sternlight, briefly describes the professional responsibility literature on how attorneys and clients ought to divide decision-making responsibilities. After reading the material presented by Professor Sternlight, consider whether, as a matter of ethics, attorneys have a duty to consult with their clients regarding the selection of mediators.

## MEDIATION OF LEGAL MALPRACTICE CASES: PREVENTION AND RESOLUTION
609 PLI/Lit 847, 860–66 Practicing Law Institute Litigation and Administrative Practice Course Handbook Series Litigation PLI Order No. H0-003Q (June 1999)*
By David Geronemus

The issue of choosing the right mediator might best be phrased as finding the mediator who is most likely to be successful in helping to resolve the dispute. There are certain clear prerequisites. Obviously any mediator should be neutral and respected by both sides. In this regard, consider how one should react to a mediator proposed by an opponent — especially one that the opponent has used before. Although some litigants reflexively reject a mediator the other side has used before, it is interesting to note that such a mediator presumably has the respect of the opposition. If the mediator agrees with you on the merits of the case, it will be difficult for your opponents to walk away from the mediator's advice. Thus, it is often worth investing the time to deter-mine whether you can become comfortable with the mediator's neutrality. If so, he or she may well be a serious candidate for your mediation. This analysis also leads to the proposition that picking a mediator because you believe he or she may be sympathetic to you on the merits can be hazardous. Even if you are able to convince the other side to use your candidate, unless the other side perceives the mediator as neutral and fair throughout the process, he or she will be able to have little impact.

The mediation process that you participate in will vary enormously depending on the mediator you choose. In picking a mediator, it is important to begin with a general understanding of the range of available options.

One useful way of classifying mediators is to consider whether they rely principally on "evaluative" techniques or on "facilitative" techniques. *See* L. Riskin, *Mediator Orientations, Strategies and Techniques*, 12 Alternatives 111 (1994). [Ed.

---

note: For the more complete article, see Leonard L. Riskin, *Understanding Mediators' Orientations, Strategies, and Techniques: A Grid For The Perplexed*, 1 Harv. Neg. L. Rev. 7 (1996), in Chapter 4, Section C.1., *supra*.] Briefly stated, a purely evaluative mediator focuses on the strengths and weaknesses of the parties' cases, while a purely facilitative mediator will not offer an opinion on these issues, focusing his or her attention on clarifying communications and issues, defusing emotion, and curing any information deficiencies that may retard settlement. In addition, mediators differ in whether they focus only on parties' legal rights or whether they also attempt to find creative solutions that satisfy the parties' underlying needs or interests.

Even within these broad categories, mediators differ widely in their approaches. For example, some evaluative mediators tend to offer their views of the case early in the proceedings; others view evaluation as one of many impasse breaking techniques, and will offer evaluative feedback only as necessary to break an impasse — typically in the latter stages of the mediation. Indeed, this distinction can be crucially important to the success of the process, since the "right" evaluation at the wrong time can cause one of the parties to decide that the process is not worth pursuing. In addition, if a mediator evaluates the case before the parties have negotiated to impasse, there is always the risk that the evaluation will itself become a barrier to settlement. For example, assume that the opening positions before a mediation are $2 million demanded and $25,000 offered. Unbeknownst to the enthusiastically evaluative mediator, the plaintiff is really willing to settle for$250,000, not much more than the defendant would be willing to pay. I suspect that if the mediator produces an early evaluation of say $500,000, the mediator will have gone a long way towards making the case more difficult to settle. On the other hand consider what might occur if the mediator withheld the evaluation until the parties had negotiated to impasse at, say, $275,000 demanded and $200,000 offered. A well-reasoned statement by the mediator that the defendant should add to her offer may well be effective in breaking the impasse.

Mediators also differ in the extent to which they will want to work with the parties in structuring the process and in the kind of process that they prefer. For example, some mediators will want to work with the parties as soon as they are retained to discuss what kind of process makes sense. Others leave the process structure entirely to the parties. Some mediators will talk to the parties or counsel prior to the mediation to gain an understanding of the problems and opportunities that they may face at the mediation; others rely on the impressions that they gain in the mediation. Some mediators rely extensively on joint sessions, others do most of their work in private caucuses. And, of course, mediators differ in the substantive legal expertise that they bring to the process. Finally, some mediators have worn a judge's robes; others have not.

These differences among mediators lead to two points about choosing the right mediator for a case. First, given the extent of these differences, at least for cases with relatively high stakes, it is important to spend time learning in some detail about prospective mediators. Relying on a mediator's general reputation for having a high settlement rate, being a distinguished and fair member of the legal community, or being a highly skilled mediator is a useful start, but operates at too great a level of generality to provide the best answers. Talking with parties who have used the mediator before is one useful tool in learning in detail about a mediator's approach. Another approach that is underutilized is a joint interview of the mediator by both parties. Most mediators are in my experience willing to be interviewed about significant cases. There is probably no better way to learn about the approach that a mediator will take than to ask him or her about it. Indeed, to at least some extent lawyers will want to determine whether the prospective mediator has the right personality to interact in a productive way with the parties to the dispute, and to a great extent an interview provides a useful forum to find out.

Second, the choice of the mediator ought to be made with reference to the barriers to the settlement of the case and to your goals in the dispute. For example, if restoration of a damaged relationship is an important goal, it will be important to choose a mediator with strong interpersonal skills. By contrast, if there are widely divergent views of the merits that are making it difficult to settle the case, a mediator with strong evaluative skills will be important. Of course, in many cases both strong evaluative and facilitative skills will be required. And, the extent to which the mediation will require evaluation should determine the extent to which the mediator need have at least some specialized substantive experience.

Following these guidelines should enhance your chances of choosing the best possible mediator for your dispute. Making sure that you design the right sort of mediation process — preferably in conjunction with the mediator — is an equally important next step in utilizing mediation effectively.

## LAWYER'S REPRESENTATION OF CLIENTS IN MEDIATION: USING ECONOMICS AND PSYCHOLOGY TO STRUCTURE ADVOCACY IN A NONADVERSARIAL SETTING
14 Ohio St. J. on Disp. Resol. 269, 349–52 (1999)*
By Jean R. Sternlight

A vast professional responsibility literature discusses the appropriate division of responsibilities in a case between lawyer and client. This literature attempts to fill in the gaps left by the rather vague strictures of both the Model Rules of Professional Conduct and the Model Code of Professional Responsibility. While both sets of rules essentially require the lawyer to defer to her client on major matters (ends) while allowing the lawyer leeway on tactical choices (means), [see Rule 1.2(a) of the Model Rules of Professional Conduct and Ethical Canon 707 of the Model Code of Professional Responsibility], this distinction leaves plenty of room for argument. One school of thought, which some have called "traditional," contends that expert attorneys should behave very directively toward their typically passive clients. The other model, which some have called "participatory," urges that because many strategic decisions involve important choices on ultimate objectives, attorneys need to work closely and consultatively with their clients. As Professor David Luban has observed:

---

[The ends-means rule] assumes a sharp dichotomy between ends and means, according to which a certain result (acquittal, a favorable settlement, *etc.*) is all that the client desires, while the legal tactics and arguments are merely routes to that result. No doubt this is true in many cases, but it need not be: the client may want to win acquittal *by* asserting a certain right, because it vindicates him in a way that matters to him; or he may wish to obtain a settlement without using a certain tactic, because he disapproves of the tactic. In that case, what the lawyer takes to be mere means are really part of the client's ends.[269]

In short, current rules, codes, cases, and commentary provide some guidance but do not provide crystal clear guidance on how, in general, lawyers and clients ought to divide decisionmaking responsibilities.

Nor do existing ethical provisions or commentary provide clear guidance on the specific question of how lawyers and their clients ought to divide negotiation and mediation responsibilities. While it is well recognized that lawyers have an obligation to convey settlement offers to their clients and to allow their clients to make the decision as to whether or not to accept a particular offer, few decisions or commentators have addressed the further questions of how lawyer and client should divide responsibilities beyond that bare minimum. One exception is Professor Robert Cochran, who has argued eloquently that lawyers ought to be required to consult with their clients extensively both as to the nature of the negotiation and as to whether a dispute would best be handled through litigation or rather through some form of alternative dispute resolution.[271] Cochran argues that such consultation is desirable to preserve parties' individual autonomy, to ensure better results, and to protect against attorney conflicts of interest.

## NOTES AND QUESTIONS

(1)   Do you believe that attorneys have an ethical obligation to consult with their clients regarding the choice of a mediator? *Should* attorneys have such an obligation? Note that some mediators say that they view their client as the attorney, rather than the attorney's client. Does this perspective raise any concerns?

(2)   As a matter of "good practice," should attorneys consult with their clients regarding the choice of a mediator?

(3)   Whether alone or in consultation with a client, what criteria should an attorney use to select a mediator for a particular dispute?

(4)   Once a lawyer and client have decided on the relevant criteria for selecting a mediator, how do they actually find a mediator who meets these criteria? Many

---

[269] David Luban, *Paternalism and the Legal Profession*, 1981 Wis. L. Rev. 454, 459 n.9; *see also* Robert F. Cochran, Jr., *Legal Representation and the Next Steps Toward Client Control: Attorney Malpractice for the Failure to Allow the Client to Control Negotiation and Pursue Alternatives to Litigation*, 47 Wash. & Lee L. Rev. 819, 827–828 (1990); Mark Spiegel, *Lawyering and Client Decisionmaking: Informed Consent and the Legal Profession*, 128 U. Pa. L. Rev. 41, 57 (1979). [Ed. note: parentheticals omitted.]

[271] *See* Cochran, *supra* note 269, at 823–24.

not-for-profit and for-profit organizations, including the American Arbitration Association, the CPR Institute for Dispute Resolution and JAMS, maintain lists of mediators and will provide information about the mediators on their list to inquiring parties. As noted previously, some courts or administrative agencies provide training and/or "certify" mediators in their jurisdiction (*see, supra*, Chapter 9) and some may make information about the mediators on their lists available to parties and counsel. Increasingly such information may be available through the Internet.

## 2.  Does the Participation of Lawyers Benefit or Harm the Mediation Process?

Some have argued that, in some contexts, mediation works best when attorneys are absent from the mediation. As an empirical matter, the extent to which attorneys attend and participate in mediation varies by jurisdiction as well as by type of mediation. For example, parties are often unrepresented in community mediations and some jurisdictions bar attorneys from small claims courts, effectively barring them from the mediation of small claims disputes. Do the policy reasons for barring lawyers from the adversarial process in small claims courts carry over to the mediation of these disputes?

Perhaps not surprisingly, the question of whether the participation of attorney/advocates in the mediation process is helpful or harmful to reaching a satisfactory resolution to the dispute has been raised most frequently in the context of dissolution of marriage cases. In these cases the mediator is often not an attorney and the issues are ones that will have long-term impact on both the parties and their children. In addition, since dissolution of marriage cases often involve high emotions, some argue that attorneys' adversarial perspective systematically undercuts the problem-solving approach of mediation. In light of these and other considerations, some states have permitted mediators to prohibit lawyers from participating in mediation in "family" mediations.

Some commentators, such as Mark Rutherford, *Lawyers and Divorce Mediation: Designing the Role of "Outside Counsel,"* Mediation Q. 17 (June 1986) have suggested that attorneys may be helpful to the mediation process: (1) during the pre-mediation referral period; (2) as an expert adviser during the mediation process; or (3) after the mediation, as a reviewer of the final mediated agreement and as a drafter of a legally binding marital agreement. He contends that to the extent the attorney participates at all, he or she should do so non-adversarially. Such a non-adversarial attorney would help to ensure that the agreement is fair, but not help his or her client secure any advantage. Others have recommended a more prominent role for attorneys arguing that the presence and active participation of attorneys is beneficial to the mediation process. In the first excerpt below, Craig A. McEwen, Nancy H. Rogers, and Richard J. Maiman suggest that it is important for lawyers to participate in mediation to protect the rights and interests of their clients.

The second reading in this section is Section 10 of the Uniform Mediation Act (Appendix F), which prohibits excluding attorneys from mediation. Note that whereas states do not necessarily adopt uniform acts in their entirety, all six jurisdictions that first adopted the UMA adopted Section 10.

# BRING IN THE LAWYERS: CHALLENGING THE DOMINANT APPROACHES TO ENSURING FAIRNESS IN DIVORCE MEDIATION

79 Minn. L. Rev. 1317, 1322, 1376–77, 1394–95 (1995)*

By Craig A. McEwen, Nancy H. Rogers & Richard J. Maiman

. . . . . [W]e argue that the debate about fairness in divorce mediation, as well as the resulting legal schemes based on either the "regulatory" or "voluntary participation" approaches, results from the view that one must choose between a "lawyered" process ending in the courtroom, and an informal, problem-solving process involving parties but not lawyers in the mediation room. In our view, this dichotomy has unnecessarily narrowed the policy choices underlying mediation schemes, because it assumes that lawyers either cause conflict or act as mouth-pieces for clients with a cause; that the divorce process is one in which, absent mediation (where lawyers do not appear), aggressive lawyers contest custody cases at hearings; and that mediators either protect parties' interests or pressure them toward a particular (and sometimes unjust) settlement.

We challenge these assumptions and the two approaches in statutes and court rules that follow from them — the "regulatory" and the "voluntary participation" approaches. We argue that the mediation scheme in Maine, where attorneys participate regularly and vigorously in mandated divorce mediation, provides a third avenue — one we call the "lawyer-participant" approach. Research evidence about this third approach undermines the assumptions that have confined the debate about fairness . . . .

. . . .

Most fairness concerns evaporate if lawyers attend mediation sessions with the parties or if the parties opt out of the process when unrepresented. Less intrusive regulations, such as judicial review of agreements, prohibition of settlement pressures, and provisions for unrepresented parties, may moderate the remaining fairness issues. The detailed rules of the "regulatory approach" largely become unnecessary to preserve fairness if lawyers are present.

By encouraging lawyer presence and permitting modification of the mediation ground rules, this scheme is more flexible and certain in responding to the problems of bargaining imbalances and mediator pressures. Especially given the unpredictability and changing situational character of these challenges to fairness, the presence of lawyers in the process can assure necessary help in those unpredictable circumstances. The Maine research shows that with lawyers present as advisors and potentially as spokespersons, the risks of unfairness decline, even in the most unbalanced situations. By permitting adjustment of the mediation process (for example, allowing shuttle mediation), mediation can be tailored to fit particular relationships and issues in each case.

Lawyers prevent or moderate the effects of a face to face encounter with an abuser, thus diminishing the likelihood of unfairness in domestic violence cases.

---

Maine lawyers attending mediation sessions with their clients report arranging separate sessions, time-outs, and other measures to protect their clients. Past violence, which may be a key factor in determining whether the parties will submit to an unfair settlement or will be forced into a frightening situation, becomes less of a bargaining factor if the parties attend with their lawyers. Lawyers can advise clients to avoid settlements that will allow further opportunities for abuse, or that are unlikely to be obeyed, or that are bad deals. Lawyers can also advise their clients to terminate mediation sessions . . . .

Issue limitations also become unnecessary if lawyers attend and can advise on economic trade-offs and legal issues. There is no more danger in combining the issues in mediation than exists if disposition of all issues occurs outside of mediation.

So, too, an assumption that lawyers will be absent underlies reliance on mediator qualifications as a means to ensure fairness. Absent lawyers, mediators must have at least some of the skills and knowledge that lawyers would otherwise provide. In fact, Maine divorce lawyers acknowledge that they sometimes get poor mediators. In these cases, the lawyers simply take charge and use the sessions as four-way negotiation sessions. Although mediator qualifications involving advanced educational degrees may help increase settlements or party confidence, they are unnecessary to protect against unfairness under the "lawyer-participant" approach, because mediators need not substitute their knowledge for that of lawyers. Lawyers can intervene (as discussed above) to compensate for inferior mediators and can request their removal.

Mediator duties to appraise [*sic*] parties of various legal rights, to terminate mediation, and to moderate bargaining imbalances also rest on the assumption that lawyers are absent in mediation. Obviously, requirements for post-mediation review of settlements by lawyers rest on the assumption that the lawyer does not take part in the give-and-take of negotiations.

In other words, lawyer participation reduces substantially the need for regulation . . . .

. . . .

With lawyers present and participating, the concern for fairness no longer justifies heavy regulation or confining mediation to voluntary participants. Lawyer participation in the mediation sessions permits intervention on behalf of clients and buffers pressures to settle. Lawyers may also counsel clients to moderate extreme demands. In addition, once lawyers become accustomed to mediation, lawyer involvement in mandated mediation does not appear to prevent the meaningful participation of parties or inhibit emotional expression between spouses.

With mediation covering a broad scope of issues and with lawyers in attendance, the parties probably will pay more for lawyers and less for mediators. Overall costs, however, will probably remain unchanged because settlements are more likely to be comprehensive and less likely to fall victim to negative reviews by a non-participating lawyer. In addition, mediation with lawyers may reduce discovery costs. What the parties will get is likely to be a fair process in which lawyers intervene to protect against pressures from the other party, the process, or the mediator. They are also likely to get a more spontaneous mediation, unfettered by a web of regulation or defensive mediators. They will enjoy, as compared with parties in a system without mandatory mediation, a greater likelihood of having the opportunity to express themselves and to listen to discussions regarding matters of utmost concern. About one-half the time, they can expect to secure a settlement earlier in the process than would otherwise be the case.

Bringing the lawyers into mandatory mediation will permit the repeal of numerous statutes and a reduction in court rules. Furthermore, it will ease fairness concerns as a reason not to compel participation in mediation. The revised regulatory approach preserves the widespread use and flexibility of the mediation process without undue risk of unfairness.

------

## UNIFORM MEDIATION ACT, SECTION 10

An attorney or other individual designated by a party may accompany that party to and participate in a mediation. A waiver of participation given before the mediation may be rescinded.

### COMMENTS

The fairness of mediation is premised upon the informed consent of the parties to any agreement reached . . . Some statutes permit the mediator to exclude lawyers from mediation, resting fairness guarantees on the lawyer's later review of the draft settlement agreement . . . At least one bar authority has expressed doubts about the ability of a lawyer to review an agreement effectively when that lawyer did not participate in the give and take of negotiation. Similarly, concern has been raised that the right to bring counsel might be a requirement of constitutional due process in mediation programs operated by courts or administrative agencies. Richard C. Reuben, *Constitutional Gravity: A Unitary Theory of Alternative Dispute Resolution and Public Civil Justice*, 47 UCLA L. Rev. 949, 1095 (April 2000).

Some parties may prefer not to bring counsel. However, because of the capacity of attorneys to help mitigate power imbalances, and in the absence of other procedural protections for less powerful parties, the Drafting Committee elected to let the parties, not the mediator, decide. Also, their agreement to exclude counsel should be made after the dispute arises, so that they can weigh the importance in the context of the stakes involved. . . .

## NOTES AND QUESTIONS

(1) Do you agree with the principle set out in Section 10 of the UMA? Do you think it is important for jurisdictions to have a uniform approach on whether or not attorneys are permitted to participate in mediation?

(2)   What do you perceive as the potential drawbacks or advantages of having attorneys participate in mediations as advocates? For another view on how lawyers can assist in the settlement process, see Robert H. Mnookin, Scott R. Peppet & Andrew S. Tulumello, *Beyond Winning: Negotiating to Create Value in Deals and Disputes* (2000).

(3)   Do you think the advantages and disadvantages of having attorneys participate in mediations vary according to the subject matter of the mediation? Why do you suppose that attorneys are less likely to participate in family mediations than in mediations involving other subjects?

(4)   Should states be permitted to require disputants to mediate their disputes without the assistance of an attorney? Do you believe that such a restriction would raise constitutional concerns, as has been suggested by Professor Reuben?

## 3.   How Lawyers Advocate for Their Clients in Mediation

This chapter began with Professor Macfarlane's thesis that the changes in the legal profession have resulted in the need for a new conception of lawyering — namely a move away from adversarial advocacy and toward conflict resolution advocacy. *See* Section B, *supra.* Many commentators have analyzed how lawyers ought to participate in mediations. Virtually all agree that good preparation by both attorney and client is essential for a productive and effective mediation session, noting that attorneys either fail to do advance planning or prepare for mediation using the same adversarial mindset as they would in preparing for a deposition or a court appearance. Instead, they urge, lawyers should prepare themselves and their clients for a very different kind of process, one that combines aspects of litigation and negotiation. In order to be an effective advocate in this distinctive setting, the lawyer should become familiar with the facts of the case and the relevant law, work with the client to decide on a theme and to develop a presentation strategy, and decide which if any exhibits or demonstrations should be used at the mediation. Since the goal of mediation is not to "win" but rather to reach a mutually acceptable settlement, the attorney must also understand her client's underlying needs and interests, anticipate the projected interests of the opposing party, begin to brainstorm possible solutions, consider settlement ranges and limits, and map out a settlement strategy. One essential aspect of attorney preparation for mediation is preparing her client for it. The client must understand the purpose of a mediation, how it differs from litigation, what the different stages of the mediation will be, and what roles the client and the client's attorney will play in the mediation.

Commentators differ, however, in their advice regarding the respective roles both attorney and client should play when an attorney accompanies the client to a mediation. Should the attorney sit quietly and let the client do most of the talking or should the attorney dominate the mediation conversation, essentially asking the client to be a silent observer?

In the first three excerpts that appear below, Professors Carrie Menkel-Meadow, Harold Abramson, and Jean Sternlight offer their views regarding the appropriate stance of advocacy in mediation. As you review these readings, remember and consider that how lawyers should approach mediation is a subset of larger professional responsibility questions such as how lawyers can best represent their clients' interests and whether lawyers have duties to persons or interests (justice) other than their clients. *See, supra,* Chapter 7.

In the second group of readings, the authors identify particular behaviors or strategies that support effective advocate conduct. Professor Jean Sternlight draws upon social science literature regarding barriers to negotiation to identify the respective roles attorneys and clients ought to take in order to capitalize on the possibility mediation offers for resolving a dispute. Tom Arnold identifies 20 errors a lawyer might make in preparing for and handling a mediation and offers practical tips for avoiding them. Finally, Professor Dwight Golann provides specific suggestions on how lawyers can advocate effectively during a mediation.

## ETHICS IN ALTERNATIVE DISPUTE RESOLUTION: NEW ISSUES, NO ANSWERS FROM THE ADVERSARY CONCEPTION OF LAWYERS' RESPONSIBILITIES
38 S. Tex. L. Rev. 407, 408–10, 426–28 (1997)[*]
By Carrie Menkel-Meadow

While one strand of ADR (the one with which I identify — "qualitative" — better processes and solutions) has always associated itself with pursuing "the good" and the "just," the other strand of ADR (quantitative, efficiency concerned, cost-reducing, docket clearing) has produced institutionalized forms of dispute resolution in the courts and in private contracts. To the extent that ADR has become institutionalized and more routine, it is now practiced by many different people, pursuing many different goals. Demonstrating another form of irony is a recent continuing education program that advertised itself as "How to Win in ADR!" Thus, lawyers as "advocates," as well as "problem-solvers" and parties now come to the wide variety of dispute resolution processes with a whole host of different intentions and behaviors, many of which may be inconsistent with the original aims of some forms of ADR. As skillful advocates try to manipulate ADR processes in order to achieve their conventional party maximization goals, the rules of behavior demanded in ADR become both less clear and in some respects even more important.

. . . .

The first and most important dilemma is one that has plagued me throughout my career as a lawyer — scholar — practitioner: the powerful heuristic of the adversary model and its concrete expressions in legal dispute resolution as a paradigm which does not aid, indeed, makes more difficult, the resolution of "ethical" dilemmas when one seeks to use other processes. To put it at its most concrete, as I have asserted in debate with many legal ethicists, the Model Rules of Professional Conduct (still based on an adversarial conception of the advocate's, including "counselor's," role) is not responsive to the needs, duties, and responsibilities of one seeking to be a "non-adversarial" problem-solver and the Code of Judicial Conduct, while perhaps helpful for arbitrators, is not responsive to the particular needs, duties, and responsibilities of the now wide variation in third-party neutral practices. Rules premised on adversarial and advocacy systems, with legal decision-makers, simply do not respond to processes which are intended to be conducted differently (in forms of communication, in sharing of information, in problem analysis and resolution) and to produce different outcomes (not necessarily win-loss, but some more complex and variegated solutions to legal and social problems).

. . . .

While we continue to debate whether ADR is a good or bad idea (supplanting or supplementing more formal judicial systems) it is important to note that the behaviors, skills and tasks of parties and their representatives may be called on in different ways in these alternative processes. The zealous advocate who jealously guards (and does not share) information, who does not reveal adverse facts (and in some cases, adverse law) to the other side, who seeks to maximize gain for his client, may be successful in arbitrations and some forms of mini-trials and summary jury trials.

However, the zealous advocate will likely prove a failure in mediation, where creativity, focus on the opposing sides' interests, and a broadening, not narrowing of issues, may be more valued skills. Indeed, in the second generation of ADR training which now focuses on training the representatives how to "be" in a mediation or other ADR setting, there is recognition that certain aspects of the conventional adversarial role may, in fact, be disadvantageous for effective behavior and the achievement of Pareto optimal solutions in settlement contexts. Such principles as "reactive devaluation" in which one side simply discounts proposals from the other side because the proposals come from the other side, teach us that we will have to relearn how to process and prepare information in a settlement-oriented setting.

Some have suggested the settlement function is sufficiently different from the adversarial function requiring different individuals, with different personalities and orientations as well as ethics. Thus, as courts struggle with such legal issues as what it means to attend a settlement proceeding "in good faith," representatives of parties (which is the term I prefer to the term "advocates") have to consider how to become effective in a different forum. A different orientation to the client and to the "adversary" may be essential in the kind of creative option generation and problem-solving that is essential in a mediation setting.

## MEDIATION REPRESENTATION: ADVOCATING IN A CREATIVE PROBLEM-SOLVING PROCESS[*]
### 1–4 (2004)
### By Harold Abramson

The mediation process is indisputably different from other dispute resolution processes. Therefore, the strategies and techniques that have proven so effective in settlement conferences, arbitrations, and judicial trials do not work optimally in mediation. You need a different representation approach, one tailored to realize the full benefits of this burgeoning and increasingly preferred forum for resolving disputes. Instead of advocating as a zealous adversary, you should advocate as a zealous problem-solver.

. . . .

The familiar adversarial strategy of presenting the strongest partisan arguments and aggressively attacking the other side's case may be effective in court where each side is trying to convince a judge to make a favorable decision. But, in mediation, there is no third-party decision-maker, only a third-party facilitator. The third party is not even the primary audience. The primary audience is the other side, who is surely not neutral and can often be quite hostile. In this different representational setting, the adversarial approach is less effective if not self-defeating.

. . . .

As a problem solver that is creative, you do more than just try to settle the dispute. You creatively search for solutions that go beyond the traditional ones based on rights, obligations, and precedent. Rather than settling for win-lose outcomes, you search for solutions that can benefit both sides. To creatively problem-solve in mediation, you develop a collaborative relationship with the other side in a way that is likely to result in solutions that are enduring as well as inventive

. . . .

Shifting between adversarial and problem-solving tactics during the course of mediation can undercut the problem-solving approach. A consistent adherence to problem-solving will more likely produce the best results for clients.

## LAWYER'S REPRESENTATION OF CLIENTS IN MEDIATION: USING ECONOMICS AND PSYCHOLOGY TO STRUCTURE ADVOCACY IN A NONADVERSARIAL SETTING
14 Ohio St. J. on Disp. Resol. 269, 291–97 (1999)*
By Jean R. Sternlight

Attorney advocacy, properly defined, is entirely consistent with and supportive of mediation. While many commentators have attacked attorneys' use of advocacy in the mediation process . . . the problem is not advocacy per se, but rather certain kinds of advocacy or adversarial behavior employed under particular circumstances. However, some attorney behavior should be proscribed in mediation (as it is in litigation), and some attorneys have a lot to learn regarding how best to advocate for their clients in a mediation.

If advocacy is defined broadly as supporting or pleading the cause of another, there is no inconsistency between advocacy and mediation. Permitting an attorney to act as an advocate for her client simply allows that attorney to speak and make arguments on her client's behalf and to help her client achieve her goals. The

---

purpose of mediation is to reach an agreement which is acceptable to and desired by all parties. To reach such an agreement, both parties may wish to share their views as to their likely success in court as well as to engage in problem-solving. While some parties may be comfortable participating pro se, others may prefer to be aided by an attorney. If a party can advocate for her own interests, this Author sees no reason why her representative should not also be permitted to "advocate" on her behalf.

Nor is it clear why "adversarial" behavior, at least broadly defined, is necessarily inconsistent with mediation. To the extent that acting adversarially means advocating only on behalf of one's own client and not on behalf of any other party or on behalf of the process or system, the conduct is easy to reconcile with mediation. The problem-solving that works well in mediation does not require sacrifice of one's self-interest, but rather allows parties to search for solutions that are mutually beneficial.

Therefore, it is not at all clear to this Author why an attorney, hired by a party, should work toward achieving mediation results that, while helpful to others or supportive of a peaceful solution, do not serve the wishes of the client. Of course, if a client chooses to direct her attorney to work toward an agreement that benefits all parties equally, rather than one that benefits the client most, she should be able to do so, but it is not clear why a client should be obliged to have her attorney represent interests other than her own. Certainly a client should not be required to have the attorney she has retained act contrary to her interests. Were we to entirely forbid attorneys from advocating on behalf of their clients, to require them to be neutral between their own clients and others or to require them to disclose all that they know about their clients' interests and positions, many people would no doubt decide not to retain attorneys to help them in mediation.

Still, it is appropriate to place certain restraints on attorney and client advocacy and adversarial behavior in mediation, just as we have placed limits on such conduct in litigation. In litigation we require that attorneys and clients have an adequate basis for positions taken in pleadings, we require attorneys to disclose the existence of relevant binding precedent to a tribunal, and we limit attorneys' ability to lie on behalf of their clients. These and other constraints may be appropriate in the mediation context as well.

Nor does this endorsement of advocacy mean that attorneys are relegated to being mere "hired guns." A vast professional responsibility literature contains many works urging that attorneys do and should have their own sense of morality, and it is entirely appropriate for attorneys to attempt to convince their clients that a particular course of action is unwise or immoral. Acceptance of such a view does not require abandonment of the principle that attorneys should serve as advocates for their clients.

Yet, while attorneys may appropriately advocate for their clients in mediation, it is certainly true that those attorneys who attempt to employ traditional "zealous" litigation tools when representing their clients in mediation may frequently (but not always) fail either to fulfill their clients' wishes or to serve their clients' interests. Those who would hoard information, rely solely on legal rather than emotional arguments, or refuse to let their clients speak freely will often have little success in mediation. This is not because attorneys ought not to advocate for their clients, but rather because attorneys ought not to advocate *poorly* on behalf of their clients . . .

The distinction between whether attorneys may advocate on behalf of their clients in mediation and how they may do so is not merely semantic. Once it is recognized that advocacy is permitted the question becomes when and how attorneys should best represent their clients in mediation. Attorneys need much more specific guidance on how to behave in mediations than the simple edict "thou shalt not advocate" or the equally simple "thou shalt advocate."

# QUESTIONS

(1)   Is advocacy the same as adversarialness? If not, how do they differ? For an argument that lawyers should advocate for their clients by learning to work effectively with mediators, see James K.L. Lawrence, *Mediation Advocacy: Partnering with the Mediator*, 15 Ohio St. J. on Disp. Resol. 425 (2000).

(2)   Is adversarialness appropriate in mediation? Is attorney advocacy appropriate in mediation? Is advocating as a zealous problem-solver (Abramson) the same as conflict resolution advocacy (Macfarlane)?

(3)   Professor Abramson argues that shifting between adversarial and problem-solving approaches during mediation can undercut the problem-solving approach. Is his view consistent with Professor Sternlight's point that attorneys can be advocates for their clients without being adversarial?

(4)   Is an attorney who does not "advocate" for a client in mediation failing adequately to represent the client? Is such failure a violation of the attorney's ethical responsibilities?

(5)   Do we need a new set of ethics rules to cover the role of the attorney in mediation and other forms of ADR?

(6)   Is it feasible to have one set of ethics rules that govern litigation and another set that govern mediation or other forms of ADR, when these processes may take place simultaneously?

## WHAT'S A LAWYER TO DO IN MEDIATION?
### 18 Alternatives to the High Cost of Litigation 1 (July/Aug. 2000)[*]
### By Jean R. Sternlight

What are lawyers supposed to do when they represent their clients in mediation? Should they act the same way many do in a deposition or trial, where they instruct the client not to volunteer information, and to carefully follow the attorney's lead? At the other extreme, should an attorney who is representing a client in a mediation even bother attending? If he or she does attend, should he or she largely sit silently, and let the client do the talking and run the show? Lawyers around the country are answering these questions in very different ways. The differences appear to stem not only from variations in individual philosophy but also from the culture of the local litigation and ADR community.

. . . .

Drawing on the psychological phenomena and strategic issues that arise in the lawyer-client relationship, set forth below are a few well-grounded tips for counsel representing a client in mediation.

. . . .

Counsel should always keep in mind some of the basic insights offered by economists and psychologists who have studied the question of why disputes often fail to settle (or take a long time to settle), even where an early settlement is seemingly desirable for all. One key factor is the psychological differences in the way attorneys and clients view the world. Empirical studies have demonstrated that most people are affected by a series of phenomena that cause them to act in a less than an objective, reasoned manner when they attempt to resolve disputes. To provide a few examples, people tend to be over optimistic as to their chances of success; they are more willing to gamble regarding perceived losses than perceived gains; and they prefer settlements that appear to be "just."

Also influential is the different way an attorney dissects a dispute as compared to a client. Parties are frequently interested not merely in monetary outcomes but also in "venting," receiving or giving an apology, or achieving vengeance or publicity. Studies have shown that lawyers, as compared to their clients, tend to be far more objective in their settlement approach. Lawyers often focus on a settlement's bottom-line dollar value rather than process issues or surrounding emotional concerns.

These differences between lawyers and their clients can impede desirable settlements. Attorneys, rooted in their hyper-rational world, may not realize the importance of non-monetary benefits or processes such as venting or apologizing. They may think they are aiding their clients by pushing them to be objective, but the client might have preferred terms that appealed to his or her nonobjective, emotional wishes.

. . . .

When attorneys attempt to settle their clients' disputes without using mediation, the clients remain very much in the background. While the attorney is ethically required to obtain the client's approval for any settlement, the attorney typically negotiates the deal on her own, merely consulting the client occasionally. The client is not present for the negotiation and therefore doesn't hear firsthand what the other side's position is; to hear the other side's anger; to assess the arguments of the opposing attorney; to explain the importance of non-monetary relief; to voice his feelings; or to give or receive an apology.

By contrast, in a mediation the client potentially can do each of these things and more, thereby enabling a settlement that would not otherwise have been possible. Mediation can permit the client to communicate directly with the opposing party and its attorney, and eliminate the erroneous transmissions that inevitably occur when one person acts as the agent for another.

Usually mediation can serve this beneficial purpose only where clients are permitted to play an active role in the mediation. If a client, while attending the mediation, does not express his or her own views in his or her own voice, neither the client nor the opposing party will secure many of the mediation's potential benefits. Where the attorneys "take over" the mediation and silence their own clients, they remove one of the mediation's primary potential benefits and convert the mediation back into a negotiation among attorneys.

Thus, in many instances it will be wise for an attorney to permit the client to participate vigorously, both by giving an opening statement and by speaking freely in other parts of the mediation. This participation will help the clients on both sides to communicate more directly, and to avoid some of the problems caused by differences between clients and their attorneys. For similar reasons, it also often will be desirable to permit much of the mediation to occur as a joint session, rather than moving immediately to caucus.

. . . .

In preparing for a mediation an attorney should try to think about why the case has not already settled. What might be some of the barriers? Perhaps the opposing party is blocking settlement because it has unrealistic expectations due to a lack of factual or legal information, or maybe the opposing party has unmet non-monetary goals. Maybe it is the opposing party's attorney who is blocking settlement, based on the attorney's lack of information or unmet monetary or non-monetary goals. Many times an attorney may realize that it is his or her own client's unrealistic expectations or unmet monetary or non-monetary needs that are preventing agreement. Occasionally an attorney may even have the insight that it is his or her own concerns that are the problem.

Once an attorney begins to understand why the dispute is not settling, the attorney often can see that clients' active participation in mediation might prove helpful. For example, if the opposing party or opposing attorney is blocking settlement because either has unrealistically high expectations regarding how the facts will play at trial, a client may be well qualified to teach the opposing party that the case is not as strong as the opposing party thought. Where the client tells his or her story compellingly and convincingly in the mediation, the opposing client and attorney may learn their case is not as strong as they believed.

Similarly, where the opposing client has unmet non-monetary needs, it may be critical for an attorney to have his or her client participate actively. The client is far better suited than the attorney to provide a meaningful apology. Where the opposing party needs to "vent" his anger or concerns, he or she may need to do so against a live opposing client, and not merely an attorney. A client also may be better than the attorney at helping to think up creative "win/win" solutions based on the disputants' mutual needs and interests.

Turning to blockages due to a client's misperceptions, active client participation on both sides can be critical in bringing a dose of reality to the client. Finally, allowing a client to participate actively can alleviate stresses due to the client's perception that an attorney may be acting out of self interest. These few examples illustrate that clients' active participation can be critical.

. . . .

There are situations in which attorneys would do their clients a real disservice by failing to attend or failing to participate actively. For example, sometimes the parties' failure to settle a dispute may be attributable not to lack of emotional or informational exchange between the parties, but rather to one party's misguided view of the law. Here, the most useful mediation may be one in which the opposing attorney or mediator finds a way to educate the misguided client — or attorney — as to his likelihood of success. As well, some clients' basic personality or circumstances may be such that it is important for their attorney to play the role of protector. It would typically be unwise to design a family mediation to encourage active participation by both a perpetrator and a victim of domestic violence.

. . . .

In sum, while there is no single recipe for mediation success, insights drawn from economics, psychology and agency theory reveal that active client participation is often critical to achieve the full benefits of mediation. Attorneys who consistently dominate the mediation, treating it like just another deposition or trial, or even allow their clients not to attend, often are doing their clients a disservice. Instead, drawing on the tools offered by social science, attorneys should attempt to assess what steps they and their clients should take to overcome whatever barriers may exist to a desirable settlement. Often this analysis will reveal that attorneys should foster rather than inhibit active client participation in mediation.

## 20 COMMON ERRORS IN MEDIATION ADVOCACY
13 Alternatives to the High Cost of Litigation 69 (May 1995)*
By Tom Arnold

Trial lawyers who are unaccustomed to being mediation advocates often miss important arguments. Here are 20 common errors, and ways to correct them.

### Problem 1: Wrong client in the room

CEOs settle more cases than vice presidents, house counsel or other agents. Why? For one thing, they don't need to worry about criticism back at the office. Any lesser agent, even with explicit "authority," typically must please a constituency which was not a participant in the give and take of the mediation. That makes it hard to settle cases.

A client's personality also can be a factor. A "Rambo," who is aggressive, critical, unforgiving, or self-righteous doesn't tend to be conciliatory. The best peace-makers show creativity, and tolerance for the mistakes of others. Of course, it also helps to know the subject.

### Problem 2: Wrong lawyer in the room

Many capable trial lawyers are so confident that they can persuade a jury of anything (after all, they've done it before), that they discount the importance of preserving relationships, as well as the exorbitant costs and emotional drain of litigation. They can smell a "win" in the court room, and so approach mediation with a measure of ambivalence.

Transaction lawyers, in contrast, tend to be better mediation counsel. At a minimum, parties should look for sensitive, flexible, understanding people who will do their homework, no matter their job experience. Good preparation makes for more and better settlements. A lawyer who won't prepare is the wrong lawyer.

### Problem 3: Wrong mediator in the room

Some mediators are generous about lending their conference rooms but bring nothing to the table. Some of them determine their view of the case and urge the parties to accept that view without exploring likely win-win alternatives.

. . . .

Masters of the process can render valuable services whether or not they have substantive expertise. When do the parties need an expert? When they want an evaluative mediator, or someone who can cast meaningful lights and shadows on the merits of the case and alternative settlements.

It may not always be possible to know and evaluate a mediator and fit the choice of mediator to your case. But the wrong mediator may fail to get a settlement another mediator might have finessed.

### Problem 4: Wrong case

Almost every type of case, from antitrust or patent infringement to unfair competition and employment disputes, is a likely candidate for mediation. Occasionally, cases don't fit the mold, not because of the substance of the dispute, but because one or both parties want to set a precedent.

. . . .

### Problem 5: Omitting client preparation

Lawyers should educate their clients about the process. Clients need to know the answers to the types of questions the mediator is likely to ask. At the same time, they need to understand that the other party (rather than the mediator) should be the focus of each side's presentation.

In addition, lawyers should interview clients about the client's and the adversary's "best alternative to negotiated agreement," and "worst alternative to negotiated agreement," terms coined by William Ury and Roger Fisher in their book, *Getting to YES*. A party should accept any offer better than his perceived BATNA and reject any offer seen as worse than his perceived WATNA. So the

BATNAs and WATNAs are critical frames of reference for accepting offers and for determining what offers to propose to the other parties. A weak or false understanding of either party's BATNA or WATNA obstructs settlements and begets bad settlements.

Other topics to cover with the client:

— the difference between their interests and their legal positions; — the variety of options that might settle the case; — the strengths and weaknesses of their case; — objective independent standards of evaluation; — the importance of apology and empathy.

### Problem 6: Not letting a client open for herself

At least as often as not, letting the properly coached client do most, or even all, of the opening and tell the story in her own words works much better than lengthy openings by the lawyer.

To prepare for mediation, rehearse answers to the following questions, which the mediator is likely to ask:

— How do you feel about this dispute — Or about the other party? — What do you really want in the resolution of this dispute? — What are your expectations from a trial? Are they realistic? — What are the weaknesses in your case?

— What law or fact in your case would you like to change? — What scares you most?

— What would it feel like to be in your adversary's shoes?

— What specific evidence do you have to support each element of your case? — What will the jury charge and interrogatories probably be? — What is the probability of a verdict your way on liability? — What is the range of damages you think a jury would return in this case if it found liability?

— What are the likely settlement structures, from among the following possibilities: Terms, dollars, injunction, services, performance, product, recision [sic], apology, costs, attorney fees, releases.

— What constituency pressures burden the other party? Which ones burden you?

### Problem 7: Addressing the mediator instead of the other side

Most lawyers open the mediation with a statement directed at the mediator, comparable to opening statements to a judge or jury. Highly adversarial in tone, it overlooks the interests of the other side that gave rise to the dispute.

Why is this strategy a mistake? The "judge or jury" you should be trying to persuade in a mediation is not the mediator, but the adversary. If you want to make the other party sympathetic to your cause, don't hurt him.

For the same reason, plenary sessions should demonstrate your client's humanity, respect, warmth, apologies and sympathy. Stay away from inflammatory issues, which are better addressed by the mediator in private caucuses with the other side.

### Problem 8: Making the lawyer the center of the process

Unless the client is highly unappealing or inarticulate, the client should be the center of the process. The company representative for the other side may not have attended depositions, so is unaware of the impact your client could have on a judge or jury if the mediation fails. People pay more attention to appealing plaintiffs, so show them off.

Prepare the client to speak and be spoken to by the mediator and the adversary. He should be able to explain why he feels the way he does, why he is or is not responsible, and why any damages he *caused* are great or only peanuts. But he should also extend empathy to the other party.

### Problem 9: Failure to use advocacy tools effectively

You'll want to prepare your materials for maximum persuasive impact. Exhibits, charts, and copies of relevant cases or contracts with key phrases highlighted can be valuable visual aids. A 90-second video showing key witnesses in depositions making important admissions, followed by a readable size copy of an important document with some relevant language underlined, can pack a punch.

### Problem 10: Timing mistakes

Get and give critical discovery, but don't spend exorbitant time or sums in discovery and trial prep before seeking mediation.

Mediation can identify what's truly necessary discovery and avoid unnecessary discovery. One of my own war stories: With a mediation under way and both parties relying on their perception of the views of a certain vice president, I leaned over, picked up the phone, called the vice president, introduced myself as the mediator, and asked whether he could give us a deposition the following morning. "No," said he, "I've got a Board meeting at 10:00."

"How about 7:30 a.m., with a one-hour limit?" I asked. "It really is pretty important that this decision not be delayed." The parties took the deposition and settled the case before the 10:00 board meeting.

### Problem 11: Failure to listen to the other side

Many lawyers and clients seem incapable of giving open-minded attention to what the other side is saying. That could cost a settlement.

### Problem 12: Failure to identify perceptions and motivations

Seek first to understand, only then to be understood. Messrs. Fisher and Ury suggest you brainstorm to determine the other party's motivations and perceptions. Prepare a chart summarizing how your adversary sees the issues . . . .

### Problem 13: Hurting, humiliating, threatening, or commanding

Don't poison the well from which you must drink to get a settlement. That means you don't hurt, humiliate or ridicule the other folks. Avoid pejoratives like "malingerer," "fraud," "cheat," "crook," or "liar." You can be strong on what your evidence will be and still be a decent human being.

All settlements are based upon trust to some degree. If you anger the other side, they won't trust you. This inhibits settlement.

The same can be said for threats, like a threat to get the other lawyer's license revoked for pursuing such a frivolous cause, or for his grossly inaccurate pleadings.

Ultimatums destroy the process, and destroy credibility. Yes, there is a time in mediation to walk out — whether or not you plan to return. But a series of ultimatums, or even one ultimatum, most often is very counterproductive.

### Problem 14: The backwards step

A party who offered to pay $300,000 before the mediation, and comes to the mediation table willing to offer only $200,000, injures its own credibility and engenders bad feelings from the other side. Without some clear and dramatic reasons for the reduction in the offer, it can be hard to overcome the damage done.

### Problem 15: Too many people

Advisors — people to whom the decision-maker must display respect and courtesy, people who feel that since they are there they must put in their two bits worth — all delay a mediation immeasurably. A caucus that with only one lawyer and vice president would take 20 minutes, with five people could take an hour and 20 minutes. What could have been a one-day mediation stretches to two or three.

This is one context in which I use the "one-martini lunch." Once I think that everyone present understands all the issues, I will send principals who have been respectful out to negotiate alone. Most come back with an expression of oral settlement within three hours. Of course, the next step is to brush up on details they overlooked, draw up a written agreement and get it signed. But usually those finishing touches don't ruin the deal.

### Problem 16: Closing too fast

A party who opens at $1 million, and moves immediately to $500,000, gives the impression of having more to give. Rightly or wrongly, the other side probably will not accept the $500,000 offer because they expect more give.

The "dance" is part of communication. Skip the dance, lose the communication, and risk losing settlement at your own figure.

Problem 17: Failure to truly close

Unless parties have strong reasons to "sleep on" their agreement, to further evaluate the deal, or to check on possibly forgotten details, it is better to get some sort of enforceable contract written and signed before the parties separate. Too often, when left to think overnight and draft tomorrow, the parties think of new ideas that delay or prevent closing.

Problem 18: Breaching a confidentiality

Sometimes parties to a mediation unthinkingly, or irresponsibly, disclose in open court information revealed confidentially in a mediation.

When information is highly sensitive, consider keeping it confidential with the mediator. Or if revealed to the adversary in a mediation where the case did not settle, consider moving before the trial begins for an order in limine to bind both sides to the confidentiality agreement.

Problem 19: Lack of patience and perseverance

The mediation "dance" takes time. Good mediation advocates have patience and perseverance.

Problem 20: Misunderstanding conflict

A dispute is a problem to be solved together, not a combat to be won.

# MEDIATION ADVOCACY:
## THE ROLE OF LAWYERS IN MEDIATION
### American Bar Association (forthcoming)*
### By Dwight Golann

This book is intended for lawyers who represent parties in mediation. It explains how attorneys can use the structure of the process and the special powers of mediators to achieve their bargaining goals.

. . .

The key lesson is not to approach the process passively, but instead to use the mediation process in an active way to advance your clients' interests. Based on the author's experience as a mediator with attorneys from Europe, Asia and North America, this book offers suggestions about how a lawyer can "borrow" a mediator's powers to achieve an optimal outcome.

. . . .

Influence the Process

---

* Reprinted with permission.

(a) Manage the flow of information

*(1) Focus discussion on specific issues*

One important skill of a good negotiator is the ability to influence how issues are discussed. To accomplish this lawyers can tell a mediator what they want stressed to an opponent, and in what manner.

. . . .

Assume, for instance, that your client is outraged at the other side's alleged fraud. You see the evidence as weak but your client refuses to abandon the fraud claim; even discussing the issue makes him angry. You might make a pre-mediation call to the mediator, alerting her that discussing this claim will inflame your client and frustrate progress on other issues. You could ask her to discourage the other side from discussing the fraud issue until later in the day, when your client may be calmer.

*(2) Gather and convey information*

. . . .

*Gathering data.* Parties are usually more willing to provide information in mediation than in negotiation. They know that they are likely to achieve a settlement through mediation, and therefore can expect to get something in return. They are also likely to trust the mediator to protect them from being exploited. . . .

Information problems arise most often between opposing parties, but this is not always the case; lawyers sometimes have difficulty getting data from their own client, for example because someone in the organization feels that they may be blamed for the problem. Co-defendants also sometimes hide data from each other in an effort to minimize their share of responsibility for a loss. Mediators can sometimes help an attorney persuade his own client to provide data, or one defendant to share information with another.

*Conveying information.* It is also possible to use mediation to convey data more effectively. Suppose, for example, you have strong evidence that an opposing witness is lying, but are concerned that if you raise the issue directly with your opponent he will become angry. One option is to give the evidence to the mediator and ask him to discuss it with the other party. Evidence presented in this way is less apt to be summarily rejected, and even if the information has no impact on the other side, the fact that you provide it will focus the mediator's attention on the issue.

Another form of information concerns a party's bargaining intentions. Imagine, for instance, that a plaintiff has decided to make its final offer. It is concerned, however, that its opponent will take offense, feeling that the offer amounts to an ultimatum. The attorney may be able to convey the offer more effectively through a mediator ("Tell them we've thought it over and 900 is our last and final offer.") At a minimum the mediator can cushion the message, making it less likely the other side will react with anger ("They agreed to make one more concession — they say they've gone as far as they can go . . . .") If the neutral believes that the offer is truly final she can say so, assuring the recipient that it is not merely a bluff ("I've been talking to them for hours. You can never be sure, but my sense is they really can't go below 900.")

### (3) Probe an opponent's state of mind

Advocates can also ask a mediator about the other side's state of mind. If, for example, a party seems agitated during the opening session, the opposing attorney might later ask the mediator, "Has he calmed down yet?" A lawyer could also inquire about the other side's decisionmaking process . . .

Questions to a mediator about what the other side is thinking pose ethical and practical issues for the neutral, because a mediator has two somewhat contradictory roles: She must preserve the confidentiality of what each side says, and at the same time facilitate communication between them. But the fact that a question is difficult for a neutral to answer does not mean a lawyer should not ask it.

Be aware, however, that if you ask a mediator for information about your opponent, the neutral is likely to feel that she has permission to give the other side the same kind of data about you. If you are concerned that information may "leak" to the other caucus room, discuss with your mediator what he will say to the other side about your side.

. . . .

### (4) Use confidentiality to manage the flow of data

Mediation is . . . a confidential process. For purposes of advocacy it is important to realize that confidentiality is not only a cloak that can protect you, but also a tool to make bargaining more effective. One way to accomplish this is to give the mediator information and either bar him from disclosing it . . . or permit disclosure only under conditions.

*Give information to the mediator alone.* The most common tactic is to describe evidence to a mediator but forbid her from disclosing it to one's opponent. In this way a lawyer can reveal evidence to persuade a mediator of the strength of his legal case without revealing the information to the other side . . .

. . . [T]he fact that you forbid a mediator from disclosing information at one point in the process does not prevent you from authorizing the mediator to reveal it later. Lawyers sometimes allow information to be disclosed on conditions ("You can show them the affidavit, but only if you think it will tie down a deal").

*Disclose information to an opponent, subject to confidentiality.* Advocates can also authorize evidence to be given to an opponent, but use the special confidentiality rules that apply to mediation to limit how the data can be used if the case does not settle.

. . . .

*Authorize partial disclosure.* Most lawyers expect a mediator to reveal at least some of what occurs in private caucus discussions. Experienced attorneys know, in other words, that while mediators will not reveal sensitive data, they will usually feel authorized to go beyond simply repeating what a party has said . . .

You can ask a mediator to convey an interpretation of your position, presenting it as his assessment of the situation and not attributing his comments specifically to you. Communicating intentions in this way has two advantages. First, the listener is left somewhat unsure about whether you have sent the signal, giving you the freedom either to reinforce it or back away . . . . Second, the fact that it is the mediator who offers the interpretation makes it appear less manipulative, and therefore less subject to devaluation by the recipient, than if you had sent the signal directly.

b. Influence the Bargaining Process

Advocates can also use mediation to improve their effectiveness in the give-and-take of bargaining.

. . . .

*(1) Support a competitive bargaining strategy*

. . . [Mediation] allows negotiators to use tougher tactics than they could apply in a direct negotiation. . . . [W]hile parties can break off negotiations and resume them later, most parties believe that if mediation fails they are unlikely to be able to resume the process. As a result participants in mediation are reluctant to walk out even when their opponent makes an "insulting" offer.

. . . [T]he mediator is present to cushion the impact of abrasive bargaining tactics, by calming a party who is angry at what an opponent has done. . . .

*(2) Explore hidden issues and creative options*

Mediators can also be used to help identify non-legal issues and support creative approaches to bargaining . . . . Mediation allows lawyers to have it both ways: they can press their legal arguments and push for the best possible monetary deal, while simultaneously asking their mediator to explore the parties' underlying interests and creative settlement terms. The effect is to have bargaining take place on two levels, one involving an exchange of money and another the parties' other priorities.
. . .

*(3) Obtain advice about tactics*

Mediators typically spend hours talking with the parties, which gives them a unique perspective on each side's bargaining style and settlement priorities. By using a mediator as a bargaining consultant lawyers can tap into this information.

. . . .

*(4) Enhance your offers*

*Authorship.* Experienced lawyers instinctively understand "reactive devaluation" — the concept that any offer by an opponent is viewed with suspicion, but the same proposal made by a neutral mediator is likely to be given respectful consideration. To take advantage of this, good attorneys sometimes seek to convince a mediator to "adopt" their offer as the mediator's own, or at least to endorse the lawyer offer as reasonable.

. . . .

*Endorsement.* If you cannot persuade a mediator to take ownership of a proposal, another alternative is to ask him to endorse it. You could, for example, ask the neutral to tell your opponent that he sees your latest offer as "a reasonable step forward." Alternatively you might offer to make a larger concession if the mediator will endorse its reasonableness and ask the other side to reciprocate ("If I could convince my client to go to 'X,' would you be willing to tell the plaintiff you think it is a significant step and ask them to go to "Y'?")

. . . .

### (5) Take advantage of a mediator's flexibility

Mediators do not need to worry about maintaining a judge's dignity or showing a litigator's toughness. As a result they have more freedom to take unusual steps to achieve a settlement. Mediators do not always know, however, what obstacles are blocking a settlement. When advocates encounter hidden barriers to agreement, they should inform the mediator, and if necessary prod the neutral to take on unusual roles ranging from "ambassador" to "scapegoat."

. . . .

### c. Overcome blockages

A mediator can also help resolve impasses . . .

### (1) Restart the bargaining

A mediator's most important quality when faced with a bargaining impasse is simple determination — the willingness to push on. The right mediator will show this quality in the face of discouragement. . . . Apart from pure determination, mediators can apply a variety of techniques when parties fall into impasse.

. . . .

*What if?* ("What if I could get them to go to one million?") is an attractive tactic for a mediator, because it encourages parties to think of compromise and at the same time gives the mediator new information. . . . If a mediator poses what-if questions:

First decide whether you want the mediator to use the technique at all.

If so, take the initiative to suggest a number favorable to you ("If you can get them to 1.5 we'll be open to moving . . .")

If the mediator puts forth a number, consider bargaining over it ("1.2 million won't do it. They'd have to go to at least 1.5").

Alternatively, you can probe the mediator about how confident is he that the other side will move — in other words, how hypothetical is the what-if number?

*Change in format.* Faced with an impasse a mediator might declare a temporary recess, adjourn to another day or "hold the parties' feet to the fire" by asking them to remain late into the evening . . . . Alternatively a mediator can change the mix of personalities in the discussion, for example by putting people from each side together (CEO with CEO, etc).

The issue for an advocate to consider is: What is the best process option for my client at this point? Is it to adjourn or press on? Remain separated in caucuses or meet together? If so, who should meet? Advocate for the option you think will most benefit your client, whether or not the mediator has suggested it. If you do not think a tactic will be helpful, make that clear to the mediator as well.

*Estimate the size of the gap.* If parties are stalled because they have taken unrealistic bargaining positions, a mediator can attempt to estimate the real gap through a process called "confidential listener." A mediator using this technique would say something like this:

"Your offers are a million euros apart, but I think you are in fact considerably closer than that. Let's try this. I will ask each of you to give me what I will call your 'next-to-last number' — an offer one step away from the farthest you would go to settle this case. "I won't reveal either side's number to the other side. Instead I will call the lawyers together and give them a verbal assessment of the difference between you — an estimate that does not lock anyone in. I'll be back in a few minutes to ask for your number."

If the parties agree to the process, on hearing their numbers the mediator might say for example: "You are closer than the cost of litigating this case, so it is worth continuing to talk" or "You are very far apart. Unless someone changes their view of what the case is worth in court, it will be hard for you to agree."

. . . [M]ediators usually do not expect this tactic to settle a case. Instead the goal is to give the parties a better estimate of the real gap between them. What should you tell a mediator playing confidential listener? You will usually want to give a number that is optimistic enough to set up a favorable compromise, but reasonable enough to motivate the other side to continue.

. . . .

One option is to ask the mediator for a candid assessment about what you must do to keep the process going, but you should do this only if you trust the neutral, since it is in a mediator's interest for each party to make a large concession.

*(2) Educate an unrealistic opponent — or client*

Parties may also fall into impasse because one or both is not realistic about the strength of their case. . . .

A mediator can deliver bad news — that a case is not as good as the party thinks it is, or even as the lawyer may have suggested in the past. By having the mediator take on the role of "devil's advocate," attorneys can continue to act as the client's champion, sometimes even arguing against a mediator who they know is correct.

. . . .

*Should you get an evaluation?* In dealing with the issue of mediator evaluation, your first challenge is again to decide whether you want one at all. Ask yourself two questions:

- Is the primary obstacle to settling the case a disagreement about the legal merits? Or is the real problem high emotion, lawyer-client disagreements, or something else? If the problem is not legal in nature then evaluation will be useless.

- If the mediator does evaluate, are you confident that it will be helpful? If you are not sure, consider sounding the neutral out privately before he issues an opinion.

Once you have decided to seek an evaluation, the next issue is how to structure the process. The questions to ask are similar to those a mediator must consider, but there are differences that flow from your roles: The mediator is focused on breaking a deadlock, while you want to end the deadlock but also achieve the best possible outcome.

. . . .

*What should be evaluated?* . . . The purpose of a mediator's evaluation . . . is . . . to break a bargaining impasse. If one thinks of an impasse as the bargaining equivalent of driving into a ditch, a mediator's evaluation would be like a truck that pulls the car back onto the road, but not to its final destination. An evaluative "tow" should therefore be as brief as possible. If disagreement on a particular issue is driving the impasse then evaluation of that issue alone is probably enough to put the parties back on the road to settlement.

The question then is: What aspect of the case do you wish evaluated? The answer lies in your diagnosis of what is causing the impasse. It may be, for example, that the disagreement turns on an argument that a lawyer knows she will lose but has made to humor a client. If you are raising an issue for a reason other than the legal merits, you will not normally want to have the issue evaluated and should make that clear to the neutral.

*How specific an opinion?* Good mediators see evaluation as a spectrum of interventions rather than a single event. They rely on their tone of voice and choice of words to convey thoughts as often as explicit statements. You are likely to know better than the mediator what level of specificity and emphasis your client needs at a certain point in the process. If, for instance, the client is not ready to hear the complete truth, ask the mediator to be diplomatic and perhaps avoid certain issues. Alternatively, some litigants may need to be hit with the mediation equivalent of a club; if so, tell the mediator. . . .

*What data should the mediator see?* . . .

Take care to insure that the mediator fully considers your key evidence before arriving at a conclusion. A mediator may not read every document that was sent to her by the parties; mediators often receive thick piles of documents in advance of mediation and cannot predict what will prove important as the case proceeds. Busy mediators skim through voluminous materials, waiting for the mediation process to tell them what is important. Mediators are also reluctant to take recesses in middle of a mediation to read long documents for fear of losing momentum.

Organize the evidence you give to a mediator much as you would for a judge. If you have important documents or decisions, bring copies to the mediation and highlight the key language. . . . If a neutral is assisted she is less likely to jump to a bad conclusion.

. . . .

### (3) Prompt a decision

When the bargaining process has ended and cannot be revived, it may still be possible to obtain agreement through a "last and final" offer. . . .

*Last-and-final offer by a party.* If either party issues a last-and-final offer it runs the risk that the other will reject it, either out of anger at being "pushed around" or simple devaluation. You can avoid some of the negative reactions to such an offer by asking a mediator to communicate it.

Ask the mediator to explain that you honestly believe that the offer is reasonable . . . .Suggest that the mediator emphasize to the other side that the offer came only after the neutral had pushed you hard to go as far as possible — in other words the offer is not an ultimatum from you, but rather a response to an ultimatum from the mediator.

Let the mediator set the deadline for consideration of your offer.

*Mediator proposal.* Another option is to allow the neutral to make a "mediator's proposal" to both sides. In doing so,

- The mediator suggests specific settlement terms.

- Each litigant must tell the mediator privately whether it can agree to the proposal, assuming the other side agrees to it.

- The terms must be accepted unconditionally; parties cannot "nibble" by changing some terms and then accepting. . . .

- Each side must answer without knowing the other's reply.

- If one party rejects the proposal it will never be told whether its opponent would have accepted it.

Mediator proposals have the disadvantage that the neutral, rather than the parties, decides on the terms of settlement. On the other hand such proposals give parties the ability to achieve complete peace with a single concession. They also have the assurance that if the effort fails, the other side will never know they were willing to compromise. A mediator's proposal also relieves parties of the "water torture" of making one concession after another without knowing whether any move will bring a resolution, and with the fear that their reasonableness will be exploited by their opponent.

Finally, mediator proposals allow parties to place the responsibility for a difficult compromise on an outsider ("This wasn't our idea, it was the mediator's!"), again using the mediator as a scapegoat. In the author's experience mediator proposals are successful at least two-thirds of the time.

. . . .

### (4) Demand further efforts

Suppose that your case does not settle at a mediation session. A good mediator will contact the parties afterward to attempt to pursue the settlement process. Some neutrals, however, do not take the initiative to do this, either because they do not think it appropriate or because they are distracted by other cases. If your client would benefit from a further effort at settlement and your mediator does not take the lead, prod him to do so.

. . . .

Sometimes settlement is unachievable despite a mediator's best efforts. Even then a mediator can be of use by helping counsel work out a more efficient process of adjudication. The mediator might, for example, facilitate negotiations to set up an efficient litigation plan or arbitration process. . . .

### In conclusion

Mediation is an active process which is capable of almost infinite variation. Good lawyers know that a mediator can help them bargain more effectively and take the initiative to ask a mediator for help.

By doing so, they are able to achieve better outcomes for their clients.

## NOTES AND QUESTIONS

(1) Several books focus explicitly on how lawyers should represent their clients in mediation. *See* Harold I. Abramson, *Mediation Representation: Advocating as a Problem-Solver* (2012); Eric Galton, *Representing Clients in Mediation* (1994); and John W. Cooley, *Mediation Advocacy* (1996). For useful articles, see Harold Abramson, *Problem-Solving Advocacy in Mediation: A Model of Client Representation*, 10 Harv. Neg. L. Rev. 103 (2005); James K. L. Lawrence, *Mediation Advocacy: Partnering with the Mediator*, 15 Ohio St. J. on Disp. Resol. 425 (2000); Lawrence M. Watson, Jr., *Effective Advocacy in Mediation: A Planning Guide to Prepare for a Civil Trial Mediation*, http://www.uww-adr.com/wp-content/uploads/pdfs/effectiveadvocacy.pdf. For a thoughtful article discussing mediation advocacy on behalf of parents in the context of dependency mediation, see Debra Ratterman Baker, *Dependency Mediation: Strategies for Parents' Attorneys*, 18 A.B.A. Child L. Prac. 124 (1999).

(2)    How do you believe lawyers and their clients should divide responsibilities in a mediation? If you believe the determination should vary from case to case, what factors do you believe are important to consider?

(3)    What are some of the "barriers" that might preclude opposing parties from reaching a settlement? How might mediation help overcome each of these barriers?

(4)    Do you believe that the degree of participation of lawyer or client in a mediation has any impact on whether the mediation ultimately results in a settlement? Why or why not? As between the attorney and the client, who should decide on their respective degrees of participation in a mediation? Are ethical rules relevant to the consideration of this question?

(5)    In his article, Professor Golann states that, "Even if a mediator proposal fails, it is not the end of the process. Good neutrals simply keep going ('If you won't take that, what would you take?' or 'What data would you have to see in order to change your mind?')." As an attorney, how would you feel about the mediation continuing after the mediator has made a proposal which is not favorable to your client? How does this suggestion comport to your understanding of mediator neutrality?

## 4.    What Ethical Constraints Apply to Lawyers in Mediation?

In Chapter 2, you considered the rules of professional conduct that govern lawyers' behavior in negotiation. In this section, we explore the ethical rules governing negotiation in the context of mediation. Existing ethical rules restrain lawyers from lying in litigation, arbitration, or negotiation. ABA Model Rule 3.3 prohibits a lawyer, *inter alia*, from knowingly "mak[ing] a false statement of material fact or law to a tribunal" or "fail[ing] to disclose a material fact to a tribunal when disclosure is necessary to avoid assisting a criminal or fraudulent act by the client," or "fail[ing] to disclose to the tribunal legal authority in the controlling jurisdiction known to the lawyer to be directly adverse to the position of the client and not disclosed by opposing counsel." ABA Model Rule 1.0(m) defines the term "tribunal" to include arbitrators who issue binding awards, as well as courts. ABA Model Rule 4.1 prohibits a lawyer, in the course of representation, from "mak[ing] a false statement of material fact or law" or "fail[ing] to disclose a material fact to a third party when disclosure is necessary to avoid assisting a criminal or fraudulent act . . ." However, the Official Comment notes that, under generally accepted negotiation conventions, statements as to price, value or a party's intentions regarding settlement would not typically be regarded as statements of material fact.

Two important excerpts on this topic appear below. In 2006, the American Bar Association issued a formal opinion stating that the dictates of Rule 4.1 (and not the higher standard of Rule 3.3) apply to mediation. Previously, Professor James Alfini had argued that there is a need to revise Rule 4.1 to create a more suitable ethics infrastructure to support mediation and other ADR proceedings. Do you think a revision to Rule 4.1 is necessary? If so, do you think the practicing bar would find Professor Alfini's revision acceptable? Why or why not?

## Formal Opinion 06-439, April 12, 2006

Lawyer's Obligation of Truthfulness When Representing a Client in Negotiation: Application to Caucused Mediation

. . .

In this opinion, we discuss the obligation of a lawyer to be truthful when making statements on behalf of clients in negotiations, including the specialized form of negotiation known as caucused mediation.

. . . [T]he ethical principles governing lawyer truthfulness do not permit a distinction to be drawn between the caucused mediation context and other negotiation settings. The Model Rules do not require a higher standard of truthfulness in any particular negotiation contexts. Except for Rule 3.3, which is applicable only to statements before a "tribunal," the ethical prohibitions against lawyer misrepresentations apply equally in all environments. Nor is a lower standard of truthfulness warranted because of the consensual nature of mediation. Parties otherwise protected against lawyer misrepresentation by Rule 4.1 are not permitted to waive that protection, whether explicitly through informed consent, or implicitly by agreeing to engage in a process in which it is somehow "understood" that false statements will be made. Thus, the same standards that apply to lawyers engaged in negotiations must apply to them in the context of caucused mediation. . . . We emphasize that, whether in a direct negotiation or in a caucused mediation, care must be taken by the lawyer to ensure that communications regarding the client's position, which otherwise would not be considered statements "of fact," are not conveyed in language that converts them, even inadvertently, into false factual representations. For example, even though a client's Board of Directors has authorized a higher settlement figure, a lawyer may state in a negotiation that the client does not wish to settle for more than $50. However, it would not be permissible for the lawyer to state that the Board of Directors had formally disapproved any settlement in excess of $50, when authority had in fact been granted to settle for a higher sum.

### Conclusion

Under Model Rule 4.1, in the context of a negotiation, including a caucused mediation, a lawyer representing a party may not make a false statement of material fact to a third person. However, statements regarding a party's negotiating goals or its willingness to compromise, as well as statements that can fairly be characterized as negotiation "puffing," are ordinarily not considered "false statements of material fact" within the meaning of the Model Rules.

# SETTLEMENT ETHICS AND LAWYERING IN ADR PROCEEDINGS: A PROPOSAL TO REVISE RULE 4.1
## 19 N. Ill. U. L. Rev. 255, 270–71 (1999)*
### By James Alfini

## RULE 4.1 TRUTHFULNESS IN STATEMENTS TO OTHERS
### [Alfini Proposal]

**In the course of representing a client a lawyer shall not knowingly: (a) make a false statement of material fact or law to a third person; or**

**(b) assist the client in reaching a settlement agreement that is based on reliance upon a false statement of fact made by the lawyer's client; or**

**(b) (c) fail to disclose a material fact to a third person when disclosure is necessary to avoid assisting a criminal or fraudulent act by a client, unless disclosure is prohibited by Rule 1.6.**

### Comment

### Misrepresentation

[1] A lawyer is required to be truthful when dealing with others on a client's behalf, but generally has no affirmative duty to inform an opposing party of relevant facts. A misrepresentation can occur if the lawyer incorporates or affirms a statement of another person that the lawyer knows is false. Misrepresentations can also occur by failure to act.

### Statements of Fact

[2] This Rule refers to statements of fact. Whether a particular statement should be regarded as one of fact can depend on the circumstances. Under generally accepted conventions in negotiation, certain types of statements ordinarily are not taken as statements of material fact. Estimates of price or value placed on the subject of a transaction and a party's intentions as to an acceptable settlement of a claim are in this category, and so is the existence of an undisclosed principal except where nondisclosure of the principal would constitute fraud.

### Alternative Dispute Resolution

[2] A lawyer's duty of truthfulness applies beyond formal tribunals (see Rule 3.3) to less formal settings. The obligation to be truthful is particularly essential with the increased use by courts of dispute resolution alternatives such as mediation, arbitration, mini-trial, and summary jury trial to effect settlement. When representing a client in these less formal settings, the lawyer may often encounter situations where both the lawyer and his or her client participate freely in open and frank discussions unconstrained by rules of evidence or procedure. The lawyer should therefore inform the client of the lawyer's duty to be truthful and the lawyer's inability to assist the client in reaching a settlement agreement that is procured in whole or

in part as a result of a false statement of material fact or law made by the client.

### Fraud by Client

[3] Paragraph (b) recognizes that substantive law may require a lawyer to disclose certain information to avoid being deemed to have assisted the client's crime or fraud. The requirement of disclosure created by this paragraph is, however, subject to the obligations created by Rule 1.6.

## NOTES AND QUESTIONS

(1)   In his thoughtful article, *Telling the Truth in Mediation: Mediator Owed Duty of Candor*, Disp. Resol. Magazine, Winter 1997, at 17, Bruce E. Meyerson quotes a prominent mediator: "Don't believe anything a lawyer will tell you during a mediation!" Meyerson goes on to argue for a higher standard of truth-telling in the mediation setting. Do you think it is feasible to have one standard of truth-telling in mediation, another in negotiation, and still another in court?

(2)   In *In re Fee*, 898 P.2d 975, 980 (Ariz. 1995), the Arizona Supreme Court held that attorneys violated their duty of candor to a tribunal by failing to disclose their complete fee agreement to a judge acting as settlement judge or mediator. If the mediator had not been a judge, should the case have been decided differently?

# Chapter 11

# CAREER DIRECTIONS IN MEDIATION

## A.  INTRODUCTION

For more than four decades, mediation has been used as a forum to resolve a broad range of interpersonal and business controversies as well as some of the most serious policy and social challenges of our times. Some mediation initiatives were experimental only; others have led to its sustained use. This history raises the following two considerations: (1) do career opportunities exist for persons who want to devote their professional lives to mediating? and (2) is mediation's use, and the need for mediators, likely to continue?

## B.  CAREERS IN MEDIATION

If someone is interested in working as a mediator as one's profession, it is possible to do it.

The development route, however, is not a straight line. As is true for shaping and advancing any career, an individual who wants to become a mediator must be persistent, dedicated, resourceful, optimistic, and patient. She must be attentive to possibilities, not constrained by "labels," and careful not to overpromise results.

In Section 1, we identify the range of substantive areas in which the use of mediation has been sustained. Section II contains interview excerpts with successful, practicing mediators who discuss how their mediation careers emerged and the challenges and rewards they find in it. We describe in Section III the general strategies one can pursue in developing a full-time career working as a mediator.

### 1.  Substantive Practice Areas: The Range of Possibilities

The substantive domain of possible mediation service is remarkable. In summary fashion, we highlight below the more salient activity arena. Not all command comparable financial remuneration; not all provide daily work. But all are areas in which mediators are regularly used, so the creative practitioner who is building or sustaining her practice should explore how to participate in multiple, related activities.

Some of these areas were referenced in Chapter 1 when discussing mediation activities during "The Foundational Years"; others have emerged more recently. In some areas, court systems serve as the intersection point for party engagement, and court personnel refer such cases to mediators; in other settings, companies, social service organizations, professional organizations, or entities such as condominium complexes develop their own mediation programs and, in appropriate instances, refer their disputing parties to a mediator; and in some contexts, disputing parties themselves invite or accept mediator assistance. And, to encourage those early in their professional careers, remember that almost none of these areas of mediation practice existed 30 years ago.

### a. Small Claims Mediation and Neighborhood Justice Center Programs

This label is a shorthand reference for those disputes, typically filed or about to be filed in a civil or criminal court system, that involve limited financial demands and, often, multiple interpersonal dynamics. Some state court systems officially create a "small claims courts" in which disputants can appear without counsel and present their cases to a judge for decision; some states or cities have developed other specialty courts, such as housing courts, for handling related conflicts. When the disputants arrive at the pretrial conference in these settings, they are encouraged (or sometimes required) to attend a mediation conference offered through that court to attempt to settle their dispute. If they resolve it through mediation the settlement is treated in the same manner as a court judgment. Neighborhood justice center complaints emerge along a different track; a complaining neighbor typically files her claims with a clerk in a prosecutor's office, and the prosecutor and court divert the case to mediation. Parties routinely appear and participate in each of these mediation settings without lawyer representation.

These disputes cover multiple topics: alleged breach of contract for failure to make timely payments on a "rent-to-own" furniture contract; alleged theft of company property by a terminated employee; landlord claims for alleged rental arrears or tenant claims for a non-refunded security deposit; or alleged failure by one tenant against a co-tenant to pay "agreed-upon shared" expenses, such as utility or internet service billings. In the neighborhood justice domain, these financial claims are often blended with such interpersonal dynamics as failed romantic relationships or disruptive, harassing or threatening conduct.

A person who mediates these cases generally performs on a volunteer basis. For many practitioners, mediating these cases constitutes the most viable, initial source for gaining robust mediation experience.

### b. Family Mediation

Our family court system, though distinctive in each state, constitutes a forum that is pressed to serve a remarkable range of family dynamics and challenges. Not surprisingly, family court personnel have been pro-active in developing innovative programs — including the provision of mediation services — to serve parties in need.

The demand is broad-based: married couples seeking a divorce; divorced couples seeking to revise parenting or financial arrangements; a divorced parent accusing the other of being unfit to parent, due to drug, alcohol, or mental health problems; parents who have lost patience with their child who systematically disobeys their parentally imposed curfew or fails to attend school regularly and are soliciting legal assistance to get their child to obey; child protective service agencies, in their effort to protect the well-being of a family member as well as, to the extent possible, preserve the family unit, petitioning family courts to establish appropriate living arrangements for children feared to be victims of parental neglect or abuse. For each of these areas, and others, mediators provide service.

### c.  "Civil Law Cases"

This "catch-all" category references the broad range of potential lawsuits that could be filed in a civil court, whether at the state or federal level. Typically, under a relevant court rule, parties must first try to resolve their dispute through mediation. This area is currently the largest public source of compensated, sustained mediating case activity. As noted in Section 2 below, many persons — almost all law-trained — who are full-time mediation practitioners today develop their professional practice by mediating these types of cases. Most successful mediators develop a professional reputation as a specialist in a targeted substantive area.

We highlight below six categories of legal claims to illustrate the potential range of cases for mediator service and to indicate those substantive legal areas in which mediation service has been particularly effective.

*1. Personal Injury Disputes.* These cases capture multiple tort actions, including the "slip and fall" injury that a grocery-store customer sustained when she slipped on a wet floor that the store owner's employee had recently mopped; the pedestrian injured by a car driver who had proceeded through an intersection against a red light; or the interested bystander at a construction site who is injured by flying debris that was accidentally dropped by project employees working on an elevated platform. While many lawyer advocates describe these legal claims as "routine," everyone involved in resolving them appreciates the complexity of the parties' feelings and judgments; thoughtful, supportive mediators effectively help parties navigate increased understanding of each person's perspective and the resolution of relevant claims.

But the PI dispute also captures the complex catastrophic tort action. These actions characteristically involve the fatal loss of a loved one, cutting short a future full of hope. Consider the following: an 18-year-old high school senior who had compiled a perfect academic record, excelled in athletics, held leadership positions in student government, participated actively and without fanfare in various religious and community service activities, and gained admittance to attend a prestigious college to pursue his dream of becoming a scientist is fatally injured in an auto accident the night before his high school graduation. The deceased was driving his car at 2:00 a.m. on a country road; his car crossed the middle line only to be met by an oncoming car driven by a 19-year-old driver — unemployed and a high-school dropout — who was traveling at a speed far exceeding the speed limit. The deceased party was the parent's only child; there is some evidence that he was intoxicated while driving.

It does not take much imagination to envision how complex and intense these discussions might be: a family grieving over the loss of their only, and remarkably talented, child; their perception that the defendant driver had failed in every way that their son had excelled; a defendant who felt very badly about the accident but did not perceive the victim to be blameless, and his parent who loves him as much as the plaintiff's parents loved their son. Managing these conversations in a constructive, empathetic way is intellectually and emotionally exhausting for everyone, including the mediator. But many prefer it to reliving the tragedy in the context of a contested jury trial.

*2. Medical Malpractice Claims.* Every dispute is important to its participants, but medical malpractice claims often invite special attention. Sometimes this is due to the complex technical and emotional environment in which treatment decisions must be made; sometimes people are concerned that the prescribed, but not yet administered, medical or hospital treatment that has been ordered for one of their loved ones is the identical course of treatment that prompted previous malpractice claims against this doctor; and sometimes the medical doctor's reputation for competence is the lingering question of her current patients. Helping to resolve the targeted cases in a constructive, effective, and responsible way, cognizant not only of the complexities often associated with catastrophic tort cases but also from these various third-party interests, is the challenge posed to the talented mediator.

*3. Construction.* Roofs leak. Buildings collapse, through faulty material, unanticipated stresses, shoddy craftsmanship, or natural disasters. Air conditioning units, heating systems, or ventilation ducts do not operate as promised. Delays in delivering materials lead to project cost overruns and significant construction delays. These controversies involve multiple players: the building owner; architects; engineers; material suppliers; skilled tradespeople; bankers; insurance companies; and many others. Whether it is building office space, apartment buildings, single-family homes, bridges, or airplanes, the construction process — and businesses — is team-dependent. Organizing and facilitating multiple conversations simultaneously among numerous stakeholders and their representatives is the significant contribution that a mediator makes to the resolution of these conflicts.

*4. Labor and Employment.* For most people, work is crucial: it importantly contributes to one's sense of self-dignity and the financial income from one's work often constitutes one's primary economic resource. If one's work life is made miserable by the harassing or belittling remarks made by one's co-worker or supervisor, one wants to take action to stop it. If one is denied an employment opportunity or promotion because of one's age or sex, one wants to correct that injustice. If a storeowner believes that an employee has stolen company property, she wants to be able to terminate that individual quickly.

Every workplace participant — owners, supervisors, and co-workers — has a stake in participating in an effective, stimulating employment environment. No one needs to wait until someone files a lawsuit before encouraging contesting parties to meet with a mediator to discuss their challenges. As noted previously in Chapter 4, the U.S. Postal Service created its REDRESS (Resolve Employment Disputes Reach Equitable Solutions Swiftly) mediation program as an organizational program targeted to encourage employees to promptly and effectively address workplace challenges with the assistance of a mediator; the Service recruits, appoints and compensates the individuals (none of who work for the postal service) who have been trained to serve as mediators in this program. Similarly, through an on-going grant, the Keybridge Foundation administers the U.S. Department of Justice' American with Disability Act Mediation Program, using specially trained private mediators to serve these cases. In growing numbers, private sector employers, colleges and universities, and other organizations, are designing their own dispute resolution systems that provide for using a mediator to promote settlement discussions before anyone files formal court papers. And, perhaps not surprisingly, many class action discrimination lawsuits are ultimately resolved through mediated negotiations.

5. *Intellectual Property.* Copyrights, patents, and trademarks are valuable. These protections exist in order to stimulate intellectual imagination, scientific and engineering creativity, and business acumen. When a person believes that others have pirated their creation, she seeks recompense and recognition. These disputants need to discuss their contentions comprehensively but in a manner that does not reveal competitive secrets. Some discussions involve complex technical matters; others involve a close analysis of the creative process. Time is often of the essence, at least to one party. Using a mediator perfectly meets these needs.

6. *Business and Contract Disputes.* Business enterprises, like marriages, can thrive and prosper, or they can fail. In either setting, disputes emerge. If success envelops the business, owners can fight over allocating profits, development plans, or employment practices; if the business fails, agreements must be reached involving such matters as creditor payoffs, asset sales, and terminating employment contracts. Whether the case comes as a court-referral of a litigated matter or because business partners and their advisors proactively seek assistance, savvy business personnel or experienced business lawyers serving as mediators provide valuable services to such disputants.

## d. Elder Care

Advances in medical science and technology enable us to live longer. For many persons, though, the quality of that expanded biological existence distinctly varies. With aging, a person's physical mobility diminishes; one's memory deterioration, whether prompted by natural causes or accelerated by Alzheimer or other diseases, compromises independence. What were once routine trips and falls generate more complex orthopedic injuries. When these and other elder care challenges arise, family members often shape and implement a supporting service network for their parents or loved ones. But developing and implementing such a network can trigger conflict: who will pay for support expenses? How is caring time by loved ones, not professionals, divided between spouse and children? How is caring time by loved ones compensated, if at all? How are different opinions among family members about appropriate treatment options resolved? What procedures are there for making significant health-care and quality of life decisions? These challenges are emotionally excruciating, take time and patience to address, and require developing sustained, supportive relationships with multiple stakeholders. Mediators are playing an enhanced, central role in developing and managing these poignant discussions among multiple stakeholders.

## e.  Probate

Death invites disputes. In the family context, those controversies may be wrapped in years of emotional and intellectual engagement; if the family member's demise was preceded by a sustained period of illness that triggered its own treatment disputes, that complex history additionally shapes the discussion and resolution of disputes over estate matters.

But probate disputes are not confined to families. Persons or organizations that expected to be beneficiaries of someone's largesse but are then informed otherwise are properly suspicious. The distribution of art collections or valued musical instruments can generate intense controversy since, by definition, persons are dealing with one-of-a-kind objects. The components of a person's estate could be more sentimental than financial, but the discussion and debate over how it should be distributed — whether it involves the decedent's extensive collection of auto repair tools, a professor's unpublished manuscripts, one's book collection, or the decedent's entertainment china — might be explosive. Persons involved in these situations often want prompt, private resolution of these controversies and they seek mediator assistance to secure it.

## f.  Peer Mediation

In the K-12 school setting, students, as do adults, get mired in conflict. The conflict can erupt over personal property — taking someone's school supplies or iPod — or involve more intense, interpersonal dynamics such as bullying, teasing, or "messing with my friend." Normally, school systems hire independent mediators to design or administer the school's "dispute resolution program," which includes training students to become peer mediators, supervising student mediator conduct, and initiating educational programs about conflict resolution processes and skills for all members of the school community.

## g.  Bioethical Disputes

The adage that life is uncertain is accurate. It is made more painful when one is forced to choose among medical care options that lead to disability, suffering, or death — and, often, to be forced to make that decision within severely curtailed time constraints. The litigated fight between the husband and parents of Terri Schiavo over whether and how her medical care should be terminated was highly publicized. But disputes similar in kind occur regularly — without the fanfare — throughout the country.

Often, these disputes arise in the context of a medical care facility — a hospital or nursing home — in which a patient either enters the care facility with a life-altering medical condition or, while receiving medical treatment, acquires such a condition. Loved ones — spouses, children, parents — of the patient must, in consultation with treating physicians, other health-care professionals, social work-ers, medical students, and perhaps medical ethicists work out an acceptable treatment plan. When there are disagreements, the challenge becomes to develop a plan acceptable to all so that a final decision can be effectively implemented. Some hospitals have established Bioethics Consultation Services (BCS) to handle such disputes; law-trained and philosophically trained individuals, each of whom is also trained as a mediator, staff these services. Their task is to facilitate conversations involving the multiple stakeholders in a manner that advances informed decision-making.

## h.  Environmental Disputes

Environmental controversies pierce geographic boundaries. Air quality; water purity; toxic waste sites; nuclear waste contamination; forest preservation or deterioration — all impact the quality of our life. But they collide with other practices that people enjoy: driving cars powered by fossil fuels; building highways that redefine and disrupt previously established neighborhood boundaries; listening to music on machines that operate with disposable batteries; snow skiing on mountain paths made possible by razing trees; or tearing down old buildings that some view as historically precious but others view as impediments to contemporary construction technology and aesthetic possibilities. The world of urban and regional planning in an era of increased environmental consciousness is a world of controversy involving multiple players, both private and governmental. Persons who mediate such controversies are knowledgeable about political processes, community organizations, and business practices. They are creative in persuading private foundations or donors to provide economic resources necessary to facilitate broad-based, sustained participation by multiple parties. They often work in teams, blending technical and professional backgrounds in service of the disputants.

## i.  Public Policy Disputes

We live in exciting times, confronting significant challenges — economic polarity, immigration policy, educational restructuring — that test the continued viability of democratic governance. For some of these public policy disputes — how to finance public educational systems — citizens can anticipate and deliberate about them; others simply erupt, such as the reaction to the proposal to build a Muslim Community Center with a mosque in New York City at a site near the World Trade Center. Is there a role for mediators in these situations? Of course. As in the Foundational years, mediated discussions of public policy controversies can enhance, not undermine, democratic governance. Constructively facilitated citizen engagement over such matters energizes civic vitality, responsibility, and pride. Recent initiatives operating under the rubric of Deliberative Democracy or the Public Conversations Project aspire to trigger such public participation. More modest initiatives, such as helping a public high school develop a viable policy to govern cell phone use by its community members, also dot the landscape. Engagement in these settings develops in multiple ways: a political or community leader may encourage it; an established, respected business or social organization may suggest it; or a dispute resolution entity — be it a bar association committee, a community dispute resolution program, or a university institute — may explore possible service, using private mediators to deliver the service.

## 2.  Independent Mediation Practices

All parties to a mediation want an experienced mediator to assist them. But the Catch-22 is: how does one gain that experience? Unlike a traditional legal practice in which law firm partners utilize associates to assist in the research and presentation of a case, mediating is primarily a solo activity. How can a mediator and potential client become linked?

There are several avenues: a person who participates in an established law practice or business activity can, over time, develop relationships with clients and other persons who might have a future need for a mediator. Alternatively, a mediator, like other professional and business personnel, may engage in networking activities by participating actively in social or community activities. Additionally, many courts, governmental agencies (both federal and state), and not-for-profit organizations develop "panels" of mediators. In some instances, that governing agency appoints a panel member to mediate a case, while in other situations the agency provides the negotiating parties with a list of selected panel members and leaves it to the parties to choose their mediator; under either scenario, becoming a panel member is the critical avenue for gaining service as a mediator. Finally, as noted above, a person can gain significant experience by providing pro bono mediation services for community-based mediation programs, school peer mediation projects, or Court-sponsored "Settlement Week" activities.

Developing an independent mediation practice requires energy and patience; because parties understandably seek mediators with experience, one must not underestimate the challenge of embarking on a solo mediation practice. While Section 3, *infra*, describes viable avenues for gaining employment opportunities in the mediation field, it is important to affirm that there is no one established avenue for pursuing this professional calling. The excerpts from Galton, Gonzalez, Curtis, and Chernick reflect the many different motivations, backgrounds, and roads they traveled to become respected practitioners.

### ADR PERSONALITIES AND PRACTICE TIPS
99, 101–02, 104–06 (James J. Alfini & Eric R. Galton, Eds., 1998)*
#### By Eric R. Galton

[Eric Galton is a mediator, arbitrator, and lecturer based in Austin, Texas and is recognized throughout the United States as a leader in the Alternative Dispute Resolution field. He has maintained a full-time ADR practice since 1997.]

My Personal Journey

. . . .

Upon reflection, I realize now that my entire early life history prepared me for my work as a neutral . . . .

In the summer before my senior year of high school, my then hometown of

Plainfield, New Jersey experienced a terrible race riot. The National Guard was called in. The town was divided. People were afraid. Many of us never saw some of our friends again. Certain parts of town were off limits. I created a project called the Plainfield Reading Program. Black and white high school seniors, at first with police escorts, would go into an inner-city youth center and work with seventh and eighth graders upgrading their reading skills. I still remember my seventh grade student, David. I helped him learn to write better and six months later David handed me a wonderful "book" of his poems. David taught me about diversity and how difficult and important it is to walk in someone else's shoes. I also remember our last month at the center. The police escorts were no longer necessary. Peace felt like a merciful and welcome rain and was so palpable that you could almost touch it and feel it.

A year later, I entered Duke at the height of the Vietnam war protests. I saw buildings taken over, the campus shut down, got on a bus to participate in the march in Washington, D.C., and got tear gassed while waiting in a church for our bus ride back to North Carolina. I understood from that experience the curse of polarization and how even fair-minded people often failed to communicate effectively; i.e., a lot of talking and not much listening.

. . . .

### My Professional Journey

If my personal experiences molded me to be a neutral, the kindness and inspiration of others and sheer dumb luck and good timing allowed me to become a neutral.

. . . .

In Texas, our founding father of ADR, and my mentor, was the Honorable Frank B. Evans, then Justice of the 14th Court of Appeals in Houston. Judge Evans was my vice-chair of the State Bar of Texas Citizens Legal Education Committee.

A visionary State Bar of Texas President, Cullen Smith, appointed me, a five-year lawyer, to chair that committee and, recognizing I needed help, gave me Frank Evans as a vice-chair. One day, Frank asked me if I knew what ADR was. I did not. Frank explained ADR to me and asked me to sit in on the initial State Bar ADR planning meetings. Somehow, Judge Evans, through his sheer force of will and determination, managed to get our comprehensive ADR Act passed. I was with him the day the Governor signed the bill. Perhaps today it is passé to have heroes; but Judge Evans was and is mine. He inspired Texas lawyers and judges to give mediation a chance. And Judge Evans opened the door which allowed me to transition from an eleven year litigator to a full-time mediator.

On a local level, the Honorable Joseph Hart, judge of the 126th Judicial District Court of Travis County, Texas, determined that Austin needed Settlement Week before it was legislatively mandated. Settlement Week is a process in which the courthouse shuts down for a week and docketed cases receive pro bono mediation from volunteer neutrals. Judge Hart named Paul Knisely and myself co-chairs of our first Settlement Week. We were generally clueless of what to do (but our colleagues in Tarrant County, who had already done several, helped us) and worried whether lawyers would submit cases and if they would settle. As it turned out, over 160 cases were submitted and well over 70% of those cases settled. Because of Judge Hart's determination and belief in the value of ADR to our citizens, Settlement Week proved to Austin lawyers that mediation actually worked. Thus, the mediation movement in Austin, and throughout Texas, was truly born.

. . . .

## Mediation "Markets"

Basically, you will enter one of three distinct ADR markets: first, a "no market situation" in which no one makes a living doing "ADR"; second, a developing ADR market; or, third, an over-saturated ADR market (yes, they really do exist). The realities of developing an ADR practice depend upon which sort of market you are entering.

. . . .

## Over-Saturated Market

An over-saturated market is one in which several generations of mediators have entrenched themselves. This market has already ferreted out mediators who are deemed "unsuccessful." The remaining mediators have identifiable sectors of loyal clients. This market may have even, perhaps not expressly, identified mediators by style and the grade of complexity of a case (routine, complex, impossible). Mediators may be perceived as interchangeable within these subgroups or strata. I am also assuming that in such a market and in court annexed cases the *lawyers* select the mediator (in some venues, this is not the case).

In such markets, I see two wildly different approaches. They are as follows:

**Develop a Niche.** Certain types of disputes require a neutral with specific skills or expertise; i.e., family law, intellectual property, tax, etc. Or, certain services, even in an over saturated market, may not be available.

. . . .

**Patience: Cream Rises to the Top.** Alternatively, you do not want to be identified in a niche and you believe that you can compete heads up with the local talent. I would suggest the following plan:

- Be patient. Do not quit your day job.

- Contact lawyers you really know well, advise them of your training and commitment, and ask for a tryout. Inevitably, their preferred neutrals will have scheduling conflicts.

- When you finally get the call, excel and resolve the dispute. As a general rule, each successful mediation creates four new ones. . . .

## Developing Market

In a developing market, others have gone before you, created the potential for the market, and have developed something of a following.

Assuming you have received your training and made an informed decision that mediation is for you, I would suggest the following approach:

- Keep your day job. You do not know how the market will respond to your efforts nor do you know whether you will succeed as a mediator or enjoy the practice.

- Do a direct mail piece to those colleagues you really know. Outline your training, your commitment, and specify your fee structure.

 . . . .

- Should the courts in your jurisdiction maintain a list of qualified mediators, do what is necessary to get on such a list.

- Consider developing an identity as a "specialist" in a particular area.

### No Market

If you think about it, the maximum opportunity and greatest difficulty in creating a mediation practice exists in a venue in which no one has established a viable mediation practice.

In these venues, most people will advise you that you cannot succeed. Depending upon your personality, such naysaying may be music to your ears. But, you need to exercise your communication skills and find out why people believe you will not succeed.

Again, my frame of reference is court-annexed mediation, so the questions I would ask are in that context and are as follows:

- Are the local judges opposed to mediation and why? If judges are opposed, you need to educate the judges about the value of the mediation process.

- Are local lawyers opposed to mediation and why? Most lawyers oppose what they do not understand. Again, your mission is to educate lawyers and explain that mediation is good for both their clients and them.

- Have others before you attempted to develop a mediation practice and failed? If so, why?

Your primary job will be to educate those who are in a position to refer cases. Anticipate skepticism, distrust, and ignorance. But, as a bright beacon in the fog, keep this one unmistakable truth in mind — most of the greatest skeptics and naysayers about the process become the most outspoken proponents of the process after a successful mediation.

# ADR PERSONALITIES AND PRACTICE TIPS
19–21, 23–27 (James J. Alfini & Eric R. Galton, Eds., 1998)*
## By Steven Gonzales

[Steven Gonzales is currently Associate Professor of Law and Director of Experiential Learning at the Phoenix School of Law. Prior to that, Mr. Gonzales was deputy city attorney of Peoria, Arizona. He had three gubernatorial administrative law judge appointments with Senate confirmation by the age of 34, serving in Arizona, Colorado, and Michigan. . . . He . . . chaired the ABA Section of Dispute Resolution's Diversity Committee and participated in the ABA's Project Outreach, a school mediation project. Mr. Gonzales received his J.D. from Wayne State University and his M.A./B.A. from Michigan State University.]

. . . .

I began my legal career as most attorneys, eager to gain courtroom seasoning. In time I became a prosecuting attorney, foe to hardened criminals in Battle Creek, Michigan, home of serial killers and far from my native and peaceful Detroit. My future distaste of litigation was signaled by one of my first cases as a young prosecutor. The case involved a riotous mob infuriated with a scrappy dog whose owner let him roam free despite his affection for scaring the bejeebers out of everyone in the county.

Unfortunately for the prisoner pooch, Michigan law permitted a judge to execute hairy felons, making this my first capital case. As fate would have it, he got off when a surprise witness, a French poodle named Fifi, testified to a hushed courtroom that he had been with *her* that night.

. . . .

Then I moved to Arizona, first living on the Navajo Indian Reservation, a land of immense beauty. As counsel to the Navajo Nation, I witnessed the impressive focus on unity of thought stressed by America's largest Indian Nation. This was a far cry from the old saying that there is not enough business in a small town for one lawyer, but there is always enough for two! Mediation it turns out, is a close cousin of Indian consultation.

. . . .

Of course there will always be a need for courts, lawyers and due process of law. That is not seriously in question. But our Republic is not so fragile that we must settle all disputes with judicial officers. The real issue is why offer a one-size-fits-all system? If every case is procedurally treated the same, then the neighborhood barking dog, requiring social unity, or a child custody case, needing sensitivity and other professional resources, are handled the same as insurance fender bender cases. Moreover, this has the effect of aggravating some smaller conflicts into bigger ones.

All this may have been tolerable when our population was smaller, lawsuits

---

comparatively rare, and time not so precious. But it certainly is not designed for the coming century.

Yet legal professionals are leading the way, despite the reluctance of a few. It is probably fair to state that conflict resolution would never have gained such strength if it were not for many supportive lawyers, judges and legal scholars over the past 25 years.

So once you have accepted that mediation is generally beneficial to communities, for the legal profession and that it can become part of your legal skillbank as well as a service your firm or organization can offer, how do you go about establishing the practice? Lawyers, never a dull lot, are learning to adapt to the changing practice.

Before practicing mediation the first lesson should be one of professional humility. Do not assume that because you have attended twenty years of settlement conferences, negotiated countless contracts, or even have judicial experience, that you are a trained mediator.

Mediation has its own training, language, professional associations, customs, ethical schemes and delivery systems. An experienced mediator can usually determine in an exchange of a few sentences whether a lawyer is trained in mediation or is deluded into thinking he or she learned mediation from participating in settlement conferences.

Start with professional training, at a minimum, the standard forty-hour basic course offered by many community mediation centers, some professional mediation firms, and a few public agencies. Then, do some volunteer mediation with another mediator, known as "co-mediation," preferably one who is well-experienced.

. . . .

Once trained, there are a variety of ways to incorporate mediation into your practice. One way I have enjoyed has been as counsel to a municipality in suburban Phoenix. This city is replete with all the familiar disputes of a rapidly growing community of 90,000.

Some of the "best" conflicts from which to learn are those neighborhood disputes that drive local police crazy. It is amazing how similar are the processes of conflict and resolution, whether involving neighborhood barking dogs (the City of Phoenix's mediation office fields an average of just over 100 barking-dog complaints per month), contentious commercial disputes, or international tensions.

. . . .

Perhaps one of the most practical uses of mediation is between disputing employees. More and more employers are complementing the old ombudsperson office or even older grievance procedures with trained in-house mediators. In one large county government in Arizona, the procedure permits every single grievance to ultimately work its way up to the county CEO. Stacks of grievances pile up, overwhelming the senior staff. The county recently hired a lawyer-mediator to try to resolve this cumbersome procedure.

Services such as these enabled my practice to expand to include mediating neighborhood and employee disputes, citizen complaints, and negotiating on behalf of the city. In effect, it created a market within existing systems, inserted before matters get to court, rather than a court connected system.

. . . .

Attorneys may also maintain a mediation practice. When this route is selected a formalized office procedure should be developed. At the outset, mediation clients must be carefully educated to understand they are not retaining you as their lawyer and you cannot provide them legal advice or later serve as their attorney in the same case. . . .

Lawyers experienced in court administration and related disciplines can become involved in research, design and administration of conflict resolution systems. In between my departure from Michigan and move to Arizona, I served two years as an administrative law judge and manager of Colorado's workers' compensation system. During these years I co-designed a multi-tiered mediation and pre-hearing procedure for workers' compensation cases. The program was generally very well received by the bench, bar and parties. This should be no surprise to those who have had the pleasure of working with Colorado's outstanding and progressive bar.

Legal professionals trained and well-experienced in mediation can also teach or train. Although the market may be shaky and varies from community to community, there are many great opportunities. In addition to my legal and mediation practice, I am a visiting professor at a university in Europe. Several times a year I must sacrifice and go to Switzerland to teach American style mediation to graduate students. I have also trained eager judges in mediation in South America.

Attorneys, particularly with business, management or related experience or advanced degrees, can develop a business consultant practice. Conflict resolution is a perfect complement to business consultant training seminars.

Once your forms are printed and you are ready to foster peace among even the most inveterate of disputants, how do you find a market? There are options supplementing the obvious use of the yellow pages and local advertisement. One of my favorites is use of pro bono time. This both serves and gets you out into the community.

In my case I have trained high school students in peer mediation, taught mediation at a local community forum and helped design mediation programs for mayors, city councils and neighborhood associations. Some municipal and occasionally higher courts use lawyer mediators and maintain a list of approved neutrals for mediating cases.

Experienced lawyers are best advised to build on contacts and strengths already established. Creating a specialized niche, especially in larger population centers, is one of the most time-honored forms of American business strategy. Mediation, at least in a widespread and formal fashion, is still new in most areas of commerce.

## ADR PERSONALITIES AND PRACTICE TIPS
49–52 (James J. Alfini & Eric R. Galton, Eds., 1998)*
By Dana L. Curtis

[Dana L. Curtis mediates civil disputes in a wide range of substantive areas. . . . She began practice as a full-time mediator in 1991 with Mediation Law Offices in Mill Valley and served as Circuit Mediator with the U.S. Court of Appeals for the Ninth Circuit in San Francisco until 1997. . . . Her solo practice is based in Sausalito, California.]

I knew I wanted to be a mediator when I was introduced to mediation in a second-year law school course. My other courses, though interesting intellectually, minimized the role of the human being behind the legal claims. Mediation focused on the individuals involved and on the meaning they attached to the dispute. The parties' priorities could be the most important reference point for resolution. In addition to, or instead of, the rule of law, their concerns, needs, fears, hopes and desires all mattered. As well as seeing how mediation could better meet the needs of the parties than a litigated resolution, I realized that mediation better utilized my strengths. As a mediator, I could use relationship and communication skills I had developed in my first career as a teacher.

Full of enthusiasm for mediation, I asked my professor where to learn about mediating as a career. He referred me to Gary Friedman, a pioneer lawyer mediator and Director of the Center for Mediation in Law in Mill Valley, California. I sought Gary's advice about mediating employment and other commercial disputes. He encouraged me, but warned that such a career would be difficult to forge, as the application of mediation in civil disputes was uncommon at that time. He also noted that I seemed to have what it would take — the commitment to mediation and an entrepreneurial spirit, evidenced by the fact that I had entered law school as a single mother after moving to California from Idaho with my three children.

Gary advised me to remain committed, to be patient and to get litigation experience to enhance my credibility with lawyers and my understanding of the legal process. Following his advice, after law school I clerked for a California Supreme Court associate justice and thereafter joined a large San Francisco law firm, practicing commercial and employment litigation in San Jose and San Francisco. I began as an enthusiastic associate and during much of my first year of practice seriously considered a long-term litigation career. Before long, my enthusiasm abated. The enormity of financial and human resources spent on litigation astounded me. The inefficiency of the discovery process (where the object, it seemed to me, was to provide the other side with as little information as possible), the lack of predictability and fairness of jury trials, and the failure of litigation to address the clients' true needs all left me disaffected.

In addition, the demands of big firm practice, the often sixty-and sometimes eighty-hour work weeks, and the isolation I experienced among 200 other big firm lawyers convinced me that I was not willing to sacrifice more years of "being" for "becoming." The idea of partnership became unthinkable. As one of my law school friends put it, partnership is like a pie eating contest where the prize is more pie.

I dreamed of mediating. Although I had trained as a mediator and had been teaching mediation for several years, I was unable to see a way to make the transition. During this time of profound dissatisfaction with my career, I spent an evening with four dear women friends, as I had been doing on a bimonthly basis for several years. That night I spoke of my life consumed with work, of the months without a day off, of the weeks in a hotel room, of the frustrations of a difficult trial and of the day-to-day failure of my career to provide deep, personal meaning for me. What followed caused me finally to initiate change in my life. One of my friends looked me in the eye and said, "Dana, you will die if you don't leave your job." I knew she was right. If not physically, I was dying spiritually. The next day, without knowing what else I would do, I gave notice that I would be leaving the firm.

A few days later, I ran into Gary Friedman on the street in San Francisco. When he discovered I was leaving my law practice, he invited me to meet with him. Over a series of meetings, I learned that he was becoming increasingly interested in mediation of civil disputes and would like to work closely with lawyers who were pursuing commercial mediation. Within a few months, I hung out my mediation shingle (literally!) at Gary's office in Mill Valley. There, I practiced mediation for two years with Laura Farrow, another lawyer who left the firm at the same time I did. It was an exciting time — the invigoration of moving from a high-rise Financial District office to a renovated house with rose bushes, even an apple tree, in the yard, where at last my whole heart was in my work, as well as the uncertainty of whether a mediation practice could actually support my family.

The years I spent at Mediation Law Offices enabled me to develop a successful practice and to build a foundation that has been important in my practice and in my teaching. By working closely with Gary, I became more effective and more reflective. Following most mediations, I would write a critique of the process and meet with Gary to reflect on the dynamic between the parties and within myself. I was also able to consult with Gary on the spot. At the outset of one early divorce mediation, for example, a couple told me they had come to ask me to write up an agreement they had already reached. Essentially, the agreement provided the husband would have custody of the children and all but $10,000 of their community property assets, which totaled about $300,000. I had been ready to launch into the first phase of mediation, discussing the process and helping the parties to decide if they wanted to go forward, but I was thrown by this request. Excusing myself to get some papers, I ducked into Gary's office and in three minutes worked out an approach that engaged the parties in discussion about the efficacy of their agreement without compromising my neutrality.

After two years at Mediation Law Offices, I had the opportunity to become a Circuit Court Mediator for the U.S. Court of Appeals for the Ninth Circuit in San Francisco. I was persuaded to leave private practice by the promise of an endless array of federal cases to mediate and steady paychecks. In the Ninth Circuit Mediation Program, I worked with five other full-time mediators to resolve cases on appeal. It was a mediator's dream come true. We selected our caseload from hundreds of diverse civil appeals. On any day, we might conduct a telephone mediation in a securities case, an employment discrimination dispute, a products liability matter, an IRS appeal, a bankruptcy case or an insurance coverage dispute. Several times a month, I would mediate in person, often in complex multi-party disputes. It was a time of applying my experience and knowledge of a face-to-face mediation model, where the parties could reach understanding in order to craft a resolution that addressed their priorities, not just their assessment of their legal positions. I sought to provide more than a settlement conference. In fact, when I began to speak of legal argument in mediation as an *option*, not a *given*, I was surprised by how frequently the parties, and even their lawyers, agreed that discussing the law would not be productive. The first time I suggested that we may not want to discuss the law, the plaintiff (in an employment discrimination case) said, "Thank God! If I had to listen for five more minutes to the company's lawyer telling me what a rotten case I have, I'd leave!"

During the three years I worked at the Ninth Circuit, I mediated hundreds of appeals. I learned that it is never too late for mediation. It was not unusual for a case to have been in litigation for ten years or more — and still settle! I also learned the approach required of an appellate mediator: how to unravel a long history of misunderstanding; how to address the harm the parties inflict upon one another in litigation, which often eclipses the original grievance; how to use the parties' experience with numerous failed negotiations, settlement conferences and mediations to structure a mediation process that avoids repeating their failures. On a more practical note, I learned how to discuss the law, and especially legal issues unique to appeals, without crowding out other reference points for decision; I learned about effective facilitation of both distributional and interest-based negotiations; and I learned how to turn mandatory mediation into a voluntary process — and to believe in it!

A year ago, I left the Ninth Circuit to return to private mediation practice and to join the Negotiation and Mediation Program at Stanford Law School, where I am a lecturer teaching two mediation courses a year.

## ADR PERSONALITIES AND PRACTICE TIPS
43–46 (James J. Alfini & Eric R. Galton, Eds., 1998)*
### By Richard Chernick

[Richard Chernick is an arbitrator and a mediator. He is currently Vice President and Managing Director of JAMS' Arbitration Practice. He is a former member of the American Arbitration Association President's Panel for the Mediation of High Stakes Cases and the Mass Tort Panel (both national) and the California Statewide Panel of Neutrals. He was formerly a partner at Gibson, Dunn & Crutcher where he specialized in commercial litigation and domestic and international arbitration. . . .]

### History

I was an associate and then a partner at Gibson, Dunn & Crutcher in Los Angeles, California from 1970 through 1994. My interest in dispute resolution grew out of a commercial litigation practice which emphasized "non-traditional" forms of litigation. As a young lawyer, I found that I was able to get significant trial experience which was not easily available to associates in large firms by working on commercial arbitrations. I was "first chair" in moderate-sized construction, commercial and entertainment arbitrations at a time when my peers were getting almost no courtroom experience at all.

I was drawn to the flexibility and informality of the arbitration process. I became familiar with the procedural rules governing arbitration, developed a reputation within my firm as having answers to difficult questions in the arbitration field and became our first ADR resource person before the term "ADR" had been coined.

Because of this expertise, I was consulted on many litigation assignments not involving traditional court processes. For example, when private judging became popular in California in the late 1970s, I was most often the person who was able to provide advice on process and procedural issues.

In the 1980s, I began to expand my arbitration practice to international matters. This was a direct outgrowth of my domestic arbitration practice. I conducted arbitrations under various institutional rules and in *ad hoc* (nonadministered) processes. I tried several matters before the Iran-U.S. Claims Tribunal in The Hague.

As part of my work in arbitration and private judging proceedings I became skilled in drafting arbitration clauses and, later, dispute resolution clauses. Here again I became a resource for my firm in drafting and reviewing clauses; I provided some informal training to the transactional lawyers on do's and don'ts of clause drafting. I came to realize that the most effective pre-dispute agreements are a cooperative effort of the responsible transactional lawyer and an experienced litigator who understands the intricacies of arbitration and other process choices. I tried (with limited success) to sell this concept to my partners at every opportunity.

As my firm's expert on dispute resolution, I became its liaison with the Center for Public Resources (now the CPR Legal Institute); I was an early participant in CPR's excellent educational programs and seminars and was exposed to some of the best neutrals and trainers in the United States through CPR. It was there that I first learned, systematically, negotiation and mediation skills. (My law school curriculum included a then-innovative trial practice course, but it would be years before law schools began to teach negotiation, mediation and "ADR.")

The more I participated in ADR processes as a lawyer, the more the role of the neutral intrigued me. I began to volunteer as a settlement officer and mediator in court programs in the Los Angeles courts and as an arbitrator at the American Arbitration Association (as well as a judge *pro tem* in the Los Angeles Municipal and Superior Courts). I found that my skills as a trial lawyer were helpful to me as a neutral and that I was comfortable in that role.

I began to be selected occasionally by lawyers who knew me for assignments as a neutral in larger matters, and was actually compensated for my work in most of these cases. It was about this time that the AAA inaugurated its Large Complex Case Program, and I was selected for the Los Angeles Panel of Neutrals. . . .

## Becoming a Neutral

It was in the early stages of this program, as I began to be selected somewhat regularly for cases as a sole arbitrator and occasionally as a mediator, that I began to think about neutral work as a full-time occupation. My firm had always been generous in allowing me to serve on volunteer panels and had voiced no objection to my increasing work as a compensated neutral in these cases. But as my calendar began to be more and more filled with neutral assignments, I realized that the potential for conflicts of interest in a firm as large as mine, and the lack of opportunity to leverage my time as a neutral, were eventually going to put me on a collision course with some of my partners who rightfully were responsible for promoting the firm's bottom line. I began to explore the possibility of withdrawing from my firm and setting up a free-standing arbitration and mediation practice.

I had been on the AAA National Board of Directors for several years and was aware of the changes that esteemed organization was undergoing. I spoke with the leadership at AAA to inform them of my intentions, and that conversation led quickly to a discussion of an exclusive relationship with AAA as a full-time neutral. Simply put, I would commit to bring all of my business to AAA and AAA would in turn agree to market my services, along with other AAA panelists, and to provide extra effort on my behalf because of my commitment of exclusivity.

I have never had a written agreement with AAA, but the relationship has been mutually beneficial from day one. I attract substantial mediation business which AAA administers for me and some arbitration submission cases; AAA promotes me through its California and national panels and provides, through the customary selection process, much of my arbitration business.

I also consult on dispute resolution issues with lawyers (clause drafting, process development, neutral selection) and companies (dispute system design); I also testify occasionally as an expert witness on dispute resolution issues. I do this work separate from AAA by mutual agreement.

## Marketing

When I decided to become a neutral, I decided not to continue to practice law. Many neutrals edge into the field by trying over time to shift their practice from lawyering to neutral work in increments. I find this "straddle" to detract from the neutral's attractiveness as a neutral. Such a person seems not to be fully committed to the practice (or not successful enough to do it exclusively), the neutral also may be in the position of seeking business on Monday from colleagues who will be litigation adversaries on Tuesday. This is particularly problematic if the neutral is an arbitrator. Moreover, many lawyers will be reluctant to recommend a competitor for a neutral assignment because the neutral will often appear in a particularly favorable light to the referring lawyers' client.

As a result of this belief, I do not use "Esq." on my stationery or business cards. I am Richard Chernick — "Arbitrator and Mediator;" not "Richard Chernick, Esq.: Lawyer — arbitrator — mediator."

I market myself to lawyers by speaking and writing on dispute resolution issues.

This is how I demonstrate my competence and knowledge as a neutral. My inclusion on many AAA specialty panels in areas in which I had litigation experience (commercial, employment, entertainment, real property, and law practice disputes) provides additional credibility.

I market myself to businesses, usually through their general counsel, much as described above. I also try to speak on programs which include business people in the audience. I teach ADR to non-lawyers and train mediators in the Los Angeles County Bar Association Dispute Resolution Services program, which includes a fair number of non-lawyers.

My most effective marketing tool is to impress the participants in each mediation and arbitration that I know my stuff: that I am experienced and comfortable in the particular process, that I am able to guide the parties through the process efficiently and effectively, and that with my assistance their objectives will be achieved. As I tried to do as a lawyer, I hope to convey the impression to each person who comes into contact with me that I am dedicated to a successful outcome.

## NOTES AND QUESTIONS

(1)   For additional, extensive interviews with persons who describe both the development of their mediation career and their approach to mediation, see *The Mediators: Views from the Eye of the Storm* (Mediate.com), a DVD recording with 64 individuals who are described in the promotional material as "the best known and most experienced mediators in the world."

(2)   When trying to develop one's practice, what types of ethical dilemmas might a mediator encounter advertising one's services? Would sending potential clients a complimentary ball-point pen or calendar bearing the mediator's name violate any ethical norms for mediators? If a mediator's website, contains, among other things, her client list, would that be acceptable? See Chapter 8,*supra*, for additional challenges posed when mediators engage in business development activities.

(3)   Given what you know about the mediation environment where you are currently attending school, or in your home town, what do you think would be the best way of trying to establish yourself as a mediator in those settings?

### 3.   Organization-Based Employment Opportunities

Many persons interested in pursuing employment opportunities in mediation do not want to operate independent solo practices; they prefer salaried jobs connected with institutions. Two such options exist: staff mediator positions with agencies or organizations, and staff positions with dispute resolution programs which include, but are not limited to, serving as a mediator. The method for gaining entry to each realm differs significantly.

### a.   Mediator Positions in Agencies and Organizations

There are some organizations, mostly governmentally based, that hire full-time staff mediators. Historically, most of these positions have been affiliated with those governmental units that provide mediation and technical assistance to participants in union-management relations. The Federal Mediation and Conciliation Service (FMCS), for example, employs staff mediators to assist private-sector labor-management representatives conduct their collective bargaining sessions. With the explosive growth of formal union-management relations involving public sector employees in the late 1960s, state governments created agencies comparable to FMCS to serve collective bargaining needs involving public sector unions and management; these are variously referred to as Public Employment Relations Boards (PERBs) or Public Employment Relations Commissions (PERCs). A limited number of governmental agencies exist at both the federal and state level that provide mediators and conciliators to help resolve controversies involving civil rights or civil disturbances; the leading example is the Community Relations Service (CRS) of the U.S. Department of Justice. Some federal government agencies, such as the Department of Defense, hire staff mediators; various state government offices, such as Worker Compensation Offices, Human Rights Agencies, or Departments of Education, now regularly recruit for staff mediators. Finally, many state and federal court systems have hired staff persons to serve as mediators both in subject-specific areas, such as family or juvenile court settings, and for cases involving general civil and appellate matters.

These agencies, in their recruiting process, seek individuals who have gained experience in the targeted domain of service. Persons hired as staff mediators for agencies servicing union-management collective bargaining normally have employment experience related to that area; persons who have held union leadership positions, served in labor-relations offices in either the private or public sector, or have represented unions or management in grievance arbitration cases are typically the kinds of persons who qualify for consideration as staff mediators with agencies such as FMCS. Similarly, persons appointed to court mediator positions have professional experience in the relevant area. As is true for those persons who establish an independent mediation practice, the route to gain appointment is indirect; one first acquires experience in the relevant practice area in a non-mediator capacity before a mediation career becomes viable.

### b.   Working for a Dispute Resolution Agency

There are multiple employment opportunities for persons who want to enter this field immediately following their formal educational training. However, most involve working in settings in which one performs various organizational activities, not just mediating. These organizational-employment opportunities fall into two categories.

### i.   Dispute Resolution Agencies That Provide Direct Service

Many not-for-profit organizations exist to provide mediation and other dispute resolution services to their communities. Some of these organizations are free-standing, privately-financed programs, such as the Community Boards Program in San Francisco. Other not-for-profit organizations have contractual relationships with their local court systems, school systems, family service agencies, and other organizations pursuant to which the agency refers cases to the dispute resolution agency, which then provides mediation services. Staff members of these dispute resolution organizations, such as New York's and Michigan's Community Dispute Resolution Centers Program, not only mediate disputes but also recruit and train community residents to serve as mediators, and engage in other community-education and outreach activity. These programs typically recruit staff members whose qualifications are predicated more heavily on their formal educational training than on their dispute resolution experience.

There are also significant employment opportunities within more traditional organizations that require mediation and dispute resolution skills but whose job title does not reflect a dispute resolution designation. Persons who work in a company's human resource department routinely deploy "dispute resolution skills"; colleges and universities often recruit administrators to supervise student judicial councils that conduct hearings ranging from allegations of student harassment to charges such as plagiarism or cheating on examinations that can result in student suspensions or dismissal. Some organizations, both for-profit and not-for-profit, hire individuals to work in their office of ombudsperson.

Persons entering the field through any of these avenues rapidly develop or sharpen multiple employment capacities, including supervisory and budgeting expertise, staff training and development presentation abilities, and program development skills; with this robust employment profile, particularly when joined with formal legal training, a person enjoys a competitive advantage in pursuing mediation employment opportunities in organizational settings, traditional law practices, or in the development of an independent mediation practice.

## ii.     Working for a DR Administrative or Provider Organization

Some institutions provide education, technical assistance, and administrative support to parties who use dispute resolution services. While these institutions want their professional staff to be persons who are knowledgeable about mediation theory and practice, staff personnel themselves do not perform an official mediating role. Working in these administrative positions, however, enables a person interested in mediation to immediately obtain employment in the dispute resolution field and to interact with multiple players, including parties to a controversy and mediators. For example, in the public sector, there are dispute resolution programs placed organizationally within the administrative offices of a state's Supreme Court. Persons employed in these offices conduct research about experimental programs in mediation, assist in developing prototype mediation programs and institutionalizing their use through the promulgation of rules and procedures, and provide technical assistance and training to courts, bar associations, judicial conferences, and community organizations who are interested in promoting mediation's use. Although these court employees do not mediate cases, they acquire experience and expertise about process design and skill development while positioning themselves, if they choose, for more direct service opportunities.

There are also entities referred to as "provider" organizations. The structure and operation of the American Arbitration Association (AAA), the oldest of such organizations, is characteristic: the AAA develops "panels" of mediators and arbitrators. When parties to a controversy want to hire a mediator, they contact the AAA and, with appropriate compensation for its administrative services, engage AAA to identify possible mediators (or select one for the parties), arrange for the conference meeting place and time, handle the transmission of all documents among the parties and mediator, and, at the case's end, close out the file by sending appropriate billings. The important contribution of the AAA staff member' to the proceeding is primarily procedural. Much like the employment experience in the administrative office of a state's supreme court, discussed previously, securing an administrative position with a private provider organization enables someone with an interest in mediation to begin working immediately in the dispute resolution field and gain valuable insights into how parties, their representatives, and mediators perform their work. While the AAA and the International Institute for Conflict Prevention and Resolution are not-for-profit provider organizations, entities such as JAMS operate on a for-profit basis.

## C.  MEDIATION'S PROMISE

Barring dramatic social and political changes, most United States residents can be confident that our basic legal institutions and processes will continue to operate in predictable form well into the future.

Many signs also point to sustained mediation activity: expansion of mandatory court-connected mediation programs in state and local courts; state and federal legislation supporting mediation's use in various sectors; courses on mediation at universities and law schools throughout the country; and a social climate in which persons and businesses demand that their dispute resolution budgets support flexible, efficient, and varied dispute resolution processes.

But a contrary vision about mediation is also plausible. Despite more than forty years of expanding mediation activity, most persons still believe suing someone is the most desirable way to resolve controversies. As depicted in television shows, movies, and courtroom novels, our role model of the heroic problem solver is the strong, aggressive courtroom advocate. Few if any television shows, movies, or novels effectively portray the power and skills of negotiators and mediators; and many lawyers continue to view mediation as only an incidental, required hurdle to jump in the litigation process.

Several dominant lessons emerge from the mediation story, though, that provide powerful reasons for believing that mediation's place in our democratic society is vital and secure. What are they?

First, wherever persons want to participate responsibly in resolving controversies in which they are a stakeholder, using mediation can help make that happen. There are important social practices within our own country that appear ripe for reconsideration and reconstruction: health care delivery, public school systems, and banking practices are just three examples of significant institutions that are undergoing significant transformations. Trained mediators can be a force for creating constructive dialogue among concerned stakeholders on such pivotal matters.

Second, we are becoming better educated about mediation. Many of today's law students, unlike their predecessors, attended a middle school or high school in which there was a peer mediation program; they might very well have served as mediators themselves. But the education initiative is much broader than a law school curriculum: workshops at professional and business organizations are replete with topics relating to negotiation and consensus-building; and academic and certificate programs in dispute resolution at both the undergraduate and graduate levels are expanding, with students in business, nursing, and natural resources being required to take mediation and facilitation courses. There is a slow, steady climate change occurring with respect to how persons choose to deal with differences, and the study and use of mediation is a part of that change.

Finally, as the biographical excerpts above so poignantly display, persons drawn to this work, by and large, are remarkably strong, energetic, thoughtful, and resourceful individuals. Their energy in, and commitment to, this work has been shaped by personal experiences and perspectives that give them confidence in the integrity and value of mediation. They are persistent, imaginative, and committed to serving the parties at the highest standards of excellence. They experience an extraordinary sense of satisfaction in helping parties overcome what had previously been perceived as insuperable barriers. They know that each mediation session involves persons with distinctive aspirations, values, and priorities — and that fact mandates their treating each party with empathy and respect. Engaging talented, compassionate individuals to do the work of mediation plays a significant role in shaping its future. As long as persons seek to be treated with dignity, as is their right, and as long as persons of character and conviction continue to assume the mediator's role, there will be a role for mediation.

# Appendix A

# MODEL STANDARDS OF CONDUCT FOR MEDIATORS

AMERICAN ARBITRATION ASSOCIATION
(ADOPTED SEPTEMBER 8, 2005)

AMERICAN BAR ASSOCIATION
(ADOPTED AUGUST 9, 2005)

ASSOCIATION FOR CONFLICT RESOLUTION
(ADOPTED AUGUST 22, 2005)

SEPTEMBER 2005

The *Model Standards of Conduct for Mediators* was prepared in 1994 by the American Arbitration Association, the American Bar Association's Section of Dispute Resolution, and the Association for Conflict Resolution.[1] A joint committee consisting of representatives from the same successor organizations revised the Model Standards in 2005.[2] Both the original 1994 version and the 2005 revision have been approved by each participating organization.[3]

## *Preamble*

Mediation is used to resolve a broad range of conflicts within a variety of settings. These Standards are designed to serve as fundamental ethical guidelines for persons mediating in all practice contexts. They serve three primary goals: to guide the conduct of mediators; to inform the mediating parties; and to promote public confidence in mediation as a process for resolving disputes.

Mediation is a process in which an impartial third party facilitates communication and negotiation and promotes voluntary decision making by the parties to the dispute.

Mediation serves various purposes, including providing the opportunity for parties to define and clarify issues, understand different perspectives, identify

---

[1] The Association for Conflict Resolution is a merged organization of the Academy of Family Mediators, the Conflict Resolution Education Network and the Society of Professionals in Dispute Resolution (SPIDR). SPIDR was the third participating organization in the development of the 1994 Standards.

[2] Reporter's Notes, which are not part of these Standards and therefore have not been specifically approved by any of the organizations, provide commentary regarding these revisions.

[3] The 2005 revisions to the Model Standards were approved by the American Bar Association's House of Delegates on August 9, 2005, the Board of the Association for Conflict Resolution on August 22, 2005 and the Executive Committee of the American Arbitration Association on September 8, 2005.

interests, explore and assess possible solutions, and reach mutually satisfactory agreements, when desired.

*Note on Construction*

These Standards are to be read and construed in their entirety. There is no priority significance attached to the sequence in which the Standards appear.

The use of the term "shall" in a Standard indicates that the mediator must follow the practice described. The use of the term "should" indicates that the practice described in the standard is highly desirable, but not required, and is to be departed from only for very strong reasons and requires careful use of judgment and discretion.

The use of the term "mediator" is understood to be inclusive so that it applies to co-mediator models.

These Standards do not include specific temporal parameters when referencing a mediation, and therefore, do not define the exact beginning or ending of a mediation.

Various aspects of a mediation, including some matters covered by these Standards, may also be affected by applicable law, court rules, regulations, other applicable professional rules, mediation rules to which the parties have agreed and other agreements of the parties. These sources may create conflicts with, and may take precedence over, these Standards. However, a mediator should make every effort to comply with the spirit and intent of these Standards in resolving such conflicts. This effort should include honoring all remaining Standards not in conflict with these other sources.

These Standards, unless and until adopted by a court or other regulatory authority do not have the force of law. Nonetheless, the fact that these Standards have been adopted by the respective sponsoring entities, should alert mediators to the fact that the Standards might be viewed as establishing a standard of care for mediators.

## STANDARD I. SELF-DETERMINATION

**A.** A mediator shall conduct a mediation based on the principle of party self-determination. Self-determination is the act of coming to a voluntary, uncoerced decision in which each party makes free and informed choices as to process and outcome. Parties may exercise self-determination at any stage of a mediation, including mediator selection, process design, participation in or withdrawal from the process, and outcomes.

    **1.** Although party self-determination for process design is a fundamental principle of mediation practice, a mediator may need to balance such party self-determination with a mediator's duty to conduct a quality process in accordance with these Standards.

    **2.** A mediator cannot personally ensure that each party has made free and informed choices to reach particular decisions, but, where appropriate, a mediator should make the parties aware of the importance of consulting other professionals to help them make informed choices.

**B.** A mediator shall not undermine party self-determination by any party for reasons such as higher settlement rates, egos, increased fees, or outside pressures from court personnel, program admin istrators, provider organizations, the media or others.

## STANDARD II. IMPARTIALITY

**A.** A mediator shall decline a mediation if the mediator cannot conduct it in an impartial manner. Impartiality means freedom from favoritism, bias or prejudice.

**B.** A mediator shall conduct a mediation in an impartial manner and avoid conduct that gives the appearance of partiality.

**1.** A mediator should not act with partiality or prejudice based on any participant's personal characteristics, background, values and beliefs, or performance at a mediation, or any other reason.

**2.** A mediator should neither give nor accept a gift, favor, loan or other item of value that raises a question as to the mediator's actual or perceived impartiality.

**3.** A mediator may accept or give *de minimis* gifts or incidental items or services that are provided to facilitate a mediation or respect cultural norms so long as such practices do not raise questions as to a mediator's actual or perceived impartiality.

**C.** If at any time a mediator is unable to conduct a mediation in an impartial manner, the mediator shall withdraw.

## STANDARD III. CONFLICTS OF INTEREST

**A.** A mediator shall avoid a conflict of interest or the appearance of a conflict of interest during and after a mediation. A conflict of interest can arise from involvement by a mediator with the subject matter of the dispute or from any relationship between a mediator and any mediation participant, whether past or present, personal or professional, that reasonably raises a question of a mediator's impartiality.

**B.** A mediator shall make a reasonable inquiry to determine whether there are any facts that a reasonable individual would consider likely to create a potential or actual conflict of interest for a mediator. A mediator's actions necessary to accomplish a reasonable inquiry into potential conflicts of interest may vary based on practice context.

**C.** A mediator shall disclose, as soon as practicable, all actual and potential conflicts of interest that are reasonably known to the mediator and could reasonably be seen as raising a question about the mediator's impartiality. After disclosure, if all parties agree, the mediator may proceed with the mediation.

**D.** If a mediator learns any fact after accepting a mediation that raises a question with respect to that mediator's service creating a potential or actual conflict of interest, the mediator shall disclose it as quickly as practicable. After disclosure, if all parties agree, the mediator may proceed with the mediation.

**E.** If a mediator's conflict of interest might reasonably be viewed as undermining the integrity of the mediation, a mediator shall withdraw from or decline to proceed with the mediation regardless of the expressed desire or agreement of the parties to the contrary.

**F.** Subsequent to a mediation, a mediator shall not establish another relationship with any of the participants in any matter that would raise questions about the integrity of the mediation. When a mediator develops personal or professional relationships with parties, other individuals or organizations following a mediation in which they were involved, the mediator should consider factors such as time elapsed following the mediation, the nature of the relationships established, and services offered when determining whether the relationships might create a perceived or actual conflict of interest.

## STANDARD IV. COMPETENCE

**A.** A mediator shall mediate only when the mediator has the necessary competence to satisfy the reasonable expectations of the parties.

**1.** Any person may be selected as a mediator, provided that the parties are satisfied with the mediator's competence and qualifications. Training, experience in mediation, skills, cultural understandings and other qualities are often necessary for mediator competence. A person who offers to serve as a mediator creates the expectation that the person is competent to mediate effectively.

**2.** A mediator should attend educational programs and related activities to maintain and enhance the mediator's knowledge and skills related to mediation.

**3.** A mediator should have available for the parties' information relevant to the mediator's training, education, experience and approach to conducting a mediation.

**B.** If a mediator, during the course of a mediation determines that the mediator cannot conduct the mediation competently, the mediator shall discuss that determination with the parties as soon as is practicable and take appropriate steps to address the situation, including, but not limited to, withdrawing or requesting appropriate assistance.

**C.** If a mediator's ability to conduct a mediation is impaired by drugs, alcohol, medication or otherwise, the mediator shall not conduct the mediation.

## STANDARD V. CONFIDENTIALITY

**A.** A mediator shall maintain the confidentiality of all information obtained by the mediator in mediation, unless otherwise agreed to by the parties or required by applicable law.

**1.** If the parties to a mediation agree that the mediator may disclose information obtained during the mediation, the mediator may do so.

**2.** A mediator should not communicate to any non-participant information about how the parties acted in the mediation. A mediator may report, if required, whether parties appeared at a scheduled mediation and whether or not the parties reached a resolution.

**3.** If a mediator participates in teaching, research or evaluation of mediation, the mediator should protect the anonymity of the parties and abide by their reasonable expectations regarding confidentiality.

**B.** A mediator who meets with any persons in private session during a mediation shall not convey directly or indirectly to any other person, any information that was obtained during that private session without the consent of the disclosing person.

**C.** A mediator shall promote understanding among the parties of the extent to which the parties will maintain confidentiality of information they obtain in a mediation.

**D.** Depending on the circumstance of a mediation, the parties may have varying expectations regarding confidentiality that a mediator should address. The parties may make their own rules with respect to confidentiality, or the accepted practice of an individual mediator or institution may dictate a particular set of expectations.

## STANDARD VI. QUALITY OF THE PROCESS

**A.** A mediator shall conduct a mediation in accordance with these Standards and in a manner that promotes diligence, timeliness, safety, presence of the appropriate participants, party participation, procedural fairness, party competency and mutual respect among all participants.

1. A mediator should agree to mediate only when the mediator is prepared to commit the attention essential to an effective mediation.

2. A mediator should only accept cases when the mediator can satisfy the reasonable expectation of the parties concerning the timing of a mediation.

3. The presence or absence of persons at a mediation depends on the agreement of the parties and the mediator. The parties and mediator may agree that others may be excluded from particular sessions or from all sessions.

4. A mediator should promote honesty and candor between and among all participants, and a mediator shall not knowingly misrepresent any material fact or circumstance in the course of a mediation.

5. The role of a mediator differs substantially from other professional roles. Mixing the role of a mediator and the role of another profession is problematic and thus, a mediator should distinguish between the roles. A mediator may provide information that the mediator is qualified by training or experience to provide, only if the mediator can do so consistent with these Standards.

6. A mediator shall not conduct a dispute resolution procedure other than mediation but label it mediation in an effort to gain the protection of rules, statutes, or other governing authorities pertaining to mediation.

7. A mediator may recommend, when appropriate, that parties consider resolving their dispute through arbitration, counseling, neutral evaluation or other processes.

8. A mediator shall not undertake an additional dispute resolution role in the same matter without the consent of the parties. Before providing such service, a mediator shall inform the parties of the implications of the change in process and

obtain their consent to the change. A mediator who undertakes such role assumes different duties and responsibilities that may be governed by other standards.

**9.** If a mediation is being used to further criminal conduct, a mediator should take appropriate steps including, if necessary, postponing, withdrawing from or terminating the mediation.

**10.** If a party appears to have difficulty comprehending the process, issues, or settlement options, or difficulty participating in a mediation, the mediator should explore the circum stances and potential accommodations, modifications or adjustments that would make possible the party's capacity to comprehend, participate and exercise self-determination.

**B.** If a mediator is made aware of domestic abuse or violence among the parties, the mediator shall take appropriate steps including, if necessary, postponing, withdrawing from or terminating the mediation.

**C.** If a mediator believes that participant conduct, including that of the mediator, jeopardizes conducting a mediation consistent with these Standards, a mediator shall take appropriate steps including, if necessary, postponing, withdrawing from or terminating the mediation.

## STANDARD VII. ADVERTISING AND SOLICITATION

**A.** A mediator shall be truthful and not misleading when advertising, soliciting or otherwise communicating the mediator's qualifications, experience, services and fees.

**1.** A mediator should not include any promises as to outcome in communications, including business cards, stationery, or computer-based communications.

**2.** A mediator should only claim to meet the mediator qualifications of a governmental entity or private organization if that entity or organization has a recognized procedure for qualifying mediators and it grants such status to the mediator.

**B.** A mediator shall not solicit in a manner that gives an appearance of partiality for or against a party or otherwise undermines the integrity of the process.

**C.** A mediator shall not communicate to others, in promotional materials or through other forms of communication, the names of persons served without their permission.

## STANDARD VIII. FEES AND OTHER CHARGES

**A.** A mediator shall provide each party or each party's representative true and complete information about mediation fees, expenses and any other actual or potential charges that may be incurred in connection with a mediation.

**1.** If a mediator charges fees, the mediator should develop them in light of all relevant factors, including the type and complexity of the matter, the qualifications of the mediator, the time required and the rates customary for such mediation services.

**2.** A mediator's fee arrangement should be in writing unless the parties request otherwise.

**B.** A mediator shall not charge fees in a manner that impairs a mediator's impartiality.

**1.** A mediator should not enter into a fee agreement which is contingent upon the result of the mediation or amount of the settlement.

**2.** While a mediator may accept unequal fee payments from the parties, a mediator should not use fee arrangements that adversely impact the mediator's ability to conduct a mediation in an impartial manner.

## STANDARD IX. ADVANCEMENT OF MEDIATION PRACTICE

**A.** A mediator should act in a manner that advances the practice of mediation. A mediator promotes this Standard by engaging in some or all of the following:

**1.** Fostering diversity within the field of mediation.

**2.** Striving to make mediation accessible to those who elect touse it, including providing services at a reduced rate or on a pro bono basis as appropriate.

**3.** Participating in research when given the opportunity, including obtaining participant feedback when appropriate.

**4.** Participating in outreach and education efforts to assist the public in developing an improved understanding of, and appreciation for, mediation.

**5.** Assisting newer mediators through training, mentoring and networking.

**B.** A mediator should demonstrate respect for differing points of view within the field, seek to learn from other mediators and work together with other mediators to improve the profession and better serve people in conflict.

# Appendix B

# REPORTER'S NOTES

## MODEL STANDARDS OF CONDUCT FOR MEDIATORS
### (September 9, 2005)

### I. Introduction

During the 1992–94 period, representatives from the American Arbitration Association, the American Bar Association's Section of Dispute Resolution, and the Association for Conflict Resolution[4] developed the Model Standards of Conduct for Mediators (hereinafter referred to as 1994 Version). These Standards had three stated functions: to serve as a guide for the conduct of mediators; to inform the mediating parties; and to promote public confidence in mediation as a process for resolving disputes.

The 1994 Version has performed these functions with remarkable success. Two salient signs of such success are that various state programs adopted it in total or with slight variations as their guide for mediator conduct,[5] and multiple educational texts reference it in their discussion of ethical norms for mediators.[6]

During the past decade, however, the use of mediation has grown exponentially. State jurisdictions authorize referrals to mediation across a broad range of cases; Florida, as a single state, reported more than 100,000 cases being mediated in a given year. At the federal level, both district and circuit courts have experimented with various mediation initiatives. Delivery systems vary: some jurisdictions support the development of private marketplace mediator service delivery while others hire staff mediators in order to provide mediation services to all parties without additional cost to them. As use has grown, so have guidelines and rules; partly in response to the phenomenon that there are now more than 2200 statutory provisions or court rules shaping mediation's use, leaders in the field initiated efforts in the late 1990s that led to the development of the Uniform Mediation Act. And in contexts other than courts, such as peer mediation programs in middle schools and high schools, mediation systems in organizational contexts, and facilitated dialogue to resolve social policy conflicts, mediation's use has become prominent.

---

[4] The Association for Conflict Resolution is the merged organization of three entities: the Academy of Family Mediators, the Conflict Resolution Education Network, and the Society of Professionals in Dispute Resolution. The Society of Professionals in Dispute Resolution was the third participating organization in the development of the 1994 Standards.

[5] Such states include Alabama, Arkansas, Arizona, California, Georgia, Kansas, Louisiana, and Virginia.

[6] Examples include Alfini, et al, MEDIATION THEORY AND PRACTICE, Goldberg, Sander, et al, DISPUTE RESOLUTION: NEGOTIATION, MEDIATION, AND OTHER Processes.

Given this expanded use, representatives from the original participating organizations believed it important to review the 1994 Version to assess whether changes were warranted. In September 2002, two designated representatives from each of the three original participating organizations convened (hereinafter referred to as Joint Committee) to initiate its review These persons included:

American Arbitration Association:

Eric P. Tuchmann

John H. Wilkinson

American Bar Association, Section of Dispute Resolution

R. Wayne Thorpe

Susan M. Yates

Association for Conflict Resolution

Sharon B. Press

Terrence T. Wheeler

## II. Guiding Principles

The members of the Joint Committee adopted the following principles to govern their work:

A. The three-fold major functions of the 1994 Version — to serve as a guide for the conduct of mediators; to inform the mediating parties; and to promote public confidence in mediation as a process for resolving disputes — should remain unchanged.

B. The Standards should retain their original function of serving as fundamental, basic ethical guidelines for persons mediating in all practice contexts while simultaneously recognizing that mediation practice in selected contexts may require additional standards in order to insure process integrity.

C. The basic architecture of the 1994 Version should be retained. Where possible, the original concepts should be retained, but changes should be made to correct, clarify or respond to new developments in mediation practice.

D Each Standard should target fundamental, ethical guidelines for mediators and exclude references to desirable behaviors or "best practices" in the statement of a Standard.

E. The process for conducting the Joint Committee's review of the 1994 Version should be accessible by the various publics interested in and affected by the practice of mediation.

F. Any changes to the Standards should be supported by a consensus of all Joint Committee members.

## III. Joint Committee Schedule of Operations

The Joint Committee convened in September 2002 to begin its work. Members discussed basic governing principles to guide both procedural and substantive issues. It agreed to recruit a Reporter to assist it in its work.

At its meeting in March 2003 at the ABA's Section of Dispute Resolution Annual Conference in San Antonio, Texas, the Joint Committee adopted the following procedural guidelines:

a) Convene a series of Joint Committee meetings during the 2003-04 period at which the Committee members, in executive session, would analyze the 1994 Version, consider input from outside the Joint Committee, raise questions or concerns about its current vitality, and, if appropriate, develop and adopt alternative format, language, and content;

b) Conduct regular public sessions at the various conferences or meetings of the sponsoring organizations with the goal of eliciting comments and insights from practitioner audiences regarding appropriate questions to raise about the project's goals or particular elements of individual Standards; and

c) Publish the Committee's work through a web site in order to elicit broad-based comments and reactions to the Joint Committee's activities.

In July 2003, the Joint Committee, through its Reporter, sent letters of invitation to more than 50 organizations in the dispute resolution field requesting them to designate a liaison to the Joint Committee. The Committee Reporter was charged with contacting these organizational liaisons in timely, regular ways to alert them to the development of the Joint Committee work. While participation and comments were desired from all persons affected by the Joint Committee's work, the Joint Committee believed that having organizations identify such liaison personnel would expedite communication.

The Joint Committee met in executive session in May 2003, October 2003, January 2004, April 2004, November 2004, and December 2004. These in-person sessions were accompanied by extensive conference call discussions. The Joint Committee conducted public forum about its work at the annual conferences of the ABA's Section of Dispute Resolution (March 2003 and April 2004) and the Association for Conflict Resolution (October 2003 and October 2004). It established its website, listing the 1994 version and inviting practitioner comment, in July 2003 (www.moritzlaw.osu.edu).

The Joint Committee posted a proposed revised Model Standards (January 2004) in January 2004. It received public comments to the posting, both via website responses and the workshop discussion at the ABA's Section of Dispute Resolution Annual Meeting in April 2004. Throughout Summer 2004, the Joint Committee engaged in extensive conference call discussions to analyze and address the various issues raised by public comment. It posted Model Standards (September 2004) at the beginning of September; this version reflected substantial changes to the Model Standards (January 2004) document, including a significant proposed revision for the role and shape of the Reporter's Notes. At the time of the posting, the Joint

Committee invited public comments for an approximate 60-day period, noting that it planned to meet in early November to begin consideration of its final draft. Public comments were received through early December 2004 and considered at the Joint Committee's final sessions on December 6-7, 2004. Through subsequent conference calls during December 2004, the Joint Committee developed its December 2004 draft, a draft designed as a final document, subject to consultation by Joint Committee members with their respective internal constituencies. The December 2004 draft and accompanying Reporter's Notes (January 17, 2005) were posted to the website for public information purposes. During the January-July, 2005 period, the Joint Committee examined targeted suggestions from constituent sources and developed the July 29, 2005 document.

The Joint Committee agreed unanimously to recommend to its respective organizations for appropriate adoption the Model Standards of Conduct (July 2005); for reasons explained below in Footnote 4, the document is referred to throughout these Reporter's Notes as Model Standards (September 2005)).[7]

### IV. Format of Model Standards (September 2005)

*General changes.* The Joint Committee has recommended several significant organizational format changes to the 1994 Version. The Joint Committee, with the aid of sustained, thoughtful public comments, concluded that the 1994 Version could be improved by adopting the following principles:

(1) separate the statement of the Standard's title from a statement of the Standard itself; (2) divide the statement of the Standard into enumerated paragraphs and sub-paragraphs, thereby facilitating clarity of exposition and public discussion of distinct, albeit related concepts; (3) eliminate the ambiguous status of the "hanging paragraphs" that follow the statement of the Standard itself by drafting the document so that all entries provide meaningful guidance for mediator conduct; (4) distinguish the level of guidance provided to the mediator by the targeted use of the verbs, "shall" and "should," thereby eliminating the need for the categorical distinction between the statement of the Standard and "Comments"; (5) shape the document so that the language of the Standards guides the mediator's conduct rather than the conduct of other mediation participants; and (6) shape the document to provide guidance for mediator conduct in situations when the operation of two or more Standards might conflict with one another.

While believing that the 1994 Version could be improved in these ways, the Joint Committee wants to state publicly its collective admiration and respect for the efforts of those individuals who crafted the 1994 Version. The quality of their work is confirmed in multiple ways, including the numbers of states that have adopted the

---

[7] The Joint Committee formatted the first page of the Model Standards (September 2005) so as to reflect an effective date. It agreed that the effective date would be that date on which, chronologically, the last of the three original participating organizations adopts the Model Standards. The Joint Committee instructed its Reporter that, once an effective date was established, he should revise the Reporter's Notes to change all references to "Model Standards (July 2005)" to reflect that adoption date. As noted on the cover page for the Standards, the adoption dates by the respective organizations were: American Arbitration Association (September 8, 2005), the American Bar Association House of Delegates (August 9, 2005), and the Association for Conflict Resolution (August 22, 2005).

1994 Version to govern its court-annexed mediation programs and the number of textbooks that cite it in discussions of mediator ethics. As the Joint Committee considered using alternative phrases and words in various Standards and Comments, it routinely returned to admiring the insight contained in the original Standards. And perhaps most significantly, the Joint Committee, after canvassing multiple codes and standards operating in courts and programs, enthusiastically confirmed that the drafters of the 1994 Version had served the public elegantly by providing a comprehensive, useable document organized around nine Standards. The Joint Committee has retained that basic architecture throughout its revisions.

*Changes in format to the Model of Standards of Conduct for Mediators.*

The Joint Committee attempted to incorporate and implement the above-noted principles throughout its multiple drafts. In the first posted revision, the Model Standards (January 2004) embraced the principles of having a title for each Standard, stating the Standard in declarative sentences targeted exclusively at guiding mediator conduct, enumerating them in appropriately separated sentences, and distinguishing the type of mediator guidance offered by a Standard or Comment by the use of "shall" and "should" respectively. Second, in terms of format, the Model Standards (January 2004) used footnotes to try to provide several types of information:

a) a definition of relevant terms; (b) examples of how a particular Standard or comment might operate at cross purposes with another Standard in a particular setting; (c) general comments regarding the significance of particular Standards, using verbatim the language of the 1994 Version; and (d) clarification, by way of example, of new elements being added to the 1994 Version. Third, the Model Standards (January 2004) suggested that the Reporter's Notes would be an official source to summarize or clarify matters relevant to the statement of the Model Standards.

Public comments to the Model Standards (January 2004) applauded the Joint Committee's effort to organize crisply the statement of the Standard and the Comment section. However, many noted that the use of footnotes was problematic: format-wise, it instantly prompted a reader to assess what status to accord them: were they binding? Were they of the same significance as a statement of a Standard or Comment? And, in the final analysis, what would be their relationship to an expanded version of the Reporter's Notes? Further, given that one of the Joint Committee's guiding principles was that substantive changes to the 1994 Version would be made only if there were evidence that current practice or policies warranted such changes, some charged that the footnotes, even in combination with enriched Reporter's Notes, did not systematically deliver on that promise. Finally, several persons suggested that the content or statement of particular footnotes needed clarification.

The Joint Committee, in its deliberations during the April-August 2004 period, found persuasive the public comments that argued that the use of footnotes created complexity and confusion rather than clarity. Accordingly, the Model Standards (September 2004), with two exceptions, contained no footnotes; those exceptions addressed two topics that the Joint Committee thought important to reflect in the document itself: first, that no participating organization had yet to consider and adopt the Model Standards (September 2004); and second, that the use of the term "mediator" in the Standards was to be understood to apply to persons operating in a co-mediator model as well as to those working in a solo capacity. In eliminating the footnotes, however, the Joint Committee proposed having the Reporter's Notes serve as the legislative history regarding the development and application of the Model Standards of Conduct for Mediators. Accordingly, it directed its Reporter to format and prepare the Reporter's Notes so that the Notes contained a discussion of the following elements: the concerns and rationale the Joint Committee found persuasive for offering substantive changes to the 1994 Version; examples of application questions that the footnotes in the Model Standards (January 2004) were designed to address; and a recounting, at least in a general way, of the types of concerns and comments raised by public participants and the manner in which the Joint Committee addressed those comments in its current draft.

In response to public and organizational comments to the Model Standards (September 2004), the Committee made three significant changes in developing the December 2004 draft. First, in response to public concerns about there being multiple documents (*i.e.*, the Model Standards and the Reporter Notes), the Joint Committee chose to develop a format for the Standards such that the document itself constituted a complete statement. The Joint Committee concluded that it would not try to integrate or weave the Reporter's Notes or any other commentary into the final statement of the Model Standards nor have the Reporter's Notes viewed as an independent but necessary component of the publication of the Standards for which formal adoption by participating organizations would be sought. Each Joint Committee member agrees, though, that these Reporter Notes accurately reflect the commentary, history and deliberations of the Revision process and hopes that they serve their intended educational role.

Second, the Joint Committee chose to eliminate organizationally the distinction between Standards and Comments, opting to address through clear language in each entry the precise guidance provided to a mediator.

Finally, the Joint Committee included explicit provisions directed to considerations of interpretative construction.

### V. Analysis of Model of Standards of Conduct for Mediators (September 2005).

#### Preamble

The Model Standards (September 2005) amends the organizational format of the 1994 Version. It identifies an effective date for the adoption of the Standards by participating organizations, begins with a paragraph describing the historical context of the document and its revision, and substitutes a *Preamble* and *Note on Construction* for the "Introductory Note" and "Preface."

The Joint Committee determined that the Model Standards, to be most effective, must operate as a single, self-contained, defining document. As a result, while it noted that that the Reporter's Notes could serve a valuable educational function for the public regarding the rationale for various changes, the Joint Committee concluded that its prior consideration to have the Reporter's Notes serve an integral role as an interpretative resource for the Standards was misdirected. Further, the Joint Committee determined that the distinction between a statement of a "Standard" and the "Comments" relevant to that Standard was ultimately not helpful; although this distinction occurs in the 1994 Version and had been retained by the Joint Committee in both the Model Standards (January 2004) and Model Standards (September 2004), the Joint Committee decided that the fundamental difference for guiding mediator conduct contained in this categorical distinction was more effectively communicated in clear language for each entry. To promote clarity, the Model Standards (September 2005) contains a new section entitled *Note on Construction* with material that explains the level of mediator guidance provided by each entry. With these significant format changes, the Joint Committee believes the Model Standards (September 2005) can operate effectively as a self-contained document.

In the *Preamble*, the Model Standards (September 2005) revises the definition of mediation in order to make it consistent with changes in Standard I that recognize that party self-determination operates over not just voluntary decision-making as to outcomes but to multiple process components as well. Since the publication of the 1994 Version, there has been significant academic and policy discussion focused on mediation style or theory. In particular, the terms, facilitative and evaluative, to describe mediator orientations have taken on particular meanings in the popular literature and approaches to mediation differently conceptualized in such frameworks as problem-solving or transformative have been trenchantly analyzed. The revised definition of mediation is not designed to exclude any mediation style or approach consistent with Standard I's commitment to support and respect the parties' decision-making roles in the process.

Note on Construction

This section is designed to provide clarity to the interpretation and application of the Standards, both individually and collectively.

The Model Standards (September 2005) retain the 9-Standard architecture of the 1994 Version. The *Note* indicates that the Standards are to be read and construed in their entirety. The interpretative principle that mandates that each Standard be read and interpreted in such a manner as to promote consistency with all other Standards is the presumed operative principle guiding the drafting of the Model Standards (September 2005).

By eliminating the structural framework that led to using "shall" and "should" in the statement of the Standard and Comment respectively, the Joint Committee believed it important to define these terms, given the purposes and goals of these Standards. The definition of "shall" prescribes mandatory mediator conduct. The definition of "should," more sharply than conventional understanding might otherwise suggest, stipulates that the recommended guidance to a mediator, though not mandated, can be discarded only for compelling reasons. The combined message is clear: the Standards, in their various statements, provide strong guidance for mediator conduct; while not presuming to be a "rule-book" that anticipates and answers every possibility, the Standards provide meaningful guidance for most situations and the burden transfers to an individual mediator to justify a departure from its prescriptions.

While some sections of the Model Standards (September 2005), such as Standards III (A-F) and IV (B), make reference to a time frame for a mediation (using language such as "during and after a mediation,") the *Note on Construction* notes clearly that the Model Standards (September 2005) do not try to provide precise definitions for the beginning and ending of a mediation. The Joint Committee recognizes that such definitional precision might be important in some contexts, such as where court rules, statutes or other regulations govern a mediation; however, in other settings, the exact beginning or end of a mediation is not always clear, yet the Model Standards (September 2005) are designed to guide mediator conduct even in such contexts of ambiguity.

The *Note* explicitly addresses the fact that a mediator's conduct may be affected by applicable law, court rules, regulations, other applicable professional rules, mediation rules to which the parties have agreed, and agreement of the parties, some of which may conflict with and take precedence over compliance with these Standards. This topic is noted here for both format and substantive reasons. Organizationally, it became clumsy to represent this conflict throughout the document with such phrases as "unless otherwise required by law"; while that phrase has been used once in the statement of a provision of Standard V dealing with Confidentiality (a significantly law-regulated area of mediator activity), the Joint Committee believed it best to state this basic proposition at the beginning of the document so that it would operate as a presumed understanding throughout.

Substantively, the Joint Committee, in response to comments, believed it important to clarify for a mediator what posture he or she should adopt when confronted with such a conflict. The basic principle, while straightforward, requires elaboration. The principle that guides mediator conduct in such contexts is: in the event of a conflict between a provision of a Standard and one or more external sources identified in the *Note*, a mediator ought to conduct oneself in a manner that retains and remains faithful to as much of the spirit and intent of the affected Standard, and all other Standards, as is possible. The following example is illustrative: Assume that a court orders a party to mediation; one party's counsel telephones the mediator and states that neither the lawyer nor client plans to attend, believing any such session to be worthless for this case. The mediator reminds the attorney of the court directive; indeed, in some jurisdictions, since the mediator may even have a duty to report participant non-attendance to the referring court, the mediator may remind the attorney of that matter, too. Here is a conflict between a court rule and Standard I: a mediator cannot consistently adhere to the court rule and simultaneously honor the prescription in Standard I that a mediator conduct the mediation based on party self-determination with regard to "participation in [a mediation.]" When a mediator in this situation recognizes that the court rule takes precedence over this provision of Standard I, a mediator still has an ethical responsibility to conduct that mediation in a manner consistent with all other aspects of Standard I — *e.g.*, respecting and promoting self-determination with respect to process design and outcomes — as well as consistent with all other Standards. The current language of the penultimate paragraph reflects the Joint Committee's decision that a mediator must act in various practice contexts in a manner that retains and advances as much of the spirit and intent of the Standards as is possible.

The Joint Committee has consistently noted that the Standards can be used in multiple ways by individuals, programs, or organizations, including requiring compliance with these Standards as a condition for continuing membership in a program or organization. The Joint Committee, however, has added a final paragraph under *Note* to clarify for mediators that courts or other entities may use these Standards to establish the expected level of care for mediator conduct.

### Standard I: Self-Determination

There are two significant changes proposed to the 1994 Version. First, the 1994 Version focuses exclusively on exercising self-determination with respect to out-come; it is silent with regard to such matters as mediator selection, designing procedural aspects of the mediation process to suit individual needs, and choosing whether to participate in or withdraw from the process. The Model Standards (September 2005) extends the scope of self-determination to these other areas.

Second, the 1994 Version does not address the question of the interplay among the Standards. In some instances, the interplay is consistent but the mediator must be cognizant of it. For example, while parties can exercise self-determination in the selection of their mediator, a mediator must consider *Standard III: Conflicts of Interests* and *Standard IV: Competence* when deciding whether to accept the invitation to serve. Alternatively, the interplay among Standards may result in a conflict; a mediator, for example, may feel pulled in conflicting directions when the mediator, duty-bound to support party self-determination (*Standard I*), recognizes that parties are trying to design a process that is not mediation but want to call it mediation to gain confidentiality protections, thereby undermining the mediator's obligation to sustain a quality process (*Standard VI*). Standard I(A)(1) and I(B) explicitly recognize this potential for conflict and indicates to the mediator that sustaining a quality process places limits on the extent to which party autonomy, external influences, and mediator self-interest should shape participant conduct.

Standard I (B) directly addresses the concern that mediators may undermine party self-determination or themselves experience conflicts of interest as a result of pressure or incentives generated by court personnel, program administrators, provider organizations, the media, or other outside influences. Many factors can operate this way, intended or not: for instance, a program administrator might suggest to one mediator that more cases shall be assigned to another mediator because that person "always gets a settlement," or a news media writer might report settlement talks as having stalled in a way that might possibly harm the reputation of the identified mediator. The result is that such pressures or influences prompt the mediator to engage in conduct to override party self-determination in an effort to gain resolution. The Joint Committee reaffirms the Comment in the 1994 Version on this point that the mediator's commitment to the parties and process must remain steadfast and a mediator must not coerce parties to settle; the language of the Model Standards (September 2005) has been sharpened to eliminate any ambiguity regarding that duty.

Several public comments raised concerns that the language of the 1994 Version stating, "Self-determination is the fundamental principle of mediation" had not been retained. The Joint Committee believes that the expanded statement of Standard I, together with the definition of mediation appearing in the Preamble, appropriately reaffirms the central responsibility that a mediator has to actively support party self-determination, prohibits conflict of interest issues from undermining a mediator's commitment to promoting party self-determination (I(B)), yet recognizes, as noted above, that Standards may conflict.

Other public comments suggested that the Standard should contain language that requires the mediator to make certain that the parties made informed decisions; given the significant controversy about whether and how a mediator might insure that a party's decisions are suitably informed, the Joint Committee reaffirmed retaining the language of the 1994 Version as I (B). Additionally, several public comments noted that parties can be effectively ordered to mediation by a judge, thereby rendering self-determination as to process irrelevant. The Joint Committee addresses this dynamic in the *Preamble* in its discussion of the potential conflict between the operation of the Model Standards (September 2005) and other sources that might govern an individual mediator's conduct. Finally, some public comments suggested that Standard I should contain guidance to a mediator regarding his or her duty to report "good faith" participation by various mediation participants. To the degree that might be required by other rules governing mediator behavior in a particular setting, the Joint Committee addresses this topic in the *Note on Construction's* statement regarding potential conflicts. However, in Standard V (A) (2) on confidentiality, the Joint Committee explicitly supports the position widely adopted in practice and program rules that a mediator can override confidentiality, if required, for only two purposes: to report whether parties appeared at a scheduled mediation or to report whether the parties reached a resolution; the Joint Committee rejected overriding the confidentiality requirement for any other purpose.

## Standard II: Impartiality

The Joint Committee believes that several developments of the past decade's growth in mediation practice warrant changes to the 1994 Version of Standard II. First, with the expanded growth of private sector mediation practices, the range of business practices and practices regarding fees raises concerns about the mediator being perceived as partial. Second, with the remarkable diversity of participants in mediation, challenges have arisen with regard to sustaining a mediator's impartiality while simultaneously respecting practices grounded in different cultures.

The Model Standards (September 2005) addresses these concerns in the following way. In Standard II (A), the Joint Committee reaffirms the central role of the need for a mediator to be impartial; disclosure of potential conflicts of interests, and parties choosing to proceed following such disclosure, is a separate consideration addressed in Standard III.

Second, the propriety and impact of fee arrangements, including success fees or practices involving unequal payment of the mediator's fee by the parties, affects several Standards; the Joint Committee chose to address these matters in *Standard VIII: Fees and Other Charges.*

In response to insightful public comment, the Joint Committee revised the language of what is now Standard II (B)(1) to reflect that the mediator must not act in a manner that favors or prejudices any mediation participant based on the

personal characteristics, background, values and beliefs, or performance at a
mediation of that individual; the proscription governs the mediator's conduct
towards any participant, not just the parties. While the Standard delineates
recognizable elements that operate to undermine mediator impartiality, the list is
not exhaustive. Additionally, the Joint Committee decided to strengthen the 1994
Version by shaping the Standards both to guide the conduct of mediators rather
than other mediation participants and to provide guidance for mediator conduct
through the defined use of "shall" and "should"; by so doing, the Joint Committee
agreed that the phrase, "should guard against," that is used in the 1994 Version in
this section was not consistent with such changes.

Some public comments urged the Joint Committee to adopt language that
required the mediator, when his or her ability to remain impartial was undermined,
to withdraw from the mediation "without harming any party's interests." Individual
members of the Joint Committee questioned whether withdrawal without harm to
at least some interests of one or more parties is always possible, even though all
agreed that the duty to withdraw in these circumstances is clear. The Joint
Committee believes that the manner of withdrawal is a matter of "best practices";
further, throughout the Standards, the Joint Committee has declined to insert
language that requires a mediator to insure a particular outcome.

Finally, potential challenges to a mediator's impartiality in private sector practice
arise with remarkable frequency. For example, if all parties, their representatives
and the mediator are immersed in discussions in an all-day mediation and they
decide to order food for lunch, does the mediator violate Standard II if the lawyer
for one of the parties offers to pay for everyone's lunch? If a mediator accepts a
small gift from a grateful party following a successful mediation, must the mediator
return it on pain of violating the impartiality requirement? And these matters
become more complex when practices grounded in cultural traditions surface: if the
cultural tradition of one party prompts that individual to bring a ceremonial gift to
the mediator in order to reaffirm the seriousness of the talks and the well-wishes
that the talks proceed constructively, can the mediator accept it? The Joint
Committee supports the individual mediator, whether in a private practice setting
or government or organizational program setting, responding sensitively and
comfortably to such contemporary practices, but with the caveat that all such
conduct be grounded in a sincere assessment as to whether accepting such benefits
or giving such gifts will raise questions as to that mediator's actual or perceived
impartiality; by using the term "*de minimis* gifts or incidental items," the Standard
signals to the practicing mediator that the threshold for questioning whether a
mediator is no longer impartial for these types of matters is low.

There were several public comments expressing concern that the following
language from the 1994 Version's Comment Section of Standard II had not been
retained in the posted Model Standards (January 2004):

> "When mediators are appointed by a court or institution, the appointing
> agency shall make reasonable efforts to ensure that mediators serve
> impartially."

Comparable comments were received regarding the role of program administrators in government or organizational mediation programs. The Joint Committee
appreciates the conviction expressed by program administrators operating in court

or other institutional settings that the cited language serves a critically important role in assisting program administrators to advance quality mediation practice. However, one goal of the Model Standards (September 2005) is to have all language focus sharply and exclusively on guiding mediator conduct; for that reason, the Joint Committee has consistently resisted suggestions that it develop language that recognized and extended coverage of the Standards to administrators of mediation programs in court, administrative and organizational contexts. That is not to suggest, however, that the Standards will not influence the conduct of these other participants, indirectly or directly; for instance, the Joint Committee explicitly addresses the concerns raised by these comments in Standard I (B): *Self-Determination* where the language of the Standard reinforces the mediator's duty to the parties and process when responding to pressure being exerted by such outside influences as court personnel or provider organizations.

## Standard III: Conflicts of Interest

Standard III (A) defines a conflict of interest as a dealing or relationship that undermines a mediator's impartiality; while Standard II and III are explicitly connected in a fundamental manner, the Joint Committee felt it important to retain the distinction in order to emphasize that a mediator's impartiality is central to the mediation process and that mediator conduct that raises questions of conflicts of interest serves to undermine public or party confidence in the central integrity of the process.

Standard III (A) notes that a conflict of interest can arise from multiple sources in multiple time dimensions. A mediator must canvass this extensive range of possible disqualifying activities, attuned to the notion that his or her immediate duty is to disclose information that might create a possible conflict of interest; if parties, with knowledge of the relationship, consent to that mediator's service, then the mediator, pursuant to Standard I, could proceed. However, the Model Standards (September 2005) retains content and language of the 1994 Version that notes that if the conflict of interest casts serious doubts on process integrity, then the mediator shall decline to proceed despite the preferences of the parties.

Public comment requested clarification of the interplay between such sections as Standard III (C) or III (D) with Standard II (C): Impartiality. As is referenced in the Reporter's Notes in *Note on Construction*, the interpretative principle mandates that each Standard be read in a manner that promotes consistency. Applying that principle, in Standard II (C), the Joint Committee supports the posture that a mediator shall not conduct a mediation if he or she is unable to conduct it in an impartial manner; even if participants, under Standard III (C) or III (D) gave consent to the mediator to proceed after a mediator disclosed an actual or potential conflict of interest, Standard II (C) prohibits the mediator from proceeding.

Some Committee members were disturbed to hear reported that a common practice among some mediators is for the mediator not to disclose with all mediation parties and their representatives that the mediator has served previously as a mediator in situations involving some of the mediation parties or their representatives; the language of III (A) seriously questions the integrity of such a practice.

Standard III (B) explicitly acknowledges that how one conducts a conflicts check varies by practice context. For a complex case that comes to a mediator through his or her law firm, best practice consists of making a firm-wide conflicts check at the pre-mediation phase. By contrast, for a mediator of an interpersonal dispute administered by a community mediation agency who is charged with mediating the case immediately upon referral, making an inquiry of the parties and participants at the time of the mediation regarding potential conflicts of interest may be sufficient.

In drafting Standard III (C), public comments highlighted one particular source of potential conflict as being that situation in which a significant portion of a mediator's work, particularly when compensated, comes from a single source; these commentators suggested that that situation be explicitly addressed. The Joint Committee, as individuals, agreed that such a situation creates a serious potential conflict and that there would be a duty minimally to disclose that situation. However, as other public comments noted, there are multiple examples of relationships between one party and a mediator that give rise to the same concern about conflicts of interest; if one attempted to catalogue a comprehensive list, then failure (through oversight) to include some relationship might be seen, incorrectly, to license that conduct. Therefore, the Joint Committee developed language of a general nature.

In performing the mediator's role, an individual displays multiple analytical and interpersonal skills; therefore, it is not surprising that a mediation participant who witnesses such talent might consider employing that mediator again. If a mediation participant, be it a party, party representative, witness or some other participant wants to employ the individual mediator in a subsequent mediation, or in another role (such as a personal lawyer, therapist, or a consultant to their business), then the individual serving as mediator must make certain that entering into such a new relationship does not cast doubt about the integrity of the mediation process. The Model Standards (January 2004) contained an explicit enumeration (Paragraph C) that prohibited a mediator from soliciting any type of future professional services; in response to public comments critical of the broad, absolutist language of that paragraph, the Joint Committee deleted that provision in the Model Standards (September 2004) and revised the language of what was then Comment 3 to address this matter. The final language appears in Model Standards (September 2005) as Standard III (F). Unlike some other Codes, Standard III (F) does not impose rigid time lines to regulate the development of such relationships but does suggest that the amount of time that has elapsed is a factor to consider.

### Standard IV: Competence

Mediators operate in many contexts and reflect a broad range of backgrounds, trainings, and competencies. The Model Standards (September 2005) retains the commitment expressed in the 1994 Version that the Standards not create artificial or arbitrary barriers to serve the public as a mediator. But to promote public confidence in the integrity and usefulness of the process and to protect the members of the public, an individual representing himself or herself as a mediator must be committed to serving only in those situations for which he or she possesses the basic competency to assist.

The Joint Committee, Standard IV (A), changes the language of the 1994 Version to use the term, "competence" in place of "qualification." In elaborating on IV (A), Standard IV (A) (1) indicates that such elements as training, experience in mediation, and cultural understandings are often necessary in order to provide effective service. But the Joint Committee understands its language to explicitly reject two notions with regard to the operations of this Standard: first, that possessing particular educational degrees is an absolute requirement to establish mediator competency, and second, that the list of desirable competencies means that each competency is required for effective service in every mediation.

Standard IV (B) recognizes the situation in which a mediator, upon agreeing to serve, learns during the course of the discussions that the matters are more complex than originally anticipated and beyond his or her competency. In such a situation, Standard IV (B) imposes a duty on that mediator to take affirmative steps with the parties to address the situation and make appropriate arrangements for serving them (perhaps through hiring co-mediators with relevant competencies or the selection of an alternative mediator).

Public comments on the Model Standards (January 2004) strongly supported language that reaffirmed, as a central feature of Standard IV, that training and experience are the necessary and sufficient conditions for service as a mediator. The Joint Committee believes that its current language reflects that commitment and that it appropriately appears in Standard IV (A) (1). The Joint Committee also wanted to emphasize that mediator competency also includes cultural understandings, a dimension that the 1994 Version does not address. Additional public comments suggested that the language of the Standards include reference to an individual's meeting the qualification requirements set forth by relevant state statutes; the Joint Committee believed that its statements in the *Note on Construction* regarding the relationship between the Standards and state law addressed this matter, together with its *Preamble* statement that the Standards are considered as fundamental ethical guidelines; particular programs or practice areas might require additional elements for service.

Standard IV (C) mandates that a mediator not conduct the mediation if she or he is impaired by drugs, alcohol, medication or otherwise. If a mediator has the ability to correct this impairment, then she or he can initiate or continue service.

### Standard V: Confidentiality

One of the most significant developments surrounding the practice of mediation that has occurred since the adoption of the 1994 Version has been the development of the Uniform Mediation Act (2003). That undertaking significantly enhanced professional conversation and awareness of the policy goals advanced by the presumption that parties should determine their own rules regarding confidentiality and that communications made for purposes of advancing a mediation conversation should not be available for use in subsequent proceedings. Discussion and debate surrounding that uniform law focused significantly on whether the parties and the mediator or just the parties should hold the privilege independently, and what exceptions to the privilege should be made a part of law. While this Standard is consistent with the confidentiality policy goals of the Uniform Mediation Act, it is not designed to match its substantive provisions and nuances in every dimension.

Standard V directs mediator conduct in two ways. First, it imposes a duty on the mediator not to share with others information obtained as a result of serving as a mediator. Even if the parties agree that the mediator shall disclose it (pursuant to Standard I (A)), Standard V (A) (1) states that the mediator may do so but is not required to do so. Second, Standard V imposes a duty on the mediator to promote participant understanding of the extent to which information shared and comments made for purposes of mediation are confidential. What is crucial to the effective operation of the Standard — and hence to the integrity of the process — is that all participants to the mediation, including the mediator, actively seek to understand the nature and extent of the confidential status of communications made during the mediation. The current language promotes that goal.

Some public comments to prior versions urged the Joint Committee to adopt language that explicitly linked or tracked the Standard to the requirements of state or Federal law; as noted above in a related matter, the Joint Committee placed references in the *Note on Construction* to the interplay between the Standards and relevant legal guidelines, in part to enhance the fluidity of the language of the Standards and in some measure to resist a perceived tendency to over regulate mediation practice. The Model Standards (September 2005) retains, in both V (A) and V (A) (2), references to recognized exceptions to the confidentiality reach.

Standard V(A)(3) tracks the concept of the 1994 Version in which its drafters sought to insure that the Confidentiality Standard did not prohibit monitoring, research, evaluation or education of mediation by responsible persons. However, since the language of the Standards is targeted to guide mediator conduct, the language of the 1994 Version required modification. Further, when reflecting on the nature of how the teaching, research and evaluation of mediation could appropriately go forward, the Joint Committee thought it appropriate to adopt a two-fold goal: first, protect the identity of individual participants, so that a mediator participating in teaching, research and evaluation could discuss aspects of the case but doing so in a way that does not readily enable people to discern the identities of the parties; second, to permit teaching, research and evaluation to proceed without imposing undue requirements for gaining party consent to every initiative — for example, if a court system sought to evaluate its mediation program, it would be an undue requirement to insist that the evaluator affirmatively obtain from every party or party representative to a mediation his or her consent to have reported such elements as the length of a mediation session.

Some public comments suggested that a mediator, when conducting a caucus, can appropriately place the responsibility on the party with whom she or he is caucusing to flag each element of information that the party wishes the mediator to keep confidential. In Standard V (B), the Joint Committee rejects that approach to the degree that it is not consistent with securing meaningful and timely party consent. At a practice level, the Joint Committee notes that some mediators advise the participants that the mediator will keep confidential those matters disclosed by a participant if the participant so requests; otherwise, the mediator shall treat comments made in the caucus as being ones that he or she could use in subsequent caucuses if doing so, in the mediator's judgment, would help advance discussion. By contrast, the practice of other mediators when conducting a caucus is to advise the participants that a mediator will treat all matters shared with him or her as confidential but shall ask at the end of a particular caucus whether the mediator has the participant's consent to use any or all of that developed information in subsequent caucuses. Whichever practice is adopted by a mediator, Standard V (B) affirms that it is a mediator's duty to insure that party consent to the approach is known, meaningful and timely.

Standard V (C) targets a mediator's responsibility to make certain that the parties understand the extent to which they, not the mediator, will maintain confidentiality of information that surface in mediation. Section V (D) is a provision that applies equally to V (A-C); while some might believe it implicit in each of the preceding paragraphs of the Standards, the Joint Committee thought it important to emphasize, even if somewhat redundant, the need for participant understanding of the confidentiality guidelines governing the conversation.

### Standard VI: Quality of the Process

The 1994 Version sets forth in the statement of the Standard and in its "hanging paragraph" a series of distinct, concrete ways in which a mediator could act to advance a quality process. The Model Standards (September 2005) captures those elements in its statement of VI(A), incorporating from public comment a revision that requires a mediator to conduct a process that advances procedural fairness, not, as in the Model Standards (January 2004), "process fairness."

Public comments to both the Model Standards (January 2004) and the Model Standards (September 2004), combined with further Joint Committee discussion, resulted in several changes reflected in the Model Standards (September 2005). In summary form, those changes include:

1. Comment 1 from the Model Standards (January 2004) read as follows: "A mediator should conduct mediation in a way that prevents one or more parties from manipulating the process to advance personal goals that are inconsistent with mediation principles and values." That comment has been deleted for two reasons: first, the Model Standards (September 2005) focus on guiding mediator behavior and not that of other participants in the mediation process; second, the Model Standards (September 2005) capture the goal of preventing such participant behavior in provisions such as VI (A) (6).

2. Standard VI (A) (1-9) is sequenced to reflect the presumptive order in which a mediator might confront these considerations in practice.

3. Standard VI (A) (4) reflects the nuanced environment in which mediation occurs. The language of Standard VI(A)(4) prohibits a mediator from knowingly misrepresenting a material fact or circumstance to a mediation participant while it acknowledges that resolving matters in mediation is not always predicated on there having been complete honesty and candor among those present. To state the matter differently, while mediation participants might engage in negotiating tactics such as bluffing or exaggerating that are designed to deceive other parties as to their acceptable positions, a mediator must not knowingly misrepresent a material fact or circumstance in order to advance settlement discussions.

4. Standard VI (A) (5-8) reflects an effort to reorganize and distinguish more sharply among related but importantly different directions to the mediator. VI (A)(5) announces that the mediator's role differs substantially from that of other professional roles; the goal is to distinguish between a mediator's role and such other roles as being a lawyer, mental health counselor, and the like. Yet, (A)(5) also recognizes that the insights and training the mediator draws upon to assist parties in mediation might

simultaneously constitute an important element of enabling a mediator to be competent and effective to serve the parties in that setting and be drawn from the mediator's training and experience in those other professional roles. So, the language of VI (A) (5) recognizes the differing roles that a mediator as an individual assumes in his or her life and then supports the mediator sharing information that he or she is qualified by training or experience to provide only if it is done in a manner consistent with other Standards, most notably promoting party self-determination and sustaining mediator impartiality.

Standard VI (A) (6) makes it explicit that a mediator cannot engage in a ruse of labeling a dispute resolution process as "mediation" in order to gain its benefits (such as confidentiality protections) when it is apparent that the participants have designed and participated in some other form of dispute resolution. (A)(7), as a stand-alone entry, notes that it certainly is plausible for a mediator to recommend, when appropriate, that the parties consider resolving their dispute through some other third-party process. This guideline makes at least two presumptions: first, that a mediator might identify such an option when it seems an appropriate track to pursue as a matter of process choice (i.e. "fitting the forum to the fuss") or after mediation efforts to resolve the issue(s) have not been successful in resolving all issues to each party's satisfaction; and second, that the mediator is qualified by training or experience to explain to the parties, if requested, how these various processes operate. Finally, (A) (8) clarifies that a mediator shall not undertake in the same matter that he or she is mediating a different intervener role (such as those described in (A)(7)) without party consent, without explaining to the parties and their representatives the implications of changing processes (e.g. a third-party decision-maker might have to make decisions regarding participant credibility that was not necessary in a mediation process), and without being cognizant that undertaking a new role might be governed by standards governing other third-party professions, such as a Code of Ethics for Arbitrators.

5. Standard VI (A)(9) reflects revised language to the 1994 Version by targeting guidance to the mediator more sharply: it guides a mediator who confronts mediation participants using mediation to further criminal conduct, not simply illegal conduct, to take appropriate steps to deter them from accomplishing that goal. Several public comments suggested that the mediator's duty in such a situation was to affirmatively report such conduct to appropriate legal authorities. The Joint Committee rejected that suggestion for two reasons. First, the subtly of such matters — including there being multi-issue cases in which only one issue raised a specter of criminal conduct — requires that a mediator be firm but flexible in addressing such a situation; second, confidentiality laws or agreements may prevent it, such that unless there were an exception in the confidentiality agreement for this situation or a mediator had a duty to report such conduct, a mediator might expose himself or herself to liability by reporting such conduct.

6. Standard VI (A) (10) reflects new language that addresses the situation involving a mediator's obligation when conducting a mediation with persons with recognized disabilities. The Joint Committee recognizes that the language of Comment 8 in its Model Standards (January 2004), while included by oversight but actually reflecting the language contained in the 1994 Version, was completely unacceptable. Public comments thoughtfully suggested a variety of possible clauses to address this situation; Comment 8 in the Model Standards (September 2004) reflected the Joint Committee's judgment as to the best expression of the multiple commitments involved in such a situation and it received positive endorsement from several public stakeholders. That September language remains unchanged and appears as (A) (10).

7. The Joint Committee believes that developments in practice regarding the mediation of cases in which allegations of domestic abuse arise must be addressed in any revision to the 1994 Version. Public comments strongly endorsed amending the 1994 Version to address this topic and

Standard VI (B) reflects that effort. The Joint Committee understands the term, "domestic abuse," to apply to acts of both physical violence and psychological coercion among persons in a domestic relationship. Standard VI (B) also provides guidance to mediators for situations in which mediation participants in non-domestic relationships have engaged in acts of violence towards one another. Mediator guidance for addressing challenges posed by the threat of violent conduct among participants is reinforced through such other provisions as Standards I and VI (A)..

Some public comments suggested that any provision targeted at mediations involving domestic abuse should contain a detailed prescription regarding the manner in which the mediator should screen participants, the requisite training to serve as a mediator in such situations, the requirement to report such matters to appropriate agencies if one is a mandatory reporter, and the like; the Joint Committee chose to retain the targeted, albeit general language of VI (B), with the notion that Standards for particular programs might choose to build in more elaborate requirements.

### Standard VII: Advertising and Solicitation

With increased private sector activity in the provision of mediation services, the Joint Committee believed that the 1994 Version required modest amendment to provide guidance to mediators in a more complex, technological world. The language of Standard VII (A) addresses the complexity that confronts a mediator who seeks to communicate effectively the nature of his or her services as a mediator and his or her expertise without making representations that are inconsistent with such principles as party self-determination and mediator impartiality. Standard VII (A) (1) reaffirms the 1994 Version's commitment that a mediator must not include any promise as to outcome.

Standard VII (A) (2) addresses the concern that a mediator representing to the public that he or she is a "certified" mediator might be misunderstood by the public as suggesting that the mediator has met a more stringent level of selectivity than is otherwise the case. The 1994 Version addresses this challenge as well. Some governmental entities, including courts or administrative agencies, and private sector organizations have developed, publicized procedures through which an individual mediator can obtain status as having been "certified" to be on that entity's mediator roster. If a person has been granted that status by a governmental entity or private organization, then he or she is free to so advertise it. The Joint Committee notes, however, that it would mislead the public — and be prohibited by VII (A)(2) — were an individual to complete a privately-offered mediator training program, receive a "Certificate" that states that he or she has successfully completed that course, and then advertise that he or she is a "Certified" mediator.

Standard VII (B) addresses the increasing challenge of blending appropriate communication and marketing of a mediator's services without soliciting business in a manner that results in compromising that individual's actual or perceived impartiality, and VII(C) prohibits a mediator from listing the names of clients or persons served in mediation without their permission.

### Standard VIII: Fees and Other Charges

The Model Standards (September 2005) amends the title of this Standard from the 1994 Version by adding the words, "and other Charges."

Several developments have prompted amendments to the 1994 Version. The language of VIII (A) and VIII (A) (1) provide guidance to a mediator regarding basic principles on which to construct a fee; the language of VIII (B), while not prohibiting the amount a person might charge for his or her mediation services, does mandate that the method or structure for fee payments cannot operate at cross purposes with such fundamental values of the mediation process as party self-determination or mediator impartiality.

Some scholars and practitioners have urged members of the "mediation field" to carefully examine the relationship between mediator fees and mediated outcomes. Recognizing that there remains significant controversy about whether or how success or contingent fees might operate consistently with other Standards, the Joint Committee, in Standard VIII (B)(1), retained the language of the 1994 Version regarding these matters.

A significant, controversial practice that has developed in private sector mediation practice during the past decade is the situation in which the mediator's fee is paid in unequal amounts by the parties. The presumptive norm had been that parties pay the mediator's fees in equal amounts, thereby insuring that the mediator's impartiality, both in perception and reality, was secured. The reality of contemporary practice in some sectors is that one party pays the entire fee and that all parties are comfortable with that arrangement. This practice occurs routinely in such areas as the mediation of employment discrimination lawsuits, where the defendant employer pays the mediator's fee, personal injury litigation, and the like. Some argue that parties would not have access to the benefits of mediation if such fee payment arrangements were not available.

The Joint Committee believed that, at the practical level, this practice of parties' paying unequal amounts of the mediator's fee creates the danger of undermining process integrity in two important ways: first, if the parties were not aware of this arrangement, one party, upon learning of it at a later date, might believe the outcomes had been skewed in favor of the party who had paid the higher percentage of the mediator's fee; second, if the payer of the higher fee percentage is that mediator's primary or exclusive client, the practice might create the impression that the mediator's financial interest in servicing that client outweighed his or her commitment to conducting a quality process in an impartial manner. For both situations, the Joint Committee believed that the appropriate stance of the Standard should, in the first instance, support disclosure of the arrangement to all participants, since unequal payments of fees almost always creates a perception of partiality; further, the Standard should require the mediator to be attentive to how that practice, even when acceptable to all parties, impacts the integrity of the process. Standard VIII (B) addresses these concerns.

The Model Standards (September 2005) eliminates the proposed language of the Model Standards (January 2004) regarding excepting administrative fees from the concept of referral fees; public comment raised important questions about the meaning of "administrative expense" and the Joint Committee refocused its comments to address the mediator, not provider agencies or other program sponsors.

### Standard IX: Advancement of Mediation Practice

The Model Standards (September 2005) changes the title of this Standard from the 1994 Version, replacing "Obligations to the Process" with "Advancement of Mediation Practice." The Joint Committee believes the proposed title more accurately reflects the Standard's intended focus.

Standard IX (A) (1-5) delineates some of the ways in which an individual can participate in advancing mediation practice. Given the targeted definitions provided to the terms "shall" and "should" in the Model Standards (September 2005), and consistent with public suggestions, the Joint Committee uses the term, "should," in the statement of Standard IX. The Joint Committee does not believe the delineated list of activities for advancing the practice of mediation is exhaustive nor that a mediator need engage in all of these initiatives all the time; the second sentence of Standard IX (A) reflects that judgment. Finally, the Joint Committee embraced as persuasive the thoughtful public comments that recommended that the language of Standard IX (B) substitute the word "respect" for "tolerate."

Joseph B. Stulberg, JD, Ph.D.
Reporter
Professor of Law
Moritz College of Law, The Ohio State University Columbus, Ohio


Membership of Joint Committee for the Model Standards of Conduct for Mediators (July 29, 2005)

Sharon B. Press, Attorney/Mediator
Director, Florida Dispute Resolution Center
Adjunct Professor, Florida State University College of Law Tallahassee, Florida

R. Wayne Thorpe Mediator/Arbitrator
JAMS Atlanta Office Director Atlanta, Georgia

Eric P. Tuchmann
General Counsel
American Arbitration Association New York, New York

Terrence T. Wheeler
Attorney/Mediator
Artz & Dewhirst, LLP
Adjunct Professor, Capital University Law School
Co-Director, Center for Dispute Resolution at CULS
Columbus, Ohio

John H. Wilkinson
Attorney/Mediator
Fulton, Rowe & Hart
New York, New York

Susan M. Yates
Mediator
Executive Director
Center for Analysis of Alternative Dispute Resolution Systems
Chicago, Illinois

# Appendix C

## MODEL STANDARDS OF PRACTICE FOR FAMILY AND DIVORCE MEDIATION* [DRAFT August 2000]

### OVERVIEW AND DEFINITIONS

Family and divorce mediation ("family mediation" or "diation") is a process in which a mediator, an impartial third party, facilitates the resolution of family disputes by promoting the participants' voluntary agreement. The family mediator assists communication, encourages understanding and focuses the participants on their individual and common interests. The family mediator works with the participants to explore options, make decisions and reach their own agreements.

Family mediation is not a substitute for the need for family members to obtain independent legal advice or counseling or therapy. Nor is it appropriate for all families. However, experience has established that family mediation is a valuable option for many families because it can:

- increase the self-determination of participants and their ability to communicate;

- promote the best interests of children; and

- reduce the economic and emotional costs associated with the reso lution of family disputes.

Effective mediation requires that the family mediator be qualified by training, experience and temperament; that the mediator be impartial; that the participants reach their decisions voluntarily; that their decisions be based on sufficient factual data; that the mediator be aware of the impact of culture and diversity; and that the best interests of children be taken into account. Further, the mediator should also be prepared to identify families whose history includes domestic abuse or child abuse.

These *Model Standards of Practice for Family and Divorce Mediation ("Model Standards")* aim to perform three major functions:

1. to serve as a guide for the conduct of family mediators;

2. to inform the mediating participants of what they can expect; and

---

* The Model Standards are the product of an effort by mediation-interested organizations and individuals to create a unified set of standards. The following organizations were among those involved in the drafting: The Family Law Section of the American Bar Association and the National Council of Dispute Resolution Organizations (an umbrella organization which includes the Academy of Family Mediators, the American Bar Association Section of Dispute Resolution, AFCC, Conflict Resolution Education Network, the National Association for Community Mediation, the National Conference on Peacemaking and Conflict Resolution, and the Society of Professionals in Dispute Resolution).

3.   to promote public confidence in mediation as a process for resolving family disputes.

The *Model Standards* are aspirational in character. They describe good practices for family mediators. They are not intended to create legal rules or standards of liability.

The *Model Standards* include different levels of guidance:

- Use of the term "may" in a *Standard* is the lowest strength of guidance and indicates a practice that the family mediator should consider adopting but which can be deviated from in the exercise of good professional judgment.

- Most of the *Standards* employ the term "should" which indicates that the practice described in the *Standard* is highly desirable and should be departed from only with very strong reason.

- The rarer use of the term "shall" in a *Standard* is a higher level of guidance to the family mediator, indicating that the mediator should not have discretion to depart from the practice described.

### Standard I

*A family mediator shall recognize that mediation is based on the principle of self-determination by the participants.*

**A.** Self-determination is the fundamental principle of family mediation. The mediation process relies upon the ability of participants to make their own voluntary and informed decisions.

**B.** The primary role of a family mediator is to assist the participants to gain a better understanding of their own needs and interests and the needs and interests of others and to facilitate agreement among the participants.

**C.** A family mediator should inform the participants that they may seek information and advice from a variety of sources during the mediation process.

**D.** A family mediator shall inform the participants that they may withdraw from family mediation at any time and are not required to reach an agreement in mediation.

**E.** The family mediator's commitment shall be to the participants and the process. Pressure from outside of the mediation process shall never influence the mediator to coerce participants to settle.

### Standard II

*A family mediator shall be qualified by education and training to undertake the mediation.*

**A.** To perform the family mediator's role, a mediator should:

**1.** have knowledge of family law;

**2.** have knowledge of and training in the impact of family conflict on parents, children and other participants, including knowledge of child development, domestic abuse and child abuse and neglect;

**3.** have education and training specific to the process of mediation;

**4.** be able to recognize the impact of culture and diversity.

**B.** Family mediators should provide information to the participants about the mediator's relevant training, education and expertise.

### Standard III

*A family mediator shall facilitate the participants' understanding of what mediation is and assess their capacity to mediate before the participants reach an agreement to mediate.*

**A.** Before family mediation begins a mediator should provide the participants with an overview of the process and its purposes, including:

**1.** informing the participants that reaching an agreement in family mediation is consensual in nature, that a mediator is an impartial facilitator, and that a mediator may not impose or force any settlement on the parties;

**2.** distinguishing family mediation from other processes designed to address family issues and disputes;

**3.** informing the participants that any agreements reached will be reviewed by the court when court approval is required;

**4.** informing the participants that they may obtain independent advice from attorneys, counsel, advocates, accountants, therapists or other professionals during the mediation process;

**5.** advising the participants, in appropriate cases, that they can seek the advice of religious figures, elders or other significant persons in their community whose opinions they value;

**6.** discussing, if applicable, the issue of separate sessions with the participants, a description of the circumstances in which the mediator may meet alone with any of the participants, or with any third party and the conditions of confidentiality concerning these separate sessions;

**7.** informing the participants that the presence or absence of other persons at a mediation, including attorneys, counselors or advocates, depends on the agreement of the participants and the mediator, unless a statute or regulation otherwise requires or the mediator believes that the presence of another person is required or may be beneficial because of a history or threat of violence or other serious coercive activity by a participant.

**8.** describing the obligations of the mediator to maintain the confidentiality of the mediation process and its results as well as any exceptions to confidentiality;

**9.** advising the participants of the circumstances under which the mediator may suspend or terminate the mediation process and that a participant has a right to suspend or terminate mediation at any time.

**B.** The participants should sign a written agreement to mediate their dispute and the terms and conditions thereof within a reasonable time after first consulting the family mediator.

**C.** The family mediator should be alert to the capacity and willingness of the participants to mediate before proceeding with the mediation and throughout the process. A mediator should not agree to conduct the mediation if the mediator reasonably believes one or more of the participants is unable or unwilling to participate.

**D.** Family mediators should not accept a dispute for mediation if they cannot satisfy the expectations of the participants concerning the timing of the process.

## Standard IV

*A family mediator shall conduct the mediation process in an impartial manner. A family mediator shall disclose all actual and potential grounds of bias and conflicts of interest reasonably known to the mediator. The participants shall be free to retain the mediator by an informed, written waiver of the conflict of interest. However, if a bias or conflict of interest clearly impairs a mediator's impartiality, the mediator shall withdraw regardless of the express agreement of the participants.*

**A.** Impartiality means freedom from favoritism or bias in word, action or appearance, and includes a commitment to assist all participants as opposed to any one individual.

**B.** Conflict of interest means any relationship between the mediator, any participant or the subject matter of the dispute, that compromises or appears to compromise the mediator's impartiality.

**C.** A family mediator should not accept a dispute for mediation if the family mediator cannot be impartial.

**D.** A family mediator should identify and disclose potential grounds of bias or conflict of interest upon which a mediator's impartiality might reasonably be questioned. Such disclosure should be made prior to the start of a mediation and in time to allow the participants to select an alternate mediator.

**E.** A family mediator should resolve all doubts in favor of disclosure. All disclosures should be made as soon as practical after the mediator becomes aware of the bias or potential conflict of interest. The duty to disclose is a continuing duty.

**F.** A family mediator should guard against bias or partiality based on the participants' personal characteristics, background or performance at the mediation.

**G.** A family mediator should avoid conflicts of interest in recommending the services of other professionals.

**H.** A family mediator shall not use information about participants obtained in a mediation for personal gain or advantage.

**I.** A family mediator should withdraw pursuant to *Standard IX* if the mediator believes the mediator's impartiality has been compromised or a conflict of interest has been identified and has not been waived by the participants.

## Standard V

*A family mediator shall fully disclose and explain the basis of any compensation, fees and charges to the participants.*

**A.** The participants should be provided with sufficient information about fees at the outset of mediation to determine if they wish to retain the services of the mediator.

**B.** The participants' written agreement to mediate their dispute should include a description of their fee arrangement with the mediator.

**C.** A mediator should not enter into a fee agreement that is contingent upon the results of the mediation or the amount of the settlement.

**D.** A mediator should not accept a fee for referral of a matter to another mediator or to any other person.

**E.** Upon termination of mediation a mediator should return any unearned fee to the participants.

### Standard VI

*A family mediator shall structure the mediation process so that the participants make decisions based on sufficient information and knowledge.*

**A.** The mediator should facilitate full and accurate disclosure and the acquisition and development of information during mediation so that the participants can make informed decisions. This may be accomplished by encouraging participants to consult appropriate experts.

**B.** Consistent with standards of impartiality and preserving participant self-determination, a mediator may provide the participants with information that the mediator is qualified by training or experience to provide. The mediator shall not provide therapy or legal advice.

**C.** The mediator should recommend that the participants obtain independent legal representation before concluding an agreement.

**D.** If the participants so desire, the mediator should allow attorneys, counsel or advocates for the participants to be present at the mediation sessions.

**E.** With the agreement of the participants, the mediator may document the participants' resolution of their dispute. The mediator should inform the participants that any agreement should be reviewed by an independent attorney before it is signed.

### Standard VII

*A family mediator shall maintain the confidentiality of all information acquired in the mediation process, unless the mediator is permitted or required to reveal the information by law or agreement of the participants.*

**A.** The mediator should discuss the participants' expectations of confidentiality with them prior to undertaking the mediation. The written agreement to mediate should include provisions concerning confidentiality.

**B.** Prior to undertaking the mediation the mediator should inform the participants of the limitations of confidentiality such as statutory, judicially or ethically mandated reporting.

**C.** As permitted by law, the mediator shall disclose a participant's threat of suicide or violence against any person to the threatened person and the appropriate authorities if the mediator believes such threat is likely to be acted upon.

**D.** If the mediator holds private sessions with a participant, the obligations of confidentiality concerning those sessions should be discussed and agreed upon prior to the sessions.

**E.** If subpoenaed or otherwise noticed to testify or to produce documents the mediator should inform the participants immediately. The mediator should not testify or provide documents in response to a subpoena without an order of the court if the mediator reasonably believes doing so would violate an obligation of confidentiality to the participants.

## Standard VIII

*A family mediator shall assist participants in determining how to promote the best interests of children.*

**A.** The mediator should encourage the participants to explore the range of options available for separation or post divorce parenting arrangements and their respective costs and benefits. Referral to a specialist in child development may be appropriate for these purposes. The topics for discussion may include, among others:

1. information about community resources and programs that can help the participants and their children cope with the consequences of family reorganization and family violence;

2. problems that continuing conflict creates for children's development and what steps might be taken to ameliorate the effects of conflict on the children;

3. development of a parenting plan that covers the children's physical residence and decision-making responsibilities for the children, with appropriate levels of detail as agreed to by the participants;

4. the possible need to revise parenting plans as the developmental needs of the children evolve over time; and

5. encouragement to the participants to develop appropriate dispute resolution mechanisms to facilitate future revisions of the parenting plan.

**B.** The mediator should be sensitive to the impact of culture and religion on parenting philosophy and other decisions.

**C.** The mediator shall inform any court-appointed representative for the children of the mediation. If a representative for the children participates, the mediator should, at the outset, discuss the effect of that participation on the mediation process and the confidentiality of the mediation with the participants. Whether the representative of the children participates or not, the mediator shall provide the representative with the resulting agreements insofar as they relate to the children.

**D.** Except in extraordinary circumstances, the children should not participate in the mediation process without the consent of both parents and the children's court-appointed representative.

**E.** Prior to including the children in the mediation process, the mediator should consult with the parents and the children's court-appointed representative about whether the children should participate in the mediation process and the form of that participation.

**F.** The mediator should inform all concerned about the available options for the children's participation (which may include personal participation, an interview with a mental health professional, the mediator interviewing the child and reporting to the parents, or a videotaped statement by the child) and discuss the costs and benefits of each with the participants.

## Standard IX

*A family mediator shall recognize a family situation involving child abuse or neglect and take appropriate steps to shape the mediation process accordingly.*

**A.** As used in these Standards, child abuse or neglect is defined by applicable state law.

**B.** A mediator shall not undertake a mediation in which the family situation has been assessed to involve child abuse or neglect without appropriate and adequate training.

**C.** If the mediator has reasonable grounds to believe that a child of the participants is abused or neglected within the meaning of the jurisdiction's child abuse and neglect laws, the mediator shall comply with applicable child protection laws.

**1.** The mediator should encourage the participants to explore appropriate services for the family.

**2.** The mediator should consider the appropriateness of suspending or terminating the mediation process in light of the allegations.

## Standard X

*A family mediator shall recognize a family situation involving domestic abuse and take appropriate steps to shape the mediation process accordingly.*

**A.** As used in these Standards, domestic abuse includes domestic violence as defined by applicable state law and issues of control and intimidation.

**B.** A mediator shall not undertake a mediation in which the family situation has been assessed to involve domestic abuse without appropriate and adequate training.

**C.** Some cases are not suitable for mediation because of safety, control or intimidation issues. A mediator should make a reasonable effort to screen for the existence of domestic abuse prior to entering into an agreement to mediate. The mediator should continue to assess for domestic abuse throughout the mediation process.

**D.** If domestic abuse appears to be present the mediator shall consider taking measures to insure the safety of participants and the mediator including, among others:

**1.** establishing appropriate security arrangements;

**2.** holding separate sessions with the participants even without the agreement of all participants;

**3.** allowing a friend, representative, advocate, counsel or attorney to attend the mediation sessions;

**4.** encouraging the participants to be represented by an attorney, counsel or an advocate throughout the mediation process;

**5.** referring the participants to appropriate community resources;

**6.** suspending or terminating the mediation sessions, with appropriate steps to protect the safety of the participants.

**E.** The mediator should facilitate the participants' formulation of parenting plans that protect the physical safety and psychological well-being of themselves and their children.

## Standard XI

*A family mediator shall suspend or terminate the mediation process when the mediator reasonably believes that a participant is unable to effectively participate or for other compelling reason.*

**A.** Circumstances under which a mediator should consider suspending or terminating the mediation, may include, among others:

**1.** the safety of a participant or well-being of a child is threatened;

**2.** a participant has or is threatening to abduct a child;

**3.** a participant is unable to participate due to the influence of drugs, alcohol, or physical or mental condition;

**4.** the participants are about to enter into an agreement that the mediator reasonably believes to be unconscionable;

**5.** a participant is using the mediation to further illegal conduct;

**6.** a participant is using the mediation process to gain an unfair advantage;

**7.** if the mediator believes the mediator's impartiality has been compromised in accordance with *Standard IV.*

**B.** If the mediator does suspend or terminate the mediation, the mediator should take all reasonable steps to minimize prejudice or inconvenience to the participants which may result.

## Standard XII

*A family mediator shall be truthful in the advertisement and solicitation for mediation.*

**A.** Mediators should refrain from promises and guarantees of results. A mediator should not advertise statistical settlement data or settlement rates.

**B.** Mediators should accurately represent their qualifications. In an advertisement or other communication, a mediator may make reference to meeting state, national, or private organizational qualifications only if the entity referred to has a procedure for qualifying mediators and the mediator has been duly granted the requisite status.

## Standard XIII

*A family mediator shall acquire and maintain professional competence in mediation.*

**A.** Mediators should continuously improve their professional skills and abilities by, among other activities, participating in relevant continuing education programs and should regularly engage in self-assessment.

**B.** Mediators should participate in programs of peer consultation and should help train and mentor the work of less experienced mediators.

**C.** Mediators should continuously strive to understand the impact of culture and diversity on the mediator's practice.

# Appendix D

## SPECIAL POLICY CONSIDERATIONS FOR STATE REGULATION OF FAMILY MEDIATORS AND COURT-AFFILIATED PROGRAMS

The *Model Standards Recognize the National Standards for Court Connected Dispute Resolution Programs* (1992). There are also state and local regulations governing such programs and family mediators. The following principles of organization and practice, however, are especially important for regulation of mediators and court-connected family mediation programs. They are worthy of separate mention.

**A.** Individual states or local courts should set standards and qualifications for family mediators including procedures for evaluations and handling grievances against mediators. In developing these standards and qualifications, regulators should consult with appropriate professional groups, including professional associations of family mediators.

**B.** When family mediators are appointed by a court or other institution, the appointing agency should make reasonable efforts to insure that each mediator is qualified for the appointment. If a list of family mediators qualified for court appointment exists, the requirements for being included on the list should be made public and available to all interested persons.

**C.** Confidentiality should not be construed to limit or prohibit the effective monitoring, research or evaluation of mediation programs by responsible individuals or academic institutions provided that no identifying information about any person involved in the mediation is disclosed without their prior written consent. Under appropriate circumstances, researchers may be permitted to obtain access to statistical data and, with the permission of the participants, to individual case files, observations of live mediations, and interviews with participants.

# Appendix E

# FLORIDA RULES FOR CERTIFIED AND COURT-APPOINTED MEDIATORS

Part I   Mediator Qualifications

Rule 10.100   Certification Requirements

(a)   General. For certification as a county court, family, circuit court, dependency, or appellate mediator, a mediator must be at least 21 years of age and be of good moral character. For certification as a county court, family, circuit court or dependency mediator, one must have the required number of points for the type of certification sought as specifically required in rule 10.105.

(b)   County Court Mediators. For initial certification as a mediator of county court matters, an applicant must have at least a high school diploma or a General Equivalency Diploma (GED) and 100 points, which shall include:

30 points for successful completion of a Florida Supreme Court certified county court mediation training program;

   (1) 10 points for education; and

   (2) 60 points for mentorship.

(c)   Family Mediators. For initial certification as a mediator of family and dissolution of marriage issues, an applicant must have at least a bachelor's degree and 100 points, which shall include, at a minimum:

   (1) 30 points for successful completion of a Florida Supreme Court certified family mediation training program;

   (2) 25 points for education/mediation experience; and

   (3) 30 points for mentorship.

Additional points above the minimum requirements may be awarded for completion of additional education/mediation experience, mentorship, and miscellaneous activities.

(d)   Circuit Court Mediators. For initial certification as a mediator of circuit court matters, other than family matters, an applicant must have at least a bachelor's degree and 100 points, which shall include, at a minimum:

   (1) 30 points for successful completion of a Florida Supreme Court certified circuit mediation training program;

   (2) 25 points for education/mediation experience; and

   (3) 30 points for mentorship.

Additional points above the minimum requirements may be awarded for completion of additional education/mediation experience, mentorship, and miscellaneous activities.

(e) Dependency Mediators. For initial certification as a mediator of dependency matters, as defined in Florida Rule of Juvenile Procedure 8.290, an applicant must have at least a bachelor's degree and 100 points, which shall include, at a minimum:

(1) 30 points for successful completion of a Florida Supreme Court certified dependency mediation training program;

(2) 25 points for education/mediation experience; and

(3) 40 points for mentorship.

Additional points above the minimum requirements may be awarded for completion of additional education/mediation experience, mentorship, and miscellaneous activities.

(f) Appellate Mediators. For initial certification as a mediator of appellate matters, an applicant must be a Florida Supreme Court certified circuit, family or dependency mediator and successfully complete a Florida Supreme Court certified appellate mediation training program.

(g) Senior Judges Serving As Mediators. A senior judge may serve as a mediator in a court-ordered mediation only if certified by the Florida Supreme Court as a mediator for that type of mediation.

(h) Referral for Discipline. If the certification or licensure necessary for any person to be certified as a family or circuit mediator is suspended or revoked, or if the mediator holding such certification or licensure is in any other manner disciplined, such matter shall be referred to the Mediator Qualifications Board for appropriate action pursuant to rule 10.800.

(i) Special Conditions. Mediators who are certified prior to August 1, 2006, shall not be subject to the point requirements for any category of certification in relation to which continuing certification is maintained.

## Rule 10.105   Point System Categories

(a) Education. Points shall be awarded in accordance with the following schedule (points are only awarded for the highest level of education completed and honorary degrees are not included):

| | |
|---|---|
| High School Diploma/GED | 10 points |
| Associate's Degree | 15 points |
| Bachelor's Degree | 20 points |
| Master's Degree | 25 points |
| Master's Degree in Conflict Resolution | 30 points |
| Doctorate (e.g., Ph.D., J.D., M.D., Ed.D., LL.M) | 30 points |
| Ph.D. from Accredited Conflict Resolution Program | 40 points |

An additional five points will be awarded for completion of a graduate level conflict resolution certificate program in an institution which has been accredited by Middle States Association of Colleges and Schools, the New England Association of Schools and Colleges, the North Central Association of Colleges and Schools, the Northwest Association of Schools and Colleges, the Southern Association of Colleges and Schools, the Western Association of Schools and Colleges, the American Bar Association, or an entity of equal status.

(b) Mediation Experience. One point per year will be awarded to a Florida Supreme Court certified mediator for each year that mediator has mediated at least 15 cases of any type. In the alternative, a maximum of five points will be awarded to any mediator, regardless of Florida Supreme Court certification, who has conducted a minimum of 100 mediations over a consecutive five-year period.

(c) Mentorship. Ten points will be awarded for each supervised mediation completed of the type for which certification is sought and five points will be awarded for each mediation session of the type for which certification is sought which is observed.

(d) Miscellaneous Points.

(1) Five points shall be awarded to applicants currently licensed or certified in any United States jurisdiction in psychology, accounting, social work, mental health, health care, education, or the practice of law or mediation. Such award shall not exceed a total of five points regardless of the number of licenses or certifications obtained.

(2) Five points shall be awarded for possessing conversational ability in a foreign language as demonstrated by certification by the American Council on the Teaching of Foreign Languages (ACTFL) Oral Proficiency Test, qualification as a court interpreter, accreditation by the American Translators Association, or approval as a sign language interpreter by the Registry of Interpreters for the Deaf. Such award shall not exceed a total of five points regardless of the number of languages in which the applicant is proficient.

(3) Five points shall be awarded for the successful completion of a mediation training program (minimum 30 hours in length) which is certified or approved by a jurisdiction other than Florida and which may not be the required Florida Supreme Court certified mediation training program. Such award shall not exceed five points regardless of the number of training programs completed.

(4) Five points shall be awarded for certification as a mediator by the Florida Supreme Court. Such award shall not exceed five points per category regardless of the number of training programs completed or certifications obtained.

**Committee Notes**

**The following table is intended to illustrate the point system established in this rule. Any discrepancy between the table and the written certification requirements shall be resolved in favor of the latter.**

| Points Needed Per Area of Certification | | Minimum Points Required in Each Area |
|---|---|---|
| County | 100 | 30 certified county mediation training; 10 education (minimum HS Diploma/GED); 60 mentorship |
| Family | 100 | 30 certified family mediation training; 25 education/mediation experience (minimum Bachelor's Degree); 30 mentorship [and requires 15 additional points] |
| Dependency | 100 | 30 certified dependency mediation training; 25 education/mediation experience (minimum Bachelor's Degree); 40 mentorship [and requires 5 additional points] |
| Circuit | 100 | 30 certified circuit mediation training, 25 education/mediation experience (minimum Bachelor's Degree); 30 mentorship; [and requires 15 additional points] |

| Education/Mediation Experience (points awarded for highest level of education received) | | | |
|---|---|---|---|
| HS Diploma/GED | 10 points | Master's Degree in Conflict Resolution | 30 |
| Associate's Degree | 15 points | Doctorate (e.g., JD, MD, PhD, EdD, LLM) | 30 |
| Bachelor's Degree | 20 points | Ph.D. from accredited CR Program | 40 |
| Master's Degree | 25 points | Graduate Certificate CR Program | +5 |
| Florida certified mediator: 1 point per year in which mediated at least 15 mediations (any type) OR any mediator: — 5 points for minimum of 100 mediations (any type) over a 5 year period | | | |

| Mentorship — must work with at least 2 different certified mediators and must be completed for the type of certification sought | |
|---|---|
| Observation | 5 points each session |
| Supervised Mediation | 10 points each complete mediation |

| Miscellaneous Points | |
|---|---|
| Licensed to practice law, psychology, accounting, social work, mental health, health care, education or mediation in any US jurisdiction | 5 points (total) |
| Florida Certified Mediator | 5 points (total) |

| Miscellaneous Points | |
|---|---|
| Foreign Language Conversational Ability as demonstrated by certification by ACTFL Oral Proficiency Test; qualified as a court interpreter; or accredited by the American Translators Association; Sign Language Interpreter as demonstrated by approval by the Registry of Interpreters for the Deaf | 5 points (total) |
| Completion of additional mediation training program (minimum 30 hours in length) certified/approved by a state or court other than Florida | 5 points (total) |

## Rule 10.110    Good Moral Character

(a)    General Requirement. No person shall be certified by this Court as a mediator unless such person first produces satisfactory evidence of good moral character as required by rule 10.100.

(b)    Purpose. The primary purpose of the requirement of good moral character is to ensure protection of the participants in mediation and the public, as well as to safeguard the justice system. A mediator shall have, as a prerequisite to certification and as a requirement for continuing certification, the good moral character sufficient to meet all of the Mediator Standards of Professional Conduct set out in rules 10.200-10.690.

(c)    Certification. The following shall apply in relation to determining the good moral character required for initial and continuing mediator certification:

(1) The applicant's or mediator's good moral character may be subject to inquiry when the applicant's or mediator's conduct is relevant to the qualifications of a mediator.

(2) An applicant for initial certification who has been convicted of a felony shall not be eligible for certification until such person has received a restoration of civil rights.

(3) An applicant for initial certification who is serving a sentence of felony probation shall not be eligible for certification until termination of the period of probation.

(4) In assessing whether the applicant's or mediator's conduct demonstrates a present lack of good moral character the following factors shall be relevant:

(A) the extent to which the conduct would interfere with a mediator's duties and responsibilities;

(B) the area of mediation in which certification is sought or held;

(C) the factors underlying the conduct;

(D) the applicant's or mediator's age at the time of the conduct;

(E) the recency of the conduct;

(F) the reliability of the information concerning the conduct;

(G) the seriousness of the conduct as it relates to mediator qualifications;

(H) the cumulative effect of the conduct or information;

(I) any evidence of rehabilitation;

(J) the applicant's or mediator's candor; and

(K) denial of application, disbarment, or suspension from any profession.

(d)   Decertification. A certified mediator shall be subject to decertification for any knowing and willful incorrect material information contained in any mediator application. There is a presumption of knowing and willful violation if the application is completed, signed, and notarized.

## Rule 10.120   Notice of Change of Address or Name

(a)   Address Change. Whenever any certified mediator changes residence or mailing address, that person must within 30 days thereafter notify the center of such change.

(b)   Name Change. Whenever any certified mediator changes legal name, that person must within 30 days thereafter notify the center of such change.

## Rule 10.130   Notification of Conviction

(a)   Definition. "Conviction" means a determination of guilt which is the result of a trial, or entry of a plea of guilty or no contest, regardless of whether adjudication of guilt or imposition of sentence was suspended, deferred, or withheld, and applies in relation to any of the following:

(1) a felony, misdemeanor of the first degree, or misdemeanor of the second degree involving dishonesty or false statement;

(2) a conviction of a similar offense described in subdivision (1) that includes a conviction by a federal, military, or tribal tribunal, including courts-martial conducted by the Armed Forces of the United States;

(3) a conviction of a similar offense described in subdivision (1) that includes a conviction or entry of a plea of guilty or no contest resulting in a sanction in any jurisdiction of the United States or any foreign jurisdiction. A sanction includes, but is not limited to, a fine, incarceration in a state prison, federal prison, private correctional facility, or local detention facility; or

(4) a conviction of a similar offense described in subdivision (1) of a municipal or county ordinance in this or any other state.

(b)   Report of Conviction. A conviction shall be reported in writing to the center within 30 days of such conviction. A report of conviction shall include a copy of the order or orders pursuant to which the conviction was entered.

(c)   Suspension. Upon receipt of a report of felony conviction, the center shall immediately suspend all certifications and refer the matter to the qualifications complaint committee.

(d)   Referral. Upon receipt of a report of misdemeanor conviction, the center shall refer the matter to the qualifications complaint committee for appropriate action. If the center becomes aware of a conviction prior to the required notification, it shall refer the matter to the qualifications complaint committee for appropriate action.

## Part II   Standards of Professional Conduct

## Rule 10.200   Scope and Purpose

These Rules provide ethical standards of conduct for certified and court-appointed mediators. They are intended to both guide mediators in the performance of their services and instill public confidence in the mediation process. The public's use, understanding, and satisfaction with mediation can only be achieved if mediators embrace the highest ethical principles. Whether the parties involved in a mediation choose to resolve their dispute is secondary in importance to whether the mediator conducts the mediation in accordance with these ethical standards.

***Committee Notes***

**2000 Revision. In early 1991, the Florida Supreme Court Standing Committee on Mediation and Arbitration Rules was commissioned by the Chief Justice to research, draft and present for adoption both a comprehensive set of ethical standards for Florida mediators and procedural rules for their enforcement. To accomplish this task, the Committee divided itself into two sub-committees and, over the remainder of the year, launched parallel programs to research and develop the requested ethical standards and grievance procedures.**

**The Subcommittee on Ethical Standards began its task by searching the nation for other states or private dispute resolution organizations who had completed any significant work in defining the ethical responsibilities of professional mediators. After searching for guidance outside the state, the subcommittee turned to Florida's own core group of certified mediators for more direct and firsthand data. Through a series of statewide public hearings and meetings, the subcommittee gathered current information on ethical concerns based upon the expanding experiences of practicing Florida certified mediators. In May of 1992, the "Florida Rules for Certified and Court Appointed Mediators" became effective.**

**In the years following the adoption of those ethical rules, the Committee observed their impact on the mediation profession. By 1998, several other states and dispute resolution organizations initiated research into ethical standards for mediation which also became instructive to the Committee. In addition, Florida's Mediator Qualifications Advisory Panel, created to field ethical questions from practicing mediators, gained a wealth of pragmatic experience in the application of ethical concepts to actual practice that became available to the Committee. Finally, The Florida Mediator Qualifications Board, the disciplinary body for mediators, developed specific data from actual grievances filed against mediators over the past several years, which also added to the available body of knowledge.**

**Using this new body of information and experience, the Committee undertook a yearlong study program to determine if Florida's ethical rules for mediators**

would benefit from review and revision. Upon reviewing the 1992 ethical Rules, it immediately became apparent to the Committee that reorganization, renumbering, and more descriptive titles would make the Rules more useful. For that reason, the Rules were reorganized into four substantive groups which recognized a mediator's ethical responsibilities to the "parties," the "process," the "profession" and the "courts." The intent of the Committee here was to simply make the Rules easier to locate. There is no official significance in the order in which the Rules appear; any one area is equally important as all other areas. The Committee recognizes many rules overlap and define specific ethical responsibilities which impact more than one area. Clearly, a violation of a rule in one section may very well injure relationships protected in another section. Titles to the Rules were changed to more accurately reflect their content. Additionally, redundancies were eliminated, phrasing tightened, and grammatical changes made to more clearly state their scope and purpose.

Finally, the Committee sought to apply what had been learned. The 2000 revisions are the result of that effort.

## Rule 10.210   Mediation Defined

Mediation is a process whereby a neutral and impartial third person acts to encourage and facilitate the resolution of a dispute without prescribing what it should be. It is an informal and non-adversarial process intended to help disputing parties reach a mutually acceptable agreement.

## Rule 10.220   Mediator's Role

The role of the mediator is to reduce obstacles to communication, assist in the identification of issues and exploration of alternatives, and otherwise facilitate voluntary agreements resolving the dispute. The ultimate decision-making authority, however, rests solely with the parties.

## Rule 10.230   Mediation Concepts

Mediation is based on concepts of communication, negotiation, facilitation, and problem-solving that emphasize:

(a) self determination;

(b) the needs and interests of the parties;

(c) fairness;

(d) procedural flexibility;

(e) confidentiality; and

(f) full disclosure.

## Rule 10.300   Mediator's Responsibility to the Parties

The purpose of mediation is to provide a forum for consensual dispute resolution by the parties. It is not an adjudicatory procedure. Accordingly, a mediator's responsibility to the parties includes honoring their right of self-determination; acting with impartiality; and avoiding coercion, improper influence, and conflicts of interest. A mediator is also responsible for maintaining an appropriate demeanor, preserving confidentiality, and promoting the awareness by the parties of the interests of non-participating persons. A mediator's business practices should reflect fairness, integrity and impartiality.

***Committee Notes***

**2000 Revision. Rules 10.300–10.380 include a collection of specific ethical concerns involving a mediator's responsibility to the parties to a dispute. Incorporated in this new section are the concepts formerly found in Rule 10.060 (Self Determination); Rule 10.070 (Impartiality/Conflict of Interest); Rule 10.080 (Confidentiality); Rule 10.090 (Professional Advice); and Rule 10.100 (Fees and Expenses). In addition, the Committee grouped under this heading ethical concerns dealing with the mediator's demeanor and courtesy, contractual relationships, and responsibility to non-participating persons.**

## Rule 10.310 Self-Determination

(a) Decision-making. Decisions made during a mediation are to be made by the parties. A mediator shall not make substantive decisions for any party. A mediator is responsible for assisting the parties in reaching informed and voluntary decisions while protecting their right of self-determination.

(b) Coercion Prohibited. A mediator shall not coerce or improperly influence any party to make a decision or unwillingly participate in a mediation.

(c) Misrepresentation Prohibited. A mediator shall not intentionally or knowingly misrepresent any material fact or circumstance in the course of conducting a mediation.

(d) Postponement or Cancellation. If, for any reason, a party is unable to freely exercise self-determination, a mediator shall cancel or postpone a mediation.

***Committee Notes***

**2000 Revision. Mediation is a process to facilitate consensual agreement between parties in conflict and to assist them in voluntarily resolving their dispute. It is critical that the parties' right to self-determination (a free and informed choice to agree or not to agree) is preserved during all phases of mediation. A mediator must not substitute the judgment of the mediator for the judgment of the parties, coerce or compel a party to make a decision, knowingly allow a participant to make a decision based on misrepresented facts or circumstances, or in any other way impair or interfere with the parties' right of self-determination.**

**While mediation techniques and practice styles may vary from mediator to mediator and mediation to mediation, a line is crossed and ethical standards are violated when any conduct of the mediator serves to compromise the parties' basic right to agree or not to agree. Special care should be taken to preserve the party's right to self-determination if the mediator provides input to the mediation process. See Rule 10.370.**

**On occasion, a mediator may be requested by the parties to serve as a decision-maker. If the mediator decides to serve in such a capacity, compliance with this request results in a change in the dispute resolution process impacting self-determination, impartiality, confidentiality, and other ethical standards. Before providing decision-making services, therefore, the mediator**

shall ensure that all parties understand and consent to those changes. See Rules 10.330 and 10.340.

Under subdivision (d), postponement or cancellation of a mediation is necessary if the mediator reasonably believes the threat of domestic violence, existence of substance abuse, physical threat or undue psychological dominance are present and existing factors which would impair any party's ability to freely and willingly enter into an informed agreement.

## Rule 10.320    Nonparticipating Persons

A mediator shall promote awareness by the parties of the interests of persons affected by actual or potential agreements who are not represented at mediation.

***Committee Notes***

**2000 Revision. Mediated agreements will often impact persons or entities not participating in the process. Examples include lienholders, governmental agencies, shareholders, and related commercial entities. In family and dependency mediations, the interests of children, grandparents or other related persons are also often affected. A mediator is responsible for making the parties aware of the potential interests of such non-participating persons.**

**In raising awareness of the interests of non-participating persons, however, the mediator should still respect the rights of the parties to make their own decisions. Further, raising awareness of possible interests of related entities should not involve advocacy or judgments as to the merits of those interests. In family mediations, for example, a mediator should make the parents aware of the children's interests without interfering with self-determination or advocating a particular position.**

## Rule 10.330    Impartiality

(a)   Generally. A mediator shall maintain impartiality throughout the mediation process. Impartiality means freedom from favoritism or bias in word, action, or appearance, and includes a commitment to assist all parties, as opposed to any one individual.

(b)   Withdrawal for Partiality. A mediator shall withdraw from mediation if the mediator is no longer impartial.

(c)   Gifts and Solicitation. A mediator shall neither give nor accept a gift, favor, loan, or other item of value in any mediation process. During the mediation process, a mediator shall not solicit or otherwise attempt to procure future professional services.

***Committee Notes***

**2000 Revision. A mediator has an affirmative obligation to maintain impartiality throughout the entire mediation process. The duty to maintain impartiality arises immediately upon learning of a potential engagement for providing mediation services. A mediator shall not accept or continue any engagement for mediation services in which the ability to maintain impartiality is reasonably impaired or compromised. As soon as practical, a mediator shall make reasonable inquiry as to the identity of the parties or other circumstances which could compromise the mediator's impartiality.**

**During the mediation, a mediator shall maintain impartiality even while**

**raising questions regarding the reality, fairness, equity, durability and feasibility of proposed options for settlement. In the event circumstances arise during a mediation that would reasonably be construed to impair or compromise a mediator's impartiality, the mediator is obligated to withdraw.**

**Subdivision (c) does not preclude a mediator from giving or accepting de minimis gifts or incidental items provided to facilitate the mediation.**

## Rule 10.340   Conflicts of Interest

(a)   Generally. A mediator shall not mediate a matter that presents a clear or undisclosed conflict of interest. A conflict of interest arises when any relationship between the mediator and the mediation participants or the subject matter of the dispute compromises or appears to compromise the mediator's impartiality.

(b)   Burden of Disclosure. The burden of disclosure of any potential conflict of interest rests on the mediator. Disclosure shall be made as soon as practical after the mediator becomes aware of the interest or relationship giving rise to the potential conflict of interest.

(c)   Effect of Disclosure. After appropriate disclosure, the mediator may serve if all parties agree. However, if a conflict of interest clearly impairs a mediator's impartiality, the mediator shall withdraw regardless of the express agreement of the parties.

(d)   Conflict During Mediation. A mediator shall not create a conflict of interest during the mediation. During a mediation, a mediator shall not provide any services that are not directly related to the mediation process.

(e)   Senior Judge. If a mediator who is a senior judge has presided over a case involving any party, attorney, or law firm in the mediation, the mediator shall disclose such fact prior to mediation. A mediator shall not serve as a mediator in any case in which the mediator is currently presiding as a senior judge. Absent express consent of the parties, a mediator shall not serve as a senior judge over any case involving any party, attorney, or law firm that is utilizing or has utilized the judge as a mediator within the previous three years. A senior judge who provides mediation services shall not preside over the same type of case the judge mediates in the circuit where the mediation services are provided; however, a senior judge may preside over other types of cases (e.g., criminal, juvenile, family law, probate) in the same circuit and may preside over cases in circuits in which the judge does not provide mediation services.

***Committee Notes***

**2000 Revision. Potential conflicts of interests which require disclosure include the fact of a mediator's membership on a related board of directors, full or part time service by the mediator as a representative, advocate, or consultant to a mediation participant, present stock or bond ownership by the mediator in a corporate mediation participant, or any other form of managerial, financial, or family interest by the mediator in any mediation participant involved in a mediation. A mediator who is a member of a law firm or other professional organization is obliged to disclose any past or present client relationship that firm or organization may have with any party involved in a mediation. The duty to disclose thus includes information relating to a mediator's ongoing finan-**

cial or professional relationship with any of the parties, counsel, or related entities. Disclosure is required with respect to any significant past, present, or promised future relationship with any party involved in a proposed mediation. While impartiality is not necessarily compromised, full disclosure and a reasonable opportunity for the parties to react are essential.

Disclosure of relationships or circumstances which would create the potential for a conflict of interest should be made at the earliest possible opportunity and under circumstances which will allow the parties to freely exercise their right of self-determination as to both the selection of the mediator and participation in the mediation process.

A conflict of interest which clearly impairs a mediator's impartiality is not resolved by mere disclosure to, or waiver by, the parties. Such conflicts occur when circumstances or relationships involving the mediator cannot be reasonably regarded as allowing the mediator to maintain impartiality.

To maintain an appropriate level of impartiality and to avoid creating conflicts of interest, a mediator's professional input to a mediation proceeding must be confined to the services necessary to provide the parties a process to reach a self-determined agreement. Under subdivision (d), a mediator is accordingly prohibited from utilizing a mediation to supply any other services which do not directly relate to the conduct of the mediation itself. By way of example, a mediator would therefore be prohibited from providing accounting, psychiatric or legal services, psychological or social counseling, therapy, or business consultations of any sort during the mediation process. Mediators establish personal relationships with many representatives, attorneys, mediators, and other members of various professional associations. There should be no attempt to be secretive about such friendships or acquaintances, but disclosure is not necessary unless some feature of a particular relationship might reasonably appear to impair impartiality.

## Rule 10.350   Demeanor

A mediator shall be patient, dignified, and courteous during the mediation process.

## Rule 10.360   Confidentiality

(a)   Scope. A mediator shall maintain confidentiality of all information revealed during mediation except where disclosure is required or permitted by law or is agreed to by all parties.

(b)   Caucus. Information obtained during caucus may not be revealed by the mediator to any other mediation participant without the consent of the disclosing party.

(c)   Record Keeping. A mediator shall maintain confidentiality in the storage and disposal of records and shall not disclose any identifying information when materials are used for research, training, or statistical compilations.

## Rule 10.370   Advice, Opinions, or Information

(a)   Providing Information. Consistent with standards of impartiality and preserving party self-determination, a mediator may provide information that the mediator is qualified by training or experience to provide.

(b)   Independent Legal Advice. When a mediator believes a party does not understand or appreciate how an agreement may adversely affect legal rights or obligations, the mediator shall advise the party of the right to seek independent legal counsel.

(c)   Personal or Professional Opinion. A mediator shall not offer a personal or professional opinion intended to coerce the parties, unduly influence the parties, decide the dispute, or direct a resolution of any issue. Consistent with standards of impartiality and preserving party self-determination however, a mediator may point out possible outcomes of the case and discuss the merits of a claim or defense. A mediator shall not offer a personal or professional opinion as to how the court in which the case has been filed will resolve the dispute.

***Committee Notes***

**2000 Revision (previously Committee Note to 1992 adoption of former rule 10.090). Mediators who are attorneys should note Florida Bar Committee on Professional Ethics, formal opinion 86-8 at 1239, which states that the lawyer-mediator should "explain the risks of proceeding without independent counsel and advise the parties to consult counsel during the course of the mediation and before signing any settlement agreement that he might prepare for them."**

**2000 Revision. The primary role of the mediator is to facilitate a process which will provide the parties an opportunity to resolve all or part of a dispute by agreement if they choose to do so. A mediator may assist in that endeavor by providing relevant information or helping the parties obtain such information from other sources. A mediator may also raise issues and discuss strengths and weaknesses of positions underlying the dispute. Finally, a mediator may help the parties evaluate resolution options and draft settlement proposals. In providing these services however, it is imperative that the mediator maintain impartiality and avoid any activity which would have the effect of overriding the parties' rights of self-determination. While mediators may call upon their own qualifications and experience to supply information and options, the parties must be given the opportunity to freely decide upon any agreement. Mediators shall not utilize their opinions to decide any aspect of the dispute or to coerce the parties or their representatives to accept any resolution option. While a mediator has no duty to specifically advise a party as to the legal ramifications or consequences of a proposed agreement, there is a duty for the mediator to advise the parties of the importance of understanding such matters and giving them the opportunity to seek such advice if they desire.**

## Rule 10.380   Fees and Expenses

(a)   Generally. A mediator holds a position of trust. Fees charged for mediation services shall be reasonable and consistent with the nature of the case.

(b)   Guiding Principles in Determining Fees. A mediator shall be guided by the following general principles in determining fees:

(1) Any charges for mediation services based on time shall not exceed actual

time spent or allocated.

(2) Charges for costs shall be for those actually incurred.

(3) All fees and costs shall be appropriately divided between the parties.

(4) When time or expenses involve two or more mediations on the same day or trip, the time and expense charges shall be prorated appropriately.

(c)  Written Explanation of Fees. A mediator shall give the parties or their counsel a written explanation of any fees and costs prior to mediation. The explanation shall include:

(1) the basis for and amount of any charges for services to be rendered, including minimum fees and travel time;

(2) the amount charged for the postponement or cancellation of mediation sessions and the circumstances under which such charges will be assessed or waived;

(3) the basis and amount of charges for any other items; and

(4) the parties' pro rata share of mediation fees and costs if previously determined by the court or agreed to by the parties.

(d)  Maintenance of Records. A mediator shall maintain records necessary to support charges for services and expenses and upon request shall make an accounting to the parties, their counsel, or the court.

(e)  Remuneration for Referrals. No commissions, rebates, or similar remuneration shall be given or received by a mediator for a mediation referral.

(f)  Contingency Fees Prohibited. A mediator shall not charge a contingent fee or base a fee on the outcome of the process.

## Rule 10.400  Mediator's Responsibility to the Mediation Process

A mediator is responsible for safeguarding the mediation process. The benefits of the process are best achieved if the mediation is conducted in an informed, balanced and timely fashion. A mediator is responsible for confirming that mediation is an appropriate dispute resolution process under the circumstances of each case.

***Committee Notes***
**2000 Revision. Rules 10.400–10.430 include a collection of specific ethical concerns involved in a mediator's responsibility to the mediation process. Incorporated in this new section are the concepts formerly found in rule 10.060 (Self-Determination), rule 10.090 (Professional Advice); and rule 10.110 (Concluding Mediation). In addition, the Committee grouped under this heading ethical concerns dealing with the mediator's duty to determine the existence of potential conflicts, a mandate for adequate time for mediation sessions, and the process for adjournment.**

## Rule 10.410  Balanced Process

A mediator shall conduct mediation sessions in an even-handed, balanced manner. A mediator shall promote mutual respect among the mediation participants throughout the mediation process and encourage the participants to conduct themselves in a collaborative, non-coercive, and non-adversarial manner.

***Committee Notes***

**2000 Revision. A mediator should be aware that the presence or threat of domestic violence or abuse among the parties can endanger the parties, the mediator, and others. Domestic violence and abuse can undermine the exercise of self-determination and the ability to reach a voluntary and mutually acceptable agreement.**

## Rule 10.420   Conduct of Mediation

(a)   Orientation Session. Upon commencement of the mediation session, a mediator shall describe the mediation process and the role of the mediator, and shall inform the mediation participants that:

(1) mediation is a consensual process;

(2) the mediator is an impartial facilitator without authority to impose a resolution or adjudicate any aspect of the dispute; and

(3) communications made during the process are confidential, except where disclosure is required or permitted by law.

(b)   Adjournment or Termination. A mediator shall:

(1) adjourn the mediation upon agreement of the parties;

(2) adjourn or terminate any mediation which, if continued, would result in unreasonable emotional or monetary costs to the parties;

(3) adjourn or terminate the mediation if the mediator believes the case is unsuitable for mediation or any party is unable or unwilling to participate meaningfully in the process,

(4) terminate a mediation entailing fraud, duress, the absence of bargaining ability, or unconscionability; and

(5) terminate any mediation if the physical safety of any person is endangered by the continuation of mediation.

(c)   Closure. The mediator shall cause the terms of any agreement reached to be memorialized appropriately and discuss with the parties and counsel the process for formalization and implementation of the agreement.

***Committee Notes***

**2000 Revision. In defining the role of the mediator during the course of an opening session, a mediator should ensure that the participants fully understand the nature of the process and the limits on the mediator's authority. See rule 10.370(c). It is also appropriate for the mediator to inform the parties that mediators are ethically precluded from providing non-mediation services to any party. See rule 10.340(d). Florida Rule of Civil Procedure 1.730(b), Florida Rule of Juvenile Procedure 8.290(o), and Florida Family Law Rule of Procedure 12.740(f) require that any mediated agreement be reduced to writing. Mediators have an obligation to ensure these rules are complied with, but are not required to write the agreement themselves.**

## Rule 10.430    Scheduling Mediation

A mediator shall schedule a mediation in a manner that provides adequate time for the parties to fully exercise their right of self-determination. A mediator shall perform mediation services in a timely fashion, avoiding delays whenever possible.

## Rule 10.500    Mediator's Responsibility to the Courts

A mediator is accountable to the referring court with ultimate authority over the case. Any interaction discharging this responsibility, however, shall be conducted in a manner consistent with these ethical rules.

***Committee Notes***

**2000 Revision. Rules 10.500–10.540 include a collection of specific ethical concerns involved in a mediator's responsibility to the courts. Incorporated in this new section are the concepts formerly found in rule 10.040 (Responsibilities to Courts).**

## Rule 10.510    Information to the Court

A mediator shall be candid, accurate, and fully responsive to the court concerning the mediator's qualifications, availability, and other administrative matters.

## Rule 10.520    Compliance with Authority

A mediator shall comply with all statutes, court rules, local court rules, and administrative orders relevant to the practice of mediation.

## Rule 10.530    Improper Influence

A mediator shall refrain from any activity that has the appearance of improperly influencing a court to secure an appointment to a case.

***Committee Notes***

**2000 Revision. Giving gifts to court personnel in exchange for case assignments is improper. De minimis gifts generally distributed as part of an overall business development plan are excepted. See also rule 10.330.**

## Rule 10.600    Mediator's Responsibility to the Mediation Profession

A mediator shall preserve the quality of the profession. A mediator is responsible for maintaining professional competence and forthright business practices, fostering good relationships, assisting new mediators, and generally supporting the advancement of mediation.

***Committee Notes***

**2000 Revision. Rules 10.600–10.690 include a collection of specific ethical concerns involving a mediator's responsibility to the mediation profession. Incorporated in this new section are the concepts formerly found in rule 10.030 (General Standards and Qualifications), rule 10.120 (Training and Education), rule 10.130 (Advertising), rule 10.140 (Relationships with Other Professionals), and rule 10.150 (Advancement of Mediation).**

## Rule 10.610    Marketing Practices

(a)    False or Misleading Marketing Practices. A mediator shall not engage in any marketing practice, including advertising, which contains false or misleading information. A mediator shall ensure that any marketing of the mediator's qualifications, services to be rendered, or the mediation process is accurate and honest.

(b) Supreme Court Certification. Any marketing practice in which a mediator indicates that such mediator is "Florida Supreme Court certified" is misleading unless it also identifies at least one area of certification in which the mediator is certified.

(c) Other Certifications. Any marketing publication that generally refers to a mediator being "certified" is misleading unless the advertising mediator has successfully completed an established process for certifying mediators that involves actual instruction rather than the mere payment of a fee. Use of the term "certified" in advertising is also misleading unless the mediator indentifies the entity issuing the referenced certification and the area or field of certification earned, if applicable.

(d) Prior Adjudicative Experience. Any marketing practice is misleading if the mediator states or implies that prior adjudicative experience, including, but not limited to, service as a judge, magistrate, or administrative hearing officer, makes one a better or more qualified mediator.

(e) Prohibited Claims or Promises. A mediator shall not make claims of achieving specific outcomes or promises implying favoritism for the purpose of obtaining business.

(f) Additional Prohibited Marketing Practices. A mediator shall not engage in any marketing practice that diminishes the importance of a party's right to self-determination or the impartiality of the mediator, or that demeans the dignity of the mediation process or the judicial system.

***Commentary***

**2010 Revision. Areas of certification in subdivision (b) include county, family, circuit, dependency and other Supreme Court certifications.**

**The roles of a mediator and an adjudicator are fundamentally distinct. The integrity of the judicial system may be impugned when the prestige of the judicial office is used for commercial purposes. When engaging in any mediation marketing practice, a former adjudicative officer should not lend the prestige of the judicial office to advance private interests in a manner inconsistent with this rule. For example, the depiction of a mediator in judicial robes or use of the word "judge" with or without modifiers to the mediator's name would be inappropriate. However, an accurate representation of the mediator's judicial experience would not be inappropriate.**

## Rule 10.620 Integrity and Impartiality

A mediator shall not accept any engagement, provide any service, or perform any act that would compromise the mediator's integrity or impartiality.

## Rule 10.630 Professional Competence

A mediator shall acquire and maintain professional competence in mediation. A mediator shall regularly participate in educational activities promoting professional growth.

## Rule 10.640   Skill and Experience

A mediator shall decline an appointment, withdraw, or request appropriate assistance when the facts and circumstances of the case are beyond the mediator's skill or experience.

## Rule 10.650   Concurrent Standards

Other ethical standards to which a mediator may be professionally bound are not abrogated by these rules. In the course of performing mediation services, however, these rules prevail over any conflicting ethical standards to which a mediator may otherwise be bound.

## Rule 10.660   Relationships with Other Mediators

A mediator shall respect the professional relationships of another mediator.

## Rule 10.670   Relationships with Other Professionals

A mediator shall respect the role of other professional disciplines in the mediation process and shall promote cooperation between mediators and other professionals.

## Rule 10.680   Prohibited Agreements

With the exception of an agreement conferring benefits upon retirement, a mediator shall not restrict or limit another mediator's practice following termination of a professional relationship.

***Committee Notes***

**2000 Revision. Rule 10.680 is intended to discourage covenants not to compete or other practice restrictions arising upon the termination of a relationship with another mediator or mediation firm. In situations where a retirement program is being contractually funded or supported by a surviving mediator or mediation firm, however, reasonable restraints on competition are acceptable.**

## Rule 10.690   Advancement of Mediation

(a)   Pro Bono Service. Mediators have a responsibility to provide competent services to persons seeking their assistance, including those unable to pay for services. A mediator should provide mediation services pro bono or at a reduced rate of compensation whenever appropriate.

(b)   New Mediator Training. An experienced mediator should cooperate in training new mediators, including serving as a mentor.

(c)   Support of Mediation. A mediator should support the advancement of mediation by encouraging and participating in research, evaluation, or other forms of professional development and public education.

## Part III   Discipline

## Rule 10.700   Scope and Purpose

These rules apply to all proceedings before all panels and committees of the mediator qualifications board involving the discipline or suspension of certified mediators or non-certified mediators appointed to mediate a case pursuant to court rules. The purpose of these rules of discipline is to provide a means for enforcing the Florida Rules for Certified and Court-Appointed Mediators.

## Rule 10.710  Privilege to Mediate

Certification to mediate confers no vested right to the holder thereof, but is a conditional privilege that is revocable for cause.

## Rule 10.720  Definitions

(a)  Board. The mediator qualifications board.

(b)  Center. The Florida Dispute Resolution Center of the Office of the State Courts Administrator.

(c)  Complaint. Formal submission of an alleged violation of the Rules for Certified and Court-Appointed Mediators, including allegations of a lack of good moral character. A complaint may originate from any person or from the center.

(d)  Complaint Committee. Three members of the board from the division in which a complaint against a mediator originates.

(e)  Counsel. Counsel appointed by the center, at the direction of the complaint committee, responsible for presenting the complaint to the panel.

(f)  Division. One of 3 standing divisions of the mediator qualifications board, established on a regional basis.

(g)  Investigator. A certified mediator, or attorney, or other qualified individual appointed by the center at the direction of a complaint committee.

(h)  Mediator. A person certified by the Florida Supreme Court or an individual mediating pursuant to court order.

(i)  Panel. Five members of the board from the division in which a complaint against a mediator originates.

(j)  Qualifications Complaint Committee. Three members of the board selected for the purpose of considering referrals pursuant to rule 10.800.

## Rule 10.730  Mediator Qualifications Board

(a)  Generally. The mediator qualifications board shall be composed of 3 standing divisions that shall be located in the following regions:

(1) One division in north Florida, encompassing the First, Second, Third, Fourth, Eighth, and Fourteenth judicial circuits;

(2) One division in central Florida, encompassing the Fifth, Sixth, Seventh, Ninth, Tenth, Twelfth, Thirteenth, and Eighteenth judicial circuits;

(3) One division in south Florida, encompassing the Eleventh, Fifteenth, Sixteenth, Seventeenth, Nineteenth, and Twentieth judicial circuits.

Other divisions may be formed by the supreme court based on need.

(b)  Composition of Divisions. Each division of the board shall be composed of:

(1) three circuit or county judges;

(2) three certified county mediators;

(3) three certified circuit mediators;

(4) three certified family mediators, at least 2 of whom shall be non-lawyers;

(5) not less than 1 nor more than 3 certified dependency mediators;

(6) not less than 1 nor more than 3 certified appellate mediators; and

(7) three attorneys licensed to practice law in Florida who have a substantial trial practice and are neither certified as mediators nor judicial officers during their terms of service on the board, at least 1 of whom shall have a substantial dissolution of marriage law practice.

(c)   Appointment; Terms. Eligible persons shall be appointed to the board by the chief justice of the Supreme Court of Florida for a period of 4 years. The terms of the board members shall be staggered.

(d)   Complaint Committee. Each complaint committee of the board shall be composed of 3 members. A complaint committee shall cease to exist after disposing of all assigned cases. Each complaint committee shall be composed of:

(1) one judge or attorney, who shall act as the chair of the committee;

(2) one mediator, who is certified in the area to which the complaint refers; and

(3) one other certified mediator.

(e)   Qualifications Complaint Committee. One member of each division shall serve as a member of the qualifications complaint committee for a period of 1 year. The qualifications complaint committee shall be composed of:

(1) one judge or attorney, who shall act as the chair of the committee; and

(2) two certified mediators.

(f)   Panels. Each panel of the board shall be composed of 5 members. A panel shall cease to exist after disposing of all assigned cases. Each panel shall be composed of:

(1) one circuit or county judge, who shall serve as the chair;

(2) three certified mediators, at least 1 of whom shall be certified in the area to which the complaint refers; and

(3) one attorney.

(g)   Panel Vice-Chair. Each panel once appointed shall elect a vice-chair. The vice-chair shall act as the chair of the panel in the absence of the chair.

*Committee Notes*

**2000 Revision. In relation to (b)(5), the Committee believes that the Chief Justice should have discretion in the number of dependency mediators appointed to the Board depending on the number of certified dependency mediators available for appointment. It is the intention of the Committee that when dependency mediation reaches a comparable level of activity to the other**

**three areas of certification, the full complement of three representatives per division should be realized.**

## Rule 10.740    Jurisdiction

(a)    Complaint Committee. Each complaint committee shall have such jurisdiction and powers as are necessary to conduct the proper and speedy investigation and disposition of any complaint. The judge or attorney presiding over the complaint committee shall have the power to compel the attendance of witnesses, to take or to cause to be taken the depositions of witnesses, and to order the production of records or other documentary evidence, and the power of contempt. The complaint committee shall perform its investigatory function and have concomitant power to resolve cases prior to panel referral.

(b)    Qualifications Complaint Committee. The qualifications complaint committee shall have jurisdiction over all matters referred pursuant to rule 10.800. The qualifications complaint committee shall have such jurisdiction and powers as are necessary to conduct the proper and speedy investigation and disposition of any good moral character complaint or other matter referred by the center. The judge or attorney presiding over the qualifications complaint committee shall have the power to compel the attendance of witnesses, to take or to cause to be taken the depositions of witnesses, and to order the production of records or other documentary evidence, and the power of contempt. The qualifications complaint committee shall perform its investigatory function and have concomitant power to resolve cases prior to panel referral.

(c)    Panel. Each panel shall have such jurisdiction and powers as are necessary to conduct the proper and speedy adjudication and disposition of any proceeding. The judge presiding over each panel shall have the power to compel the attendance of witnesses, to take or to cause to be taken the depositions of witnesses, to order the production of records or other documentary evidence, and the power of contempt. The panel shall perform the adjudicatory function, but shall not have any investigatory functions.

(d)    Contempt. Should any witness fail, without justification, to respond to the lawful subpoena of the complaint committee, the qualifications complaint committee, or the panel or, having responded, fail or refuse to answer all inquiries or to turn over evidence that has been lawfully subpoenaed, or should any person be guilty of disorderly or contemptuous conduct before any proceeding of the complaint committee, the qualifications complaint committee, or the panel, a motion may be filed by the complaint committee, the qualifications complaint committee, or the panel before the circuit court of the county in which the contemptuous act was committed. The motion shall allege the specific failure on the part of the witness or the specific disorderly or contemptuous act of the person which forms the basis of the alleged contempt of the complaint committee, the qualifications complaint committee, or the panel. Such motion shall pray for the issuance of an order to show cause before the circuit court why the circuit court should not find the person in contempt of the complaint committee, the qualifications complaint committee, or the panel and the person should not be punished by the court therefor. The circuit court shall issue such orders and judgments therein as the court deems appropriate.

Rule 10.750    Staff

The center shall provide all staff support to the board necessary to fulfill its duties and responsibilities under these rules.

Rule 10.800    Good Moral Character; Professional Discipline

(a)    Good Moral Character.

(1) Prior to approving an applicant for certification or renewal as a mediator the center shall review the application to determine whether the applicant appears to meet the standards for good moral character. If the center's review of an application for certification or renewal raises any questions regarding the applicant's good moral character, the center shall request the applicant to supply additional information as necessary. Upon completing this extended review, the center shall forward the application and supporting material as a complaint to the qualifications complaint committee.

(2) If the center becomes aware of any information concerning a certified mediator which could constitute credible evidence of a lack of good moral character, the center shall refer such information as a complaint to the qualifications complaint committee.

(3) The qualifications complaint committee shall review all documentation relating to the good moral character of any applicant or certified mediator in a manner consistent, insofar as applicable, with rule 10.810. In relation to an applicant, the qualifications complaint committee shall either recommend approval or, if it finds there is probable cause to believe that the applicant lacks good moral character, it shall refer the matter to a hearing panel for further action. In relation to a certified mediator, the qualifications complaint committee shall dismiss or, if there is probable cause to believe that the mediator lacks good moral character, refer the matter to a hearing panel for further action.

(4) The panel shall take appropriate action on the issue of good moral character by dismissing the charges, denying the application in relation to an applicant, or imposing sanctions against a certified mediator pursuant to rule 10.830.

(5) All such hearings shall be held in a manner consistent, insofar as applicable, with rule 10.820.

(b)    Professional Licenses and Certifications.

(1) A certified mediator shall inform the center, in writing, of the change in status of any professional license held by the mediator within 30 days of such change.

(2) Upon becoming aware that a certified mediator has been disciplined by a professional organization of which that mediator is a member, the center shall refer the matter to the qualifications complaint committee.

Rule 10.810    Committee Process

(a)    Initiation of Complaint. Any individual wishing to make a complaint alleging that a mediator has violated one or more provisions of these rules shall do so in writing under oath. The complaint shall state with particularity the specific facts that form the basis of the complaint.

(b)   Filing. The complaint shall be filed with the center, or, in the alternative, the complaint may be filed in the office of the court administrator in the circuit in which the case originated or, if not case specific, in the circuit where the alleged misconduct occurred.

(c)   Referral. The complaint, if filed in the office of the court administrator, shall be referred to the center within 5 days of filing.

(d)   Assignment to Committee. Upon receipt of a complaint in proper form, the center shall assign the complaint to a complaint committee or the qualifications complaint committee within 10 days.

(e)   Facial Sufficiency Determination. The complaint committee or the qualifications complaint committee shall convene, either in person or by conference call, to determine whether the allegation(s), if true, would constitute a violation of these rules. If the committee finds a complaint against a certified mediator to be facially insufficient, the complaint shall be dismissed without prejudice and the complainant and the mediator shall be so notified. If the qualifications complaint committee finds a complaint against an applicant to be facially insufficient, the complaint shall be dismissed and the application approved if all other requirements are met. If the complaint is found to be facially sufficient, the committee shall prepare a list of any rule or rules which may have been violated and shall submit such to the center.

(f)   Service. The center shall serve a copy of the list of alleged rule violations prepared by the committee, a copy of the complaint, and a copy of these rules to the mediator or applicant in question. Service on the mediator or applicant shall be made by certified mail addressed to the mediator or applicant at the mediator's or applicant's place of business or residence on file with the center. Mailing to such an address shall constitute service.

(g)   Response. Within 20 days of the receipt of the list of violations prepared by the committee and the complaint, the mediator or applicant shall send a written, sworn response to the center by registered or certified mail. If the mediator or applicant does not respond, the allegations shall be deemed admitted.

(h)   Preliminary Review. Upon review of the complaint and the mediator's or applicant's response, the committee may find that no violation has occurred and dismiss the complaint. The committee may also resolve the issue pursuant to subdivision (j) of this rule.

(i)   Appointment of Investigator. The committee, after review of the complaint and response, may direct the center to appoint an investigator to assist the committee in any of its functions. Such person shall investigate the complaint and advise the committee when it meets to determine the existence of probable cause. In the alternative to appointing an investigator, the committee or any member or members thereof may investigate the allegations, if so directed by the committee chair. Such investigation may include meeting with the mediator, the applicant and the complainant.

(j)   Committee Meeting with the Mediator or Applicant. Notwithstanding any other provision in this rule, at any time while the committee has jurisdiction, it may meet with the complainant and the mediator or applicant, jointly or separately, in an effort to resolve the matter. This resolution may include sanctions if agreed to by the mediator or applicant. If sanctions are accepted, all relevant documentation shall be forwarded to the center. Such conferences shall be in person, by video-conference or teleconference at the discretion of the committee.

(k)   Review. If no other disposition has occurred, the committee shall review the complaint, the response, and any investigative report, including any underlying documentation, to determine whether there is probable cause to believe that the alleged misconduct occurred and would constitute a violation of the rules.

(l)   No Probable Cause. If the committee finds no probable cause, it shall dismiss the complaint and so advise the complainant and the mediator or applicant in writing.

(m)   Probable Cause Found. If probable cause exists, the committee may draft formal charges and forward such charges to the center for assignment to a panel. In the alternative, the committee may decide not to pursue the case by filing a short and plain statement of the reason or reasons for non-referral and so advise the complainant and the mediator or applicant in writing.

(n)   Formal Charges and Counsel. If the committee refers a complaint to the center, the committee shall submit to the center formal charges which shall include a short and plain statement of the matters asserted in the complaint and references to the particular sections of the rules involved. After considering the circumstances of the complaint and the complexity of the issues to be heard, the committee may direct the center to appoint a member of The Florida Bar to investigate and prosecute the complaint. Such counsel may be the investigator appointed pursuant to this rule if such person is otherwise qualified.

(o)   Dismissal. Upon the filing of a stipulation of dismissal signed by the complainant and the mediator with the concurrence of the complaint committee, the action shall be dismissed. If an application is withdrawn by the applicant, the complaint shall be dismissed with or without prejudice depending on the circumstances.

## Rule 10.820   Hearing Procedures

(a)   Assignment to Panel. Upon referral of a complaint and formal charges from a committee, the center shall assign the complaint and formal charges or other matter to a panel for hearing, with notice of assignment to the complainant and the mediator or applicant. No member of the committee shall serve as a member of the panel.

(b)   Hearing. The center shall schedule a hearing not more than 90 days nor less than 30 days from the date of notice of assignment of the matter to the panel. At any time prior to the hearing, the panel may accept an admission to any or all charges and impose sanctions upon the mediator. The panel shall not be required to physically meet in person to accept such admission.

(c)   Dismissal. Upon the filing of a stipulation of dismissal signed by the complainant and the mediator, and with the concurrence of the panel, a complaint shall be dismissed.

(d)   Procedures for Hearing. The procedures for hearing shall be as follows:

(1) No hearing shall be conducted without 5 panel members being physically present.

(2) The hearing may be conducted informally but with decorum.

(3) The rules of evidence applicable to trial of civil actions apply but are to be liberally construed.

(4) Upon a showing of good cause to the panel, testimony of any party or witness may be presented over the telephone.

(e)   Right to Defend. A mediator or applicant shall have the right to defend against all charges and shall have the right to be represented by an attorney, to examine and cross-examine witnesses, to compel the attendance of witnesses to testify, and to compel the production of documents and other evidentiary matter through the subpoena power of the panel.

(f)   Mediator or Applicant Discovery. The center shall, upon written demand of a mediator, applicant, or counsel of record, promptly furnish the following: the names and addresses of all witnesses whose testimony is expected to be offered at the hearing, together with copies of all written statements and transcripts of the testimony of such witnesses in the possession of the counsel or the center which are relevant to the subject matter of the hearing and which have not previously been furnished.

(g)   Panel Discovery. The mediator, applicant, or counsel of record shall, upon written demand of the counsel or the center, promptly furnish the following: the names and addresses of all witnesses whose testimony is expected to be offered at the hearing, together with copies of all written statements and transcripts of the testimony of such witnesses in the possession of the mediator, applicant, or counsel of record which are relevant to the subject matter of the hearing and which have not previously been furnished.

(h)   Failure to Appear. Absent a showing of good cause, if the complainant fails to appear at the hearing, the panel may dismiss a complaint for want of prosecution.

(i)   Mediator's or Applicant's Absence. If the mediator or applicant fails to appear, absent a showing of good cause, the hearing shall proceed.

(j)   Rehearing. If the matter is heard in the mediator's or applicant's absence, the mediator or applicant may petition for rehearing, for good cause, within 10 days of the date of the hearing.

(k)   Recording. Any party shall have the right, without any order or approval, to have all or any portion of the testimony in the proceedings reported and transcribed by a court reporter at the party's expense.

(l)   Dismissal. Upon dismissal, the panel shall promptly file a copy of the dismissal order with the center.

(m)   Sanctions. If, after the hearing, a majority of the panel finds that there is clear and convincing evidence to support a violation of the rules, the panel shall impose such sanctions included in rule 10.830 as it deems appropriate and report such action to the center.

(n)   Denial of Application for Certification. If, after a hearing, a majority of the panel finds by the preponderance of the evidence that an applicant should not be certified as a mediator, the panel shall deny the application and report such action to the center.

## Rule 10.830   Sanctions

(a)   Generally. The panel may impose one or more of the following sanctions:

(1) Imposition of costs of the proceeding.

(2) Oral admonishment.

(3) Written reprimand.

(4) Additional training, which may include the observation of mediations.

(5) Restriction on types of cases which can be mediated in the future.

(6) Suspension for a period of up to 1 year.

(7) Decertification or, if the mediator is not certified, bar from service as a mediator under Florida Rules of Civil Procedure.

(8) Such other sanctions as are agreed to by the mediator and the panel.

(b)   Conviction of Felony. If the panel finds that a certified mediator has a felony conviction, it shall decertify the mediator for a period of not less than two years or until restoration of civil rights, whichever comes later. In order to become a reinstated, such decertified mediator must comply with the requirements of subdivision (h).

(c)   Failure to Comply. If there is reason to believe that the mediator failed to timely comply with any imposed sanction, a hearing shall be held before a panel convened for that purpose within 60 days of the date when the center learned of the alleged failure to comply. The hearing shall also include any additional alleged failures to comply of which the center becomes aware prior to the date of the hearing. The holding of a hearing shall not preclude a subsequent hearing on an alleged failure occurring after the first alleged failure. Any suspension in effect at the time of discovery of the violation by the center shall continue in effect until a decision is reached at the hearing. A finding of the panel that there was a willful failure to substantially comply with any imposed sanction shall result in the decertification of the mediator.

(d)   Decertified Mediators. If a mediator has been decertified or barred from service pursuant to these rules, the mediator shall not thereafter be certified or assigned to mediate a case pursuant to court rule or be designated as mediator pursuant to court rule unless reinstated.

(e)   Decision to be Filed. Upon making a determination that discipline is appropriate, the panel shall promptly file with the center a copy of the decision including findings and conclusions certified by the chair of the panel. The center shall promptly mail to all parties notice of such filing, together with a copy of the decision.

(f) Notice to Circuits. The center shall notify all circuits of any mediator who has been decertified or suspended unless otherwise ordered by the Supreme Court of Florida.

(g) Publication. Upon the imposition of sanctions, the center shall publish the name of the mediator, a short summary of the rule or rules which were violated, the circumstances surrounding the violation, and any sanctions imposed.

(h) Reinstatement after Suspension. Except if inconsistent with rule 10.110, a mediator who has been suspended shall be reinstated as a certified mediator upon the expiration of the imposed or accepted suspension period and satisfaction of any addition renewal obligations.

(i) Reinstatement after Decertification. Except if inconsistent with rule 10.110, a mediator who has been decertified may be reinstated as a certified mediator. Except as otherwise provided in the decision of the panel, no application for reinstatement may be tendered within 2 years after the date of decertification. The reinstatement procedures shall be as follows:

(1) A petition for reinstatement, together with 6 copies, shall be made in writing, verified by the petitioner, and filed with the center.

(2) The petition for reinstatement shall contain:

(A) the name, age, residence, and address of the petitioner;

(B) the offense or misconduct upon which the decertification was based, together with the date of such decertification; and

(C) a concise statement of facts claimed to justify reinstatement as a certified mediator.

(3) The center shall refer the petition for reinstatement to a hearing panel in the appropriate division for review.

(4) The panel shall review the petition and, if the petitioner is found to be unfit to mediate, the petition shall be dismissed. If the petitioner is found fit to mediate, the panel shall notify the center and the center shall reinstate the petitioner as a certified mediator contingent on the petitioner's completion of a certified mediation training program of the type for which the petitioner seeks to be reinstated. Successive petitions for reinstatement based upon the same grounds may be reviewed without a hearing.

## Rule 10.840 Subpoenas

(a) Issuance. Subpoenas for the attendance of witnesses and the production of documentary evidence for discovery and for the appearance of any person before a complaint committee, a panel, or any member thereof, may be issued by the chair of the complaint committee or panel or, if the chair of the panel is absent, by the vice-chair. Such subpoenas may be served in any manner provided by law for the service of witness subpoenas in a civil action.

(b) Failure to Obey. Any person who, without adequate excuse, fails to obey a duly served subpoena may be cited for contempt of the committee or panel in accordance with rule 10.740.

## Rule 10.850 Confidentiality

(a) Generally. Until sanctions are imposed, whether by the panel or upon agreement of the mediator, all proceedings shall be confidential. After sanctions are imposed by a panel or an application is denied, all documentation including and subsequent to the filing of formal charges shall be public with the exception of those matters which are otherwise confidential under law or rule of the supreme court, regardless of the outcome of any appeal. If a consensual agreement is reached between a mediator and a complaint committee, only the basis of the complaint and the agreement shall be released to the public.

(b) Witnesses. Each witness in every proceeding under these disciplinary rules shall be sworn to tell the truth and not disclose the existence of the proceeding, the subject matter thereof, or the identity of the mediator until the proceeding is no longer confidential under these disciplinary rules. Violation of this oath shall be considered an act of contempt of the complaint committee or the panel.

(c) Papers to be Marked. All notices, papers, and pleadings mailed prior to formal charges being filed shall be enclosed in a cover marked "confidential."

(d) Breach of Confidentiality. Violation of confidentiality by a member of the board shall subject the member to removal by the chief justice of the Supreme Court of Florida.

***Committee Notes***
**1995 Revision. The Committee believed the rule regarding confidentiality should be amended in deference to the 1993 amendment to section 44.102, Florida Statutes that engrafted an exception to the general confidentiality requirement for all mediation sessions for the purpose of investigating complaints filed against mediators. Section 44.102(4) specifically provides that "the disclosure of an otherwise privileged communication shall be used only for the internal use of the body conducting the investigation" and that "[Prior] to the release of any disciplinary files to the public, all references to otherwise privileged communications shall be deleted from the record."**
**These provisions created a substantial potential problem when read in conjunction with the previous rule on confidentiality, which made public all proceedings after formal charges were filed. In addition to the possibly substantial burden of redacting the files for public release, there was the potentially greater problem of conducting panel hearings in such a manner as to preclude the possibility that confidential communications would be revealed during testimony, specifically the possibility that any public observers would have to be removed prior to the elicitation of any such communication only to be allowed to return until the next potentially confidential revelation. The Committee believes that under the amended rule the integrity of the disciplinary system can be maintained by releasing the results of any disciplinary**

**action together with a redacted transcript of panel proceedings, while still maintaining the integrity of the mediation process.**

**2008 Revision. The recent adoption of the Florida Mediation Confidentiality and Privilege Act, sections 44.401–44.406, Florida Statutes, renders the first paragraph of the 1995 Revision Committee Notes inoperative. The second paragraph explains the initial rationale for the rule, which is useful now from a historical standpoint.**

## Rule 10.860  Interested Party

A mediator is disqualified from serving on a committee or panel proceeding involving the mediator's own discipline or decertification.

## Rule 10.870  Disqualification of Members of a Panel or Committee

(a)  Procedure. In any case, any party may at any time before final disciplinary action show by a suggestion filed in the case that a member of the board before which the case is pending, or some person related to that member, is a party to the case or is interested in the result of the case or that the member is related to an attorney or counselor of record in the case or that the member is a material witness for or against one of the parties to the case.

(b)  Facts to be Alleged. A motion to disqualify shall allege the facts relied on to show the grounds for disqualification and shall be verified by the party.

(c)  Time for Motion. A motion to disqualify shall be made within a reasonable time after discovery of the facts constituting grounds for disqualification.

(d)  Action by Chair. The chair of the appropriate committee or panel shall determine only the legal sufficiency of the motion. The chair shall not pass on the truth of the facts alleged. If the motion is legally sufficient, the chair shall enter an order of disqualification and the disqualified committee or panel member shall proceed no further in the action. In the event that the chair is the challenged member, the vice-chair shall perform the acts required under this subdivision.

(e)  Recusals. Nothing in this rule limits a board member's authority to enter an order of recusal on the board member's own initiative.

(f)  Replacement. The center shall assign a board member to take the place of any disqualified or recused member.

(g)  Qualifications. Each assignee shall have the same qualifications as the disqualified or recused member.

## Rule 10.880  Supreme Court Chief Justice Review

(a)  Right of Review. Any mediator or applicant found to have committed a violation of these rules or otherwise sanctioned by a hearing panel shall have a right of review of that action. Review of this type shall be by the chief justice of the Supreme Court of Florida or by the chief justice's designee. A mediator shall have no right of review of any resolution reached under rule 10.810(j).

(b)  Rules of Procedure. The Florida Rules of Appellate Procedure, to the extent applicable and except as otherwise provided in this rule, shall control all appeals of mediator disciplinary matters.

(1) The jurisdiction to seek review of disciplinary action shall be invoked by submitting an original and one copy of a Notice of Review of Mediator Disciplinary Action to the chief justice within 30 days of the panel's decision. A copy shall also be provided to the Center.

(2) The notice of review shall be substantially in the form prescribed by rule 9.900(a), Florida Rules of Appellate Procedure. A copy of the panel decision shall be attached to the notice.

(3) Appellant's initial brief, accompanied by an appendix as prescribed by rule 9.220, Florida Rules of Appellate Procedure, shall be served within 30 days of submitting the notice of review. Additional briefs shall be served as prescribed by rule 9.210, Florida Rules of Appellate Procedure.

(c)   Standard of Review. The review shall be conducted in accordance with the following standard of review:

(1) The chief justice or designee shall review the findings and conclusions of the panel using a competent substantial evidence standard, neither reweighing the evidence in the record nor substituting the reviewer's judgment for that of the panel.

(2) Decisions of the chief justice or designee shall be final upon issuance of a mandate under rule 9.340, Florida Rules of Appellate Procedure.

## Rule 10.900   Mediator Ethics Advisory Committee

(a)   Scope and Purpose. The Mediator Ethics Advisory Committee shall provide written advisory opinions to mediators subject to these rules in response to ethical questions arising from the Standards of Professional Conduct. Such opinions shall be consistent with supreme court decisions on mediator discipline.

(b)   Appointment. The Mediator Ethics Advisory Committee shall be composed of 9 members, 3 from each geographic division served by the Mediator Qualifications Board. No member of the Mediator Qualifications Board shall serve on the committee.

(c)   Membership and Terms. The membership of the committee shall be composed of 1 county mediator, 1 family mediator, and 1 circuit mediator from each division and shall be appointed by the chief justice. At least one of the 9 members shall also be a certified dependency mediator, and at least one of the 9 members shall also be a certified appellate mediator. All appointments shall be for 4 years. No member shall serve more than 2 consecutive terms. The committee shall select 1 member as chair and 1 member as vice-chair.

(d)   Meetings. The committee shall meet in person or by telephone conference as necessary at the direction of the chair to consider requests for advisory opinions. A quorum shall consist of a majority of the members appointed to the committee. All requests for advisory opinions shall be in writing. The committee may vote by any means as directed by the chair.

(e)   Opinions. Upon due deliberation, and upon the concurrence of a majority of the committee, the committee shall render opinions. A majority of all members shall be required to concur in any advisory opinion issued by the committee. The opinions shall be signed by the chair, or vice-chair in the absence of the chair, filed with the Dispute Resolution Center, published in the Dispute Resolution Center newsletter, and be made available upon request.

(f)   Effect of Opinions. While reliance by a mediator on an opinion of the committee shall not constitute a defense in any disciplinary proceeding, it shall be evidence of good faith and may be considered by the board in relation to any determination of guilt or in mitigation of punishment.

(g)   Confidentiality. Prior to publication, all references to the requesting mediator or any other real person, firm, organization, or corporation shall be deleted from any request for an opinion, any document associated with the preparation of an opinion, and any opinion issued by the committee. This rule shall apply to all opinions, past and future.

(h)   Support. The Dispute Resolution Center shall provide all support necessary for the committee to fulfill its duties under these rules.

*Committee Notes*

**2000 Revision. The Mediator Ethics Advisory Committee was formerly the Mediator Qualifications Advisory Panel.**

# Appendix F

# UNIFORM MEDIATION ACT

**UNIFORM MEDIATION ACT**
**(Last Revised or Amended in 2003)**

Drafted by the
NATIONAL CONFERENCE OF COMMISSIONERS
ON UNIFORM STATE LAWS
and by it
APPROVED AND RECOMMENDED FOR ENACTMENT
IN ALL THE STATES
at its
ANNUAL CONFERENCE
MEETING IN ITS ONE-HUNDRED-AND-TENTH YEAR
WHITE SULPHUR SPRINGS, WEST VIRGINIA
AUGUST 10-17, 2001 AMENDMENTS APPROVED
at its
ANNUAL CONFERENCE
MEETING IN ITS ONE-HUNDRED-AND-TWELFTH YEAR
IN WASHINGTON, DC
AUGUST 1-7, 2003

**SECTION 1. TITLE.**
This [Act] may be cited as the Uniform Mediation Act.

**SECTION 2. DEFINITIONS.**
In this [Act]:

(1) "Mediation" means a process in which a mediator facilitates communication and negotiation between parties to assist them in reaching a voluntary agreement regarding their dispute.

(2) "Mediation communication" means a statement, whether oral or in a record or verbal or nonverbal, that occurs during a mediation or is made for purposes of considering, conducting, participating in, initiating, continuing, or reconvening a mediation or retaining a mediator.

(3) "Mediator" means an individual who conducts a mediation.

(4) "Nonparty participant" means a person, other than a party or mediator, that participates in a mediation.

(5) "Mediation party" means a person that participates in a mediation and whose agreement is necessary to resolve the dispute.

(6) "Person" means an individual, corporation, business trust, estate, trust, partnership, limited liability company, association, joint venture, government;

governmental subdivision, agency, or instrumentality; public corporation, or any other legal or commercial entity.

(7) "Proceeding" means:

(A) a judicial, administrative, arbitral, or other adjudicative process, including related pre-hearing and post-hearing motions, conferences, and discovery; or

(B) a legislative hearing or similar process.

(8) "Record" means information that is inscribed on a tangible medium or that is stored in an electronic or other medium and is retrievable in perceivable form.

(9) "Sign" means:

(A) to execute or adopt a tangible symbol with the present intent to authenticate a record; or

(B) to attach or logically associate an electronic symbol, sound, or process to or with a record with the present intent to authenticate a record.

## SECTION 3. SCOPE.

(a) Except as otherwise provided in subsection (b) or (c), this [Act] applies to a mediation in which:

(1) the mediation parties are required to mediate by statute or court or administrative agency rule or referred to mediation by a court, administrative agency, or arbitrator;

(2) the mediation parties and the mediator agree to mediate in a record that demonstrates an expectation that mediation communications will be privileged against disclosure; or

(3) the mediation parties use as a mediator an individual who holds himself or herself out as a mediator or the mediation is provided by a person that holds itself out as providing mediation.

(b) The [Act] does not apply to a mediation:

(1) relating to the establishment, negotiation, administration, or termination of a collective bargaining relationship;

(2) relating to a dispute that is pending under or is part of the processes established by a collective bargaining agreement, except that the [Act] applies to a mediation arising out of a dispute that has been filed with an administrative agency or court;

(3) conducted by a judge who might make a ruling on the case; or

(4) conducted under the auspices of:

(A) a primary or secondary school if all the parties are students or

(B) a correctional institution for youths if all the parties are residents of that institution.

(c) If the parties agree in advance in a signed record, or a record of proceeding reflects agreement by the parties, that all or part of a mediation is not privileged, the privileges under Sections 4 through 6 do not apply to the mediation or part agreed upon. However, Sections 4 through 6 apply to a mediation communication made by a person that has not received actual notice of the agreement before the communication is made.

*Legislative Note: To the extent that the Act applies to mediations conducted under the authority of a State's courts, State judiciaries should consider enacting conforming court rules.*

## SECTION 4. PRIVILEGE AGAINST DISCLOSURE; ADMISSIBILITY; DISCOVERY.

(a) Except as otherwise provided in Section 6, a mediation communication is privileged as provided in subsection (b) and is not subject to discovery or admissible in evidence in a proceeding unless waived or precluded as provided by Section 5.

(b) In a proceeding, the following privileges apply:

(1) A mediation party may refuse to disclose, and may prevent any other person from disclosing, a mediation communication.

(2) A mediator may refuse to disclose a mediation communication, and may prevent any other person from disclosing a mediation communication of the mediator.

(3) A nonparty participant may refuse to disclose, and may prevent any other person from disclosing, a mediation communication of the nonparty participant.

(c) Evidence or information that is otherwise admissible or subject to discovery does not become inadmissible or protected from discovery solely by reason of its disclosure or use in a mediation.

*Legislative Note: The Act does not supersede existing state statutes that make mediators incompetent to testify, or that provide for costs and attorney fees to mediators who are wrongfully subpoenaed. See, e.g., Cal. Evid. Code Section 703.5 (West 1994).*

## SECTION 5. WAIVER AND PRECLUSION OF PRIVILEGE.

(a) A privilege under Section 4 may be waived in a record or orally during a proceeding if it is expressly waived by all parties to the mediation and:

(1) in the case of the privilege of a mediator, it is expressly waived by the mediator; and

(2) in the case of the privilege of a nonparty participant, it is expressly waived by the nonparty participant.

(b) A person that discloses or makes a representation about a mediation communication which prejudices another person in a proceeding is precluded from asserting a privilege under Section 4, but only to the extent necessary for the person prejudiced to respond to the representation or disclosure.

(c) A person that intentionally uses a mediation to plan, attempt to commit or commit a crime, or to conceal an ongoing crime or ongoing criminal activity is precluded from asserting a privilege under Section 4.

## SECTION 6. EXCEPTIONS TO PRIVILEGE.

(a) There is no privilege under Section 4 for a mediation communication that is:

(1) in an agreement evidenced by a record signed by all parties to the agreement;

(2) available to the public under [insert statutory reference to open records act] or made during a session of a mediation which is open, or is required by law to be open, to the public;

(3) a threat or statement of a plan to inflict bodily injury or commit a crime of violence;

(4) intentionally used to plan a crime, attempt to commit or commit a crime, or to conceal an ongoing crime or ongoing criminal activity;

(5) sought or offered to prove or disprove a claim or complaint of professional misconduct or malpractice filed against a mediator;

(6) except as otherwise provided in subsection (c), sought or offered to prove or disprove a claim or complaint of professional misconduct or malpractice filed against a mediation party, nonparty participant, or representative of a party based on conduct occurring during a mediation; or

(7) sought or offered to prove or disprove abuse, neglect, abandonment, or exploitation in a proceeding in which a child or adult protective services agency is a party, unless the

[Alternative A: [State to insert, for example, child or adult protection] case is referred by a court to mediation and a public agency participates.]

[Alternative B: public agency participates in the [State to insert, for example, child or adult protection] mediation].

(b) There is no privilege under Section 4 if a court, administrative agency, or arbitrator finds, after a hearing in camera, that the party seeking discovery or the proponent of the evidence has shown that the evidence is not otherwise available, that there is a need for the evidence that substantially outweighs the interest in protecting confidentiality, and that the mediation communication is sought or offered in:

(1) a court proceeding involving a felony [or misdemeanor]; or

(2) except as otherwise provided in subsection (c), a proceeding to prove a claim to rescind or reform or a defense to avoid liability on a contract arising out of the mediation.

(c) A mediator may not be compelled to provide evidence of a mediation communication referred to in subsection (a)(6) or (b)(2).

(d) If a mediation communication is not privileged under subsection (a) or (b), only the portion of the communication necessary for the application of the exception from nondisclosure may be admitted. Admission of evidence under subsection (a) or (b) does not render the evidence, or any other mediation communication, discoverable or admissible for any other purpose.

　　*Legislative Note: If the enacting state does not have an open records act, the following language in paragraph (2) of subsection (a) needs to be deleted: "available to the public under [insert statutory reference to open records act] or."*

## SECTION 7.　PROHIBITED MEDIATOR REPORTS.

　　**(a)** Except as required in subsection (b), a mediator may not make a report, assessment, evaluation, recommendation, finding, or other communication regarding a mediation to a court, administrative agency, or other authority that may make a ruling on the dispute that is the subject of the mediation.

　　**(b)** A mediator may disclose:

　　　　**(1)** whether the mediation occurred or has terminated, whether a settlement was reached, and attendance;

　　　　**(2)** a mediation communication as permitted under Section 6; or

　　　　**(3)** a mediation communication evidencing abuse, neglect, abandonment, or exploitation of an individual to a public agency responsible for protecting individuals against such mistreatment.

　　**(c)** A communication made in violation of subsection (a) may not be considered by a court, administrative agency, or arbitrator.

## SECTION 8.　CONFIDENTIALITY.

　　Unless subject to the [insert statutory references to open meetings act and open records act], mediation communications are confidential to the extent agreed by the parties or provided by other law or rule of this State.

## SECTION 9.　MEDIATOR'S DISCLOSURE OF CONFLICTS OF INTEREST; BACKGROUND.

　　**(a)** Before accepting a mediation, an individual who is requested to serve as a mediator shall:

　　　　**(1)** make an inquiry that is reasonable under the circumstances to determine whether there are any known facts that a reasonable individual would consider likely to affect the impartiality of the mediator, including a financial or personal interest in the outcome of the mediation and an existing or past relationship with a mediation party or foreseeable participant in the mediation; and

　　　　**(2)** disclose any such known fact to the mediation parties as soon as is practical before accepting a mediation.

　　**(b)** If a mediator learns any fact described in subsection (a)(1) after accepting a mediation, the mediator shall disclose it as soon as is practicable.

　　**(c)** At the request of a mediation party, an individual who is requested to serve as a mediator shall disclose the mediator's qualifications to mediate a dispute.

　　**(d)** A person that violates subsection [(a) or (b)][(a), (b), or (g)] is precluded by the violation from asserting a privilege under Section 4.

(e) Subsections (a), (b), [and] (c), [and] [(g)] do not apply to an individual acting as a judge.

(f) This [Act] does not require that a mediator have a special qualification by background or profession.

(g) A mediator must be impartial, unless after disclosure of the facts required in subsections (a) and (b) to be disclosed, the parties agree otherwise.]

## SECTION 10. PARTICIPATION IN MEDIATION.

An attorney or other individual designated by a party may accompany the party to and participate in a mediation. A waiver of participation given before the mediation may be rescinded.

## SECTION 11. INTERNATIONAL COMMERCIAL MEDIATION.

(a) In this section, "Model Law" means the Model Law on International Commercial Conciliation adopted by the United Nations Commission on International Trade Law on 28 June 2002 and recommended by the United Nations General Assembly in a resolution (A/RES/57/18) dated 19 November 2002, and "international commercial mediation" means an international commercial conciliation as defined in Article 1 of the Model Law.

(b) Except as otherwise provided in subsections (c) and (d), if a mediation is an international commercial mediation, the mediation is governed by the Model Law.

(c) Unless the parties agree in accordance with Section 3(c) of this [Act] that all or part of an international commercial mediation is not privileged, Sections 4, 5, and 6 and any applicable definitions in Section 2 of this [Act] also apply to the mediation and nothing in Article 10 of the Model Law derogates from Sections 4, 5, and 6.

(d) If the parties to an international commercial mediation agree under Article 1, subsection (7), of the Model Law that the Model Law does not apply, this [Act] applies.

> Legislative Note. The UNCITRAL Model Law on International Commercial Conciliation may be found at www.uncitral.org/en-index.htm. Important comments on interpretation are included in the Draft Guide to Enactment and Use of UNCITRAL Model Law on International Commercial Conciliation. The States should note the Draft Guide in a Legislative Note to the Act. This is especially important with respect to interpretation of Article 9 of the Model Law.

## SECTION 12. RELATION TO ELECTRONIC SIGNATURES IN GLOBAL AND NATIONAL COMMERCE ACT.

This [Act] modifies, limits, or supersedes the federal Electronic Signatures in Global and National Commerce Act, 15 U.S.C. Section 7001 et seq., but this [Act] does not modify, limit, or supersede Section 101(c) of that Act or authorize electronic delivery of any of the notices described in Section 103(b) of that Act.

## SECTION 13. UNIFORMITY OF APPLICATION AND CONSTRUCTION.

In applying and construing this [Act], consideration should be given to the need to promote uniformity of the law with respect to its subject matter among States that enact it.

## SECTION 14. SEVERABILITY CLAUSE.

If any provision of this [Act] or its application to any person or circumstance is held invalid, the invalidity does not affect other provisions or applications of this [Act] which can be given effect without the invalid provision or application, and to this end the provisions of this [Act] are severable.

## SECTION 15. EFFECTIVE DATE.

This [Act ] takes effect

. . . . . . . . . . . . . . . . .

## SECTION 16. REPEALS.

The following acts and parts of acts are hereby repealed:

(1)

(2)

(3)

## SECTION 17. APPLICATION TO EXISTING AGREEMENTS OR REFERRALS.

(a) This [Act] governs a mediation pursuant to a referral or an agreement to mediate made on or after [the effective date of this [Act]].

(b) On or after [a delayed date], this [Act] governs an agreement to mediate whenever made.

# REFERENCES

## CHAPTER 1

ABRAMSON, Harold I. (2004) *Mediation Representation: Advocating in a Problem-Solving Process*. South Bend: The Nat'l Inst. for Trial Advocacy.

AUERBACH, Jerold S. (1983) *Justice Without Law?* New York: Oxford Univ. Press.

BUSH, Robert A. Baruch, and FOLGER, Joseph. (1994) *The Promise of Mediation*. San Francisco: Jossey-Bass.

CARPENTER, Susan C., and KENNEDY, W.J.D. (1988) *Managing Public Disputes*. San Francisco: Jossey-Bass.

COLE, Sara et al., eds. (2011) Mediation: Law, Policy and Practice (2012 ed.) St. Paul: Thompson-West.

DANZIG, Richard. (1973) *Toward the Creation of a Complementary, Decentralized System of Criminal Justice*, 26 Stan. L. Rev. 1

DEUTSCH, Martin. (1973) *The Resolution of Conflict*. New Haven: Yale Univ. Press.

FELSTINER, William, ABEL, Richard L., and SARAT, Austin. (1980-81) *The Emergence and Transformation of Disputes: Naming, Blaming, Claiming*, 15 L. & Soc'y Rev. 631.

FISHER, Roger, and URY, William. (1981) *Getting to Yes*. Boston: Houghton Mifflin.

FOLBERG, Jay, and TAYLOR, Alison. (1984) *Mediation*. San Francisco: Jossey-Bass.

FULLER, Lon. (1971) *Mediation: Its Forms and Functions*, 44 S. Cal. L. Rev. 305.

GALTON, Eric R., and LOVE, Lela P., eds. (2012) Stories Mediators Tell. Washington, D.C.: Am. Bar Ass'n Sec. on Disp. Resol.

GOLANN, Dwight. (1997) *Mediating Legal Disputes: Effective Strategies for Lawyers and Mediators*. New York: Aspen Publishers.

GOLDMANN, Robert. (1980) *Roundtable Justice*. Boulder: Westview Press.

HAYNES, John. (1994) *The Fundamentals of Family Mediation*. Albany: State Univ. of New York Press.

KATSH, Ethan, RIFKIN, Janet, and GAITENBY, Alan. (2000) *E-Commerce, E-Disputes, and E-Dispute Resolution: In the Shadow of "eBay Law,"* 15 Ohio St. J. on Disp. Resol. 705.

KOLB, Deborah. (1994) *When Talk Works: Profiles of Mediators*. San Francisco: Jossey-Bass.

LAX, David, and SEBENIUS, James. (1986) *The Manager as Negotiator*. New York: The Free Press.

MAGGIOLO, Walter. (1985) *Techniques of Labor Mediation*. New York: Oceana Publications.

McGILLIS, Daniel, and MULLEN, Joan. (1977) *Neighborhood Justice Centers: An Analysis of Potential Models*. Washington, D.C.: U.S. Department of Justice.

MNOOKIN, Robert H. (2000) *Beyond Winning: Negotiating to Create Value in Deals and Disputes*. Cambridge: Harvard Univ. Press.

MOORE, Christopher. (2003) The Mediation Process: Practical Strategies for Resolving Conflict (3d ed.). San Francisco: Jossey-Bass.

PODZIBA, Susan L. (2012) Civic Fusion: Mediating Polarized Public Disputes. Washington, D.C.: Am. Bar Ass'n Sec. on Disp. Resol.

RAIFFA, Howard. (1982) *The Art and Science of Negotiation*. Cambridge: Harvard Univ. Press.

RISKIN, Leonard L. (1996) *Understanding Mediators' Orientations, Strategies, and Techniques: A Grid for the Perplexed*, 1 Harv. Negot. L. Rev. 7.

ROGERS, Nancy, and McEWEN, Craig. (1994) Mediation: Law, Policy, Practice (2d ed.). St. Paul: West Publishing Co.

SCHELLING, Thomas. (1960) *The Strategy of Conflict*. Cambridge: MA: Harvard Univ. Press.

SIMKIN, William, and FIDANDIS, Nicolas. (1986) Mediation and the Dynamics of Collective Bargaining (2d ed.). Washington, D.C.: Bureau of Nat'l Affairs.

STULBERG, Joseph B. (1987) *Taking Charge/Managing Conflict*. Lexington, MA: Lexington Press.

STULBERG, Joseph B. (1981) *The Theory and Practice of Mediation: A Reply to Professor Susskind*, 6 Vt. L. Rev. 85.

STULBERG, Joseph B. and LOVE, Lela P. (2013) The Middle Voice: Mediating Conflict Successfully (2d ed.). Durham: Carolina Acad. Press.

SUSSKIND, Lawrence, and CRUIKSHANK, Jeffrey. (1985) *Breaking the Impasse*. New York: Basic Books.

SUSSKIND, Lawrence. (1981) *Environmental Mediation and the Accountability Problem*, 6 Vt. L. Rev. 1.

WALTON, Richard, and MCKERSIE, Robert. (1991) A Behavioral Theory of Labor Negotiations (2d ed.). Ithaca, N.Y.: ILR Press.

WAHRHAFTIG, Paul, and ASSEFA, Hizkias. (1988) *Extremist Groups and Conflict Resolution: the MOVE crisis in Philadelphia*. New York: Praeger.

# CHAPTER 2

ALFINI, James J. (1999) *Settlement Ethics and Lawyering in ADR Proceedings: A Proposal to Revise Rule 4.1*, 19 N. Ill. U. L. Rev. 255.

ARROW, Kenneth, ed. (1995) *Barriers to Conflict Resolution.* New York: W. W. Norton.

BIRKE, Richard, and FOX, Craig R. (1999) *Psychological Principles in Negotiating Civil Settlements*, 4 Harv. Negot. L. Rev. 1.

BOK, Sissela. (1978) *Lying: Moral Choice in Public and Private Life.* New York: Pantheon Books.

BRESLIN, J. William, and RUBIN, Jeffrey Z., eds. (1991) *Negotiation Theory and Practice.* Cambridge, MA.: Program on Negotiation.

BROWN, Jennifer Gerarda. (1997) *The Role of Hope in Negotiation*, 44 UCLA L. Rev. 1661.

BUSH, Robert A. Baruch. (1997) *"What Do We Need a Mediator For?": Mediation's "Value-Added" for Negotiators*, 12 Ohio St. J. on Disp. Resol. 1.

CIALDINI, Robert B. (1993) Influence: The Psychology of Persuasion (rev. ed.). New York: Morrow.

CRAVER, Charles B. (2002) *The Intelligent Negotiator: What to Say, What to Do, and How to Get What You Want — Every Time.* Roseville, Calif.: Prima Publishing.

CRAVER, Charles B. (1997) Symposium: *The Lawyer's Duties and Responsibilities in Dispute Resolution: Article: Post-Conference Reflection: Negotiation Ethics: How to be Deceptive Without Being Dishonest/How to Be Assertive Without Being Offensive*, 38 S. Tex. L. Rev. 713.

CRAVER, Charles B. (1997) Effective Legal Negotiation and Settlement (3d ed.). Charlottesville: Michie.

EBNER, Noam, and KAMP, Adam. (2010) Relationship 2.0, in Rethinking Negotiation Teaching: Venturing Beyond the Classroom (Christopher Honeyman et al., eds.). St. Paul: DRI Press.

EBNER, Noam et al., eds. (2012) *Rethinking Negotiation Teaching: Assessing Our Students, Assessing Ourselves.* St. Paul: DRI Press.

EBNER, Noam, et al. (2009) You've Got Agreement: Negotiating via Email, in Rethinking Negotiation Teaching: Innovations for Context and Culture (Christopher Honeyman et al., eds.). St. Paul: DRI Press.

FISHER, Roger, URY, William, and PATTON, Bruce. (1981, 1991) *Getting to Yes: Negotiating Agreement Without Giving In* (2d. ed.). New York: Penguin Books.

FISHER, Roger. (1984) *Comment*, 34 J. Legal. Educ. 120.

FRESHMAN, Clark et al. (2002) *The Lawyer-Negotiator as Mood Scientist:*

*What We Know and Don't Know About How Mood Relates to Successful Negotiation*, 2002 J. Disp. Resol. 1.

GIFFORD, Donald G. (1989) *Legal Negotiation.* St. Paul: West Publishing Co.

GOODPASTER, Gary. (1996) *A Primer on Competitive Bargaining*, 1996 J. Disp. Resol. 325.

GUERNSEY, Thomas F., and ZWIER, Paul J. (2005) *Advanced Negotiation and Mediation Theory and Practice: A Realistic Integrated Approach. National Institute for Trial Advocacy.*

HINSHAW, Art, and ALBERTS, Jess K. (2011) *Doing the Right Thing: An Empirical Study of Attorney Negotiation Ethics*, 16 Harv. Negot. L. Rev. 95.

HOFLING, Charles, et al. (1966) *An Experimental Study of Nurse-Physician Relationships*, 143 J. Nervous & Mental Disease 171.

HONEYMAN, Christopher et al., eds. (2009) *Rethinking Negotiation Teaching: Innovations for Context and Culture.* St. Paul: DRI Press.

HONEYMAN, Christopher et al., eds. (2010) *Rethinking Negotiation Teaching: Venturing Beyond the Classroom.* St. Paul: DRI Press.

HONEYMAN, Christopher et al., eds. (forthcoming 2013) *Rethinking Negotiation Teaching: Educating Negotiators for a Connected World.* St. Paul: DRI Press.

HSU, Shi-Ling. (2002) *A Game-Theoretic Approach to Regulatory Negotiation and a Framework for Empirical Analysis*, 26 Harv. Envtl. L. Rev. 33.

JOLLS, Christine et al. (1998) *A Behavioral Approach to Law and Economics*, 50 Stan. L. Rev. 1471.

KAHNEMAN, Daniel et al., eds. (1982) *Judgment Under Uncertainty: Heuristics and Biases.* Cambridge: Cambridge University Press.

KAHNEMAN, Daniel, and TVERSKY, Amos. (1995) *Conflict Resolution: Cognitive Perspective, in Barriers to Conflict Resolution* (K. Arrow, ed.). New York: W. W. Norton.

KOLB, Deborah M., and WILLIAMS, Judith. (2003) Everyday Negotiation: Navigating the Hidden Agendas in Bargaining (Rev. ed.). San Francisco: Jossey-Bass.

KOROBKIN, Russell. (2008) *Against Integrative Bargaining*, 58 Case W. Res. L. Rev. 1323.

KOROBKIN, Russell. (2002) *A Positive Theory of Legal Negotiation*, 88 Geo. L.J. 1789.

KOROBKIN, Russell et al. (1997) *Psychology, Economics, and Settlement: A New Look at the Role of the Lawyer*, 76 Tex. L. Rev. 77.

KOROBKIN, Russell, and GUTHRIE, Chris. (1994) *Psychological Barriers to Litigation Settlement: An Experimental View*, 93 Mich. L. Rev. 107.

KRAMER, Henry S. (2001) *Game Set, Match: Winning the Negotiations Game.* New York: ALM Publishing.

KRITEK, Phyllis Beck. (2002) Negotiating at an Uneven Table: Developing Moral Courage in Resolving Our Conflicts (2d ed.). San Francisco: Jossey-Bass.

LAX, David A., and SEBENIUS, James K. (1986) The Manager as Negotiator: Bargaining for Cooperation & Competitive Gain. New York: Free Press.

LEWICKI, Roy J. et al. (2004) Essentials of Negotiation (3d ed.). New York: McGraw-Hill/Irwin.

LEWICKI, Roy J. et al. (2009) Negotiation: Readings, Exercises, and Cases (6th ed.). New York: McGraw-Hill/Irwin.

LUBAN, David. (1988) *The Quality of Justice, Institute for Legal Studies,* Working Papers Series 8.

LUM, Grande et al. (2002) *Expand the Pie: How to Create More Value in Any Negotiation.* Seattle: Castle Pac. Publ'g.

MENKEL-MEADOW, Carrie. (1984) *Toward Another View of Legal Negotiation: The Structure of Problem Solving,* 31 UCLA L. Rev. 754.

MEYERSON, Bruce. (1997) *Telling the Truth in Mediation: Mediator Owed Duty of Candor,* Disp. Resol. Magazine, Vol. 4, No. 17 (Winter 1997).

MILGRAM, Stanley. (1974) *Obedience to Authority: An Experimental View.* New York: Harper & Row.

MNOOKIN, Robert H. (2003) Strategic Barriers to Dispute Resolution: A Comparison of Bilateral and Multilateral Negotiations, 8 Harv. Negot. L. Rev. 1.

MNOOKIN, Robert H., PEPPET, Scott, and TULUMELLO, Andrew. (2000) *Beyond Winning: Negotiating to Create Value in Deals and Disputes.* Cambridge: Belknap Press of Harvard Univ. Press.

MNOOKIN, Robert H., and ROSS, Lee. (1995) Introduction to Barriers to Conflict Resolution 3 (Kenneth J. Arrow, ed.). New York: W. W. Norton.

MNOOKIN, Robert H. (1993) *Why Negotiations Fail: An Exploration of Barriers to the Resolution of Conflict,* 8 Ohio St. J. on Disp. Resol. 235.

MNOOKIN, Robert H., and WILSON, Robert R. (1989) *Rational Bargaining and Market Efficiency: Understanding* Pennzoil v. Texaco, 75 Va. L. Rev. 295.

NELKEN, Melissa L. (2001) *Understanding Negotiation.* Cincinnati: Anderson Publishing Co.

PRUITT, Dean G., and LEWIS, Steven A. (1977) The Psychology of Integrative Bargaining (in) Negotiations: Social-Psychological Perspectives (D. Druckman, ed.). Beverly Hills: Sage.

RACHLINSKI, Jeffrey J. (1996) *Gains, Losses, and the Psychology of Litigation,* 70 S. Cal. L. Rev. 113.

RAIFFA, Howard et al. (2007) *Negotiation Analysis: The Science and Art of Collaborative Decision Making*. Cambridge: Belknap Press of Harvard Univ. Press.

RAIFFA, Howard. (1982) *The Art & Science of Negotiation*. Cambridge: Harvard Univ. Press.

RAMBO, Lynne H. (2000) *Impeaching Lying Parties With Their Statements During Negotiation: Demysticizing the Public Policy Rationale Behind Evidence Rule 408 and the Mediation-Privilege Statutes*, 75 Wash. L. Rev. 1037.

ROBINSON, Rob J. et al. (June 1990) *Misconstruing the Views of the "Other Side": Real and Perceived Differences in Three Ideological Conflicts*, Stanford Center on Conflict and Negotiation Working Paper No. 18.

ROSS, Lee, and STILLINGER, Constance. (1991) *Barriers to Conflict Resolution*, 7 Negot. J. 389.

SCHNEIDER, Andrea Kupfer. (2002) *Shattering Negotiation Myths: Empirical Evidence on the Effectiveness of Negotiation Style*, 7 Harv. Negot. L. Rev. 143.

SCHNEIDER, Andrea Kupfer. (1994) *Effective Responses to Offensive Comments*, 1994 Negot. J. 107.

SCHNEIDER, Andrea Kupfer. (2012) *Teaching a New Negotiation Skills Paradigm*, 39 Wash. U. J.L. & Pol'y 13.

SCHNEIDER, Andrea Kupfer, and HONEYMAN, Christopher, eds. (2006) The Negotiator's Fieldbook: The Desk Reference for the Experienced Negotiator. Washington, D.C.: Am. Bar Ass'n Sec. on Disp. Resol.

SIMONS, Herbert W. (1986) *Persuasion: Understanding, Practice and Analysis*. New York: McGraw-Hill College.

STERNLIGHT, Jean R. (1999) *Lawyers' Representation of Clients in Mediation: Using Economics and Psychology to Structure Advocacy in an Nonadversarial Setting*, 14 Ohio St. J. on Disp. Resol. 259.

STILLINGER, Constance A. et al. (1988) *The Reactive Devaluation Barrier to Conflict Resolution*, Stanford Center on Conflict and Negotiation, Working Paper No. 3. *Symposium: The Emerging Interdisciplinary Canon of Negotiation*, 87 Marq. L. Rev. 637 (2004).

THURMAN, Ruth Fleet. (1990) *Chipping Away at Lawyer Veracity: The ABA's Turn Toward Situation Ethics in Negotiations*, 1990 J. Disp. Resol. 103.

TVERSKY, Amos et al. (1990) *The Causes of Preference Reversals*, 80 Am. Econ. Rev. 204.

TVERSKY, Amos, and KAHNEMAN, Daniel. (1991) *Loss Aversion in Riskless Choice: A Reference-Dependent Model*, 106 Q.J. Econ. 1038.

TVERSKY, Amos, and THALER, Richard. (1990) *Anomalies: Preference Reversals*, 4 J. Econ. Persp. 201.

WHITE, James J. (1984) *The Pros and Cons of Getting to Yes*, 34 J. Legal Educ. 115.

WHITE, James. (1980) *Machiavelli and the Bar: Ethical Limitations on Lying in Negotiation*, 1980 Am. B. Found. Res. J. 926.

WILLIAMS, Gerald R. (1983) *Legal Negotiation and Settlement*. St. Paul: West Publishing Co.

ZOGHBY, Marguerite. (2001) *The Prohibition of Communication with Adverse Parties in Civil Negotiations: Protecting Clients or Preventing Solutions?* 14 Geo. J. Legal Ethics 1165.

## CHAPTER 3

AARON, Marjorie Corman. (2005) *Do's and Don'ts for Mediation Practice*, Disp. Resol. Magazine, Vol. XI, No. II (Winter 2005).

BUSH, Robert A. Baruch, and FOLGER, Joseph P. (1996) *Transformative Mediation and Third-Party Intervention: Ten Hallmarks of a Transformative Approach to Practice*, 13 Mediation Q. 263.

FOLBERG, Jay, and TAYLOR, Alison. (1988) *Mediation: A Comprehensive Guide to Resolving Conflicts without Litigation*. San Francisco: Jossey-Bass.

HAYNES, John M., and HAYNES, Gretchen L. (1989) *Mediating Divorce*. San Francisco: Jossey-Bass.

MOORE, Christopher W. (1991) *The Mediation Process: Practical Strategies for Resolving Conflict*. San Francisco: Jossey-Bass.

PRESS, Sharon, and KOSCH, Kimberly. (2013) *County Mediator's Manual*. Tallahassee, FL: Florida Disp. Resol. Center.

STULBERG, Joseph B. and LOVE, Lela P. (2013) The Middle Voice: Mediating Conflict Successfully (2d ed.). Durham: Carolina Acad. Press.

THE TEST DESIGN PROJECT. (1995) *Performance-Based Assessment: A Methodology, for Use in Selecting, Training and Evaluating Mediators*. Washington, DC: Nat'l Inst. for Disp. Resol.

## CHAPTER 4

AARON, Marjorie Corman. (1996) Evaluation in Mediation (in) Mediating Legal Disputes (Dwight Golann, ed.). New York: Aspen Law and Business.

ALFINI, James J. (1991) *Trashing, Bashing, and Hashing It out: Is This the End of "Good Mediation"?*, 19 Fla. St. U. L. Rev. 47.

ANDERSON, Jonathan F., and BINGHAM, Linda. (1997) *Upstream Effects from Mediation of Workplace Disputes: Some Preliminary Evidence from the USPS*, 48 Lab. L.J. 601.

ANTES, James R., FOLGER, Joseph P., and DELLA NOCE, Dorothy J. (2001) *Transforming Conflict Interactions in the Workplace: Documented Effects of the USPS REDRESS Program*, 18 Hofstra Lab. & Emp. L.J. 429.

BERNARD, Sydney E. et al. (1984) *The Neutral Mediator: Value Dilemmas in Divorce Mediation*, 4 Mediation Q. 61.

BICKERMAN, John. (2012) *Adapting Mediation to What Users Want*, 45 Md. Bar J. 55.

BICKERMAN, John. (1996) *Evaluative Mediator Responds*, 14 Alternatives to the High Cost of Litigation 70.

BINGHAM, Linda, KIM, Kiwhan, and RAINES, Susan Summers. (2002) *Exploring the Role of Representation in Employment Mediation at the USPS*, 17 Ohio St. J. on Disp. Resol. 341.

BRETT, Jeanne M. et al. (1986) *Mediator Style and Mediation Effectiveness*, 1986 Negot. J. 277.

BUSH, Robert A. Baruch, and FOLGER, Joseph P. (2005) The Promise of Mediation: The Transformative Approach to Mediation (2d ed.). San Francisco: Jossey-Bass.

BUSH, Robert A. Baruch, and FOLGER, Joseph. (1994) *The Promise of Mediation: Responding to Conflict Through Empowerment and Recognition.* San Francisco: Jossey-Bass.

BUSH, Robert A. Baruch. (1989) *Efficiency and Protection, or Empowerment and Recognition?: The Mediator's Role and Ethical Standards in Mediation*, 41 Fla. L. Rev. 253.

COBB, Sara, and RIFKIN, Janet. (1991) *Practice and Paradox: Deconstructing Neutrality in Mediation*, 16 Law & Soc'y Inquiry 35.

FEERICK, John et al. (1995) *Standards of Professional Conduct in Alternative Dispute Resolution*, 1995 J. Disp. Resol. 95.

FOLBERG, Jay, and TAYLOR, Alison. (1984) *Mediation: A Comprehensive Guide to Resolving Conflicts Without Litigation.* San Francisco: Jossey-Bass.

FOLGER, Joseph P., and BUSH, Robert A. Baruch. (1996) *Transformative Mediation and Third-Party Intervention: Ten Hallmarks of a Transformative Approach to Practice*, 13 Mediation Q. 263.

FOLGER, Joseph P., BUSH, Robert A. Baruch, and DELLA NOCE, Dorothy J., eds. (2010) *Transformative Mediation: A Sourcebook.* Reston, VA: Ass'n for Conflict Resol. & Inst. for the Study of Conflict Transformation.

FRIEDMAN, Gary J. (1993) *A Guide to Divorce Mediation.* New York: Workman Publications.

FRIEDMAN, Gary J. and HIMMELSTEIN, Jack. (2008) Challenging Conflict Mediation Through Understanding. Washington, D.C.: Am. Bar Ass'n Sec. on Disp. Resol.

FRIEDMAN, Gary J. and HIMMELSTEIN, Jack (2006) *Resolving Conflict Together: The Understanding-Based Model of Mediation*, 2006 J. Disp. Resol. 523.

FULLER, Lon L. (1971) *Mediation: Its Forms and Functions*, 44 S. Cal. L. Rev. 305.

GAYNIER, Lisa P. (2005) *Transformative Mediation: In Search of a Theory of Practice*, 22 Conflict Resol. Q. 397.

GOLANN, Dwight, ed. (1996) *Mediating Legal Disputes*. New York: Aspen Law and Business.

HAYNES, John M. (1992) *Mediation and Therapy: An Alternative View*, 10 Mediation Q. 21.

HANSEN, Toran. (2004) *The Narrative Approach to Mediation*, 4 Pepp. Disp. Resol. L.J. 297.

KOLB, Deborah. (1994) *When Talk Works: Profiles of Mediators*. San Francisco: Jossey-Bass.

KOLB, Deborah. (1983) The Mediator *s*. Cambridge: MIT Press.

KOVACH, Kimberlee, and LOVE, Lela. (1996) *Evaluative Mediation Is an Oxymoron*, 14 Alternatives to the High Cost of Litigation 31.

KRESSEL, Kenneth et al. (1994) *The Settlement-Orientation vs. the Problem-Solving Style in Custody Mediation*, 50 J. Soc. Issues 67.

KRESSEL, Kenneth. (1994) Frances Butler: Questions That Lead to Answers in Child Custody Mediation (in) When Talk Works: Profiles of Mediators (Deborah M. Kolb ed.). San Francisco: Jossey-Bass.

LANG, Michael, guest ed. (1996) *Transformative Approaches to Mediation: Special Issue*, 13 Mediation Q. 4.

LOVE, Lela P. (1997) *The Top Ten Reasons Why Mediators Should Not Evaluate*, 24 Fla. St. U. L. Rev. 937.

MAUTE, Judith. (1991) *Public Values and Private Justice: A Case for Mediator Accountability*, 4 Geo. J. Legal Ethics 503.

McCRORY, John. (1981) *Environmental Mediation — Another Piece for the Puzzle*, 6 Vt. L. Rev. 49.

MENKEL-MEADOW, Carrie. (1995) *The Many Ways of Mediation: The Transformation of Traditions, Ideologies, Paradigms, and Practices*, 11 Negot.. J. 217.

NAUSS EXON, Susan. (2008) *The Effects That Mediator Styles Impose on Neutrality and Impartiality Requirements of Mediation*, 42 U.S.F. L. Rev. 577.

NOLAN-HALEY, Jacqueline. (1999) *Informed Consent in Mediation: A Guiding Principle for Truly Educated Decisionmaking*, 74 Notre Dame L. Rev. 775.

RISKIN, Leonard L. (2003) *Decisionmaking In Mediation: The New Old Grid and the New New Grid System*, 79 Notre Dame L. Rev. 1.

RISKIN, Leonard L. (1996) *Understanding Mediators' Orientations, Strategies, and Techniques: A Grid for the Perplexed*, 1 Harv. Negot. L. Rev. 7.

RISKIN, Leonard L. (1994) *Mediator Orientations, Strategies and Techniques*, 12 Alternatives to the High Cost of Litigation 111.

RISKIN, Leonard L. (1982) *Mediation and Lawyers*, 43 Ohio St. L.J. 29.

RISKIN, Leonard L. (1984) *Toward New Standards for the Neutral Lawyer in Mediation*, 26 Ariz. L. Rev. 329.

SIBLEY, Susan S., and MERRY, Sally E. (1986) *Mediator Settlement Strategies*, 8 Law & Pol'y 7.

STARK, James. (1997) *The Ethics of Mediation Evaluation: Some Troublesome Questions and Tentative Proposals, from an Evaluative Lawyer Mediator*, 38 S. Tex. L. Rev. 769.

STIPANOWICH, Thomas J. (1998) *The Multi-Door Contract and Other Possibilities*, 13 Ohio St. J. on Disp. Resol. 303.

STULBERG, Joseph B. (1987) *Taking Charge/Managing Conflict*. Lexington, MA: Lexington Press.

STULBERG, Joseph B. (1981) *The Theory and Practice of Mediation: A Reply to Professor Susskind*, 6 Vt. L. Rev. 85.

STULBERG, Joseph B. and SUSSKIND, Lawrence. (2012) *Core Values of Dispute Resolution: Is Neutrality Necessary?*, 95 Marq. L. Rev. 805.

SUSSKIND, Lawrence. (1981) *Environmental Mediation and the Accountability Problem*, 6 Vt. L. Rev. 1.

WECKSTEIN, Donald T. (1997) *In Praise of Party Empowerment — And of Mediator Activism*, 33 Willamette L. Rev. 501.

WILLIAMS, Michael. (1997) *Can't I Get No Satisfaction?: Thoughts on The Promise of Mediation*, 15 Mediation Q. 143.

WINSLADE, John, and MONK, Gerald. (2000) *Narrative Mediation: A New Approach to Conflict Resolution*. San Francisco: Jossey-Bass.

# CHAPTER 5

BROWN, Jennifer Gerarda, and AYRES, Ian. (1994) *Economic Rationales for Mediation*, 80 Va. L. Rev. 323.

BRUNET, Edward. (1987) *Questioning the Quality of Alternative Dispute Resolution*, 62 Tul. L. Rev. 1.

COLE, Sara et al., eds. (2011) Mediation: Law, Policy and Practice (2012 ed.). St. Paul: Thompson-West.

MAX, Rodney. (1998) Confidentiality Agreement of Rodney Max, in ADR Personalities and Practice Tips (James J. Alfini and Eric Galton, eds.). Washington, D.C.: Am. Bar Ass'n Sec. on Disp. Resol.

DEASON, Ellen E. (2002) *Predictable Mediation Confidentiality in the U.S. Federal System*, 17 Ohio St. J. on Disp. Resol. 239.

DEASON, Ellen E. (2002) Uniform Mediation Act — Law Ensures Confidentiality, Neutrality of Process, Disp. Resol. Magazine (Summer 2002), at 7, 9.

EHRHARDT, Charles W. (1999) *Confidentiality, Privilege and Rule 408: the Protection of Mediation Proceedings in Federal Court*, 60 La. L. Rev. 91.

FEINBERG, Kenneth R. (1989) *A Preferred Method of Dispute Resolution*, 16 Pepp. L. Rev. 55.

FREEDMAN, Lawrence R., and PRIGOFF, Michael. (1986) *Confidentiality in Mediation: The Need for Protection*, 2 Ohio St. J. on Disp. Resol. 37.

HARTER, Phillip J. (1989) *Neither Cop Nor Collection Agent: Encouraging Administrative Settlements by Ensuring Mediator Confidentiality*, 41 Admin. L.J. 315.

HUGHES, Scott H. (1998) *A Closer Look: The Case for a Mediation Confidentiality Privilege Still Has Not Been Made*, Disp. Resol. Magazine, Vol. 5, No. 14 (Winter 1998).

IZUMI, Carol. (1995) Remarks in *Symposium on Standards of Professional Conduct in Alternative Dispute Resolution*, 1995 J. Disp. Resol. 95.

KATZ, Lucy V. (1988) *Enforcing an ADR Clause — Are Good Intentions All You Have?* 26 Am. Bus. L.J. 575.

KIRTLEY, Alan. (1995) *The Mediation Privilege's Transition from Theory to Implementation: Designing a Mediation Privilege Standard to Protect Mediation Participants, the Process and the Public Interest*, 1995 J. Disp. Resol. 1.

PERINO, Michael A. (1995) *Drafting Mediation Privileges: Lessons from the Civil Justice Reform Act*, 26 Seton Hall L. Rev. 1.

PRIGOFF, Michael L. (1988) *Toward Candor or Chaos: The Case of Confidentiality in Mediation*, 12 Seton Hall Legis. J. 1.

REUBEN, Richard C. (2003) *The Sound of Dust Settling: A Response to Criticisms of the UMA*, 2003 J. Disp. Resol. 99.

SHANNON, Brian D. (2003) *Dancing with the One That "Brung Us" — Why the Texas ADR Community Has Declined to Embrace the UMA*, 2003 J. Disp. Resol. 197.

SHERMAN, Edward F. (1997) *Confidentiality in ADR Proceedings: Policy Issues Arising From the Texas Experience*, 38 S. Tex. L. Rev. 541.

WELSH, Nancy A. (2011) *Musings on Mediation, Kleenex, and (Smudged) White Hats*, 33 U. La Verne L. Rev. 5.

## CHAPTER 6

AMERICAN BAR ASSOCIATION. (2004) *Resolution on Good Faith Requirements for Mediators and Mediation Advocates in Court-Mandated*

*Mediation Programs*, ABA Section of Dispute Resolution, Approved by Section Council, August 7, 2004.

CARTER, Roger L. (2002) *Oh Ye of Little [Good] Faith: Questions, Concerns and Commentary on Efforts to Regulate Participant Conduct in Mediations*, 2002 J. Dis. Res. 367.

COBEN, James R., and THOMPSON, Peter N. (1999) *The Haghighi Trilogy and the Minnesota Civil Mediation Act: Exposing a Phantom Menace Casting a Pall Over the Development of ADR in Minnesota*, 20 Hamline J. Pub. L. & Pol'y 299.

COLE, Sara et al., eds. (2011) Mediation: Law, Policy and Practice (2012 ed.). St. Paul: Thompson-West.

DEASON, Ellen E. (2001) *Enforcing Mediated Settlement Agreements: Contract Law Collides with Confidentiality*, 35 U.C. Davis L. Rev. 33.

IZUMI, Carol L., and LA RUE, Homer C. (2003) *Prohibiting "Good Faith" Reports Under the Uniform Mediation Act: Keeping the Adjudication Camel out of the Mediation Tent*, 2003 J. Disp. Resol. 67.

KOVACH, Kimberlee K. (1997) *Good Faith Mediation — Requested, Recommended, or Required? A New Ethic*, 38 S. Tex. L. Rev. 575.

KOVACH, Kimberlee K. (1997) *Lawyer Ethics in Mediation: Time for A Requirement of Good Faith in Mediation*, Disp. Resol. Magazine (Winter 1997), at 9.

LANDE, John. (2002) *Using Dispute System Design Methods to Promote Good-Faith Participation in Court-Connected Mediation Programs*, 50 UCLA L. Rev. 69.

SHERMAN, Edward F. (1993) *Court-Mandated Alternative Dispute Resolution: What Form of Participation Should Be Required?*, 46 SMU L. Rev. 2079.

SHERMAN, Edward F. (1997) *"Good Faith" Participation in Mediation: Aspirational, Not Mandatory*, Disp. Resol. Magazine (Winter 1997), at 14.

THOMPSON, Peter N. (2011) *Good Faith Mediation in the Federal Courts*, 26 Ohio St. J. on Disp. Resol. 363.

# CHAPTER 7

ADLER, Robert. (1988) Sharing the Children: How to Resolve Custody Problems and Get On with Your Life.

ALFINI, James J. (1991) *Trashing, Bashing, and Hashing It Out: Is This The End of "Good Mediation"?*, 19 Fla. St. U. L. Rev. 47.

ASSOCIATION FOR CONFLICT RESOLUTION ANNUAL CONFERENCE 2003. (2004) *The World of Conflict Resolution: A Mosaic of Possibilities*, 5 Cardozo J. Conflict Resol. 190.

AUGSBURGER, D.W. (1992). *Conflict Mediation Across Cultures*. Louis ville, KY: Westminister/John Knox Press.

BABCOCK, Linda, and LASCHEVER, Sara. (2003) *Women Don't Ask: Negotiation and the Gender Divide*. Princeton, NJ: Princeton Univ. Press.

BARNES, Bruce. (1994) *Conflict Resolution Across Cultures: A Hawaii Perspective and a Pacific Mediation Model*, 12 Mediation Q. 117.

BRYAN, Penelope E. (1992) *Killing Us Softly: Divorce Mediation and the Politics of Power*, 40 Buff. L. Rev. 441.

COBB, Sara, and RIFKIN, Janet. (1991) *Practice and Paradox: Deconstructing Neutrality in Mediation*, 16 Law & Soc. Inquiry 35.

CHALMERS, W. Ellison. (1974) *Racial Negotiations: Potentials & Limitations*. Ann Arbor: Inst. of Lab. and Indus. Rel.

COKER, Donna. (1999) *Enhancing Autonomy for Battered Women: Lessons from Navajo Peacemaking*, 47 UCLA L. Rev. 1.

DAHL, Robert A. (1989) *Democracy and Its Critics*. New Haven: Yale Univ. Press.

DELGADO, Richard et al. (1985) *Fairness and Formality: Minimizing the Risk of Prejudice in Alternative Dispute Resolution*, 1985 Wis. L. Rev. 1359.

DODD, Carley H. (1987) *Dynamics of Intercultural Communication*. Dubuque: W.C. Brown.

DURYEA, Michelle LeBaron, and GRUNDISON, J. Bruce. (1993) *Conflict and Culture: Research in Five Communities in Vancouver, British Colombia*. Victoria, BC: UVic. Inst. for Disp. Resol.

FELSTINER, William, ABEL, Richard L., and SARAT, Austin. (1980–81) *The Emergence and Transformation of Disputes: Naming, Blaming, Claiming*, 15 Law & Soc'y Rev. 631.

FISS, Owen. (1984). *Against Settlement*, 93 Yale L.J. 1073.

FOLBERG, Jay, and TAYLOR, Alison. (1984) *Mediation*. San Francisco: Jossey-Bass.

FULLER, Lon. (1958) *Positivism and Fidelity to Law — A Reply to Professor Hart*, 71 Harv. L. Rev. 630.

GAGNON, Andree G. (1992) *Ending Mandatory Divorce Mediation for Battered Women*, 15 Harv. Women's L.J. 272.

GILLIGAN, Carol. (1982) *In a Different Voice*. Cambridge: Harvard Univ. Press.

GOLDBERG, Stephen B., SANDER, Frank E.A., ROGERS, Nancy H., and COLE, Sarah Rudolph. (2007) Dispute Resolution: Negotiation, Mediation, and Other Processes (5th ed.). New York: Wolters Kluwer.

GRILLO, Trina. (1990) *Process Dangers for Women*, 100 Yale L.J. 1545.

GULLIVER, P.H. (1979) *Disputes and Negotiations: A Cross-Cultural Perspective*. San Diego: Academic Press.

GUTMANN, Amy, and THOMPSON, Dennis. (1996) *Democracy and*

*Disagreement*. Cambridge: Belknap Press of Harvard Univ.

HALL, Edward T., and HALL, Mildred R. (1987) *Hidden Differences*. Garden City, N.Y.: Anchor Press.

HART, H.L.A. (1994) *The Concept of Law* (2d ed.). Oxford: Clarendon Press.

HART, H.L.A. (1958) *Positivism and the Separation of Law and Morals*, 71 Harv. L. Rev. 593.

HENSLER, Deborah R. (2002) *Suppose It's Not True: Challenging Mediation Ideology*, 2002 J. Disp. Resol. 81.

HERMANN, Michelle, et al. (1993) *An Empirical Study of the Effects of Race and Gender on Small Claims Adjudication and Mediation*. Albuquerque: Inst. of Pub. L., Univ. of New Mexico.

HUGHES, Scott. (1995) *Elizabeth's Story*, 8 Geo. J. Legal Ethics 553.

HYMAN, Jonathan M. (2004) *Swimming in the Deep End: Dealing with Justice in Mediation*, 6 Cardozo J. Conflict Resol. 19.

HYMAN, Jonathan M., and LOVE, Lela P. (2002) *If Portia Were a Mediator: An Inquiry Into Justice in Mediation*, 9 Clinical L. Rev. 159.

IZUMI, Carol. (2010) *Implicit Bias and the Illusion of Mediator Neutrality*, 34 Wash. U. J.L. & Pol'y 71.

KELLY, Joan B. (1989) *Mediated and Adversarial Divorce: Respondents' Perception of Their Processes and Outcomes*, 24 Mediation Q. 71.

KOLB, Deborah M. (2009) *Too Bad for the Women or Does It Have to Be? Gender and Negotiation Research over the Past Twenty-Five Years*, 2009 Negot. J. 515.

KOLB, Deborah M., and COOLIDGE, Gloria C. (1991) Her Place at the Table: A Consideration of Gender Issues in Negotiation, in Negotiation Theory and Practice (William Breslin & Jeffrey Z. Rubin, eds.). Cambridge: The Harvard Program on Negot. Books.

KOLB, Deborah M., and WILLIAMS, Judith. (2000) *The Shadow Negotiation: How Women Can Master the Hidden Agendas That Determine Bargaining Success*. New York: Simon & Shuster.

LANDRUM, Susan. (2011) *The On-Going Debate About Mediation in the Context of Domestic Violence: A Call for Empirical Studies of Mediation's Effectiveness*, 12 Cardozo J. Conflict Resol. 425.

LOVE, Lela, and MCDONALD, Cheryl B. (1997) *A Tale of Two Cities: Day Labor and Conflict Resolution for Communities in Crisis*. Disp. Resol. Magazine (Fall 1997), at 8.

LUBAN, David. (1995) *Settlement and the Erosion of the Public Realm*, 83 Geo. L.J. 2619.

MACKINNON, Catherine A. (1993) *Only Words*. Cambridge: Harvard Univ. Press.

MATSUDA, Mari J. (1989) *Public Response to Racist Speech: Considering the Victim's Story*, 87 Mich. L. Rev. 2320.

MCEWEN, Craig A., and MAIMAN, Richard M. (1984) Mediation in Small Claims Court: Achieving Compliance Through Consent, 19 Law & Soc'y Rev. 11.

MCEWEN, Craig A., and MAIMAN, Richard M. (1986) *The Relative Significance of Disputing Forum and Dispute Characteristics for Outcome and Compliance*, 20 Law & Soc'y Rev. 439.

MCEWEN, Craig A., and WILLIAMS, Laura. (1998) *Legal Policy and Access to Justice Through Courts and Mediation*, 13 Ohio St. J. on Disp. Resol. 865.

MENKEL-MEADOW, Carrie. (1995) *Whose Dispute is it Anyway? A Philosophical and Democratic Defense of Settlement (In Some Cases)*, 83 Geo. L.J. 2663.

NOLAN-HALEY, Jacqueline. (1999) *Informed Consent in Mediation: A Guiding Principle for Truly Educated Decisionmaking*, 74 Notre Dame L. Rev. 775.

O'CONNELL CORCORAN, Kathleen, and MELAMED, James C. (1990) *From Coercion to Empowerment: Spousal Abuse and Mediation*, 7 Mediation Q. 303.

PEARSON, Jessica. (1991) *The Equity of Mediated Agreements*, 9 Mediation Q. 179.

PEARSON, Jessica. (1997) *Mediating When Domestic Violence Is a Factor: Policies and Practices in Court-Based Divorce Mediation Programs*, 14 Mediation Q. 319.

PENA-GRATEREAUX, Mary E., and JESSOP, Maria I. (2000) *Mediation and Culture: Conversations with New York Mediators from Around the World.* New York: Washington Heights Inwood Coalition Mediation Program.

REISMAN, W. Michael. (1983*) Looking, Staring, and Glaring: Microlegal Systems and Public Order*, 12 Denv. J. Int'l L. & Pol'y 165.

RIMELSPACH, Rene. (2001) *Mediating Family Disputes in a World With Domestic Violence: How to Devise a Safe and Effective Court-Connected Mediation Program*, 17 Ohio St. J. on Disp. Resol. 95.

ROSENBERG, Joshua D. (1991) *In Defense of Mediation*, 33 Ariz. L. Rev. 467.

ROTHMAN, Jay. (2003) *Improving Police-Community Relations in Cincinnati: A Collaborative Approach.* Cincinnati Enquirer (Fall 2003).

RUBIN, Jeffrey Z., and SANDER, Frank E.A. (1991) *Culture, Negotiation, and the Eye of the Beholder*, 7 Negot. J. 249.

SAPOSNEK, Donald T. (1983) *Mediating Child Custody Disputes.* San Francisco: Jossey-Bass.

STULBERG, Joseph B. (1998) *Mediation and Fairness*, 13 Ohio St. J. on Disp. Resol. 909.

STULBERG, Joseph B., and LOVE, Lela P. (1996) Community Dispute Resolution Training Manual (rev. ed.). Lansing: Mich. Sup. Ct.

TANNEN, Deborah. (1990) *You Just Don't Understand*. New York: HarperCollins.

TANNEN, Deborah. (1995) *Talking 9 to 5: Women and Men at Work*. New York: HarperCollins.

VIDMAR, Neil. (1984) The Small Claims Court: A Reconceptualization of Disputes and an Empirical Investigation, 18 Law & Soc'y Rev. 515.

VIDMAR, Neil. (1987) Assessing the Effects of Case Characteristics and Settlement Forum on Dispute Outcomes and Compliance, 21 Law & Soc'y Rev. 155.

WELSH, Nancy A. (2002) *Disputant's Decision Control in Court-Annexed Mediation: A Hollow Promise Without Procedural Justice*, 2002 J. Disp. Resol. 179.

WISSLER, Roselle. (1995) *Mediation and Adjudication in the Small Claims Court: The Effects of Process and Case Characteristics*, 29 Law & Soc'y Rev. 323.

## CHAPTER 8

BUSH, Robert A. Baruch. (1992) *The Dilemmas of Mediation Practice: A Study of Ethical Dilemmas and Policy Implications*, National Institute for Dispute Resolution.

COBEN, James R., and LOVE, Lela P. (2010) *Trick or Treat: The Ethics of Mediator Manipulation*. Disp. Resol. Magazine, Vol. 17, No. 18 (Fall 2010).

LAFLIN, Maureen E. (2000) *Preserving the Integrity of Mediation Through the Adoption of Ethical Rules for Lawyer Mediators*, 14 Notre Dame J.L. Ethics & Pub. Pol'y 479.

MAUTE, Judith. (1991) *Public Values and Private Justice: A Case for Mediator Accountability*, 4 Geo. J. Legal Ethics 503.

MENKEL-MEADOW, Carrie. (1996) *Mediation and the Legal System: Is Mediation the Practice of Law?*, 14 Alternatives 57.

MEYERSON, Bruce. (1996) *Lawyers Who Mediate Are Not Practicing Law*, 14 Alternatives 74.

MOFFITT, Michael. (2003) *Ten Ways to Get Sued: A Guide for Mediators*, 8 Harv. Negot. L. Rev. 81.

PEPPET, Scott. (2003) *Contractarian Economics and Mediation Ethics: The Case for Customizing Neutrality Through Contingency Fee Mediation*, 82 Tex. L. Rev. 227.

PLIMPTON, David. (2000) *Liability Pitfalls May Be Waiting for Lawyer-Neutrals*, 18 Alternatives to the High Cost of Litigation 65.

RAVINDRA, Geetha. (2000) *The Response: The Goal is to Inform, Not Impede, ADR*, 18 Alternatives 124.

RUBIN, Melvin. (2010) *Mediatory Malpractice: A Proposed Defensive Path Through the Minefield*, Disp. Resol. Magazine (Fall 2010), at 24–25.

STEMPEL, Jeffrey W. (1997) *Beyond Formalism and False Dichotomies: The Need for Institutionalizing a Flexible Concept of the Mediator's Role*, 24 Fla. St. U. L. Rev. 949.

WELSH, Nancy. (2001) *The Thinning Vision of Self-Determination in Court-Connected Mediation: the Inevitable Price of Institutionalization?*, 6 Harv. Negot. L. Rev. 1 (2001).

WING, Leah, and RIFKIN, Janet. (2001) Racial Identity Development and the Mediation of Conflicts, in New Perspectives on Racial Identity Development (Charmaine L. Wijevesinghe and Bailey W. Jackson III, eds.). New York: New York Univ. Press.) *With Conflicts at Issue, Florida Firm and Its Former Partners Restructure ADR* — Again (1997), 15 Alternatives to the High Cost of Litigation 131.

YOUNG, Paula M. (2008) *A Connecticut Mediator in a Kangaroo Court?: Successfully Communicating the "Authorized Practice of Mediation" Paradigm to "Unauthorized Practice of Law" Disciplinary Bodies*, 2008 S. Tex. L. Rev. 1047.

YOUNG, Paula M. (2006) *Take It or Leave It. Lump It or Grieve It: Designing Mediator Complaint Systems That Protect Mediators, Unhappy Parties, Attorneys, Courts, the Process, and the Field*, 21 Ohio St. J. on Disp. Resol. 721.

## CHAPTER 9

ALFINI, James J. et al. (1994) *What Happens When Mediation Is Institutionalized?: To the Parties, Practitioners, and Host Institutions*, 9 Ohio St. J. on Disp. Resol. 307.

ALFINI, James J., and McCABE, Catherine G. (2001) *Mediating in the Shadow of the Courts: A Survey of the Emerging Case Law*, 54 Ark. L. Rev. 171.

BINGHAM, Lisa A. (1997) *Mediating Employment Disputes: Perceptions of REDRESS at the United States Postal Service*, 20 Rev. of Pub. Personnel Admin. 20 (Spring 1997).

BRAZIL, Wayne D. (2002) *Court ADR 25 Years After Pound: Have We Found a Better Way?*, 18 Ohio St. J. on Disp. Resol. 93.

BUSH, Robert. A. Baruch. (1989) *Mediation and Adjudication, Dispute Resolution and Ideology: An Imaginary Conversation*, 3 J. Contemp. Legal Issues 1.

COLE, Sara et al., eds. (2011) Mediation: Law, Policy and Practice (2012 ed.). St. Paul: Thompson-West.

CRATSLEY, John C. (2006) *Judicial Ethics and Judicial Settlement Practices:*

*Time for Two Strangers to Meet*, 21 Ohio St. J. on Disp. Resol. 569.

FOLGER, Joseph P. et al. (2001) A Benchmarking Study of Family, Civil and Citizen Dispute Mediation Programs in Florida, http://www.transformativemediation.org/cart/proddetail.php?prod=Benchmark.

JOHNSON, Earl. (2012) The Pound Conference Remembered. Disp. Resol. Magazine (Fall 2012).

KELLY, Joan B. (2004) *Family Mediation Research: Is There Empirical Support for the Field?*, 22 Conflict Resol. Q. 3.

LANDE, John. (2000) *Getting the Faith: Why Business Lawyers and Executives Believe in Mediation*, 5 Harv. Negot. L. Rev. 137.

MACFARLANE, Julie, and KEET, Michaela. (2005) *Civil Justice Reform and Mandatory Civil Mediation in Saskatchewan: Lessons from a Maturing Program*, 42 Alberta L. Rev. 677.

McADOO, Bobbi, and HINSHAW, Art. (2002) *The Challenge of Institutionalizing Alternative Dispute Resolution: Attorney Perspectives on the Effect of Rule 17 on Civil Litigation in Missouri*, 67 Mo. L. Rev. 473.

McADOO, Bobbi et al. (2004) *Institutionalization: What Do Empirical Studies Tell Us About Court Mediation?*, Disp. Resol. Magazine (Winter 2003).

McADOO, Bobbi. (2002) *A Report to the Minnesota Supreme Court: The Impact of Rule 114 on Civil Litigation Practice in Minnesota*, 25 Hamline L. Rev. 401.

McCRORY, John P. (1999) *Mandated Mediation of Civil Cases in State Courts: A Litigant's Perspective on Program Model Choices*, 14 Ohio St. J. on Disp. Resol. 813.

MENKEL-MEADOW, Carrie. (1991) *Pursuing Settlement in an Adversary Culture: a Tale of Innovation Co-Opted or "The Law of ADR,"* 19 Fla. St. L. Rev. 1.

PRESS, Sharon. (1992–93) *Building and Maintaining a Statewide Mediation Program: A View from the Field*, 81 Ky. L.J. 1029.

PRESS, Sharon. (1997) *Institutionalization: Savior or Saboteur of Mediation?*, 24 Fla. St. U. L. Rev. 903.

PRESS, Sharon. (2003) *Institutionalization of Mediation in Florida: At the Crossroads*, 108 Penn St. L. Rev. 43.

PRESS, Sharon. (2011) *Mortgage Foreclosure Mediation in Florida — Implementation Challenges for an Institutionalized Program*, 11 Nev. L. Rev. 306.

ROBINSON, Peter. (2012) *Opening Pandora's Box: An Empirical Exploration of Judicial Settlement Ethics and Techniques*, 27 Ohio St. J. on Disp. Resol. 53.

SANDER, Frank E.A. (2000) *The Future of ADR*, 2000 J. Disp. Resol. 3.

SCHNEIDER, Andrea Kupfer, and FLEURY, Natalie. (2011) *There's No Place*

*Like Home: Applying Dispute Systems Theory to Create a Foreclosure Mediation System*, 11 Nev. L.J. 368.

SHACK, Jennifer. (2003) *Efficiency: Mediation in Courts Can Bring Gains, But Under What Conditions?* Disp. Resol. Magazine 11 (Winter 2003).

WALDMAN, Ellen. (1996) *The Challenge of Certification: How to Ensure Mediator Competence While Preserving Diversity*, 30 U.S.F. L. Rev. 723.

WECKSTEIN, Donald T. (1996) *Mediator Certification: Why and How*, 30 U.S.F. L. Rev. 757.

WELSH, Nancy A. (2004) *The Place of Court-Connected Mediation in a Democratic Justice System*, 5 Cardozo J. Conflict Resol. 117.

WISSLER, Roselle L. (2004) *The Effectiveness of Court-Connected Dispute Resolution in Civil Cases*, 22 Conflict Resol. Q. 3.

# CHAPTER 10

ABRAMSON, Harold I. (2011) Mediation Representation (2d rev. ed.) New York: Oxford Univ. Press.

ABRAMSON, Harold I. (2004) *Mediation Representation: Advocating in a Problem-Solving Process*. South Bend: The Nat'l Inst. for Trial Advocacy.

ABRAMSON, Harold I. (2005) *Problem-Solving Advocacy in Mediation: A Model of Client Representation*, 10 Harv. Negot. L. Rev. 103.

ALFINI, James J. (1999) *Settlement Ethics and Lawyering in ADR Proceedings: A Proposal to Revise Rule 4.1*, 19 N. Ill. U. L. Rev. 255.

ARNOLD, Tom. (1995) *20 Common Errors in Mediation Advocacy*, 13 Alternatives to the High Cost of Litigation 69.

BAKER, Debra Ratterman. (1999) *Dependency Mediation: Strategies for Parents' Attorneys*, 18 ABA Child L. Prac. 124.

BECKWITH, Sandra S., and SLOVIN, Sherri. (2003) *The Collaborative Lawyer as Advocate: A Response*, 18 Ohio St. J. on Disp. Resol. 497.

BREGER, Marshall J. (2000) *Should an Attorney be Required to Advise a Client of ADR Options?*, 13 Geo. J. Legal Ethics 427.

COCHRAN, Robert F. Jr. (1999) *ADR, the ABA, and Client Control: A Proposal that the Model Rules Require Lawyers to Present ADR Options to Clients*, 41 S. Tex. L. Rev. 183.

COCHRAN, Robert F. Jr. (1990) *Legal Representation and the Next Steps Toward Client Control: Attorney Malpractice for the Failure to Allow the Client to Control Negotiation and Pursue Alternatives to Litigation*, 47 Wash. & Lee L. Rev. 819.

COOLEY, John W. (1996) *Mediation Advocacy*. South Bend: Nat'l Inst. for Trial Advocacy.

FAIRMAN, Christopher M. (2003) *Ethics and Collaborative Lawyering: Why*

*Put Old Hats on New Heads?*, 18 Ohio St. J. on Disp. Resol. 505.

FISHER, Roger, URY, William, and PATTON, Bruce. (1981, 1991) Getting to Yes: Negotiating Agreement Without Giving in (2d ed.). New York: Penguin Books.

GALTON, Eric. (1994) *Representing Clients in Mediation.* Dallas: American Lawyer Media.

GERONEMUS, David. (1999) *Mediation of Legal Malpractice Cases: Prevention and Resolution,* Practicing Law Institute Litigation and Administrative Practice Course Handbook Series Litigation PLI Order No. H0-003Q, 609 PLI/Lit 847 (June 1999).

GOLANN, Dwight. (forthcoming) *Mediation Advocacy: The Role of Lawyers in Mediation.* Washington, D.C.: Am. Bar Ass'n Sec. on Disp. Resol.

GUTHRIE, Chris. (2001) *The Lawyer's Philosophical Map and the Disputant's Perceptual Map: Impediments to Facilitative Mediation and Lawyering,* 6 Harv. Negot. L. Rev. 145.

LANDE, John. (1997) *How Will Lawyering and Mediation Transform Each Other?,* 24 Fla. St. U. L. Rev. 839.

LAWRENCE, James K.L. (2002) *Collaborative Lawyering: A New Deve opment in Conflict Resolution,* 17 Ohio St. J. on Disp. Resol. 431.

LAWRENCE, James K.L. (2000) *Mediation Advocacy: Partnering with the Mediators,* 15 Ohio St. J. on Disp. Resol. 425.

LUBAN, David. (1981) *Paternalism and the Legal Profession,* 1981 Wis. L. Rev. 454.

MACFARLANE, Julie. (2008) *The Evolution of the New Lawyer: How Lawyers are Reshaping the Practice of Law,* 2008 J. Disp. Resol. 61.

MACFARLANE, Julie, and KEET, Michaela. (2005) *Civil Justice Reform and Mandatory Civil Mediation in Saskatchewan: Lessons from a Maturing Program,* 42 Alberta L. Rev. 677.

McADOO, Bobbi. (2002) *A Report to the Minnesota Supreme Court: The Impact of Rule 114 on Civil Litigation Practice in Minnesota,* 25 Hamline L. Rev. 401.

McADOO, Bobbi, PRESS, Sharon, and GRIFFIN, Chelsea. (2012) *It's Time to Get it Right: Problem-Solving in the First-Year Curriculum,* 39 Wash. U. J.L. Pol'y 39.

McADOO, Bobbi, and HINSHAW, Art. (2002) *The Challenge of Institutionalizing Alternative Dispute Resolution: Attorney Perspectives on the Effect of Rule 17 on Civil Litigation in Missouri,* 67 Mo. L. Rev. 473.

McEWEN, Craig A. et al. (1995) *Bring in the Lawyers: Challenging the Dominant Approaches to Ensuring Fairness in Divorce Mediation,* 79 Minn. L. Rev. 1317.

MENKEL-MEADOW, Carrie. (1997) *Ethics in Alternative Dispute Resolution:*

*New Issues, No Answers from the Adversary Conception of Lawyers' Responsibilities*, 38 S. Tex. L. Rev. 407.

MEYERSON, Bruce. (1997) *Telling the Truth in Mediation: Mediator Owed Duty of Candor*, 4 Disp. Resol. Magazine 17.

MNOOKIN, Robert H., and KORNHAUSER, Lewis. (1979) *Bargaining in the Shadow of the Law: The Case of Divorce*, 88 Yale L.J. 950.

MNOOKIN, Robert H. (2000) *Beyond Winning: Negotiating to Create Value in Deals and Disputes*. Cambridge: Harvard Univ. Press.

NOLAN-HALEY, Jacqueline M. (1998) *Lawyers, Clients and Mediation*, 73 Notre Dame L. Rev. 1369.

PEDONE, Nicole. (1998) *Lawyer's Duty to Discuss Alternative Dispute Resolution: In the Best Interest of Children*, 36 Fam. & Conciliation Cts. Rev. 65.

PRIGOFF, Michael L. (1990) At Issue: *Professional Responsibility: Should There Be a Duty to Advise of ADR Options? NO: An Unreasonable Burden*, 76 A.B.A. J. 51 (Nov. 1990).

REUBEN, Richard C. (2000) *Constitutional Gravity: A Unitary Theory of Alternative Dispute Resolution and Public Civil Justice*, 47 UCLA L. Rev. 949.

RISKIN, Leonard. (1982) *Mediation and Lawyers*, 43 Ohio St. L.J. 29.

RISKIN, Leonard L. (1994) Mediator Orientations, Strategies and Techniques, 12 Alternatives to the High Cost of Litigation 111.

RISKIN, Leonard L. (1996) *Understanding Mediators' Orientations, Strategies, and Techniques: A Grid for the Perplexed*, 1 Harv. Negot. L. Rev. 7.

ROGERS, Nancy H., and McEWEN, Craig A. (1998) *Employing the Law to Increase the Use of Mediation and to Encourage Direct and Early Negotiations*, 13 Ohio St. J. on Disp. Resol. 831.

RUBINSON, Robert. (2004) *Client Counseling, Mediation, and Alternative Narratives of Dispute Resolution*, 10 Clinical L. Rev. 833.

RUTHERFORD, Mark C. (1986) *Lawyers and Divorce Mediation: Designing the Role of "Outside Counsel,"* Mediation Q. (June 1986), at 17.

SANDER, Frank E.A. (1990) *At Issue: Professional Responsibility Should There be a Duty to Advise of ADR Options? Yes: An Aid to Clients*, 76 A.B.A. J. 50 (Nov. 1990).

SCHMITZ, Suzanne J. (1999) *Giving Meaning to the Second Generation of ADR Education: Attorney's Duty to Learn about ADR and What They Must Learn*, 1999 J. Disp. Resol. 29.

SPIEGEL, Mark. (1979) *Lawyering and Client Decisionmaking: Informed Consent and the Legal Profession*, 128 U. Pa. L. Rev. 41.

STERNLIGHT, Jean R. (1999) *Lawyers' Representation of Clients in Mediation:*

*Using Economics and Psychology to Structure Advocacy in an Nonadversarial Setting*, 14 Ohio St. J. on Disp. Resol. 259.

STERNLIGHT, Jean R. (2005) *Separate and Not Equal: Integrating Civil Procedure and ADR in Legal Academia*, 80 Notre Dame L. Rev. 681.

STERNLIGHT, Jean R. (2000) *What's a Lawyer to Do in Mediation?* 18 Alternatives to the High Cost of Litigation 1.

WARMBROD, Monica L. (1996–7) *Could an Attorney Face Disciplinary Actions or Even Legal Liability for Failure to Inform Clients of Alternative Dispute Resolution?* 27 Cumb. L. Rev. 791.

WIDMAN, Stuart M. (1993 symposium issue) *Attorneys' Ethical Duties to Know and Advise Clients About Alternative Dispute Resolution*, Prof. Law. 18.

WISSLER, Roselle L. (2004) *Barriers to Attorneys' Discussion and Use of ADR*, 19 Ohio St. J. on Disp. Resol. 460.

WISSLER, Roselle L. (2002) *When Does Familiarity Breed Content? A Study of the Role of Different Forms of ADR Education and Experience in Attorneys' ADR Recommendations*, 2 Pepp. Disp. Resol. L.J. 199.

# CHAPTER 11:

ALFINI, James J., and GALTON, Eric R. (1998) ADR Personalities and Practice Tips. Washington, D.C.: Am. Bar Ass'n Sec. on Disp. Resol. The Mediators: Views from the Eye of the Storm (Mediate.com 2006).

# TABLE OF CASES

[References are to pages]

[References are to pages]

[References are to pages]

# INDEX

[References are to sections.]

## A

**ADR MOVEMENT** (See ALTERNATIVE DISPUTE RESOLUTION (ADR) MOVEMENT)

**ADVERTISING** (See ETHICAL ISSUES FOR MEDIATORS, subhead: Advertising/solicitation)

**AGREEMENTS**
Confidentiality . . . 5[C]
Enforceability of mediated agreements . . . 6[E]
Mediate, to . . . 6[B]

**ALTERNATIVE DISPUTE RESOLUTION (ADR) MOVEMENT**
Challenges
    Generally . . . 1[B][1]
    Diagnosing . . . 1[B][2][a]
    Hot city night . . . 1[B][1][a]
    Local government, working for . . . 1[B][1][c]
    Neighborhood citizenship . . . 1[B][1][b]
    Working for local government . . . 1[B][1][c]
Grand experiment
    Generally . . . 1[B][3]
    Diagnosing challenge . . . 1[B][2][a]
    Mediation services, building blocks of . . . 1[B][2][b]
Hot city night . . . 1[B][1][a]
Local government, working for . . . 1[B][1][c]
Mediation services, building blocks of . . . 1[B][2][b]
Neighborhood citizenship . . . 1[B][1][b]
Working for local government . . . 1[B][1][c]

**ATTORNEYS**
Generally . . . 10[A]
Advantages and disadvantages of participation in mediation . . . 10[C][2]
Advocate, lawyer as
    Generally . . . 10[A]
    Advantages and disadvantages of participation in mediation . . . 10[C][2]
    Advocating for client . . . 10[C][3]
    Ethical constraints . . . 10[C][4]
    Mediation and litigation, relationship between . . . 10[B]
    Mediator, role in selection of . . . 10[C][1]
    Role in mediation, lawyers'
        Generally . . . 10[C]
        Advantages and disadvantages of participation in mediation . . . 10[C][2]
        Advocating for client . . . 10[C][3]
        Clients, advocating for . . . 10[C][3]
        Ethical constraints . . . 10[C][4]
        Mediator selection . . . 10[C][1]
Advocating for client . . . 10[C][3]
Attorney-mediator, issues facing (See MEDIATION (GENERALLY), subhead: Attorney-mediator, issues facing)

**ATTORNEYS**—Cont.
Ethical constraints . . . 10[C][4]
Mediation and litigation, relationship between . . . 10[B]
Mediator, confusing role of attorney and . . . 8[D][2]
Mediator, role in selection of . . . 10[C][1]

## B

**BIOETHICAL DISPUTES**
Generally . . . 11[B][1][g]

## C

**CAREER DIRECTIONS IN MEDIATION**
Generally . . . 11[A]; 11[B]
Bioethical disputes . . . 11[B][1][g]
Civil law cases . . . 11[B][1][c]
Dispute resolution agency, working for
    Generally . . . 11[B][3][b]
    Direct service, agency providing . . . 11[B][3][b][i]
    DR administrative or provider organization, working for . . . 11[B][3][b][ii]
Elder care . . . 11[B][1][d]
Employment opportunities, organization-based
    Generally . . . 11[B][3]
    Agencies, mediator positions in . . . 11[B][3][a]
    Dispute resolution agency, working for (See subhead: Dispute resolution agency, working for)
    Mediator positions in agencies and organizations . . . 11[B][3][a]
    Organizations, mediator positions in . . . 11[B][3][a]
    Working for dispute resolution agency (See subhead: Dispute resolution agency, working for)
Environmental disputes . . . 11[B][1][h]
Family mediation . . . 11[B][1][b]
Independent mediation practices . . . 11[B][2]
Neighborhood justice center programs, small claims mediation and . . . 11[B][1][a]
Organization-based employment opportunities (See subhead: Employment opportunities, organization-based)
Peer mediation . . . 11[B][1][f]
Possibilities, range of
    Generally . . . 11[B][1]
    Bioethical disputes . . . 11[B][1][g]
    Civil law cases . . . 11[B][1][c]
    Elder care . . . 11[B][1][d]
    Environmental disputes . . . 11[B][1][h]
    Family mediation . . . 11[B][1][b]
    Neighborhood justice center programs, small claims mediation and . . . 11[B][1][a]
    Peer mediation . . . 11[B][1][f]

[References are to sections.]

[References are to sections.]

**GOVERNMENT, LOCAL**
Working for . . . 1[B][1][c]

# H

**HEALTH CARE DISPUTES**
Bioethical disputes . . . 11[B][1][g]

# I

**INSTITUTIONALIZATION OF MEDIATION IN COURTS**
Generally . . . 9[A]
Criticism of . . . 9[E]
Development of . . . 9[B]
Empirical evaluations . . . 9[D]
Judicial mediation . . . 9[F]
Policy development . . . 9[C]

**INTEGRATIVE NEGOTIATION**
Distributive negotiation versus . . . 2[B][1]

# J

**JUDICIAL MEDIATION**
Generally . . . 9[F]

**JUSTICE**
Generally . . . 7[A]
Mediation
    Growth and impact on justice system (See MEDIATION (GENERALLY), subhead: Justice system, mediation's growth and impact on)
    Rule of law, and . . . 7[D]
Rule of law, mediation and . . . 7[D]
System (See MEDIATION (GENERALLY), subhead: Justice system, mediation's growth and impact on)

# L

**LEGAL ISSUES**
Generally . . . 6[A]
Agreements
    Enforceability of mediated agreements . . . 6[E]
    Mediate, to . . . 6[B]
Enforceability of mediated agreements . . . 6[E]
"Good faith," mediation in . . . 6[D]
Judicial power to compel mediation . . . 6[C]
Statutory requirements to mediate . . . 6[B]

**LEGAL SYSTEM** (See MEDIATION (GENERALLY), subhead: Legal system, and)

**LITIGATION AND MEDIATION** (See ATTORNEYS)

**LOCAL GOVERNMENT**
Working for . . . 1[B][1][c]

# M

**MEDIATION (GENERALLY)**
Generally . . . 1[A][1]; 3[B][1][a]
Accumulation of information
    Generally . . . 3[B][1][b]; 3[C][2]
    Case file, reviewing . . . 3[C][2][a]
    Disputants' opening statements . . . 3[C][2][b]
    Listening skills . . . 3[C][2][d]
    Non-verbal communication . . . 3[C][2][f]
    Notes . . . 3[C][2][c]
    Pre-mediation information . . . 3[C][2][a]
    Questions, use of . . . 3[C][2][e]
Advocate, mediation and lawyer as (See ATTORNEYS, subhead; Advocate, lawyer as)
Agenda development
    Generally . . . 3[B][1][c]; 3[C][3]
    Characterizing issues . . . 3[C][3][a]
    Priorities . . . 3[C][3][b]
    Structuring discussion . . . 3[C][3][c]
Alternative Dispute Resolution (ADR) movement, foundational years of contemporary (See ALTERNATIVE DISPUTE RESOLUTION (ADR) MOVEMENT)
Attorney-mediator, issues facing
    Advertising and solicitation issues . . . 8[D][5]
    Fee sharing issues . . . 8[D][4]
    Interest issues, conflict of . . . 8[D][3]
    Solicitation issues, advertising and . . . 8[D][5]
Beginning mediation process . . . 3[B][4]
Career directions in (See CAREER DIRECTIONS IN MEDIATION)
Case file, reviewing . . . 3[C][2][a]
Caucus (See subhead: Separate session)
Characterizing issues . . . 3[C][3][a]
Conclusion of mediation
    Generally . . . 3[B][1][e]; 3[C][6]
    Agreement
        Generally . . . 3[C][6][b]
        Enforcement of . . . 3[C][6][b][ii]
        Format of . . . 3[C][6][b][i]
    Enforcement of agreement . . . 3[C][6][b][ii]
    No agreement . . . 3[C][6][a]
Confidentiality (See CONFIDENTIALITY)
Disputants' opening statements . . . 3[C][2][b]
Divorce mediation, model standards of practice for family and . . . Appendix C
Ending mediation (See subhead: Conclusion of mediation)
Evaluative mediation . . . 3[D][2]
Family mediation (See FAMILY MEDIATION)
Historical perspective . . . 1[A][2]
Institutionalization of mediation in courts (See INSTITUTIONALIZATION OF MEDIATION IN COURTS)
Justice system, mediation's growth and impact on
    Generally . . . 1[C][1]
    Challenges of growth . . . 1[C][5]
    Emerging and expansive growth, areas of . . . 1[C][3][a]

[References are to sections.]

# N